COLLEGE COSTS & FINANCIAL AID HANDBOOK

1997

SEVENTEENTH EDITION

College Scholarship Service

College Entrance Examination Board
New York

The College Scholarship Service (CSS) is an activity of the College Board concerned with improving equal educational opportunity. The CSS, through the determination of financial need, assists in the equitable distribution of financial assistance to students. Its services are offered to students and their parents, to secondary schools, to noncollegiate sponsors of financial aid programs, and to all institutions of postsecondary education.

This publication contains material related to Federal Title IV student aid programs. While the College Board believes that the information contained herein is accurate and factual, this publication has not been reviewed or approved by the U.S. Department of Education.

Copies of this book may be ordered from your local bookseller or from College Board Publications, Box 886, New York, New York 10101-0886. The price is $16.95.

Editorial inquiries regarding this book should be addressed to the College Scholarship Service, The College Board, 45 Columbus Avenue, New York, New York 10023-6992; or telephone (212) 713-8120.

Photo credits: page 4, left, Martin Dixon, Forsyth Technical Community College; page 4, right, Martin Dixon, Vassar College; page 19, Hugh Rogers; page 27, Emile Wamsteker, Syracuse University; page 66, Equity 2000 site, Providence, RI; page 67, Hugh Rogers; page 68, Hugh Rogers, Piscataway High School.

Library of Congress Catalog Number: 80-648095

International Standard Book Number: 0-87447-544-9

Printed in the United States of America

Contents

Mission Statement

The College Board champions educational excellence for all students through the ongoing collaboration of member schools, colleges, universities, educational systems, and organizations. It promotes—by means of responsive forums, research, programs, and policy development—universal access to high standards of learning, equity of opportunity, and sufficient financial support so that every student is prepared for success in college and work.

The College Board

Educational Excellence for *All* Students

Preface

This book is based on a simple premise: without advance planning, almost no one can afford to pay for college. With planning, *anybody* can. It is true for families whose children are already high school juniors and seniors—and even truer for families whose children are still quite young.

You may have doubted that education or training after high school is within your family's reach. *That is probably not true.*

You may have assumed that there is nothing you can do to help yourself or improve your chances of finding the outside help you need. *That is definitely not true.*

This book is designed to help students and their families meet college costs. If you are worried about your family's ability to pay future educational expenses, early planning *can* help. The *purpose* of planning is twofold:

- to get as much mileage as you can out of your own resources
- to secure the additional outside help—the "financial aid"—you may need

Planning ahead to meet college costs involves several different kinds of activities. This book will

- show you how to estimate the full costs of attending the colleges you are considering
- help you to estimate what share of those costs you and your family will probably be expected to bear
- prove that you can make time work *for* you in covering your share of the costs
- describe different ways that families can make their costs more manageable
- help you estimate your own probable need and eligibility for financial aid
- explain the various types and sources of financial aid available and what you need to do to apply
- assist you in developing a personal financing plan and timetable for gathering the resources *you* need

Next to buying a home, the money that you and your family pay toward college costs may well be the largest financial investment you ever make in your lifetime. You owe it to yourself to investigate all your options beforehand, and then to manage that investment as carefully as you would any other.

The author gratefully acknowledges the contributions of the many individuals who assisted in the development of the 1997 edition of *College Costs and Financial Aid Handbook*. Data in Parts II and III were collected by the editorial staff of Guidance Publishing under the direction of Renée Gernand, using information collected through the College Board's Annual Survey of Colleges. The book was edited by Karen Dubno.

Mary Gaffney, Norma Hammond, Jack Joyce, Jacqueline King, and Debbie Ranjeet provided valuable assistance in various aspects of research and statistical analysis.

At the time this book went to press, a few aspects of financial aid delivery for academic year 1997-98 had not yet been finalized. Changes in program, application, and eligibility rules are always possible. Thus, it is very important that students seeking aid for the fall of 1997 take steps, early on, to ensure that they fully understand and comply with all application requirements.

To improve your chances of getting the help you need, you must know *what* you have to do, *when* you have to do it, and *how* to do it right—the first time. Missed deadlines, incomplete or inaccurate answers, and messy or illegible forms can hurt you. *If you have any doubts at all about which forms to file or which questions to complete, contact the financial aid offices at the colleges to which you are applying.*

Developments in computer technology are rapidly changing the college-going process for students, parents, and counselors. Increasingly colleges provide direct electronic links for student inquiries and applications, whether through the Internet or via institutional software programs like the College Board's EXPAN Guidance and Application Network.

The College Board, too, has developed an online website where students and educational professionals can get continuously updated information about the college-going process and fast responses to questions or concerns about College Board programs and services. If you have access to the Internet, we invite you to stop by the College Board Online at http://www.college-board.org and let us know what you think about the *College Costs and Financial Aid Handbook* and about our new electronic college transition services. While you are there, you can also register for the SAT, sample actual SAT questions, search for and apply to colleges, calculate financial need, or order publications.

If you do not have access to the Internet, we would like to hear from you by mail or phone. We welcome any comments and suggestions that will help us make our publications and services useful to you.

Kathleen Brouder
Director, CSS Information and Training
The College Scholarship Service

Part I.
Paying
for college

1. What does college cost?

Some of the best things in life may be free, but unfortunately, college is not one of them.

In fact, it costs even more than you may think. High as the prices may seem to the family that is facing them, the truth is, they represent only part of the real costs. Only a very few colleges charge you the *full* costs of providing an education.

Public colleges and universities receive large operating subsidies from state and local taxes. Most independent or private colleges and universities meet at least some of their operating expenses through endowments, contributions from graduates, and government or foundation grants. Virtually all of them invest money and use the return to help pay for their activities. The influx of federal and state institutional aid for research, facilities, and special programs is an important part of most colleges' operating budgets, helping to hold down the amounts that must be charged to students and their families.

However, all of this may not be much consolation to students and parents like you who actually have to find a way to pay the bills. Average annual costs of attendance continue to climb for virtually every postsecondary educational option, from commuting to a low-cost community college to living on campus at a high-cost private institution.

The purpose of this book is to help you plan to meet college costs. Because every family's personal and financial circumstances are different, each family's plan for meeting college costs will be different, too. The worksheets in Chapter 10 follow three sample students from different family and financial backgrounds—Andrea, Beth, and Carlos—as they plan to meet college costs. Space is also provided for you to make some preliminary plans.

Your first step in planning is to learn what college costs. Part II of this book lists the average student expenses at 3,100 colleges and universities for the 1996-97 academic year (AY). The average expenses at different kinds of colleges for 1995-96 (the most recent year for which averages are available) are listed in Chapter 10.

The components of college costs

Regardless of where you enroll, your expenses include both direct educational expenses *and* living expenses, and typically consist of five parts:

- tuition and fees
- books and supplies
- room and board
- personal expenses
- transportation

Many students have additional expenses not covered under any of these categories, such as costs arising from medical care or a disability. Be sure to include these extra expenses in estimating the costs of attending the particular colleges you are considering.

Do not let the costs scare you! As this book explains, you may not have to pay the whole amount yourself, *and* there are ways of making more manageable the part you do have to pay.

Tuition and fees

Tuition is the charge for instruction. Fees may be charged for services such as the library, student activities, or the health center. The amount of tuition and fees charged by a particular college depends on many factors, but the most significant factor is what kind of college it is.

Because they receive funds from taxes, tuition and fees at public institutions are generally the lowest, particularly for legal residents of the state or district in which they are located. Most two- and four-year public colleges charge higher tuition for nonresidents, however. This "out-of-state" tuition (or "out-of-district"

The budget for maintaining, staffing, and operating college facilities is met by federal and state aid, endowments, and investments in addition to charges to students.

tuition, in the case of two-year community colleges) often can make the cost of attending a public institution as high as the cost of attending many private institutions. (In rare instances, religiously affiliated colleges may add a surcharge for students who are not members of that religious group.) Tuition at private colleges is usually much higher than at public institutions because private colleges must charge a larger percentage of the real costs. Tuition at proprietary or profit-making institutions (such as many trade and technical schools) is usually set at a level to recover all of their operating costs plus a profit.

The tables in Part II of this book show the tuition and fees charged to most first-time, full-time students. Part-time charges, usually set by credit or semester hour, may work out to be higher per unit. Tuition and fees for upper-division students and graduate or professional students may also vary.

Books and supplies

Every college student has to buy books, pencils, paper, and other supplies. The amount you spend for books

and supplies will vary only slightly by type of institution but is generally related to the curriculum or courses you select. In some academic fields, for instance, students may have to spend a good deal more than the averages cited in Part II of this book.

Art students, for example, may need more extensive supplies, such as canvases, paints, brushes, and clay. Engineering students may need calculators or slide rules. Students in the sciences may have additional expenses for lab work. Computer science students may need to buy more computer time, or even purchase personal computers. In some programs, the textbooks are more expensive simply because the "information explosion" causes rapid changes in the field.

Room and board

Room and board means basic living expenses for food and housing. Regardless of the kind of institution you choose, you will have to consider these expenses.

You may choose to live in a dormitory on campus or in other college-operated housing located near campus

4

(such as college-owned apartments). Although some private two-year colleges have college-operated housing available, most public community colleges do not.

Or you may want to live in privately owned housing, such as an apartment or rooming house near campus. At many large colleges and universities where on-campus housing is limited, students often live in dormitories for the first year or two and then shift to off-campus private housing.

Or you may choose to live at home with your parents and commute to campus.

The terms "resident student" and "commuter student" can be confusing. In this book, students who live in dormitories or in off-campus, college-owned housing away from their families are called "resident students" (not to be confused with the term "legal resident" used in the discussion of tuition and fees). "Commuter students" are those who live at home with their families. Many colleges have additional budget categories designed to cover students who live off campus in private housing; information about estimated expenses for such students is available in college catalogs and financial aid bulletins. Students who live off campus in private housing generally have expenses that are more like the resident budgets in this book than the commuter budgets.

Colleges with their own housing typically charge residents on a nine-month basis for room rental and most meals, excluding holiday and vacation periods. The room and board charge is built into the student expense budget. Colleges also expect that students living in privately owned, off-campus housing have a similar level of expense (although this is sometimes estimated as somewhat higher or lower than the college's own room and board costs, depending on the local housing market).

Commuter students, on the other hand, are generally assumed to have somewhat lower expenses than resident students because they do not have to pay for housing. However, families should remember that they will still need to buy food for the student and pay for other normal living expenses. For example, if classes start early in the morning and go on until late at night, commuter students will need to buy at least one meal a day, and possibly additional snacks, in the student union or coffee shop. Therefore, the estimated cost of food and other expenses at home is usually built into commuter student expense budgets for financial aid purposes. Take these costs into account in your planning.

Personal expenses

No matter what kind of institution you choose, you will have some personal expenses for such things as clothing, laundry, toiletries, recreation, medical insurance and care, and perhaps incidental furnishings for your dormitory room. This is an area in which you can economize, but colleges usually estimate that students spend at least $1,100 to $1,500 per academic year on such items.

Transportation

All students spend some money for travel. Resident students who live on or near campus must travel to get there at the start of the academic year and return home at the end; most also go home at least once during the year. If you plan to live at college but expect to travel home frequently, your transportation costs may be considerably higher than the averages shown in this book or reported by individual colleges. Include estimated travel costs in your planning. For financial aid purposes, colleges often budget students for two round-trips home per year by the lowest-cost means of travel possible.

Commuter students who travel to and from campus daily also have travel expenses, whether they use public transportation or a private car. The costs of gasoline and daily parking can add up quickly, so estimate carefully. These costs, too, are built into student expense budgets by colleges for financial aid purposes.

Total expense budget

The total expense budget for a particular college is determined by adding up these five categories of expenses. The tables, sample cases, and worksheets in Chapter 10 reflect sample total expenses for resident and commuter students. For your own estimates, remember to consider any additional costs that might result from medical bills or other extraordinary personal expenses.

The total budgets at public colleges are lower than those at private colleges largely because tuition and fees tend to be lower at the former. There is not, however, a lot of difference in the other costs. So do not rule out a private college because of its higher tuition. Private institutions often have more financial aid resources that can help you make up the difference between costs and financial aid. *The greater your overall expense, the greater is the possibility of your demonstrating need for financial aid.*

Questions and answers about college costs

Q All of these costs look greater than anything we can afford. How can we possibly manage to pay for college?

A First, you may be eligible for some financial aid to help you meet part of the costs. What *you* pay for college is not necessarily what the price tag says. Second, you may be able to cut your costs and stretch your resources, as described in later chapters, but be prepared to contribute *something*. In very rare cases, parents are judged too poor to contribute anything toward the costs. Third, remember that you and your family are already paying some of these expenses right now—your food, clothing, and personal expenses, for example.

That is not to say that your expenses as a member of the household are not putting a strain on the household budget; they may well be. If you can manage it now, however, ask yourself seriously if your family cannot manage it for another two or four years.

Q With college costs so high, as well as the rising cost of living in general, shouldn't I just look for the cheapest alternative?

A Not necessarily. Higher cost colleges often have more financial aid to help families bridge the gap between the costs and what they can afford to pay.

Q How do I know that the costs at a particular college won't keep going up during the years I'm enrolled?

A You do not. In fact, they probably *will* continue to rise. However, your family's income will probably rise, too. Whether your family's ability to pay will increase at the same rate as college costs depends on a lot of factors, including the overall state of the economy.

2. How much will you be expected to pay?

You should regard your family as the first—and probably primary—source of funds for education (see Table 2.1 on page 8). Virtually all colleges, government agencies, and private student aid programs expect you to pay *something* toward college costs, according to your ability. Financial aid often makes up the difference between the costs of attendance and what a family can afford to pay. You may not have to pay as much as the prices listed in a college's catalog if you are eligible for financial aid. Thus, estimating how much your family can reasonably be expected to pay toward educational expenses is a major part of understanding financial aid—and a critical aspect of goal setting.

Whether your family's share of the total costs amounts to 5 percent or 100 percent, you have a better chance of achieving the goal if you know how much you are aiming for.

To help them evaluate a family's financial strength, most college financial aid administrators and aid sponsors use a set of federal formulas that take into consideration income, assets, expenses, family size, and other factors.

In addition, many colleges use an alternate set of formulas for awarding their own *institutional* student aid funds. This alternate guideline, informally known as the "Institutional Methodology," differs from the "Federal Methodology" in several respects. For instance, the Institutional Methodology takes home equity into account and includes a minimum expected contribution from students in calculating a family's ability to pay, but also permits more generous treatment of medical/dental expenses, elementary and secondary school tuition payments, and child support paid. In Chapter 10, you will see how the formulas actually work. But the two methodologies share some common general principles.

Evaluating a family's income

A family's total income for the previous calendar year is added up. Parents' wages and all other income (such as dividends, social security, or welfare benefits) are included, but not all of this income can be used to pay for college. For most families, the largest part of its annual income must be used to provide for basic living expenses—housing, food, medical care, clothing, and so forth.

In evaluating a family's financial strength, aid administrators also take into account other demands on the parents' income, such as taxes or unusually large medical or dental bills. Even the costs of working must be taken into consideration—clothing, transportation, meals away from home, and so forth. Elementary and secondary school tuition payments for other children may also be considered.

After all these family expenses are taken into account, the amount remaining to a family for other uses is quite a bit smaller than its original income. This remaining amount is called "available income." A family would be expected to use some of this remaining income to help pay college costs. The more available income a family has, the more would be expected of them.

Evaluating a family's assets

Many family's assets are considered, too, because a family with assets is in a stronger financial position than a family with similar income but no assets. All of the assets are added up—the value of a business or farm, cash, savings and checking accounts, stocks and bonds, and so forth. At lower income levels, home equity is not considered in the *federal* aid formulas.

In the same way that a family cannot be expected to spend all its income on education, neither is it expected to use all its assets to pay for college. The system "protects" a portion of parents' assets for their use in retirement. The amount parents are allowed to protect gets larger as the age of the primary wage earner increases, because an older worker has fewer years to save for retirement than a younger one. The system also "protects" a substantial portion of family assets tied up in a business or farm, since a business or farm is also a source of income. If it were all used up to pay for college, there would be nothing left to generate income in the future.

Even when the various allowances are subtracted from total assets, a family is not expected to convert all its remaining assets into cash for college—only a portion called "income supplement from assets."

Available income (the discretionary part of a family's annual income) is added to the income supplement from assets to get a dollar amount called "adjusted available income." Not all the adjusted available income is tapped for educational expenses, only a percentage. A family with a higher adjusted available income is expected to pay a greater share of college costs than is a family with a lower adjusted available income.

If more than one family member is attending college at the same time, the amount parents are expected to pay is divided by the number attending, in order to find the expected contribution per student. This means that sometimes a family is not eligible for aid when the first child goes to college but becomes eligible in subsequent years when a younger brother or sister starts college.

Evaluating a student's ability to pay

A student is usually expected to contribute toward college expenses, too, from savings and summer earnings. While *federal* student aid rules do not prescribe a minimum expected contribution from students, many colleges expect a freshman to contribute at least $900 a year from summer job earnings when it comes to awarding their own private funds. Upper-division students are often expected to contribute even more from summer and part-time jobs—upward of $1,100 a year at many colleges, and more than that at some.

Estimating your expected family contribution

Your family's "share" is the sum of what your parents can contribute from their income and assets *and* what

Table 2.1. Sources for educational expenses

Resources	Percentage of students having resource	Percentage of students receiving $1,500 or more from resource
Parents' assistance	76.2%	52.4%
Federal Pell Grant	22.7	5.4
Federal Supplemental Educational Opportunity Grant	5.8	1.0
State scholarship or grant	16.2	3.6
Other college grant	26.0	14.8
Other private grant	9.9	2.9
Federal Stafford Loan	28.8	14.5
Federal Perkins Loan	8.9	2.5
College loan	9.9	5.8
Other loan	7.2	4.5
College Work-Study Program	12.9	3.6
Part-time job on campus	22.5	2.3
Part-time job off campus	23.5	2.2
Full-time job	3.0	.9
Savings from summer work	49.7	8.3
Other savings	29.8	7.2
Student's spouse	1.5	0.4
Other government aid	3.0	1.8
Vocational rehabilitation funds	1.1	.5
Other aid	4.2	2.1

Source: Adapted from *The American Freshman: National Norms for Fall, 1995* (Los Angeles: American Council on Education and University of California at Los Angeles, 1995).

you can contribute from your earnings, savings, and so forth. In the financial aid process, this amount is also referred to as the "expected family contribution":

What parents can contribute from income
+ What parents can contribute from assets
+ What a student can contribute from income
+ What a student can contribute from assets
= Expected family contribution.

If you are simply curious about what magnitude of expense this represents, the estimated Parents' Contribution table in Chapter 10 gives you a sense of what is expected of *parents* at different income and asset levels, assuming they meet the specifications as to age, family size, and other characteristics. Pick the combination of annual income and asset figures that most resembles your own, and you will have a *very* crude approximation of how your parent's share might work out.

You can make a much closer estimate of what might be expected of you and your family by fully completing the worksheets in Chapter 10. By subtracting your expected family contribution from the average costs of attendance at different kinds of colleges, you can get a sense of your remaining financial need. (In addition, computer software, such as the College Board's *College Cost Explorer/FUND FINDER*, can be helpful when you are trying to determine how to pay for college. It provides a scholarship data base, detailed information about costs at 2,800 colleges, and also explains how expected family contribution is calculated and then translated into eligibility. Check to see if your guidance office or library has a copy of *FUND FINDER* for you to use.)

You are usually eligible for financial aid equal to the amount of your demonstrated financial need. (Whether you are able to obtain all of the financial aid you are eligible for depends on a variety of factors, such as the availability of funds in any given year.)

Setting a goal

Your estimate of your expected family contribution—be it 5 percent or 100 percent of college costs—should be your goal. Your plan should be organized to help you achieve, or even exceed, that goal. If the goal seems too *big* in relation to your household budget, do not panic! Chapters 3 and 4 give some ideas about ways to finance your share of the costs. If your goal seems too *small* in relation to actual college costs, do not worry! Chapters 5 and 6 demonstrate how financial aid can bridge the gap. Whatever your goal, write it down on a piece of paper and refer to it occasionally. *Writing goals down on paper helps to make them real.*

Special note on independent (self-supporting) students

So far the discussion has focused on students who are dependent on their parents for financial support. If you are truly financially independent of your parents, you are called an "independent," or "self-supporting," student. This does not mean that your resources are always sufficient to pay your direct educational costs as well as living expenses (for yourself and your family).

What it *does* mean is that, in considering your need for financial aid, colleges and other aid providers assume that your parents will not provide you with any support. (When it comes to awarding their own *institutional* funds, some colleges will expect parents to supply *information*, however, regardless of the student's dependency status.)

Your ability as a self-supporting student to contribute toward college costs is evaluated on the basis of your own income, assets, and expenses. Expenses are typically higher than a dependent student's because self-supporting students must provide for maintenance and living expenses year-round. You may also have extra expenses, such as child care, which may be considered in the student expense budget developed by a college for self-supporting financial aid applicants. Because they do not get help from their parents and because their expenses are usually higher than dependent students' expenses, self-supporting students often have a greater financial need. (They may also be expected to contribute more toward their own educational expenses.)

Who is considered self-supporting and who is not? There are certainly many students who really are self-supporting, such as younger students who no longer have financial support of their parents, or older students with families of their own. The problem is defining what really constitutes self-supporting status.

At the time this book went to press, it was assumed that for the 1997-98 academic year the federal definition of independence, as outlined in the Higher Education Amendments of 1992, will be used to determine eligibility for the Federal Pell Grant, Federal Stafford Loan, and campus-based programs. Most state, institutional, and private aid sponsors are expected to use a similar definition.

Under this definition, you are *automatically* considered to be self-supporting if

- you are at least 24 years old by December 31 of the award year (e.g., by December 31, 1997, for the 1997-98 award year)
- you are a veteran of the United States Armed Forces, regardless of age
- you are an orphan or a ward of the court
- you have legal dependents of your own *other than* a spouse
- you are married
- you are a graduate or a professional student

Financial aid administrators can make exceptions for students who do not meet these criteria but are nonetheless self-supporting. Contact the financial aid offices at the colleges you are considering if you need more information about dependency status.

Even if you meet the federal criteria for self-supporting status, however, you may be required to submit parents' financial data as part of the aid application process at some colleges. Some colleges may also ask you to provide additional documentation of your income and expenses if you claim self-supporting status. Also, some private sponsors may use different definitions than the federal government for determining self-supporting status. Contact the financial aid offices at the colleges from which you are seeking help if you think you may qualify as a self-supporting student and wish further information.

Questions and answers about how much you will be expected to pay

Q We have special expenses that aren't talked about in this chapter that affect our ability to pay (for example, a handicapped child who requires special medical care or education). Does anybody take this into account?

A Colleges try to take into account the unique circumstances of each applicant. In Chapter 6, where applying for financial aid is discussed, you will learn about ways in which you can make sure that the colleges you are considering at least understand your situation fully. Whether they will be able to give you extra help depends on a variety of factors, one of the most important being how much money they have available to help students in any given year.

Q We live in a big city and the rents for apartments are very high. Does the need analysis system take this into account?

A The formulas do take housing costs into account, along with food, clothing, and other family living expenses. Financial aid administrators at some colleges also may consider the high cost of living in your particular residential area.

Q I've calculated our expected family contribution, and it's more money than we can possibly afford. How can we pay this out of our current earnings?

A You aren't necessarily expected to pay it out of your current earnings alone. The next chapter will explain that no matter how large that expectation may appear to you, it can be made smaller if you break it into monthly amounts. The earlier you start planning, the more choices you have about how to finance your share of the costs.

3. How to make time work for you

If you have estimated how much you may be expected to pay toward college costs, you may wonder how you can possibly squeeze that much out of current income.

In fact, you probably *cannot* squeeze it all out of current income. Few people are wealthy enough to pay cash for houses, cars, or major appliances. Most of us save or borrow, sometimes both, to finance the purchase of "big-ticket" items. In fact, we may not even be able to figure out whether we can afford something until we see how it breaks down in terms of monthly payments.

The more time you give yourself, the more choices you will have about how to finance your share. If you still have several years left before enrollment, you have many more options than families who are facing enrollment within the next year or two. But even if you were to enroll next month, you would still have some choices.

What does "expected family contribution" actually mean?

Your expected family contribution is *not* a prediction of how much extra cash you actually have on hand, or even an assumption of how much you "ought to" be able to pull from current income. Rather, the expected family contribution is a measure of your family's overall capacity to absorb some portion of educational expenses, and you can cover your share in any number of ways.

If you start early enough, you may be able to *save* your entire share, and more. One of the advantages of starting early is that you *earn* interest toward your goal. If you start late, you may have to *borrow*. The downside is that you are *paying* interest, not earning it. You could use a combination of saving *and* borrowing—or even "leverage" your money by borrowing against your own savings. The toughest way to cover your share of educational expenses, though, is

to force them into your current household budget. Some families do it, but it is not easy.

Financing the parents' contribution

Students can get summer or part-time jobs to help finance their portion of the expected family contribution. Accommodating the parents' portion, or "parents'

Table 3.1. Relationship of family income to parental contribution (1996-97 Federal Methodology)

Annual family income	Net income (after tax)	Parents' contribution (annual)	Percentage of total	Percentage of net
$ 10,000	$ 8,435	$ 0	0.0%	0.0%
15,000	12,653	0	0.0	0.0
20,000	16,353	0	0.0	0.0
25,000	19,820	0	0.0	0.0
30,000	23,288	668	2.2	2.9
35,000	26,755	1,431	4.1	5.3
40,000	30,223	2,194	5.5	7.3
45,000	33,690	2,319	5.2	6.9
50,000	37,158	4,148	8.3	11.2
55,000	40,625	5,464	9.9	13.4
60,000	43,514	6,799	11.3	15.6
65,000	45,680	7,817	12.0	17.1
70,000	48,807	9,287	13.3	19.0
75,000	51,935	10,757	14.3	20.7
80,000	55,062	12,227	15.3	22.2
85,000	58,190	13,697	16.1	23.5
90,000	61,317	15,166	16.9	24.7
95,000	64,445	16,636	17.5	25.8
100,000	67,572	18,106	18.1	26.8

Note: Estimated parents' contributions in Tables 3.1-3.4 assume four family members; one family member in college as an undergraduate; older parent (age 45) is employed; the other parent is not employed; income only from employment; no unusual circumstances; standard deductions on U.S. income tax; asset neutrality (assets equal to Asset Protection Allowance). Values are approximate.

Table 3.2. Parents' contribution related to monthly net income (1996-97 Federal Methodology)

Annual family income	Annual net income (after tax)	Parent's contribution (annual)	Monthly net income (after tax)	Monthly net required to pay contribution
$ 10,000	$ 8,435	$ 0	$ 703	$ 0
15,000	12,653	0	1,054	0
20,000	16,353	0	1,363	0
25,000	19,820	0	1,652	0
30,000	23,288	668	1,941	56
35,000	26,755	1,431	2,230	119
40,000	30,223	2,194	2,519	183
45,000	33,690	2,319	2,808	193
50,000	37,158	4,148	3,096	346
55,000	40,625	5,464	3,385	455
60,000	43,514	6,799	3,626	567
65,000	45,680	7,817	3,807	651
70,000	48,807	9,287	4,067	774
75,000	51,935	10,757	4,328	896
80,000	55,062	12,227	4,589	1,019
85,000	58,190	13,697	4,849	1,141
90,000	61,317	15,166	5,110	1,264
95,000	64,445	16,636	5,370	1,386
100,000	67,572	18,106	5,631	1,509

Table 3.3. Financing parents' contribution (PC) under four different scenarios: percentage impact on monthly budgets

Annual family income	Parents' contribution (annual)	Percentage of gross income required each month to finance PC			
		Pay from current income (0-4-0)	Borrow in full (0-4-10)	Borrow and save (4-4-4)	Save in full (8-4-0)
$ 10,000	$ 0	0.0%	0.0%	0.0%	0.0%
15,000	0	0.0	0.0	0.0	0.0
20,000	0	0.0	0.0	0.0	0.0
25,000	0	0.0	0.0	0.0	0.0
30,000	668	2.2	0.8	0.7	0.7
35,000	1,431	4.1	1.5	1.3	1.2
40,000	2,194	5.5	2.0	1.8	1.6
45,000	2,319	5.2	1.9	1.7	1.5
50,000	4,148	8.3	3.1	2.7	2.4
55,000	5,464	9.9	3.7	3.3	2.9
60,000	6,799	11.3	4.2	3.7	3.3
65,000	7,817	12.0	4.4	3.9	3.5
70,000	9,287	13.3	4.9	4.3	3.9
75,000	10,757	14.3	5.3	4.7	4.2
80,000	12,227	15.3	5.6	5.0	4.5
85,000	13,697	16.1	5.9	5.3	4.7
90,000	15,166	16.9	6.2	5.5	5.0
95,000	16,636	17.5	6.5	5.7	5.1
100,000	18,106	18.1	6.7	5.9	5.3

Values are approximate.

contribution," in the current household budget can be much harder, simply because the amount represents a large portion of annual income, as Table 3.1 illustrates.

At any point on the chart, you can see that the expected parents' share would require a pretty large percentage of income—*if* you were trying to take it all out of current income. At the $55,000 annual income level, for example, the expected parents' contribution would require nearly *10 percent* of gross income, and a whopping *13 percent* of net (after-tax) income. As Table 3.2 demonstrates, that translates into a pretty big chunk of the monthly household budget.

You do not have to finance your share that way. You can if you want to and are able to, but spreading the expense out over time has a much smaller impact on your monthly budget. This is true whether you save, borrow, or both.

By way of illustration, consider these four very different scenarios for financing the *same* parents' contribution:

- Pay the entire contribution out of current income during the four years of enrollment.
- Borrow the full amount of the same contribution,

starting at the point of enrollment and spreading repayment out over the four years of enrollment and the 10 years following graduation.

- Save some of the amount during the four years preceding enrollment, and then borrow the balance, with repayments spread out over the four years of enrollment and the four years following graduation.
- Save the full amount in the eight years preceding and the four years of enrollment.

The four approaches yield the same parents' contribution, but their respective effects on a household's monthly budget differ. Table 3.3 displays parents' contributions as constant percentages of total (pre-tax) income under each of the four scenarios.

To get a feel for how the percentages in Table 3.3 work out in dollar terms, see Table 3.4.

Look again at the $55,000 annual income band in Tables 3.3 and 3.4. Paying the parents' contribution entirely from current income would require modifying consumption by approximately $454 a month. Spreading the expense over time by any of the other

Table 3.4. Financing parents' contribution (PC) under four different scenarios: dollar impact on monthly budgets

		Percentage of gross income required each month to finance PC			
Annual family income	Parents' contribution (annual)	Pay from current income	Borrow in full	Borrow and save	Save in full
$ 25,000	$ 0	$ 0	$ 0	$ 0	$ 0
30,000	668	55	20	18	18
35,000	1,431	120	44	38	35
40,000	2,194	183	67	60	53
45,000	2,319	195	71	64	56
50,000	4,148	346	129	113	100
55,000	5,464	454	170	151	133
60,000	6,799	565	210	185	165
65,000	7,817	650	238	211	190
70,000	9,287	776	286	251	228
75,000	10,757	894	331	294	263
80,000	12,227	1,020	373	333	300
85,000	13,697	1,140	418	375	333
90,000	15,166	1,268	465	413	375
95,000	16,636	1,385	515	451	404
100,000	18,106	1,508	558	492	442

scenarios could reduce the effect on the monthly budget by more than half.

The other important point about Tables 3.3 and 3.4 is that it is *never too late* to plan. If you were to enroll tomorrow and had not yet saved any money, you could still make time work for you by borrowing. The differences in the monthly payouts between the borrowing, saving, and borrowing/saving options in Tables 3.3 and 3.4 are nowhere near as large as the difference between all three of them and the pay-from-current-income options.

However, when you are actually at the point of determining what your family should do, analyze the total *costs* associated with each option. Depending on the length of time you will be making loan payments, the amount of interest you will be paying, the rate of inflation, and the general state of the economy, some borrowing options may be a lot more expensive than others.

NOTE: The values in Tables 3.3 and 3.4 are calculated by a computer model using standard annuity formulas to create a monthly "outlay" computed as a constant percentage of family income. The model also assumes a 7 percent yield on investments, an 11 percent interest rate on borrowed money, and 5 percent annual increases in income and parents' contributions over the period of years associated with each scenario. The model is designed to compare the relative effects of various financing scenarios on a monthly household budget. It cannot be used to compare the relative *costs* associated with those scenarios; borrowing, for instance, typically costs more than saving (except when inflation is high). Furthermore, the model deliberately fixes the monthly outlay as a constant percentage of income for comparison purposes, and thus Tables 3.3 and 3.4 cannot be used as amortization tables.

Questions and answers about making time work for you

Q My child will start college in less than a year. is not it too late to start saving?

A It is *never* too late to make plans. First of all, check your current finances to ensure you are getting as high a rate of return as possible. Second, take steps to make sure that you are creditworthy. If you are going to have to borrow, make sure that your credit history is accurate and that you have not exhausted your borrowing capacity. Third, look at the next chapters for some ideas about ways to finance your share—and reduce your costs. Fourth, investigate financial aid. Remember, even if your child *does* start college next year, he or she will be enrolled for four or more years. You do not just have one year to plan ahead; you have several.

Q Is it wise to borrow for education?

A Borrowing is an honorable way of paying for education; many students *and* parents take out loans to cover college costs. The important thing is not to get in over your head. Chapters 5 and 6 describe some current loan programs designed to help students and parents cover expenses, and Chapter 7 includes consumer advice about responsible borrowing.

Q How do I actually start saving for future educational expenses?

A The worksheets in Chapter 10 will help you estimate probable future college costs and what might be expected of your family toward paying those expenses. Once you have set an overall goal, break it down into annual, monthly, or even weekly goals.

The next chapter describes a variety of approaches to financing your share of the costs. If you have many resources already, you may wish to consult your financial adviser to make sure that your savings and investment programs are achieving your objectives.

4. Making the most of your own resources

Are you concerned that your family cannot come up with enough cash to cover the contribution a college believes you should be able to make? What if a college cannot give you any aid or cannot give you enough to meet your need fully? What if you decide to attend college late in the year, and financial aid has already run out by the time you apply for admission?

Remember that colleges and most other student aid sponsors regard the student and his or her family as the primary source of funds for meeting the cost of education or training after high school. There are rare instances where parents are considered unable to contribute anything whatsoever toward college costs, but even then, the student would be expected to contribute something from savings and summer earnings.

This chapter will review some of the strategies that students and families have used to meet their share of college costs. Not all of these ideas will be applicable to your unique family situation, of course, but perhaps one or two will provoke some creative thinking. (Several commercial and not-for-profit organizations' programs are described in this chapter. Their inclusion is intended to illustrate the wide and growing array of options available to families in meeting college costs but does not imply any endorsement whatsoever.) The next chapter will describe how financial aid—grants and scholarships, loans, and jobs—can cover the gap between your best efforts and the costs of attendance.

If there is a "silver lining" to the rising costs, it is that colleges are working harder than ever not only to contain the costs but also to develop new mechanisms to assist students and families in meeting the costs. This chapter also describes some of the ways that colleges are trying to help families finance education after high school. Not all of these approaches will be available at the particular col- leges you are considering, but they are worth asking about. Make sure that you review the lists in Part III of this book; you will find the names of many colleges that offer special kinds of help to families in financing educational expenses.

Strategies for stretching your resources

Many students and families have used a variety of strategies for getting the most out of the resources they *do* have for meeting college costs. Some of these ideas may work for you, and some may make you angry! This section describes some possible strategies for getting more mileage out of family resources. Remember, the point is to do your share, *not* necessarily to cover the whole expense.

Rearranging your personal finances

Few families can cover their expected share from current earnings only, never mind bridge the gap that could be created by insufficient financial aid resources. To minimize the impact on your household budget when the time comes to start paying college bills, you should start planning as early as possible.

For instance, you might want to think about how your current assets can be resources for paying educational bills. Ask yourself, What are they worth now? What are they most likely to be worth when I want to use them? You may want to talk to your banker, a financial adviser, or an investment specialist about the best way of "saving" for college, given your financial situation. These professionals can offer you advice on financial planning for college based on your present situation, how much time you have left to save, and the risks involved in selecting certain financing alternatives.

The long-range approach

The earlier you start, the more time you have to arrange your personal finances to the greatest advantage. Families with young children, for instance, should think about creating a regular savings plan against the day when their children start college. Starting earlier rather than later really does make a difference. Deposited funds accrue interest, and the effect of compounding can be astonishing over a long period of time.

Many banks, savings and loan organizations, credit unions, investment firms, and other financial institutions market programs designed to help families accumulate resources for their children's future education. Under some programs, families make regular deposits to a savings account at interest rates that increase with the amount of the balance in savings; other programs provide for one-time or periodic payments into various kinds of investment funds or other financial products. Sometimes counseling and financial planning services are included as part of the program.

Tax laws govern several of the ways in which families can accumulate money for college. Consumer guides to the tax laws are widely available in bookstores, and you can also pose questions directly to the local office of the Internal Revenue Service (IRS). Or you may want to seek the help of a professional adviser, such as a Certified Financial Planner (CFP), a Certified Public Accountant (CPA), or a tax attorney. In any case, carefully investigate all the features of the programs offered by banks and investment firms. There is considerable variety in the safety, the yield, and the requirements of college savings programs and products now on the market. Shop around before you invest your hard-earned dollars.

More immediate options

Even if you have to start paying bills within the next year, it is worth your time to talk to your banker about your current savings and investment arrangements. Banks, savings and loan associations, credit unions, and investment firms never have been more eager for your money or have offered so many varieties of plans. The family with several thousand dollars in a passbook savings account is almost certainly not getting the most mileage out of its money.

No college expects you to sell the family homestead to pay for education, but when it comes to awarding their own institutioal funds, some colleges *are* quite explicit about their expectations of families with assets. The Higher Education Amendments of 1992 eliminated consideration of home equity in the case of families at lower income levels for purposes of determining eligibility for federal Title IV student aid. You may find that a college financial aid office wants to know your net return on investments, for instance. Others may suggest that you refinance the mortgage on your home. Others may inquire about the contribution that other members of the extended family (such as grandparents) might make to a student's educational expenses. Such observations from colleges may startle or even anger you, but they reflect a renewed emphasis on the family's central responsibility for financing education or training after high school.

There are some respects in which the family homestead has taken on potential new importance in paying educational expenses. Under the Tax Reform Act of 1986, the consumer interest deduction was phased out over a period of five years, effective December 31, 1986. One important exception is interest on indebtedness securing a taxpayer's principal residence or a second residence, up to the amount of the original purchase price plus improvements. (Taxpayers cannot take out home equity loans on the appreciated value to make consumer purchases and deduct the interest, except in strictly limited cases where loans are to be used for education, medical expenses, or home improvements. Make sure you understand how the IRS rules are applied before you act.)

Many banks are marketing new loans and lines of credit based on home equity. Some of the new programs are geared specifically to educational expenses. As with most financial services, there is considerable variation in the terms of such programs, so you will want to shop both widely and cautiously. Make sure you understand all the implications of using your home this way, not just the tax-related ones.

Here are some other ideas.

Federal Parent Loan
for Undergraduate Students

The Higher Education Amendments of 1992 expanded an important financial resource for families—the Federal Parent Loan for Undergraduate Students (PLUS) Program. (The Federal Stafford Loan Program will be described in the next chapter.)

As of July 1, 1994, parents may borrow up to the

total cost of education *minus* any student aid awarded, per child. (There is no longer an annual limit or aggregate total.) The interest rate on a Federal PLUS Loan is variable, based on the 52-week T-Bill (treasury-bill) rate plus 3.1 percent, and is capped at 9 percent. Monthly repayment begins within 60 days of disbursement although some lenders may permit borrowers to make interest-only payments while the child is still enrolled. Federal PLUS loans are made without regard to financial need, but borrowers must demonstrate that they do not have an adverse credit history.

Because repayment generally must begin within 60 days, Federal PLUS loans are primarily assistance in meeting the cash-flow problems caused by college bills. Some parents borrow under the Federal PLUS program to meet all or part of the expected parental contribution, while others borrow to make up the difference between costs and their contribution plus available financial aid.

Federal PLUS loans are widely available through programs like CollegeCredit™, sponsored by the College Board, as well as many banks, credit unions, and savings and loan associations.

Privately sponsored supplemental loans

Many organizations, banks, and credit unions sponsor special education loan programs that have more favorable interest rates and/or other special features that make the loans more attractive than other consumer borrowing options. Eligibility generally relates more to demonstrated creditworthiness than demonstrated financial need, and parents rather than students are generally the borrowers under such programs (although creditworthy students may be eligible as well).

For example, the College Board sponsors two privately insured supplemental loan programs as part of its CollegeCredit Program. The ExtraCredit™ Loan works like a line of credit for families who want to plan ahead for meeting up to four full years of college costs. Borrowers have up to 15 years to repay; competitive interest rates, high loan limits, fixed monthly payments, and a one-time application process afford families both convenience and control. The EXTRATIME™ Loan provides funds for families who need help in paying for up to the total costs of attendance for a single year of college. Borrowers have up to 15 years to repay. An optional feature of EXTRATIME Loans is that the borrower may choose to pay only the *interest* while the student is enrolled, so that monthly payments are lower when the parents'

expenses are the highest. (For more information about ExtraCredit and EXTRATIME Loans, call 1-800-874-9390.)

A few private supplemental loan programs permit students and parents to borrow *jointly*. For instance, under the MassPlan℠ sponsored by the Massachusetts Educational Financing Authority, parents *and* students from any state may jointly borrow up to 100 percent of the costs of attendance minus any financial aid at 63 participating Massachusetts colleges and universities. Two options are available: a fixed-interest-rate plan and a variable-interest-rate plan. Both have repayment terms of 15 years. Borrowers who secure their loans with a home mortage option may be able to take advantage of the tax deductibility of interest payments. (For information about MassPlan, call 1-800-449-MEFA [6332].)

Chapter 7 contains extensive information about responsible borrowing, and includes some advice about evaluating the terms and features of private supplemental loan programs.

Combination savings/loan plans

This approach to financing a child's education is becoming more widely available. Under such plans, a participating bank will "leverage," or multiply, a customer's balance to give a family a line of credit for meeting college costs that is, in effect, a long-term loan, with the interest on savings offsetting to a substantial degree the interest on the loan.

Terms and conditions of these and similar programs can vary considerably from sponsor to sponsor, so prospective users will want to shop around. Inquire about the availability of programs at banks in your community.

College-sponsored financing programs

Many institutions of higher education participate in a tuition budgeting plan that permits families to spread out their payments over a longer period of time. Some colleges finance the programs themselves, while others participate in commercially available options. Because of the interest, insurance, and service fees involved in such programs, a family will typically end up spending more money than if the charges had been paid outright. However, for families with cash-flow problems or insufficient reserves, as well as for families who prefer to preserve their capital, such programs can be very helpful. Information about the options available at a particular college usually can be found in its catalog or financial aid bulletin; if you do not find it, ask.

Some insurance companies offer tuition budgeting programs to families. Insurance features on plans like these generally guarantee that the tuition will continue to be paid in the event of a parent's death or total disability. Some colleges offer variations on plans like this, financed through their own resources.

In evaluating these approaches to stretching your resources, get all the facts before you sign any contracts, promissory notes, or loan agreements. You should evaluate both what you pay and what you get back to ensure that you are getting the best possible deal.

Do not assume that you can always find financing plans or tuition installment plans at every college and university. Some public institutions, for instance, are prohibited by state law from extending credit to anyone. However, they may be able to direct you to commercial budgeting or installment plans offered by outside companies. Information about programs designed to help you manage educational expenses at a particular college can usually be found in the college's catalog or financial aid bulletin.

Strategies for cutting costs

In the absence of sufficient personal resources and financial aid, one obvious approach to financing a college education is to reduce the overall costs. There are many different ways to cut expenses, and your personal situation and ambitions will determine whether any of these approaches can work for you.

Reducing the time involved in earning a degree

By reducing the length of time involved in earning a degree, you can reduce the overall costs. (Reducing the amount of time you spend in education or training may also reduce your "forgone income," or the amount of money you could otherwise have earned if you were employed.) There are several approaches to cutting time and thus cutting costs.

For instance, many colleges award advanced placement and/or academic credit to students who can demonstrate proficiency in college-level studies through examinations such as those sponsored by the Advanced Placement (AP) Program and the College-Level Examination Program (CLEP) of the College Board. Credit-by-examination means the number of courses required to earn a degree is reduced, so the overall costs are cut. As you investigate colleges, you may want to ask about credit-by-examination policies.

Some colleges also grant advanced placement and/or academic credit to students who can demonstrate proficiency because of prior independent study and "life experience." A student might demonstrate particular competencies or skills, for example, by compiling a portfolio that documents prior learning experiences. College requirements for documenting prior learning tend to be quite rigorous, but if you can meet them, you can reduce both your time and your financial investment. You may find that this approach is less commonly available than credit-by-examination options. You may also find that some colleges offering such opportunities restrict their use to older, "nontraditional" students who have spent several years working or raising a family.

Some students also compress the time required to earn their degrees by taking more courses than the average student and/or attending summer school. (Attending summer classes will cut down on your ability to work during the summer to earn money for college.) Some students successfully complete a bachelor's degree in less than four years, thus reducing their overall costs, but this requires a high degree of motivation. You may want to ask colleges you are considering whether it is possible to earn a degree in less than four years, since some colleges have policies limiting the number of credits a student can carry per semester.

Sometimes students can earn some college credit without actually attending classes, thus reducing transportation and possibly some living expenses. This approach would also allow a student to work and save for full-time attendance later. Check with the colleges you are considering if this appeals to you.

Reducing indirect costs

Living at home instead of on campus has helped many students reduce their overall costs. Some students live at home and commute to campus for the entire course of their studies, while others alternate between living in college housing (or off-campus private housing) and living at home with their families. Other students elect to attend a local, lower cost college (such as a community college) for the first two years and then transfer to a higher cost public or private college to complete their degrees.

Dormitory residents at some colleges have also discovered that savings can be achieved in the choice of college-sponsored meal plans. Investigate carefully the options open to you before you select a particular meal plan.

Some students work in return for room and board in private homes. Information about such opportunities is often available through a college's placement or student affairs office.

Students at many colleges have banded together to provide services for each other that can reduce both their direct educational expenses and their living expenses. The range of student-sponsored services is enormous and well worth investigating as part of your college-search process. Secondhand bookshops enable students to reduce textbook expenses. Food co-ops enable residents in private, off-campus housing to cut their food bills and still get adequate nutrition. Daycare programs provide help to students with dependents of their own. Revolving emergency loan funds can provide short-term financial assistance. Housing referral services or guides can help students to locate private housing, while tenant organizations protect and advocate their rights with landlords. Entertainment programs are specifically designed to provide free or low-cost recreation to students living on a budget.

College administrators, too, have instituted programs at many institutions, usually in conjunction with the student affairs or financial aid offices. The financial aid office may conduct workshops on money management, for instance, or the student activities office may issue guides to low-cost housing and shopping in the community. As the effects of rising costs and declining aid begin to be felt more widely, the number and range of such programs to help students live on a tight budget can be expected to grow.

Guaranteed or stabilized tuition plans

You can expect increases in tuition charges at least once, and probably annually, during your enrollment at a particular college. A few colleges guarantee their tuition for four years at the time of enrollment, at no obligation to the student. Under other plans, families can prepay tuition for four years in one lump sum and escape subsequent tuition increases.

Taking advantage of such programs could reduce your overall expenses, although you may want to consider whether you can get a return on your investments that is equivalent to or better than the rate of tuition increases, while still having the use of your money. For families who do not have enough disposable income to pay the entire sum at once, some colleges offer a borrowing option whereby payment is made in monthly installments over a period of years. However, with the gradual phaseout of consumer interest deductibility, you may want to make some calculations to ensure that this option still makes financial sense for you.

Strategies for working your way through college

Working your way through college is certainly possible, but it is not easy, particularly if you want to attend college on a full-time basis. The problems include both money and time. Educational and living expenses are sufficiently high to make it difficult to earn enough money to cover them fully while maintaining a full course load, but here again, there are a variety of approaches to working your way through. One or more of them may work for you. An estimated half of all college students now hold jobs of some sort.

Part-time employment

Some students find that they can earn enough money through part-time employment to meet their costs. Many students work part time while enrolled full time, and find that a part-time job does not hamper their studies. The Federal Work-Study Program described in Chapter 5 provides employment opportunities for many students with demonstrated financial need. Other students work in jobs, on or off campus, that they find themselves.

Some colleges have made a special commitment to helping students pay some of their educational expenses through working. For example, Cornell University in New York sponsors a unique program that assists students in meeting their educational costs. The Cornell Tradition, a loan-forgiveness fellowship program, recognizes students committed to the work ethic and service. Tradition Fellows receive awards that reduce the amount of their student loans up to $2,500 per year. Since the program's inception, over $10 million has been awarded in recognition of student work and service; about 600 students are recognized annually.

At Babson College in Massachusetts, students are encouraged to own and operate their own businesses, both to earn needed funds and develop hands-on business skills. A student Chamber of Commerce serves as a forum for exchanging ideas and sharing skills, while the Babson Entrepreneurial Exchange links students with alumni and nonalumni business people.

Some colleges have instituted special programs

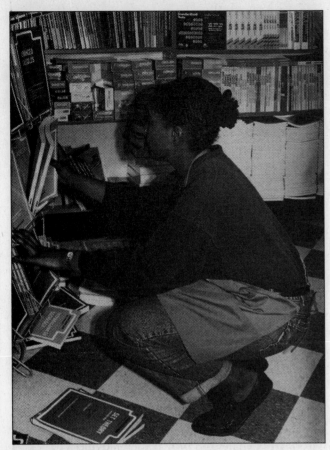

To find out about employment opportunities, such as working in the campus bookstore, contact the job placement office or consult the job bulletin board.

to help students find part-time employment. Check with the financial aid and student employment offices at the colleges you are considering.

You should begin lining up summer job prospects as soon as you are old enough to work. You might also think about acquiring and cultivating skills that will be useful in finding part-time jobs to help finance your education. As you investigate colleges, you may want to inquire about the availability of part-time jobs on and off campus. Admission recruiters, financial aid counselors, and job placement counselors may be able to give you some clues about the kinds of jobs most frequently available. If you are visiting a college, pick up copies of the student newspaper as well as local newspapers to check out the help-wanted ads.

You might be able to tailor some of your precollege courses or summer job experiences to improve your chances in the job market once enrolled. For example, if there is a typically heavy demand for typing term papers at the college you are aiming for, it may be worth your while to take a word processing

course. If there are usually openings on campus and in the community for experienced waiters and waitresses, that might be useful to know when you are looking for summer and part-time jobs in high school.

Unless you have truly unusual and marketable skills, part-time work is not likely to earn you enough money to cover all your expenses, but, depending on your overall costs and your family's ability to contribute toward your education, plus financial aid, you may be able to cover the difference through part-time employment.

Cooperative education

Some students have found that alternating periods of full-time employment and full-time enrollment works best for them. Many colleges have even formalized such arrangements through cooperative education programs. In cooperative education programs, students alternate semesters of academic enrollment with semesters of full-time employment, usually in jobs directly related to their field of study. In addition to helping them finance their studies, cooperative education programs give students a chance to develop concrete job skills and experience that enhance their employability after graduation. About 1,000 colleges and universities across the country offer some form of cooperative education opportunities; inquire about the possibility at the colleges you are considering.

Deferred enrollment

Some students take a year or two off before going to college to get some money in their pockets. Some colleges have formalized this, too—it is called "deferred enrollment." You are accepted, but you do not actually start going to college until the following year. You might keep this in mind as a question to ask about the various colleges you investigate.

Employee fringe benefits

Some students decide to work full time and attend college part time at their employer's expense. Many employers offer educational opportunities as fringe benefits. Sometimes workers are reimbursed, in whole or in part, for successfully completed course work; other programs pay tuition expenses up front. (Check with the Internal Revenue Service for the most current tax treatment of employee educational expense benefits.)

Keep in mind, too, that some unreimbursed educational expenses may be considered tax deductible.

However, under the Tax Reform Act of 1986, they can be deducted only if they meet specific criteria. Check with the IRS for more information.

Managing your time if you work

There have not been many studies of students who combine work and school. The information that does exist, however, tends to show that students who work part time do not usually seem to suffer academically for the time they put into their jobs. Some studies have indicated, in fact, that students who work part time achieve higher grade-point averages than their nonemployed fellow students. For most students who work, the discipline required to juggle their responsibilities and manage their time effectively pays off in academic work, too. (At the same time, some colleges try to minimize the necessity of part-time work for some groups of students, particularly freshmen, in order to ease their transition into college life.) Some students also like the opportunity to develop employment experience in anticipation of job hunting after graduation.

Questions and answers about making the most of your resources

Q My parents have scrimped and saved for my college education, but because we have savings, we won't have as much eligibility for financial aid. Aren't we being penalized for being thrifty?

A You and your parents *will* be expected to contribute something toward the cost of college from the money you and they have saved, but as subsequent chapters will illustrate, the system *also* takes into account your parents' ages and corresponding need to save for retirement. Remember, too, that a student whose parents have no savings must rely much more heavily on financial aid than you. That family may have a heavier work or loan burden than yours will have to carry. In a time when public appropriations for student aid programs are not keeping pace with increases in college costs, your reduced reliance on financial aid may give you a wider range of choices.

Q Didn't tax reform knock out all the incentives for college saving?

A The Tax Reform Act of 1986 affected many of the "income transfer" strategies that some parents have used in the past to accumulate college savings and shelter some assets from taxation by putting them in their children's names. "Clifford Trusts," for instance, were eliminated entirely, and new restrictions were imposed on "generation-skipping" bequests from grandparents.

The experts still have lots of ideas about how families can build up money for college, with or without tax advantages. The more time you give yourself to study the various ideas, the better off you will be. The important thing is to take advantage of whatever time you and your family have before enrollment. The loss of a specific tax break that may have existed in previous years is no reason to stop saving for college.

Q Is the interest on educational loans tax-deductible?

A The Tax Reform Act of 1986 initiated a gradual phaseout of the deductibility of consumer interest on all nonmortgage loans, including loans assumed by students and parents to pay for education, such as Federal Stafford Loans (formerly Guaranteed Student Loans) and Federal PLUS loans. However, interest on home mortgages, including second mortgages up to the fair market value of the house, is still deductible, and interest on debt *in excess* of a house's value may still be deductible if used for educational or medical expenses. Always check with the IRS or your tax adviser before making any personal financial decisions on the basis of tax treatment. Laws change and so do regulations.

Since the passage of the Tax Reform Act of 1986, legislation that would *reinstate* the tax deductibility of student loans has often been contemplated, but is not yet enacted. This could change.

Q Is it better to take out a Federal PLUS Loan or a private supplemental loan?

A Like many financial questions, this one does not have a black-and-white answer.

The interest rate on Federal PLUS Loans will sometimes be lower than supplemental loans, and the rate is always capped by law, making it a better choice for some borrowers.

Other borrowers may prefer the comfort of fixed monthly payments and/or the security of a four-year credit line, available with some private loans, such as ExtraCredit™. "Shop around" before you borrow. Terms and conditions vary widely from program to program. (See Chapter 7 for more advice on responsible borrowing.)

5. How financial aid can help

Financial aid is help for meeting college costs: both direct educational costs (such as tuition, fees, and books) and personal living expenses (such as food, housing, and transportation). People are sometimes surprised that students can get financial aid to help them pay for living expenses. Even colleges with comparatively low tuition, such as community colleges, can give qualified students some help in paying for food, rent, commuting, and other personal expenses.

Many students do not realize that financial aid is available to pay for noncollegiate education and training programs, too. If you are thinking about vocational or trade school after high school, financial aid could be a possibility for you.

Who gets financial aid?

While many scholarships are based on criteria other than demonstrated need, most financial aid today is awarded on the basis of need. (Sometimes factors such as academic performance, career plans, or special abilities are considered in addition to demonstrated need.) Chapter 2 explained that "need" is the difference between what it costs to attend a particular college and what you and your family can afford to pay toward those costs. Students are usually eligible for aid equal to the amount of their demonstrated financial need.

Since the amount a family can afford to pay stays the same whether the costs are high or low, you can see that you would be eligible for different amounts of aid at different colleges. In fact, if you get all the financial aid you are eligible for, you could end up paying the same amount at a high-cost college as you would at a low-cost one.

That is a pretty big "if." In academic year 1994-95, more than 5 million students received an estimated $47 billion in various forms of student assistance

to help them meet the costs of education or training after high school. Large as that amount may seem, it still was not enough fully to meet the need of all the students who could have used some help.

You can improve your chances of getting the outside help you need. Financial aid does not just happen to you. You have to take an active part in the process—by identifying all possible sources of assistance for which you might be eligible (the topic of this chapter) and by applying in the right way at the right time (discussed in Chapter 6).

Types of financial aid

There are three types of financial aid generally offered to undergraduate students in college.

Grants and scholarships. Grants and scholarships are sometimes called gift aid, because you do not have to repay them or work to earn them. Grants are usually awarded on the basis of need alone, while scholarship recipients may have to meet criteria other than or in addition to need (academic achievement, for example).

Educational loans. A form of self-help aid, educational loans are usually subsidized by the state or federal government or by colleges themselves and carry lower interest rates than commercial loans. They have to be repaid, generally after you have graduated or left college.

Student employment or work aid. Another form of self-help aid is student employment or work aid. The Federal Work-Study Program is perhaps the best known example of this kind of assistance. Students work, usually 10 to 15 hours a week, to "earn" their aid.

Financial aid comes from a variety of sources: the federal government, the state government, colleges themselves, and a wide range of private organizations. Most students get a combination of gift aid and self-help aid from a variety of sources. This is called a financial aid package. The financial aid administrator at the college you attend or apply to will help you put your package together.

Eligibility for financial aid

While each program has its own special criteria, certain basic eligibility requirements are common to almost all programs. For instance, to be eligible for many programs, you must be at least a half-time student (usually defined as six semester hours of courses per semester or the equivalent). In some cases, less-than-half-time students may be eligible for some federal funds, but other programs, such as those sponsored by colleges and private organizations, require recipients to attend on a full-time basis, usually at least 12 hours per semester.

You must be enrolled in an eligible program at an eligible institution, according to the aid program's definition. For some federal student aid programs, you can receive aid to attend more than 9,500 eligible institutions, including colleges, universities, and vocational and technical schools. State aid programs are sometimes limited only to accredited colleges and universities. Some programs have restrictions on providing aid to students in certain fields of study (for example, religious studies) or in vocational or technical courses (those that are shorter than six months in duration). Most programs require that you maintain satisfactory academic progress toward a degree or certification and that you be in good standing with the institution you attend.

Federal student aid programs require that a recipient be either a United States citizen, or a noncitizen who is a permanent resident; refugees or persons granted political asylum may be eligible, too. State student aid programs are usually restricted to legal residents of their particular state, although exceptions to this rule do exist, especially in loan programs. College-sponsored and private assistance programs usually require recipients to be citizens of the United States, too, except for a few programs designed for foreign students.

Financial aid from the federal government

The federal government is the largest single source of student assistance, providing over $35 billion—or about 75 percent of all available financial aid

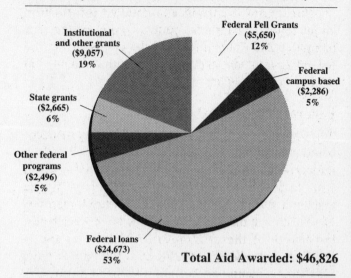

Figure 5.1. Estimated student aid by source for academic year 1994-95 (current dollars in millions)

Institutional and other grants ($9,057) 19%

Federal Pell Grants ($5,650) 12%

Federal campus based ($2,286) 5%

State grants ($2,665) 6%

Other federal programs ($2,496) 5%

Federal loans ($24,673) 53%

Total Aid Awarded: $46,826

Note: "Federal Loans" includes Federal Family Education Loans and Ford Direct Student Loans. "Other Federal Programs" includes SSIG, Military, Other Grants, and Other Loans.

dollars—in academic year 1994-95 (see Figure 5.1). About 74 percent of federal dollars were concentrated in the Federal Family Education Loans Program, and another 16 percent in the Pell Grant Program.

This massive commitment of taxpayer dollars to financial aid reflects the bipartisan national commitment to equalizing postsecondary educational opportunity that has prevailed in the United States since the 1950s—a commitment unparalleled anywhere in the world.

Despite real growth over the past decade, however, federal funding of student aid programs has not kept pace with educational costs. There are many reasons why: the rate at which college costs have been increasing annually, competing demands on the federal budget, the downward pressure of the federal deficit, and the effects of a recessionary economy on families' ability to contribute to educational expenses. But the net result is that federal funds—and indeed, *all* student aid funds—are being stretched further and further to meet growing needs.

In the summer of 1992, Congress "reauthorized" the Higher Education Act. The configuration of federal Title IV student aid programs remained fundamentally the same, but the authorized maximums for some programs were increased. Whether the authorized maximums will actually be available in any given year depends on whether Congress subsequently appropriates more funds.

The Higher Education Amendments of 1992 also modified the formulas for determining eligibility for federal Title IV funds. The result is expanded eligibility for many families.

For the most current and detailed information about federal programs, obtain a copy of the free pamphlet *The Student Aid Guide,* published by the federal government and cited in "Further reading" at the end of this chapter.

Federal Pell Grant Program

The Federal Pell Grant Program is the largest need-based student aid program. An estimated 3.7 million undergraduates received Pell Grants ranging from $100 to $2,300 for the 1994-95 academic year. The amount a student receives depends on need, the costs of education at the particular college he or she attends, the length of the program in which he or she is enrolled, and whether enrollment is full or part time. Graduate students are not eligible, nor are students who have previously received a bachelor's degree. The maximum Pell Grant for 1996-97 is $2,470.

Federal Supplemental Educational Opportunity Grant Program

The Federal Supplemental Educational Opportunity Grant Program (SEOG) is one of three federal campus-based programs. "Campus-based" means that while the money comes from the federal government, the colleges distribute the money to students who demonstrate need. Recipients must be United States citizens enrolled at least half time in an undergraduate program at an accredited college or university. Grants of up to $4,000 a year are awarded on the basis of need. About 991,000 students received Federal SEOGs in 1994-95.

Federal Perkins Loan Program

The Perkins Loan Program is another federal campus-based program administered by colleges and universities. Undergraduate and graduate students enrolled at least half time may borrow up to $3,000 a year for each year of undergraduate study, to a total of $15,000 for an undergraduate degree and $30,000 for graduate and professional study (including any amount borrowed as an undergraduate). Approximately 724,000 students borrowed Perkins Loans in 1994-95.

Federal Perkins Loans carry the lowest interest rate of any educational loans (5 percent) and repayment is deferred until a student graduates or leaves school. Nine months after a student leaves school, regular repayments are required over a maximum period of 10 years until the total amount (including interest) is repaid. A minimum monthly payment of $30 is usually required, unless the college agrees to a lower amount.

Repayment can sometimes be further deferred for up to three years for service in the military, the Peace Corps, or approved comparable organizations, or if study is resumed on at least a half-time basis. (In such instances, however, the student does not get another six-month grace period in which to defer payment.) A student who wants to have repayment of a Federal Perkins Loan deferred for any reason must complete a request form and submit it to the college from which the loan was originally borrowed. Perkins Loans are cancelled outright in the event of a student's death or total disability. (See Chapter 7 for more information about borrowing money from this and other programs, including legal requirements and advice.)

Federal Work-Study Program

The Federal Work-Study Program (FWSP) is also a federal campus-based program. Participating colleges provide employment opportunities for students with demonstrated need who are enrolled for at least half-time study at either the undergraduate or graduate level. Students are almost always employed on campus, although occasionally jobs are arranged off campus. In assigning work-study to aid recipients, financial aid administrators typically take into account their employable skills, class schedule, and academic progress.

Students are generally paid at least the prevailing federal minimum wage. Students may work as many as 40 hours a week under the program, although 10 to 15 hours is far more typical. The only limitation on Federal Work-Study is a student's demonstrated financial need.

Examples of on-campus jobs for students are faculty aide, dining hall worker, library assistant, grounds keeper, office secretary, and financial aid peer counselor. About 713,000 students received help under the Federal Work-Study Program in 1994-95.

Federal Stafford Loan Program

The Federal Stafford Loan Program (formerly called the Guaranteed Student Loan Program) permits students with demonstrated need to borrow money for educational expenses from private sources such as banks, credit unions, savings and loan associations, and educational organizations. For example, the CollegeCredit™ program sponsored by the College Board is a coordinated array of subsidized and unsubsidized educational loans available through participating colleges and universities. In some states, a public agency also acts as a lender; some colleges also participate in the program as lenders.

Because Federal Stafford Loans are subsidized by the government, the interest rate is lower than most commercially available loans (although higher than Perkins Loans). The government pays the interest while the student is enrolled—another big advantage. For new borrowers after July 1, 1994, the interest rate is variable, based on the 91-day Treasury-bill rate plus 3.1 percent, capped at 8.25 percent. Repayment on both interest and principal is deferred until six months after a student graduates or leaves school. In most states, a state government guaranty agency (or a private organization authorized by the state government) insures the loans; in those states where there is no guaranty agency, the federal government insures them, in which case they are called Federally Insured Student Loans. An estimated 4.6 million students borrowed under the subsidized Federal Stafford Loan Program in 1994-95.

Although some states permit half-time students to borrow under the Stafford Loan Program, most states require that borrowers be full-time students. Freshmen may borrow up to $2,625 a year, and upperclassmen may borrow larger amounts annually, to a maximum of $23,000 for dependent undergraduates ($46,000 for independent undergraduates). Graduate and professional students are currently eligible to borrow a maximum of $65,500 in *subsidized* federal Stafford Loans; they may also be able to borrow additional sums under the unsubsidized Stafford Loan program (see below).

If you borrow money under the Stafford Loan Program, you are charged an origination fee or service charge of 3 percent. Your guaranty agency may also charge you an insurance premium of up to 1 percent. This amount is subtracted from the amount of your loan money before you receive payment.

Stafford Loans are insured against the student's death or total disability, but there are no provisions for cancellation of any part of a loan for other reasons. Under certain circumstances (such as full-time study or service in the military or Peace Corps), repayment can be deferred temporarily. The schedule for repayment is worked out between the student and the lender; the borrower usually has between 5 and 10 years to repay, with the amount of monthly payments and the length of the repayment period depending on the total amount borrowed.

The Higher Education Amendments of 1992 created a new resource for students—the *unsubsidized*

Federal Stafford Loan Program. Unsubsidized Stafford Loans are intended for use by students who *do not* qualify for a Federal Stafford Loan and/or who need additional funds. The amounts, interest rates, and terms are generally the same as for subsidized Federal Stafford Student Loans, with a couple of important differences. For example, repayment begins when the loan is disbursed instead of when the student borrower graduates or leaves school; the borrower may opt to postpone payments until leaving school, but interest begins to accrue immediately. An estimated 2.1 million students borrowed from the unsubsidized Stafford Loan Program in 1994-95.

Students at some postsecondary institutions can borrow subsidized and unsubsidized Federal Stafford Loans from the federal government through the new Federal Direct Student Loan Program (FDSLP). If the college you attend is participating in the FDSLP, the financial aid office will tell you how to apply for these loans. (Parents of students enrolled at participating institutions will also be able to borrow Federal PLUS Loans under FDSLP.) The interest rates, maximums, and other terms and conditions of Stafford and PLUS Loans available through the FDSLP are the same as described above.

For more information about Stafford Loans, contact the financial aid office at the colleges you are considering, your guidance counselor, or the guaranty agency for your state listed in Part II of this book. (See Chapter 6 for information about applying and Chapter 7 for advice on responsible borrowing.)

Military options

Military service options are a way of paying for education as you go. Service academies offer a college education at no cost to students, while the Reserve Officers' Training Corps (ROTC) programs help pay for your education at participating colleges and universities. (Still another approach is described elsewhere in this chapter under the heading "Assistance from benefit programs.")

Service academies

The United States service academies prepare both men and women for careers in the military, merchant marine, or Coast Guard. Students attending one of the academies have all expenses paid by the federal government and receive a monthly stipend for incidental expenses as well. Appointments to the academies (with the exception of the Coast Guard) are made through nominations from members of Congress. If you are interested, contact your senator or congressional representative early in the spring of your junior year in high school. Appointments to the Coast Guard Academy are based on national competition for admission. For more information write

Director of Admission
United States Air Force Academy
2304 Cadet Drive, Suite 200
United States Air Force Academy,
Colorado 80840-5025

Director of Admission
United States Military Academy
West Point, New York 10996

Dean of Admission
United States Naval Academy
117 Decatur Road
Annapolis, Maryland 21402-5018

Director of Admission
United States Merchant Marine Academy
Kings Point, New York 11024

Director of Admission
United States Coast Guard Academy
15 Mohegan Avenue
New London, Connecticut 06320-4195

Reserve Officers' Training Corps

Reserve Officers' Training Corps (ROTC) programs are located at approximately 600 colleges and universities across the country; in addition to the institutions that serve as hosts or extensions, there are about 1,800 other institutions in which an ROTC student can cross-enroll. Graduating high school seniors may qualify for competitive four-year ROTC scholarships that typically cover the costs of tuition, fees, and books, and provide a monthly stipend. Students who receive ROTC scholarships must meet certain physical and academic requirements and agree to accept appointment as commissioned officers in the military after graduation. (A minimum of four years' active and two years' reserve duty is required.)

In addition, some ROTC in-college scholarships may be available for students who decide to join as sophomores or even juniors, as well as for students who originally joined ROTC units as nonscholarship

students. The requirements and obligations are somewhat different than for four-year scholarship students.

There are different procedures, requirements, and benefits associated with the ROTC programs operated by the different military services. In addition to ROTC programs, there are also other special programs providing financial assistance for education to students who promise to fulfill a term of military service after graduation; the officer training occurs during summer vacations or after college. A good source for students interested in exploring the various military-related options for college assistance is *How the Military Will Help You Pay for College*, by Don M. Betterton (see "Further reading"), which describes each service's ROTC program, the service academies, and several other programs available to military personnel who want to continue with their education. The book also contains a comprehensive list of host and cross-enrollment institutions. Contact the ROTC units at the colleges you are considering, or write or telephone

HQ AFROTC/RREC
551 East Maxwell Boulevard
Maxwell Air Force Base
Montgomery, Alabama 36112-6106

Army ROTC Scholarship Program
HQ—Cadet Command
Building 56/Scholarship Branch
Fort Monroe, Virginia 23651
Telephone: 1-800-USA-ARMY, ext. 499

Navy-Marine Corps NROTC Scholarship Program
Chief of Naval Education and Training
Code N-2/081
Naval Air Station
250 Dallas Street
Pensacola, Florida 32508-5220
Telephone: 1-800-USA-NAVY

Assistance from the Bureau of Indian Affairs

Students who can demonstrate financial need and are registered as being at least one-fourth Native American or Alaskan native of a federally recognized tribe are eligible for assistance through the Bureau of Indian Affairs (BIA). Scholarship assistance may be used at any accredited postsecondary institution. For more information, contact your tribal education officer, BIA Area Office.

Assistance from benefit programs

Benefit programs are not quite the same as financial aid programs, but they provide many students with assistance in meeting college costs.

Assistance for military personnel and veterans

There are several programs designed to help servicemen and women pursue higher education, as well as to assist veterans. Defense Activity for Non-Traditional Education Support (DANTES) permits military personnel to demonstrate job proficiency, qualify for college admission, or earn college-level credits by taking correspondence courses and/or examinations. Each of the services operates programs in which active duty personnel can take courses on an off-duty basis, and you also may be able to translate some of your on-the-job technical training into college credits later on. If you are thinking about enlisting, carefully explore the educational possibilities associated with the various services, including the requirements and obligations of each.

If you think you may want to go to college eventually but are also interested in the military, investigate the major initiative launched on July 1, 1985, called the Montgomery G.I. Bill, which replaced the former Veteran's Educational Assistance Plan (VEAP). Although an enlisted service person could use the plan to pay for college work while on active duty, it is more likely that people will use the Montgomery G.I. Bill to accumulate benefits for use after discharge. Funds are automatically deducted from your paycheck during your years of active duty. (You can choose not to participate when you enlist, in which case the deduction would not be made.) Depending on how many years you serve on active duty, you could earn several thousand dollars for later use in paying for education.

The "College Fund" currently offers additional benefits beyond those cited. You could earn up to $30,000 in combined G.I. Bill and College Fund benefits. Men and women serving in the reserves can also participate in return for a service commitment, earning up to to $24,000 in combined benefits. Because these programs are still new and subject to modification, they may be changed by the time you are ready to go to college; the most current information can be obtained from military recruiting offices.

If you are already a veteran and want to know whether you or your spouse or dependents qualify for educational assistance, contact your local Veterans Administration (VA) office.

Vocational rehabilitation benefits

Since 1977 the federal Rehabilitation Act has prohibited discrimination on the basis of a handicap and has provided for equal participation by handicapped people in programs and activities of postsecondary educational institutions that receive federal funds. The intent of the law is to assure qualified handicapped students of access to educational programs, including financial aid. Many colleges have tried to expand opportunities, particularly in the Federal Work-Study area.

State vocational rehabilitation agencies in most states can help students with handicaps meet the costs of education or job training after high school. In many states, these agencies are working with groups of financial aid administrators to develop cooperative agreements about financial aid and other assistance for handicapped students enrolled in postsecondary institutions. In developing an aid package for a handicapped student, the financial aid administrator at the college typically will consider both the amount of assistance and the type of services provided by the vocational rehabilitation agency. A handicapped student's expense budget may be larger than a nonhandicapped student's budget, in order to take into account greater expenditures for such things as special equipment, noninsured and nonroutine medical expenses, assistants or attendants, and special transportation. To find out about special help for handicapped students, contact your state department of vocational rehabilitation.

Financial aid from state governments

Every state has a scholarship or grant program that provides some form of financial aid to eligible students who are legal residents of the state. Eligibility criteria vary from state to state. Most state programs award aid to students with demonstrated need, although a few states have some funds available to assist students who meet criteria other than or in addition to need (such as academic performance). Most programs require that students attend a postsecondary institution within the state. Nearly 2 mil-

State vocational rehabilitation agencies can help students with handicaps to meet the costs of a college education.

dents who meet criteria other than or in addition to need (such as academic performance, proposed field of study, or special talents or abilities). See Part III of this book for lists of colleges offering various types of scholarships.

Student employment programs are also provided on many campuses to supplement employment provided through the Federal Work-Study Program. These college-funded job programs usually are not based on financial need but on the special skills of the student employees. Examples include laboratory assistant, business office aide, and dormitory resident adviser. At some colleges, need is also considered in addition to skills and experience.

Short-term and emergency loans usually are available to all students. The repayment period generally is confined to an academic year, and interest is either quite low or not charged at all.

The criteria and application procedures for college programs vary considerably, and your best source of information is the catalog or financial aid bulletin published by the college you are considering. Private colleges often have more college-sponsored aid available to assist students than do public institutions; proprietary or profit-making institutions generally have very little or none at all.

Financial aid from private sources

While aid from the federal government, state governments, and colleges and universities constitutes most of the financial assistance received by students, private student aid programs can offer important assistance. The total amount of funds available through such private programs is comparatively small. For an individual student, however, these programs can mean the difference between attending the college one likes best and the college one can afford. So it is well worth investigating the private programs for which you may be eligible.

There are literally thousands of private student aid programs in the United States that award grants, scholarships, and low-interest loans to students to help them further their education or training after high school. One of the best known programs is the National Merit Scholarship Program, which awards over $37 million each year to about 8,000 students. High school juniors enter the competition for these awards by taking the Preliminary SAT/National Merit

lion students received some form of state grant or scholarship in 1994-95.

Your high school guidance counselor can provide you with additional information about the programs and requirements in your state. Part II of this book contains summaries of the major scholarship and grant programs in each of the 50 states, with an address to which you may write for additional information.

Financial aid from colleges

Assistance programs sponsored and administered by colleges and universities themselves are another important resource. College-sponsored financial aid usually comes from one of two sources: tuition revenues and contributions from private donors.

Some scholarships and grants-in-aid are based on demonstrated need, while others are awarded to stu-

Scholarship Qualifying Test (PSAT/NMSQT) each October at more than 20,000 high schools around the country that offer the test.

Eligibility criteria, application procedures, number of awards given annually, and average award amounts vary tremendously from program to program. Some programs base their awards on financial need, others on need plus other criteria, and still others do not consider need at all. You might qualify because of your

- academic achievement
- religious affiliation
- ethnic or racial heritage
- community activities
- artistic talents
- leadership potential
- athletic ability
- career plans
- proposed field of study
- hobbies and special interests
- parents' employers or union membership
- parents' membership in a civic or fraternal group.

Since virtually everyone can claim to meet one of these general criteria, some perspective on the subject seems important. Frequently, stories appear in the press about the "millions of scholarship dollars that go begging every year." Strictly speaking, that is true, but that does not mean that if *you* go begging for some of them, you will necessarily get any!

Many of the scholarships are tied to particular colleges and universities, or programs of study within those institutions. For instance, there actually may be an obscure little scholarship fund for students with a particular last name, but it has to be used at the particular college that administers that bequest. That means you have to be admitted to that college before you can claim any of the funds. If that happens to be a college you have been accepted to and want to attend anyway, terrific! But trying to finance your education in this way is a little like using coupons to get a discount on a product you do not really want and would never buy under normal circumstances.

Many of the scholarships have very detailed and restrictive eligibility requirements—you might, for instance, have to live in a certain state or region, attend a particular college, pursue a particular course of study, meet certain high academic standards, and demonstrate financial need. If you do not meet them all, you do not qualify.

Nevertheless, it makes good sense to investigate all possible sources of assistance for which you might be eligible. Check with your guidance counselor, and periodically look for notices on your school bulletin board. If you are not yet a senior, read your hometown newspapers (especially in April, May, and June) for the names of scholarships given to graduating seniors in your area. If you think you might qualify, check with the sponsor.

Contact your church or synagogue to see if either the local unit or national organization offers any student aid programs. Contact local civic and fraternal organizations, religious groups, and veterans' posts; many local, state, and national units sponsor some scholarship programs, especially for members' children.

Ask your parents to check with their employers. Many employers have some form of scholarship or grant aid available to help employees' children meet educational expenses; sometimes these programs are competitive, with awards based on academic achievement, while others are based on demonstrated need alone. Some employer programs are even offered as employee fringe benefits, particularly in educational institutions and nonprofit organizations.

If your parents are members of labor unions or trade and professional associations, they may discover that these organizations have some type of aid available to assist members' children. If one of your parents is a military veteran, you might also qualify for some help.

Investigate programs that may be underwritten by local businesses and industries. Community-based Education Opportunity and Upward Bound programs sometimes can assist you in identifying private sources of aid, too.

Scholarship search services

The microcomputer is a powerful tool that can help you in your search for financial aid. Should you use the services of a company that matches you to appropriate scholarships? The Student Advisory Committee of the College Scholarship Service looked at that question a few years ago. Here are the questions that the committee suggests you ask when evaluating a service:

- If the company suggests that large amounts of aid currently are not being used, how does it document the statement?
- How many financial aid sources exist in the com-

pany's computer file? Does the company maintain its own file of sources, or does it use the file of some other company or service?

- Is there a minimum number of sources provided by the company? Are the listings in the form of scholarships, work, loans, or contests? Do they include federal and state programs for which the student will be considered through the regular financial aid application process?

- How often does the company update its list of aid sources? Does the company check to confirm that the source still exists, and that data concerning application deadlines and eligibility criteria are current?

- Can the student apply directly to the aid sources provided by the company, or must he or she be recommended for consideration by some other person or group? Are there application fees for the sources provided?

- How long will the student have to wait for the information? Will the list of aid sources be received prior to application deadlines?

- What characteristics are used to match students with aid sources?

- How successful have previous participants been in obtaining funds from aid sources identified by the company?

- Will the company refund the program fee if aid sources are incorrectly matched with the student's qualifications, if aid sources no longer exist or fail to reply to the student, or if application deadlines for aid sources have already passed when the information is received?

The College Board, in the interest of enabling families to get scholarship information *without* paying a fee, developed a software program that includes a scholarship search. *College Cost Explorer/FUND FINDER*, annually updated software developed in collaboration with the Education Resources Institute and American Student Assistance Corporation, enables you to

- Search a data base of private and public scholarships for ones you are eligble for

- Get detailed cost and scholarship information about 2,800 undergraduate institutions

- Calculate your family's Expected Family Contribution to college costs under the federal methodology.

Students cannot be charged for using *FUND FINDER*.

Check with your library or guidance office to see if they have the program.

You could be pleasantly surprised to discover that there is a local, regional, or national scholarship program aimed specifically at someone with your particular experiences, talents, part-time employment history, career plans, or proposed field of study. Realize that there is no guarantee that you will receive any funds, even if through reputable sources you find and apply for scholarships that you are eligible for.

There are also many helpful publications that describe sources of financial aid. (Some are listed at the end of this chapter.) You may also find some leads on the World Wide Web.

Questions and answers about financial aid

Q With fewer scholarship and loan dollars available and jobs so hard to find, is financial aid available only to people with very low incomes?

A No. You do not have to be poor to receive financial aid, but you have to prove you need it. You are eligible for financial aid equal to the difference between college costs (tuition, living expenses, and so forth) and what you and your family can afford to contribute toward those costs.

Q I've done an estimate of my expected family contribution and financial need on the worksheets in Chapter 10. Can I count on getting this much money to help me?

A Not necessarily. You may be eligible for a certain amount, but you may not be able to get all you are eligible for simply because there is not enough to go around. If you have done the estimate, you have a rough idea of your financial need, but you should be aware of some important limitations on this estimate.

The methods and formulas used in analyzing a family's financial need can and often do change from year to year.

Family situations change. Your family may have unusual personal or financial circumstances that could not be taken adequately into account in these calculations, but would affect your family's ability to pay for education. (An example might be unusually high expenses associated with an illness or a disability.) When the time comes for you actually to apply for financial aid, you can provide more detailed information than you used in completing these worksheets. At that time, you can explain your financial situation in more detail, and note any special family circumstances.

You should be aware that financial aid administrators at colleges can—and often do—adjust the family share calculated by CSS if a change in circumstances or additional information about your situation warrants a revision. This is because a national need analysis system can never accommodate all the special circumstances that make each family's situation unique. For any of these reasons, your expected family contribution and financial need could be different from your current estimate when the time actually comes for you to apply for financial aid. Use the estimates as a tool for planning, but count on doing as much as you can to help yourself.

Q If I am awarded aid, when will I actually get my money?

A You should get your money when you enroll (although not necessarily "on the spot") or at the start of the term or semester for which you enroll. The financial aid officer can tell you exactly when you will receive your award. Note that awards are not necessarily cash grants but may also be in the form of loans and jobs; most students get a combination or "package."

Q I plan to attend school half time, but I'll still need help with expenses. Will going to college part time lessen my chances of receiving aid?

A In awarding aid, many institutions give priority to full-time students; however, you may be eligible for some aid on a half-time basis. Depending on the priorities and availability of funds at a particular college, half-time students could be eligible for virtually all forms of federal aid. Depending on your financial situation, you could be eligible for a Pell Grant. Ask the financial aid office at the colleges you are considering whether part-time students are given any assistance.

Q Are noncitizens eligible for financial aid?

A In most cases noncitizens are not eligible for tax-supported financial aid (such as federal or state assistance). Usually, however, noncitizens who are permanent residents are eligible, as are some refugees. Some colleges may have limited private funds to assist foreign students.

Q Will I receive special consideration if I have brothers and sisters who are continuing their education beyond high school?

A Generally speaking, yes. Your parents will not be expected to contribute as much to your college costs if you have brothers and sisters whom they are also assisting.

Q My older brother was turned down for financial aid last year. Is there any point in my trying for financial aid?

A Definitely! College costs, institutional policies, and your family's financial circumstances change from one year to the next. The only way to know for sure whether you are eligible for financial aid is to apply for it. (See Chapter 6 for details.)

Q My older sister and my next-door neighbor both applied for financial aid at the same school last year. Their house is bigger than ours, and they make more money than our parents, so why did my neighbor get more financial aid than my sister?

A The formulas used to assess family financial strength are designed to treat families in similar circumstances equally. There are many reasons why your neighbor may have received more money than your sister:

1. Although her family has a larger house and a greater total income, they may also owe substantially more money on their home mortgage. If so, they would be able to contribute less to college costs and would be eligible for more aid.

2. The family might have financial circumstances of which you are unaware (more family members, extraordinary medical expenses, and so forth).

3. Your neighbor may have met the criteria for some financial aid award that your sister did not meet. For instance, the college may have been able to award her some aid because of her proposed academic major or because of her past academic achievement.

4. The college did not have enough money to fully meet the needs of all the students who needed some assistance. Unfortunately, when the overall student need at a college exceeds the funds available, the financial aid administrator has to make difficult choices in deciding how much to give each recipient.

But *you* are not your sister. The only way to find out if you are eligible and how much you can receive is to apply for financial aid.

Q Do I have to pay income tax on my student aid award? How about FICA tax on my earnings from work-study jobs?

The Tax Reform Act of 1986 included some new provisions related to the taxation of scholarships and fellowships. Under the new law, grants, scholarships, and fellowships *in excess of* the amount needed for tuition and fees plus related expenses must be included in taxable income. The Internal Revenue Service has ruled that this means that amounts of awards used for tuition, fees, and required books, supplies, and equipment are nontaxable, but amounts used for other indirect expenses—such as room and board—are subject to taxation.* (However, remember that even these portions of your student aid package would be taxable only if you make enough money overall that you are required to pay income taxes.) Ask at your financial aid office or local IRS office if you have questions about the taxability of your aid award.

Under current law, students are *not* required to pay social security (FICA) tax on wages they earn in jobs provided by the colleges and universities they attend, such as jobs in the Federal Work-Study Program. (Jobs with *other* employers are subject to FICA tax withholding.)

Further reading
Many of these publications are available in public and/or school libraries.

General
Annual Register of Grant Support, 1997. 30th ed. New Providence, N.J.: R.R. Bowker. Lists over 3,000 programs providing grant support in the humanities, international affairs, race and minority concerns, education, environment and urban affairs, social sciences, physical sciences, life sciences, technology, and other areas. Revised annually. $199.95 plus $13.30 shipping and handling. R.R. Bowker, 121 Chanlon Rd., New Providence, NJ 07974. Order ISBN 0-8352-3671-4.

Chronicle Financial Aid Guide, 1995-96. Moravia, N.Y.: Chronicle Guidance Publications, Inc., 1995. Information on more than 1,600 financial aid programs for students at high school and undergraduate levels of study, including those offered by noncollege organizations, labor unions, and federal and state governments. Revised annually (1996-97 edition available September 1996). $22.47 plus $2.50

*Department of the Treasury, Internal Revenue Service, Public Affairs Division, News Release IR-87-55, April 13, 1987, page 1.

postage and handling. Contact Chronicle Guidance Publications, 66 Aurora St., P.O. Box 1190, Moravia, NY 13118-1190. Telephone: 1-800-521-8110.

College Blue Book: Scholarships, Fellowships, Grants, and Loans. 25th ed. New York: Macmillan Publishing Co., 1993. Lists sources of financial aid assistance for high school seniors through students in advanced professional programs. One of a set of five volumes, $47 per volume. Simon & Schuster Publishing. Telephone: 1-800-223-2336.

College Costs and Financial Aid Handbook, 1997. 17th ed. New York: College Board Publications, 1996. This how-to reference for students and parents outlines major aid programs, discusses how financial need is determined, and lists current costs and scholarship opportunities at 3,100 two- and four-year public, private, and proprietary institutions. Indexes to colleges that award scholarships for achievement in academics, visual and performing arts, and sports. Revised annually. $16.95 plus $3.95 handling. Order item #005449 from College Board Publications, Box 886, New York, NY 10101-0886.

Financial Aids for Higher Education, 1997. Keeslar, Oreon, ed. 17th ed. Dubuque, Ia.: Wm. C. Brown Company, 1996. Updated biennially. Lists more than 3,000 programs for students entering as college freshmen. Information includes title, sponsor, nature of program, monetary value, rules for eligibility, basis for selection, application procedures, deadline dates, and addresses. $58 plus $2.50 shipping and handling. Order from Brown & Benchmark, a division of Times-Mirror Higher Education, 2460 Kerper Blvd., Dubuque, IA 52001.

Foundation Grants to Individuals. Mills, Carlotta, R., ed. 10th ed. New York: The Foundation Center, 1995. Lists undergraduate and graduate scholarship sources by general and specific requirements. Also includes fellowships, residencies, internships, and grants by U.S. foundations to foreign nationals and citizens and company-sponsored aid. $65 plus $4.50 postage and handling. Order from The Foundation Center, 79 Fifth Ave., 8th Floor, New York, NY 10003.

Fulbrights and Other Grants for Study Abroad, 1996-97. New York: Institute of International Education, 1994. Information on Mutual Educational Exchange, Fulbright, and other grants offered by foreign governments, universities, and private donors. Free. Write U.S. Student Programs Division, IIE, 809 United Nations Plaza, New York, NY 10017.

Need a Lift? Educational Opportunities, Careers,

Loans, Scholarships, Employment. 45th ed. Indianapolis: The American Legion Education Program. Updated annually. Sources of career, scholarship, and loan information for all students, with emphasis on scholarships for veterans, their dependents, and children of deceased or disabled veterans. $3 prepaid. Order from Emblem Sales, Attn.: Need a Lift, P.O. Box 1050, Indianapolis, IN 46206.

The Official Handbook for the CLEP *Examinations.* New York: College Board Publications, 1996. Information about earning college credit for college-level learning acquired elsewhere. Includes questions from general and subject CLEP exams, a description of each examination, test preparation advice, and a list of 1,200 CLEP test centers by city and state. $15 plus $3.95 shipping and handling. Order item #005546 from College Board Publications, Box 886, New York, NY 10101-0886.

The Scholarship Book: The Complete Guide to Private Sector Scholarships, Grants, and Loans for Undergraduates. 5th ed. Cassidy, Daniel J., and Michael J. Alves. Upper Saddle River, N.J.: Prentice Hall, Inc., 1996. Lists over 50,000 private-sector scholarships, grants, loans, fellowships, internships, and contest prizes covering major fields of study. Includes sample form letters requesting information on scholarship application requirements and tips on applying for scholarship money. $24.95 plus $4.29 postage and sales tax where applicable. Order from Prentice Hall, Order Processing Center, P.O. Box 11071, Des Moines IA 50336-1070; or telephone 1-800-947-7700.

The Student Guide. 1996-97. Washington, D.C.: U.S. Department of Education, Office of Student Financial Assistance, 1995. Detailed information on federal student aid programs, eligibility rules, application procedures. Free. Order from Federal Student Aid Programs, P.O. Box 84, Washington, DC 20044, or call 1-800-433-3243. (See also http://www.ed.gov./prog-info/SFA/studentguide/.)

Specific population groups

Directory of Financial Aids for Minorities, 1995-97. 5th ed. Schlacter, Gail Ann. San Carlos, Ca.: Reference Service Press, 1995. Biennial. Over 2,000 references and cross-references to scholarships, fellowships, grants, loans, awards, and internships set aside for ethnic minorities. $47.50, plus $4 for shipping. Order from Reference Service Press, 1100 Industrial Rd., Suite 9, San Carlos, CA 94070.

Directory of Financial Aids for Women, 1995-97. Schlacter, Gail Ann. San Carlos, Ca.: Reference Service Press, 1995. Over 1,500 scholarships, fellowships, grants, loans, awards, and internships set aside for women. $45 plus $4 postage and handling. Order from Reference Service Press, 1100 Industrial Rd., Suite 9, San Carlos, CA 94070.

Educational Assistance and Opportunities Information for Army Family Members. Alexandria, Va.: Department of the Army. A general guide available to the Department of the Army on educational financial assistance of particular interest to dependents of active duty, retired, or deceased Army personnel. Free. Order from Commander U.S. Army Pers. Comm., Attn: TATC-POE, 2461 Eisenhower Ave., Alexandria, VA 22331.

Federal Benefits for Veterans and Dependents. Washington, D.C.: Veterans Administration, 1993. Comprehensive summary of benefits, updated every January. $3.25, prepaid. Order Fact Sheet IS-1 from Superintendent of Documents, U.S. Government Printing Office, Washington, D.C. 20402.

Financial Aid for the Disabled and Their Families. 1996-98. Schlacter, Gail Ann, & R. David Weber. San Carlos, Ca.: Reference Service Press, 1996. Lists hundreds of scholarships, fellowships, loans, grants-in-aid, and awards established for the disabled and their children or parents. 900 entries. Also identifies state educational offices and agencies concerned with the disabled. $39.50 plus $4 for shipping. Order from Reference Service Press, 1100 Industrial Rd., Suite 9, San Carlos, CA 94070.

Financial Aid for Minorities in Business and Law. Garrett Park, Md.: Garrett Park Press, 1994. Lists financial aid sources for minority students specifically in business and legal fields. Other books in the *Financial Aid for Minorities* series cover allied health, education, engineering, science, mass communications and journalism, and sources available regardless of major. $4.95 each *or* $27 for the series. Order from Garrett Park Press, P.O. Box 190, Garrett Park, MD 20896.

Financial Aid for Veterans, Military Personnel and Their Dependents, 1996-98. Schlacter, Gail Ann, and R. David Weber. San Carlos, Ca.: Reference Service Press, 1996. Identifies scholarships, fellowships, loans, grants-in-aid, awards, and internships for military-related personnel. More than 900 references to programs open to applicants at all levels (from high school through postdoctoral) for education, research, travel, training, career development, or emergency situations. $39.50 plus $4 postage and handling. Order from Reference Service Press, 1100 Industrial Rd., Suite 9, San Carlos, CA 94070.

Higher Education Opportunities for Minorities and Women. Washington, D.C.: U.S. Government Printing Office, 1991. Select listing of opportunities for minorities and women in higher education, including some information on scholarships, fellowships, and loans. $8. Order document #065-000-00458-5 from Superintendent of Documents, U.S. Government Printing Office, Washington, DC 20402-9325.

How the Military Will Help You Pay for College. 2nd ed. Betterton, Don M. Princeton, N.J.: Peterson's Guides, 1990. Information about scholarship and financial aid for students going directly to college after high school, including the service academies, ROTC, and other special programs, as well as scholarship and tuition-payment programs for members of the armed forces. $9.95. Available in bookstores.

Fields of study

Allied Health Education Directory, 1996-97. 22nd ed. Chicago: American Medical Association, 1995. Contains a section on financial aid and a listing of allied health education programs. $54.95 plus $11.95 postage and handling. Order from American Medical Association, P.O. Box 109050, Chicago, IL 60610-9050.

Directory of Grants in the Humanities, 1995-96. 9th ed. Phoenix, AZ: Oryx Press, 1995. $84.50 plus $7.00 postage and handling. Contains more than 3,500 current funding programs that support research and performance in literature, language, anthropology, philosophy, ethics, sculpture, crafts, mime, etc. Order from Oryx Press, 4041 N. Central, Suite 700, Phoenix, AZ 85012-3397 or call 1-800-279-6799.

Financial Assistance for Library and Information Studies, Academic Year 1995-96. Chicago: American Library Association, 1995. Produced by Office of Library Personnel Resources. Lists assistance administered by state library agencies and associations, local libraries, and academic institutions. $1 (postage and handling). Order from Office for Library Personnel Resources, American Library Association, 50 East Huron St., Chicago, IL 60611.

Grants and Awards Available to American Writers 1996-97. 19th ed. New York: PEN American Center, 1995. Updated annually. Lists awards granted to American writers to use in the United States or abroad. $13.00. Order from PEN American Center, 568 Broadway, New York, NY 10012.

Grants, Fellowships and Prizes, 1995-96.

Washington, D.C.: American Historical Association, 1995. Lists over 400 history-oriented sources of humanities grants, fellowships, prizes, internships, and awards from undergraduate to senior postdoctoral level. $8 to members; $10 to nonmembers. Updated annually. Order from American Historical Association, 400 A St. SE, Washington, DC 20003.

A Journalist's Road to Success: A Career and Scholarship Guide. Princeton, N.J.: Dow Jones Newspaper Fund, 1996. Updated annually. Information on journalism programs, scholarships, and minority grants. $3.00. Order from Dow Jones Newspaper Fund, P.O. Box 300, Princeton, NJ 08543-0300 or call 1-800-DOW-FUND.

Medical School Admissions Requirements, U.S. and Canada, 1997-98. 45th ed. Washington, D.C.: Association of American Medical Colleges, 1996. Updated annually. Describes U.S. and Canadian medical schools, detailing entrance requirements of each school, selection factors, and curriculum features. It includes up-to-date information on medical education, premedical planning, choosing a medical school, the Medical College Admission Test (MCAT), the American Medical College Application Service (AMCAS), financing a medical education and other aspects of the medical school application and admission process. Information for minority students, high school students, and applicants not admitted to medical school. $15 plus $5 for shipping and handling. Order from Association of American Medical Colleges, 2450 N St. NW, Washington, DC 20037. Attn: Membership and Publication Orders.

The National Directory of Grants and Aid to Individuals in the Arts. 8th ed. Fandel, Nancy A. Des Moines, IA: Washington International Arts Letter, 1993. Lists grants, prizes, and awards for professional work in the U.S. and abroad. Includes information about universities and schools offering aid to students in the arts, as well as retreats and residencies. $30. Order from Washington International Arts Letter, Box 12010, Des Moines, IA 50312.

Scholarships and Loans in Nursing Education, 1996-97. New York: National League for Nursing, 1996. Lists fellowships, scholarships, traineeships, and loans for nursing education, including public funding—federal and state scholarships and loans and work study programs. Outlines packages offered by selected schools and universities; scholarships from community groups and membership organizations for specific purposes and constituencies; fellowships, traineeships, and grants for research and postdoctoral studies; and aid for minority students. Includes tips on how to apply for aid. Bibliography. Appendix of state boards of nursing and brief explanation of the licensing process and types of nursing programs. $16.95 plus $3.95 postage. Order from National League for Nursing, Publications Order Unit, 350 Hudson St., New York, NY 10014. Order No. 41-6789.

Scholarships for Architecture Students. New York: American Institute of Architects, 1993. Poster. Lists major scholarship programs in architecture; accredited schools of architecture; programs for minorities, post-graduates, and professionals. Free. Order from the American Institute of Architects, 1735 New York Ave. NW, Washington, DC 20006.

Student Financial Aid: Speech-Language Pathology and Audiology. Rockville, Md.: American Speech and Hearing Association, 1996. Mimeographed list of general information about grants, scholarships, and loans at the graduate level and aid for graduate education in the field. Free. Order from American Speech-Language Hearing Association, 10801 Rockville Pike, Rockville, MD 20852.

Graduate study

Graduate Guide to Grants 1996-97. Verba, Cynthia. Cambridge, Mass: Harvard University, 1996. Annual publication prepared by the Harvard Graduate School of Arts and Sciences. Designed to help graduate students locate grants and fellowships applicable to a wide range of fields in the arts and sciences. Most grants listed are to support specific research projects—usually dissertation research—but some support earlier stages of graduate study during course work. $25, including postage. Order from Harvard University, Byerly Hall, 8 Garden St., Cambridge, MA 02138.

Graduate Study in Psychology and Associated Fields, 1996. Washington, D.C.: American Psychological Association, 1996. Information about financial assistance and foundations and agencies accepting fellowship applications, as well as information about graduate programs in psychology. $17.95 to members, $19.95 to nonmembers, plus $3.50 for shipping and handling. For charge card orders call 1-800-374-2721. Order from American Psychological Association, 750 First St. NE, Washington, DC 20002-4242.

Grants Register, 1995-97. New York: St. Martin's Press, 1995. Updated biennially. Lists scholarships and fellowships at all levels of graduate study. Includes specific awards for refugees,

war veterans, minorities, and students in unexpected financial difficulties. $95 plus $2.50 postage and handling from St. Martin's Press, Attn.: Cash Sales, 175 Fifth Ave., New York, NY 10010.

Selected List of Fellowship Opportunities and Aids to Advanced Education for U.S. Citizens and Foreign Nationals. Washington, D.C.: The National Science Foundation, 1993. Prepared by the National Research Council of the National Academy of Sciences. Lists organizations, federal and private, offering fellowships at advanced levels of education. International sources included. Free. Order NSF 93-147 from the Publications Office, National Science Foundation, 4201 Wilson Boulevard, Arlington, VA 22230.

The Directory of Biomedical and Health Care Grants, 1995. 9th Ed. Taken from the files of *The Grants* Database. Contains more than 3,100 sources. From pure research and health care services to facility expansion and in-service training programs, the directory features more than 200 sources for *graduate* scholarships and assistantships, fellowships, etc. Order from Oryx Press, 4041 No. Central #700, Phoenix, AZ 85012-3397, 1-800-279-6799.

The Graduate Scholarship Directory. Daniel J. Cassidy. 4th Ed. A guide to scholarships, fellowships, grants, and loans for graduate and professional study. Compiled from the data base of the National Scholarship Research Service (NSRS), this guide lists sources of financial aid in all areas of study: business, education, engineering, and humanities. $24.95 plus $3.50 postage and handling. Order from Career Press, 3 Tica Road, P.O. Box 687, Franklin Lakes, NJ 07417.

Study abroad

Financial Aid for Research and Creative Activities Abroad, 1996-1998. Schlachter, Gail Ann, and R. David Weber. San Carlos, Ca.: Reference Service Press, 1996. Approximately 1,300 opportunities in every major subject area to support research, lectureships, exchange programs, work assignments, conference attendance and creative activities at the high school through postdoctorate and professional level. $45 plus $4.50 shipping. Order from Reference Service Press, 1100 Industrial Rd., Suite 9, San Carlos, CA 94070.

Financial Aid for Study and Training Abroad, 1996-1998. Schlachter, Gail Ann, and R. David Weber. San Carlos, Ca.: Reference Service Press,

1996. More than 900 scholarships, fellowships, loans, and grants to support structured and unstructured study abroad for applicants at any educational level. $38.50 plus $4.50 shipping. Order from Reference Service Press, Suite 9, 1100 Industrial Rd., San Carlos, CA 94070.

Fulbrights and Other Grants for Graduate Study Abroad, 1997-98. New York: Institute of International Education, 1996. Mutual Educational Exchange, Fulbright and other grants offered by foreign governments, universities, and private donors. Free. Order from U.S. Student Programs Division, Institute of International Education, 809 United Nations Plaza, New York, NY 10017-3580.

The Worldwide Scholarship Directory. 4th ed. Cassidy, Daniel J., Santa Rosa, Ca.: National Scholarship Research Service. 1995. Guide to financial aid for worldwide study. Lists scholarships, fellowships, grants, internships, and loans available for graduates and undergraduates in every major field of study. Can be used in many countries by both Americans and international students seeking educational opportunities anywhere in the world. $19.99 (subject to change) plus postage and sales tax where applicable. Order from National Scholarship Research Service, 2280 Airport Blvd., Santa Rosa, CA 95403 or call 1-707-546-6781.

6. Applying for financial aid

If you have estimated your expenses at the colleges that interest you, evaluated your family's financial situation, and concluded that you will need some extra help in meeting educational expenses, then you should apply for financial aid. Even if you are not certain that you will qualify, you should apply—that is the only way to find out if you are eligible. Simply applying for admission to college is not enough. If you think you need financial aid, you *must apply* for aid.

The process of applying for financial aid can be confusing and time-consuming, especially to the first-time applicant. (Yes, you must reapply for aid every year, but it really does seem a lot simpler and less confusing the second time around.) In Chapter 5, you learned about the various types and sources of financial aid. Application requirements differ from college to college (and program to program), but the good news is that you do not really have to file separate applications for each and every one.

In order to improve your chances of getting the aid you need, you must know *what* you have to do, *when* you have to do it, and how to do it right—the first time.

What do you need to do?

Financial aid does not just *happen* to you. You have to provide information about yourself and your family as the first step in the application process.

The process begins with identifying which form or forms you need to complete in order to meet the requirements of the various sources from which you are seeking financial aid. Do not guess! Find out for sure.

All applicants for *federal* student aid, including Federal Stafford Loans, *must* complete the Free Application for Federal Student Aid (FAFSA). The

FAFSA is available from high school guidance offices and college financial aid offices, generally in the late fall. Depending on where you are applying for admission, this may be the *only* form you need to complete.

Your high school counselor can probably tell you what form you need to complete to apply for assistance from your *state* scholarship or grant program. In some states, your FAFSA information is enough to establish your eligibility; in other states, a separate form may be required. If your counselor does not know what is required in your state, contact the appropriate agency at the address listed in Part II of this book.

The FAFSA may also be sufficient to apply for aid at many colleges and universities. However, many other colleges and most private scholarship programs require the completion of *additional* forms. Check with each college and private scholarship program from which you are looking for assistance.

Details about the form requirements for both colleges and private scholarship programs are generally found in the descriptive material they send to applicants, such as college catalogs and special financial aid information packets or brochures. If you do not see the information in these materials or are not certain what it means, contact the college or program and ask.

For purposes of awarding their own private funds, many colleges and universities require the submission of a form in addition to the FAFSA, such as the CSS/Financial Aid PROFILE. If a college you are considering advises you to complete the PROFILE process, ask your guidance counselor or the financial aid office for information about how to register with the College Scholarship Service (CSS).

When you register for PROFILE, you will answer a few questions about yourself and where you are

The starting point in applying for financial aid is getting information about the need analysis form or forms required by the colleges that interest you. Make sure you meet the financial aid application deadlines.

applying for aid. That information forms the basis for your personal record in the CSS processing system, and also permits CSS to customize a package of forms and instructions for you personally.

That package, which you will receive in the mail two to three weeks after you have registered, includes important information about how to complete the PROFILE form and when to return it to CSS for processing in order to meet all your deadlines. The first part of the PROFILE form itself contains questions for all filers, but Section Q includes questions unique to the particular colleges and private scholarship programs to which you are applying. If a particular college or program wants you to complete additional CSS supplemental forms, copies will be included in your package. A sample PROFILE application form for 1996-97 appears at the end of this book on pages 331-337. It is similar to the form that will be available for 1997-98.

Most of the institutions that require or accept the CSS/Financial Aid PROFILE will be listed on a special CSS code list available to registrants. Some colleges may use PROFILE only for certain subsets of their populations, such as Early Admission candidates.

Read the college's material carefully to determine whether and when you need to complete a PROFILE form. Use the four-digit CSS codes when you register for PROFILE (not the six-digit federal codes you list on the FAFSA).

Other colleges and universities do not accept or require PROFILE. Do not list a college, university, or private scholarship program on your PROFILE registration *unless* it appears on the CSS code list *or* the institution or agency has supplied a four-digit CSS code to you privately.

You pay a fee for the CSS/Financial Aid PROFILE service to cover the costs of processing your information and sending it to the colleges and programs from which you are seeking aid. The fee is payable at the time you register, but you may subsequently add more colleges or programs to your list for an additional charge.

Note that PROFILE is *not* the same as a federal form and may not be used to establish eligibility for federal student aid programs. All students who want to apply for federal student aid must complete a FAFSA.

Some colleges, universities, and private scholarship programs may ask you to complete their own financial aid application in order to be considered for private funds. Institutional applications do not usually carry a fee, although a few do. If a college wants you to complete its own institutional application, it will send you the form directly. Private programs sometimes have other requirements as well, such as personal essays or biographical statements.

If you are not sure what forms a particular college wants you to complete, do not guess. *Contact the financial aid office and ask.*

Later in the process, you may receive requests from colleges or other aid sponsors for clarification of information you provided on your original forms. For example, you may be asked to provide copies of your own or your parents' most recent tax return. Or you may receive a letter asking for additional information about some aspect of your application.

Respond to any such inquiries promptly and in as much detail as is requested. Do not assume that something is "wrong" with your application just because you are asked for additional detail. Colleges that administer federal funds are required to verify information from at least a portion of their applicants; some routinely request tax returns from all their aid applicants.

When do you need to do it?

Here again the key is to find out what colleges and programs want from you, and to follow their instructions as closely as possible. Some colleges have deadlines for the receipt of all application materials; others have preferred filing dates; still others will accept applications at any time.

For most types of aid, you start the application process in the fall or winter *preceding* the academic year for which help is needed. Try to submit your FAFSA at least four weeks before the earliest college deadline you need to meet. However, do not file your FAFSA before January 1.

If one or more of the colleges and programs from which you are seeking aid requires completion of a PROFILE form, determine what your earliest deadline is and plan accordingly. Count on two to three weeks between the time you register and the time you receive your customized package; add a minimum of a week to fill out the enclosed form and supplements (if any); then assume another two to three weeks for processing and reporting. In other words, you will want to start the registration process about seven to eight weeks before the earliest college deadline for completed applications on your list.

Some colleges may establish different PROFILE completion deadlines for different sets of applicants. For instance, a college may request Early Decision candidates to submit a PROFILE form to CSS by November 15, all other first-time applicants by January 15, and all renewal applicants by April 15. If you are in doubt about when a college wants you to submit forms, *ask the financial aid office.*

Many private scholarship programs use CSS/Financial Aid PROFILE, including the National Merit Scholarship Corporation. Some programs may decide *not* to be listed on the CSS code list, but will provide applicants with the four-digit CSS code privately.

Still other private scholarship programs use their own applications, and some have deadlines that are far earlier than college deadlines. Some entail substantial effort, such as writing an essay, entering a competition, or compiling a portfolio or dossier of materials. Private sponsors will provide the information to you directly, but do not hesitate to contact the sponsor if you have questions.

After you have started the application process, the important thing is to respond promptly to any follow-up requests for information that you receive from a college or a program.

Generally speaking, it is unwise to wait until you have found out whether you are *admitted* to a college before you apply for financial aid. There are two reasons for not waiting.

First, most colleges try to tell you what financial aid is available before you have to accept their offers of admission; if you *need* financial aid, the colleges understand that you need information about what is available before you can make informed decisions about where to enroll.

Second, if you wait until after you have heard from colleges about your admission applications, their grant and scholarship funds may be exhausted. Colleges do not have enough money to meet fully the needs of all the students who could use some help, and grants and scholarships usually run out first.

How do you do it *right*?

The forms you complete as part of the application process collect information about your family and finances much like that reviewed in Chapter 2—information about income, assets, family size, unusual circumstances, and so forth. Detailed step-by-step instructions are provided.

Read the instructions. Then read them again. If you

do not understand what an instruction means, ask your counselor or call the financial aid office. Enough said.

Get organized. Before you sit down to complete your forms, gather together your most recent income tax returns, W-2 forms, pay stubs, interest statements, home mortgage debt information, records of medical and dental expenses, business or farm records, notices of social security payments for veterans benefits, and other financial records. You will need the records for the calendar year preceding the academic year for which you are seeking assistance. For example, for the 1997-98 academic year, you will need to collect information for calendar year 1996.

Know which federal income tax forms you plan to file, and draft your responses. The tax form you are eligible to file—an IRS 1040, 1040A, or 1040EZ—is one of the factors that influences how your eligibility for federal aid programs will be determined. You do not actually have to *file* your income tax return before you complete financial aid applications, but it is a good idea to at least rough it out. Some questions on the FAFSA are cross-referenced to the most common IRS forms in order to make them easier to complete. Besides, figuring out your answers to your IRS forms in advance—even if you do not actually file your tax return until later—increases the likelihood that if your case is verified, the answers on the financial aid applications will match up with the answers on your tax forms.

Complete all forms accurately, completely, and legibly. Inaccurate or missing information, or unreadable answers, could cause costly delays in the processing of your documents.

Provide all the information requested in the form it is requested. For instance, if the answer calls for a zero, enter a zero. Do not just leave the question blank. (A blank and a zero and a "not applicable" may seem like the same thing to you, but the computers may not interpret them the same way.)

At the same time, do not provide more information than you are asked for. If there is something you want to communicate to a college, for example, and there does not appear to be any place to enter it on the form you are completing, do not try to *force* the information into another answer. Send the college a letter. (If you are completing a CSS/Financial Aid PROFILE form, a blank space is provided in which you can explain special circumstances.)

Keep photocopies of every form you complete. If you are asked for follow-up information, you may need to refer to your original answers. Do not trust your memory.

Identify yourself consistently on all forms you complete. Do not call yourself "John James Doe" on one form and "Jack Doe" on another. Take special care to check that you always write social security numbers correctly. Colleges and programs sometimes need to match up records from multiple sources in order to complete your file, and incorrect social security numbers and variations on your name can slow the process down.

Review carefully all the communications that you receive back from programs and colleges. For example, within a few weeks of completing a FAFSA, you will receive back a Student Aid Report (SAR). If there are errors in the information, make corrections directly on the special page provided, and mail it back to the processor; within another few weeks, you will get a revised SAR. If you complete a CSS/Financial Aid PROFILE form, within a few weeks you will receive from CSS an Acknowledgment. Check the Acknowledgment carefully and follow the instructions provided about correcting information or adding more listings to your original request. You may also receive letters from colleges or private programs requesting additional information.

Respond promptly. If additional information is needed, send it as soon as possible. If you find errors, fix them quickly. When it comes to applying for aid, time *is* money.

Chapter 8—*"Pulling it all together"*—describes what happens to your forms in the final stages of the application process. Do not skip it! It includes some important information about what *you* need to do to nail down your financial aid award.

Questions and answers about applying for financial aid

Q Must I be accepted for admission before I apply for financial aid?

A You should apply for financial aid at the time you apply for admission. Remember, too, that simply applying for admission is not the same as applying for financial aid. To receive aid, you must *apply* for aid; this means that you must file the appropriate form(s). In some cases, you may also be required to submit a separate institutional or state application as well. You will not actually receive aid until you have enrolled.

Q Is it necessary for me to apply for financial aid every year?

A Yes. At most colleges you must apply each academic year, but applying is almost always easier the second time around because there is less paperwork and you are familiar with the process.

Q I want to apply for a scholarship only. Do I have to fill out the FAFSA or the CSS/Financial Aid PROFILE form or both?

A Check with the sponsor of the scholarship and/or the financial aid office at the institution to which you are applying. Find out what forms should be completed and when they are due.

Q How can I find out what the deadline is for applying for aid at the college I am interested in?

A Look for the deadline in Part II of this book or in the college's catalog. If you cannot find it there, ask the college's financial aid office. Be aware that many institutions have "priority filing dates," which you should meet if you possibly can. After that date, some aid may still be available; check with the financial aid office if you are applying later than the deadline or priority date given.

Q One college I'm applying to *requires* the FAFSA plus the CSS/Financial Aid PROFILE form and another *requires* only a FAFSA. What should I do?

A List the college that requires the FAFSA plus the PROFILE form on both forms. List the college that requires *only* the FAFSA on the FAFSA only.

Q My parents are divorced. Who should complete the form?

A The parent with whom you lived for the longest period in the last 12 months should fill out the form. If you did not live with either parent, or lived with each parent for an equal number of days, the form should be filled out by the parent who provided things such as housing, food, clothes, car, medical and dental care, and college costs.

Q Can a college legally require each of my divorced or separated parents to fill out forms?

A To be considered for financial aid, you need to provide FAFSA information only from the parent with whom you live. However, an aid administrator at a particular college can make his or her decision about whether to require both parents to file the PROFILE or other need analysis forms when you are being considered for institutional aid. The current marital status and other obligations of the parent who does not have custody would be considered in this situation.

Q My parents are divorced, but the parent who qualifies and who must complete the form doesn't want to provide the necessary data. However, the parent who doesn't qualify is willing. What should I do?

A According to criteria established by federal programs, the qualifying parent *must* provide information unless an exception is made by a financial aid administrator. However, for purposes of qualifying for aid administered by colleges, the aid administrator at the college may resolve the problem. The administrator may determine, for instance, that there are sufficiently adverse home circumstances that information from the responsible parent cannot be obtained and that information from the other parent is acceptable. This situation should be explained in a letter to your college's financial aid administrator.

Q My parents refuse to file any forms. What should I do?

A In order to be considered for financial aid, you must file a need analysis form. However, aid administrators will sometimes consider special circumstances if they are documented by your cleric, counselor, or social worker. You must realize that resources will be limited because no state or federal funds can be distributed without documented financial need. (You also may be asked to provide a notarized statement of parent nonsupport.)

Q I plan to start college in the fall of 1997. So why do all the forms ask questions about my parents' income from *this* year when I need the money next year?

A 1996 is the last complete year for which your parents' income can be verified through tax returns. If your parents' income in 1997 will differ substantially from their 1996 income, explain this situation. The financial aid administrator may be able to take these special circumstances into consideration in making your award.

Q Will anyone else see the information we provide on a FAFSA or CSS/Financial Aid PROFILE form?

A Information is shared with the colleges and programs you list as recipients because you are seeking financial aid from them. (You should be aware, however, that the federal government *does* routinely perform some data base matches of federal student aid applicants' records with the Selective Service and Immigration and Naturalization Service, for instance.)

Q Should I attach receipts? Will anyone ever ask for receipts? Should I attach my IRS Form 1040 to my FAFSA or CSS/Financial Aid PROFILE form?

A No. Do not enclose receipts. However, financial aid offices at colleges to which you apply may ask for documentation of unusually high expenses that occur during the academic year. It is more likely that they will request a copy of your tax returns to verify expenses that occurred in the prior calendar year. More and more colleges are requesting tax returns to validate information reported on applicants' forms. Do *not* attach a copy of your tax returns to the PROFILE or other need analysis document. If a college or program wants to see your tax returns, send them directly to the address indicated.

Note: A copy of the 1996-97 CSS/Financial Aid PROFILE is reproduced at the back of this book. It is similar to the PROFILE that will be available for 1997-98.

7. Borrowing for education

As costs rise and financial aid resources get tighter, fewer and fewer students will be able to escape the necessity of borrowing some amount of money to complete their education.

Almost half of the student aid dollars available today are in the form of loan dollars, predominantly in the Federal Stafford Student Loan Program. Other federal loans available to students include Federal Perkins Loans and Federal Supplemental Loans for Students. (See Chapters 4 and 5.)

Parents, too, are increasingly turning to public and private loan programs to help finance some or all of their "expected contribution." Federal PLUS Loans and private supplemental loans are among the options available to parents of college students. (See Chapter 4.)

Keep borrowing in perspective

The idea of borrowing to pay for college makes some students and parents anxious. This is especially understandable among people who have never before borrowed money, or who have had a negative experience with borrowing.

But without borrowing, few people could afford houses or cars or major appliances—*or* college. Borrowing can be a useful and appropriate way to help meet college expenses.

If you are worried about your ability to repay a student loan, remember that education usually makes people more employable and thus increases their earning power. U.S. Census data make it clear that the average lifetime earnings of *college* graduates far exceed the average lifetime earnings for high school graduates. By earning a degree or certificate, you will be better prepared to find a job that allows you to repay your student loan.

At the same time, remember that a loan *is* a loan, and not a gift. You are legally responsible for *repay-ing* student loans when you graduate or leave school, and you will have to repay both the *principal*—or the total amount you borrow—and *interest,* which is a fee that you pay for using someone else's money. (There are provisions for certain loans that allow the fulfillment of some or all of the obligation through specific kinds of service.)

How serious are you?

When you borrow, you commit a portion of your *future* income to pay for a *current* expense. That makes it a serious business, so it is important to know how serious *you* are about your education.

If you have grave doubts about your ability to do college-level work, or if you are honestly not sure you are interested in education or training after high school, you might want to hold off on borrowing until you have a clearer sense of what you really want. Taking out a large student loan just to "see how you like college" may not be as sensible as taking courses part time at a low-cost institution or working for a while to save the first semester's tuition.

On the other hand, if you *are* sure about your desire for education, a student loan can be a wise investment in your own future. The education that you purchase with your student loan dollars is something that you will have forever—not a product that will wear out or get used up.

Credit where credit is due

Thinking of your loan as "credit," rather than as "debt," may ease your mind a little. When people lend you money, they extend credit to you because they believe you will be willing and able to repay the money, with interest. That makes it a good deal on both sides of the transaction—and it is why the federal government has put so much money into subsidized student loans.

And, contrary to the headlines, the vast majority of citizens *do* repay their student loans. Furthermore, they go on to participate fully in the social and economic life of the country in a way that justifies the nation's investment in them.

Repayment of student loans *does* leave borrowers with less money in their pockets than they would like, especially in the first few years out of college—but they manage. And as their salaries grow over time, repaying their student loans becomes less burdensome. If financial setbacks occur, they can and do take steps to arrange for temporary relief of student loan payments until their financial situations improve again.

Educate yourself about loans

Your student loan may be the first big legal obligation you have assumed. And it may well be the largest single financial obligation you ever take on, short of a home mortgage. Many students borrow during their undergraduate years, and then borrow more funds for graduate or professional school as well.

Protect yourself by becoming an informed consumer. Take the time to educate yourself about loans in advance of applying for them. Familiarize yourself with the key terms and concepts, and know what questions you should ask *before* you sign on the dotted line.

Learn the language

Know your terms. The amount of money you borrow is called the *principal*. When you pay back a loan, you pay both principal and the *interest*—which is the fee you pay for using someone else's money. Interest is expressed as a percentage.

When you investigate the interest rates on different loans, look for the annual percentage rate (APR). (This is also sometimes called the *simple interest rate*.) Your lender is required by law to tell you what this rate is. Do not be confused by a description that talks about *compound monthly interest*. A 1 1/2 percent monthly compounded interest rate may sound like a better deal than a 10 percent annual interest rate, but spread out over one year, that 1 1/2 percent compounded monthly amounts to nearly 18 percent (12 x 1 1/2 = 18).

How much you pay each month is called the *minimum monthly payment*. Your lender or your financial aid office can help you estimate your minimum monthly payment, which varies by the amount borrowed and the number of years for which you have borrowed it.

The *term* of a loan is how long you have to repay the obligation. This can vary substantially, up to 10 years or more. Some loan programs, such as the Federal Stafford and Federal PLUS Programs, permit you to *prepay* your loan, or pay it off early; that can save you considerable interest. (In other programs, you may pay a penalty if you pay off early.)

The *grace period* is how long you can wait before you have to *start* repaying; this, too, varies by program. With Federal Stafford Loans, for example, you have a grace period of six months after you graduate, leave school, or drop below half-time status. With some supplemental loans, including several privately sponsored loan programs, the borrower (usually the parent) has to begin making payments within 30 to 60 days of the date the loan is *disbursed* (made available).

An *origination fee* is a charge deducted from a loan to pay for the costs of making the loan; some programs have an origination fee and others do not. Some programs also charge an *insurance premium* or a *guaranty fee* to insure your loan, while others may charge an *application fee*, which may or may not be refundable, depending on whether you qualify for the loan. Read the lender's literature carefully to make sure you understand what costs you may be incurring.

Subsidized loans—such as Federal Stafford, Perkins, and PLUS Loans—are loans backed by a guarantor; they usually have a lower interest rate and/or other more favorable features than *commercial* loans. A *guarantor* (or *guarantee agency*) is an organization that agrees to pay the loan if the student does not; state agencies, the federal government, and authorized private organizations are the most typical guarantors for student loans. Some loans are *privately insured* rather than backed by a guarantor.

A *lender* may be a bank, a savings and loan association, a credit union, a finance company, a college or university, a public or quasi-public agency, or a private organization.

Check out several lenders before you make a decision about where to borrow. Even in the case of the government-backed loans, there are some important differences among lenders, such as what kind of *repayment options* they offer. Repayment options can include *graduated repayment*, where payments are smaller in the first few years after you leave school (when earning power is less), and increase later on; and *consolidation*, where you combine multiple loans into a single obligation for smaller monthly payments but a longer repayment term. (Knowing that these *options* are available is important. You should also be aware, however, that exercising such repayment options can add to the *overall* cost of borrowing.)

Regardless of where you borrow or from what loan program you borrow, you will have to provide some information about yourself on a *loan application*; this information may be checked before a loan is actually made to you. A *promissory note* is another name for a legal agreement or contract you sign when you borrow money.

A *cosigner* or *cosignatory* is a person who signs for your loan with you. You do not need a cosigner for Federal Stafford or Perkins Loans, but you may be asked for one if you borrow from other loan programs, particularly if you are a minor.

If you *default*, or fail to repay your loan when it comes due, a cosigner is legally responsible for your debt. There are other things that can happen, too, if you default on a loan. Your *credit record* (or *credit history*) will most likely be damaged, which will create problems for you if you want to borrow money for other purchases, like a car or a house (or more education). Your salary may be *attached* (or *garnished*), which means that your employer is legally required to turn over part of your earnings to your lender; your federal income tax refund may also be withheld.

People sometimes default because they do not know that other options are available to them—options that would protect their credit records and help them meet their obligations. Under certain circumstances, for example, you may qualify for *deferment*, or temporary postponement of payments (*forbearance*); interest may or may not continue to *accrue* (or add up) during this time.

Evaluate how much you need

Make a realistic but conservative estimate of how much you really *need* to borrow. Remember, you do not have to borrow the maximum amount available. Have you exhausted other alternatives for meeting your expenses? Could you cut your expenses a little, or perhaps work a bit more and borrow a bit less?

Borrowing *more* than you really need just because the yearly or aggregate maximums are higher than your immediate need can be risky. It could impede your eventual ability to repay your loans, or at least reduce your borrowing capacity at a point in the future when you genuinely need more money.

At the same time, borrowing *less* than you really need can also be risky, but in a different way. You do

Table 7.1. Selected average starting salaries[1]

College major	Starting salary
Chemical engineering	$ 41,516
Electrical engineering	37,662
Mechanical engineering	36,907
Computer engineering	36,591
Industrial engineering	36,258
Computer science	34,565
Allied health	34,061
Management information systems	32,476
Civil engineering	31,775
Nursing	31,632
Accounting	28,971
Economics/finance	27,789
Business administration	27,032
Marketing	26,217
Political science/government	23,943
English	21,973
Psychology	20,932
Sociology	20,041

[1] Excerpted from the National Association of Colleges and Employers March 1996 *Salary Survey*. Data are compiled from offers extended to students graduating between September 1, 1995, and March 13, 1996, as reported by 365 college and university career service offices nationwide.

not want to jeopardize your enrollment by trying to get by on a lot less money than is really required to meet your educational expenses. For one thing, if you drop out of school *before* achieving your degree, you will be at a disadvantage in the job market, but you will still have a loan to repay!

Estimate how much you can repay

Estimating how much debt you can manage becomes more critical every time you borrow (and many students borrow more than once, and from more than one program). Take into account the amounts you have already borrowed, how much more you will need to complete your education (including graduate or professional school, if that is in your plans), your estimated monthly payments, and starting salaries for the kinds of jobs you are likely to get once you graduate.

According to the U.S. Census Bureau, the average monthly income for persons with a bachelor's degree is $2,109, while monthly incomes for persons with professional degrees average $4,323. Of course, those figures are for all workers with degrees. A somewhat better frame of reference for estimating your own future earnings are the data in Table 7.1, which displays average starting salary data for stulater on; that is not the case, although sometimes it may be possible.

Whether you are considering a subsidized government loan or a commercial loan, you should know the answers to all of these questions before you commit yourself:

- What is the simple interest rate?
- When will you have to begin repayment?
- How large will the monthly payments be, and how long will you be paying back the loan?
- Are there any extra charges involved in borrowing the money? (For instance, you may have to pay an origination fee, service fee, or insurance charges up front.)
- Are there any restrictions?
- Can the lender terminate the loan, and under what conditions?
  Do you have to be notified before cancellation?
- Can you terminate the loan before the contract is up? How much notice must you give the lender? Are there any prepayment penalties, such as additional costs for paying the loan off early?
- Does the loan agreement contain a "balloon clause"—one payment, usually larger than the rest, that is tacked onto the end of the contract? (Sometimes borrowers cannot afford to pay this larger sum when the time comes and must get their loans refinanced.)
- Does the contract include a clause allowing wage assignments or garnisheeing? Such a clause allows the lender to ask your employer to take out a specified sum from your monthly earnings and send it to the lender if you default on your loan for any reason, and without any legal procedure. Most banks have eliminated such clauses from their loan contracts, and you should avoid any contract with such a clause.
- What kind of repayment options does the lender offer? Can you count on graduated repayment and/or consolidation options later on?
- Have you taken out other loans from this lender already? If you plan to borrow under the Federal Stafford Student Loan Program for each of your years in school, it makes sense to borrow from a single lender. That will make it easier for you to manage your obligations when you go into repayment, as well as to request consolidation if you decide you want it.

Before you sign any contract or promissory note, make sure you understand what it is all about. If something is unclear, do not be embarrassed to ask for an explanation. You have the right to seek outside counsel and advice before entering into any binding legal agreement.

Questions and answers about borrowing for education

Q Our family didn't qualify for need-based aid. Is any help available?

A A Federal PLUS Loan is a possibility, because you do not have to demonstrate financial need. A Federal PLUS Loan is a government-sponsored loan for *parents* of dependent students. Parents at all income levels may apply; these are "signature loans" that require no collateral. You may borrow from any lender approved by the U.S. Department of Education.

If you are creditworthy, you may also be able to qualify for a privately insured supplemental loan. These programs take many forms, from lines of credit and tuition budgeting plans to more conventional installment loans for students and/or parents. (See Chapter 4 for some examples, or ask your financial aid office for suggestions.)

Q My child is taking out a Federal Stafford Loan. May I take out a Federal PLUS Loan, too?

A Yes. In many families, both students and parents help to pay for college. Your child is legally responsible for Federal Stafford Loan repayment, and you are legally responsible for Federal PLUS Loan repayment. (You may also borrow under a private supplemental loan program, if you are creditworthy.) In some loan programs, both the student and the parent(s) are actually co-signatories on the loan, and legally share the obligation for repayment.

Q How much should I borrow?

A Ask yourself two questions: How much do I really need, and how much can I eventually repay?

Estimating how much debt you can manage becomes more critical each time you borrow. Take into account amounts you have already borrowed, how much more you will need to complete your education (including graduate or professional school, if that is in your plans), your estimated monthly payments, and starting salaries for the kinds of jobs you are likely to get. (If you are a *parent*, and you are thinking about a Federal PLUS Loan or a privately sponsored supplemental loan, you may want to consider how much you have already borrowed for education as well as for other purposes, how much more you are likely to need to educate other children, other family needs and goals, your current salary and your prospects over the next several years, and how much debt you can handle for a sustained period.)

Q Can I borrow more than once, or from more than one program?

A Yes, many students borrow under the Federal Stafford Loan Program for each year in school; many also borrow from other loan programs.

Keep in mind, though, that each time you borrow from a new loan program, you create a new repayment obligation. Unless you eventually consolidate your loans, you may have separate minimum monthly payments to make on *each* loan program.

Q What is consolidation?

A Once you have entered your grace period or actually started repayment, you may be able to combine your Federal Stafford Loans and most other government-sponsored student loans into one debt. The result is a single monthly payment for the consolidated debt, which is smaller than the total of the separate monthly payments, at least in the initial years. You generally get more time to pay off the consolidated debt, but you'll also pay more in interest.

Investigate consolidation options before you borrow. The option is not available with all lenders.

8. Pulling it all together

Most of this book has been about how you interact with other people and agencies and institutions in the process of planning to pay for college. (That is partly because most of this book has been about getting other people's help for meeting college costs!) You have read about *guidelines*—for estimating costs, for demonstrating need, for determining eligibility. You have learned about *questions* you will be asked—questions about your income and your assets, your hopes, and your needs. You have heard about *decisions*—how colleges, the federal government, state student assistance agencies, and private scholarship programs make them.

In the end it comes down to the student and his or her family. There are a lot of people who will help you to pull together a personal financing strategy, get financial aid, or offer you advice. But advice is cheap—college is not. At some point in the process (the earlier the better), you need to develop your own guidelines, ask yourself some questions, and make some personal decisions.

Understanding financial aid awards

On page 50 you will see a sample financial aid award letter. In mid-spring of your senior year of high school, you will begin to receive notices from financial aid administrators at the colleges to which you applied. Most selective institutions tell you about their admission and aid decisions at the same time, often around April 15. Other institutions may have a "rolling" admission schedule—that is, they make admission decisions as soon as applications are complete—and use either a rolling or a fixed schedule for telling admitted students about their financial aid awards.

Sometimes financial aid administrators will not know exactly how much money is available in the aggregate to help their applicants; uncertainty about state or federal student aid appropriations, for example, can make estimating difficult. Many colleges issue tentative or preliminary award notices in the spring, which are subsequently confirmed in the summer when more information becomes available. In such a circumstance, a college will try to meet its original commitment to a student, but if government funds are reduced, the college may have to adjust the original award offer. The colleges find this process just as frustrating as do families, but in a time of uncertainty, it may simply be unavoidable.

Comparing award offers

If you are considering more than one college, you may want to compare the financial aid awards offered by the colleges. Resist the temptation to look only at the amount of the awards! College A may offer you $1,500 and College B may offer you $3,000. You need to look at the total student expense budgets at College A and College B before you can determine which award comes closer to meeting your need. The smaller award from College A may be all the extra help you need to attend, while the award from College B may not be enough to bridge the gap.

Here are some points to consider in comparing financial aid awards:

- What is the budget that the college used in determining your award offer? Does it coincide with your estimated budget for that college?
- What is the amount determined by the college that you and your family can be expected to pay toward college costs?
- How much of your need is met at each college—costs minus family contribution?
- What portion of each financial aid package is made up of gift aid (scholarships and grants) and

BROOKDALE COLLEGE

Ms. Juanita L. Student
21 Cornwall Lane
Centerville, CA 95007

Date   06/28/96

ID#   123-45-6789

Dear Juanita:

We have completed our review of your application for financial assistance from Brookdale College. Listed below is the financial aid that we can offer to you at this time, showing how it will be paid to you during the year.

SOURCE:	FALL	WINTER	SPRING	TOTAL
Jacobson Family Grant	667	667	666	2,000
Federal Work-Study Employment	779	778	778	2,335
Federal Pell Grant (ESTIMATED)	284	283	283	850
State Award: Cal Grant	367	367	366	1,100
	2,097	2,095	2,093	6,285

Our decision was based on an analysis of your estimated costs and projected family and other resources. In addition to the awards listed above we recommend that you apply for a Federal Stafford Loan in the amount of $2,625. For information or an application for the loan, contact the Financial Aid Office.

The Jacobson Family Grant was provided by Mr. E.C. Jacobson. If you wish to write him a thank you letter, it should be addressed to him care of my office. We will forward it to him with our annual accounting for the fund.

Please read the enclosed financial aid brochure carefully. If you wish to accept these awards, please complete and return the form enclosed within 30 days. If you have any questions or would like further information, please telephone my office.

Kathleen M. Brouder
Dean of Admission and Financial Aid

A FICTIONAL, NON-DEGREE-GRANTING INSTITUTION

what portion consists of self-help aid (loan and work)?

- Which college would you most like to attend from an educational standpoint? From a financial standpoint, is this college also your best choice? If not, is the aid offered sufficient to permit you to attend?

Worksheet 6 in Chapter 10 provides a simple framework in which to analyze and compare your financial aid awards from various colleges. Remember, the point is not so much how many dollars you are awarded as how much of your need is met.

Accepting a financial aid award

After you have received award letters from the colleges to which you applied and have compared the offers, accept the award at the college you choose by signing the award letter. Complete and return any additional forms that were sent with the award letter. Also notify the other colleges that you are declining their aid offers, so that the funds can be distributed to other students.

If you have any questions about your award, contact the financial aid office at the college. Sometimes revisions in the composition of your award package are possible. For example, you may be able to shift a loan to a work opportunity. You are usually not required to accept the entire financial aid package as offered. If you decide not to accept a part of your aid offer, it may not be possible for the financial aid office to restore that aid later, should you change your mind.

Particularly in a time of declining resources, you should understand that if you need financial aid to meet college costs, you will almost certainly have to accept some of that aid in the form of self-help aid— that is, loans and/or jobs—during the course of your education. Many colleges gradually increase the self-help portion of a student's financial aid package over the four years he or she is enrolled, so you cannot necessarily expect the same package every year, even if your need is the same. For instance, some colleges try to minimize the Federal Work-Study awards offered to freshmen so that they can devote more time to studying and adjusting to college life, but colleges that do this may replace some of the grant aid in the freshman packages with jobs in subsequent years.

Appealing your award package

If you believe that your financial aid package is insufficient to meet your needs, you may want to contact the financial aid office at the college. Inquire about how your expense budget was put together and how your family contribution and financial need were determined. If there are special circumstances that you think have been overlooked, bring these to the aid administrator's attention. It may be that the aid administrator can take your particular situation into account and adjust your award offer.

After visiting with the aid administrator, if you still feel that you have unmet needs or that you have been treated unfairly, you may want to consider appealing your award. Some colleges have a formal administrative procedure with a review board to hear your appeal. Others have a much less formal process: usually the award decision is reviewed by the aid administrator's superior to see that institutional policies have been followed. Contact the financial aid office to find out what the appeal procedures are, and follow them.

Understand, though, that a college's inability to meet your full need probably reflects nothing more than insufficient funds. There has never been enough aid to meet the needs fully of all the students who could use some extra help, and when this book was written, resources were shrinking, not expanding. You have a right to a full explanation of a college's policies and practices with regard to determining need, eligibility, and priorities for distribution of funds, and a college will probably be happy to provide you with this information. The answers to your questions will not necessarily provide the answers to your financial problems. (You may want to review Chapter 4 for some ideas on getting the most mileage out of your own resources.)

Loans and your aid award package

Your financial aid award letter may include the recommendation that you borrow from the Federal Stafford Student Loan Program as part of your aid package.

You will need to complete a separate application for the Federal Stafford Student Loan Program. Your award letter will tell you how to proceed. Some colleges send applications directly to their students; in other situations, you may receive a loan application from your state guaranty agency or be directed to pick one up from your local bank.

The processing of Federal Stafford Student Loan applications varies somewhat from state to state, but the basics are the same. As the borrower, you complete one section of the application. Your financial aid administrator completes another, certifying that you are enrolled or have been admitted and providing other information about the cost of education and the financial aid awarded. The application is sent to your lender, and once the loan has been made, the application is sent on (either by mail or electronically) to your guarantor for approval.

At some colleges and universities, students may now apply directly to the government for subsidized and unsubsidized Federal Stafford and Federal PLUS Loans. If the college or university you choose to attend is a participant in the Federal Direct Student Loan Program (FDSLP), the financial aid office will explain to you exactly how and when to apply for loans through the institution. (Note that the terms and conditions of the Federal Stafford and Federal PLUS Loans are the same, regardless of whether you borrow from a private lender or through your college.)

Read carefully any information about how to borrow from the Federal Stafford Student Loan Program that accompanies your award letter. Follow the instructions completely and promptly. If you are uncertain how to proceed, call or write the aid office for additional details.

Your aid package may also contain an award of a Federal Perkins Loan. If you are awarded a Federal Perkins Loan, you will not have to complete a separate loan application. However, you will be required to sign a promissory note for each loan advance. A copy of the promissory note and other loan information is provided to recipients in accordance with federal loan disclosure laws. Recipients may also have to provide additional information at some point in the process, such as a list of personal references.

When you review your award letter, make sure you understand exactly what kind of aid you are being offered and what you must do to receive it. Take particular notice of any loans you are awarded, and whether you need to file separate applications in order to get the funds. (And remember the advice in Chapter 7 about borrowing only as much as you *really* need.)

Work and your aid award package

Many students receive a work-study job as part of their aid packages, generally through the Federal Work-Study Program (although some colleges also sponsor work-study programs of their own). Your aid award will tell you how much of your package you are expected to earn through your work-study job, but will not typically tell you what kind of job you will get. The aid award notice will explain to you how to find out about and apply for eligible jobs, usually on campus.

A student who receives funding under the Federal Work-Study Program will be required to file a federal income tax witholding form (Form W-4) or witholding exemption form (Form W-4E) with the college before he or she can earn any funds. The financial aid office will provide you with full information and copies of the necessary forms.

Private scholarships and your aid award package

Thousands of organizations other than colleges and universities and state and federal governments provide scholarships to thousands of students every year. The way that these outside awards "fit" into a financial aid package can sometimes cause confusion—or even bad feelings—among recipients *and* donors. Often students receive outside scholarships *after* they have already received notification about colleges' financial aid awards. If a student's package was designed to meet demonstrated financial need fully, as discussed earlier in this book, then the college *must* make adjustments in the original award to comply with federal regulations that prohibit recipients of federal aid from getting *more* money than they need. Even if their original awards from colleges did not fully meet their demonstrated need, outside scholarship winners sometimes find that their packages are nonetheless reduced; this might occur because the colleges have a policy of reducing packages to maximize limited resources. A review of the institution's policy in advance can prevent disappointment about the nature of the reduction.

A few years ago, the New England Regional Office of the College Board asked an advisory committee of college financial aid administrators, high school guidance counselors, and foundation personnel to look at some of the problems that were occurring in that particular region of the country. The advisory committee discovered wide differences in colleges' policies regarding financial aid packaging, the percentage of demonstrated financial need met, and how outside awards were treated—a diversity repeated across the country. The committee helped create a pamphlet addressed to high school students who were applying for or had received outside scholarship assistance. Here is some of the good advice included in that pamphlet:

Q. *If I receive financial aid from the college I'm planning to attend, and then I am awarded a scholarship from a civic group or business organization, how do I know if the college will change its financial aid award?*

A. The only way to be sure if your financial aid award will be adjusted is to check the policy of the institution you plan to attend. The financial aid officer at the college or university is your best source of information. A quick review of the institution's financial aid materials might also provide the answers. Remember, policies differ greatly from one institution to another. What may be true for your classmate's college may not be true for yours.

Q. *Is it true that my institutional financial aid can be reduced by as much as the full amount of any outside scholarship I receive? That seems really unfair.*

A. The answer depends primarily on whether or not your institution has already met your financial need (as measured by the institution). The answer: probably yes if your need has been met; probably no if your need has not been met.

Q. *What if I decide to avoid all this and do not report an outside scholarship to my college?*

A. That is a bad idea. Institutional policies and state and federal regulations require that if you are a candidate for financial aid, you must report your outside scholarships to the financial aid office of the institution you are planning to attend. Remember, the information you and your parents provide about your financial situation and your outside scholarships must be complete and accurate. If it is not, you risk losing your entire financial aid package.

So what happens if a student's need has already been fully met and he or she receives an outside scholarship? The advisory committee noted that different colleges have different ways of handling the situation. Some reduce the gift aid (grants or scholarships) in the institutional offer by the same amount as the outside award. Others reduce the self-help (work and/or loan) portion of the package, while still others adjust both the gift and the self-help portions. If a student's need has *not* been fully met, however,

the committee noted that many colleges would apply the amount of the outside award against the student's remaining unmet need, and not reduce the aid package until the student's need was fully met.

The advisory committee noted that students were still better off receiving outside scholarships even if their institutional awards were reduced, simply because "only a small number of New England institutions will reduce your institutional gift aid by the full value of your outside scholarship," a situation that holds true in most areas of the country. Investigating institutional policies in advance is certainly advisable, as the committee recommended, and high school counselors and college financial aid administrators continue to be good sources of information and advice on this subject.

Your rights and responsibilities

Education or training after high school requires an investment of time, money, and energy. Some people think of students as consumers, and feel that students, like other consumers, have both rights and responsibilities. The federal government has outlined a series of rights and responsibilities that you may want to keep in mind as you develop a personal financial plan and pursue financial aid opportunities.

Student rights

You have a right to receive the following information from a college:

- what financial aid is available, including information about federal, state, and institutional programs
- what the deadlines are for applying for each kind of aid
- what the cost of attendance is, and what the refund policies are if you withdraw
- what criteria the college uses to select aid recipients
- how the college determines your financial need, including how student expenses are figured in your budget
- what resources, such as parents' contribution, other financial aid and benefits, assets, and so on, are considered in determining your need
- how much of your financial need has been met
- what aid resources make up your financial package
- what part of the aid received must be repaid and what part is grant aid
- if you receive a student loan, what the interest rate is, what the total amount is that must be repaid,

what the procedures are for paying back the loan, how long you have to repay, and when repayment is to begin

- what the procedures are for appealing a financial aid decision if you feel you have been treated unfairly
- how the college determines whether or not you are making satisfactory academic progress, and what happens if you are not

Student responsibilities

You have a responsibility to

- review and consider all information about a college's program before you enroll
- pay special attention to your application for student financial aid, including completing it accurately and submitting it on time to the right place. (Errors can delay your getting aid, and intentional misreporting of information is a violation of law subject to penalties under the United States Criminal Code.)
- return all additional documentation, verification, corrections, and/or new information requested either by the financial aid administrator or the agency to which you submitted your application, read and understand all forms that you are asked to sign and keep copies of them, accept responsibility for all agreements signed by you
- notify the lender of a loan you receive of any change in your name, address, or school status
- perform in a satisfactory manner the work that is agreed upon in accepting the aid if you are assigned student employment
- know and comply with the deadlines for applying and for reapplying for aid
- know and comply with your college's refund policies and procedures.

Questions and answers about pulling it all together

Q If I accept a college's financial aid offer, how can I be sure of getting the same amount of money next year? How do I renew my award?

A The terms and conditions of your award will be spelled out in your award letter and/or accompanying literature from the aid office. Review this information carefully to make sure you understand exactly what you have to do to maintain your eligibility.

For several reasons, you may not receive exactly the same financial aid package next year. Your parents' income could go up (or down), or the college's tuition and room and board charges could increase. The college may have more or fewer aid dollars to distribute, or government funding could increase or decrease. Factors like these could influence the amount for which you qualify.

It is also possible that the *contents* of your financial aid package may change somewhat, even if its overall value stays approximately the same. Some colleges do not like to give first-year students too much work-study, for example, lest jobs distract them from academics in the critical first year. Others try to minimize loans until students have demonstrated their persistence by successfully completing a year or two.

The important thing to remember is that the financial aid office is there to *help* you. The staff are as anxious to see you make it—academically and financially—as you are. If you are worried about getting help for future years, or have any questions at all about what your package means or what you need to do to maintain your eligibility, call the aid office and *ask*.

Q I decided really late in the school year that I want to go to college in the fall. Is there any chance that I can still get some financial aid?

A It is possible, but you will have to act quickly!

If you have already initiated the *admission* application process, call the aid office to find out what you need to do to apply for assistance. If you have not taken any action whatsoever yet, call the admission office and explain that you need information about applying for admission and financial aid.

If you are eligible for a Federal Pell Grant and/or a Federal Stafford Student Loan, you can still apply. However, you are likely to find that you have missed the deadline for state aid, college scholarships, and other programs administered by the college, like work-study. (You *may* be able to get consideration for some of these during the second semester.)

Q My parents say they just can't (or won't) come up with the amount of the expected contribution, and the aid offer from the college I like best just doesn't go far enough. What should I do?

A You can call or write the aid office to explain your situation and see if the staff have any suggestions. Some colleges have installment payment programs or tuition budgeting plans that might make it easier for your parents to finance their contribution. You could also investigate Federal PLUS Loans (for parents) or one of the privately sponsored supplemental loan programs.

If you truly have extenuating circumstances that affect your family's ability to contribute to your educational expenses, the aid office *may* be willing to reconsider your application. Just keep in mind that an aid administrator is likely to be more interested in factors that influence your family's *ability* to pay, not its *willingness* to do so.

It is not always easy—for the aid administrator or the family—to tell the difference between ability and willingness. Another child with exceptional needs or continuing medical expenses, or a parent who has lost a job, affect ability. Not wanting to spend a child's educational trust fund, or wanting more grants in order to avoid borrowing, may reflect more on willingness than on ability. Be prepared to answer some questions.

Q I didn't get nearly as much aid as I needed to attend the college I like best. What now?

A You still have options. Find out if your preferred college will defer your enrollment for a year, giving you time to earn some money. Or consider enrolling in a less expensive college for a year or two, and transferring to your preferred college later on.

You could also go to college part time while you work. Look for an employer that offers tuition payment or reimbursement as a fringe benefit. (As a matter of fact, colleges and universities often give their staffs free or reduced tuition as a benefit of employment. The advantage is, you are already on campus.)

Financial aid checklist

❑ **Develop a list of colleges that interest you** and that seem to match your educational and career goals. You may want to use a comprehensive guide, such as *The College Handbook* or *Index of Majors and Graduate Degrees*, to help you do this. Software packages like *College Cost Explorer/FUND FINDER* can also help; see if it is available in your counselor's office, or obtain a copy to use at home.

❑ **Write to the admission office** at each college on your list for an admission application form.

Remember also to inquire about financial aid opportunities and application procedures. It is best to do this early in the fall of your senior year of high school.

❑ **Make certain you know what forms to file.** You can usually get forms from your high school guidance office or a college financial aid office.

❑ **Register for CSS/Financial Aid PROFILE if one or more of the colleges to which you are applying requests it.** You may register by calling 1-800-778-6888 (toll-free) or via EXPAN or College Board Online (http://www.collegeboard.org). Within two or three weeks of registering, you will receive a personalized package of forms and instructions. If possible, complete and return your PROFILE form to CSS for processing four weeks in advance of your earliest deadline.

❑ **Mail your completed FAFSA as soon after January 1 as possible.** The form should be sent for processing at least four weeks before the earliest financial aid deadline set by the colleges or state scholarship or grant programs to which you are applying (but no earlier than January 1). Carefully follow the instructions for filling out the form. Make sure your answers are complete and correct.

❑ **Apply for all forms of student financial aid.** Determine early on whether you must fill out additional application forms. Find this out well in advance and make certain you file the appropriate forms by the deadlines.

❑ **Supply additional information promptly.** If you or your parents receive requests for additional information about your need analysis form, respond promptly so that there will be no further delay in processing your request for aid.

❑ **Review the acknowledgment you get back.** After submitting your need analysis form, you will receive some type of acknowledgment from the processor. Make certain that all entries on the acknowledgment are correct.

❑ **Review your award letters carefully.** The director of financial aid at each college and scholarship program is responsible for determining a student's need, knowing which funds a student is eligible for, and making a decision about who will receive financial aid and how much. Once that decision is made, you will receive an award letter describing the contents of your financial aid package and outlining any conditions attached to the award.

❏ **Check to see if other financial aid application forms are required** by the colleges to which you are applying and find out the deadline dates for each. Complete these forms as early as possible.

❏ **Check with your guidance counselor, high school library, and public library** for books and pamphlets about other aid sources. Follow the directions for applying. You may qualify for a private scholarship, grant, or loan program because of your

    academic achievement
    religious affiliation
    ethnic or racial heritage
    community activities
    hobbies or special interests
    organizational memberships
    artistic talents, athletic abilities, or
        other special skills
    career plans or proposed field of study

❏ **Find out if your parents' employers, professional associations, or labor unions** sponsor any aid programs.

❏ **Investigate community organizations and civic, cultural, and fraternal groups** to see if they sponsor scholarship programs at the local, state, or national level. Also check with local religious organizations, veterans' posts, businesses, and industries.

❏ **If you or either of your parents is a military veteran,** you may be eligible for special assistance. Contact the nearest office of the Veterans Administration for information.

❏ **Ask about benefits from vocational rehabilitation or other social service agencies** if you think you qualify for assistance.

❏ **Pay close attention to award notices from state and federal student financial aid programs.** Review your federal Student Aid Report (SAR) carefully.

❏ **Learn how the payments from each aid source will be made.** Generally, payment of financial aid awards is made at the time you actually enroll. Also find out if there are additional procedures you should be aware of or forms you must fill out in order to receive aid.

❏ **Explore alternatives.** Some colleges offer tuition and/or fee waivers to certain categories of students, such as adults, children of alumni, or family members enrolled simultaneously. If you qualify, you may want to take advantage of this type of discount. (See Part III of this book for lists of colleges that offer tuition and/or fee waivers.) Colleges that offer special tuition payment plans—installment, deferred, or credit card—or tuition discounts for prepayment also are listed in Part III of this book.

❏ **Educate yourself about loans.** Investigate all the options before you borrow, and make sure that you understand the interest rates, repayment requirements, and other terms and conditions for each loan program you are considering. Give yourself plenty of time—at least six weeks—before the start of the semester to have your loan application processed.

❏ **Make a decision about which college to attend on the basis of your education and career goals.** Remember to notify the college whose offer you are accepting and to communicate your decision to other colleges so that the financial aid they reserved for you can be freed for other applicants.

9. Long-range planning:
A special message to parents

If your child will not be enrolling in college for several years, or if you have one enrolling now but others coming up. you have more time to plan. This chapter is written especially for you.

If you have not already done so, turn now to the tables in the next chapter showing average costs, or look up the average expenses for a few colleges with which you are familiar. Then think about this question:

When it is time to enroll in college, will you have enough ready cash to cover these expenses, in a single lump-sum payment, at the start of the semester?

Most people do not. Even what is generally regarded as the *least* expensive of the various educational options—living at home and commuting to a nearby community college—requires over $5,700 a year on average. The budget for students living on campus now averages about $9,300 per year at an in-state public college or university and more than $19,700 at a private one. And no one is sure how much higher the costs are going to go.

If your family saves little or no money before enrollment, it will be almost impossible to change your household budget fast enough or radically enough to pay for all your college expenses out of current income alone. People with low or fixed incomes do not have the extra money to spend. Even people with high incomes cannot afford to divert large chunks of current income to make big payments once or twice a year. However, if you do the best you can for yourself, you may be able to get enough outside help to cover the difference between what you can afford and what college costs.

The purpose of planning

Remember that the purpose of financial planning to meet educational costs is twofold:

- to get as much mileage as you can out of your own resources
- to secure the additional outside help—the "financial aid"—you may need in order to make up the difference between what you can afford and what it costs to attend the college of your choice

The two objectives are inseparable. The entire financing system for American postsecondary education is based on the assumption that you and your family have the *primary* responsibility for meeting college costs, to the extent of your ability.

You may wonder, Why should we use *our* resources at all if financial aid is available? Why not "plan" to have financial aid pay for it all?

The answer is that the bulk of financial aid awarded in the United States is, and always has been, based on "demonstrated need"; that is, it comes into play only after a family has done as much as it can reasonably be expected to do for itself, according to formulas that are applied to all aid applicants. Also, every dollar that you save in advance is probably one less that your child will have to borrow.

Some students come from families that have few or no resources to contribute toward college expenses. Others come from families that can easily foot the bill for even the most expensive educational options. But most students come from families that fall somewhere between the two extremes.

The Smiths and the Joneses

Imagine two families whose overall income pictures have been very similar over time and whose current

The Smiths

Two parents, both working outside the home, older parent age 45. Two children, one in junior high school, the other starting college in the fall. No unusual expenses; standard U.S. income tax deductions and exemptions

The Smiths saved $75,000.

Income before taxes	$60,000
Total assets	75,000
Expected from parents	
from income:	$7,946
from savings:	2,019
First-year costs	$15,000
– Expected from parents	9,965
= Demonstrated need	$5,035

The Joneses

Two parents, both working outside the home, older parent age 45. Two children, one in junior high school, the other starting college in the fall. No unusual expenses; standard U.S. income tax deductions and exemptions

The Joneses saved $15,000.

Income before taxes	$60,000
Total assets	15,000
Expected from parents	
from income:	$6,502
from savings:	0
First-year costs	$15,000
– Expected from parents	6,502
= Demonstrated need	$8,498

*Parental expectations are based on the Federal Methodology formulas for the 1996-97 academic year. Values are approximate.

incomes are identical. Both the Smiths and the Joneses have two children, one of whom will be in college, and the parents are of the same age.

The one big difference between the families is that the Smiths have done a much better job of saving over the years. They started saving a portion of both incomes each month when their children were very young, in anticipation of needing some of those assets to pay for college. They have accumulated $75,000 in savings, while the Joneses have spent more of their current income each year and have saved only $15,000.

It is obvious that when the time comes for their respective children to enroll in college, the Smiths will have more money available to put toward college costs than the Joneses. But, will not the Joneses simply qualify for more financial aid?

The answer is, to a degree, yes—but the Smiths will be much better off than the Joneses. Here is why.

Assets, such as savings, *are* considered in the formulas for estimating a family's ability to pay for educational expenses. A family with assets is considered to be in a much stronger financial position than a family without assets. Despite this, the contribution from *income*

has a much greater influence on the expected contribution, as demonstrated with the Smiths and Joneses.

As shown above, the Federal Methodology will assume that the Smiths will be able to contribute $2,019 from their assets for the first year of their child's college expenses. That's only $2,019 out of the $75,000 saved! The Joneses, however, are not expected to make a contribution from assets since their assets are so low. Both families will be expected to contribute several thousand dollars toward educational expenses from their current incomes.

While some might argue that the Smiths are being "penalized" for saving, let us take a closer look. The Smiths have options the Joneses do not have.

Many families find it difficult to contribute the amount assumed available from current income. Families often accumulate financial obligations related to choices they have made in selecting a home or car, or in acquiring more consumer debt than they would like. These obligations can make it difficult to divert enough current income to educational expenses.

Because they have saved, the Smiths have the option of substituting some of their savings for part of the contribution expected from income, thus freeing up current income and lessening their need to borrow to meet educational expenses. This is a choice the Joneses can make for a year or two for their first child's college expenses, but doing so would leave them without that option for their second child and would leave the parents with very little savings toward their retirement.

In addition, both the Smiths' and Joneses' college-bound children will be asked to take out student loans to meet part of their expenses. The Smiths are in a much better position to use more of their savings to reduce the need for their child to go into debt.

If the families do find it difficult to contribute the amounts expected from their incomes, the availability of assets can make the difference between selecting a college on the basis of *educational value* rather than on the basis of *cost*.

Saving for college makes good sense. It puts a family in a strong position when decisions about college are to be made. It provides a family with options that might not otherwise be available. And as far as being "penalized" for saving is concerned, it is important to note that under the current Federal Methodology, the maximum amount that parents can be expected to contribute from their assets in a given year is *less than 6 percent of their total assets*. And, home equity is excluded. That leaves a great deal of a family's wealth unassessed by the formula, giving the family a real chance for receiving financial aid while leaving them with the ability to make sound educational decisions.

How to plan

The *basics* are the same for long-range planning as for short-range planning, and have been described earlier in this book: educating yourself about college costs, estimating what you will be expected to pay toward those costs, developing a timetable, choosing strategies to get the most mileage out of your family resources, and finding out about financial aid programs.

The details of your plan to meet college costs will necessarily be very different from a family whose child will enroll within the next few months. If your children are still quite young, time is on your side—a big advantage. On the other hand, you also have the disadvantage of uncertainty about what circumstances will influence both college costs and your ability to pay between now and enrollment. However, you still can—and should—plan.

Setting realistic goals

Setting realistic goals is the first step. A goal is not a wish but a statement of purpose, a description of an objective to be achieved. It should be as concrete and specific as possible.

Reviewing Chapters 1 and 2 will help you

- learn what college costs today
- estimate what share of those costs *you* would be expected to pay if your child were enrolling in the near future

Once you have done so, you will have to make some *additional* assumptions about what college costs and family expectations will look like when it is time for your children to enroll.

No one is really sure what college will cost in 5 or 10 or 15 years, and the further into the future you look, the murkier becomes the crystal ball. In the short run, at least, the prices charged by institutions for tuition, room, and board are *not* likely to go down, because operating costs continue to rise. Although colleges and universities are working harder than ever to achieve economies in their operating budgets, higher education continues to be very labor intensive. That means that one of their largest continuing expenses is salaries and benefits for employees—faculty members, administrators, librarians, cafeteria and maintenance workers, health service and security personnel, and so on.

Does that mean that the costs charged to students and parents will continue to rise at the same rate as they have in recent years? For the last several years, overall increases have averaged 6 to 8 percent, a somewhat slower rate of increase than the double-digit annual increases that characterized the early 1980s.

A family whose children will start college in the fall of 1997 will probably not be too far off in their estimates of total expense if they add 7 or 8 percent *per year* to the 1995-96 averages in Chapter 10. Beyond that, you will have to keep track of annual increases and revise your own projections.

Nor is anyone certain that the formulas for assessing a family's ability to contribute will remain stable over time. However, the basic *principles* embodied in the current methodology have been in place for over 30 years. The same kinds of factors will probably continue to be considered in evaluating a family's financial strength as are discussed in this chapter, although they may be treated or weighted differently.

If you are trying to make some ballpark estimate of what will be expected of you when the time comes, you might want to complete the worksheets in Chapter 10, estimating what you think your income, assets, and so on will be at the time of enrollment. Subtract that estimate from your estimate of future college costs. Alternately, use current figures for estimating both total costs and family share, and inflate the resulting goal statement by your assumption of annual inflation between now and the point of enrollment.

Update your assumptions and goals annually. Revise your estimates of probable future expenses by incorporating new data about actual college costs and periodic changes in the formulas for assessing family ability to contribute. Keep your eye on changes in other leading economic indicators, too.

Developing a timetable

Developing a realistic timetable is closely related to goal-setting. The amount of time—in months or years—that is left before your children *start* college is an important factor. It represents the period in which you can *save* money and *look* for extra outside help. However, your plans could also include assumptions about the periods of time *during and after* college in which you may *spend* money to repay loans. Developing a timetable also lets you translate big goals into more manageable terms. To save $1,200 in one year you have to put aside $100 a month or $25 a week or $3.50 a day—actually a little less, assuming your money earns some interest.

Review Chapter 3 to prove to yourself that time really *is* on your side. It demonstrates that the longer the time period over which you finance any purchase, the smaller its impact will be on your monthly budget. For most families, the hardest possible way to finance their fair share of college costs—whether that share is 5 percent or 100 percent—is by cramming it into their household budget during the four-year period of enrollment. Do not assume, however, that you can, or should, defer saving with the intention of relying on loans when your children are ready to enroll.

Under some economic conditions, borrowing is certainly a feasible and even sensible way of making major purchases, but planning to borrow may not be your wisest strategy. The farther into the future you look, the harder it is to be sure about credit availability, your borrowing capacity, the state of the economy, and so on.

If you are fortunate enough to have many years before your children enter college and considerable discretionary income, consult your financial adviser for recommendations about various savings and investment strategies to achieve your goals for meeting college costs. A lot is going to be expected of you. Even if you do not have much to spare, plan to save as much as you can in advance. Regular, systematic savings—even of small amounts—add up, and compounding of interest increases your money powerfully.

Strategies for paying your fair share

Deciding how to pay your fair share is the next step, once you have established goals and timetables. Review Chapter 4 for descriptions of many of the options that are available today. Some are used far in advance of enrollment to save money, while others are designed to make the burden more manageable at the time of enrollment. To keep education affordable, many colleges and universities have instituted new financing programs in the last several years.

Not every choice is appropriate for—or even available to—every student and family. But the earlier you start, the more choices you will have, and the more time to investigate the potential benefits and risks.

The dilemma, of course, is that other concerns and expenses may push college savings to the back burner. In particular, you may not feel as though there is much to be saved at the end of the month, once the basic bills have been paid.

Financial planning to meet college costs *is not* just for wealthy people. It is true that particular financial accounts or products may be appropriate for (or even available only to) families at higher income levels. But financial planning itself is not a product. It is a *process*, a way of thinking about how to organize whatever resources you do have—including your own time and energy—to meet college costs. In fact, the fewer financial resources you have, the more you need to plan the most effective way of using those you do.

- If you can afford to invest several hundred dollars a month to cover future college costs, *do it*. You will need every penny of the principal *and* interest when the time comes.
- If you can carve $50 or $75 a month out of your household budget to save toward future college costs, *do it*. You may not be able to finance the whole amount that way, but you will be able to

manage a good piece of it. If you cover your fair share, then financial aid may be available to cover the rest.

■ If your best effort is only $2 or $5 a week, *do it*. Even a few dollars a week in the jar beside the kitchen sink is important, not just in a financial sense, but as a statement of faith in the future. The important thing is to make it *regularly*.

Evaluating savings and prepayment plans

Should you use one of the many new public and private plans that have recently been developed to help families engage in long-term saving for college costs? The answer will be different for each family, depending on its resources and its goals.

To help families assess the strengths and weaknesses of the different options, the College Board issued a set of guidelines, some of which are cited below.*

1. Is there a minimum contribution required to enter the program? Are incremental additions possible?
2. Is there a maximum annual amount that can be contributed? Will any such maximum restrict the accumulation below a realistic projection of future college costs?
3. Can anyone in the family, or an agent of the family, contribute to the plan? Are there exclusions?
4. Can the proceeds from the plan be transferred to another family member if educational plans change?
5. Are there eligibility restrictions to a particular class of institutions, either within a state or within an institutional sector, such as independent colleges? Are there penalties associated with these restrictions?
6. Is the yield from the plan guaranteed? How is it guaranteed? How is the family protected from investment deficits below college cost levels?
7. Is the plan insured? Can the investment be recovered if the plan sponsor ceases to exist?
8. Does the plan cover all college costs, or just tuition?
9. Are there any residency requirements for eligibility? What happens if the family moves during the plan years?
10. Are there age restrictions or time limits on use? Do proceeds from the plan have to be used within a certain number of years after high school?
11. How many years of study are covered by the proceeds? Undergraduate only? Is graduate study possible? Full time only? Is part-time attendance possible?
12. Are there restrictions as to who might match funds contributed to the plan? Could an employer or state contribute?
13. What are the refund conditions in the event of a student's nonadmission to college, disability, or death?
14. Does the family benefit from any investment surplus over the necessary cost levels, or is that a profit to the sponsor?
15. Will the plan benefits be taxable, either for federal or state taxes? Will any tax accrue to the contributor, plan sponsor, or student?

Finding extra outside help

Will financial aid continue to be available to help families cover the gap between their best efforts and the costs of attendance? Probably, although its form may change over time. Federal funding of student assistance programs has not kept pace with rising costs in recent years, but Congress has consistently resisted proposals to reduce the level of federal support. Many colleges, states, and private organizations actually have increased their support of student aid programs.

There is not very much you can do in advance of your child's senior year in high school about finding financial aid, beyond educating yourself about it (and expressing your continuing support of it to your legislators). The vast majority of federal, state, and institutional programs do not permit you to apply before January 1 of the year in which your child will actually enroll in college.

Private scholarship programs constitute one exception to this general rule. Review the section on private aid sources in Chapter 5. Competition for some of these private awards begins in the junior year of high school, or even earlier. One of the things you *can* do in advance of your child's senior year is check out the terms, conditions, and application procedures of any private aid source for which you think he or she might be eligible.

A closing note

A college education *is* within the reach of every qualified student in the United States. Paying for it is hard—but planning for it makes the paying easier.

---

*The *College Board Review*, Spring 1988, No. 147, p. 11.

If you do as much as you can for yourself, chances are you will find the extra outside help—the financial aid—you need to take care of the rest.

The other kind of planning you should do is academic. Watch what courses your children are taking in school, and make sure that they are taking the right courses for college. This can save time and money in the future—the curricular choices that children make, as early as the seventh grade, can either open doors or close them.

The College Scholarship Service wishes you well in your planning, and looks forward to serving you when the time comes to apply for financial aid.

Questions and answers about planning

Q Isn't educational financial planning complicated?

A A little. Certainly some savings and investment programs can be pretty complicated! The more money you have, the more sophisticated are the options that may be open to you, and the more you may want to get professional advice.

The basic principles are simple. Dr. Karl E. Case, a professor of economics at Wellesley College who has done a lot of thinking about how families can prepare themselves to meet future educational expenses, cites three important ideas:

1. If you pay over more years, your payment is lower.
2. If you decide to pay early, you will earn some interest on this investment.
3. Compound interest can yield surprisingly large gains (8% compounded annually doubles your money in nine years).*

Besides, educational financial planning is not as complicated as figuring out how to pay for college when you *have not* done any planning at all.

Q I've done some calculations, and I do not think we're going to be able to save our full share between now and the time of enrollment. Can we count on loans being available?

A Review Chapter 4 for some insight into the kinds of financing options available today. You will

note that most of the loan programs aimed at parents (as distinct from many of the student loan programs) require a credit check. So it is important that you not arrive at the point of enrollment with your borrowing capacity already exhausted.

Also, do not assume that installment payment plans are necessarily going to be available at all colleges; state laws may even prohibit them at some public institutions. (Remember that installment plans and budgeting plans typically carry some additional costs, too.)

---

*Case, Karl E. "The Office of Family Finance and Planning" (formerly "The Financial Aid Office") in *Educational Financial Planning: A New Concept for the Financial Aid Office.* Columbus, Ga.: Southern Association of Student Financial Aid Administrators, 1986, page 34.

10. Tables, sample cases, and worksheets

Table 10.1 provides average college costs for the 1995-96 academic year. These costs are based on information from all colleges that provided data for two consecutive years. Average tuition and fees are weighted by total undergraduate enrollment; room and board charges for resident students are weighted by the percentage of undergraduates living in college housing. Additional out-of-state tuition and fees are the mean charges reported by public institutions; they are not weighted by enrollment. (Private colleges rarely have additional nonresident tuition and fees.)

All other figures are average student expenses in each category. Average costs for books and supplies are weighted by total undergraduate enrollment; transportation and other expenses for resident students are weighted by the percentage of undergraduates living in college housing; and board, transportation, and other expenses for commuters are weighted by the percentage of undergraduates who commute.

The next table, Table 10.2, provides sample expense budgets based on the average 1995-96 costs for resident students and commuters at different types of colleges.

By the time that *you* are ready to enroll in college, these costs will almost certainly be higher, but the patterns will probably be similar.

The table on estimated parents' contribution, Table 10.3, shows estimates used to determine how much parents would be expected to pay based on income and family size according to the 1996-97 Federal Methodology. (Average costs and estimated parental contributions are likely to be different for students enrolling in subsequent years. The 1997-98 Federal Methodology may be similar to the 1996-97 Federal Methodology, but is adjusted for inflation.) See Chapter 3 for a discussion of how you can use this in your early financial planning.

Sample cases and worksheets

Meet our three sample students—Carlos, Beth, and Andrea—whose family backgrounds, financial situations, and educational goals have been made up from many of the characteristics of students who are facing the choices of a college education and how to pay for it. Following them through the process of determining financial need and applying for aid may help you develop your own financial plan.

All three begin their planning by estimating on Worksheet 1 their probable expenses at the colleges that interest them. Carlos, Beth, and Andrea come from families with very different financial situations. Before they can tell how much they will be expected to pay toward these educational expenses, they need to evaluate their own circumstances in relation to the costs of attending the particular colleges they are interested in. You will see that Worksheets 2-5 have been completed to help in this process. Worksheet 6 is a record of financial aid they are offered.

You can use Worksheets 1-6 for your personal plan.

Table 10.1 Average student expenses, 1995-96

	Tuition and fees	Add'l out-of-state tuition	Books and supplies	Resident Room and board	Resident Trans-portation	Resident Other costs	Commuter Board only	Commuter Trans-portation	Commuter Other costs
National									
2-year public	1,387	2,775	577	—	—	—	1,752	894	1,142
2-year private	6,350		567	4,243	578	972	1,796	902	1,220
4-year public	2,860	4,508	591	3,963	565	1,304	1,721	929	1,348
4-year private	12,432		601	5,199	521	1,009	1,845	863	1,169
New England									
2-year public	2,230	3,492	518	—	—	—	1,918	949	1,139
2-year private	10,801		559	—	—	—	1,655	902	2,404
4-year public	4,272	5,044	560	4,591	413	1,167	1,712	986	1,138
4-year private	16,416		588	6,325	435	917	1,771	1,032	996
Middle States									
2-year public	2,202	2,836	558	—	—	—	1,437	900	1,313
2-year private	8,001		586	4,821	401	1,017	2,015	849	1,398
4-year public	3,876	4,094	605	4,593	481	1,169	1,644	895	1,457
4-year private	13,201		585	5,950	386	940	1,707	780	1,160
South									
2-year public	*1,028*	2,423	*523*	—	—	—	1,761	1,022	907
2-year private	*7,426*		*524*	4,152	619	968	1,751	*1,047*	*1,019*
4-year public	2,337	4,104	595	3,491	613	1,177	1,695	1,025	1,258
4-year private	10,777		598	4,488	667	1,014	1,686	847	1,020
Midwest									
2-year public	1,632	2,902	572	—	—	—	1,753	997	1,068
2-year private	6,361		597	3,477	514	966	1,451	1,208	988
4-year public	3,104	4,154	541	3,636	471	1,381	1,574	903	1,314
4-year private	11,875		593	4,335	510	992	1,871	885	1,218
Southwest									
2-year public	*812*	1,302	*633*	—	—	—	*1,759*	*916*	*1,093*
2-year private	4,008	—	453	2,945	287	673	*1,577*	859	*1,225*
4-year public	1,910	4,257	581	3,570	1,000	1,425	1,605	*1,205*	1,322
4-year private	9,019		588	3,957	707	1,316	1,732	1,063	1,269
West									
2-year public	*808*	3,453	*615*	—	—	—	*1,947*	*718*	*1,210*
2-year private	*3,404*		—	—	—	—	—	678	1,062
4-year public	2,561	6,141	651	4,753	625	1,504	1,979	762	1,456
4-year private	12,245		710	5,406	629	1,242	2,386	859	1,314

Note: Calculations are enrollment-weighted and utilize only those institutions for which two consecutive years' worth of price and enrollment data are available. Institutions do not necessarily report cost data in all fields. A blank indicates that the data are not generally applicable for the type of institution. A dash (—) indicates that the number of institutions reporting data on this item was too small to support an analysis. Averages in *italicized* type indicate that while the number of institutions reporting data on this item was large enough to support an analysis, the sample size was marginal.

Table 10.2 Sample expense budgets

	Resident	Commuter
2-year public	—	$ 5,752
2-year private	$12,710	10,835
4-year public	9,285	7,449
4-year private	19,762	16,910

Table 10.3 1996-97 Estimated parents' contribution

Net assets	$25,000				$50,000			
Family size	3	4	5	6	3	4	5	6

1995 income before taxes

	$25,000				$50,000			
$20,000 . . . . $	0 $	0 $	0 $	0	$ 84 $	0 $	0 $	0
30,000	1,325	668	51	0	1,610	953	336	0
40,000	2,933	2,194	1,577	833	3,309	2,508	1,862	1,168
50,000	5,271	4,148	3,265	2,428	5,824	4,595	3,641	2,752
60,000	8,049	6,799	5,633	4,480	8,658	7,408	6,243	4,985
70,000	10,537	9,287	8,121	6,791	11,146	9,896	8,730	7,400
80,000	13,477	12,227	11,061	9,731	14,086	12,836	11,670	10,340
90,000	16,417	15,166	14,001	12,671	17,026	15,776	14,610	13,280
100,000	19,357	18,106	16,941	15,611	19,966	18,715	17,550	16,220

Net assets	$100,000				$150,000			
Family size	3	4	5	6	3	4	5	6

1995 income before taxes

	$100,000				$150,000			
$20,000 . . . . $	1,404 $	748 $	131 $	0	$ 2,787 $	2,068 $	1,451 $	705
30,000	3,037	2,274	1,656	962	5,041	3,953	3,098	2,284
40,000	5,415	4,271	3,369	2,518	8,204	6,801	5,499	4,285
50,000	8,644	7,241	5,922	4,611	11,464	10,061	8,742	7,259
60,000	11,478	10,228	9,063	7,699	14,298	13,048	11,883	10,519
70,000	13,966	12,716	11,550	10,220	16,786	15,536	14,370	13,040
80,000	16,906	15,656	14,490	13,160	19,726	18,476	17,310	15,980
90,000	19,846	18,596	17,430	16,100	22,666	21,416	20,250	18,920
100,000	22,786	21,535	20,370	19,040	25,606	24,355	23,190	21,860

Note: The figures shown are parents' contribution under Federal Methodology (FM), assuming the older parent is age 45; both parents are employed (equal wages); income is only from employment; no unusual circumstances; standard deductions on U.S. income tax; 1040 tax return filed; and one undergraduate child enrolled in college. Net assets exclude primary place of residence and family farms.

Carlos, Beth, and Andrea plan for college costs

Worksheet 1: Estimating student expenses

	Carlos
1. Tuition and fees	$ 1,400
2. Books and supplies	600
3. Student's room	Not applicable
4. Student's board/meals*	1,800
5. Personal (clothing, laundry, recreation, medical)	1,200
6. Transportation**	900
7. Other (such as costs of child care, extra expenses because of handicap)	0
A. Total budget (add 1-7)	$ 5,900

* You will want to consider these expenses to your family if you live at home.

** If you are planning to live on campus, estimate the costs of the round-trips you will have to make to your home. Colleges usually estimate a student makes two or three round-trips during the year. Students living at home should figure the costs of daily tranportation to college.

Carlos Fernandez age 18, graduated from high school in June 1996. He wanted to live with his family and attend a nearby community college to pursue an Associate of Arts degree in chemistry. He hopes to transfer to a four-year college of engineering when he completes his AA degree and eventually to become a chemical engineer.

Carlos' father, age 42, earns $23,000 per year as a maintenance worker; his mother, age 41, earns $9,500 as a part-time beautician at a local salon. His younger brother, age 16, is a junior in high school and also hopes to attend college after he finishes high school. The family owns a cooperative apartment and files IRS form 1040. They earn about $260 a year in interest from their savings of $5,320. Carlos earned $2,750 in 1995 working as a grocery clerk after school and full time during the summer. He expects to continue working part time at the grocery store while enrolled in college. He has saved $1,500 toward his college education.

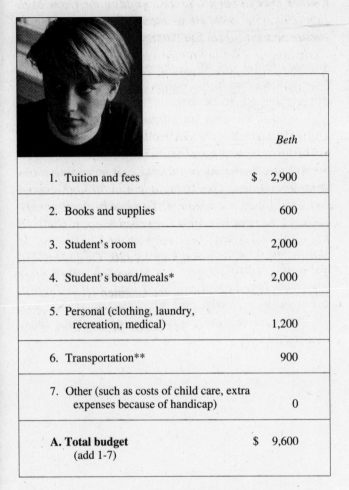

	Beth
1. Tuition and fees	$ 2,900
2. Books and supplies	600
3. Student's room	2,000
4. Student's board/meals*	2,000
5. Personal (clothing, laundry, recreation, medical)	1,200
6. Transportation**	900
7. Other (such as costs of child care, extra expenses because of handicap)	0
A. Total budget (add 1-7)	$ 9,600

* You will want to consider these expenses to your family if you live at home.

** If you are planning to live on campus, estimate the costs of the round-trips you will have to make to your home. Colleges usually estimate a student makes two or three round-trips during the year. Students living at home should figure the costs of daily tranportation to college.

Beth Edwards is 17 and graduated from high school in June 1996. She hoped to attend the state university to study journalism and plans to live on campus.

Beth's mother, age 45, does not work outside the home, but is kept busy looking after Beth's 5-year-old twin sisters. Beth's father passed away unexpectedly in December, 1994. The family is now supported by social security benefits of $17,350 (which will be reduced when Beth starts college). Her mother also receives about $950 in interest income from her savings of $30,000, the proceeds of Beth's father's life insurance policy. The family rents an apartment and Beth's mother files IRS form 1040A.

Beth earned $1,500 during the summer of 1995 as a summer camp counselor and spent the school year doing volunteer work. She has been unable to save since she has contributed most of her earnings to her mother for household expenses.

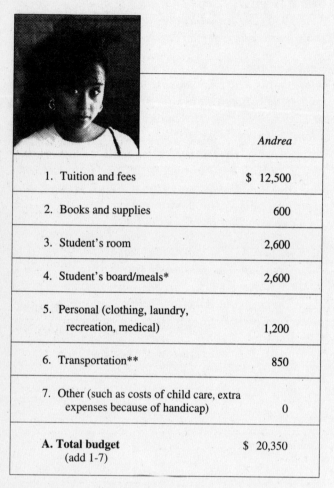

	Andrea
1. Tuition and fees	$ 12,500
2. Books and supplies	600
3. Student's room	2,600
4. Student's board/meals*	2,600
5. Personal (clothing, laundry, recreation, medical)	1,200
6. Transportation**	850
7. Other (such as costs of child care, extra expenses because of handicap)	0
A. Total budget (add 1-7)	$ 20,350

* You will want to consider these expenses to your family if you live at home.

** If you are planning to live on campus, estimate the costs of the round-trips you will have to make to your home. Colleges usually estimate a student makes two or three round-trips during the year. Students living at home should figure the costs of daily tranportation to college.

Andrea Daley, age 18, graduated from high school in June 1996. She planned to attend a private college to pursue premedical studies. She will live on campus.

Andrea's father, age 49, is the pastor of the community's Baptist Church and earns $19,500 per year. Her mother, age 50, is an assistant principal at the local high school, earning an annual salary of $49,750. Andrea's parents have additional income of $750 in interest from savings and also receive $1,000 per year from a part-ownership in a family dry-cleaning business. The Daley's assets include $25,000 in savings and $55,000 in home equity. Their part of the family business is worth $62,500. They file IRS form 1040.

Andrea has a sister, age 20, who is a junior in college. Her younger brother, age 14, is a freshman in high school. Andrea earned $1,050 in 1996 as the organist at her father's church and has saved $500. She has also been selected to receive two local scholarships totalling $1,000.

Worksheet 2: Parents' expected contribution (Federal Methodology[1])

	Carlos	Beth[2]	Andrea
A. 1995 income:			
1. Father's yearly wages, salaries, tips, and other compensation	$23,000	$ 0	$ 19,500
2. Mother's yearly wages, salaries, tips, and other compensation	9,500	0	49,750
3. All other income of mother and father (dividends, interest, social security, pensions, welfare, child support, etc.) *Include IRA/Keogh payments and 401(K) and 403(B) contributions.*	260	18,300	1,750
4. IRS allowable adjustments to income (business expenses, interest penalties, alimony *paid,* etc.) *Do not include IRA/Keogh payments.*	0	0	0
B. Total income (Add 1, 2, 3 and subtract 4.)	32,760	18,300	71,000
Expenses:			
5. U.S. income tax parents paid on their 1995 income (not amount withheld from paycheck)	$ 2,807	$ 0	$ 10,330
6. Social Security (FICA) tax (See Table 10.4 for 6.)	2,487	0	5,298
7. State and other taxes (Enter 8% of B.)[3]	2,621	1,464	5,680
8. Employment allowance. If 2-parent family and both parents work, allow 35% of lower salary to a maximum of $2,600; if 1-parent family, allow 35% of salary to a maximum of $2,600. No allowance for a 2-parent family in which only one parent works.	2,600	0	2,600
9. Income Protection Allowance (See Table 10.5 for 9)	17,650	17,650	18,860
C. Total allowance against income (Add 5, 6, 7, 8, 9.)	28,165	19,114	42,768
D. Available income (Subtract C from B.)	4,595	(814)	28,232
Assets:			
10. Other real estate equity (value minus unpaid balance on mortgage)	0	$ 0	0
11. Business or farm (Figure total value minus indebtedness and then take percentage shown in Table 10.6 for 11.) If your family is only part owner of the farm or business, list only your share of the net value.	0	0	25,000
12. Cash, savings, and checking accounts	5,320	30,000	25,000
13. Other investments (current net value)	0	0	0
E. Total assets	5,320	30,000	50,000
Deductions:			
F. Asset protection allowance (See Table 10.7 for F.)	36,400	27,200	43,700
G. Remaining assets (Subtract F from E.)	(31,080)	2,800	6,300
H. Income supplement from assets (Multiply G by 12%, if negative, enter 0.)	0	336	756
I. Adjusted available income (Add D and H.)	4,595	(478)	28,988
J. Parents' expected contribution (Multiply I by taxation rate amount given in Table 10.8 for J.)	1,011	0	9,489
K. Parents' expected contribution if more than one family member is in college (Divide J by number of family members in college at least half-time.)	0	0	4,745

1. Note that this and subsequent worksheets are based on the 1996-97 Federal Methodology (FM), and reflect the procedures that would have been used to estimate contributions in the 1996-97 academic year. Average student expenses displayed in Table 10.1 on page 64 reflect 1995-96 college costs. Average costs *and* average contributions are likely to be different for students enrolling in subsequent years.

2. Federal need analysis provisions provide a "simple needs test" treatment for families with total Adjusted Gross Income or earned income of $50,000 or less, who file the 1040A or 1040EZ federal income tax return or do not file taxes. Therefore, if neither Beth *nor* her parent filed a Form 1040 federal tax return, family assets would not be considered in the "simple needs test," and only available income ($314) shown in line D would be used to compute a $69 expected contribution for line J.

3. Note that state taxes vary substantially from state to state. This is a national average. The FM itself uses a state-specific average.

Tables used for completion of Worksheets 2 and 3

Table 10.4 Social Security (FICA) Tax Allowance (Items 6 and 19)

When individual's yearly wage total equals	Allowance per wage earner for Social Security (FICA) tax is:
$ 1 to $ 61,200	7.65% of income earned by each wage earner (maximum $4,682 per person)
$ 61,201 or more	$4,682 + 1.45% of income earned above $61,200 by each wage earner

Table 10.5 Income protection allowance (Item 9)

Family size* (including student)	Number in college**				
	1	2	3	4	5
2	$11,480	$ 9,510			
3	14,290	12,340	$10,380		
4	17,650	15,690	13,740	$11,770	
5	20,830	18,860	16,910	14,950	$12,990
6	24,360	22,400	20,450	18,480	16,530

* For each additional family member, add $2,750.
** For each additional college student, subtract $1,950.

Table 10.6 Business or farm adjustments (Item 11)

Net worth (NW)	Adjusted net worth
Less than $ 1	$ 0
$ 1 to 80,000	$ 0 + 40% of NW
$ 80,001 to 245,000	$ 32,000 + 50% of NW over $ 80,000
$245,001 to 410,000	$114,500 + 60% of NW over $245,000
$410,001 or more	$213,000 + 100% of NW over $410,000

Table 10.8 Parents' expected contribution (Item J)

Adjusted available income (AAI) (Item I)	Total parents' contribution
Less than $-3,409	$ -750
$ -3,409 to 10,300	22% of AAI
$ 10,301 to 12,900	$ 2,266 + 25% of AAI over $ 10,300
$ 12,901 to 15,500	$ 2,916 + 29% of AAI over $ 12,900
$ 15,501 to 18,100	$ 3,670 + 34% of AAI over $ 15,500
$ 18,101 to 20,700	$ 4,554 + 40% of AAI over $ 18,100
$ 20,701 or more	$ 5,594 + 47% of AAI over $ 20,700

Table 10.7 Asset protection allowance (Item F)

Older parent's age	Two-parent family	One-parent family
25 or under	$ 0	$ 0
26	2,300	1,600
27	4,600	3,300
28	7,000	4,900
29	9,300	6,500
30	11,600	8,200
31	13,900	9,800
32	16,200	11,400
33	18,600	13,100
34	20,900	14,700
35	23,200	16,300
36	25,500	18,000
37	27,800	19,600
38	30,200	21,200
39	32,500	22,900
40	34,800	24,500
41	35,500	25,000
42	36,400	25,600
43	37,300	26,100
44	38,300	26,700
45	39,200	27,200
46	40,300	27,900
47	41,300	28,600
48	42,300	29,300
49	43,700	29,800
50	44,800	30,500
51	45,900	31,300
52	47,400	32,000
53	48,500	33,000
54	50,100	33,700
55	51,600	34,500
56	53,200	35,500
57	54,800	36,400
58	56,500	37,400
59	58,200	38,300
60	60,000	39,400
61	62,100	40,500
62	64,300	41,700
63	66,200	42,900
64	68,400	44,100
65 or more	70,800	45,500

Worksheet 3: Student's expected contribution

	Carlos	Beth	Andrea
L. Student's 1995 income:			
14. Student's yearly wages, salaries, tips, and other compensation	$ 2,750	$ 1,500	$ 1,050
15. Spouse's yearly wages, salaries, tips, and other compensation	0	0	0
16. All other income of student (dividends, interest, untaxed income, and benefits)	30	0	21
M. Total income (Add 14, 15, and 16.)	2,780	1,500	1,071
Allowances:			
17. U.S. income tax student (and spouse) paid on 1995 income (not amount withheld from paychecks)	0	0	0
18. State and other taxes (enter 4% of M.)	111	60	43
19. Social security (FICA) tax (See Table 10.4 for 19.)	210	115	80
20. Dependent student offset	1,750	1,750	1,750
N. Total allowances against student's income (Add 17, 18, 19, and 20.)	2,071	1,925	1,873
O. Available income (Subtract N from M.)	709	0	0
Resources:			
21. Contribution from income (Line O x 50%. Cannot be less than $0.)	355	0	0
22. Contribution from assets (Multiply the total savings and other assets—such as stocks and bonds excluding home equity by 35%.)	525	0	175
23. Other gifts and scholarships already received	0	0	1,000
Q. Total student resources (Add 21, 22, and 23.)	$ 880	$ 0	$ 1,175

Worksheet 4: Total family contribution

	Carlos	Beth	Andrea
J. Parents' expected contribution (Use figure for K instead of J if there is more than one family member in college.)	$ 1,011	$ 69*	$ 4,745
Q. Student's expected contribution from resources	880	0	1,175
R. Total family contribution (Add J and Q.)	$ 1,891	$ 69	$ 5,920

Worksheet 5: Student need

	Carlos	Beth	Andrea
S. Total college expense budget	$ 5,900	$ 9,600	$ 20,350
R. Total family contribution	1,891	0	5,920
T. Student need (Subtract R from S.)	$ 4,009	$ 9,600	$ 14,430

* Assumes that Beth qualified for the federal "simple needs test."

Worksheet 6: Financial aid awards

	Carlos
A. Total student budget	$ 5,900
R. Total family contribution	1,891
T. Demonstrated financial need	4,009
1. Federal Pell Grant	800
2. State scholarship	700
3. Institutional grant	0
4. Federal Work-Study	0
5. Federal Perkins Loan	0
6. Federal Supplemental Educational Opportunity Grant	500
7. Federal Stafford Loan	2,009
8. Private scholarships	0
Total resources for college	$ 5,900

	Beth
A. Total student budget	$ 9,600
R. Total family contribution	0
T. Demonstrated financial need	9,600
1. Federal Pell Grant	2,470
2. State scholarship	1,500
3. Institutional grant	800
4. Federal College Work-Study	1,205
5. Federal Perkins Loan	0
6. Federal Supplemental Educational Opportunity Grant	1,000
7. Federal Stafford Loan	2,625
8. Private scholarships	0
Total resources for college	$ 9,600

Carlos received a financial aid award from the community college that fully met his need. He received a Federal Pell Grant and a Federal Supplemental Educational Opportunity Grant along with a state scholarship The combined total of his grants was enough to cover his tuition and books. Since Carlos has an off-campus job at a grocery store, the college did not offer him a campus job, instead recommending that he take out a Federal Stafford Loan to meet his remaining need. Before applying for the loan, Carlos planned to evaluate carefully how much he might need to borrow. He might decide to increase his hours at the grocery store in an effort to mimimize his borrowing.

The financial aid award offer **Beth** received met her demonstrated need and included a wide variety of sources. Beth received a Federal Pell Grant from the federal government, a scholarship from her state student assistance agency, and—because her family income is quite low—a Federal Supplemental Educational Opportunity Grant. Beth also received a scholarship from the college based on the Federal Methodology for determining need. In addition, like almost all financial aid recipients, Beth will be expected to assume some "self-help" aid. In her case, she took out a Federal Stafford Loan, which she will repay after she graduates or leaves college, and she accepted the offer of a campus job through the Federal Work-Study Program.

	Andrea	
	Federal Methodology	Institutional Methodology
A. Total student budget	$ 20,350	$ 20,350
R. Total family contribution	5,920	8,360
T. Demonstrated financial need	14,430	11,990
1. Federal Pell Grant	0	0
2. State scholarship	0	0
3. Institutional grant	6,765	6,765
4. Federal Work-Study	1,400	1,400
5. Federal Perkins Loan	1,200	1,200
6. Federal SEOG	0	0
7. Federal Stafford Loan	2,625	2,625
8. Private scholarships	1,000*	1,000*
Total resources for college	$ 17,910	$ 20,350

*included in R (above).

*Even though **Andrea's** family has the greatest resources of the three students, she also has the greatest need because the college she wanted to attend has the highest costs. The financial aid award Andrea received included awards from three federal programs, a scholarship from the college's own scholarship fund, as well as two local scholarships from her hometown. The federal funds Andrea received included a campus job through the Federal Work-Study program, and two loans, including a Federal Perkins Loan and a Federal Stafford Loan. Because Andrea's parents' income was higher than average, she was not eligible for the Federal Pell Grant or a state scholarship, and the college was unable to offer her a Federal Supplemental Educational Opportunity Grant.*

All colleges awarding federal financial aid funds must determine need by using a mandatory Federal Methodology. Although this methodology establishes eligibility for federal funds, most colleges, particularly higher cost schools, do not have enough federal funds to meet their students' full federally determined need. Many colleges that award substantial amounts of their own funds use a need analysis methodology that differs from the Federal Methodology. Colleges using an institutional methodology to award institutional funds do so because they feel that it is a better means of assessing a family's true ability to pay for college costs. In Andrea's case, her eligibility for a scholarship from the college was based on an institutional methodology, which unlike the Federal Methodology, took into account her parents' home equity and depreciation-based business losses. Under the institutional methodology, her parents' contribution to costs is higher and the college also assumes that Andrea will make a minimum contribution of $900 from her summer savings.

Based on the college's own assessment of Andrea's need, Andrea received a scholarship from the college, which in addition to her awards from the federal programs and her local scholarships, met her institutionally determined need in full. Because Andrea's college uses an institutional methodology in awarding its own scholarship funds, two breakdowns of need are shown above.

Your personal plan

Now that you have followed Carlos, Beth, and Andrea through the financial aid application process, complete your own need analysis estimate. You can begin to make your own plans by filling in Worksheet 1 for the colleges you are considering. You can use the college cost information in Part II of this book, but *remember* that these costs are for the 1995-96 academic year; you should make a somewhat higher estimate. (Some colleges will have a greater increase, others a smaller one.) When you are actually applying for aid, the college catalog or financial aid bulletins for the colleges to which you are applying are the most authoritative sources of information about costs that will apply to you.

You can begin to get a sense of your need at these colleges by completing your own Worksheets 2-5. These will take you through the steps of estimating parents' expected contribution (Worksheet 2), estimating your own contribution (Worksheet 3), combining the total family contribution (Worksheet 4), and finding the difference between the contribution and the costs at each of the colleges you are considering (Worksheet 5)—that is, your financial need.

Worksheet 1: **Estimating student expenses**	*College A*	*College B*	*College C*
1. Tuition and fees	$	$	$
2. Books and supplies			
3. Student's room			
4. Student's board/meals*			
5. Personal (clothing, laundry, recreation, medical)			
6. Transportation**			
7. Other (such as costs of child care, extra expenses because of handicap)			
A. Total budget (Add 1–7.)	$	$	$

*You will want to consider these expenses to your family if you live at home.

**If you are planning to live on campus, estimate the costs of the round-trips you will have to make to your home. Colleges ususally estimate a student makes two or three round-trips during the year. Students living at home should figure the costs of daily transportation to college.

Parents' expected contribution

See Worksheet 2 for Carlos, Beth, and Andrea, and use the tables following their worksheet (Tables 10.4-10.8) to help you estimate your parents' expected contribution toward your total resources for college.

Worksheet 2: Parents' expected contribution (Federal Methodology)

A. 1995 income:

1. Father's yearly wages, salaries, tips, and other compensation $

2. Mother's yearly wages, salaries, tips, and other compensation

3. All other income of mother and father (dividends, interest, social security, pensions, welfare, child support, etc.) *Include IRA/Keogh payments and 401(K) and 403(B) contributions.*

4. IRS allowable adjustments to income (business expenses, interest penalties, alimony *paid,* etc.) *Do not include IRA/Keogh payments.*

B. Total income (Add 1, 2, 3 and subtract 4.)

Expenses:

5. U.S. income tax parents paid on their 1995 income (not amount withheld from paycheck) $

6. Social Security (FICA) tax (See Table 10.4 for 6.)

7. State and other taxes (Enter 8% of B.)

8. Employment allowance. If 2-parent family and both parents work, allow 35% of lower salary to a maximum of $2,600; if 1-parent family, allow 35% of salary to a maximum of $2,600. No allowance for a 2-parent family in which only one parent works.

9. Income Protection Allowance (See Table 10.5 for 9.)

C. Total allowance against income (Add 5, 6, 7, 8, 9.)

D. Available income (Subtract C from B.)

Assets:

10. Other real estate equity (value minus unpaid balance on mortgage) $

11. Business or farm (Figure total value minus indebtedness and then take percentage shown in Table 10.6 for 11.) If your family is only part owner of the farm or business, list only your share of the net value.

12. Cash, savings, and checking accounts

13. Other investments (current net value)

E. Total assets

Deductions:

F. Asset protection allowance (See Table 10.7 for F.)

G. Remaining assets (Subtract F from E.)

H. Income supplement from assets (Multiply G by 12%; if value is negative, enter 0.)

I. Adjusted available income (Add D and H.)

J. Parents' expected contribution (Multiply I by taxation rate amount given in Table 10.8 for J.)

K. Parents' expected contribution if more than one family member is in college
(Divide J by number of family members in college at least half-time.)

Student's expected contribution

Students, too, are expected to contribute toward college costs when they are employed and/or have accumulated assets. Worksheet 3 will allow you to estimate what your contribution will be for your first year in college based on the Federal Methodology. It is important to note, however, that many colleges will expect a minimum contribution, such as $900 for a freshman and $1,100 for an upperclassman, when consideration is given for nonfederal funds.

Worksheet 3: Student's expected contribution	
L. Student's 1995 income:	
14. Student's yearly wages, salaries, tips, and other compensation	$
15. Spouse's yearly wages, salaries, tips, and other compensation	
16. All other income of student (dividends, interest, untaxed income, and benefits)	
M. Total income (Add 14, 15, and 16.)	
Allowances:	
17. U.S. income tax student (and spouse) paid on 1995 income (not amount withheld from paychecks)	
18. State and other taxes (enter 4% of M.)	
19. Social security (FICA) tax (See Table 10.4 for 19.)	
20. Dependent student offset	
N. Total allowances against student's income (Add 17, 18, 19 and 20.)	
O. Available income (Subtract N from M.)	
Resources:	
21. Contribution from income (Line O x 50%. Cannot be less than $0.)	
22. Contribution from assets (Multiply the total savings and other assets, such as stocks and bonds, excluding home equity, by 35%.)	
23. Other gifts and scholarships already received	
Q. Total student resources (Add lines 21, 22, and 23.)	$

Total family contribution

Use Worksheet 4 to transfer figures from Worksheet 2 (line J, or line K if there will be more than one family member in college) and Worksheet 3 (line Q). By adding together these two figures, you can determine your total estimated family contribution.

Worksheet 4: Total family contribution	
J. Parents' expected contribution (Use figure for K instead of J if there is more than one family member in college.)	$
Q. Student's expected contribution from resources	
R. Total family contribution (Add J and Q.)	$

Estimated financial need

Are you potentially eligible for financial aid? Use Worksheet 5 to compare your family contribution with the cost of going to college. Record the student expense budgets at the colleges that interest you. Enter your total family contribution (from line R in Worksheet 4) and subtract it from each of the student expense budgets. If your family contribution is less than the student expense budget, you have demonstrated financial need and may be eligible for financial aid equal to this estimate of your need.

It is important to remember that the figure you arrive at in line T is only an estimate, and you should consider this figure to be only a rough approximation of your eligibility for financial aid. It is also important to remember that this estimate of need is based on 1996-97 need analysis methodology for *federal* financial aid programs. Colleges that award significant amounts of nonfederal funds may use a different methodology, as demonstrated in Andrea's case.

Your eligibility for financial aid, and the amount and type of aid you receive, will be determined by the financial aid administrator at each college. Many colleges lack sufficient funds to meet the need of all needy students, regardless of the methodology used. So it is most important that you apply for financial aid as early as possible and meet all deadlines. The only way you can find out how much you might receive is to apply for financial aid!

Worksheet 5: Student need	College A	College B	College C
S. Total college expense budget	$	$	$
R. Total family contribution			
T. Student need (Subtract R from S.)	$	$	$

Financial aid awards

Use Worksheet 6 to record your own aid awards. Your aid award letter will provide detail about the types and amounts of aid a particular college or university offers you. Compare the "total student budget" at each institution you are considering with the "total resources for college" to assess the extent to which the aid you are offered *plus* your total family contribution meets your expected expense. Using a chart like this will also help you compare the "gift" and "self-help" components of your packages from different schools.

Worksheet 6: Financial aid awards	College A	College B	College C
A. Total student budget	$	$	$
R. Total family contribution			
T. Demonstrated financial need			
1. Federal Pell Grant			
2. State scholarship			
3. Institutional grant			
4. Federal Work-Study			
5. Federal Perkins Loan			
6. Federal Supplemental Educational Opportunity Grant			
7. Federal Stafford Loan			
8. Private scholarships			
Total resources for college	$	$	$

11. Glossary

The definitions given here of terms commonly used by colleges to describe their programs, admission procedures, and financial aid policies are necessarily general. Students should consult the catalogs of specific colleges and financial aid programs to get more detailed and up-to-date descriptions of their programs and procedures.

Accelerated program. A college program of study completed in less time than is usually required, most often by attending in summer or by taking extra courses during the regular academic terms. Completion of a bachelor's degree program in three years is an example of acceleration.

ACT. *See* American College Testing Program Assessment.

Advanced placement. Admission or assignment of a freshman to an advanced course in a certain subject on the basis of evidence that the student has already completed the equivalent of the college's freshman course in that subject. In some cases, the college also grants academic credit for the college-level work that has been completed.

Advanced Placement (AP) Program. A service of the College Board that provides high schools with course descriptions in college subjects and Advanced Placement Examinations in those subjects. High schools implement the courses and administer the examinations to interested students, who are then eligible at many colleges for advanced placement, college credit, or both, on the basis of satisfactory grades.

American College Testing Program Assessment (ACT). Test battery of the American College Testing Program, given at test centers in the United States and other countries on specified dates throughout the year. It includes tests in English, mathematics, reading, and science reasoning.

Bachelor's degree. The degree awarded after completion of an undergraduate college program that normally takes four years. Also called the baccalaureate degree.

Campus-based programs. The three federally funded student financial aid programs that are directly administered by colleges: Federal Supplemental Educational Opportunity Grant Program, Federal Perkins Loan Program, and Federal Work-Study Program.

Candidates Reply Date Agreement (CRDA). A college subscribing to this agreement will not require any applicants offered admission as freshmen to notify the college of their decision to attend (or to accept an offer of financial aid) before May 1. The purpose of the agreement is to give applicants time to hear from all the colleges to which they have applied before having to make a commitment to any one of them.

Certificate. An award for completing a particular program or course of study, sometimes given by two-year colleges or vocational or technical schools.

College-Level Examination Program (CLEP). A service of the College Board that provides examinations in undergraduate college courses so that students and other adults may demonstrate achievement at the first- and second-year college levels. The examinations are used by colleges to award credit by examination to adult applicants who have not attended college (or have not done so recently), students transferring from other colleges, and entering freshmen. They are also used by business, industries, government agencies, and professional groups to satisfy education requirements for advancement, licensing, admission to further training, and other purposes.

College Scholarship Service (CSS). A division of the College Board that assists postsecondary institutions, state scholarship programs, and private scholarship organizations in the equitable and efficient distribution of student financial aid funds.

College Work-Study Program. *See* Federal Work-Study Program.

Consumer Price Index (CPI). A measure of inflation or deflation at the consumer level, updated monthly by the U.S. Bureau of Labor Statistics. The index is determined by comparing the current price of a "market basket" of goods to the price at which the same "basket" could have been purchased during a given base year. The goods include food, shelter, clothing, transportation, and other items.

Cooperative education. A college program in which a student alternates between periods of full-time study and full-time employment in related work. Students are paid for their work at the prevailing rate. Typically, five years are required to complete a bachelor's degree program, but graduates have the advantage of having completed about a year's practical experience in addition to their studies. Some colleges refer to this sort of program as work-study, but it should not be confused with the federally sponsored Federal Work-Study Program.

CRDA. *See* Candidates Reply Date Agreement.

Credit by examination. Academic credit granted by a college for a student's having demonstrated proficiency in a subject as measured by an examination.

CSS. *See* College Scholarship Service.

CSS/Financial Aid PROFILE. A need analysis form required by many colleges, universities, and private scholarship programs in addition to the FAFSA. PROFILE is used in awarding private financial aid funds. Students pay a fee to register for PROFILE and send reports to institutions and programs that use it. Students register with CSS by calling a toll-free telephone service (1-800-778-6888), or by connecting to EXPAN in their high school (if their school is a subscriber to EXPAN) or to College Board Online on the World Wide Web (http://www.collegeboard.org).

Dependent student. A student dependent on his or her parents for financial support. A student's dependency status is determined by guidelines established by the federal government.

Early decision. Early decision admission plans are offered to applicants who are sure of the college they want to attend and are likely to be accepted by that college. An early decision admission application is initiated by the student, who is then notified of the college's decision earlier than usual—generally by December 15 of the senior year.

Early Decision Plan (EDP-F, EDP-S). Colleges that subscribe to this plan agree to follow a common schedule for early decision applicants. Colleges may offer either of two plans. A student applying under the first-choice plan (EDP-F) must withdraw applications from all other colleges as soon as he or she is notified of acceptance by the first-choice college. A student applying under the single-choice plan (EDP-S) may not apply to any colleges other than his or her first choice unless rejected by that institution. If a college follows either type of plan, applications (including financial aid applications) must be received by a specified date no later than November 15, and the college agrees to notify the applicant by a specified date no later than December 15. While many colleges subscribe to the agreement, many others offer a variation on the plan.

FAFSA. *See* Free Application for Federal Student Aid.

Family contribution. The total amount a student and his or her family are expected to pay toward college costs from their income and assets. The amount is derived from a need analysis of the family's overall financial circumstances. A Federal Methodology is used in determining a student's eligibility for federal student aid. Colleges, state agencies, and private aid programs may use a different methodology in determining eligibility for nonfederal sources of financial aid.

Federal Parent Loan for Undergraduate Students. The federal PLUS loan program permits parents of undergraduate students to borrow up to the full cost of education less any other financial aid the student may have received. The interest rate is variable, set at 3.1 percent above the one-year Treasury-bill, capped at 9 percent. The rate is adjusted annually each July 1.

Federal Pell Grant Program. A federally sponsored and administered program that provides grants based on need to undergraduate students. Congress annually sets the dollar range. Currently a Pell Grant cannot exceed $2,470 per year.

Federal Perkins Loan Program. A federally funded program based on need, administered by colleges, that provides low-interest (5%) loans of up to $3,000 per year during undergraduate study and up to $15,000 for the total undergraduate program. The combined cumulative total of loan funds available to an individual for undergraduate and graduate education is $30,000. Repayment need not begin until completion of the student's education or after limited periods of service in the military, Peace Corps, or approved comparable organizations.

Federal Stafford Loan Program. A federal program that allows students to borrow to meet educational expenses. Funds are borrowed directly from banks or other lending institutions, or, for colleges participating in the Federal Direct Loan Program, from the U.S. Government.

The federal government pays the full interest on subsidized Stafford Loans while students are enrolled in college if the loan is made on the basis of demonstrated need. For students who have not demonstrated need, unsubsidized Federal Stafford Loans are available. For unsubsidized loans, students will usually be asked to make interest payments while enrolled in school. Following a grace period, all students borrowing in the Federal Stafford Loan Program must begin repaying principal and interest after graduating or leaving school.

Federal Stafford Loans have a variable interest rate set at 3.1 percent above the federal 91-day Treasury-bill rate with a cap of 8.25 percent. The rate is adjusted annually on July 1.

The amounts that may be borrowed depend on the student's year in school. The undergraduate loan limits are as follows: first year, $2,625; second year, $3,500; third and fourth years, $5,500; to a total amount as an undergraduate of $23,000. Graduate and professional students may borrow $8,500 per year in subsidized funds and up to $10,000 in unsubsidized, to an aggregate limit, including undergraduate borrowing, of $65,000 in subsidized Federal Stafford Loans plus $13,000 in unsubsidized Stafford Loans.

Federal Supplemental Educational Opportunity Grant Program (SEOG). A federal program administered by colleges to provide need-based aid to undergraduate students. Grants of up to $4,000 a year may be awarded.

Federal Work-Study Program. A federally sponsored campus-based program. Participating colleges provide employment opportunities for students with demonstrated need who are enrolled for study at either the undergraduate or graduate level. Students are usually employed on campus, although occasionally jobs are arranged off campus. In assigning work-study to aid recipients, financial aid administrators typically take into account the recipient's employable skills, class schedule, and academic progress.

Financial aid award letter. A notice from a college or other financial aid sponsor that tells a student how much aid is being offered. The award letter also usually explains how a student's financial need was determined, describes the contents of the financial aid package, and outlines any conditions attached to the award.

Financial aid package. The total financial aid award received by a student. It may be made up of a combination or "package" of aid that includes both gift aid and self-help. Many colleges try to meet a student's full financial need, but availability of funds, institutional aid policies, and the number of students needing assistance all influence the composition of a financial aid package.

Financial need. The amount by which a student's family contribution falls short of covering the student expense budget. Assessments of need may differ depending on the need-analysis methodology used. (*See* Family contribution.)

Free Application for Federal Student Aid (FAFSA). A form completed by all applicants for federal student aid. In many states, completion of the FAFSA is also sufficient to establish eligibility for state-sponsored aid programs. There is no charge to students for completing the FAFSA. Forms are widely available in high schools and colleges, and may be filed any time *after* January 1 of the year for which one is seeking aid (e.g., after January 1, 1997, for academic year 1997-98 assistance).

Gift aid. Student financial aid, such as scholarships and grants, that does not have to be repaid and that does not require a student's being employed.

Independent student. *See* Self-supporting student.

Need analysis form. The starting point in applying for financial aid. All students must file the federally sponsored Free Application for Federal Student Aid (FAFSA) to apply for the federal financial aid programs. For many colleges, this may be the only need analysis form you will need to file. For other schools, particularly private colleges, other forms may also be required. To apply for state financial aid programs, the FAFSA may be all that you will need to file, but you should check with your state agency to learn if any other application forms need to be submitted.

Open admission. The college admission policy of admitting high school graduates and other adults generally without regard to conventional academic qualifications, such as high school subjects, high school grades, and admission test scores. Virtually all applicants with high school diplomas or their equivalent are accepted.

Parents' contribution. The amount a student's parents are expected to pay toward college costs from their income and assets. The amount is derived from need analysis of the parents' overall financial situation. The parents' contribution and the student's contribution together constitute the total family contribution, which, when subtracted from the student expense budget, equals financial need. Generally, students are eligible for financial aid equal to their financial need.

Pell Grant Program. *See* Federal Pell Grant Program.

Perkins Loan Program. *See* Federal Perkins Loan Program.

Parent Loan for Undergraduate Students (PLUS). *See* Federal Parent Loan for Undergraduate Students.

Preliminary SAT/National Merit Scholarship Qualifying Test (PSAT/NMSQT). A shorter version of the College Board's SAT I administered by high schools each year in October. The PSAT/NMSQT aids high schools in the early guidance of students planning for college and serves as the qualifying test for scholarships awarded by the National Merit Scholarship Corporation.

Reserve Officers' Training Corps (ROTC). Programs conducted by certain colleges in cooperation with the U.S. Air Force, Army, and Navy. Local recruiting offices of the services themselves can supply detailed information about these programs. Information is also available from participating colleges.

SAR. *See* Student Aid Report.

SAT I: Reasoning Test. The College Board's test of developed verbal and mathematical reasoning abilities, given on specified dates throughout the year at test centers in the United States and other countries. The SAT I is required by many colleges and sponsors of financial aid programs.

SAT II: Subject Tests. College Board tests in specific subjects, given at test centers in the United States and other countries on specified dates throughout the year.

Used by colleges not only to help with decisions about admission but also in course placement and exemption of enrolled freshmen. Formerly called Achievement Tests.

Self-help. Student financial aid, such as loans and jobs, that require repayment or a student's being employed.

Self-supporting student. For financial aid purposes, a student who is independent of support from his or her parents.

Stafford Loan Program. *See* Federal Stafford Loan Program.

Student Aid Report (SAR). A report produced by the U.S. Department of Education and sent to students who have applied for federal student financial aid. The SAR must be submitted to the college that the student attends to certify his or her eligibility for Federal Pell Grants and other federal financial programs such as the Federal Work-Study Program, Federal Perkins Loan Program, Federal Supplemental Educational Opportunity Grants, and the Federal Family Education Loan Programs.

Student expense budget. A calculation of the annual cost of attending college that is used in determining a student's financial need. Student expense budgets usually include tuition and fees, books and supplies, room and board, personal expenses, and transportation. Sometimes additional expenses are included for students with special education needs, students who have a disability, or students who are married or have children.

Student's contribution. The amount students are expected to pay toward college costs from their income, assets, and benefits. The amount is derived from need analysis of the student's resources. The student's contribution and parents' contribution constitute the total family contribution, which, when subtracted from the student budget, equals financial need. Generally, students are eligible for financial aid equal to their financial need.

Supplemental Educational Opportunity Grant Program. *See* Federal Supplemental Educational Opportunity Grant Program (FSEOG).

Tuition and fee waivers. Some colleges waive the tuition or tuition and fees for some categories of students, such as adults, senior citizens, or children of alumni. Colleges with such plans are listed in a separate section in this book.

Part II. College costs and financial aid

12. Table of college information

Introduction

The Table of College Information provides detailed lists of expenses and financial aid at 3,100 colleges, universities, and proprietary schools. The data were compiled from information supplied by the institutions themselves on the College Board's Annual Survey of Colleges, 1996-97. The lists are alphabetical by state, and include the information provided by all participating institutions through the end of May 1996. Every effort is made to ensure that the data are as complete and accurate as possible. However, students are urged to contact institutions directly to confirm the information.

Institutions were asked to give expense figures for the academic year beginning fall 1996. If the 1996-97 tuition and fees were not yet set but a reliable forecast was available, the estimated tuition and fees are given with a single dagger next to them. If these figures were not yet available, the 1995-96 tuition and fees are listed with a double dagger next to them.

Details on each category of expenses and financial aid and what these figures can mean to applicants are explained here.

In an effort to collect comparable cost information, the College Board asked institutions to provide data for specifically budgeted items. The figures supplied under each column heading represent the following.

Educational costs
Tuition and fees

This figure indicates the annual tuition and general fees an institution charges most first-year, full-time students. Colleges were asked to report these costs based on a nine-month academic year of 30 semester hours or 45 quarter hours.

Additional out-of-state/district tuition

This item represents only the *additional* charges made to students who do not meet state or district residency requirements. The figure to the left of the diagonal mark shows additional charges for out-of-state students; the figure to the right shows additional out-of-district charges. These charges added to the tuition and fees in the first column will give you the total tuition and fees for out-of-state and out-of-district students, respectively.

Books and supplies

This figure is the average cost of books and supplies for the normal course load for full-time students. Supplies may be more expensive for students in certain areas of study (art, architecture, or engineering, for example) and institutions did not include these special costs unless the majority of their students are in these fields.

Living costs: Campus residents
Room and board for campus residents

For resident students, room and board includes the charge for living and eating for nine months in facilities operated by or for the college. These are average charges based on double-room occupancy and 21 meals a week in college facilities.

Transportation for campus residents

These figures include typical costs for two round-trips between home and campus during the nine-month academic year. If you anticipate more frequent trips between home and campus during the academic year, you should adjust this figure accordingly.

Other costs for campus residents

This column shows typical costs for miscellaneous

personal expenses, such as clothing, laundry, entertainment, snacks, medical insurance, and furnishings.

Living costs: Students living at home

Board for students at home

This column shows average costs for dependent students living at home, including three meals a day, seven days a week.

Transportation for students at home

The figures in this column represent the typical costs for daily travel to and from college for students who commute.

Other costs for students at home

This column shows miscellaneous personal expenses for students living at home. These include clothing, laundry, entertainment, and medical insurance.

Financial aid information

Total freshmen enrolled

This is the total freshman enrollment for fall 1995 on which the percentage of freshman students receiving aid is based.

Percentage receiving aid

This figure represents the percentage of enrolled freshmen (preceding column) who received some form of financial aid in fall 1995. The aid could be based on financial need or on other criteria such as talent or athletic ability. The financial aid could be in the form of grants, scholarships, loans, or jobs.

Freshmen judged to have financial need

This column shows the number of freshmen in fall 1995 who were judged to have financial need.

Percent offered aid

This figure is the percentage of freshmen with financial need (preceding column) who were offered aid. The financial aid could be grants, loans, or jobs.

Grants and scholarships

Need-based scholarships

An X in these columns indicates that the college awards scholarships on the basis of financial need combined with exceptional academic ability or talent in music or drama, art, or athletics.

Non-need scholarships

An X in these columns indicates that the college awards scholarships, without regard for financial need, on the basis of exceptional academic ability or talent in music or drama, art, or athletics.

Financial aid deadlines

Priority deadline for financial aid

The priority deadline is the date by which the college prefers that you submit your financial aid application. Missing this deadline may mean that most or all financial aid may have already been awarded, but it does not necessarily mean that *all* aid has been given out. It is best to meet the college's priority deadline in order to have the best chance of receiving aid if you qualify.

Closing deadline for financial aid

This is the final date by which the college will accept your application for financial aid.

Institutional aid form

An X in this column indicates that the college has its own financial aid form that you will have to complete if you are applying for aid. This requirement is in addition to the FAFSA. Be sure to verify with the college what it requires. (See "Need analysis form" in the Glossary for more information.)

Notes

Use this page to make notes about the colleges that interest you.

Alabama

Institution	Tuition and fees	Add'l out-of-state/district tuition	Books and supplies	Costs for campus residents			Costs for students at home		
				Room and board	Trans-portation	Other costs	Board only	Trans-portation	Other costs
Alabama Agricultural and Mechanical University	† 2,358	1,886/—	615	2,218	1,000	950	1,530	1,000	950
Alabama Aviation and Technical College	‡ 1,080	990/—	1,625		1,000	1,300	2,700	1,000	1,000
Alabama Southern Community College	‡ 1,305	1,080/—	750					600	
Alabama State University	2,052	1,800/—	600	3,000	900	1,200	2,070	1,200	1,500
Athens State College	† 1,959	1,884/—	450		564	900	1,783	989	1,021
Auburn University									
Auburn *7,470*	‡ 2,250	4,500/—	600	4,098	693	1,413	1,848	771	1,413
Montgomery	‡ 2,025	4,050/—	720		1,040	1,300	2,780	1,700	1,300
Bessemer State Technical College	‡ 1,080	990/—	717				1,500	900	750
Bevill State Community College	‡ 1,125	990/—	600				1,500	1,125	750
Birmingham-Southern College	‡ 12,524		500	4,585	500	900	1,500	1,500	900
Bishop State Community College	‡ 1,350	1,125/—	532				1,500	853	1,033
Calhoun Community College	‡ 1,215	990/—	500		1,000	500	1,900	1,000	500
Central Alabama Community College	‡ 1,350	1,125/—	300				1,800	600	500
Chattahoochee Valley Community College	‡ 1,305	1,080/—	600				1,800	1,125	750
Community College of the Air Force	0								
Douglas MacArthur State Technical College	‡ 990	900/—	595				1,800	1,560	668
Draughons Junior College	5,110		600						
Enterprise State Junior College	‡ 1,350	1,125/—	450				1,900	650	550
Faulkner University	6,600		1,084	3,500	1,200	1,200	830	1,200	1,200
Gadsden State Community College	‡ 1,350	1,125/—	525	2,250	150	525	1,500	790	525
George C. Wallace State Community College									
Dothan	‡ 1,350	1,125/—	600				2,000	720	300
Selma	‡ 1,260	1,035/—	690				1,500	577	976
Harry M. Ayers State Technical College	‡ 1,035	900/—	400				2,400	1,200	
Huntingdon College	10,140		500	4,410	500	745		300	545
International Bible College	† 4,650		450		700	1,500	2,100	1,000	1,500
J. F. Drake State Technical College	‡ 1,170	1,080/—	500					550	
Jacksonville State University	1,940	970/—	600	2,870	900	1,200	930	1,500	1,200
James H. Faulkner State Community College	‡ 1,350	1,125/—	450	2,175	550	800	1,500	950	700
Jefferson Davis Community College	‡ 1,170	990/—	525	2,100			1,500	300	600
Jefferson State Community College	† 1,350	1,125/—	495				2,250	1,155	540
John M. Patterson State Technical College	‡ 1,260	1,125/—	400					300	200
Judson College	‡ 6,400		650	3,950	400	1,600		650	1,600
Lawson State Community College	‡ 1,215	990/—	450				1,600	850	900
Lurleen B. Wallace State Junior College	‡ 1,193	990/—	375				1,800	600	600
Marion Military Institute	7,740		644	2,800	625	1,962		400	1,575
Miles College	4,500		400	2,750	500	1,000		500	1,000
Northeast Alabama Community College	‡ 1,125	900/—	600	225			1,200	750	1,500
Northwest-Shoals Community College	‡ 1,350	1,125/—	600				1,200	800	900
Oakwood College	7,340		600	4,326	2,400	1,500	2,500	600	800
Reid State Technical College	‡ 990	900/—	400						
Samford University	9,070		550	4,106	700	1,650	2,066	990	1,650
Selma University	‡ 5,340		400		350	650			600
Shelton State Community College	‡ 1,305	1,080/—	450				1,000	500	200
Snead State Community College	‡ 1,035	900/—	600	1,643	540	700	1,500	925	700
Southeastern Bible College	5,040		300	2,940	400		2,000	720	

†Figures are projected for 1996-97. ‡Figures are for 1995-96.

All aid		Need-based aid		Grants and scholarships								Financial aid deadlines		Inst	
				Need-based				Non-need-based						aid	
Total fresh-men	Percent receiving aid	Freshmen judged to have need	Percent offered aid	Acad	Music/drama	Art	Athl	Acad	Music/drama	Art	Athl	Priority	Closing	form	Notes
853	90			X				X	X		X	4/1	6/1	X	
60	65							X					none	X	
													none		
1,158	90	1,058	100					X	X	X	X	6/1	none	X	
							X	X	X	X	X		none		
3,592	52	800	100	X	X			X	X	X	X	4/15	none	X	
741	40	289	100					X	X		X	4/15	4/15	X	
711	65	115	91	X				X				9/1	none		
2,361	68							X	X		X	5/1	8/25		
247	99	111	100	X	X	X	X	X	X	X	X	3/1	none	X	
729	42			X	X	X	X	X			X	6/15	none		
4,976	21	675	100	X	X	X	X	X	X	X	X	5/1	none	X	
								X	X	X	X	7/15	none		
773	63							X	X	X	X	6/1	none		
													none		
390	80							X				6/1	none		
													none		
				X				X	X	X	X	4/1	none		
223	90							X			X	5/1	none		
								X	X		X	4/15	none	X	
													none		
528	60							X	X		X	6/1	none		
													none		
163	97	117	100	X	X	X	X	X	X	X	X	5/1	none	X	
11	61	8	88	X								7/1	none		
230	75			X				X					none		
927	49	435	100	X	X	X	X	X	X	X	X	3/15	none	X	
1,220	63							X	X	X	X	7/1	8/1		
													none		
911	39			X	X		X	X	X		X	5/1	none	X	
373	60							X					none		
													none		
481	81	267	100	X	X	X	X			X	X	6/1	none		
349	70			X	X	X	X	X	X	X	X	6/1	none		
135	95			X				X	X		X	6/15	none		
250	84			X			X	X				4/15	none		
512	60							X	X	X			none		
		350	100					X	X	X	X	6/1	none	X	
374	67	255	94	X				X				4/15	5/15		
272	89			X									none		
650	76	253	97	X	X			X	X	X	X	3/1	none		
													none		
													none		
								X	X	X	X	4/15	none		
84	90	59	100	X	X			X	X			5/1	9/10	X	

Institution	Tuition and fees	Add'l out-of-state/ district tuition	Books and supplies	Costs for campus residents			Costs for students at home		
				Room and board	Trans-portation	Other costs	Board only	Trans-portation	Other costs
Southern Christian University	6,660		696				5,240	1,233	1,610
Southern Union State Community College	‡ 1,350	1,125/—	400		600	1,100	1,800	600	600
Sparks State Technical College	‡ 1,080	990/—	820						
Spring Hill College	13,140		600	4,960	900	900	1,500	900	900
Stillman College	5,200		500	3,100	300	1,000	1,500	300	1,000
Talladega College	6,084		1,000	2,964	900	500	750	900	500
Troy State University									
Dothan	2,325	2,100/—	600				3,060	1,080	1,425
Montgomery	‡ 1,887	1,887/—	600					1,785	7,953
Troy	† 2,205	1,980/—	600	3,330	500	600			
Tuskegee University	7,424		665	3,620	700	1,207	2,100	300	210
University of Alabama									
Birmingham	2,700	2,400/—	750		850	1,350	2,500	1,725	1,350
Huntsville	3,750	4,140/—	720	3,570	900	1,200	1,800	1,350	900
Tuscaloosa	† 2,470	3,798/—	650	3,285	586	1,400	2,250	1,654	1,400
University of Alabama at Birmingham:									
Walker College	1,976	1,800/—	480	2,460	2,400	4,180	2,620	4,215	2,816
University of Mobile	6,910		500	3,880	250	1,000	1,500	450	400
University of Montevallo	2,780	2,640/—	600	3,142	1,000	1,000	1,750	1,000	1,000
University of North Alabama	‡ 1,885	1,266/—	550	3,010	800	1,556	1,975	800	1,556
University of South Alabama	‡ 2,541	1,050/—	450	2,940					
University of West Alabama	† 2,145		570	2,634	900	1,200	1,500	1,500	1,200
Virginia College	6,400		300				1,700	100	100
Wallace State College at Hanceville	‡ 990	900/—	450		675	2,650	1,500	1,155	900
Alaska									
Alaska Bible College	3,300		400	3,400	1,000	1,000		750	700
Alaska Pacific University	8,040		800	4,300	500	1,500	1,500	1,500	1,500
Prince William Sound Community College	2,150	4,200/—	500		936	1,125	2,520	936	1,125
Sheldon Jackson College	9,250		550	4,800	2,000	1,000	2,800	500	1,000
University of Alaska									
Anchorage	2,263	4,200/—	800		1,080	1,260	2,520	1,080	1,260
Fairbanks	2,890	4,200/—	550	3,690	324	1,980	4,010	1,710	1,980
Southeast	2,134	4,200/—	610		162	990	2,025	585	990
Arizona									
Academy of Business College	‡ 5,200								
Al Collins Graphic Design School	15,300		1,400						
American Indian College of the Assemblies of God	3,300		450	3,000	1,100	1,400		1,100	1,400
Arizona College of the Bible	5,886		450		540	900	1,500	1,000	900
Arizona State University *8,678	‡ 1,950	6,028/—	700			2,500	2,390		2,500
Arizona Western College	‡ 780	4,800/—	350	2,930	350	952	1,100	924	950
CAD Institute	† 10,125		1,005						
Central Arizona College	700	4,284/—	400	3,020	700	1,500	1,500	700	1,500
Cochise College	‡ 810	4,284/—	600	2,930	680	1,125	1,800	800	675
DeVry Institute of Technology: Phoenix	‡ 6,335		550				2,217	1,831	2,045
Eastern Arizona College	‡ 628	3,412/—	400	2,952	950	900	1,700	950	900
Embry-Riddle Aeronautical University:									
Prescott Campus	8,675		600	3,640	1,800	1,220	1,300	1,860	1,220
Gateway Community College	‡ 1,030	3,750/—	700				2,500	1,150	1,150
Glendale Community College	‡ 1,030	3,412/—	700				2,504	1,150	1,150
Grand Canyon University	‡ 7,240		600	3,100	612	1,125	1,530	612	1,125
Lamson Junior College at Mesa	10,120		1,288						

†Figures are projected for 1996-97. ‡Figures are for 1995-96.

| All aid | | Need–based aid | | Grants and scholarships | | | | | | | | Financial aid deadlines | | Inst aid form | Notes |
| Total freshmen | Percent receiving aid | Freshmen judged to have need | Percent offered aid | Need–based | | | | Non–need–based | | | | | | | |
				Acad	Music/drama	Art	Athl	Acad	Music/drama	Art	Athl	Priority	Closing		
				X				X				5/1	6/30		
													none		
380	88			X				X				8/1	none		
232	87	147	100	X				X			X	3/1	7/15	X	
226	90			X	X			X	X			6/15	none		
223	94			X			X	X			X	4/1	6/10		
20	15			X				X				5/1	8/1		
102	30												none		
891	35			X	X	X	X	X	X	X	X	5/1	none		
624	90			X				X	X		X	3/15	3/31	X	
1,182	53	675	90	X			X	X	X	X	X	5/1	none	X	
561	49			X			X	X	X	X	X	4/1	none		
2,531	50	825	97	X				X	X	X	X	3/1	none	X	
301	61	172	93	X		X	X	X		X	X	7/1	none		
372	96	250	100	X				X		X	X	3/31	none		
549	31	207	100				X	X	X		X	4/15	none		
788	40	270	100	X				X	X		X	4/1	none		
													none	X	
468	77	154	100					X	X	X	X	4/20	5/15		
1,688	50							X	X	X	X		none	X	
21	72	9	100	X				X	X				8/1	X	
30	100	20	100	X				X					none		
22	55			X				X				4/1	none		
													none		
1,279	34			X				X	X	X	X	4/1	none	X	
				X	X	X			X	X	X	5/15	none		
108	75			X				X				6/1	none		
													none		
18	99			X				X				4/1	8/23		
10	70	7	100	X	X			X	X			4/15	9/15		
				X	X			X	X	X	X	3/1	none		
								X	X	X		4/20	none		
													none		
989	45			X			X	X			X	4/15	none		
								X					none		
													none		
285	74	196	96	X				X				4/15	none		
				X				X				4/15	none		
				X				X		X	X	5/15	none	X	
													none		
													none		

Institution	Tuition and fees	Add'l out-of-state/district tuition	Books and supplies	Costs for campus residents			Costs for students at home		
				Room and board	Transportation	Other costs	Board only	Transportation	Other costs
Mesa Community College	‡ 1,030	3,750/—	400					350	
Mohave Community College	‡ 580	2,900/—	680				2,020	900	1,100
Navajo Community College	† 620		450	2,940	400		1,500	600	
Northern Arizona University	‡ 1,950	6,028/—	620	3,206	880	1,350	1,120	650	1,130
Northland Pioneer College	‡ 660	1,650/—	520	2,085	670	1,150	1,730	920	1,150
Paradise Valley Community College	1,040	3,750/—	700					1,185	1,185
Phoenix College	‡ 1,032	3,750/—	700					1,150	3,654
Pima Community College	‡ 734	3,630/—	500					250	3,000
Prescott College	11,105		400				660	729	807
Rio Salado Community College	† 1,030	4,770/—	400					1,000	800
Scottsdale Community College	‡ 1,030	3,750/—	700				2,579	1,185	1,185
South Mountain Community College	‡ 1,030	3,750/—	800				1,500	800	
Southwestern College	6,300		400	2,650	700	700			700
University of Arizona *12,788*	‡ 1,950	6,028/—	620	4,190	900	1,750	1,500	1,200	1,750
University of Phoenix	‡ 6,290		525					300	
Western International University	4,950		900						
Yavapai College	‡ 666	5,000/—	500	2,830	600	1,050	700	600	900
Arkansas									
Arkansas Baptist College	‡ 2,025		600	2,926	860	850	1,100	860	860
Arkansas State University									
Beebe Branch	‡ 1,210	—/744	500	1,980	560	500		800	500
Jonesboro	‡ 1,960	1,920/1,650	500	2,620	780	630	1,500	1,200	400
Arkansas Tech University	2,007	1,902/—	550	2,732	480	1,000	2,700	1,000	750
Central Baptist College	4,406		600	3,032	600	800	1,664	800	800
East Arkansas Community College	792	372/168	400					700	1,000
Garland County Community College	860	1,484/238	600				1,500	930	2,980
Harding University	6,825		700	3,799	900	945	1,935	900	945
Henderson State University	2,032	1,860/—	650	2,720	1,400	2,000	1,280	2,000	1,600
Hendrix College	10,118		500	3,807	500	625	1,935	562	563
John Brown University	8,308		600	4,224	1,500	1,350	2,500	600	1,130
Lyon College	9,470		500	4,238					
Mississippi County Community College	1,090	1,800/300	500				5,548	985	3,032
North Arkansas Community/Technical College	‡ 912	1,272/216					925	933	1,415
Ouachita Baptist University	7,650		500	2,970	650	1,530	1,600	650	1,130
Philander Smith College	‡ 3,048		400	2,540	700	750		700	750
Phillips County Community College	‡ 840	1,128/216	450				1,350	841	1,925
Rich Mountain Community College	1,110	3,030/270	500				2,500	600	500
Shorter College	2,150		400	2,400	200	200		200	300
South Arkansas Community College	† 898	1,152/216	500				1,500		450
Southern Arkansas University									
Magnolia	‡ 1,758	936/—	500	2,500	900	1,585	2,685	1,400	1,585
Tech	‡ 1,032	516/—	500		500	1,250		900	1,250
University of Arkansas									
Fayetteville	‡ 2,190	3,192/—	650	3,618	1,250	2,000			2,000
Little Rock	‡ 2,518	3,468/—	800		800	800	2,100	800	800
Medical Sciences	‡ 2,004	3,000/—	470		831	1,600	3,874	1,152	2,413
Monticello	‡ 1,818	2,112/—	450	2,410	475	850	1,150	950	850
Pine Bluff	‡ 1,773	2,112/—	600	2,900	700	800		800	700
University of Central Arkansas	2,342	1,972/—	600	2,730	745	1,064	1,800		1,064
University of the Ozarks	7,140		600	3,400	1,800	2,700	1,400	1,300	1,215
Westark Community College	† 860	1,176/264	425				1,500	600	450
Williams Baptist College	4,970		600	2,522	700	600	1,500	700	800

†Figures are projected for 1996-97. ‡Figures are for 1995-96.

All aid		Need-based aid		Grants and scholarships								Financial aid deadlines		Inst aid form	Notes
				Need-based				Non-need-based							
Total fresh-men	Percent receiving aid	Freshmen judged to have need	Percent offered aid	Acad	Music/ drama	Art	Athl	Acad	Music/ drama	Art	Athl	Priority	Closing		
				X	X	X	X	X	X	X	X	5/15	none		
1,830	20			X	X	X		X	X	X		4/15	none		
				X				X			X	4/15	none	X	
2,330	65			X	X	X	X	X	X	X	X	4/15	none		
		1,000	100					X	X	X	X	6/1	none		
				X				X					none		
													none		
4,873	20							X			X	4/1	none		
		20	100	X				X				4/15	none		
8,379	2			X								4/15	none	X	
3,389	32	1,155	46	X	X	X	X	X	X	X	X	6/30	none		
				X	X	X	X	X	X	X	X	5/1	none		
47	95											4/15	8/31		
4,557	59			X	X	X	X	X	X	X	X	3/1	none		
													none		
453	56												none		
526	44			X	X	X	X	X	X	X	X	4/15	none		
567	60	365	96					X	X		X	5/1	none		
1,517	60			X				X	X	X	X	5/1	none		
810	58			X	X		X	X	X		X	4/1	none		
97	98	55	100	X	X			X	X			7/1	none		
367	82			X								4/15	none		
635	63			X	X	X		X	X	X	X	3/1	none		
878	82	732	100	X	X		X	X	X	X	X	4/1	none		
623	53	332	99	X				X	X	X	X	4/15	none		
274	94	155	100	X				X	X	X		2/15	none	X	
252	78	156	100	X	X		X	X	X	X	X	2/1	5/1		
193	98	135	100	X				X	X	X	X	4/1	none		
251	51	190	94	X				X	X	X	X	4/15	none	X	
								X	X	X	X	5/1	none	X	
380	95	188	100	X	X		X	X	X		X	5/1	none	X	
				X				X				5/1	none		
				X				X	X		X	4/1	5/1		
734	46			X				X				7/31	none		
85	70	25	100	X							X	5/1	none		
297	50			X				X	X		X	7/1	none		
477	63	192	100					X	X		X	6/1	none	X	
								X	X	X		7/15	none		
2,246	60	628	50	X	X			X	X	X	X	4/1	none		
962	60			X				X	X	X	X	5/1	7/1		
													none		
503	56			X				X	X		X		none		
582	83			X	X	X	X					4/15	none		
1,527	51							X	X	X	X	2/15	none		
175	71			X				X	X		X	5/1	none		
				X				X				6/1	none		
108	92			X	X	X	X	X	X	X	X	5/1	none		

Institution	Tuition and fees	Add'l out-of-state/district tuition	Books and supplies	Costs for campus residents			Costs for students at home		
				Room and board	Trans-portation	Other costs	Board only	Trans-portation	Other costs
California									
Academy of Art College	12,435		648	5,742	738	1,566		594	1,620
Allan Hancock College	‡ 414	3,210/—	648				2,196	594	1,620
American Academy of Dramatic Arts: West	9,200		460				1,652	448	1,232
American College: Los Angeles	‡ 10,230		750		800		800	800	2,000
American River College	‡ 390	3,600/—	500				2,160	400	756
Antelope Valley College	‡ 390	3,180/—	630				2,124	576	1,548
Antioch Southern California									
Los Angeles	‡ 9,600		1,050						
Santa Barbara	‡ 8,850		450						
Armstrong University	7,545		450						
Art Center College of Design	15,440		3,462					856	1,696
Art Institute of Southern California	10,500		1,216				4,587	1,327	2,312
Azusa Pacific University	13,076		600	4,020	700	1,250		1,000	
Bakersfield College	‡ 415	3,210/—	650				1,600	670	1,420
Barstow College	‡ 390	3,210/—	630				2,124	576	1,500
Bethany College	7,860		1,079	3,900	2,247	2,136	1,690	2,247	2,136
Biola University	13,408		648	4,932	540	1,278	1,062	576	1,548
Brooks College	‡ 7,140		800	4,480	1,300	1,100	1,100	900	1,100
Brooks Institute of Photography	† 14,225		6,000						
Butte College	‡ 544	4,294/—	630				907	684	1,430
Cabrillo College	‡ 484	3,270/—	630				1,512	600	1,595
California Baptist College	8,680		630	4,494	576	1,278	1,566	720	1,530
California College of Arts and Crafts	15,050		648		560	1,315	2,210	612	1,670
California Culinary Academy	‡ 12,470		1,315				7,000		
California Institute of the Arts	16,410		1,000	5,900	592	1,976		704	1,656
California Institute of Technology	18,216		795	5,478	600	1,493	1,800		1,493
California Lutheran University	14,355		630	5,640	540	1,584	2,400	720	1,530
California Maritime Academy	2,444	7,380/—	700	5,170	640	1,500			
California Polytechnic State University: San Luis Obispo	‡ 2,042	7,380/—	648	5,044	576	1,692	2,196	594	1,818
California State Polytechnic University: Pomona	‡ 1,789	7,380/—	630	4,837	540	1,638	2,124	576	1,764
California State University									
Bakersfield	‡ 1,897	7,380/—	630	4,248	530	1,164	2,124	530	925
Chico	‡ 2,002	7,380/—	648	5,150	573	1,634	2,124	682	1,700
Dominguez Hills	‡ 1,791	7,380/—	630		540	1,600	2,124	576	1,600
Fresno	‡ 1,808	7,380/—	612	4,517	558	1,206	2,124	702	1,060
Fullerton *$9,926*	‡ 1,916	7,380/—	630		540	1,638	2,124	576	1,764
Hayward	‡ 1,774	7,380/—	648		738	1,692	2,196	594	1,638
Long Beach	‡ 1,769	7,380/—	630	5,300	540	1,638	1,512	576	1,764
Los Angeles	‡ 1,772	7,380/—	630	4,763	720	1,584	2,124	576	1,584
Northridge	‡ 1,970	7,380/—	630	5,820	640	1,588	2,124	576	1,398
Sacramento	‡ 1,928	7,380/—	612	5,342	558	1,206	2,100	810	1,737
San Bernardino	‡ 1,821	7,380/—	630	5,256	576	1,584	2,124	720	1,530
San Marcos	‡ 1,720	7,380/—	648		702	1,710	2,196	576	1,710
Stanislaus	‡ 1,865	7,380/—	630	5,409	720	1,458	2,124	576	1,458
Canada College	‡ 450	3,390/—	630					650	1,450
Cerritos Community College	‡ 425	3,048/—	648				2,196	594	1,764
Cerro Coso Community College	‡ 390	3,210/—	630				2,124	720	900
Chabot College	‡ 396	3,300/—	750				2,196	750	500
Chaffey Community College	‡ 390	3,480/—	650				2,196	900	1,620

†Figures are projected for 1996-97. ‡Figures are for 1995-96.

| All aid | | Need–based aid | | Grants and scholarships | | | | | | | | Financial aid deadlines | | Inst aid form | Notes |
| Total freshmen | Percent receiving aid | Freshmen judged to have need | Percent offered aid | Need–based | | | | Non–need–based | | | | | | | |
				Acad	Music/drama	Art	Athl	Acad	Music/drama	Art	Athl	Priority	Closing		
906	40	174	100	X		X		X		X		5/1	none	X	
				X	X	X	X	X	X	X	X	5/1	none		
60	60				X			X	X			7/1	none	X	
95	20											3/2	none		
3,500	12			X				X				3/2	none		
				X	X	X		X	X	X		3/2	none		
												8/8	none		
													none		
200	63	123	100									3/1	none	X	
27	45			X		X		X		X		3/2	8/26		
501	80			X	X		X	X	X		X	3/1	none		
3,300	20			X				X				3/2	none		
77	88			X				X	X	X	X	3/2	none	X	
556	80							X	X	X	X	3/2	none	X	
													none		
96	39	30	100	X		X		X		X		3/2	none	X	
													none		
3,077	58			X	X	X	X					3/2	none		
181	88	161	100	X	X		X	X	X		X	4/1	none	X	
79	69	55	100	X		X		X		X		3/2	none	X	
650	70												none	X	
97	89				X	X			X	X		3/2	none		
218	75	151	100	X				X				1/15	none		
248	93	197	100	X	X			X	X	X		3/2	none		
38	66			X				X				3/2	none		
2,508	74	1,247	100	X	X	X	X	X	X	X	X		3/2		
1,948	56	1,336		X	X	X	X	X			X	3/2	none		
421	19			X	X	X	X	X	X	X	X	3/2	none		
1,425	24			X	X	X	X	X				3/1	none		
508	70							X	X	X	X	4/15	none		
1,616	33			X	X	X	X	X	X	X	X	3/2	none		
3,727	17			X				X	X	X	X	3/2	none		
584	51			X				X				3/2	none		
2,216	48	1,296	100		X		X	X	X	X	X	3/2	none		
1,319	55	1,043	97	X				X	X	X	X	3/1	none		
				X	X	X	X	X	X	X	X	3/2	none		
1,338	42			X	X	X	X	X	X	X	X	3/2	3/2	X	
878	62			X	X	X		X				3/20	3/2		
45	48			X				X				3/2	none		
432	25			X				X	X	X		3/2	none		
													none		
													none		
975	6			X	X	X		X	X	X		5/15	none		
													none		
				X				X				3/1	none		

Institution	Tuition and fees	Add'l out-of-state/district tuition	Books and supplies	Costs for campus residents			Costs for students at home		
				Room and board	Trans-portation	Other costs	Board only	Trans-portation	Other costs
Chapman University	18,520		600	6,644	650	1,100	2,000	650	1,100
Charles R. Drew University: College of Allied Health	3,850		2,268		1,683	2,832	1,440	720	1,460
Christian Heritage College	9,240		600	4,120	500	1,700	1,200	600	1,700
Citrus College	415	4,300/—	648				2,124	666	1,746
City College of San Francisco	‡ 410	3,584/—	645					580	4,490
Claremont McKenna College	18,460		600	6,510		900	3,600		900
Coastline Community College	‡ 328	3,084/—	648				2,196	576	1,566
Cogswell Polytechnical College	7,370		600					620	1,232
Coleman College	‡ 5,050		425					1,000	1,000
College of Alameda	‡ 394	3,810/—	630				2,124	720	1,584
College of the Canyons	‡ 410	3,120/—	630				2,124	684	1,584
College of the Desert	‡ 410	3,440/—	630				2,124	684	1,584
College of Marin: Kentfield	‡ 412	4,050/—	650				1,700	680	2,021
College of Notre Dame	† 14,400		612	6,200	558	1,392	2,322	558	1,392
College of Oceaneering	13,650						750	300	750
College of the Redwoods	‡ 405	3,630/—	630	4,565	540	1,638	2,124	576	1,550
College of San Mateo	‡ 410	3,540/—	648				2,196	594	1,818
College of the Sequoias	‡ 412	3,570/—	648				1,890	594	900
College of the Siskiyous	‡ 410	3,210/—	630	3,700	720	1,584	2,124	720	1,584
Columbia College	‡ 418	3,360/—	650		400	1,200	2,124	500	900
Columbia College: Hollywood	† 6,750		525				4,356	549	5,049
Compton Community College	‡ 390	3,120/—	650						
Concordia University	13,130		600	4,920	560	1,010	1,980	860	1,010
Contra Costa College	‡ 390	3,420/—	648				2,196	684	1,620
Cosumnes River College	‡ 390	3,750/—	630				1,750	715	1,183
Crafton Hills College	‡ 422	3,452/—	648				2,196	738	1,764
Cuesta College	‡ 450	3,470/—	630				1,566	720	1,530
Cuyamaca College	‡ 420	3,120/—	450				1,500	600	700
Cypress College	‡ 415	3,420/—	630				2,124	750	750
De Anza College	‡ 471	3,420/—	648				834	576	1,584
Deep Springs College	0				1,250	350			
DeVry Institute of Technology: Pomona	6,560		560				1,896	2,411	1,770
Diablo Valley College	‡ 402	3,432/—	630				2,124	684	1,548
Dominican College of San Rafael	14,670		680	6,700	624	1,460		740	1,675
Dominican School of Philosophy and Theology	8,450		535				2,000	1,275	1,930
Don Bosco Technical Institute	† 3,250		400					450	400
D-Q University	‡ 3,800		500	4,352	517	1,622	1,680	550	1,402
East Los Angeles College	‡ 405	3,420/—	630				2,124	576	1,300
El Camino College	‡ 410	3,510/—	612				1,998	684	1,728
Empire College	5,100								
Evergreen Valley College	‡ 410	3,620/—	612				1,998	684	1,548
Fashion Institute of Design and Merchandising									
Los Angeles	12,415								
San Francisco	‡ 12,240		1,875				1,410	612	1,512
Feather River College	‡ 434	3,750/—	550				2,196	684	1,638
Foothill College	‡ 475	3,330/—	750				600	750	1,150
Fresno City College	‡ 410	3,620/—	648				1,804		1,450
Fresno Pacific College	11,430		648	3,920	558	1,170	1,602	810	1,566
Fullerton College	‡ 413	3,420/—	648				2,196	594	1,818

†Figures are projected for 1996-97. ‡Figures are for 1995-96.

Total freshmen	Percent receiving aid	Freshmen judged to have need	Percent offered aid	Need-based Acad	Music/drama	Art	Athl	Non-need Acad	Music/drama	Art	Athl	Priority	Closing	Inst aid form	Notes
356	74	281	99	X				X	X	X		3/2	none	X	
121	35			X				X				5/1	none		
73	85			X	X		X	X	X		X	3/2	none	X	
				X	X	X	X	X	X	X	X	3/2	none		
				X	X	X	X	X				3/2	none		
288	63	148	100					X				2/1			
												3/2	none	X	
40	40			X				X				5/1	6/1		
								X				3/2	none		
1,500	15											3/2	none		
													none		
				X	X	X		X	X	X		3/1	none		
													none		
115	78	85	100	X	X			X	X	X	X	3/2	none		
													none		
1,241	50			X				X		X		4/15	none		
2,069	38	550	100									3/2	none	X	
2,038	38			X	X		X	X				3/2	none	X	
500	25							X				5/2	none		
				X	X	X		X	X	X		3/2	12/1		
80	35	35	100	X								2/1	none	X	
228	85	105	100	X	X		X	X	X		X	3/15	6/30	X	
2,016	37											3/2	none		
				X		X	X						none		
				X				X				6/1	none		
				X				X				3/2	none		
													none		
													none		
8,495	13			X	X	X		X	X	X		3/2	none		
								X					none		
4,456	10			X				X				3/2	none		
75	85	67	100	X	X	X	X	X	X	X	X	3/1	none	X	
														X	
													none		
													none		
		1,200	100	X	X	X	X					6/15	none		
4,371	8							X	X	X	X	6/1	none		
				X				X	X	X	X	5/31	none		
1,050	74											3/2	none		
													none		
480	40			X				X				3/2	none		
4,000	11			X	X	X	X	X	X	X	X	4/30	none		
5,469	80			X				X	X	X		4/15	none		
120	90	105	100	X	X	X	X	X	X	X	X	1/31	none	X	
2,736	3			X				X	X	X	X	5/1	none		

Institution	Tuition and fees	Add'l out-of-state/district tuition	Books and supplies	Costs for campus residents			Costs for students at home		
				Room and board	Transportation	Other costs	Board only	Transportation	Other costs
Gavilan Community College	‡ 390	3,840/—	648				2,835	738	1,866
Glendale Community College	‡ 408	3,276/—	408				2,196	594	1,620
Golden Gate University	8,302		400				2,050	2,176	3,330
Golden West College	‡ 410	3,210/—	630				2,124	720	1,584
Grossmont Community College	‡ 410	3,330/—	630				2,124	700	800
Hartnell College	‡ 390	3,300/—	630				2,124	576	1,380
Harvey Mudd College	19,426		700	7,197		900			
Heald Business College									
Concord	8,000		800						
Fresno	5,760		900						
San Jose	6,000								
Heald Business College: Hayward	8,050								
Heald Business College: Oakland	‡ 5,850		675						
Heald Business College-Salinas	5,850		250						
Heald Business College-Stockton	5,400		180						
Heald College									
Sacramento	‡ 5,850		525						
Santa Rosa	7,850		800						
Heald Institute of Technology	8,400		1,000						
Heald Institute of Technology-Hayward	8,450		1,100						
Heald Institute of Technology-Sacramento	9,600								
Heald Institute of Technology-San Francisco	6,350		795						
Heald Institute of Technology-San Jose	† 6,350		795						
Hebrew Union College: Jewish Institute of Religion	7,500		750						
Holy Names College	13,450		612	5,522	558	1,170	4,050	810	1,566
Humboldt State University	‡ 1,858	7,380/—	648	4,933	576	1,634	2,196	576	1,754
Humphreys College	† 5,870		630		540	1,530	1,566	720	1,530
Imperial Valley College	‡ 390	3,810/—	630				1,500	650	1,548
Irvine Valley College	‡ 410	3,210/—	630				2,124	1,040	1,784
John F. Kennedy University	‡ 8,439		504					675	
Kelsey-Jenney College	‡ 8,388						2,124	576	1,584
Kings River Community College	‡ 410	3,620/—	648	3,170	738	1,550	1,804	684	1,450
La Sierra University	13,545		450	3,990	522	1,314	1,512	612	1,458
Lake Tahoe Community College	‡ 432	3,735/—	658				2,124	576	1,386
Laney College	‡ 394	3,810/—	648				5,760	738	1,620
Las Positas College	‡ 398	3,300/—	648				2,124	720	1,530
Lassen College	‡ 405	3,668/—	648	4,588	576	1,314	2,196	594	1,620
LIFE Bible College	4,760		400	2,600		475		225	475
Lincoln University	‡ 6,475		400				5,600	360	3,600
Loma Linda University	8,400		975		700	1,500	2,200	1,500	
Long Beach City College	‡ 415	3,420/—	648				2,262	702	1,845
Los Angeles City College	‡ 405	3,720/—	840					768	2,040
Los Angeles Harbor College	‡ 390	4,140/—	648				2,196	594	1,620
Los Angeles Mission College	‡ 416	3,570/—	364				1,723	810	1,566
Los Angeles Pierce College	‡ 405	3,765/—	630				2,124	576	1,748
Los Angeles Southwest College	‡ 405	3,510/—	630				2,124	576	1,530
Los Angeles Trade and Technical College	‡ 416	4,000/—	648				2,196	594	1,620
Los Angeles Valley College	‡ 416	3,500/—	648				2,196	594	1,620
Los Medanos College	‡ 392	3,420/—	612				2,322	702	1,440

†Figures are projected for 1996-97. ‡Figures are for 1995-96.

All aid		Need-based aid		Grants and scholarships								Financial aid deadlines		Inst aid form	Notes
				Need-based				Non-need-based							
Total freshmen	Percent receiving aid	Freshmen judged to have need	Percent offered aid	Acad	Music/drama	Art	Athl	Acad	Music/drama	Art	Athl	Priority	Closing		
				X				X	X	X	X	6/30	none		
2,313	20											7/1	none		
17	51	4	75	X				X					none	X	
2,500	29			X		X		X		X		6/1	none		
4,754	15			X	X	X	X					4/1	none		
													none		
177	81	116	100										2/1		
													none		
													none		
													none		
150	90			X				X				6/30	none		
													none		
													none		
				X				X					none		
53	54			X	X	X	X	X	X	X	X	3/2	none		
931	49	465	97	X	X	X		X	X	X		3/1	none		
67	72							X					4/4		
1,400	60							X	X	X	X	3/2	none		
				X				X				4/1	none		
													none		
2,330	30	1,510	99	X	X		X	X	X		X	6/1	none		
314	65			X	X	X	X	X	X	X	X	5/1	none	X	
													none		
												4/15	none		
1,320	2			X	X	X		X	X	X		5/1	none	X	
													none		
66	35	10	100	X	X	X	X	X	X	X	X	8/1	none		
													none		
													none		
3,949	27			X	X	X		X	X	X		5/1	none	X	
													none		
3,855	14			X				X				3/2	none		
									X				8/1	none		
				X				X				7/7	none		
				X				X				7/1	none		
												5/1			
1,600	5											6/12	none		
1,529	28			X				X	X			3/2	none		

Institution	Tuition and fees	Add'l out-of-state/district tuition	Books and supplies	Costs for campus residents			Costs for students at home		
				Room and board	Transportation	Other costs	Board only	Transportation	Other costs
Louise Salinger Academy of Fashion	‡ 12,180		1,000						
Loyola Marymount University	15,313		612	6,492	50	1,320	1,602	594	1,464
Marymount College	13,080		630	6,400	540	1,278	2,300	576	1,584
Master's College	‡ 9,992		612	4,314	576	1,000		684	1,548
Mendocino College	‡ 410	4,310/—	630				2,124	684	1,584
Menlo College	16,180		612	6,500	558	1,170	1,750	594	1,200
Merced College	‡ 418	3,424/—	630				2,124	576	1,728
Merritt College	‡ 394	3,814/—	650				2,500	750	1,584
Mills College	15,712		600	6,480		1,410	1,620	810	1,410
MiraCosta College	‡ 440	3,470/—	600				2,223	585	1,287
Mission College	‡ 394	3,360/—	648				2,196	594	1,630
Modesto Junior College	‡ 390	3,420/—	630				2,124	576	1,584
Monterey Institute of International Studies	16,245		450				5,200	700	1,400
Monterey Peninsula College	‡ 430	3,418/—	630				2,124	720	1,548
Moorpark College	‡ 410	3,300/—	630				2,124	684	1,000
Mount St. Mary's College	14,490		648	6,100	558	1,170	2,285	702	1,440
Mount San Antonio College	‡ 428	3,420/—	630				2,124	684	1,728
Mount San Jacinto College	‡ 395	3,390/—	630				2,124	576	1,584
Napa Valley College	‡ 392	3,602/—	648				2,196	594	1,566
National University	‡ 6,435		500					650	
New College of California	8,299		600					800	2,268
New School of Architecture	9,500		600						
Occidental College	19,076		648	5,660		1,152			1,152
Ohlone College	‡ 392	3,302/—	630				2,124	576	1,584
Orange Coast College	‡ 436	3,460/—	630				2,150	700	1,600
Otis College of Art and Design	15,350		1,800		550	1,375		550	1,375
Oxnard College	‡ 420	3,300/—	600				1,800	700	1,300
Pacific Christian College	8,440		630	3,584	540	1,278	2,124	576	1,584
Pacific Oaks College	13,740		525				3,000	2,600	3,600
Pacific Union College	12,960		612	4,050	576	1,350	1,500	578	1,350
Palo Verde College	‡ 390	3,420/—	648				2,124	594	1,600
Palomar College	‡ 410	3,440/—	612				2,322	702	1,440
Pasadena City College	‡ 410	3,530/—	630				2,124	576	900
Patten College	6,672		550		440	1,100	1,650	330	1,595
Pepperdine University 27,470	20,210		900	6,860	750	750	2,450	1,660	726
Phillips College Inland Empire Campus	11,300								
Phillips Junior College: San Fernando Valley Campus	6,315								
Pitzer College	21,086		700	6,454		900			900
Point Loma Nazarene College	11,824		650	4,730	580	1,316	2,326	810	1,620
Pomona College	19,710		850	7,860	750	1,000	2,000	750	1,000
Porterville College	‡ 405	3,210/—	648				3,950	500	1,620
Queen of the Holy Rosary College	‡ 2,500		150						
Rancho Santiago Community College	‡ 415	3,210/—	630				2,124	576	1,764
Rio Hondo College	‡ 410	3,270/—	630				2,124	576	
Riverside Community College	‡ 417	3,060/—	792				2,124	648	1,008
Sacramento City College	‡ 390	3,750/—	630				1,971	648	1,383
Saddleback College	‡ 410	4,110/—	630				1,188	1,080	1,836
St. John's Seminary College	6,540		630	2,500	540	1,278			
St. Mary's College of California	15,098		612	6,909	558	1,170	2,322	702	1,440
Samuel Merritt College	13,930		1,112		1,845	3,100	3,150	1,845	3,100

†Figures are projected for 1996-97. ‡Figures are for 1995-96.

Total freshmen	Percent receiving aid	Freshmen judged to have need	Percent offered aid	Acad	Music/drama	Art	Athl	Acad	Music/drama	Art	Athl	Priority	Closing	Inst aid form	Notes
	All aid		**Need-based aid**	**Grants and scholarships**								**Financial aid deadlines**		**Inst aid form**	**Notes**
				Need-based				**Non-need-based**							
798	80	602	97	X	X	X	X	X	X		X	2/15	none		
310	50	165	100	X	X			X				3/2	none		
													none		
87	74	73	100	X				X				3/2	none		
1,534	35			X				X				6/1	none		
1,084	28			X								4/1	none		
133	80	95	100	X	X	X		X	X	X		2/15	none	X	
													none		
4,204	30							X	X	X		3/2	none		
								X							
1,800	40			X	X	X	X	X	X	X	X	3/2	none		
													none		
				X	X	X	X	X				3/1	none	X	
													none		
1,500	40			X				X	X	X	X	3/2	none		
						X	X	X	X	X	X	4/1	none		
				X								3/2	none		
12	75											3/1	8/1		
15	70	10	100	X		X		X		X		3/2	none		
407	83			X				X	X				2/1		
1,879	7	351	100	X	X	X		X	X	X		7/1	none		
6,980	3			X	X	X	X	X	X		X	6/1	none		
115	85			X	X							3/1	none	X	
													none		
86	98			X	X			X	X			3/2	none	X	
				X				X				3/15	none	X	
456	87							X	X			3/2	none		
300	50			X									none	X	
4,978	20	550	82	X				X				4/1	none	X	
4,755	15			X	X	X	X	X	X	X	X	5/13	none		
130	89	84	95	X	X		X	X	X		X	3/2	7/15		
584	70			X	X	X	X	X	X	X	X	2/15	4/1	X	
													none		
221	52	102	100	X									2/1		
463	72			X	X	X	X	X	X	X	X	4/10	none	X	
392	55	197	100										2/11		
472	50			X				X				3/30	none		
												3/1	7/1		
													none		
3,500	11			X	X	X	X	X	X	X	X	7/15	none		
4,000	38			X	X	X		X	X	X		3/2	none		
2,600	35			X	X	X						3/2	none		
4,041	9			X				X	X	X		3/2	5/2		
14	50											4/30	none		
487	74	319	100	X				X			X	3/2			
13	93	10	100	X				X				3/2	none		

Institution	Tuition and fees	Add'l out-of-state/district tuition	Books and supplies	Costs for campus residents			Costs for students at home		
				Room and board	Transportation	Other costs	Board only	Transportation	Other costs
San Bernardino Valley College	‡ 430	3,150/—	630				2,124	576	1,584
San Diego City College	‡ 410	3,320/—	630				2,124	684	1,548
San Diego Mesa College	‡ 390	3,300/—	648				1,537	738	1,620
San Diego Miramar College	‡ 395	3,300/—	648				2,322	756	1,503
San Diego State University	‡ 1,902	7,380/—	648	5,624	583	1,715	2,225	602	1,843
San Francisco Art Institute	16,416		1,400		315	1,305	5,600	315	1,305
San Francisco College of Mortuary Science	† 9,725		800				3,600	1,800	1,200
San Francisco Conservatory of Music	15,050		600				2,000	700	1,800
San Francisco State University	‡ 1,978	7,380/—	648	7,002	540	1,638	2,124	576	1,764
San Joaquin Delta College	‡ 390	3,420/—	700				2,200	650	1,300
San Joaquin Valley College Inc.	6,500								
San Jose Christian College	6,663		612	3,551	558	1,170	2,322	702	1,440
San Jose City College	‡ 410	3,620/—	630					576	
San Jose State University	‡ 1,966	7,380/—	630	5,340	540	1,548	2,124	684	1,548
Santa Barbara City College	‡ 408	3,210/—	648				1,998	648	1,260
Santa Clara University	15,624		612	6,780	558	1,170	2,322	702	1,440
Santa Monica College	‡ 430	3,750/—	650				2,124	585	
Santa Rosa Junior College	‡ 410	4,010/—	648		738	1,566	2,196	594	1,620
Scripps College	18,800		700	7,650		900			1,566
Shasta College	‡ 416	3,180/—	630		540	1,350	2,124	684	1,350
Sierra College	‡ 405	3,600/—	630	3,934	300	1,500	1,500	800	1,500
Simpson College	8,424		648	3,800	576	1,314	4,050	738	1,566
Skyline College	412	3,600/—	648				2,124	594	1,818
Solano Community College	‡ 400	3,540/—	630				2,124	576	1,386
Sonoma State University	‡ 2,070	7,380/—	612	5,396	292	1,370	2,124	292	1,121
Southern California College	11,126		648	4,752	576	1,314		594	1,314
Southern California Institute of Architecture	‡ 13,030		1,470				2,720	900	
Southwestern College	‡ 408	2,880/—	648				2,196	594	1,818
Stanford University	20,490		900	7,337		1,970			1,970
Taft College	‡ 460	3,420/—	250	2,600	576	1,566	2,196	576	1,566
Thomas Aquinas College	13,900		300	5,300	650	850		800	850
United States International University	11,000		630	4,530	774	1,836	2,124	900	1,836
University of California									
Berkeley	‡ 5,541	7,699/—	720	6,820	300	1,734	2,004	300	1,734
Davis	‡ 4,174	7,699/—	858	5,283	799	1,637	1,500	838	1,439
Irvine	‡ 4,052	7,699/—	850	5,536	540	1,890	2,124	576	1,584
Los Angeles	3,894	8,394/—	904	6,181	172	1,165	1,372	2,777	1,791
Riverside	‡ 4,098	7,699/—	882	5,430	576	1,260	1,500	684	1,260
San Diego	‡ 4,200	7,699/—	612	6,557	552	1,261	1,613	1,032	1,546
San Francisco	‡ 4,241	7,699/—	3,341		800	2,200	2,000	800	2,200
Santa Barbara	‡ 4,097	7,698/—	648	5,990	576	1,827	2,196	738	1,566
Santa Cruz	‡ 4,138	7,698/—	633	5,691	474	1,191	1,620	474	1,191
University of Judaism	13,358		650	6,653	800	1,800	3,100	800	1,800
University of La Verne	14,650		648	5,080	720	1,644	2,196	720	1,644
University of the Pacific	18,260		710	5,526	720	1,240			1,240
University of Redlands	17,830		600	6,775					
University of San Diego	14,965		650	7,150	555	1,170	1,170	703	1,440
University of San Francisco	15,020		750	6,934	600	1,900	2,000	600	1,900
University of Southern California	‡ 18,598		600	6,482	580	1,630	1,610	940	1,630
University of West Los Angeles	5,145		300					1,000	1,500

†Figures are projected for 1996-97. ‡Figures are for 1995-96.

| All aid | | Need-based aid | | Grants and scholarships | | | | | | | | Financial aid deadlines | | Inst aid form | Notes |
| | | | | Need-based | | | | Non-need-based | | | | | | | |
Total freshmen	Percent receiving aid	Freshmen judged to have need	Percent offered aid	Acad	Music/drama	Art	Athl	Acad	Music/drama	Art	Athl	Priority	Closing		
													none		
													none		
				X				X				3/2	none		
777	7	316	99									3/2	5/30		
3,189	77			X	X	X	X	X	X	X	X	3/2	none		
136	65	57	77								X	4/1	none	X	
30	38												9/5		
28	82	19	84	X	X				X			3/1	none	X	
1,640	73			X				X	X			5/1	none		
3,257	22			X	X	X		X	X	X		4/15	none		
73	80			X	X		X	X	X		X	3/2	8/1	X	
3,000	6											5/31	none		
1,566	30	655	100	X							X	3/2	none		
				X				X					5/1		
1,043	72	665	100	X	X	X		X	X		X	2/1	none		
3,500	23	611	87	X	X	X	X	X	X	X	X		none	X	
2,677	57			X				X	X	X	X	3/2	none		
215	53	113	100	X				X					2/1		
				X	X	X	X	X	X	X	X	3/2	none	X	
9,205	5			X	X	X	X	X	X	X	X		3/2		
175	86	142	99	X				X	X			3/2	none	X	
1,646	8			X								3/2	none		
1,371	4											6/1	none		
711	48	299	100					X	X			3/2	none		
228	80	192	100	X	X		X	X				3/2	none		
40	49			X		X		X		X		3/2	5/1	X	
4,000	25	726	84					X	X	X		3/2	none		
1,595	68	752	100	X	X	X	X				X		2/1		
				X				X				8/1	none		
72	88	63	100									3/1	9/1	X	
								X			X	3/2	none	X	
3,405	70	1,728	95	X	X	X		X	X	X	X	3/2	3/2		
				X				X				3/2	none		
2,926	61							X	X	X	X	3/2	5/1		
3,530	73			X				X	X	X	X	3/2	none	X	
1,596	55			X				X	X	X	X	3/2	none		
4,230	40			X				X				3/2	5/1		
				X				X				7/1	none	X	
3,361	69			X	X	X	X	X	X	X	X	3/2	none		
1,825	42	1,002	100	X	X	X		X	X	X		3/2	none		
12	100	11	100					X				3/2	none	X	
181	80			X	X			X				3/2	none	X	
603	70	448	100	X	X	X	X	X	X	X	X	3/2	none		
288	82			X	X	X		X	X	X		2/15	none		
981	67	498	100	X				X	X		X	2/20	none	X	
566	73	361	99	X			X	X			X	2/15	none	X	
2,608	60			X	X			X	X	X	X	2/15	3/2		
				X								6/1	none		

Institution	Tuition and fees	Add'l out–of–state/ district tuition	Books and supplies	Costs for campus residents			Costs for students at home		
				Room and board	Trans-portation	Other costs	Board only	Trans-portation	Other costs
Ventura College	‡ 384	3,192/—	600				1,800	700	1,300
Victor Valley College	‡ 400	3,420/—	648				2,124	738	1,566
Vista Community College	‡ 394	3,510/—	630				2,124	720	1,584
West Coast University	‡ 10,355		630				2,124	576	1,584
West Hills Community College	‡ 390	3,000/—	630				1,566	576	1,530
West Los Angeles College	‡ 390	3,750/—	630				2,124	684	1,748
West Valley College	‡ 444	3,300/—	630				2,124	648	1,548
Westmont College	17,150		510	5,748	630	830		630	830
Whittier College	18,088		500	6,047	548	1,450			
Woodbury University	14,115		612	5,685	558	1,170	1,636	662	1,607
Yeshiva Ohr Elchonon Chabad/West Coast Talmudical Seminary	† 7,000		125	3,200		100	2,322	702	1,440
Yuba College	‡ 412	3,750/—	648	3,400	576	1,614	2,196	594	1,662

Colorado

Institution	Tuition and fees	Add'l out–of–state/ district tuition	Books and supplies	Room and board	Trans-portation	Other costs	Board only	Trans-portation	Other costs
Adams State College	‡ 1,845	3,608/—	560	3,990	820	1,500	750	820	1,500
Aims Community College	‡ 1,065	4,590/765	500					580	1,050
Arapahoe Community College	‡ 1,693	5,445/—	450				2,385	900	274
Bel-Rea Institute of Animal Technology	5,300		800				1,584	990	1,080
Beth-El College of Nursing	5,485		450					450	200
Blair Junior College	‡ 5,355								
Colorado Christian University	8,855		700	3,930	800	1,475		1,386	
Colorado College	19,026		550	4,824	300	900	1,500	300	900
Colorado Institute of Art	‡ 9,545		1,500	4,920				675	1,250
Colorado Mountain College									
Alpine Campus	‡ 1,120	4,860/870	700	3,700	570	2,050	1,500	280	900
Spring Valley Campus	1,150	6,000/870	450	3,700	570	2,050	1,600	280	900
Timberline Campus	‡ 1,120	4,860/900	400	3,700	570	2,050	1,600	280	900
Colorado Northwestern Community College	† 1,505	—/2,945	500	3,740	800	2,365	2,050	207	3,260
Colorado School of Mines	† 4,890	8,970/—	850	4,550		1,450	2,000	1,100	1,450
Colorado State University	‡ 2,778	6,608/—	500	4,356	300	1,500			1,900
Colorado Technical University	6,468						800	800	200
Community College of Aurora	‡ 1,636	5,445/—	400						
Community College of Denver	‡ 1,782	5,445/—	415				1,115	720	916
Fort Lewis College	‡ 1,904	5,560/—	550	3,778	860	1,627	900	860	1,627
Front Range Community College	‡ 1,709	5,445/—	500				2,000	2,000	1,000
Lamar Community College	‡ 1,758	3,982/—	520	3,982	210	420	2,540	473	394
Mesa State College	‡ 1,872	3,768/—	560	4,218	500	1,855	650	360	750
Metropolitan State College of Denver	‡ 1,996	4,957/—	560				3,906	990	1,205
Morgan Community College	‡ 1,653	5,445/—	475				1,200	855	750
Naropa Institute	10,358		540						
National College	‡ 7,755		828					1,092	
Nazarene Bible College	‡ 4,220		500				1,600	750	600
Northeastern Junior College	1,802	—/2,860	500	3,840	748	832	2,021	610	832
Otero Junior College	‡ 1,728	3,690/—	400	3,920	600			800	1,200
Pikes Peak Community College	‡ 1,659	5,445/—	500					900	1,350
Pueblo College of Business and Technology	9,957		900						
Pueblo Community College	‡ 1,759	5,445/—	560				3,150	1,000	980
Red Rocks Community College	‡ 1,744	5,445/—	450				2,000	805	875
Regis University	14,240		540	5,980	495	1,170	1,440	675	1,170
Rocky Mountain College of Art & Design	6,910		1,200				5,420	800	300
Technical Trades Institute	10,500		1,000						

†Figures are projected for 1996-97. ‡Figures are for 1995-96.

All aid		Need–based aid		Grants and scholarships								Financial aid deadlines		Inst aid form	Notes
				Need–based				Non–need–based							
Total freshmen	Percent receiving aid	Freshmen judged to have need	Percent offered aid	Acad	Music/drama	Art	Athl	Acad	Music/drama	Art	Athl	Priority	Closing		
				X				X				3/2	none		
													none		
				X									6/1		
720	68			X	X	X						3/2	none		
													none		
													none		
291	83	206	100					X	X	X	X	3/1	none	X	
336	81	240	100	X	X	X		X	X	X		2/15	none		
117	76	93	100	X				X				3/2	none	X	
16	60	12	100									1/15	3/1	X	
2,546	12			X				X				3/2	none		
519	88	442	100	X				X	X	X	X	4/15	none		
				X				X				4/1	none		
5,695	10	643	100	X				X				3/15	none		
88	55							X				8/31	none		
1	2			X								6/1	none		
													none		
191	87	149	100	X	X		X	X	X		X	3/15	none	X	
623	57	262	97	X				X			X	2/15			
526	80	491	100	X	X	X		X	X	X			none	X	
198	46							X			X	3/31	none		
222	46							X			X	3/31	none		
114	46							X			X	3/31	none		
154	95			X			X	X			X	5/1	none	X	
452	85	360	100	X	X			X	X		X	3/1	none	X	
2,594	55	1,530	100					X	X	X	X	3/1	none		
149	42	84	100	X				X					none		
													none		
1,600	66	534	100	X	X	X	X	X	X	X	X	4/15	none		
5,740	25			X				X				5/1	none		
216	80			X		X	X	X		X	X	5/1	none	X	
976	75			X	X	X	X	X	X	X	X	3/1	none		
1,416	48	451	100	X			X	X	X		X	3/1	none		
													none		
				X				X				3/31	none		
													none		
144	95			X				X				6/1	none		
941	40			X	X	X	X	X	X	X	X	4/1	none	X	
698	70	304	94	X					X		X	5/1	none		
								X				7/1	none		
1,781	51			X				X				3/15	none		
1,490	18							X				6/1	none		
272	51			X				X			X	3/15	none	X	
110	90	78	100	X	X			X		X		7/31	none	X	
		81	100											X	

Institution	Tuition and fees	Add'l out-of-state/district tuition	Books and supplies	Costs for campus residents			Costs for students at home		
				Room and board	Trans-portation	Other costs	Board only	Trans-portation	Other costs
Trinidad State Junior College	‡ 1,745	3,690/—	470	3,702	600	1,125	1,800	450	900
United States Air Force Academy	0								
University of Colorado									
Boulder	‡ 2,716	11,122/—	560	4,162	990	2,383	2,515	990	2,383
Colorado Springs	† 2,594	8,740/—	576				2,388	990	464
Denver	‡ 2,137	7,780/—	560				2,313	1,422	1,980
Health Sciences Center	† 5,296	11,196/—	865				1,575	100	2,340
University of Denver	17,088		555	5,433	540	1,350		540	1,350
University of Northern Colorado	‡ 2,480	6,198/—	560	4,270	353	1,916			
University of Southern Colorado	† 2,092	5,730/—	500	4,180	950	1,500	800	800	1,500
Western State College of Colorado	‡ 1,708	4,746/—	550	4,279	685	800	1,100	500	650
Yeshiva Toras Chaim Talmudical Seminary	‡ 4,250			4,600					

Connecticut

Institution	Tuition and fees	Add'l out-of-state/district tuition	Books and supplies	Room and board	Trans-portation	Other costs	Board only	Trans-portation	Other costs
Albertus Magnus College	13,000		600	5,836	570	920	1,850	800	1,050
Asnuntuck Community-Technical College	‡ 1,646	2,976/—	600				2,000	1,500	950
Briarwood College	‡ 10,012		500		900	1,400	1,500	1,350	1,400
Capital Community-Technical College	‡ 1,646	2,976/—	500				2,000	820	1,700
Central Connecticut State University	‡ 3,266	5,092/—	750	4,848	312	1,300	1,500	614	1,300
Connecticut College	27,375 (comprehensive)		600			500	1,500		500
Eastern Connecticut State University	‡ 3,202	5,092/—		4,486					
Fairfield University	17,360		500	6,800	300	700	1,500	700	700
Gateway Community-Technical College	‡ 1,646	2,976/—	600				2,654	500	1,400
Holy Apostles College and Seminary	5,030		630	6,450	420	735		890	580
Housatonic Community-Technical College	‡ 1,646	2,976/—	600				1,500	300	700
Katharine Gibbs School	8,105		600						
Manchester Community-Technical College	‡ 1,646	2,976/—	800				1,645	1,390	1,495
Middlesex Community-Technical College	‡ 1,646	2,976/—					2,000	1,500	700
Mitchell College	12,795			5,720			2,920		
Naugatuck Valley Community-Technical College	‡ 1,646	2,976/—	800					1,100	
Northwestern Connecticut Community-Technical College	‡ 1,646	2,976/—	600				700	930	900
Norwalk Community-Technical College	‡ 1,646	2,976/—	600				1,200	2,400	2,000
Paier College of Art	10,595						3,500	1,200	600
Quinebaug Valley Community-Technical College	‡ 1,646	2,976/—	700				2,000	1,200	1,000
Quinnipiac College	14,120		500	6,770	300	800	1,500	500	800
Sacred Heart University	12,712		600	6,380	700	700	1,500	700	700
St. Joseph College	13,800		750	6,000	200	1,000	1,600	750	1,000
Southern Connecticut State University	† 3,474	4,498/—	750	5,312	300	300	1,600	1,300	300
Teikyo-Post University	12,300		650	5,600			2,862		
Three Rivers Community-Technical College	‡ 1,646	2,976/—	450						
Trinity College	21,410		600	6,130		730			730
Tunxis Community-Technical College	1,646	2,976/—	420				1,800	1,400	1,210
United States Coast Guard Academy	0								
University of Bridgeport	13,144		550	6,810	300	500	778	600	500
University of Connecticut 18,546	4,974	8,270/—		5,302		100	2,608	1,100	1,000
University of Hartford	16,416		650	6,580	500	1,150	2,400	950	1,150
University of New Haven	12,100		750	5,910	200	1,000	1,500	1,080	1,000
Wesleyan University	21,910		1,500	6,030					
Western Connecticut State University	‡ 3,168	5,092/—	800	4,088	400	1,300	1,832	800	1,300
Yale University	22,200		655	6,680	579	1,565		1,050	1,565

†Figures are projected for 1996-97. ‡Figures are for 1995-96.

All aid		Need–based aid		Grants and scholarships								Financial aid deadlines		Inst aid form	Notes
				Need–based				Non–need–based							
Total freshmen	Percent receiving aid	Freshmen judged to have need	Percent offered aid	Acad	Music/drama	Art	Athl	Acad	Music/drama	Art	Athl	Priority	Closing		
320	83							X	X	X	X	5/1	none		
4,182	41	1,487	100	X	X	X	X	X	X	X	X	4/1	none		
388	42	170	86	X			X	X			X	4/1	none		
290	38			X	X	X		X	X	X		3/31	none	X	
				X				X							
658	58			X				X	X	X	X	2/21	none		
1,789	76	858	95	X				X	X	X	X	3/1	none		
1,172	55			X				X	X	X	X	3/1	none		
601	67	275	100	X	X	X	X	X	X	X	X	4/1	none		
99	92	95	100	X				X				2/15	none		
												6/1	none	X	
231	81	172	98	X				X				4/30	none		
259	45			X				X				7/15	none		
1,113	47					X		X			X	4/22			
453	85	228	100									2/1		X	
971	65			X				X				3/15			
798	69	489	100	X	X	X	X	X	X		X	2/15			
1,433	19							X				none			
												none			
786	46	590	100									6/1	none		
136	75											none			
1,079	20			X				X				4/1	none	X	
				X								6/1	none	X	
480	70			X		X		X			X	3/1	7/15	X	
				X				X				4/7	none	X	
400	40			X				X				6/15	none		
1,602	25			X				X				4/15	none	X	
79	62	50	100	X		X						5/1	none		
357	27	135	100					X		X		10/1			
1,004	70	621	99					X			X	3/1	none	X	
632	89	478	100	X		X		X		X	X	3/1	none		
184	92	146	100	X				X				2/15	none	X	
909	33							X				3/15	none		
70	85			X				X			X	3/15	none	X	
1,134	25											7/15	none		
509	51	255	100									2/1			
550	20			X				X				7/1	none		
131	98	123	100			X		X	X		X	4/15	none		
2,021	67	1,400	100	X	X	X	X	X	X	X	X	3/1	none	X	
1,294	85	1,050	100	X	X	X	X	X	X	X	X	2/1	none	X	
459	70	262	100	X				X			X	3/15	none	X	
711	49											2/1		X	
973	67			X	X	X	X	X				4/15		X	
1,364	69	583	100									2/1		X	

Institution	Tuition and fees	Add'l out-of-state/district tuition	Books and supplies	Room and board	Trans-portation	Other costs	Board only	Trans-portation	Other costs
Delaware									
Delaware State University	‡ 2,430	3,482/—	1,000	4,310	1,000	1,000		1,000	1,000
Delaware Technical and Community College									
Owens Campus	‡ 1,275	1,800/—	450				1,500	500	300
Stanton/Wilmington Campus	‡ 1,275	1,800/—	450				1,500	500	300
Terry Campus	‡ 1,275	1,800/—	450				1,500	500	300
Goldey-Beacom College	6,780		547		819	1,068	1,817	819	1,068
University of Delaware	‡ 4,286	6,870/—	550	4,230		1,350			1,350
Wesley College	11,284		500	4,674	450	900	2,500	2,500	1,000
Wilmington College	5,750		800				1,900	2,000	1,500
District of Columbia									
American University	17,744		450	7,018	700	600	1,600	700	600
Catholic University of America	16,002		500	6,846	500	1,600	1,700	500	1,600
Corcoran School of Art	12,200		1,800		1,050	1,800	1,700	1,050	1,800
Gallaudet University	5,990		700	6,270	947	2,232	741	947	1,945
George Washington University	19,980		700	6,970		950		600	950
Georgetown University	20,388		715	7,760	413	1,350	2,216	500	1,182
Howard University	8,725		700	5,292	250	2,250	2,000	1,000	2,250
Mount Vernon College	15,430		500	7,340	1,000	1,100	2,750	500	1,100
Oblate College	5,060		500					200	
Southeastern University	8,700		600				1,000	600	850
Strayer College	7,200		600				4,000	600	2,500
Trinity College	12,490		500	6,580	600	800		500	
University of the District of Columbia	‡ 1,118	2,880/—	600					800	1,400
Florida									
Art Institute of Fort Lauderdale	† 10,375		990		1,017	1,386	1,000	1,017	1,386
Barry University	13,050		600	5,680	900	900	750	1,260	900
Bethune-Cookman College	6,780		550	3,879	520	1,660	1,500	842	920
Brevard Community College	‡ 1,050	2,850/—	550				1,800	640	600
Broward Community College	‡ 1,073	2,917/—	800				1,620	1,552	1,080
Caribbean Center for Advanced Studies:									
Miami Institute of Psychology	7,014		600						
Central Florida Community College	‡ 1,093	2,977/—	540		2,025	1,125	1,620	1,773	1,125
Chipola Junior College	‡ 1,053	2,979/—	600	2,375	1,300	800	1,400	1,300	800
Clearwater Christian College	7,000		500	3,400	800	800	2,000	1,800	2,000
Daytona Beach Community College	‡ 1,074	2,953/—	485				1,700	1,000	1,000
Eckerd College	16,625		640	4,450	745	715	1,600	500	400
Edison Community College	‡ 1,073	2,917/—	450				1,500	876	732
Edward Waters College	‡ 4,400		500	4,300	500	750		600	550
Embry-Riddle Aeronautical University	8,740		600	3,640	1,800	1,220	750	1,240	1,220
Flagler College	5,530		600	3,460	750	1,520	1,680	800	1,520
Florida Agricultural and Mechanical University	‡ 1,853	4,933/—	600	3,278	718	2,000	1,120	740	2,000
Florida Atlantic University	‡ 1,807	4,902/—	600	3,830	1,300	1,120	1,700	1,920	1,120
Florida Baptist Theological College	2,784		700		1,200	800	2,000	1,500	
Florida Bible College	5,248		425		500	3,000	1,500	500	1,000
Florida Christian College	4,795		675		955	1,580	2,365	1,172	1,580
Florida College	6,270		900	3,580	1,250	1,600	1,800	500	1,600
Florida Community College at Jacksonville	‡ 1,074	3,051/—	450				804	727	1,149

†Figures are projected for 1996-97. ‡Figures are for 1995-96.

Total freshmen	Percent receiving aid	Freshmen judged to have need	Percent offered aid	Need-based Acad	Need-based Music/drama	Need-based Art	Need-based Athl	Non-need Acad	Non-need Music/drama	Non-need Art	Non-need Athl	Priority	Closing	Inst aid form	Notes
624	83	204	75	X	X		X	X	X		X	4/1	none		
622	33			X			X	X			X	6/15	none		
1,204	25			X			X	X			X	7/1	none		
345	40			X				X					none		
326	89	206	100	X				X			X	4/1	none		
3,179	78	1,396	100	X				X	X	X	X	3/15	5/1		
495	70	240	100					X				4/15	none		
316	50	91	97					X			X	4/15	none		
1,274	60			X			X	X			X	3/1	none	X	
570	79	399	100	X	X			X	X			1/15	none	X	
74	64			X		X		X		X		5/1	none		
														X	
1,395	69	698	98	X				X	X	X	X	1/31	3/15		
1,446	47	665	100	X			X				X	2/1	none		
1,094	89			X				X	X	X	X		4/1		
134	93	110	100	X				X				3/1	8/15		
													none		
66	45							X					8/15		
1,015	45	349	100	X				X					none		
105	81			X				X				3/1	none		
713	30							X	X		X	3/15	none	X	
													none		
				X			X	X	X		X	4/1	none		
745	96	650	92	X	X		X	X	X		X		none		
2,616	27	1,450	100	X	X	X	X	X	X	X	X	6/8	none		
								X	X	X	X	4/15	none		
				X				X	X	X	X	5/1	none		
811	60							X	X	X	X	5/1	none		
													none		
								X	X	X	X		none		
335	82	216	100	X	X	X	X	X	X	X	X	4/1	none		
1,500	35							X	X	X	X	6/1	none		
													none		
650	79	628	99	X			X	X			X	4/15	none		
378	75	168	100	X		X	X	X	X		X	3/15	none	X	
								X	X		X	4/1	none		
907	50	428	89	X				X	X	X	X	4/1	none		
				X	X							5/1	none		
23	62							X	X			5/31	none		
30	98			X	X			X	X			5/15	7/15	X	
216	80	129	100	X	X			X	X		X	6/1	4/1	X	
2,107	44							X	X	X	X	3/1	none	X	

Institution	Tuition and fees	Add'l out-of-state/district tuition	Books and supplies	Costs for campus residents			Costs for students at home		
				Room and board	Transportation	Other costs	Board only	Transportation	Other costs
Florida Institute of Technology	15,295		700	4,392	1,600	1,600	2,546	1,600	1,600
Florida International University	‡ 1,791	4,902/—	900		1,410	1,826	1,650	1,934	1,826
Florida Keys Community College	‡ 1,058	2,947/—	500				2,000	800	1,000
Florida Memorial College	5,850		550	3,236	1,000	2,140	1,170	1,000	2,140
Florida National College	4,080		400						
Florida Southern College	9,970		500	5,300	650	650	2,300	650	650
Florida State University	‡ 1,798	4,902/—	702	4,500	776	2,358		1,190	2,530
Fort Lauderdale College	4,503		150			360	1,600	1,075	360
Gulf Coast Community College	‡ 1,083	2,979/—	700				1,400	750	2,200
Hillsborough Community College	‡ 1,028	2,917/—					1,800	1,640	2,000
Hobe Sound Bible College	4,300		450	2,600	1,000	2,000	1,350	500	2,000
Indian River Community College	‡ 1,074	2,982/—	450					350	400
International Academy of Merchandising and Design	7,128		1,021					974	2,689
International College	† 7,398		250						
International Fine Arts College	‡ 9,975		1,000			1,000			1,200
Jacksonville University	12,510		700	4,750	600	800	1,000	600	800
Jones College	4,350		750					950	1,700
Keiser College of Technology	10,035								
Lake City Community College	‡ 1,013	2,902/—	500	3,057	500	750	2,901	500	750
Lake-Sumter Community College	‡ 1,088	2,955/—	500				1,600	980	500
Lynn University	15,850		600	6,250	1,100	1,100		550	550
Manatee Community College	‡ 1,050	2,940/—	585				6,850	1,197	1,108
Miami-Dade Community College	‡ 1,073	2,917/—	920				2,146	2,566	2,726
New College of the University of South Florida	‡ 2,066	5,887/—	700	3,848	490	2,290		1,760	2,290
New England Institute of Technology	8,950		300				1,500	850	1,190
North Florida Junior College	‡ 930	2,610/—	450				1,700	300	475
Nova Southeastern University	9,970		877	5,912	2,219	2,520		2,219	2,520
Okaloosa-Walton Community College	‡ 924	2,590/—	665				2,606	1,020	1,750
Palm Beach Atlantic College	9,300		660	4,310	1,000	800	2,800	1,000	800
Palm Beach Community College	‡ 1,074	2,922/—	650					1,061	800
Pasco-Hernando Community College	‡ 1,092	2,976/—	600				1,500	792	1,451
Pensacola Junior College	‡ 1,073	2,917/—	500				1,920	640	1,100
Polk Community College	‡ 1,084	2,980/—	400					1,000	600
Ringling School of Art and Design	12,500		1,650	6,300	500	500	2,000	500	500
Rollins College	19,075		400	5,885	750	550	1,500	350	51
St. John Vianney College Seminary	7,100		550	4,000	900	990			
St. Johns River Community College	‡ 1,091	3,002/—	625				1,800	700	800
St. Leo College	10,496		525	5,140	840	780	2,340	950	315
St. Petersburg Junior College	‡ 1,074	2,877/—	600				2,106	1,015	915
St. Thomas University	11,220		600	4,000	990	900	2,200	990	900
Santa Fe Community College	‡ 1,074	2,925/—	690					800	800
Schiller International University	13,100		350	8,500	990	3,000			
Seminole Community College	‡ 1,075	2,877/—	600				1,705	720	960
South College: Palm Beach Campus	6,780		750						
South Florida Community College	‡ 1,080	2,786/—	700	1,425				1,300	1,830
Southeastern College of the Assemblies of God	4,000		700	3,000	700	800		500	800
Southern College	5,577		585				2,500	720	300
Stetson University	14,735		600	5,090	550	850	1,100		1,050
Tallahassee Community College	‡ 1,043	2,782/—	600					804	2,276

†Figures are projected for 1996-97. ‡Figures are for 1995-96.

All aid		Need–based aid		Grants and scholarships								Financial aid deadlines		Inst aid form	Notes
				Need–based				Non–need–based							
Total freshmen	Percent receiving aid	Freshmen judged to have need	Percent offered aid	Acad	Music/drama	Art	Athl	Acad	Music/drama	Art	Athl	Priority	Closing		
338	79	212	100	X				X			X	2/1	none		
1,166	40			X	X	X		X	X	X	X	3/15	5/1		
115	40	91	100	X				X		X		5/1	none	X	
450	95			X			X	X	X			4/1	none	X	
527	95	351	100	X			X	X	X	X	X		3/1	X	
3,175	52	2,605	100	X				X	X	X	X	3/1	none	X	
													none		
4,309	60	545	100	X				X	X	X	X	4/15	none		
								X	X	X	X	4/15	none		
26	90	26	100	X	X			X				6/1	none		
1,100	22	507	100					X	X	X	X		none		
														X	
													none		
358	60			X	X	X	X	X	X	X	X	3/15	none		
													none		
													none		
861	25			X	X		X	X			X	6/1	none		
600	23							X	X	X		6/1	none		
548	34	66	100	X			X	X			X	2/15	none		
1,044	40			X	X	X	X	X	X	X	X	7/5	none		
7,719	60			X	X	X	X	X	X	X	X	4/15	none		
143	66	55	93	X				X				2/1	none		
													none	X	
435	28	334	100	X				X	X	X	X	7/1	none		
149	87			X				X			X	4/1	none	X	
556	60							X	X	X	X	4/1	none		
341	90			X	X	X		X	X		X	5/1	none	X	
				X				X	X		X	7/1	none	X	
975	43			X			X	X			X	5/1	none	X	
1,681	60			X				X	X	X		4/1	none		
2,190	65			X	X	X		X	X	X	X		5/15		
243	70					X				X		3/1	none	X	
412	50	175	100	X	X	X	X	X	X	X	X	3/1	none		
10	3	3	100										none		
								X	X	X	X	5/15	none		
186	78	152	100	X			X	X			X	3/1	none	X	
2,889	40			X				X	X	X	X	4/15	none		
73	97	160	100	X			X	X			X	4/1	none	X	
1,340	30			X	X	X	X	X	X	X	X	3/15	6/30		
				X				X				4/1	none		
				X	X	X	X	X	X	X	X	5/15	none		
													none		
1,068	30			X	X		X	X	X		X	6/1	none	X	
								X	X			5/1			
54	87			X									none		
474	90	294	99	X	X		X	X	X		X	3/15	none		
1,882	29			X			X	X	X		X	6/1	none		

Institution	Tuition and fees	Add'l out-of-state/district tuition	Books and supplies	Costs for campus residents			Costs for students at home		
				Room and board	Trans-portation	Other costs	Board only	Trans-portation	Other costs
Talmudic College of Florida	4,700		900	3,600					
Tampa College	4,464							600	700
Trinity International University	7,808		700				2,250	540	1,800
University of Central Florida	‡ 1,840	4,902/—	700	4,004	400	1,710	1,710	1,720	1,710
University of Florida	‡ 1,705	4,902/—	620	4,310	460	1,080	2,200	790	1,080
University of Miami	18,583		855	7,101	1,051	1,029	1,800	1,120	980
University of North Florida	‡ 1,748	4,902/—	600	3,650	1,836	660		1,836	660
University of South Florida	‡ 1,877	4,902/—	700	3,909	960	2,180	1,800	960	2,180
University of Tampa	14,132		600	4,640	1,000	1,100		800	1,100
University of West Florida	‡ 1,723	4,902/—	560		556	1,352	1,784	1,038	
Valencia Community College	‡ 1,073	2,782/—	600					3,014	200
Warner Southern College	7,690		600	3,700	600	1,500	2,500	800	2,600
Webber College	6,950		600	3,200	808	2,481	2,160	808	2,780
Georgia									
Abraham Baldwin Agricultural College	‡ 1,314	2,403/—	750	2,790	680	1,500	1,011	680	1,500
Agnes Scott College	14,460		450	6,020	850	500	1,500	850	500
Albany State College	‡ 1,899	3,210/—	675	3,045	535	800	1,855	405	800
American College: Atlanta	9,825		600		560	960		560	960
Andrew College	5,832		600	4,104	700	1,200	950	200	1,100
Armstrong State College	† 1,719	3,210/—	450	3,726	500	750	1,575	800	1,425
Art Institute of Atlanta	‡ 9,514		1,500		500	500	1,100	200	500
Athens Area Technical Institute	801	756/—	600				3,000	750	750
Atlanta Christian College	‡ 5,312		400	3,030		500			4,490
Atlanta College of Art	11,500		850		450	1,245	1,525	450	1,245
Atlanta Metropolitan College	‡ 1,140	2,403/—	500						
Augusta College	‡ 1,710	3,210/—	480				975	975	1,950
Augusta Technical Institute	1,100	1,008/—	450						
Bainbridge College	‡ 1,065	2,403/—	600				1,800	1,734	450
Bauder College	‡ 7,550		750		1,000	1,100	1,100	1,000	1,100
Berry College	9,770		600	5,432	390	1,708	1,070	900	1,570
Brenau University	10,680		600	6,330	575	800	1,500	775	800
Brewton-Parker College	5,520		750	2,565		1,200	1,200	600	1,200
Brunswick College	‡ 1,155	2,403/—	600				1,600	1,000	500
Chattahoochee Technical Institute	840	756/—	950					900	1,200
Clark Atlanta University	8,830		630	5,170	840	945	1,970	378	945
Clayton State College	‡ 1,692	3,210/—	600				1,700	945	1,080
Columbus College	‡ 1,740	3,210/—	650	3,468			1,500	600	600
Columbus Technical Institute	871	816/—	500				9,126	1,200	1,034
Covenant College	11,930		470	3,960	560	200	2,003	560	200
Dalton College	‡ 1,050	2,403/—	800				2,500	1,000	200
Darton College	‡ 1,140	2,403/—	450				1,100	450	600
DeKalb College	‡ 1,143	2,081/—	900					1,500	
DeKalb Technical Institute	1,176	1,008/—	400				2,000	660	600
DeVry Institute of Technology: Atlanta	6,560		560				1,689	2,097	2,069
East Georgia College	‡ 1,065	2,403/—	600				1,800	700	350
Emmanuel College	5,560		600	3,300	500	900	2,000	700	750
Emory University	20,110		650	7,540	390	490	2,400		480
Floyd College	‡ 1,065	2,403/—	400				1,150	200	250
Fort Valley State College	‡ 1,920	3,210/—	750	2,775	1,200	1,425	1,600	1,904	945
Gainesville College	‡ 1,080	2,403/—	630					1,900	1,000
Georgia Baptist College of Nursing	† 6,048		1,200	4,739	990	1,500	2,500	2,475	1,500

†Figures are projected for 1996-97. ‡Figures are for 1995-96.

Total freshmen	Percent receiving aid	Freshmen judged to have need	Percent offered aid	Need-based Acad	Music/drama	Art	Athl	Non-need Acad	Music/drama	Art	Athl	Priority	Closing	Inst aid form	Notes
280	75			X				X					none		
102	80			X	X		X	X				4/1	none		
2,250	57	831	100					X	X	X	X	3/1	none	X	
3,699	30	1,246	99	X			X	X	X		X	4/15	none		
1,701	79	1,231	97	X	X			X	X		X	2/15	none	X	
890	32			X	X		X	X	X		X	4/1	5/30	X	
2,027	74	1,005	88	X				X	X	X	X	3/1	none		
331	83	203	100					X	X	X			none		
516	44			X				X	X	X	X	4/1	none		
3,534	30			X	X	X	X	X	X	X	X		5/1	X	
59	98			X			X	X			X	4/1	8/1		
165	79	47	100	X			X	X			X	3/31	none		
940	76	600	100	X	X	X	X	X	X	X	X	5/1	none	X	
125	95	82	100	X	X			X	X			2/15	none	X	
1,219	88			X	X		X	X				6/1	none		
44	75			X				X				6/1	none		
127	90			X	X	X	X	X	X	X	X	6/1	none		
1,228	25			X	X	X	X	X	X	X	X	5/31	none	X	
													none		
				X									none		
130	72	50	100	X		X		X		X		3/15	none	X	
375	30			X	X		X						7/19		
849	61			X	X	X		X	X	X	X	4/15	none		
790	25			X				X					none	X	
321	50							X				7/1	none	X	
													none		
483	97	327	100	X				X	X	X	X	4/1	none	X	
175	77	74	100					X	X	X	X	5/1	none	X	
458	85							X	X	X	X	4/1	none		
				X				X			X	5/1	5/30		
1,183	40	420	100	X				X				4/1	none	X	
710	78			X	X		X	X	X		X	4/1	4/15		
642	25	192	100	X				X	X	X	X	4/1	none		
1,031	39							X	X	X	X	6/1	none	X	
502	90												none		
178	88	117	100					X	X		X	3/31	none	X	
				X				X				8/1	none		
				X				X	X		X	8/1	none		
				X		X							7/1		
				X				X				7/15	8/20	X	
								X					none		
236	18			X				X					none		
307	92	208	100	X	X		X	X	X		X	3/15	none		
1,268	54	595	100	X				X	X			2/15	4/1		
				X				X				4/30	6/30	X	
512	93			X	X		X	X		X	X	4/15	5/1		
1,603	42							X	X	X		4/15	none	X	
78	91	47	100	X				X				5/1	none	X	

113

Institution	Tuition and fees	Add'l out-of-state/district tuition	Books and supplies	Costs for campus residents			Costs for students at home		
				Room and board	Transportation	Other costs	Board only	Transportation	Other costs
Georgia College	‡ 1,820	3,210/—	750	3,270	721	1,352	600	720	1,228
Georgia Institute of Technology	‡ 2,457	5,181/—	795	5,700		1,164	2,265	1,062	1,050
Georgia Military College	‡ 4,130		475	3,915		1,025		550	1,025
Georgia Southern University	‡ 1,965	3,210/—	540	3,543	525	735	1,761	705	735
Georgia Southwestern College	‡ 1,869	3,210/—	750	2,940					
Georgia State University	‡ 2,249	5,175/—	980				2,150	324	800
Gordon College	‡ 1,140	2,403/—	486	2,220	521	903	1,500	1,130	903
Gupton Jones College of Funeral Service	5,625								
Gwinnett Technical Institute	900	1,656/—	550				550	950	
Kennesaw State College	‡ 1,776	3,210/—	600				2,500	900	935
LaGrange College	9,114		600	3,990	900	900		600	600
Macon College	‡ 1,107	2,403/—	525				2,416	902	998
Meadows College of Business	‡ 2,825								
Medical College of Georgia	3,152	6,908/—	700		315	1,170	1,173	495	1,170
Mercer University									
Atlanta	7,650		450				1,607	675	800
Macon	13,896		475	4,840	500	672	1,500	300	672
Middle Georgia College	‡ 1,260	2,403/—	550	2,540	288	600	2,700	309	600
Morehouse College	9,254		700	5,976		2,772	1,766		2,272
Morris Brown College	8,576		600	4,750	500	650	1,982	500	650
North Georgia College	‡ 1,827	3,210/—	540	2,853	750	1,200	1,545	1,530	660
Oglethorpe University.	15,170		600	4,790	1,720	2,390	1,500	1,720	2,390
Oxford College of Emory University	‡ 13,500		450	4,631	350	750		750	750
Paine College	6,640		500	3,020	2,564	1,850	1,756	2,553	1,850
Piedmont College	6,360	200/—	575	3,930	650	900	1,870	900	900
Reinhardt College	5,442		500	4,536	70	1,000	1,200	600	400
Savannah College of Art and Design	11,700		1,200	6,025	1,000	900	2,780	400	500
Savannah State College	‡ 1,965	3,210/—	750	2,700	700	700	1,300	700	700
Savannah Technical Institute	1,104	908/—	300						
Shorter College	7,860		520	4,050	630	1,470	1,750	1,350	1,400
South College	5,110		600				2,317	1,109	1,305
South Georgia College	‡ 1,128	2,403/—	600	2,970	600	750	2,100	600	750
Southern College of Technology	‡ 1,761	3,210/—	528	3,375	498	1,206	1,548	843	1,206
Spelman College	9,500		750	6,130	950	1,550		950	1,550
Thomas College	4,830		600				2,738	813	1,800
Toccoa Falls College	7,040		500	3,708	1,163	1,422	2,602	1,032	1,422
Truett-McConnell College	‡ 5,100		525	2,775	500	800	1,500	650	700
University of Georgia	‡ 2,542	4,287/—	525	3,820		1,338	1,830		1,797
Valdosta State University	‡ 1,887	3,210/—	600	3,045	1,142	964	895	1,142	1,087
Waycross College	‡ 1,073	2,403/—	500				1,500	600	900
Wesleyan College	13,400		515	5,100	412	957	1,500	412	957
West Georgia College	‡ 1,884	3,210/—	495	3,084	750	1,100	1,800	1,125	1,100
Young Harris College	6,900		600	3,405	450	900	1,500	750	600
Hawaii									
Brigham Young University-Hawaii	2,563		450	4,725		1,000			1,000
Chaminade University of Honolulu	10,600		600	5,200	225	1,087	1,950	225	1,087
Hawaii Pacific University	7,100		600	6,510	1,000	900	1,950	400	900
Heald Business College: Honolulu	8,400		1,000				180	180	1,200
University of Hawaii									
Hawaii Community College	‡ 554	2,592/—	500	4,270	225	1,000	2,414	225	1,000
Hilo	‡ 554	2,592/—	780	4,066	225	1,120	2,515	225	1,120
Honolulu Community College	‡ 524	2,592/—	582				1,524	180	953

†Figures are projected for 1996-97. ‡Figures are for 1995-96.

All aid		Need-based aid		Grants and scholarships								Financial aid deadlines		Inst aid form	Notes
				Need-based				Non-need-based							
Total freshmen	Percent receiving aid	Freshmen judged to have need	Percent offered aid	Acad	Music/drama	Art	Athl	Acad	Music/drama	Art	Athl	Priority	Closing		
911	62	580	95	X	X	X	X	X	X		X	4/15	none	X	
1,823	42	1,113	100	X				X			X	3/1	none		
													none		
3,729	75			X				X	X			3/1	none		
377	78							X	X	X	X	4/1	6/1	X	
1,451	62	592	100	X				X	X	X	X	4/1	none		
								X	X	X	X	6/1	none		
													none		
				X				X					7/1		
900	30	624	83	X	X		X	X	X	X	X	3/31	none		
178	78	112	100	X				X	X	X		5/1	none	X	
				X			X	X	X	X	X	4/1	none		
													none		
				X				X				2/15	none	X	
				X				X				5/1			
623	96	364	100	X	X		X	X	X	X	X	4/1	none	X	
666	32			X				X	X		X	4/1	none	X	
700	70			X				X	X		X		4/1		
481	81			X			X	X	X	X	X	4/1	6/15		
524	89			X			X	X	X	X	X	5/1	none	X	
193	84	133	100	X				X	X			3/1	none	X	
329	90	141	100	X				X				4/1	none		
195	85			X	X		X	X	X		X	5/15	none	X	
243	92			X				X	X	X	X	6/1	none		
312	90			X	X	X	X	X	X	X	X	5/1	none		
													none		
678	71			X			X	X	X		X	5/1	8/1	X	
													none		
172	99	134	100	X	X	X	X	X	X	X	X	4/1	none	X	
33	85							X				9/1	none	X	
													none	X	
282	38	90	70	X			X	X			X	3/15	5/31	X	
				X	X			X	X			4/1	4/15	X	
133	85			X	X		X	X				9/1	none		
													none		
													none		
3,669	90			X	X		X	X	X			3/1	none	X	
1,847	45	1,092	95	X	X	X	X	X	X	X	X	5/1	none	X	
													none		
136	97	126	100	X				X	X	X		3/1	none	X	
1,425	51	1,136	100	X				X	X	X	X	3/15	none	X	
304	70	180	100	X				X	X	X	X	5/1	none	X	
556	80			X				X	X	X	X		7/31		
126	50	75	99	X			X	X			X	3/29	none		
1,113	25	350	100					X	X		X	3/1	none		
													none		
													none		
391	49			X	X	X	X	X	X	X	X	3/1	none		
													none		
													none		

Institution	Tuition and fees	Add'l out-of-state/ district tuition	Books and supplies	Costs for campus residents			Costs for students at home		
				Room and board	Trans-portation	Other costs	Board only	Trans-portation	Other costs
Kapiolani Community College	783	4,344/—	582				2,112	217	816
Kauai Community College	778	4,344/—	611				2,515	225	953
Leeward Community College	‡ 514	2,592/—	560				2,414	180	914
Manoa	2,422	5,448/—	780	4,720	225	1,120	2,515	225	953
Maui Community College	788	4,344/—	611		896		2,414	896	
West Oahu	1,402	4,344/—	780				2,987	225	953
Windward Community College	‡ 788	4,344/—	554				1,524	225	953

Idaho

Institution	Tuition and fees	Add'l out-of-state/ district tuition	Books and supplies	Room and board	Trans-portation	Other costs	Board only	Trans-portation	Other costs
Albertson College	† 14,805		500	3,225	400	675	2,100	400	675
Boise Bible College	4,190		450	3,424	700	750	2,000	1,000	800
Boise State University	‡ 1,964	5,346/—	600	3,730	832	1,800	1,660	832	900
College of Southern Idaho	‡ 1,000	1,400/1,000	900	3,250	1,400	1,800		1,400	1,800
Eastern Idaho Technical College	‡ 1,132	2,620/—	1,000					1,300	630
Idaho State University	‡ 1,930	5,430/—	500	3,280	360	1,575	1,800	360	1,575
Lewis-Clark State College	‡ 1,478	4,522/—	560	3,130	852	1,116	1,864	756	796
North Idaho College	‡ 980	2,306/1,000	500	3,410	200	830	2,290	500	830
Northwest Nazarene College	11,685		1,000	3,270	700	800	1,749	700	800
Ricks College	1,870		600	3,500	900	1,000	1,920	900	1,000
University of Idaho	‡ 1,620	5,380/—	866	3,680	930	1,836	1,946	930	1,836

Illinois

Institution	Tuition and fees	Add'l out-of-state/ district tuition	Books and supplies	Room and board	Trans-portation	Other costs	Board only	Trans-portation	Other costs
American Academy of Art	11,980		800					540	
American Conservatory of Music	† 11,200		500				800		1,200
Augustana College	14,700		450	4,449	400	650	900		650
Aurora University	10,925		600	4,497	1,187	1,473	2,450	1,355	905
Barat College	‡ 11,190		800	4,680	1,100	1,700	1,600		1,700
Belleville Area College	1,290	3,480/1,440	500				1,500	1,200	1,320
Benedictine University	11,790		650	4,470		1,500	2,580		1,500
Black Hawk College									
East Campus	1,590	5,250/2,310	530				1,334	700	1,418
Moline	‡ 1,590	4,200/1,680	500				1,334	677	1,418
Blackburn College	6,850		500	2,850	250	800	1,500	50	800
Blessing-Reiman College of Nursing	9,000		400	4,000	250	500	1,725	500	500
Bradley University	12,090		500	4,800	200	1,410	500	600	2,110
Carl Sandburg College	1,560	3,750/1,650	450				1,600	1,400	500
Chicago College of Commerce	‡ 8,170		450				4,536	540	1,305
Chicago State University	‡ 2,356	3,936/—	825				2,000	1,200	2,000
City Colleges of Chicago									
Harold Washington College	‡ 1,120	4,860/900	600				1,500	540	1,761
Harry S. Truman College	‡ 1,225	3,224/2,381	600				1,500	702	1,761
Kennedy-King College	‡ 1,300	3,224/2,381	600				1,600	560	1,280
Malcolm X College	‡ 1,285	3,224/2,381	600				1,500	540	1,800
Olive-Harvey College	‡ 1,285	3,224/2,381	600				1,500	540	1,761
Richard J. Daley College	‡ 1,225	3,224/2,381	600				1,500	540	1,761
Wright College	‡ 1,225	3,224/2,381	600				1,600	600	1,280
College of DuPage	† 1,305	4,007/2,792	962		1,604	1,190	1,500	1,604	1,190
College of Lake County	1,530	5,837/4,380	500				1,500		
College of St. Francis	‡ 10,770		410	4,340	340	900	1,500	710	900
Columbia College	8,120		700				1,560	700	1,652
Concordia University	10,835		400	4,623	400	600	1,500	400	600
Danville Area Community College	‡ 1,140	3,300/1,865	500				1,500	1,392	1,350
De Paul University	‡ 11,886		600	5,233	660	1,300	1,500	400	1,100

†Figures are projected for 1996-97. ‡Figures are for 1995-96.

All aid		Need–based aid		Grants and scholarships — Need–based				Non–need–based				Financial aid deadlines		Inst aid form	Notes
Total freshmen	Percent receiving aid	Freshmen judged to have need	Percent offered aid	Acad	Music/drama	Art	Athl	Acad	Music/drama	Art	Athl	Priority	Closing		
1,268	20			X				X				5/1	none		
				X	X			X	X			4/1	5/1		
													none		
1,778	17			X				X	X		X	3/1	none		
													none		
				X				X	X	X		5/1	none		
850	15			X				X				4/1	none		
157	91	126	100	X	X	X	X	X	X	X	X	2/15	none	X	
64	91	46	100	X				X				5/1	5/1	X	
				X	X	X		X		X	X	4/1	none		
1,838	65	1,500	93	X	X	X	X	X	X	X	X	3/30	none		
128	81			X				X				6/1	none		
1,578	80			X	X	X	X	X	X	X	X	3/15	none		
419	65	215	93	X	X	X	X	X	X			3/1	none		
1,175	39			X	X	X		X	X	X	X	4/15	none		
330	94			X	X	X		X	X	X	X	3/1	none		
2,328	78			X				X	X	X	X	5/1	none		
1,260	65			X	X	X	X	X	X	X	X	2/15	none		
142	50										X		none	X	
									X				none		
668	92	491	99					X	X	X		4/15	none	X	
127	100	98	100	X				X				5/1	9/1		
													none		
8,500	31			X				X	X	X	X	5/31	none		
260	89	187	100					X	X	X		4/15	none		
													none		
				X	X	X	X	X	X	X	X	5/15	none		
161	98			X				X				4/1	none		
				X				X				3/1	none		
1,016	82	496	100					X	X	X	X	3/1	none		
1,847	70			X	X	X	X	X	X	X	X	5/1	none		
49	65	37	100					X					none	X	
719	80			X				X	X	X	X	3/15	none	X	
													none		
													none		
				X				X			X	5/1	none		
955	80			X				X			X	6/1	none	X	
668	70						X	X			X	8/15	none		
													none		
4,894	30			X				X			X	6/1	none		
6,829	10			X	X	X		X	X	X		5/1	none		
								X	X	X	X		none		
													none	X	
				X				X				5/1	none	X	
207	92	149	100	X	X	X		X	X	X		6/1	6/1	X	
481	80							X			X	6/1	none		
1,209	68			X	X	X	X	X	X	X	X	5/1			

Institution	Tuition and fees	Add'l out-of-state/ district tuition	Books and supplies	Costs for campus residents			Costs for students at home		
				Room and board	Trans-portation	Other costs	Board only	Trans-portation	Other costs
DeVry Institute of Technology									
Addison	6,560		560				2,030	2,035	1,858
Chicago	6,560		560				2,030	2,035	1,843
Eastern Illinois University	2,905	4,104/—	120	3,434	430	1,300	1,800	810	1,160
East-West University	6,510						1,200	500	1,800
Elgin Community College	‡ 1,280	4,489/3,709	578				1,500	2,781	1,298
Elmhurst College	10,976		550	4,660		2,200	1,600	1,150	1,600
Eureka College	13,216		330	4,142	160	510	1,840	675	295
Finch University of Health Sciences/The Chicago Medical School	‡ 14,279		2,470				1,760	1,060	2,666
Gem City College	‡ 3,600		600					400	1,350
Governors State University	‡ 2,098	3,936/—	500				1,600	800	800
Greenville College	11,760		500	4,750	400	900	2,700	400	900
Harrington Institute of Interior Design	9,970		925					1,000	2,000
Highland Community College	1,260	3,640/2,640	600				1,800	1,800	1,000
Illinois Central College	‡ 1,350	3,330/2,170	500				2,225	1,344	2,335
Illinois College	‡ 8,600		500	4,000	300	1,000		700	600
Illinois Eastern Community Colleges									
Frontier Community College	‡ 895	4,580/3,484	600				1,500	1,200	800
Lincoln Trail College	‡ 895	4,580/3,484					1,500	1,200	800
Olney Central College	‡ 895	4,580/3,484	600				1,500	1,200	800
Wabash Valley College	‡ 895	4,580/3,484	600				1,500	1,200	800
Illinois Institute of Technology	15,840		500	4,795		1,700	1,600		2,200
Illinois State University	‡ 3,544	5,382/—	590	3,627	538	2,100	1,800	900	1,937
Illinois Valley Community College	1,208	3,360/—	500				1,800	1,440	1,296
Illinois Wesleyan University	16,410		400	4,424	100	550	1,500	310	600
International Academy of Merchandising and Design	† 9,300		905				1,000	750	1,428
ITT Technical Institute: Hoffman Estates	‡ 6,165		1,100						
John A. Logan College	1,074	3,200/1,609	800				1,500	1,728	1,000
John Wood Community College	‡ 1,470	4,416/2,006	550				1,500	864	720
Joliet Junior College	‡ 1,270	3,090/2,120	450				1,780	1,110	1,325
Judson College	‡ 10,200		500	4,600	300	1,200	2,500	500	1,200
Kankakee Community College	1,216	5,327/2,252	500				1,008	800	900
Kaskaskia College	‡ 1,007	3,810/1,500	500				900	672	648
Kendall College	9,465		850	5,091	260	630	2,850	625	630
Kishwaukee College	‡ 1,153	3,419/2,466	500				1,500	1,200	1,000
Knox College	17,778		400	4,662	200	600	2,589	200	600
Lake Forest College	19,000		500	4,400	300	120		500	1,240
Lake Land College	† 1,290	4,513/1,299	318				1,800	1,530	884
Lakeview College of Nursing	‡ 6,475		475						
Lewis and Clark Community College	‡ 1,200	4,890/2,280	400				4,000	900	1,100
Lewis University	10,830		500	5,000	570	1,200	1,800	1,350	1,200
Lexington College	‡ 5,700		600	3,400	1,200	400		800	400
Lincoln Christian College and Seminary	4,850		500	3,560	500	1,700	1,000	500	1,700
Lincoln College	9,120		450	4,150	200	1,000	2,300	500	1,000
Lincoln Land Community College	† 1,095	3,300/1,590	475					650	500
Loyola University of Chicago	14,820		700	6,510	220	1,550	1,840	930	1,550
MacCormac Junior College	7,530		600				1,650	444	1,200
MacMurray College	10,940		550	4,000	500	600		500	600
McHenry County College	† 1,184	3,907/3,032	500				1,900	1,160	1,400

†Figures are projected for 1996-97. ‡Figures are for 1995-96.

| All aid | | Need–based aid | | Grants and scholarships | | | | | | | | Financial aid deadlines | | Inst aid form | Notes |
| Total freshmen | Percent receiving aid | Freshmen judged to have need | Percent offered aid | Need-based | | | | Non-need-based | | | | | | | |
				Acad	Music/drama	Art	Athl	Acad	Music/drama	Art	Athl	Priority	Closing		
								X					none		
								X					none		
				X				X	X		X	4/15	none		
								X					none		
		1,095	100					X	X	X	X		5/14	X	
267	88	225	100	X	X			X	X			4/15	none	X	
148	90	146	100	X	X	X		X	X	X		5/1	none		
													none		
				X				X	X	X			none		
210	96	147	100					X	X			5/1	none		
165	39											6/1	none		
774	40			X	X	X	X	X	X	X	X	6/1	none	X	
													none		
306	94	259	100	X				X	X			5/1	none		
				X	X	X		X					none		
				X	X	X	X	X					none		
				X	X	X	X						none		
				X	X	X	X	X					none		
234	100	161	100	X				X				5/1	none	X	
								X	X	X	X	3/1	none		
								X	X	X		5/1	none		
505	90	374	100	X	X	X		X	X	X		3/1	none	X	
296	65	114	100					X				9/1	none	X	
153	95												none		
1,273	65			X				X	X	X	X	5/1	none		
													none		
2,571	25	800	75					X	X	X		7/1	none		
													none		
													none	X	
				X				X	X		X		none		
62	60			X				X					none		
				X			X	X			X	6/1	none	X	
308	90	255	100					X	X	X		3/1	none	X	
266	72	187	100	X	X			X	X			3/1	none	X	
1,427	46			X			X	X	X	X	X	5/1	none		
													4/1	X	
1,670	42			X	X	X	X	X	X	X	X	6/1	none	X	
575	85	252	100					X	X	X	X	5/1	none		
28	64	17	94	X				X				6/1	none		
140	90			X				X				8/10	none		
290	85			X	X	X	X	X	X	X	X		none		
7,215	47							X	X	X	X	5/1	none		
1,247	78	464	100	X				X	X	X	X	3/1	none		
271	80							X					none		
179	87	177	100	X	X	X		X				5/1	8/1		
3,469	10	300	83					X	X	X	X	6/1	none	X	

Institution	Tuition and fees	Add'l out-of-state/district tuition	Books and supplies	Costs for campus residents			Costs for students at home		
				Room and board	Transportation	Other costs	Board only	Transportation	Other costs
McKendree College	‡ 8,100		500	4,190	250	800	250	600	800
Mennonite College of Nursing	8,834		648	2,556	555	1,306	1,500	1,296	766
Midstate College	‡ 5,006		940		400	690	2,500	1,500	
Millikin University	13,381		600	4,828	200	765	2,000	1,578	765
Monmouth College	14,175		500	4,275	370	400	2,000	400	
Moody Bible Institute	‡ 800		600	4,200	250	500		500	500
Moraine Valley Community College	‡ 1,322	3,960/3,570	400				1,500	1,110	1,340
Morrison Institute of Technology	† 6,810		575	1,800	400	1,200	1,000	800	1,200
Morton College	1,722	3,240/2,052	400				2,000	500	900
NAES College	‡ 4,220		250						
National College of Chiropractic	‡ 8,352		830		950	1,945		1,160	2,130
National-Louis University	11,250		700	4,866	400	1,171	2,230	1,316	1,116
North Central College	13,194		500	4,854	320	1,180	1,500	1,050	1,180
North Park College	13,990		900	4,780	550	900	1,870	850	900
Northeastern Illinois University	‡ 2,523	3,936/—	552				2,007	810	2,178
Northern Illinois University	‡ 3,746	5,382/—	520	3,416	368	1,440	2,446	368	1,440
Northwestern Business College	6,545		800				900	720	1,134
Northwestern University	18,108		813	6,054		1,143	2,325	984	1,143
Oakton Community College	1,108	3,540/2,790	400				1,820	1,100	1,000
Olivet Nazarene University	10,166		600	4,460	400	800		400	800
Parkland College	1,290	4,597/3,033	600				1,800	900	900
Prairie State College	1,728	4,996/3,936	750				2,300	1,100	1,700
Principia College	13,452		450	5,586		750			
Quincy University	11,510		560	4,370	600	620	2,130	600	660
Ray College of Design	‡ 8,880		1,000				2,241	540	1,260
Rend Lake College	1,020	2,850/1,830	380				878	1,189	1,053
Richland Community College	1,185	3,155/1,169	400					1,000	
Robert Morris College: Chicago	9,750		600				1,313	540	1,145
Rock Valley College	1,460	6,016/3,248	500					1,100	
Rockford Business College	‡ 5,430		720				2,500	916	2,855
Rockford College	14,100		800	4,500	500	1,440	1,500	792	1,440
Roosevelt University	‡ 9,770		600	5,866	600	1,456	1,580	600	1,456
Rosary College	‡ 12,230		550	4,740	50	900	1,500	500	900
Rush University	‡ 10,460		500		235	1,200		510	1,200
St. Augustine College	4,920		835				1,570	650	750
St. Francis Medical Center College of Nursing	‡ 7,971		850	4,500	350	1,557	1,500	350	1,937
St. Joseph College of Nursing	‡ 7,844		750				1,800	1,200	1,500
St. Xavier University	‡ 11,600		600	4,800	340	794	2,030	830	794
Sauk Valley Community College	‡ 1,200	2,498/299	500					1,000	900
School of the Art Institute of Chicago	16,320		1,980		880	1,300	2,800	880	1,300
Shawnee Community College	‡ 844	4,380/1,530	300				1,500	1,632	540
Shimer College	‡ 12,600		700			1,300			
South Suburban College of Cook County	‡ 1,357	4,349/2,664	500				1,500	300	1,000
Southeastern Illinois College	900	3,390/2,250	450				2,500	1,200	1,400
Southern Illinois University									
Carbondale	‡ 3,338	4,800/—	600	3,369	700	1,908	1,500	700	1,208
Edwardsville	‡ 2,353	3,557/—	228	3,684	1,350	1,077	2,280	1,550	1,077
Spoon River College	‡ 1,320	4,159/218	500						
Springfield College in Illinois	‡ 5,540		400		276	3,225	390	1,700	878
State Community College	‡ 1,044	3,600/—	200				1,550	425	1,300
Telshe Yeshiva-Chicago	‡ 7,300			2,400					

†Figures are projected for 1996-97. ‡Figures are for 1995-96.

| All aid | | Need–based aid | | Grants and scholarships | | | | | | | | Financial aid deadlines | | Inst aid form | Notes |
| | | | | Need–based | | | | Non–need–based | | | | | | | |
Total fresh-men	Percent receiving aid	Freshmen judged to have need	Percent offered aid	Acad	Music/drama	Art	Athl	Acad	Music/drama	Art	Athl	Priority	Closing		
136	90			X	X	X	X	X	X	X	X	6/1	none	X	
				X				X							
495	94	405	100	X	X	X		X	X	X		5/1	none	X	
324	97	300	100	X	X	X		X	X	X		4/30	none		
265	2			X	X								none		
								X				6/1	none	X	
96	60							X					none		
		92	100	X				X	X	X	X	6/1	none	X	
													none		
													none		
				X	X			X	X			7/15	none		
330	95	252	100					X	X	X		4/1	none	X	
211	90	148	100	X	X	X		X	X	X		4/1	8/1	X	
889	22							X	X	X	X	4/1	none		
2,460	71	2,256	61	X				X	X	X		3/1	5/1	X	
								X				8/15	none	X	
1,950	49	938	100						X		X		2/15		
				X				X	X	X	X	6/1	none		
389	77			X	X	X	X	X	X	X	X	3/1	none		
2,206	63							X	X	X		3/1	none	X	
													none		
132	82	100	100	X	X			X				3/1	none	X	
260	93	227	100	X	X	X		X	X	X	X	2/15	none	X	
													none		
1,275	66							X			X		none		
				X				X			X		none		
1,847	90							X			X	6/1	none		
4,800	46							X	X			6/1	none		
													none		
128	95			X				X				4/15	none	X	
													none		
132	80	97	100	X			X	X			X	5/1	none		
				X				X				5/15	none	X	
								X					none		
225	85			X	X		X	X	X		X	3/1	none		
													none		
226	74	167	100	X		X					X	4/1	none	X	
													none		
													none		
1,169	70			X	X	X	X	X	X	X	X	5/1	none	X	
2,338	85							X	X	X	X	4/1	none		
1,147	70	697	93	X	X	X	X	X	X	X	X	3/1	6/1		
1,337	80			X	X	X	X	X	X	X			none		
													none		
373	85											7/1	none		

Institution	Tuition and fees	Add'l out-of-state/ district tuition	Books and supplies	Costs for campus residents			Costs for students at home		
				Room and board	Trans-portation	Other costs	Board only	Trans-portation	Other costs
Trinity Christian College	11,250		600	4,435	715	1,110	1,956	1,185	1,110
Trinity International University	11,918		600	4,560	400	900	2,030	400	900
Triton College	‡ 1,404	4,590/2,670	450				1,465	1,470	
University of Chicago	21,300		675	7,275		637	2,550		637
University of Illinois									
Chicago	‡ 3,974	5,131/—	630	5,188	702	3,100	1,800	702	2,526
Springfield	‡ 2,833	4,914/—	625		740	1,475	1,500	1,220	854
Urbana-Champaign	‡ 3,956	5,174/—	540	4,736	400	1,966		710	1,966
VanderCook College of Music	‡ 9,350		300	4,600	450	400	3,300	500	250
Waubonsee Community College	1,198	5,406/4,500	500				1,712	1,584	1,000
West Suburban College of Nursing	‡ 8,720		400	4,191	400	600	2,736	400	600
Western Illinois University	2,810	4,080/—	650	3,613	735	1,461	1,002	1,125	1,402
Wheaton College	13,100		580	4,350		1,500	2,000		1,500
William Rainey Harper College	1,316	—/5,670	502				1,924	920	1,492

Indiana

Institution	Tuition and fees	Add'l out-of-state/ district tuition	Books and supplies	Room and board	Trans-portation	Other costs	Board only	Trans-portation	Other costs
Ancilla College	‡ 3,060		450				1,600	450	900
Anderson University	12,040		550	3,980	400	700	2,500	400	700
Ball State University	‡ 3,048	4,776/—	630	3,768	352	1,200	1,500	1,078	1,200
Bethel College	10,650		600	3,300	600	700	1,900	1,000	700
Butler University	14,900		500	5,020	340	1,260	2,650	340	1,260
Calumet College of St. Joseph	‡ 5,300		600				1,545	775	1,130
DePauw University	16,180		550	5,400	250	700	1,500	600	350
Earlham College	17,898		600	4,412	650	700	2,280	200	600
Franklin College	11,370		590	4,390	455	895		750	895
Goshen College	10,950		650	3,880	360	960	1,503	360	960
Grace College	‡ 9,230		300	4,070	600	800	1,500	750	800
Hanover College	9,200		700	3,710	500	800	2,100	500	800
Holy Cross College	6,400		500				1,900	2,060	1,460
Huntington College	† 11,420		550	4,340	850	750	2,100	850	750
Indiana Business College	‡ 7,180		900				2,500	504	1,143
Indiana Institute of Technology	10,800		700	4,130		600		1,050	600
Indiana State University	‡ 2,928	4,296/—	600	3,860	600	1,100	1,700	968	600
Indiana University									
Bloomington	‡ 3,582	7,188/—	600	4,465	410	1,528	1,500	962	1,436
East	‡ 2,444	3,981/—	606				1,953	1,115	1,086
Kokomo	‡ 2,704	3,981/—	658				1,584	990	1,108
Northwest	‡ 2,685	3,981/—	500				2,050	1,705	1,436
South Bend	‡ 2,742	4,413/—	574				1,810	1,356	1,356
Southeast	‡ 2,585	3,981/—	576				1,890	910	1,225
Indiana University—Purdue University									
Fort Wayne	‡ 2,708	3,737/—	500				1,800	810	900
Indianapolis	‡ 3,209	6,067/—	528	3,260	378	1,359	1,827	1,233	1,359
Indiana Wesleyan University	10,260		700	4,044	700	2,000		700	
International Business College	‡ 8,240		725						
Ivy Tech State College									
Central Indiana	‡ 1,809	1,484/—	492		640	1,600	2,124	640	1,392
Columbus	‡ 1,809	1,484/—	561				1,997	640	1,392
Eastcentral	‡ 1,809	1,484/—	561				1,997	640	1,372
Kokomo	‡ 1,809	1,484/—	561				1,997	640	1,392
Lafayette	‡ 1,809	1,484/—	561				1,997	640	1,392
Northcentral	‡ 1,809	1,484/—	561					640	1,392
Northeast	‡ 1,809	1,484/—	561				1,997	640	1,392

†Figures are projected for 1996-97. ‡Figures are for 1995-96.

| All aid | | Need–based aid | | Grants and scholarships | | | | | | | | Financial aid deadlines | | Inst aid form | Notes |
| | | | | Need–based | | | | Non–need–based | | | | | | | |
Total freshmen	Percent receiving aid	Freshmen judged to have need	Percent offered aid	Acad	Music/drama	Art	Athl	Acad	Music/drama	Art	Athl	Priority	Closing		
210	96	126	94					X	X	X	X	2/15	8/15		
164	87			X	X		X	X	X		X	4/1	none		
				X				X				4/15	none	X	
986	75	608	100					X	X	X			2/1		
2,533	66	2,250	100	X			X	X	X		X	3/1	none		
				X				X			X	4/1	none		
6,113	76			X				X	X	X	X	3/15	none		
													none		
													none		
1,562	72	872	96					X	X	X	X	3/1	none		
549	84	308	100					X	X			3/15	none	X	
3,396	74			X				X	X	X		5/1	none	X	
534	60	210	100	X		X	X	X			X	5/1	none	X	
513	88			X	X	X		X	X	X		3/1	none		
3,848	60	2,162	100	X	X	X		X	X		X	3/1	none		
205	90							X	X	X	X	3/1	none	X	
849	80	484	82				X	X	X		X	3/1	none		
110	52			X				X				3/1	9/1		
613	89	359	100	X				X	X	X		2/15	none	X	
261	81	150	100	X	X	X		X				3/1	none		
283	95	239	100	X				X	X	X		3/1	none	X	
257	86	150	100	X	X	X	X	X	X		X	3/1	none	X	
162	88	125	100					X	X	X	X	4/1	none		
311	80	188	100	X				X				3/1	none		
321	47											3/1	none		
200	90	154	100	X				X	X	X	X	3/1	none	X	
186	92			X			X	X			X	3/1	none		
2,726	80							X	X	X	X		3/1	X	
5,751	70	2,283	97	X	X	X	X	X	X	X	X	3/1	none	X	
200	72			X				X				3/1	none	X	
626	45			X				X				4/30	none		
775	21			X				X				3/1	none	X	
900	40							X	X	X	X	3/1	none		
1,615	60			X	X	X	X	X	X	X	X	3/1	Closing	X	
1,590	55			X				X	X	X	X	3/1	none		
2,519	45	1,270	72					X		X	X	3/1	none		
396	90	322	100	X				X	X	X	X	3/1	none	X	
								X				3/1	none		
								X				3/1	none		
								X				3/1	none		
								X				3/1	none		
								X				3/1	none		
								X				3/1	none		
								X				3/1	none		

Institution	Tuition and fees	Add'l out-of-state/district tuition	Books and supplies	Costs for campus residents			Costs for students at home		
				Room and board	Transportation	Other costs	Board only	Transportation	Other costs
Northwest	‡ 1,809	1,484/—	561				1,997	640	1,392
Southcentral	† 1,809	1,484/—	561				1,997	640	1,392
Southeast	‡ 1,809	1,484/—	561				1,997	640	1,392
Southwest	‡ 1,809	1,484/—	561				1,997	640	1,392
Wabash Valley	‡ 1,809	1,484/—	561				1,997	640	1,392
Whitewater	‡ 1,809	1,484/—					1,997	640	1,372
Lutheran College of Health Professions	6,290		826		1,500	1,050	1,920	1,500	1,050
Manchester College	12,170		525	4,280	550	900	1,090	550	900
Marian College	† 11,582		550	4,225	700	1,000	1,500	640	1,000
Martin University	† 6,980		600				2,700	300	2,400
Oakland City University	7,996		800	3,146	1,500	1,800	2,700	1,500	1,800
Purdue University									
Calumet	‡ 2,658	3,787/—	505				1,916	1,086	1,204
North Central Campus	‡ 2,640	3,787/—	600				3,000	1,300	1,200
West Lafayette	‡ 3,056	7,072/—	600	4,110	270	1,110	1,950	1,280	1,110
Rose-Hulman Institute of Technology	15,600		1,600	4,700	300	600	1,500	800	600
St. Francis College	10,020		500	4,020				1,000	500
St. Joseph's College	12,590		600	4,640	350	600		1,840	3,750
St. Mary-of-the-Woods College	‡ 12,360		775	4,570	750	900	2,620	1,000	700
St. Meinrad College	‡ 6,725		500	4,226	1,100	900			
Saint Mary's College	15,150		500	4,966	275	1,250	1,800	425	1,250
Sawyer College, Inc.	5,135								
Taylor University	12,774		450	4,220		1,250	1,800		1,250
Tri-State University	11,106		468	4,644	441	882	1,701	831	1,032
University of Evansville	13,270		700	4,710	400	690	1,650	1,570	690
University of Indianapolis	12,350		540	4,330	430	1,030	1,675	860	980
University of Notre Dame #24,460	19,010		600	4,850	500	850	2,500	500	850
University of Southern Indiana	‡ 2,310	2,770/—	625		700	1,570	1,660	1,100	1,570
Valparaiso University	13,980		500	3,450	200	760		500	760
Vincennes University	‡ 2,286	3,150/1,050	500	3,902	700	550	1,360	700	550
Wabash College	14,825			4,620		635			
Iowa									
American Institute of Business	6,025		720	3,015	480	990	630		990
American Institute of Commerce	6,375		950				2,439	1,161	1,440
Briar Cliff College	11,430		600	4,017	500	1,000	2,000	500	1,000
Buena Vista University	14,458		500	4,125	500	1,000	1,900	500	1,000
Central College	12,304		650	3,808	550	76	2,022	550	76
Clarke College	11,966		500	4,480	200		2,500	200	600
Clinton Community College	‡ 1,582	735/—	900				1,500	900	900
Coe College	15,535		500	4,455	500	1,200	890	500	1,200
Cornell College	17,220			4,670		1,050		500	1,050
Des Moines Area Community College	1,650	1,410/—	500				1,360	1,200	640
Divine Word College	‡ 6,500		400	1,200	800	800			
Dordt College	10,900		600	2,900	1,100	1,800	2,400	1,500	1,800
Drake University	14,380		700	5,100		1,800			1,500
Ellsworth Community College	‡ 2,196	1,740/—	400	3,036		1,800		1,000	1,800
Emmaus Bible College	2,470		450	4,360	850	850	2,000	550	850
Faith Baptist Bible College and Theological Seminary	6,220		550	3,276	1,100	1,450	2,450	1,100	1,450
Graceland College	10,340		600	3,310	370	1,000	2,070		800
Grand View College	10,970		570	3,630	400	2,000	1,333	800	2,000
Grinnell College	17,134		400	4,926	500	400			400

†Figures are projected for 1996-97. ‡Figures are for 1995-96.

All aid		Need-based aid		Grants and scholarships								Financial aid deadlines		Inst aid form	Notes
				Need-based				Non-need-based							
Total freshmen	Percent receiving aid	Freshmen judged to have need	Percent offered aid	Acad	Music/drama	Art	Athl	Acad	Music/drama	Art	Athl	Priority	Closing		
556	47							X				3/1	none		
								X				3/1	none		
								X				3/1	none		
				X				X				8/31	none		
								X				3/1	none		
								X				3/1	none		
68	51	38	100	X				X				3/1	4/15	X	
323	94	292	100	X				X	X	X		3/1	none		
276	94	203	100	X	X	X	X	X	X	X	X	8/15	none	X	
286	97	263	100	X	X	X	X	X	X	X	X		3/1		
1,792	41			X			X	X			X		3/1		
989	25	675	100					X				3/1	none		
7,285	59	3,842	84	X				X			X	3/1	5/1	X	
461	90	368	100	X				X				12/1	4/1		
134	84	90	100	X				X		X	X	3/1	none	X	
215	92	181	100	X				X	X		X	5/1	8/1	X	
89	90							X	X	X	X	3/1	none	X	
27	100			X				X				3/1	none		
386	73	248	100	X	X	X		X	X			3/1	none		
472	79	251	100	X				X	X	X	X		3/1	X	
298	88	240	100					X			X	3/1	none		
785	98	560	100					X	X	X	X	3/1	none	X	
478	83	306	99	X				X	X	X	X	3/1	none	X	
1,906	77	970	100	X			X				X		2/15		
1,535	66	855	87	X				X	X	X	X	3/1	none	X	
674	79	450	100	X				X	X	X	X	3/1	none		
4,000	60			X	X	X	X	X	X	X	X	3/1	none		
227	90	168	100	X	X	X		X	X	X		2/15	none	X	
290	78	275	100					X				4/1	none		
274	80												none	X	
161	99			X	X	X	X	X	X	X	X	3/1	none		
351	99	345	100	X	X	X		X	X	X		4/20	none		
407	99	332	100	X	X	X		X	X	X		3/1	none		
187	95	128	100	X				X	X	X		3/15	none		
429	50			X		X	X			X	X	4/20	none	X	
292	88			X	X	X		X	X	X		3/1	none	X	
387	95	360	100	X	X	X		X	X	X			3/1	X	
2,598	60			X				X			X	3/1	none		
													none		
401	98	300	100	X	X	X	X	X	X	X	X	4/1	none	X	
742	95	483	100	X				X	X	X	X	3/1	none		
614	66			X	X		X	X	X		X	4/1	none		
98	92	72	100	X	X			X				4/1	none		
298	91	259	100	X				X	X	X	X	3/1	none		
275	75							X	X	X	X	3/1	none	X	
307	81	209	100	X				X					2/1	X	

Institution	Tuition and fees	Add'l out-of-state/district tuition	Books and supplies	Costs for campus residents			Costs for students at home		
				Room and board	Transportation	Other costs	Board only	Transportation	Other costs
Hamilton Technical College	5,250								
Hawkeye Community College	‡ 2,190	1,920/—	1,000				1,237	1,710	2,916
Indian Hills Community College	1,455	480/—	675	2,115	1,361	750	2,016	1,361	750
Iowa Central Community College	1,898	825/—	600	2,860	630	1,240	750	630	945
Iowa Lakes Community College	2,044	1,080/—	600	2,825	850	500	1,645	850	500
Iowa State University	‡ 2,574	5,618/—		3,382	388	1,980			
Iowa Wesleyan College	11,300		500	3,840	600	1,200	2,600	900	1,200
Iowa Western Community College	2,070	945/—	800	2,800	470		1,400	2,800	1,000
Kirkwood Community College	1,650	1,650/—	450					1,000	900
Loras College	12,660		600	4,545	500	450	3,550	300	450
Luther College	14,900		600	3,650	400	400	2,000	400	400
Maharishi University of Management	13,976		500	4,800	600	1,100	2,288	600	1,100
Morningside College	11,226		500	4,070	500	1,000	1,812	500	1,000
Mount Mercy College	11,370		560	3,900	600	1,710	1,800	1,100	2,940
Mount St. Clare College	‡ 10,300		600	3,750	350	700	2,000	400	500
Muscatine Community College	‡ 1,582	735/—	900				1,500	900	900
North Iowa Area Community College	1,875	831/—	600	2,916	325	1,216	2,050	1,012	1,216
Northeast Iowa Community College	‡ 2,130	1,860/—	1,000				1,500	1,155	945
Northwest Iowa Community College	1,920	810/—	550			710	1,000	1,900	710
Northwestern College	10,850		600	3,250	400	1,200	2,000	800	1,200
St. Ambrose University	11,739		600	4,410	600	1,300	3,300	1,300	500
Scott Community College	‡ 1,582	735/—	900				1,500	900	900
Simpson College	12,650		550	4,145	300	1,100			2,500
Southeastern Community College									
North Campus	‡ 1,613	721/—	600	2,600				1,000	
South Campus	‡ 1,575	690/—					1,350	500	700
Southwestern Community College	1,860	780/—	600	2,760	648	1,500	1,240	2,400	1,500
Teikyo Marycrest University	11,056		525	4,128	630	700	1,800	630	700
University of Dubuque	12,320		600	4,340	250	1,500	2,110	900	1,500
University of Iowa	‡ 2,558	6,250/—	694	3,780	440	2,158	668	602	1,876
University of Northern Iowa	† 2,650	4,218/—	674	3,268	622	2,344	1,774	622	2,344
University of Osteopathic Medicine and Health Sciences	10,070		450				832	445	843
Upper Iowa University	9,372		900	3,560	490	1,120	1,700	1,344	1,120
Vennard College	‡ 6,458		500	3,220	690	1,280	2,500	800	1,280
Waldorf College	10,575		600	3,825	600	1,150	3,200	600	1,150
Wartburg College	13,000		300	3,970	430	520	1,500	500	450
Western Iowa Tech Community College	1,810	1,710/—	425		150	800		825	660
Westmar University	‡ 10,276		560	3,750	800	880	1,740	800	880
William Penn College	‡ 10,290		500	3,240	500	750	1,130	1,000	800
Kansas									
Allen County Community College	‡ 1,020	1,620/—	300	2,700	500	1,620	1,200	500	1,670
Baker University	10,300		750	4,400	1,010	1,440	2,250	1,560	1,440
Barclay College	4,695		430	2,750	625	1,340	1,500	375	1,340
Barton County Community College	† 1,184	1,600/—	500	2,500	800	1,000	1,500	800	1,000
Benedictine College	‡ 10,600		550	4,350	570	1,200	2,000	570	1,200
Bethany College	9,980		550	3,560	600	1,215	1,200	990	1,474
Bethel College	9,900		500	4,030	550	1,478	1,500	760	840
Brown Mackie College	‡ 7,115		750				1,500	952	1,008
Butler County Community College	‡ 1,110	1,380/—	600	2,930	600	1,200	1,700	600	900
Central College	8,550		400	3,300	500	500	1,600	400	500

†Figures are projected for 1996-97. ‡Figures are for 1995-96.

All aid		Need–based aid		Grants and scholarships								Financial aid deadlines		Inst aid form	Notes
				Need–based				Non–need–based							
Total fresh-men	Percent receiving aid	Freshmen judged to have need	Percent offered aid	Acad	Music/ drama	Art	Athl	Acad	Music/ drama	Art	Athl	Priority	Closing		
120	90												none		
1,179	75			X				X				4/20	6/30		
1,242	85			X				X	X	X	X	4/1	none		
1,847	75			X	X	X	X	X	X		X		none		
940	80			X	X	X	X	X	X	X	X	4/22	none		
3,412	75	1,900	100	X	X	X	X	X	X	X	X	2/15	none		
101	95	100	100	X	X	X		X	X	X	X	4/22	none		
1,525	76	703	91	X				X			X	5/1	none		
3,550	46			X	X		X					3/15	none		
325	89	307	100	X				X	X	X	X		4/15		
591	73	431	100	X	X	X		X	X	X		3/1	6/1		
45	97	44	100	X				X				4/15	7/15		
204	96	144	100					X	X	X	X	3/1	none		
160	97	73	100					X	X	X		3/1	none		
427	40			X	X		X	X	X		X	4/20	none		
1,866	60			X	X		X	X	X	X	X	3/1	none		
				X				X				4/1	none		
557	70	278	100	X				X				4/20	none	X	
420	98	351	100	X	X	X	X	X	X	X	X	4/1	none	X	
306	92	230	100	X	X	X	X	X	X	X	X	3/15	none		
1,272	49			X				X				4/20	none		
412	99			X	X	X		X	X	X		4/20	none		
				X				X					none	X	
227	63			X				X					none		
399	75			X	X		X	X	X		X	4/15	none	X	
121	90			X	X	X	X	X		X	X	3/1	none		
175	97	128	100	X				X	X			4/1	none		
3,578	65			X				X	X	X	X	1/1	none		
2,044	59	1,236	98	X				X	X	X	X	2/15	none		
														X	
257	93			X	X	X		X	X	X		4/20	none		
													none		
365	95	218	100		X	X	X	X	X	X	X	4/20	none		
359	92	271	100	X	X	X		X	X	X		3/1	none		
													none		
129	85	78	100					X	X		X	4/1	none		
													none		
218	92			X				X	X	X	X	3/1	none	X	
24	100	19	100	X	X			X	X			4/1	none	X	
2,746	30			X	X	X	X	X	X	X	X	3/1	none	X	
256	96	198	100					X	X		X	4/1	none		
217	95	135	100	X				X	X	X	X	3/15	none		
134	93	105	100					X	X	X	X	2/1	none		
													none		
1,730	20							X	X	X	X	4/1	none	X	
													none		

Institution		Tuition and fees	Add'l out-of-state/ district tuition	Books and supplies	Costs for campus residents			Costs for students at home		
					Room and board	Trans-portation	Other costs	Board only	Trans-portation	Other costs
Cloud County Community College	‡	1,230	1,680/—	475	2,650	475	875	1,600	475	875
Coffeyville Community College	‡	1,080	1,380/—	350	2,650	300	1,200		200	900
Colby Community College	‡	1,080	1,620/—	500	2,816	640	612	1,500	740	612
Cowley County Community College	‡	1,140	1,620/—	500	2,625	450	1,000	1,800	1,000	1,000
Dodge City Community College	‡	1,260	1,800/—	400	3,100	400	900	1,080	400	900
Donnelly College		2,800		600					720	
Emporia State University	‡	1,782	3,982/—	464	3,220	515	1,515		515	1,515
Fort Hays State University	‡	1,842	3,982/—	700	3,214	1,200	1,250	1,500	400	1,000
Fort Scott Community College	‡	1,080	1,560/—	500	2,214	700	2,100	1,450	700	1,800
Friends University		9,505		600	3,140		2,300			2,300
Garden City Community College	†	1,050	1,110/—	550	2,850	700	1,125	1,500	700	1,125
Haskell Indian Junior College	‡	130		175	25	870	1,400		668	
Hesston College	‡	9,750		700	3,900	500	1,000	2,340	300	1,100
Highland Community College	‡	1,110	1,620/—	350	2,438	425	800	900	775	800
Hutchinson Community College	‡	1,080	1,740/—	500		600	900	1,800	1,388	900
Independence Community College	‡	1,050	1,500/—	300						
Kansas City Kansas Community College		1,080	1,710/—	700				1,800	1,000	1,350
Kansas Newman College		8,500		597	3,626	1,221	1,487		1,668	1,487
Kansas State University	‡	2,199	5,718/—	656	3,370	524	2,000	2,000	524	2,000
Kansas Wesleyan University	‡	9,120		500	3,300	400	500	1,500	400	500
Labette Community College		1,110	1,650/—	400	2,200	400	450	1,300	750	450
Manhattan Christian College		5,300		800	3,094	500	2,200	1,967	450	2,200
McPherson College		9,518		600	3,800	700	2,182	2,200	700	4,652
MidAmerica Nazarene College		8,668		1,000	4,202	231	1,050	1,776	756	1,050
Neosho County Community College	‡	1,110	1,560/—	350	2,700	224	360	2,700	224	360
Ottawa University	‡	8,490		700	3,620	250	900			900
Pittsburg State University	‡	1,806	3,982/—	500	3,126	500	1,000	1,600	700	1,000
Pratt Community College	‡	1,110	1,560/—	450	2,720	600	1,430		800	1,430
St. Mary College		9,750		600	4,200	600	950	1,500	600	950
Southwestern College		8,560		600	3,796	600	900	1,500	600	900
Sterling College		9,596		550	4,004		650	1,972	1,250	
Tabor College		9,900		600	3,750	750	1,160	1,200	750	1,160
University of Kansas										
Lawrence	‡	2,182	5,718/—	700	3,544	1,059	1,695	2,835	1,165	1,695
Medical Center	‡	1,908	5,718/—	600				1,500	1,170	2,385
Washburn University of Topeka		2,896		450	3,800	963	1,000		773	950
Wichita State University ⌐12,293	‡	2,376	5,752/—	700	3,465	1,450	1,300	1,710	1,450	1,310

Kentucky

Institution		Tuition and fees	Add'l out-of-state/ district tuition	Books and supplies	Room and board	Trans-portation	Other costs	Board only	Trans-portation	Other costs
Alice Lloyd College	‡	360	—/3,800	500	2,560	350	885	1,350	640	885
Asbury College		10,595		500	2,984	800	800	1,606	950	
Ashland Community College	‡	980	1,960/—	450					500	920
Bellarmine College		10,320		750	3,480	490	800	1,620	580	700
Berea College		195		450	3,168	250	800	1,400	975	800
Brescia College		8,650		700	3,456	600	1,000	2,200	755	1,000
Campbellsville College	‡	6,420		650	3,210	300	1,000	2,400	900	1,000
Centre College		14,000		650	4,600	250	600	1,625	150	600
Clear Creek Baptist Bible College		2,420		200	2,480		100			100
Cumberland College		7,930		500	3,676	400	600		400	600
Eastern Kentucky University	‡	1,900	3,360/—	275	3,300	475	625	1,725	625	625
Elizabethtown Community College	‡	980	1,960/—	450				1,500	500	920
Georgetown College		9,740	100/—	550	4,050	650	550	1,800	900	550
Hazard Community College	‡	980	1,960/—	450				1,500	460	848

†Figures are projected for 1996-97. ‡Figures are for 1995-96.

All aid		Need–based aid		Grants and scholarships								Financial aid deadlines		Inst aid form	Notes
				Need–based				Non–need-based							
Total freshmen	Percent receiving aid	Freshmen judged to have need	Percent offered aid	Acad	Music/drama	Art	Athl	Acad	Music/drama	Art	Athl	Priority	Closing		
													none		
													none		
1,279	78							X	X	X	X	6/1	none		
													none		
													none		
77	85			X				X				6/1	8/1		
734	85			X	X	X	X	X	X	X	X	3/15	none		
811	70			X	X	X	X	X	X	X	X	3/15	none		
1,714	40	500	100	X	X	X	X					5/1	none		
283	93							X	X	X	X	4/1	none	X	
484	75							X	X	X	X	6/1	none	X	
													none		
198	95	135	100					X				5/1	none		
													none		
2,080	38	618	90	X	X	X	X	X	X	X	X	2/15	none		
437	35			X	X	X	X	X	X	X	X	4/1	none		
1,567	22	444	70	X			X	X	X		X	5/1	none		
117	70	71	100	X	X		X	X	X		X	3/15	none	X	
3,267	70			X	X	X	X	X	X	X	X	3/1	none	X	
131	44			X	X	X	X						none		
79	62			X	X			X				3/1	none		
													none		
255	84	211	100	X	X		X	X	X		X	3/1	none	X	
250	65			X	X	X	X	X	X	X	X	7/15	none		
146	94			X	X	X	X	X	X	X	X	4/1	none		
826	53	540	100	X	X	X	X	X	X	X	X	3/15	none		
194	65	175	100	X				X	X	X	X	5/1	none	X	
75	92	65	100	X			X	X	X	X	X	4/1	none		
106	88	89	100	X				X	X	X	X	3/1	none	X	
													none		
128	100	110	100	X	X		X	X			X	5/15	none	X	
3,555	33	1,190	93	X				X	X	X	X	3/1	none		
				X				X				4/1	none		
697	80			X	X		X	X	X	X	X	3/1	none		
1,119	25	1,026	49	X				X	X	X	X	3/15	none		
298	77	230	100	X	X	X		X	X	X		3/1	none	X	
617	40	294	100	X				X				3/1	5/1	X	
342	85	213	100					X	X	X	X	3/15	none		
418	100	418	100									2/28	none		
76	98	76	100	X	X	X	X	X	X	X	X	4/1	none		
													none	X	
302	88	168	100	X				X					3/1	X	
16	95	12	100	X				X	X			7/15	none		
373	97	342	100					X	X	X	X	3/15	none		
4,187	71							X	X	X	X	4/15	none		
960	60			X				X				4/1	none		
309	95	228	100	X	X	X	X	X	X	X	X	3/1	none		
													none		

Institution		Tuition and fees	Add'l out-of-state/ district tuition	Books and supplies	Costs for campus residents			Costs for students at home		
					Room and board	Trans-portation	Other costs	Board only	Trans-portation	Other costs
Henderson Community College	‡	980	1,960/—	500						
Hopkinsville Community College	‡	980	1,960/—	450						2,808
Institute of Electronic Technology	‡	5,910		50				1,500	727	2,000
Jefferson Community College	‡	980	1,960/—	450				1,500	460	848
Kentucky Christian College		5,504		700	3,708	800	1,575	1,650	1,110	1,075
Kentucky College of Business		5,496		495						
Kentucky Mountain Bible College		3,420		400	2,780	900	400			
Kentucky State University	‡	1,860	3,360/—	510	2,984	300	800		350	800
Kentucky Wesleyan College		9,175		700	4,400	350	1,000	1,300	850	1,000
Lexington Community College	‡	1,954	3,240/—	450		484	987	1,573	484	987
Lindsey Wilson College		7,680		350	3,950	200	900	1,575	900	900
Louisville Technical Institute		8,905		800		800	1,830		1,200	
Madisonville Community College		980	1,960/—	475				1,725	550	300
Maysville Community College	‡	980	1,960/—	450				1,500	460	848
Mid-Continent Baptist Bible College		1,740		250	2,832	250	600		900	600
Midway College	‡	7,810		600	4,250	320	500	1,100	640	500
Morehead State University	†	2,000	3,200/—	600	2,950	200	850	1,500	1,050	850
Murray State University	‡	1,960	3,360/—	700	3,100	350	790	1,390	350	790
Northern Kentucky University	‡	1,980	3,360/—	500	3,070	700	800	2,500	700	800
Owensboro Community College	‡	980	1,960/—	500						
Owensboro Junior College of Business	‡	4,550		600					493	
Paducah Community College	‡	980	1,960/—	400				1,325	975	425
Pikeville College		6,500		500	3,000	400	800	1,800	1,000	800
Prestonsburg Community College	‡	1,145	1,960/—	450					400	2,808
RETS Electronic Institute	‡	5,005						2,608	750	896
St. Catharine College		5,200		500	3,100	538	1,080	1,800	538	1,080
Somerset Community College	‡	980	1,960/—	450						
Southeast Community College	‡	980	1,960/—	450				1,500	500	920
Spalding University		9,696		600	2,680	500	1,000	1,500	500	800
Sue Bennett College	†	7,063		1,000	4,239	1,050	740	2,604	2,100	1,050
Sullivan College		8,905		700	2,610	814	1,305	1,161	814	1,305
Thomas More College	‡	10,094		530	4,086	600	1,020	1,000	1,000	1,020
Transylvania University		12,690		500	4,810	200	800	1,000	600	800
Union College		8,750		500	3,120	900	600	1,500	1,000	600
University of Kentucky ⟋11,040	‡	2,594	4,520/—	450	3,476	460	850	850	460	850
University of Louisville	‡	2,470	4,520/—	550	3,500	550	1,700	1,800	900	1,900
Western Kentucky University	‡	1,910	3,360/—	500	2,986	400	1,100	1,812	1,400	1,100

Louisiana

Institution		Tuition and fees	Add'l out-of-state/ district tuition	Books and supplies	Room and board	Trans-portation	Other costs	Board only	Trans-portation	Other costs
Bossier Parish Community College		780	840/80	650				1,700	1,000	1,100
Centenary College of Louisiana		10,722		650	3,800	700	1,250	2,000	1,150	1,250
Delgado Community College	‡	1,136	1,560/—	500				1,500	860	930
Delta School of Business & Technology		6,575		500						
Dillard University		7,500		600	3,950	442	1,200	1,882	1,076	1,166
Grambling State University	‡	2,088	2,150/—	600	2,613	450	1,300	1,500	1,050	1,300
Louisiana College		5,542		535	3,024	410	1,040		970	1,040
Louisiana State University										
Agricultural and Mechanical College	‡	2,663	3,300/—	634	3,610	1,699			2,369	
Alexandria	‡	1,060	1,104/—	650				2,000	1,150	1,200
Eunice	‡	1,056	1,200/—	850					1,500	1,600
Medical Center	‡	2,702	2,500/—	1,658		385		880	979	2,492
Shreveport	‡	2,080	2,700/—	634				1,989	1,137	1,232
Louisiana Tech University	‡	2,274	1,995/—	634	2,595	623	1,430	1,989	1,137	1,430

†Figures are projected for 1996-97. ‡Figures are for 1995-96.

| All aid | | Need-based aid | | Grants and scholarships | | | | | | | | Financial aid deadlines | | Inst aid form | Notes |
Total freshmen	Percent receiving aid	Freshmen judged to have need	Percent offered aid	Need-based Acad	Music/drama	Art	Athl	Non-need-based Acad	Music/drama	Art	Athl	Priority	Closing		
								X				4/1	none		
													5/1		
													none		
													none		
184	92	128	100	X				X	X			4/1	none		
													none		
410	85							X	X		X	4/15	5/1		
151	93	137	100	X				X	X	X	X	3/1	none	X	
1,236	10							X				4/1	none	X	
380	96			X	X	X	X	X	X	X	X	4/15	none		
													none		
1,227	74			X				X				3/15	10/1		
265	94	145	100	X				X				4/1	6/30		
15	61	7	100	X				X				5/1	none	X	
1,140	70	911	95	X	X	X	X	X	X	X	X	4/1	none		
1,234	65	650	92					X	X	X	X	4/1	none	X	
1,715	42	982	79					X	X	X	X	4/1	none	X	
													none		
				X				X			X	4/1	none		
229	80	218	100	X		X		X			X	3/15	none		
624	60			X				X				4/1	none		
													none		
													none		
1,340	80			X	X			X	X			4/1	none		
1,506	73			X				X				4/15	none		
107	89			X	X	X	X	X	X	X	X	3/1	none	X	
128	93			X				X					none		
1,543	73	285	100	X			X	X			X	9/30	none		
													none		
272	94	184	100	X				X	X	X	X	3/1	none		
220	85	147	100					X	X		X	4/1	none		
2,610	48			X				X	X	X	X	4/1	none		
1,893	50	1,300	85					X	X	X	X	4/15	none		
2,537	60	1,301	94					X	X	X	X	4/1	none	X	
2,360	40			X	X		X	X	X		X	6/1	6/30	X	
215	91	137	100	X				X	X	X	X	3/15	none	X	
				X			X	X			X	4/15	6/1	X	
2,600	95							X	X		X	4/15	none		
271	80	160	100					X	X		X		5/15		
3,428	71	1,294	95	X				X	X	X	X	3/1	none		
205	44			X				X		X		6/15	none		
2,556	60			X				X					7/1		
													none		
				X				X					none	X	
1,390	77	983	99	X				X	X	X	X	4/1	none	X	

Institution	Tuition and fees	Add'l out-of-state/district tuition	Books and supplies	Costs for campus residents			Costs for students at home		
				Room and board	Transportation	Other costs	Board only	Transportation	Other costs
Loyola University New Orleans	12,750		650	5,680	500	1,264		500	1,264
McNeese State University	‡ 2,008	3,200/—	660	2,310	442	1,166	1,882	1,076	1,166
New Orleans Baptist Theological Seminary: School of Christian Education	‡ 1,350		500						
Nicholls State University	‡ 2,016	2,592/—	600	2,664	400	1,000		859	930
Northeast Louisiana University	‡ 1,926	2,400/—	648	2,060	478	1,260	2,034	1,162	1,260
Northwestern State University	‡ 2,067	2,430/—	550	2,320	981	1,051	1,696	981	
Nunez Community College	1,013	2,070/—	617				3,900	1,107	1,200
Our Lady of Holy Cross College	4,932		650				2,041	1,167	1,264
Phillips Junior College: New Orleans	‡ 3,630					25			
St. Joseph Seminary College	5,840		800	4,450	650				
Southeastern Louisiana University	‡ 1,930	2,232/—	550	2,390	900	1,000		900	1,000
Southern University									
New Orleans	‡ 1,662	1,770/—	400						
Shreveport	‡ 1,110	1,130/—	500				1,700	1,076	1,420
Southern University and Agricultural and Mechanical College	2,028	2,780/—		2,952	400	600	750	250	300
Tulane University	21,236		350	6,314		800		560	555
University of New Orleans	‡ 2,362	2,792/—	800	3,386	650	1,358	5,779	1,137	1,358
University of Southwestern Louisiana	‡ 1,898	3,600/—	634	2,218	442	1,166	1,500	1,076	1,166
Xavier University of Louisiana	8,200		617	4,500	458	1,200	1,937	1,107	1,200

Maine

Institution	Tuition and fees	Add'l out-of-state/district tuition	Books and supplies	Costs for campus residents			Costs for students at home		
				Room and board	Transportation	Other costs	Board only	Transportation	Other costs
Andover College	‡ 5,050		700				4,570	1,100	1,000
Bates College	27,415 (comprehensive)		685		250	900			
Beal College	‡ 3,945		725				1,200	1,500	700
Bowdoin College	21,750		620	6,010		875			875
Casco Bay College	6,025		650	3,800	100		800	400	1,300
Central Maine Medical Center School of Nursing	5,598		843			700	1,500	766	700
Central Maine Technical College	‡ 1,980	2,190/—	500	3,350	1,000	1,000	2,600	1,050	1,000
Colby College	22,190		500	5,710	200	800	600	300	
College of the Atlantic	16,341		450	4,850		350	1,800		350
Eastern Maine Technical College	‡ 2,065	2,190/—	600	3,400	500	1,200	1,700	1,000	1,200
Husson College	8,500		375	4,490	650	1,100		1,200	1,400
Kennebec Valley Technical College	‡ 1,890	2,190/—	400						
Maine College of Art	13,905		1,575	5,810	530	1,025		2,045	1,130
Maine Maritime Academy	5,360	3,225/1,025	700	4,895	650	720	3,000	650	720
Northern Maine Technical College	‡ 1,965	2,190/—	750	3,300	500	3,285	1,600	1,050	900
St. Joseph's College	‡ 10,925		500	5,380	300	1,200		1,000	1,200
Southern Maine Technical College	‡ 1,960	2,190/—	600	2,395	423	832	1,800	714	950
Thomas College	10,455		600	4,950	800	1,000	800	1,500	1,000
Unity College	10,955		450	5,050	400	600	1,950	225	600
University of Maine									
Augusta	‡ 2,685	3,660/—	520				800	1,100	600
Farmington	† 3,340	4,130/—	448	4,150	450	1,287	2,016	1,395	1,116
Fort Kent	‡ 2,930	3,960/—	650	3,600	800	1,000	900	1,000	1,000
Machias	‡ 2,935	3,960/—	650	3,835	900	1,600	650	1,980	1,600
Orono	‡ 3,925	6,150/—	500	4,678	400	1,150	1,455	1,100	650
Presque Isle	† 3,000	3,960/—	400	3,704	700	975	850	1,050	850
University of New England	13,560		800	5,495	450	650	500	1,000	1,500
University of Southern Maine	3,230	5,278/—	780	4,813	725	1,250	1,850	725	1,250
Westbrook College	11,650		550	4,900	450	800		800	800

†Figures are projected for 1996-97. ‡Figures are for 1995-96.

All aid		Need-based aid		Grants and scholarships								Financial aid deadlines		Inst aid form	Notes
Total freshmen	Percent receiving aid	Freshmen judged to have need	Percent offered aid	Need-based Acad	Music/drama	Art	Athl	Non-need-based Acad	Music/drama	Art	Athl	Priority	Closing		
686	86	370	100					X	X	X		5/1	8/1		
1,492	60			X				X	X	X	X	5/1	none		
													none		
2,672	56			X				X	X		X	3/1	none		
1,947	65			X				X	X	X	X	4/1	none		
1,783	68			X	X		X	X	X	X	X	4/1	none		
556	61	339	100	X				X				4/1	6/1	X	
163	65			X				X				4/15	none		
													none		
11	100	6	100	X				X				5/1	none		
2,445	55			X	X			X	X		X	5/1	none		
500	80											5/1			
													none		
													none		
1,238	66	692	100	X				X			X	1/15	2/1		
1,677	56	625	90	X	X		X	X	X		X	5/1	none	X	
2,763	75							X	X	X	X	3/1	none	X	
690	92	581	82	X	X	X	X	X	X	X	X	4/1	none		
								X					none		
437	51	192	100										2/10		
													none		
449	44	197	100									3/1	3/1	X	
		120	100										none		
47	80	33	100									3/15	7/1		
				X								5/1	none		
542	75	173	100									1/15	2/1	X	
61	72	40	100	X				X				2/15	5/1	X	
													none		
363	90	305	100	X			X	X				3/15	none		
112	89	93	100		X			X		X		3/1	none		
177	82							X				4/15	none		
													none		
254	88	220	100	X				X				3/15	none	X	
877	55	450	100	X								4/1	none		
138	93			X				X				2/15	none		
198	81	152	100					X			X	4/15	none	X	
510	80							X	X	X		4/1	none		
476	92	382	99					X				3/1	none		
100	80	73	100	X				X				3/15	none		
159	90	140	100	X	X	X	X					3/1	none		
1,595	60			X				X	X	X	X	3/1	none		
246	65	140	100	X		X		X	X	X	X	4/1	none	X	
200	85			X	X	X	X	X	X	X	X	4/1	none	X	
798	73	504	90					X	X			3/1	none		
80	86			X								5/1	none		

Institution	Tuition and fees	Add'l out-of-state/district tuition	Books and supplies	Costs for campus residents			Costs for students at home		
				Room and board	Trans-portation	Other costs	Board only	Trans-portation	Other costs
Maryland									
Allegany College	‡ 2,235	1,380/570	600				1,530	1,056	966
Anne Arundel Community College	† 1,504	1,728/576	500				1,700	950	1,200
Baltimore City Community College	‡ 1,648	3,690/—	500					400	2,000
Baltimore Hebrew University	4,520		400					400	1,300
Baltimore International Culinary College	13,560		1,200	4,797	270	3,627	3,312	270	
Bowie State University	‡ 3,019	3,142/—	750	4,075	750	1,500	3,000	1,000	1,150
Capitol College	‡ 8,781		600		800	1,350	1,600	1,600	1,500
Carroll Community College	2,040	4,125/1,848	600				1,500	1,500	1,000
Catonsville Community College	1,854	3,180/1,380	500					1,500	900
Cecil Community College	† 1,860	2,760/1,710	525				1,900	1,100	1,100
Charles County Community College	2,000	3,660/1,830	650				2,000	900	900
Chesapeake College	† 1,755	5,250/2,100	475				600	950	720
College of Notre Dame of Maryland	‡ 11,840		600	5,845	250	700	1,600	300	700
Columbia Union College	† 11,050		750	3,850	1,000	1,000	1,200	750	1,000
Coppin State College	‡ 2,894	3,214/—	500	4,640			1,500	2,050	1,031
Dundalk Community College	‡ 1,566	1,222/1,118	600				2,720	1,500	1,000
Essex Community College	1,958	3,180/1,380	500					1,500	
Frederick Community College	2,190	3,900/1,950	700				1,650	1,100	750
Frostburg State University	† 3,280	3,710/—	700	4,836	500	900	1,800	900	750
Garrett Community College	‡ 1,770	2,040/540	600	4,125	1,233	750	1,700	1,233	750
Goucher College	17,635		680	6,570	350	1,300	1,500	700	400
Hagerstown Business College	‡ 4,038		650		480	1,260	1,630	1,950	960
Hagerstown Junior College	† 2,130	1,590/780	480				1,800	380	200
Harford Community College	† 1,980	2,310/1,020	500				1,500	800	500
Hood College	15,522		500	6,592		686	2,178		
Howard Community College	‡ 2,409	2,310/1,320	450				2,500	675	700
Johns Hopkins University	20,740		500	7,200		1,045	1,500		1,045
Johns Hopkins University: Peabody Conservatory of Music	19,250		450	6,940	1,500	800	1,700	1,500	800
Loyola College in Maryland	15,460		650	6,900	250	750	1,750	650	750
Maryland College of Art and Design	‡ 8,430		1,000				1,800	1,460	1,200
Maryland Institute College of Art	16,100		1,400	5,490	500	600	600	1,000	600
Montgomery College									
Germantown Campus	‡ 2,102	3,120/1,680	644				1,100	1,700	1,000
Rockville Campus	‡ 2,102	3,120/1,680	644				1,100	1,700	1,000
Takoma Park Campus	‡ 2,102	3,120/1,680	644				1,100	1,700	1,000
Morgan State University	‡ 2,832	3,630/—	1,500	4,840	350	2,300	750	650	1,150
Mount St. Mary's College	14,885		600	6,250	300	700	2,100	650	800
Prince George's Community College	‡ 2,740	4,320/1,890	515					825	825
St. John's College	20,040		275	5,950	350	800			
St. Mary's College of Maryland	6,005	3,550/—	750	5,220	240	1,500	1,650	840	1,500
Salisbury State University	‡ 3,440	3,114/—	600	4,790	800	900	1,195	850	850
Sojourner-Douglass College	‡ 3,510		400				3,200	416	2,800
Towson State University	‡ 3,530	3,402/—	700	4,610	420	1,110	2,500	420	710
United States Naval Academy	0								
University of Baltimore	‡ 3,260	3,400/—	650				2,000	1,625	1,800
University of Maryland									
Baltimore	‡ 3,932	5,647/—	1,260		1,208	1,313		1,208	1,313
Baltimore County	‡ 3,852	4,828/—	556	4,674	521	1,220	1,500	2,425	1,200
College Park	‡ 3,794	5,944/—	586	5,311	565	1,702	1,493	565	1,702

†Figures are projected for 1996-97. ‡Figures are for 1995-96.

Total freshmen	Percent receiving aid	Freshmen judged to have need	Percent offered aid	Acad (NB)	Music/drama (NB)	Art (NB)	Athl (NB)	Acad (NNB)	Music/drama (NNB)	Art (NNB)	Athl (NNB)	Priority	Closing	Inst aid form	Notes
664	62			X			X	X			X	3/15	none		
				X		X	X	X			X	4/15	none		
													none		
												7/1		X	
269	90							X				7/1	none		
479	70	390	92	X	X	X	X	X	X		X	1/1	4/1	X	
40	39			X				X				3/1	none		
				X				X					none	X	
2,332	10							X			X	3/1	none		
310	29	32	100	X	X	X	X	X	X	X	X	8/1	none	X	
				X				X	X	X	X	4/1	none	X	
763	35	105	84	X				X			X	6/1	none	X	
													none	X	
165	85							X	X		X	3/31	5/31		
													none		
				X			X	X			X	4/15	none		
				X	X	X		X	X		X	7/1	none		
1,144	15			X	X	X		X	X	X	X	6/15	none	X	
949	58	645	100	X				X	X	X		4/1	none		
													none		
284	80	162	100	X				X	X	X		2/15	none	X	
165	84	115	100					X					none	X	
2,425	24			X			X	X			X	6/1	none		
				X	X		X	X	X		X	3/1	none	X	
186	98	136	100	X				X				3/31	none		
834	30			X	X							5/15	none	X	
876	50	444	100	X				X	X		X	1/15	2/1	X	
60	97				X				X				2/1	X	
800	67	409	99					X			X		2/1		
34	50	9	100	X		X		X		X		4/1	none		
207	78	114	100	X		X		X		X		3/1	none	X	
												2/15	none		
												2/15	none		
												2/15	none		
1,125	80	940	96	X				X			X	4/1	none		
319	78	224	99	X				X	X	X	X		3/15		
1,929	46	900	100	X			X	X	X		X	5/31	none	X	
112	60	75	100									2/15	none		
352	75	163	100					X	X				3/1		
650	40	325	100	X				X				3/1	none		
													none		
1,503	42	980	100	X	X	X	X	X	X	X	X	3/15	none		
								X						X	
999	60			X	X	X	X	X	X	X	X	3/1	none		
3,632	42	1,723	85	X	X	X	X	X	X	X	X	2/15	none		

Institution	Tuition and fees	Add'l out-of-state/district tuition	Books and supplies	Costs for campus residents			Costs for students at home		
				Room and board	Transportation	Other costs	Board only	Transportation	Other costs
Eastern Shore	‡ 2,855	4,681/—	525	4,030	525	1,025	1,825	1,025	1,025
University College	† 5,280	810/—	1,100					600	
Villa Julie College	8,610		800				920	1,200	
Washington Bible College	6,028		400	3,800	500	1,000		500	1,000
Washington College	17,250		500	5,740		300	750		300
Western Maryland College	16,125		400	5,560	400	500	1,500	600	500
Wor-Wic Community College	1,760	2,740/2,170	500				1,700	1,000	450
Massachusetts									
American International College	10,365		550	5,265	575	900	1,475	675	600
Amherst College	22,007		660	5,820		1,358			
Anna Maria College	11,780		526	5,128	503	1,039	1,865	1,117	1,095
Aquinas College at Milton	‡ 7,950		450				1,500	1,200	9,000
Aquinas College at Newton	‡ 7,550		500				1,900	1,000	1,600
Assumption College	13,845		500	6,020	400	715	2,000	400	715
Atlantic Union College	11,500		600	3,600	600	800		600	800
Babson College	18,835		520	7,530		1,225	1,500	1,000	1,225
Bay Path College	† 11,300		600	6,350	300	900	600	1,000	900
Bay State College	† 9,800		500	6,700	675	2,405	2,500	810	2,180
Becker College									
Leicester Campus	9,320		500	4,630	300	600	1,500	700	600
Worcester Campus	9,320		500	4,630	300	600	1,500	700	600
Bentley College	15,745		630	7,310	420	1,450	1,590	1,320	1,450
Berklee College of Music	13,770		530	7,390	975	1,100	3,050	1,235	1,100
Berkshire Community College	‡ 2,400	4,500/—	480				1,800	900	900
Boston Architectural Center	4,990		1,210				1,800	1,430	1,100
Boston College	19,298		500	7,530	500	1,000	1,500	1,000	500
Boston Conservatory	15,050		500	6,675	500	1,000	1,500	800	1,000
Boston University	20,864		511	7,050	275	1,000	2,525	700	1,000
Bradford College	15,380		425	6,590	450	950	1,650	550	950
Brandeis University	21,917		410	7,080		1,000	1,800	2,400	1,000
Bridgewater State College	‡ 3,462	4,134/—	500	4,221	500	1,250	2,490	1,250	1,250
Bunker Hill Community College	‡ 2,400	4,440/—	540				3,700	1,117	2,959
Cape Cod Community College	‡ 2,328	4,440/—	400				2,000	500	1,000
Clark University	20,040		500	4,250	100	700	1,780	250	700
College of the Holy Cross	20,070		400	6,750	100	900	1,500	300	1,815
Curry College	15,458		650	5,740	365	6,985	2,600	1,425	1,125
Dean College	12,485		600	6,300	300	600	2,500	800	600
Eastern Nazarene College	10,816		500	3,750	350	700		350	700
Elms College	12,950		500	5,000	500	900	1,500	800	700
Emerson College	17,040		500	8,050		937	1,500		1,577
Emmanuel College	14,000		500	6,525	200	900		200	900
Endicott College	‡ 12,220		400	6,400	600	1,000		1,000	1,000
Essex Agricultural and Technical Institute	‡ 2,115	—/3,700	500				3,000	1,700	3,000
Fisher College	11,900		735	6,500	840	945	2,153	735	635
Fitchburg State College	‡ 3,234	4,134/—	500	4,030	350	1,538	590	1,000	1,538
Forsyth School for Dental Hygienists	14,568		400	8,911	175	450		675	450
Framingham State College	‡ 3,308	4,134/—	500	3,919	500	1,200	750	1,000	1,200
Franklin Institute of Boston	9,015		700	6,800	600		660	600	1,390
Gordon College	14,690		500	4,760	600	400	1,600	400	400
Greenfield Community College	‡ 2,218	4,500/—	550				2,153	1,030	1,351
Hampshire College	22,900		375	6,090		1,120	1,665		1,120

†Figures are projected for 1996-97. ‡Figures are for 1995-96.

Total freshmen	Percent receiving aid	Freshmen judged to have need	Percent offered aid	Need-based Acad	Music/drama	Art	Athl	Non-need-based Acad	Music/drama	Art	Athl	Priority	Closing	Inst aid form	Notes
778	80							X	X	X	X	3/1	none		
				X		X		X					5/1		
288	81	170	98	X				X				3/1	none	X	
37	30				X		X	X	X		X	3/1	5/19	X	
242	85	121	100	X				X	X	X		2/15	none		
318	80	296	96	X	X	X		X	X	X		3/1	none	X	
432	35	260	100					X				6/1	7/1		
272	70	202	100	X			X	X			X	4/15	none		
426	55	190	100	X									2/1	X	
82	66			X	X			X	X			3/1	none	X	
72	88			X				X				3/1	none		
70	64			X				X					none		
453	90	349	100	X							X		3/1		
120	90							X	X		X	4/15	none	X	
399	54	204	100	X				X					2/15		
189	86	134	99	X	X		X	X	X		X	3/15	none	X	
258	85							X				3/1	none		
229	89			X				X			X	4/1	none	X	
491	89			X				X			X	4/1	none	X	
725	77	425	99	X			X	X			X	12/1	2/1	X	
765	59			X	X			X	X			3/31	none		
515	29							X				5/1	none		
19	47							X		X		6/1	none	X	
2,140	69	999	100	X				X			X	2/1	none	X	
92	72	65	94		X				X				3/1	X	
4,348	71	2,762	96	X	X	X		X	X	X	X	2/15	none		
223	75			X	X			X		X		2/15	none	X	
885	73			X				X				2/15	4/15		
1,144	73	634	100					X				3/1	none		
												5/1	none	X	
1,136	48											4/1	none		
517	81	344	100	X				X					2/1		
712	66	452	100				X	X				2/1	none		
311	60	238	100					X				3/1	none	X	
400	70			X	X	X	X	X			X	3/1	none	X	
210	95			X	X			X	X			3/1	none	X	
133	84	98	100	X				X				2/15	none	X	
530	80	309	100	X	X			X	X			3/1	none	X	
104	93	96	100	X		X		X				3/1	9/15	X	
406	86	271	100	X								3/15	none		
205	25	119	88									5/1	8/15		
233	80							X				3/1	none		
590	82			X				X	X	X		3/30	none	X	
40	70			X				X				3/1	none	X	
625	55	324	100					X				4/1	none		
190	90			X								4/1	none		
333	94			X	X			X	X			3/15	none	X	
				X								4/15	none		
314	55	183	98					X				2/15	none	X	

Institution	Tuition and fees	Add'l out-of-state/district tuition	Books and supplies	Costs for campus residents			Costs for students at home		
				Room and board	Transportation	Other costs	Board only	Transportation	Other costs
Harvard and Radcliffe Colleges	21,901			6,995					
Hebrew College	8,940		300				1,000	300	
Hellenic College	‡ 7,700		800	5,600	1,000	1,500	2,000	1,000	1,500
Holyoke Community College	‡ 2,290	4,770/—	520				2,500	1,170	1,600
Katharine Gibbs School	8,970		600					1,200	1,920
Laboure College	9,900		800				1,200	960	900
Lasell College	13,275		750	6,425	500	2,000	2,000	500	2,000
Lesley College	13,820		550	6,440	350	850	1,900	735	850
Marian Court College	8,000		465				1,742	1,240	1,695
Massachusetts Bay Community College	‡ 2,490	4,440/—	400				2,015	800	860
Massachusetts College of Art	‡ 4,078	4,959/—	1,800	5,839	600			600	2,200
Massachusetts College of Pharmacy and Allied Health Sciences	13,350		500	7,250	320	1,600	1,700	750	1,600
Massachusetts Institute of Technology	22,000		850	6,350	500	1,700			1,700
Massachusetts Maritime Academy	‡ 3,120	4,959/—	450	3,680	350	1,250		1,300	1,200
Massasoit Community College	‡ 2,490	4,440/—	508				1,700	900	900
Merrimack College	13,980		600	6,900	1,000	450	1,600	1,000	450
Middlesex Community College	‡ 2,820	4,440/300	500				1,850	900	400
Montserrat College of Art	10,532		500		800	900	1,600	800	900
Mount Holyoke College	21,390		750	6,250		750	2,310		750
Mount Ida College	11,830		715	8,130	580	525		990	525
Mount Wachusett Community College	‡ 3,150	4,440/600	500				1,500	1,305	1,165
New England Banking Institute	2,322		300						
New England Conservatory of Music	17,200		500	8,000	550	1,350	1,700	800	1,800
Newbury College	† 11,780		630	6,650	680	1,000	2,500	680	1,000
Nichols College	10,869		500	6,200	250	650		500	650
North Adams State College	‡ 3,854	4,134/—	500	4,293	407	1,246	1,900	1,172	1,246
North Shore Community College	‡ 2,490	4,440/—	500				1,200	825	1,100
Northeastern University	15,236		600	7,905	750	900	2,250	750	900
Northern Essex Community College	‡ 2,430	4,440/—	500				1,700	1,175	1,400
Pine Manor College	16,350		500	6,900	500	450	1,500	315	450
Quincy College	‡ 2,334		400				500	200	400
Quinsigamond Community College	‡ 2,280	4,440/—	560				2,475	720	1,575
Regis College	14,500		450	6,600		750	1,500	900	750
Roxbury Community College	‡ 2,400	4,440/—	600				1,600	1,075	1,470
St. Hyacinth College and Seminary	4,100		425	5,000	400	725	1,300	800	700
St. John's Seminary College	‡ 5,000		400	2,600	400	600			
Salem State College	‡ 3,408	4,134/—	450	3,980	450	900	1,422	1,233	900
School of the Museum of Fine Arts	† 14,990		1,000		1,000	1,500	1,800	1,000	1,500
Simmons College	18,040		500	7,228		1,149	1,500	948	1,149
Simon's Rock College of Bard	20,795		400	5,860	400	450	3,000	250	400
Smith College	20,538		550	6,920		550			550
Springfield College	12,830		900	5,800	400	1,000	1,800	1,500	1,200
Springfield Technical Community College	‡ 2,490	4,440/—	400				1,450	800	1,500
Stonehill College	14,170		522	6,660	180	508	1,500	1,014	508
Suffolk University	12,106		500	7,950			1,500	700	2,400
Tufts University	21,957		600	6,540		1,003			3,543
University of Massachusetts									
Amherst	‡ 5,514 *16,458	6,346/—	500	4,188	400	1,000	1,800	600	1,000
Boston	‡ 4,405	6,348/—	568				2,000	1,026	1,231
Dartmouth	‡ 4,122	5,083/—	600	4,855	450	1,000	2,026	1,275	1,000
Lowell	‡ 4,606	5,144/—	400	4,499	200	1,160	1,695	900	1,010

†Figures are projected for 1996-97. ‡Figures are for 1995-96.

Total fresh-men	Percent receiving aid	Freshmen judged to have need	Percent offered aid	Acad	Music/drama	Art	Athl	Acad	Music/drama	Art	Athl	Priority	Closing	Inst aid form	Notes
All aid		**Need–based aid**		**Grants and scholarships**								**Financial aid deadlines**			
				Need–based				**Non–need–based**							
1,618	78	953	100									2/1	none		
												6/15	none	X	
22	80	8	100	X				X				5/1	none	X	
				X				X	X	X	X	5/15	none	X	
44	75			X				X					none	X	
59	97			X				X				5/1	none	X	
272	91	208	100	X				X				5/1	none	X	
98	100			X				X				2/15	none	X	
59	83	91	100	X				X				4/1	none	X	
2,053	40			X				X					5/1		
230	41	94	100									5/1	none		
131	75							X				4/1	none		
1,116	83	674	100									1/19	none	X	
232	79			X				X				5/1	none		
1,002	65			X			X	X			X	4/15	none		
481	82			X	X		X	X			X	2/1	3/1		
1,053	40	750	88										none	X	
72	60	48	100	X		X		X		X		3/15	2/15		
500	70												1/15	X	
906	70			X		X	X			X	X	5/1	none	X	
831	63											4/1	none	X	
61	70				X				X			1/15	none		
1,252	76	326	100					X			X	5/1	none		
288	80	192	100	X				X				4/1	none		
301	66	156	100					X				4/1	none	X	
877	72	634	100									4/1	none	X	
2,783	72	2,012	100	X				X			X	3/1	none		
1,556	50											4/1	none		
96	45	36	100	X				X				3/15	none		
1,522	60							X				4/1	5/15		
910	54							X	X	X	X	7/1	none	X	
228	90	190	100	X				X				2/15	none		
700	85							X				5/1	none		
5	60			X				X				6/1	none		
11	60	3	100										none		
1,225	63			X	X	X		X	X	X		4/15	none		
207	53	178	100			X						3/15	none	X	
240	81			X				X					2/1	X	
124	90	112	100					X					none		
631	47	357	100										2/1		
503	74	369	100	X								4/1	none	X	
												4/1	none	X	
547	84	338	100	X				X	X		X	2/1	none		
428	76	281	100	X				X				3/1	none	X	
1,158	48	510	100	X				X					2/1		
3,852	67	2,800	93	X	X	X	X	X	X	X	X	3/1	none		
691	55			X				X				6/1	none	X	
1,009	60			X				X				3/1	none		
							X					3/1	none		

Institution	Tuition and fees	Add'l out-of-state/district tuition	Books and supplies	Costs for campus residents			Costs for students at home		
				Room and board	Trans-portation	Other costs	Board only	Trans-portation	Other costs
Wellesley College	20,554		600	6,416	450	1,000	1,000		1,000
Wentworth Institute of Technology	11,000		850	6,350		500	1,500	850	
Western New England College	10,810		500	5,914	300	840	1,625	925	1,140
Westfield State College	‡ 3,194	4,134/—	450	3,631	400	1,280	750	1,350	1,280
Wheaton College	19,890		740	6,250		860	1,500		860
Wheelock College	14,784		400	5,916		850	2,500		850
Williams College	21,910		500	6,140	350	800			
Worcester Polytechnic Institute	18,060		590	5,940		760	1,500		760
Worcester State College	‡ 2,753	4,134/—	500	4,000	500	1,150	1,250	1,000	1,150

Michigan

Institution	Tuition and fees	Add'l out-of-state/district tuition	Books and supplies	Room and board	Trans-portation	Other costs	Board only	Trans-portation	Other costs
Adrian College	12,350		400	3,880	545	710	1,870	545	710
Albion College	16,000		600	4,890	350	350	2,445		
Alma College	13,824		600	4,905	400	800	1,300	700	800
Alpena Community College	1,660	1,430/715	500				1,500	420	600
Andrews University	11,121		1,050	3,360	675	765		675	765
Aquinas College	12,534		380	4,198	545	730	2,500	955	730
Baker College									
Auburn Hills	5,850		750					1,600	
Cadillac	5,850		750				1,675	2,000	
Flint	5,850		650		1,000	2,500	1,575	900	2,494
Jackson	‡ 6,070		650				1,575	1,825	2,000
Mount Clemens	5,850							900	2,494
Muskegon	5,850		750		1,675	2,000	1,600	2,000	2,000
Owosso	5,850		750		1,600	2,000	1,650	1,600	2,000
Port Huron	5,850		650				1,575	1,825	2,000
Bay de Noc Community College	† 1,653	1,920/600	580		470	500	1,650	940	500
Bay Mills Community College	‡ 2,130		200	1,875					
Calvin College	11,655		420	4,160	560	720	1,960	1,560	720
Center for Creative Studies: College									
of Art and Design	13,276		1,925		1,100	1,125	1,550	1,650	975
Central Michigan University	‡ 3,142	4,586/—	650	4,036	500	983	1,800	750	1,208
Cleary College	‡ 6,840		840				2,100	1,575	1,000
Concordia College	11,450		550	4,650	154	1,100	2,460	154	1,055
Cornerstone College and Grand Rapids									
Baptist Seminary	8,174		600	4,266	679	1,500	3,800	1,414	1,500
Davenport College of Business	8,010		675		1,041	894	1,987	1,041	894
Delta College	‡ 1,757	1,387/487	585					930	600
Detroit College of Business	7,605		675				2,650	1,011	868
Eastern Michigan University	† 3,292	4,380/—	500	4,200	600	600	1,500	1,200	600
Ferris State University	3,630	3,734/—	650	4,631	438	714	1,920	704	714
Glen Oaks Community College	2,658	714/248	480				800	1,320	775
GMI Engineering & Management Institute	13,122		600	3,602	3,130	2,320	1,325	3,130	2,320
Gogebic Community College	1,246	—/434	500		750	700	1,350	750	700
Grace Bible College	5,800		300	3,600	1,115	650		915	650
Grand Rapids Community College	1,680	1,110/780	1,110				2,730	970	500
Grand Valley State University	‡ 3,140	3,682/—	600	4,180	550	450		950	550
Great Lakes Christian College	5,626		600	3,200	500	1,500		500	1,500
Great Lakes Junior College of Business	5,760		300					2,400	490
Henry Ford Community College	† 1,837	1,172/846	500				2,730	940	585
Highland Park Community College	1,700	300/—	250				1,650	675	1,300
Hillsdale College	12,320		600	5,180	1,000	900	2,600	1,000	900
Hope College	14,310		500	4,516	255	900	1,500	480	500

†Figures are projected for 1996-97. ‡Figures are for 1995-96.

140

Total freshmen	Percent receiving aid	Freshmen judged to have need	Percent offered aid	Need-based Acad	Need-based Music/drama	Need-based Art	Need-based Athl	Non-need Acad	Non-need Music/drama	Non-need Art	Non-need Athl	Priority	Closing	Inst aid form	Notes
585	47	277	100										1/15	X	
449	62			X				X				3/1	none	X	
588	80			X								4/1	none		
745	86							X				3/1	none	X	
372	70	235	100	X									2/1		
161	88	142	100	X									3/1	X	
525	45	211	100										2/1		
589	80	471	100	X				X					3/1		
485	42							X				3/15	none		
243	91	204	100	X	X	X		X	X	X		3/15	none		
474	94	353	100					X	X	X		2/15	none	X	
371	95	287	100					X	X	X		2/15	5/1		
608	55	375	96	X				X			X	5/15	none		
368	94	276	100	X				X	X			3/31	none	X	
241	99	207	100	X	X	X	X	X	X	X	X	2/15	none		
				X				X				2/15	none		
				X				X				3/15	none		
				X				X				3/15	9/1		
				X				X					9/1		
				X				X				9/1	none		
				X				X					none		
				X				X				9/1	none		
570	75							X				4/15	none		
														X	
1,015	89	708	100	X				X	X	X		2/15	none	X	
164	91			X	X					X		2/21	none	X	
2,779	63	1,651	98	X				X	X	X	X	2/21	none		
252	64	32	100	X				X				3/1	8/31	X	
94	95	88	100	X			X	X	X	X	X	3/15	5/15		
272	90	180	100					X	X		X	3/1	9/1	X	
655	75							X				3/15	none		
2,176	25							X				8/1	none		
1,428	82	897	99	X				X			X	2/15	none	X	
2,275	58			X	X	X	X	X	X	X	X	3/15	none		
1,935	70	1,437	100	X			X	X	X		X	4/1	none		
262	23			X				X	X	X	X	5/15	none		
618	83			X				X				3/15	none		
563	75			X			X	X			X	5/1	none		
48	96	45	100					X	X			4/1	none		
8,742	15	743	99	X	X	X	X	X	X	X	X	4/1	none		
1,860	68	1,258	100	X	X	X	X	X	X	X	X	2/15	none		
40	91							X	X			8/1	none		
711	76							X					none		
4,493	40	2,400	100	X	X	X	X	X	X	X	X	4/1	none		
152	85											3/15	5/1		
371	76	300	100	X	X	X	X	X	X	X	X	3/15	none		
695	87	425	100	X				X	X	X		2/15	none		

Institution	Tuition and fees	Add'l out-of-state/district tuition	Books and supplies	Costs for campus residents			Costs for students at home		
				Room and board	Trans-portation	Other costs	Board only	Trans-portation	Other costs
Jackson Community College	1,471	660/435	430				2,650	940	650
Kalamazoo College	17,214		525	5,241	210	615	918	210	615
Kalamazoo Valley Community College	1,140	1,980/990	528				3,722	993	993
Kellogg Community College	1,380	2,059/852	543				3,511	970	600
Kendall College of Art and Design	10,550		1,750				3,790	935	990
Kirtland Community College	‡ 1,602	1,140/540	450						
Lake Michigan College	‡ 1,440	600/300	500		915	1,150	1,800	1,875	1,150
Lake Superior State University	‡ 3,396	3,282/—	600	4,290	375	675	1,900	375	675
Lansing Community College	1,320	1,740/870	540				2,250	945	945
Lawrence Technological University	8,630		1,300		1,000	800	2,200	1,200	800
Lewis College of Business	5,000		500						
Macomb Community College	1,560	1,215/765	465				2,330	890	740
Madonna University	5,770		425	4,168		655		940	655
Marygrove College	8,836		500	3,840	560	1,325		1,178	1,325
Michigan Christian College	6,120		300	3,500	455	640	1,500	1,000	640
Michigan State University *16,518	† 4,921	7,035/—	608	3,954	296	936	1,500	2,414	1,176
Michigan Technological University	‡ 3,843	4,890/—	900	4,136	450	750	1,500	450	750
Mid Michigan Community College	1,480	1,500/840	500				1,500	1,200	1,000
Monroe County Community College	1,330	960/720	700				2,200	750	560
Montcalm Community College	1,458	1,361/759	700				1,391	987	500
Mott Community College	1,734	1,530/720	668					1,175	703
Muskegon Community College	1,380	1,035/585	500				1,600	1,000	800
North Central Michigan College	1,515	930/480	600	3,710	545	510	2,000	970	510
Northern Michigan University	† 2,800	2,252/—	500	4,100	410	800	1,800	400	1,800
Northwestern Michigan College	1,627	1,298/990	555	4,190	545	555		940	540
Northwood University	10,565		750	4,734			1,600		
Oakland Community College	1,450	1,890/960	630				1,365	1,110	480
Oakland University	3,487	6,292/—	450	4,250	550	650	1,800	975	650
Olivet College	12,292		550	3,920	500	530	1,820	500	530
Reformed Bible College	6,776		410	3,350	545	700		545	780
Sacred Heart Major Seminary	4,855		500	4,220	600	1,500	5,400	1,000	1,350
Saginaw Valley State University	† 3,270	3,303/—	600	4,072	420	884	2,372	810	894
St. Clair County Community College	1,705	1,665/795	600				2,500	940	500
St. Mary's College	6,350		500	4,500					
Schoolcraft College	† 1,535	1,710/690	500				2,000	850	800
Siena Heights College	9,990		530	4,220	545	580		545	580
Spring Arbor College	10,386		400	4,070	530	680	2,090	530	680
Suomi College	9,500		500	3,700	700	800	1,800	1,125	600
University of Detroit Mercy	‡ 11,838		616	4,612	578	382	1,930	1,052	382
University of Michigan									
Ann Arbor *22,479	‡ 5,548	11,524/—	510	4,897	212	1,594		212	1,594
Dearborn	‡ 3,852	6,570/—	440				1,500	850	1,040
Flint	‡ 3,304	6,270/—	600				1,816	1,110	970
Walsh College of Accountancy and Business Administration	‡ 6,525							800	900
Washtenaw Community College	1,636	1,230/660	550				2,100	600	600
Wayne County Community College	1,730	1,050/480	400				2,575	915	495
Wayne State University	‡ 3,200	3,750/—	510		1,283	831	2,067	1,283	1,008
West Shore Community College	1,432	1,350/750	400				1,900	1,015	650
Western Michigan University	‡ 3,180	4,240/—	530	4,100	410	1,270	1,800	410	1,270
William Tyndale College	† 5,900		500		425	550		810	550

†Figures are projected for 1996-97. ‡Figures are for 1995-96.

| All aid | | Need–based aid | | Grants and scholarships | | | | | | | | Financial aid deadlines | | Inst aid form | Notes |
| Total freshmen | Percent receiving aid | Freshmen judged to have need | Percent offered aid | Need–based | | | | Non–need–based | | | | | | | |
				Acad	Music/drama	Art	Athl	Acad	Music/drama	Art	Athl	Priority	Closing		
				X				X	X			4/1	none		
338	90	206	100	X				X	X	X		2/15	none		
				X				X			X	6/1	none		
618	60			X	X	X	X	X	X	X	X	5/1	none		
78	93	60	100	X		X		X		X		2/15	none		
													none		
													none		
643	75	403	100	X				X			X	4/1	none		
1,275	35			X	X	X	X	X	X	X	X	8/1	none		
298	60			X				X				6/1	9/1		
73	90														
4,026	15			X	X		X	X	X		X	5/1	none	X	
211	62	109	100	X	X	X	X	X	X	X	X		2/21	X	
													none		
								X	X		X	8/1	none		
6,602	71	3,081	99	X	X	X	X	X	X	X	X		6/30		
1,074	71	555	97	X				X			X	3/1	none		
901	50	630	63	X				X				5/1	none	X	
2,850	45			X	X	X		X	X	X		6/1	none		
358	70							X	X			8/1	none		
								X	X	X	X		none		
4,559	60			X				X	X	X	X	5/1	none	X	
638	65			X				X				4/15	none	X	
1,171	75	813	100	X	X	X	X	X	X	X	X	2/1	none		
1,580	34	380	92	X	X	X		X	X	X		4/1	none		
295	79			X			X	X			X	3/15	none		
				X				X			X	5/19	none		
1,416	53	431	99	X				X	X		X	4/1	none		
202	92	184	100	X	X	X		X	X	X		4/1	8/15		
30	88			X				X				4/1	6/1	X	
												2/15	none		
806	70	523	100					X	X	X	X	4/1	none		
1,135	45			X	X	X		X	X	X	X	6/1	none		
68	60	32	78	X				X					3/15		
1,432	25			X	X	X	X	X	X	X	X		none	X	
212	97	180	100	X		X	X	X	X	X		2/15	none		
184	92							X	X	X	X	2/15	none		
213	94	148	100	X	X	X		X	X	X		5/1	none		
5,149	42	2,500	100	X				X	X	X	X	2/1	9/30		
													none		
531	55	284	100	X	X			X	X			4/15	none	X	
				X				X				8/1	none		
2,754	52	2,700	100	X				X		X		6/1	none	X	
													none		
1,784	45			X	X	X	X	X	X	X	X		5/1		
799	50	290	84	X				X	X			5/1	none		
3,249	76	2,395	100	X	X	X	X	X	X	X	X	3/1	none		
82	60	44	100	X	X			X	X			2/15	5/1	X	

Institution	Tuition and fees	Add'l out-of-state/ district tuition	Books and supplies	Costs for campus residents			Costs for students at home		
				Room and board	Trans-portation	Other costs	Board only	Trans-portation	Other costs
Yeshiva Beth Yehuda-Yeshiva Gedolah of Greater Detroit	3,500		500	3,000		500			200
Minnesota									
Alexandria Technical College	2,300	2,120/—	500				1,800	1,350	900
Anoka-Ramsey Community College	‡ 1,901	1,800/—	600				1,500	500	600
Augsburg College	13,286		540	4,794	100	850	1,500	100	850
Austin Community College	‡ 1,901	1,800/—	625				1,620	900	450
Bemidji State University	‡ 2,646	2,747/—	660	3,043	525	1,291	1,600	689	1,000
Bethany Lutheran College	‡ 8,563		450	3,554	150	900	2,142		900
Bethel College	13,180		500	4,690	800	1,500		3,250	1,500
Carleton College	21,120		550	4,290	500	550			
Central Lakes College	‡ 1,901	1,800/—	510				1,500	720	1,230
College of St. Benedict	13,996		500	4,541	100	600	1,000	600	500
College of St. Catherine: St. Catherine Campus	13,702		500	4,402	200	800	515	300	600
College of St. Catherine-Minneapolis	‡ 9,490		600		500	900	500	750	900
College of St. Scholastica	13,206		450	3,807	456	721	720	456	721
College of Visual Arts	9,060		1,600				2,200	300	1,200
Concordia College: Moorhead	11,570		450	3,400	200	600	1,830	200	600
Concordia College: St. Paul	‡ 11,355		500	42,000	150	800	1,950	150	800
Crown College	‡ 8,386		500	3,920	700	700	2,000	600	700
Dunwoody Industrial Institute	‡ 4,310		90					1,170	2,340
Fergus Falls Community College	† 2,203	2,028/—	550				1,773	500	622
Gustavus Adolphus College	15,420		450	3,900	500	750	1,985		750
Hamline University	14,344		450	4,536		700			700
Hibbing Community College	‡ 1,901	1,800/—	600				900	900	900
Inver Hills Community College	‡ 1,901	1,800/—	500				2,000	550	590
Itasca Community College: Arrowhead Region	‡ 1,901	1,800/—	600		1,244		1,500	535	1,125
Lakewood Community College	‡ 1,901	1,800/—	640				1,590	1,030	680
Macalester College	17,708		550	5,275		700	2,390		700
Mankato State University	‡ 9,695	2,600/—	570	2,923	650	1,500	760	650	1,500
Martin Luther College	‡ 4,225		655	2,100	645	755	2,100	435	755
Mesabi Community College: Arrowhead Region	‡ 1,901		510	1,800			1,700	470	1,000
Metropolitan State University	‡ 2,658	3,110/—	700					960	2,180
Minneapolis College of Art and Design	14,786		1,200		300	500	1,500	300	500
Minneapolis Community College	‡ 1,901	1,800/—	525				900	1,800	1,350
Minnesota Bible College	5,004		375		320	1,200	1,200	320	1,200
Moorhead State University	‡ 9,697	2,768/—	600	2,958	600	1,734	850	600	1,734
National College	‡ 6,600		675				1,080		
National Education Center: Brown Institute Campus	‡ 7,007				648	1,330			
NEI College of Technology	‡ 5,440		700				2,500	1,430	2,000
Normandale Community College	‡ 1,901	1,800/—	531				1,890	1,266	1,878
North Central Bible College	‡ 6,370		638	3,450	500	1,190	1,095	500	1,190
North Hennepin Community College	‡ 1,901	1,800/—	650				1,725	1,000	600
Northland Community & Technical College	‡ 1,901	1,800/—	550				1,950	500	975
Northwest Technical Institute	8,905		300						
Northwestern College	12,750		430	4,080	700	825	1,500	883	500
Oak Hills Bible College	‡ 6,390		530	2,475		4,000	2,300		4,000
Pillsbury Baptist Bible College	5,490		935	2,800	808	1,722	2,835	808	1,155

†Figures are projected for 1996-97. ‡Figures are for 1995-96.

All aid – Total freshmen	All aid – Percent receiving aid	Need-based aid – Freshmen judged to have need	Need-based aid – Percent offered aid	Need-based Acad	Need-based Music/drama	Need-based Art	Need-based Athl	Non-need-based Acad	Non-need-based Music/drama	Non-need-based Art	Non-need-based Athl	Financial aid deadlines Priority	Financial aid deadlines Closing	Inst aid form	Notes
				X									8/1		
684	85							X				5/1	none		
1,596	50			X				X				6/1	none	X	
275	90			X	X			X	X			4/15	none	X	
435	67							X	X			5/15	none		
573	78	355	100	X				X	X	X	X	8/15	none		
229	91							X	X	X	X	5/1	none		
547	90			X	X	X		X	X	X		4/15	none		
463	78	256	100	X				X				2/15	3/15		
770	79	460	100	X	X	X	X	X	X	X	X	6/1	none	X	
495	89	360	100	X				X	X	X		4/1	8/15	X	
201	91	174	100	X	X			X	X			4/1	none	X	
437	77			X				X				6/1	none	X	
274	94	298	100	X	X			X	X			3/15	none	X	
34	91	34	97					X		X		5/1	none	X	
797	88	680	100					X	X			5/1	none	X	
154	95	145	100	X	X	X		X	X			4/15	none	X	
90	95							X	X			4/1	none		
													none		
624	85							X	X	X		6/1	none	X	
638	86	508	99	X	X			X	X			4/15	5/1	X	
358	81	289	100	X	X	X		X				3/15	none	X	
446	64			X	X			X	X			7/1	none	X	
2,584	50											5/1	none	X	
393	70	350	100	X				X				5/1	none		
1,651	40	675	100	X				X				6/15	6/30	X	
437	78	289	100	X				X				1/15	3/1		
1,691	65			X				X	X	X	X	3/15	none		
213	98	149	100	X	X			X	X			5/1	none	X	
378	82							X				4/22	none		
76	1	39	56	X								5/1	8/1	X	
86	72	105	100			X		X		X		4/1	none	X	
				X				X				6/1	none		
25	94	16	100	X				X	X			6/1	none	X	
1,140	88	870	100	X				X	X	X	X	3/1	none	X	
								X				8/21	none		
													none		
174	68	61	100					X					none		
2,326	33			X								5/15	none		
								X	X	X		4/1	5/1		
1,725	26	775	100	X	X	X		X	X			8/15	none	X	
206	75			X	X	X	X	X	X	X	X	5/1	none		
													none	X	
364	95	345	100	X	X	X	X	X	X	X	X	3/1	8/1	X	
49	98	39	100		X				X			4/1	none	X	
66	88	36	100	X				X	X			3/1	none	X	

Institution	Tuition and fees	Add'l out-of-state/district tuition	Books and supplies	Costs for campus residents Room and board	Trans-portation	Other costs	Costs for students at home Board only	Trans-portation	Other costs
Rainy River Community College	‡ 1,901	1,800/—	510	2,295	650	1,200	1,500	400	900
Rasmussen College-Minnetonka	‡ 6,625		750				1,275	1,200	1,575
Rochester Community College	‡ 1,901	1,800/—	651				2,100	750	950
St. Cloud State University	‡ 2,663	2,610/—	600	2,937	645	1,284	1,350	900	1,160
St. Cloud Technical College	‡ 2,081	1,920/—	850				1,800	515	515
St. John's University	13,996		600	4,392	100	600	2,400	100	600
St. Mary's University of Minnesota	12,045		600	3,920	110	795	1,265	110	710
St. Olaf College	15,780		550	3,850		550		300	550
St. Paul Technical College	‡ 1,968	1,920/—	700	4,300	405	900	4,300	450	900
Southwest State University	‡ 2,653	2,767/—	750	2,820	500	1,500	1,600	600	1,500
University of Minnesota									
Crookston	‡ 9,663	5,535/—	500	3,492	400	800	1,500	400	800
Duluth	‡ 3,745	6,487/—	693	3,612	663	1,401		663	1,401
Morris	‡ 4,189	7,346/—	465	3,474	500	1,200	1,200	350	1,200
Twin Cities	‡ 3,857	6,487/—	714	3,999	660	2,250	1,980	660	2,250
University of St. Thomas	13,778		500	4,559	500	953	1,922	500	953
Vermilion Community College	‡ 1,901	1,800/—	510	3,384	365	1,160	1,400	200	1,865
Willmar Community College	‡ 1,901	1,800/—	650				2,450	525	380
Willmar Technical College	‡ 2,070	1,960/—	470				1,800	1,800	900
Winona State University	‡ 2,613	2,585/—	400	3,342	300	600		300	600
Worthington Community College	‡ 1,901	1,800/—	500						
Mississippi									
Alcorn State University	† 4,128	2,502/—	650	2,299	950	1,035	955	1,800	1,035
Belhaven College	‡ 8,580		1,400	3,190	900	4,110		900	4,110
Blue Mountain College	4,090		500	2,170	300	1,500	1,390		
Coahoma Community College	‡ 910	1,900/—	500	2,168	200	200		200	200
Copiah-Lincoln Community College	1,000	1,200/—	500	1,800					
Delta State University	† 2,294	2,594/—	500	2,180	500	3,190	1,500	500	1,000
East Central Community College	‡ 1,000	1,200/—	500	1,840	640	800	1,000	960	800
East Mississippi Community College	‡ 1,000	1,000/—	500	1,960	800	400			
Hinds Community College	‡ 1,070	2,206/—	420	1,800	500	1,500	1,531	1,500	1,200
Holmes Community College	1,010	1,200/—	500	1,500	1,600			600	1,600
Itawamba Community College	900	1,200/—	600	1,740	400	800		600	800
Jackson State University	‡ 2,380	2,594/—	500	2,672	750	750	1,500	750	750
Jones County Junior College	† 792	1,260/—	400	1,782	350	1,272		900	1,008
Magnolia Bible College	3,760		400	1,390	500	4,990	1,000	750	2,200
Mary Holmes College	‡ 4,100		400	3,890	500	700	1,000	1,500	500
Meridian Community College	‡ 1,000	1,040/—	600	2,200				620	
Millsaps College	13,080		550	4,915	450	900	1,900	550	900
Mississippi College	6,942		770	3,300	770	1,650	1,650	1,650	1,650
Mississippi Delta Community College	‡ 770	1,280/90	400	1,450		400	1,410	320	240
Mississippi Gulf Coast Community College									
Jackson County Campus	‡ 880	900/—	150				1,600	1,100	
Jefferson Davis Campus	‡ 880	900/—	150				1,600	1,300	260
Perkinston	‡ 880	900/—	150	1,524			365		
Mississippi State University	‡ 2,591	2,820/—	480	3,084		1,579	2,018		1,579
Mississippi University for Women	‡ 2,244	2,502/—	600	2,457	500	1,200	1,500	500	1,200
Mississippi Valley State University	‡ 2,278	2,502/—	450	2,425	450	800	1,800	875	700
Northeast Mississippi Community College	‡ 950	1,100/—	600	1,900			1,100	600	600
Northwest Mississippi Community College	‡ 1,000	1,000/—	300	1,000		375			375
Pearl River Community College	870	1,200/—	200	1,650	300	1,085		550	1,085

†Figures are projected for 1996-97. ‡Figures are for 1995-96.

| All aid | | Need-based aid | | Grants and scholarships | | | | | | | | Financial aid deadlines | | Inst aid form | Notes |
Total freshmen	Percent receiving aid	Freshmen judged to have need	Percent offered aid	Need-based Acad	Music/drama	Art	Athl	Non-need-based Acad	Music/drama	Art	Athl	Priority	Closing		
221	82	167	100	X	X	X	X	X	X	X	X	8/1	none	X	
													none	X	
1,098	50							X					none	X	
1,926	59	817	100	X	X	X	X	X	X	X	X		none	X	
1,153	70											5/15	none	X	
430	85	321	100	X	X	X		X	X	X		3/1	none		
387	87	301	100	X	X	X		X	X	X		3/15	none		
748	80	479	100	X	X			X	X			3/1	none	X	
													none	X	
588	81			X	X	X	X	X	X		X	4/15	none		
376	90	218	100	X				X			X	4/30	none		
1,694	80	1,280	100	X	X	X	X	X	X	X	X	3/31	none		
535	79			X	X			X	X			4/1	none	X	
4,356	55	2,025	95	X	X	X	X	X	X	X	X	2/15	none		
857	77	546	100	X				X	X			4/1	none		
398	93			X				X				4/30	none	X	
562	84							X	X	X	X	4/23	none	X	
1,340	80	471	98	X								5/1	none	X	
1,275	72	720	100	X	X	X	X	X	X	X	X	4/1	none		
													none		
703	79	678	100	X	X		X	X	X		X	4/1	none	X	
143	90	90	100	X	X	X	X	X	X	X	X	4/1	none		
58	70			X	X		X	X	X		X	5/1	none		
													none	X	
				X				X	X	X	X	4/1			
491	83	338	100	X				X	X	X	X	5/1	none	X	
1,176	80	400	100					X	X	X	X	5/1	none	X	
				X				X	X		X	4/30	6/30		
3,817	40							X	X	X	X	4/1	none		
943	85			X	X	X	X	X	X	X	X		none		
2,050	73							X	X	X	X	6/1	none		
1,650	90			X	X	X	X	X	X	X	X	4/15	8/1		
1,473	80			X	X		X	X	X	X	X	5/1	none	X	
13	100	2	100	X				X				8/1	none		
157	98			X	X		X					4/1	none		
1,544	45							X	X	X	X	3/15	none		
260	90	149	100	X	X	X		X	X	X		3/1	none	X	
226	75			X	X	X	X	X	X	X	X	4/1	none	X	
				X	X		X	X	X	X	X		none		
1,712	50			X	X			X	X			6/1	none		
2,141	50	1,364	100	X				X	X		X	6/1	none	X	
								X	X	X	X	6/1	none	X	
1,807	80			X	X		X	X	X		X	4/1	none	X	
386	91							X	X	X	X	4/1	none		
580	96	375	99	X	X		X	X	X		X	4/1			
1,000	75							X	X	X	X	5/1		X	
2,670	75			X	X		X					3/1			
1,195	70	944	100	X				X	X		X	5/1	none		

Institution	Tuition and fees	Add'l out-of-state/district tuition	Books and supplies	Costs for campus residents			Costs for students at home		
				Room and board	Trans-portation	Other costs	Board only	Trans-portation	Other costs
Phillips Junior College of Jackson	‡ 4,975						660	1,040	1,612
Rust College	4,725		350	2,275	350	150	1,100	500	300
Southeastern Baptist College	2,220		300	1,800	200	350	500	300	350
Southwest Mississippi Community College	850	1,050/—	400	1,650		1,300	1,100	1,300	
Tougaloo College	6,212		500	2,696	300	800	1,500	300	500
University of Mississippi									
Medical Center	‡ 2,106	2,709/—	660		450	4,950		900	2,250
University	‡ 2,546	2,820/—	500	3,000	650	1,500	1,900	950	1,300
University of Southern Mississippi	‡ 2,468	2,820/—	750	2,465	250	1,380	800	970	1,380
Wesley College	2,120		400	2,400	400	650		500	1,150
William Carey College	‡ 5,760		900	2,565	1,500	1,440	1,463	1,500	1,440
Wood College	‡ 3,050		400	2,560	100	1,000		1,100	1,000
Missouri									
Avila College	10,200		650	4,150	600	1,600		1,200	1,450
Baptist Bible College	‡ 2,602		300	2,812	450	1,300	1,000	500	1,300
Berean College	2,095		500						
Calvary Bible College	‡ 3,924		450	2,950	800	350	1,750	800	350
Central Bible College	4,420		550	3,100	850	1,000	1,300	850	2,000
Central Christian College of the Bible	3,790		350	2,470	400	1,300	1,330	150	2,600
Central Methodist College	9,840		650	3,770	400	1,900	1,635	400	1,400
Central Missouri State University	2,520	2,520/—	325	3,980	500	1,750	650	750	1,000
College of the Ozarks	150		500	2,200		1,200		800	1,200
Columbia College	8,974		800	4,024	500	900		500	900
Conception Seminary College	7,042		400	3,274	550	800	1,750	550	800
Cottey College	6,800		500	3,600	1,000	800			1,500
Crowder College	1,200	1,110/420	500	2,750	900	1,000	960	900	1,000
Culver-Stockton College	8,800		400	4,000	500	1,200	1,500	500	1,200
Deaconess College of Nursing	7,340		953	3,700	300	300	1,600	400	300
DeVry Institute of Technology: Kansas City	6,560		560				1,802	2,035	1,808
Drury College	10,010		500	3,856	300	300	2,000	300	300
East Central College	1,326	1,086/476	600				1,865	1,312	500
Electronics Institute	6,180		965						
Evangel College	7,580		500	3,340	800	1,500	1,700	800	500
Fontbonne College	9,660		620	4,400	380	1,100	3,126	1,350	1,100
Hannibal-LaGrange College	7,140		500	2,610		1,300		300	1,300
Harris Stowe State College	2,250	2,154/—	750				3,000	1,000	1,600
Hickey School	7,580		500						
Jefferson College	‡ 1,217	720/360	460				1,800	800	1,070
Kansas City Art Institute	15,820		1,600	4,470	980	800	3,740	980	800
Kemper Military School and College	11,100		600	3,600		1,000			
Lincoln University	‡ 2,076	4,032/—	480	2,698	926	1,200	1,300	1,466	1,200
Lindenwood College	9,800		1,050	5,000	1,250	2,975	1,500	2,050	3,575
Longview Community College	1,350	1,860/900	550				1,627	1,639	1,306
Maple Woods Community College	1,410	1,860/900	550				1,627	1,627	1,972
Maryville University of Saint Louis	10,280		500	4,900	700	1,000	2,250	1,930	1,000
Mineral Area College	1,050	—/450	650				1,500	1,950	
Missouri Baptist College	7,880		600	3,770	275	1,500	1,800	1,500	1,500
Missouri Southern State College	2,190	2,100/—	400	3,170	460	900	1,500	600	600
Missouri Technical School	15,921		1,021					1,565	
Missouri Valley College	9,950		1,000	5,000	1,500	3,030	9,480		
Missouri Western State College	2,414	1,944/—	350	2,919	600	1,500	1,600	500	1,500

†Figures are projected for 1996-97. ‡Figures are for 1995-96.

Total freshmen	Percent receiving aid	Freshmen judged to have need	Percent offered aid	Need-based Acad	Need-based Music/drama	Need-based Art	Need-based Athl	Non-need-based Acad	Non-need-based Music/drama	Non-need-based Art	Non-need-based Athl	Priority	Closing	Inst aid form	Notes
217	95	196	100	X	X	X	X	X	X			5/1	none	X	
9	100	7	100	X	X							7/1	none		
750	45											8/5	none		
218	92			X	X		X	X	X		X	4/15	none		
				X				X				4/1	none		
1,645	70			X				X	X	X	X	4/1	none		
1,275	83	975	98	X				X	X	X	X	3/15	none	X	
43	22	19	100	X	X			X	X				5/15		
156	75			X				X	X		X	9/1	4/1		
													none		
105	98	81	100					X	X	X	X	7/1	none	X	
207	75							X				5/1			
													none		
				X				X					3/31		
203	63	144	100	X	X			X	X			5/1	none		
43	82			X	X			X	X			3/15	4/1		
232	95			X	X		X	X	X		X	4/1	none		
1,545	42						X	X	X	X	X	3/1	none		
267	100	232	100	X	X	X	X	X	X	X	X	4/1	none		
197	64							X	X	X	X	3/15	8/22	X	
								X	X	X		5/1	none		
246	60							X	X	X	X	8/1	none		
262	98	204	100	X				X	X	X	X	3/1	none		
70	85			X				X				4/15	7/1		
								X					none		
377	83	280	99	X	X	X	X	X	X	X	X	4/1	6/15	X	
598	30			X	X	X	X	X	X	X	X	3/30	none		
486	79	310	98					X	X	X	X	4/1	none		
144	92	121	99	X	X	X		X	X	X			none	X	
								X	X	X	X		7/1		
177	55	78	100	X			X	X	X		X	4/1	none		
													none		
1,945	37							X	X	X			none	X	
148	80	110	100	X		X		X		X		2/1	8/25		
								X	X	X	X		none		
								X	X	X	X	3/1	none		
478	90			X	X	X	X	X	X	X	X	4/30	none		
1,254	22							X	X	X	X	5/31	none	X	
720	20							X	X	X	X	5/31	none	X	
198	89	78	100	X		X		X		X		2/1	none	X	
967	50	812	100	X	X	X	X	X	X	X	X	4/15	none		
175	85							X	X		X	4/1	none	X	
2,109	71	643	100					X	X	X	X	2/15	none		
								X					none		
418	95	375	100	X	X	X		X	X	X		4/15	none		
				X	X	X	X	X	X		X	4/1	none		

Institution	Tuition and fees	Add'l out-of-state/ district tuition	Books and supplies	Costs for campus residents			Costs for students at home		
				Room and board	Trans-portation	Other costs	Board only	Trans-portation	Other costs
Moberly Area Community College	† 1,090	2,280/780	600	1,200	980	1,500		2,200	1,500
National College	‡ 7,730		800					500	
North Central Missouri College	1,875	720/—	500	2,290	890	976	1,640	1,000	976
Northwest Missouri State University	2,475	1,793/—	300	3,690	750	1,350	1,290	750	1,350
Ozark Christian College	‡ 3,865		450	3,100	720			650	
Ozarks Technical Community College	1,315		1,500						
Park College	4,200		840	4,220	420	2,415	1,890	370	1,260
Penn Valley Community College	1,410	1,860/900	550				1,627	1,627	1,972
Phillips Junior College	3,498		305				1,700	2,025	1,260
Ranken Technical College	5,550		1,700						
Research College of Nursing	11,530		720	4,350	825	915	2,600	1,250	915
Rockhurst College	11,240		525	4,490	600	695	1,800	1,000	1,235
St. Charles County Community College	1,440	1,500/600	600					900	500
St. Louis Christian College	4,136		350	2,650	400	600	1,500	405	1,200
St. Louis College of Pharmacy	‡ 10,510		350	5,650	400	1,400		1,100	2,100
St. Louis Community College									
Florissant Valley	‡ 1,260	750/330	600				3,000	960	2,000
Forest Park	‡ 1,260	750/330	600				3,000	960	2,000
Meramec	‡ 1,260	750/330	600				2,800	960	2,000
St. Louis University	13,980		800	5,260	2,600	4,700	4,200	2,600	4,700
St. Luke's College	7,370		900						
Southeast Missouri State University	‡ 2,880	2,310/—	350	3,895	700	1,650		1,700	1,650
Southwest Baptist University	7,873		500	2,623	900	600			
Southwest Missouri State University	2,888	2,670/—	650	2,910	790	2,080	1,830	790	2,080
State Fair Community College	1,230	2,460/1,320	900				2,250	1,800	750
Stephens College	14,830		450	5,440	700	1,450	2,550	700	1,450
Three Rivers Community College	1,215	1,230/390	250				900	1,421	940
Truman State University	3,008	2,408/—	600	3,808	734	1,800		798	2,700
University of Missouri									
Columbia	‡ 3,771	6,624/—	700	3,457		1,926	2,674		1,926
Kansas City	‡ 3,799	6,624/—	700	3,875			1,500	2,160	1,780
Rolla	‡ 3,900	6,624/—	765	3,290		1,542			1,542
St. Louis	‡ 3,761	6,624/—	790	3,948	530	926	1,000	992	992
Washington University	20,200		780	6,210	550	2,442	1,500	736	4,170
Webster University	10,292		800	4,614	1,500	1,500	2,500	500	1,500
Wentworth Military Academy	‡ 11,250		700	3,125	1,350	1,800	600	1,350	900
Westminster College	11,940		630	4,330	350	1,300		350	1,300
William Jewell College	11,130		600	3,270	800	1,800	1,650	1,000	1,800
William Woods University	11,850		600	5,000	1,000	2,700		700	3,050
Montana									
Blackfeet Community College	‡ 1,523		600	4,950			900	1,200	1,200
Carroll College	10,574		450	4,190	350	700	1,500	350	700
Dawson Community College	‡ 1,344	2,653/602	550		1,049	1,048	1,500	1,049	1,048
Dull Knife Memorial College	‡ 1,134		600	4,150	455	656	3,950	455	656
Flathead Valley Community College	‡ 1,260	2,328/552	500				1,170	900	600
Fort Belknap College	‡ 1,854		450				4,680	1,540	1,430
Fort Peck Community College	1,230		440	3,000					700
Helena College of Technology of the University of Montana	‡ 1,880	2,040/—	400					1,260	
Little Big Horn College	‡ 1,650		420					1,092	468
Miles Community College	1,392	2,904/600	600	2,600	600	650	1,100	600	650

†Figures are projected for 1996-97. ‡Figures are for 1995-96.

All aid		Need-based aid		Grants and scholarships								Financial aid deadlines		Inst aid form	Notes
Total freshmen	Percent receiving aid	Freshmen judged to have need	Percent offered aid	Need-based				Non-need-based				Priority	Closing		
				Acad	Music/drama	Art	Athl	Acad	Music/drama	Art	Athl				
				X				X	X		X		6/30		
30	100			X				X					none		
364	75						X	X			X	3/28	none		
1,272	79	913	100	X				X	X	X	X	3/1	none		
								X	X				5/1	X	
														X	
144	80	70	100					X	X	X	X	4/1	8/1	X	
719	33							X			X	5/31	none	X	
													none		
370	80			X				X					none		
23	90			X				X			X	4/1	none	X	
289	97	199						X			X	4/1	none	X	
941	20							X	X			4/15	none	X	
36	85			X	X			X	X			7/1	none	X	
158	76			X				X				5/31	none		
1,475	22							X	X	X	X	8/1	none		
1,170	50	1,000	70					X	X	X	X	3/15	5/15		
2,517	25	2,142	100	X	X	X	X	X	X	X	X	3/15	none	X	
1,049	93	821	100	X	X	X	X	X	X	X	X	1/1	6/1		
														X	
1,184	45			X	X	X	X	X	X	X	X	3/1	none		
647	85							X	X	X	X	4/30	none	X	
2,512	50			X	X	X	X	X	X	X	X	3/31	none		
495	63			X				X	X	X	X	7/1	none		
168	90	132	100	X	X	X		X	X			1/15	none		
1,465	75			X	X	X	X	X	X	X	X	4/1	none	X	
1,504	92	756	100	X	X	X	X	X	X	X	X	4/1	none		
3,845	60							X	X	X	X	3/1	none		
627	63	416	91	X	X	X		X	X	X	X	3/15	none	X	
828	70	580	100					X	X		X	3/1	none	X	
715	31	270	100	X				X			X	4/1	10/3		
1,184	58	550	97	X		X		X		X			2/15		
249	85	161	100	X	X	X		X	X	X		4/1	none		
		52	100	X				X				4/30	6/30		
191	85	119	100					X	X	X		3/31	none		
279	99	192	100					X	X	X	X	3/1	none	X	
181	95	162	100					X	X	X	X	3/1	5/1		
														X	
296	94							X	X		X	3/1	none		
168	70	141	100					X	X	X	X	3/1	none		
													none		
351	90	300	100	X			X	X			X	5/1	none	X	
													none		
													none	X	
119	75			X				X				4/1	none	X	
				X				X					none		
155	93			X	X		X	X	X		X	3/1	none		

Institution	Tuition and fees	Add'l out-of-state/district tuition	Books and supplies	Room and board	Trans-portation	Other costs	Board only	Trans-portation	Other costs
				Costs for campus residents			Costs for students at home		
Montana State University									
Billings College of Technology	‡ 2,038	1,968/—	500		600		1,800	600	
College of Technology-Great Falls	‡ 1,624	1,974/—	1,200			1,800		800	1,800
Billings	‡ 2,304	4,014/—	500	2,960	480	1,200	1,246	480	1,200
Bozeman	‡ 2,378	4,418/—	600	3,858	525	1,825	1,700	525	1,825
Northern	‡ 2,221	4,005/—	600	3,540	639	558	729	532	558
Montana Tech of The University of Montana	‡ 2,293	4,193/—	550	3,456	800	1,400	1,000	500	
Montana Tech of the University of Montana: College of Technology	‡ 1,708	2,058/—	550				1,500	1,500	1,000
Rocky Mountain College	† 10,079		620	3,822	400	650	2,036	400	650
Salish Kootenai College	‡ 1,883	4,284/504	600				1,350	550	
Stone Child College	‡ 1,640	450/—	400						
University of Great Falls	† 7,200		600	4,500	750	900	850	750	900
University of Montana-Missoula	‡ 2,460	4,147/—	550	4,092		2,500	1,850		2,200
University of Montana College of Technology	† 2,050	1,100/—	500	4,000					
Western Montana College of the University of Montana	‡ 2,091	3,803/—	600	3,700	1,200	1,200			2,000
Nebraska									
Bellevue University	3,610		500				5,400	900	1,800
Central Community College	1,302	579/—	450	2,250	600	700	1,350	750	700
Chadron State College	‡ 1,873	1,425/—	600	2,870	500	450	750	250	352
Clarkson College	8,308		435		1,104	1,440	3,314	1,568	1,440
College of St. Mary	11,354		400	4,080	486	1,681	1,098	971	1,852
Concordia College	10,150		500	3,540	900	1,200	1,900	900	1,200
Creighton University	12,210		650	4,726	525	1,530	1,500	950	1,530
Dana College	10,950		450	3,730	300	1,150		300	1,150
Doane College/Lincoln Campus	10,950		500	3,290	550	1,000	975	550	1,000
Gateway Electronics Institute	5,350								
Grace University	7,120		650	3,030	600	1,700		1,100	1,700
Hastings College	10,724		650	3,594	400	1,364		400	1,364
Lincoln School of Commerce	‡ 5,985		450		450	800	1,450	450	800
McCook Community College	1,050	135/—	500	2,800	610	550	560	610	550
Metropolitan Community College	1,224	287/—	450				1,500	353	
Mid Plains Community College	1,155	135/—	500	1,175	550	500	1,000	700	500
Midland Lutheran College	11,600		400	3,100	400	900	1,000	400	900
Nebraska Christian College	† 4,080		320	2,660	400	1,715	2,015	400	1,715
Nebraska College of Technical Agriculture	† 1,863	1,728/—	600	2,970	500	1,100	1,500	1,000	1,100
Nebraska Indian Community College	‡ 2,550		400				1,860	710	800
Nebraska Methodist College of Nursing and Allied Health	7,800		570		553	987	1,656	1,105	987
Nebraska Wesleyan University	10,714		500	3,520		2,000		300	2,000
Northeast Community College	1,530	306/—	600		650	900	1,260	500	900
Peru State College	‡ 1,798	1,425/—	600	2,844	510	1,200	1,500	630	1,200
Southeast Community College									
Beatrice Campus	‡ 1,148	203/—	450		650	500		900	500
Lincoln Campus	‡ 1,139	225/—	900		1,200	1,200	2,200	1,200	1,200
Milford Campus	‡ 1,139	225/—	675	2,241	900	900	1,650	900	
Spencer School of Business	4,992		1,250	1,712					
Union College	9,550		600	3,120	1,100			900	900

†Figures are projected for 1996-97. ‡Figures are for 1995-96.

Total freshmen	Percent receiving aid	Freshmen judged to have need	Percent offered aid	Acad	Music/drama	Art	Athl	Acad	Music/drama	Art	Athl	Priority	Closing	Inst aid form	Notes
													none		
													none		
740	55							X	X	X	X	3/1	none	X	
1,893	75	1,075	100	X				X	X	X	X	3/1	none		
171	52			X	X		X	X	X		X		none	X	
652	60	235	100	X			X	X			X	4/1	none		
81	65			X				X				4/1	none		
125	80	83	100								X	4/1	none	X	
													none		
				X				X				3/1	none		
261	95	120	100	X				X				4/1	none	X	
1,670	62	788	100	X	X	X	X	X	X	X	X	3/1	none	X	
388	85			X				X				3/1	none		
236	81	182	100	X		X	X	X	X	X	X	3/1	5/1		
131	61	63	100	X			X	X			X	4/15	none	X	
477	59			X	X	X	X	X	X	X	X	7/1	none	X	
585	70	260	100	X				X	X	X	X	6/1			
79	85	28	100	X								4/1	none	X	
264	100	78	100					X	X	X	X	4/1	none	X	
297	99	198	100					X	X	X	X	5/1	8/15	X	
797	82	429	100	X				X			X	4/1	none	X	
176	100	157	100		X	X	X	X	X	X	X	4/1	none	X	
240	93	213	100	X				X	X	X	X	3/15	none	X	
				X	X			X	X			3/15	none		
271	99	214	100		X	X	X	X	X	X	X	5/1	8/15	X	
180	95			X				X					none		
262	56	200	100	X	X	X	X	X		X	X	5/1	none		
1,067	18			X				X				3/30	none	X	
822	70			X				X	X	X	X	4/15	none		
283	93			X	X	X	X	X	X	X	X	5/1	none	X	
51	97	51	100	X				X				6/1	none		
172	67	105	100	X				X				4/1	none		
37	90			X								7/15	none		
63	82	41	100					X				5/1	none	X	
362	98	284	100					X	X	X		11/1	none		
566	71			X	X	X	X	X	X	X	X		4/15	X	
229	81	229	100	X	X	X	X	X	X	X	X	3/1	none	X	
238	60	170	97	X	X	X	X	X	X	X	X	4/1	none		
956	50			X				X					none	X	
110	60			X				X				4/1	none		
133	80			X	X			X	X			6/15	none		

Institution	Tuition and fees	Add'l out-of-state/district tuition	Books and supplies	Costs for campus residents Room and board	Costs for campus residents Transportation	Costs for campus residents Other costs	Costs for students at home Board only	Costs for students at home Transportation	Costs for students at home Other costs
University of Nebraska									
Medical Center	‡ 2,534	4,014/—	800				1,650	500	1,500
Kearney	‡ 2,061	1,560/—	500	2,804	436	1,400	1,800	436	1,400
Lincoln	‡ 2,562	3,750/—	545	3,350		2,230	1,885		2,035
Omaha	‡ 2,188	3,390/—	650				1,080	600	650
Wayne State College	‡ 1,840	1,425/—	540	2,740	675	1,040	1,500	765	962
Western Nebraska Community College	1,230	135/—	600	2,560	400	660	1,800	400	550
York College	6,465		600	2,785	800	1,600	1,095	350	1,600
Nevada									
Community College of Southern Nevada	‡ 1,020	3,100/—	600				4,672	1,500	2,480
Great Basin College	‡ 1,020	3,100/—	500				1,350	960	1,195
Morrison College: Reno	6,309		690						1,800
Phillips Junior College: Las Vegas Campus	4,900								
Sierra Nevada College	‡ 8,850		500		500	2,820	2,000	500	820
Truckee Meadows Community College	‡ 1,020	3,100/—	800						
University of Nevada									
Las Vegas	‡ 1,830	4,900/—	700	5,206	400	1,000	1,000	700	1,000
Reno	1,792	5,100/—	650	6,024	556	2,078	2,065	1,104	501
Western Nevada Community College	‡ 1,020	3,100/—	450				900	680	1,230
New Hampshire									
Castle College	5,485		500				2,400	1,161	1,541
Colby-Sawyer College	15,530		600	5,950	100	900	1,500	900	900
College for Lifelong Learning	‡ 3,970	420/—	650						
Daniel Webster College	‡ 13,072		500	5,262	500	500	1,500	450	500
Dartmouth College	21,951		1,745	6,282					
Franklin Pierce College	15,375		600	4,930	360	905	2,500	600	905
Hesser College	† 8,500		700	4,200	500	550	720	495	450
Keene State College	‡ 3,623	5,490/—	600	4,350	350	800	1,500	600	525
McIntosh College	‡ 3,976		400	3,300		1,536	4,576		1,536
New England College	15,071		450	5,892	450	1,050	2,500	450	1,000
New Hampshire College	12,346		600	5,112	300	900	1,500	700	900
New Hampshire Technical College									
Berlin	‡ 2,506	3,112/1,148	450				1,575	1,000	1,800
Claremont	‡ 2,530	3,112/—	550				1,800	1,600	1,100
Laconia	‡ 2,506	3,112/—	500				1,000	1,400	800
Manchester	‡ 2,506	3,112/—	500				1,700	1,000	1,770
Nashua	‡ 2,482	3,112/—	500				1,100	1,000	500
Stratham	‡ 2,554	3,112/—	600				2,680	1,500	1,000
New Hampshire Technical Institute	‡ 2,626	3,112/—	400	3,699	750	1,600	1,500	1,500	1,600
Notre Dame College	‡ 10,690		500	5,050	400	1,000	1,800	1,000	1,000
Plymouth State College of the University System of New Hampshire	‡ 3,754	5,490/—	600	4,192	254	894	1,500	1,000	700
Rivier College	11,700		600	5,250	200	900	3,465	900	900
St. Anselm College	14,950		550	5,710	200	1,000	1,500	1,400	1,000
Thomas More College of Liberal Arts	8,200		400	6,000	1,500		500		
University of New Hampshire									
Durham	‡ 5,041	8,670/—	500	4,150	300	1,100	1,200	600	1,100
Manchester	‡ 3,436	6,740/—	500				1,700	1,000	1,000
White Pines College	‡ 7,950		600	4,000	500	1,000	4,200	1,000	1,000

†Figures are projected for 1996-97. ‡Figures are for 1995-96.

| All aid | | Need–based aid | | Grants and scholarships | | | | | | | | Financial aid deadlines | | Inst aid form | Notes |
Total freshmen	Percent receiving aid	Freshmen judged to have need	Percent offered aid	Need–based Acad	Music/drama	Art	Athl	Non–need–based Acad	Music/drama	Art	Athl	Priority	Closing		
				X				X					none	X	
1,407	76							X	X	X	X	3/1	none		
3,984	54	2,400	100	X	X		X	X	X		X	3/1	5/6		
3,483	55			X	X	X	X	X	X	X	X	3/1	none		
742	85	504	98	X				X	X	X	X	5/1	none		
733	75	622	89	X	X		X	X	X	X	X	4/1	none		
168	92	101	100					X	X		X	6/30	none		
2,481	13			X								4/15	5/1		
1,368	55			X		X		X				6/1	none		
28	81	17	100	X				X					5/1		
													none		
70	70			X				X	X	X	X		none		
4,797	18											4/10	none		
1,577	54	1,309	67	X	X	X	X	X	X	X	X	2/15	none		
1,136	65	278	99					X	X	X	X	4/15	3/1	X	
1,873	32			X				X				6/1	none		
148	81	123	100					X				3/31	8/1	X	
241	62	198	100	X	X	X		X	X	X		3/1		X	
													none		
183	92	123	100	X				X					none		
1,048	60	530	100										2/1		
493	93			X			X	X			X		none		
430	75			X			X	X			X	3/1	none	X	
								X	X	X	X		3/1		
				X				X				7/1	8/15		
239	65	140	100	X	X	X		X				3/1	none	X	
981	73	392	100	X			X	X			X	3/15	none		
		353	100	X								5/1	none	X	
													none		
													none		
684	75	202	100	X								5/1	none		
				X								5/1	none		
													none		
													none		
140	90	105	100	X				X		X	X	3/15	none	X	
879	76	665	100					X	X			3/1	none		
123	80			X				X				4/1	none		
629	82	495	92	X			X	X			X	3/1	4/15		
2,440	78	1,576	97	X			X	X	X	X	X	3/1	none		
98	27	62	98	X				X					5/1		
35	50	19	100	X				X		X		3/15	5/1	X	

155

Institution	Tuition and fees	Add'l out-of-state/ district tuition	Books and supplies	Costs for campus residents			Costs for students at home		
				Room and board	Trans-portation	Other costs	Board only	Trans-portation	Other costs
New Jersey									
Assumption College for Sisters	1,200		400	1,100					
Atlantic Community College	‡ 1,501	3,149/1,267					1,550	1,425	370
Bergen Community College	‡ 2,085	3,910/1,956	850						
Berkeley College of Business	10,950		700		1,765	2,050	1,575	1,765	2,050
Beth Medrash Govoha	‡ 3,100		450	4,200					
Bloomfield College	9,250		500	4,650	300	1,440	2,829	1,095	1,275
Brookdale Community College	2,398	4,170/2,085	700				1,500	1,248	1,065
Burlington County College	‡ 1,465	2,300/440	800				2,400	2,300	
Caldwell College	‡ 9,560		425	4,900	500	1,000	2,400	1,200	1,000
Camden County College	1,790	—/1,740	600				570	1,006	1,496
Centenary College	‡ 12,094		500	5,500	300	600	2,500	1,500	600
College of St. Elizabeth	‡ 12,010		380	5,700	350	650	1,700	850	650
County College of Morris	‡ 2,195	2,920/1,920	600				2,100	1,200	950
Cumberland County College	1,782	4,842/1,614	600				1,500	727	1,429
DeVry Technical Institute	6,560		560				2,103	1,995	1,932
Drew University	20,402		520	5,972	230	370	1,500	600	500
Essex County College	‡ 2,131	3,705/1,862	600				1,500	900	1,061
Fairleigh Dickinson University									
Edward Williams College	‡ 11,480		623	5,550	588	1,553		1,944	4,523
Teaneck	13,280		623	5,864	588	1,396		1,944	4,326
Felician College	‡ 8,900		500					500	
Georgian Court College	10,492		500	4,450	800	800	1,900	1,600	800
Gloucester County College	‡ 1,740	4,740/30	600					1,000	800
Jersey City State College	‡ 3,158	1,290/—	427	4,800	400	1,400	1,600	1,045	1,040
Katharine Gibbs School	‡ 7,545		500						
Kean College of New Jersey	‡ 3,089	1,200/—	500	4,250	650	800	1,000	875	800
Mercer County Community College	‡ 1,890	3,165/1,215	880				1,500	1,120	970
Middlesex County College	1,824	—/1,824	500					657	2,954
Monmouth University	13,800		560	5,810	400	1,450	2,550	710	1,450
Montclair State University	‡ 2,969	1,312/—	700	5,060	500	950	1,700	1,375	950
New Jersey Institute of Technology	‡ 5,220	4,344/—	800	5,600	500	1,000	2,500	950	1,000
Ocean County College	1,968	1,712/315	500				1,400	1,450	900
Princeton University	22,000		730	6,325	420	1,635			
Rabbinical College of America	‡ 7,000			6,500					
Ramapo College of New Jersey	‡ 3,513	1,380/—	600	5,200	800	855	1,700	1,800	602
Raritan Valley Community College	1,656	4,320/1,440	750				1,500	1,080	1,000
Richard Stockton College of New Jersey	‡ 3,152	816/—	750	4,456	809	1,200	1,500	1,005	1,100
Rider University	14,800		700	6,030		1,200			1,200
Rowan College of New Jersey	‡ 3,392	2,490/—	600	4,768	230	1,000	1,500	800	1,000
Rutgers, The State University of New Jersey									
Camden College of Arts and Sciences	‡ 4,681	3,921/—		4,936					
College of Engineering	‡ 5,244	4,348/—		4,936					
College of Nursing	‡ 4,627	3,921/—		4,936					
College of Pharmacy	‡ 5,244	4,348/—		4,936					
Cook College	‡ 5,231	4,348/—		4,936					
Douglass College	‡ 4,798	3,921/—		4,936					
Livingston College	‡ 4,862	3,921/—		4,936					
Mason Gross School of the Arts	‡ 4,828	3,921/—		4,936					
Newark College of Arts and Sciences	‡ 4,644	3,921/—		4,936					
Rutgers College	‡ 4,836	3,921/—		4,936					

†Figures are projected for 1996-97. ‡Figures are for 1995-96.

Total fresh-men	Percent receiving aid	Freshmen judged to have need	Percent offered aid	Need-based Acad	Music/drama	Art	Athl	Non-need-based Acad	Music/drama	Art	Athl	Priority	Closing	Inst aid form	Notes
													none		
												5/1	none		
				X				X				5/15	none		
764	85			X				X					none		
319	90	266	100	X			X	X			X	6/1	none	X	
3,476	43			X				X			X	6/1	none		
1,209	50			X			X	X			X		none		
185	78	145	100	X		X	X	X		X	X	4/15	7/15	X	
2,786	25	1,259	84	X				X				7/1	12/2	X	
77	80	64	100	X				X				5/1	none	X	
144	94	57	100	X				X		X		4/1	none		
2,284	25	1,100	82	X	X	X		X			X	3/15	none		
												6/1	none		
								X					none		
434	89	258	100	X				X					3/1		
3,071	65			X				X			X	6/30	none		
314	80	211	100	X	X	X	X	X				3/15	none		
526	87	219	100	X	X	X	X				X	3/15	none		
													none		
143	76	139	100	X	X	X	X	X	X	X	X	3/1	10/1	X	
													none		
669	62	400	96					X	X	X		4/15	4/15	X	
													none		
													none		
2,454	23	572	81	X	X	X	X	X	X		X	5/1	none		
5,000	33							X			X	3/1	none		
777	92	499	100	X				X			X	3/1	none		
1,240	75	810	100					X					3/1		
564	81	390	100	X				X				3/15	none		
								X				5/31	none		
1,209	70	588	100										2/1	X	
													none		
365	56	177	94	X				X				3/15	5/1		
				X								4/1	none	X	
763	90	645	100	X				X	X	X		3/1	none		
552	80			X			X	X	X		X	3/1	none		
933	70			X	X	X		X	X	X			5/1		
250	63	194	98	X	X	X		X				3/15	none	X	
542	35	259	98	X	X		X	X			X	3/15	none	X	
48	56	34	100	X			X	X				3/15	none	X	
198	63	84	99	X			X	X			X	3/15	none	X	
629	65	321	97	X	X		X	X			X	3/15	none	X	
603	65	353	96	X	X		X	X	X		X	3/15	none		
561	56	363	98	X	X		X	X	X		X	3/15	none	X	
106	71	66	91	X	X		X	X	X	X	X	3/15	none	X	
454	51			X	X		X	X			X	3/15	none	X	
2,056	64	971	97	X	X		X	X	X		X	3/15	none		

Institution	Tuition and fees	Add'l out-of-state/district tuition	Books and supplies	Costs for campus residents			Costs for students at home		
				Room and board	Transportation	Other costs	Board only	Transportation	Other costs
St. Peter's College	12,325		700	5,530	400	600	1,500	650	600
Salem Community College	‡ 2,176	—/213	600				1,500	1,000	800
Seton Hall University	12,850		650	6,710	630	1,200	2,270	1,020	1,330
Stevens Institute of Technology	18,640		700	6,400	180	750	1,500	1,500	750
Sussex County Community College	† 2,627	4,340/2,170	680				1,500		998
Talmudical Academy of New Jersey	‡ 6,500 (comprehensive)								
Trenton State College	‡ 4,168	2,417/—	700	5,600	200	1,100	1,500	1,200	1,100
Union County College	‡ 2,180	5,670/1,890	585				1,980	962	2,573
University of Medicine and Dentistry of New Jersey: School of Nursing	‡ 2,251	593/—	478				2,187	2,908	2,223
Warren County Community College	2,094	5,670/3,780	500				1,080	864	900
Westminster Choir College of Rider University	‡ 14,015		500	6,100	150	700	2,280	1,000	700
William Paterson College of New Jersey	‡ 3,120	1,880/—	500	4,830	1,000	1,500	2,000	1,000	1,500

New Mexico

Institution	Tuition and fees	Add'l out-of-state/district tuition	Books and supplies	Room and board	Transportation	Other costs	Board only	Transportation	Other costs
Albuquerque Technical-Vocational Institute	‡ 629	1,701/—	573				1,785	1,629	1,480
Clovis Community College	678	177/30	750					978	1,467
College of Santa Fe	12,714			4,566	508	984	1,500	508	984
College of the Southwest	4,515		650	2,800	1,000	685	1,910	1,380	685
Dona Ana Branch Community College of New Mexico State University	768	1,288/120	300	3,024			1,560	500	
Eastern New Mexico University									
Portales	1,652	4,502/—	500	2,838	1,000	1,200		1,000	1,200
Roswell Campus	‡ 654	1,212/24	659	2,700	1,470	907		1,300	950
Institute of American Indian Arts	‡ 9,000		1,700	3,200	500	1,144	1,800	1,400	1,144
National College	‡ 5,965		600					2,184	
New Mexico Highlands University	‡ 1,646	4,698/—	600	4,668	1,133	824	2,000	2,060	824
New Mexico Institute of Mining and Technology	1,997	4,407/—	600	3,426	500	1,100	2,600	250	1,100
New Mexico Junior College	‡ 506	528/240	700	3,100	720	1,575	1,500	1,060	1,575
New Mexico Military Institute	‡ 1,570	1,751/—	700	2,800	500	1,000			
New Mexico State University									
Alamogordo	768	1,224/60	580	4,532	1,104	1,300		1,104	1,300
Carlsbad	768	1,206/120	580					1,104	1,300
Grants	‡ 624	1,224/120	400				1,214	754	
Las Cruces	2,196	4,956/—	550	3,288					
Northern New Mexico Community College	638	900/—	505	2,768	852	1,740	2,128	852	1,740
Parks College	6,687		675						
St. John's College	18,720		275	6,055	600	900	1,700	100	
San Juan College	360	240/—	440				2,000	900	650
Santa Fe Community College	† 550	400/72	500				2,500	650	440
Southwestern Indian Polytechnic Institute	‡ 60			3,450	600	1,000	2,000	1,000	1,000
University of New Mexico	2,071	5,750/—	568	4,000	963	1,889	1,966	884	1,215
Western New Mexico University	1,516	3,965/—	600	2,514	805	1,155	1,000	915	1,000

New York

Institution	Tuition and fees	Add'l out-of-state/district tuition	Books and supplies	Room and board	Transportation	Other costs	Board only	Transportation	Other costs
Adelphi University	† 13,530		800	6,490	1,100	1,000		3,000	3,300
Adirondack Community College	‡ 2,235	2,050/—	600				1,000	800	800
Albany College of Pharmacy	10,215		700	4,700	300	700	1,500	1,600	100
Alfred University	18,972		550	6,042	350	575	1,500	1,350	525
American Academy of Dramatic Arts	9,200		400				3,500	1,120	875

†Figures are projected for 1996-97. ‡Figures are for 1995-96.

| All aid | | Need-based aid | | Grants and scholarships | | | | | | | | Financial aid deadlines | | Inst aid form | Notes |
| | | | | Need-based | | | | Non-need-based | | | | | | | |
Total freshmen	Percent receiving aid	Freshmen judged to have need	Percent offered aid	Acad	Music/drama	Art	Athl	Acad	Music/drama	Art	Athl	Priority	Closing		
597	88	522	100					X			X	3/1	none		
				X				X			X		9/1	X	
967	74	790	95	X				X			X	4/1	none		
392	75	340	100					X				2/1	none	X	
741	40			X								3/1	8/1		
													none		
1,088	53	513	100					X	X				4/1		
1,338	17	669	91	X		X		X		X	X	3/15	none		
												3/1	none		
479	8	55	75	X				X				11/1	none		
													none		
855	49			X	X			X	X			4/1	none		
				X								3/1	none		
517	71			X				X				9/1	none		
150	91	100	100					X	X	X		3/1	none	X	
28	98	26	100					X	X		X	4/1	6/1	X	
1,050	21			X								3/1	none		
481	80			X	X	X	X	X	X	X	X	3/1	none		
422	70			X				X				5/1	none		
32	94											3/15	none	X	
36	75			X				X					none	X	
326	85			X	X	X		X	X	X	X	3/1	5/1		
195	88	106	100	X				X				3/1	none	X	
1,616	46			X	X	X	X	X	X		X	6/1	none		
314	86	83	100	X				X	X		X	5/1	none		
				X				X				3/1	none		
													none		
1,444	60			X	X		X	X	X		X	3/1	none	X	
													none		
225	96							X					none		
116	85	91	100	X								2/15	none	X	
890	25	594	82	X	X			X	X			5/1	none		
5,459	20	125	80	X				X	X			3/1	none	X	
													none		
1,727	60	679	100	X				X	X		X	3/1	none	X	
382	87	248	100	X				X	X	X	X	2/15	none		
937	48			X	X	X		X				4/15	none	X	
131	81	115	100									2/15	4/15	X	
485	90			X	X	X		X		X			none	X	
138	85			X	X								none		

Institution	Tuition and fees	Add'l out-of-state/district tuition	Books and supplies	Costs for campus residents			Costs for students at home		
				Room and board	Trans-portation	Other costs	Board only	Trans-portation	Other costs
American Academy McAllister Institute of Funeral Service	5,625		500				2,850	1,000	1,500
Audrey Cohen College	8,670		300				1,000	690	640
Bard College	21,509		550	6,520	400	450	3,232	600	600
Barnard College	20,324		520	8,374		850	660	630	830
Berkeley College	10,950		700	7,200					
Berkeley College of New York City	10,950		700						
Beth Hamedrash Shaarei Yosher Institute	3,800			1,200		2,000			1,600
Boricua College	‡ 5,925		450				6,515	560	844
Bramson ORT Technical Institute	6,130		360						
Briarcliffe: The College for Business and Technology	7,720		700				1,500	1,600	1,500
Broome Community College	‡ 1,990	1,890/—	600				750	600	750
Bryant & Stratton Business Institute									
Albany	‡ 6,589		750				1,600	450	1,100
Buffalo	‡ 6,192		750				2,241	450	1,305
Rochester	‡ 6,192		750						
Syracuse	6,780		900	3,800	450	1,305		450	1,305
Canisius College	12,926		450	5,825	430	700	1,500	430	630
Catholic Medical Center of Brooklyn and Queens School of Nursing	† 5,040		900				2,500		1,450
Cayuga County Community College	‡ 2,593	2,400/—	750				900	720	500
Cazenovia College	‡ 10,485		850	5,100	250	250	750	250	750
Central City Business Institute	5,400		600				1,500		
Central Yeshiva Tomchei Tmimim-Lubavitch	4,800			2,300					
City University of New York									
Baruch College	‡ 3,320	3,600/—	500				1,750	675	2,100
Borough of Manhattan Community College	‡ 2,590	576/—	500				1,802	675	2,100
Bronx Community College	‡ 2,610	576/—	500				1,802	675	2,100
Brooklyn College	‡ 3,387	3,600/—	500				1,802	675	2,100
City College	‡ 3,305	3,600/—	500				1,802	675	2,171
College of Staten Island	‡ 3,316	3,600/—	500				1,802	675	2,100
Hostos Community College	‡ 2,552	576/—	500				1,500	675	2,161
Hunter College	‡ 3,313	3,600/—	500		675	2,455	1,937	675	2,360
John Jay College of Criminal Justice	‡ 3,309	3,600/—	500				1,802	675	2,100
Kingsborough Community College	‡ 2,602	576/—	500				1,802	675	2,100
La Guardia Community College	‡ 2,612	576/—	500				1,802	675	2,100
Lehman College	‡ 3,320	3,600/—	500				1,802	675	2,100
Medgar Evers College	‡ 2,582	576/—	500				3,400	675	2,262
New York City Technical College	‡ 3,260	3,600/—	500				1,802	675	2,100
Queens College	‡ 3,393	3,600/—	500				1,802	675	2,100
Queensborough Community College	‡ 2,610	576/—	500				1,802	675	2,100
York College	‡ 3,292	3,600/—	600				1,835	676	2,262
Clarkson University	17,843		750	6,064	500	870	3,200		807
Clinton Community College	‡ 2,185	2,075/—	500				600	750	800
Cochran School of Nursing-St. John's Riverside Hospital	‡ 6,345		1,200				2,200	1,541	2,050
Colgate University	21,675		575	5,935	50	800			
College of Aeronautics	8,100		1,050				700	1,350	1,950
College of Insurance	13,090		550	8,200	175	1,110	3,300	480	1,110
College of Mount St. Vincent	13,060		500	6,240	150	850	1,500	600	850

†Figures are projected for 1996-97. ‡Figures are for 1995-96.

Total freshmen	Percent receiving aid	Freshmen judged to have need	Percent offered aid	Need-based Acad	Music/drama	Art	Athl	Non-need-based Acad	Music/drama	Art	Athl	Priority	Closing	Inst aid form	Notes
46	70							X					none		
122	85			X				X				8/15	none		
296	68	201	100	X	X	X		X	X	X		2/15	2/28		
531	60	276	100										2/1	X	
138	87			X				X					none		
													none	X	
500	95	288	100	X				X					none	X	
447	93			X		X		X			X		none		
1,426	60			X				X				4/1	none	X	
117	85	99	100	X				X				9/1	10/1		
													none		
													none		
187	95	159	100	X				X					none		
719	90	607	100	X			X	X			X	2/1	none	X	
4	34												none		
404	75			X				X				5/15	none		
364	91	255	100	X				X		X	X	3/1	none		
													none		
1,480	70			X				X					5/1		
3,009	85												none	X	
													none		
1,276	65	960	100	X	X	X		X	X	X		4/1	5/1		
939	80	715	99	X				X					5/15		
1,708	33											5/25	9/30		
907	95			X				X				6/1	none	X	
1,186	72			X				X				5/1	none		
1,624	80	1,461	85					X				6/1	none		
2,179	90											8/1	none		
													none		
585	75							X				6/30	none		
755	90											6/1	8/31		
2,050	87											5/15	none	X	
1,657	60							X				5/31	8/1		
2,101	92	1,500	100					X				5/1	7/12	X	
542	80											4/1	8/1		
645	92	499	100	X	X	X	X	X	X	X	X		none		
536	82			X				X				6/1	none		
													none		
729	50	306	100	X	X	X	X						2/1		
248	82	248	100	X				X				3/15	5/1		
		7	100	X				X					none		
217	89	172	100	X				X				3/15	none	X	

Institution	Tuition and fees	Add'l out-of-state/ district tuition	Books and supplies	Costs for campus residents			Costs for students at home		
				Room and board	Trans-portation	Other costs	Board only	Trans-portation	Other costs
College of New Rochelle									
New Rochelle	11,100		500	5,700	250	250	1,500	250	250
School of New Resources	‡ 4,162		500					250	250
College of St. Rose	11,174		800	5,856	500	1,600	2,000	500	1,000
Columbia University									
Columbia College	21,444		800	7,160		1,060	1,680	400	750
School of Engineering and Applied Science	21,444		800	7,160		1,060	1,680	400	700
School of General Studies	‡ 17,784		900				2,529	414	400
School of Nursing	‡ 23,075		1,600		800	1,200	2,730	800	1,200
Columbia-Greene Community College	‡ 2,178	2,066/—	450				1,320	900	950
Concordia College	11,400		600	5,310	350	850	715	350	850
Cooper Union	‡ 8,700		1,255	5,015	150	1,260	1,350	500	1,260
Cornell University	20,974		510	7,035		1,060			
Corning Community College	‡ 2,466	2,300/—	600				1,880	850	400
Culinary Institute of America	13,720		200		1,200	2,000	1,600	600	2,000
Daemen College	10,320		700	5,200	700	800		700	800
Darkei Noam Rabbinical College	‡ 4,150		300				1,800		3,000
Dominican College of Blauvelt	10,040		600	6,000	900	900	1,800	1,000	900
Dowling College	‡ 10,860		450		800	1,413	2,105	1,106	1,413
Dutchess Community College	‡ 2,095	2,000/—	560				1,785	850	750
D'Youville College	9,690		680	4,600	640	680	1,500	640	680
Eastman School of Music of the University of Rochester	18,245		600	6,930	650	700	2,670	650	700
Elmira College	17,950		450	5,880		550	1,500		550
Erie Community College									
City Campus	‡ 2,340	2,270/—	500				1,008	750	750
North Campus	‡ 2,340	2,270/—	500				1,380	750	750
South Campus	‡ 2,340	2,270/—	500				1,008	750	750
Eugene Lang College/New School for Social Research	17,065		750	8,862				600	975
Fashion Institute of Technology	‡ 2,510	3,150/—	1,200	5,174	600	1,050	1,600	800	900
Finger Lakes Community College	‡ 2,330	2,200/—	550				1,800	740	480
Five Towns College	8,650		650	4,800			2,500	2,100	2,100
Fordham University	16,015		600	7,250	600	1,735	1,850	775	3,450
Fulton-Montgomery Community College	‡ 2,284	2,150/—	500				1,800	600	500
Genesee Community College	‡ 2,472	250/—	550					680	550
Hamilton College	21,750		450	5,450	200	675			
Hartwick College	20,805		800	5,570	350	250	1,550	1,100	250
Helene Fuld College of Nursing	‡ 8,887		1,000				2,700	400	1,620
Herkimer County Community College	‡ 2,300	3,450/—	500				500	600	660
Hilbert College	8,900		600	4,450	400	660	1,500	500	660
Hobart and William Smith Colleges	21,370		600	6,315	200	600	1,500	300	
Hofstra University	‡ 12,360			6,180					
Holy Trinity Orthodox Seminary	‡ 1,400		100	1,400					
Houghton College	12,060		750	3,998	500	750	800	500	750
Hudson Valley Community College	‡ 2,031	2,600/—	550				1,700	900	800
Institute of Design and Construction	4,255		600					200	400
Interboro Institute	5,525		450				450	425	1,000
Iona College	† 12,490		600	7,200	580	1,220	1,700	1,000	1,220
Ithaca College	16,130		618	6,990		932			932
Jamestown Business College	6,000		600				525	1,845	1,427

†Figures are projected for 1996-97. ‡Figures are for 1995-96.

*Tuition and fees for Cornell Statutory Division:
$9,388 in-state, $18,262 out-of-state

Total freshmen	Percent receiving aid	Freshmen judged to have need	Percent offered aid	Need-based Acad	Need-based Music/drama	Need-based Art	Need-based Athl	Non-need-based Acad	Non-need-based Music/drama	Non-need-based Art	Non-need-based Athl	Priority	Closing	Inst aid form	Notes
148	84	136	100					X	X	X			none	X	
675	96	620	100					X	X				none	X	
260	84			X	X	X		X	X	X	X		3/1		
883	58												2/10		
278	64												2/10	X	
				X									5/30	X	
				X				X				1/1	none		
438	75							X				5/1	none		
133	92			X				X	X		X	3/31	4/15		
193	43	88	100	X				X				2/15	5/1		
3,204	65	1,585	100	X				X					2/15		
940	85							X				5/1	none	X	
				X				X					none		
541	91	364	100	X		X	X	X			X	2/15	none		
105	78	80	100	X			X	X			X	3/1	none	X	
463	80	236	100	X	X	X	X	X	X		X	5/1	none	X	
1,120	50			X				X				5/1	none	X	
286	88	192	100	X			X	X			X	4/15	none		
139	88	111	100		X			X	X			1/15	none	X	
296	90	227	100					X	X	X			none		
609	82											4/30	none		
				X								4/30	none		
981	53			X								4/30	none		
80	70			X				X				4/1	none	X	
1,994	77							X					3/15		
1,279	75							X	X	X	X	4/1	none	X	
														X	
1,096	79	965	99	X	X	X	X	X	X	X	X		2/1	X	
673	75			X				X				4/1	none		
1,434	75			X	X	X	X	X	X	X		3/1	5/1		
491	53	257	100										2/1	X	
451	88	309	100	X	X	X	X	X	X		X		2/15		
35	60	30	100	X				X					none		
963	80			X			X	X			X		4/1		
101	68			X				X				2/28	none		
494	69	311	100	X	X	X		X					2/15		
1,547	78	981	100	X				X	X	X	X	3/1	none		
295	94			X	X	X	X	X	X	X	X	3/15	none	X	
2,593	60			X								5/30	none		
94	60												none		
570	80			X									none		
593	83			X			X	X		X	X	4/15	none		
1,626	84	1,182	100	X	X			X	X			3/1	none		
144	98			X				X					none		

Institution	Tuition and fees	Add'l out-of-state/district tuition	Books and supplies	Costs for campus residents			Costs for students at home		
				Room and board	Transportation	Other costs	Board only	Transportation	Other costs
Jamestown Community College	‡ 2,900	2,600/—	600				2,500	500	550
Jamestown Community College: Olean	‡ 2,700	2,400/—	600				2,500	500	550
Jefferson Community College	‡ 2,286	1,992/—	600				1,500	310	500
Jewish Theological Seminary of America	7,440		500	4,000	400	5,000		450	2,500
Juilliard School	13,600		2,400	6,300	500	6,500	2,300	1,300	
Katharine Gibbs School									
Melville	‡ 8,546		550				1,100	1,315	1,053
New York	‡ 8,400		500					1,300	
Kehilath Yakov Rabbinical Seminary	4,000			2,000					
Keuka College	10,800		600	5,040	750	750	1,500	750	750
Laboratory Institute of Merchandising	10,950		440				1,500	1,500	1,500
Le Moyne College	12,750		300	5,390		1,000	700	250	300
Long Island College Hospital School of Nursing	7,498		1,100				2,500	911	1,863
Long Island University									
Brooklyn Campus	‡ 11,377		700	6,820	450	800	2,000	450	800
C. W. Post Campus	‡ 12,990		500	5,860	500	1,150	1,800	900	800
Southampton College	‡ 13,030		420	6,410	210	880	1,660	380	880
Machzikei Hadath Rabbinical College	5,000			1,800					
Manhattan College	15,400		500	7,350	500	1,000	1,800	800	1,000
Manhattan School of Music	16,330		650	9,000	1,000	1,000	4,000	1,000	1,000
Manhattanville College	16,745		550	7,680	400	700	3,070	1,000	700
Mannes College of Music	14,730		1,200		600	1,000	2,850	600	1,000
Maria College	5,270		600					500	500
Marist College	12,390		600	6,600	400	550	2,000	600	550
Marymount College	13,140		565	7,200	440	670	1,642	1,026	670
Marymount Manhattan College	† 11,650		400	6,000	600	1,000	1,750	600	1,000
Mater Dei College	6,225		700	4,005	150	800	1,500	300	800
Medaille College	9,950		800	4,600	1,050	1,000		1,050	1,000
Mercy College	7,200		500	6,600			1,500	700	800
Mesivta Torah Vodaath Seminary	‡ 4,665		200	4,500			2,175		
Mirrer Yeshiva Central Institute	4,400			1,000					
Mohawk Valley Community College	‡ 2,465	2,350/—	750	3,890	510	1,262	1,698	660	750
Molloy College	10,000		700				1,500	1,700	1,200
Monroe College	8,880		555				1,500	520	680
Monroe Community College	‡ 2,439	2,240/—	480				1,590	675	960
Mount St. Mary College	9,625		300	5,300	300	750	1,500	1,000	750
Nassau Community College	‡ 2,220	2,120/—	536				2,196	836	1,052
Nazareth College of Rochester	12,151		550	5,420	150	900	1,500	650	900
New York Institute of Technology	10,180		500	6,060	410	1,200	1,500	1,270	1,200
New York School of Interior Design	11,150		1,000				5,000	800	
New York University	20,756		450	7,856		1,000	1,500		
Niagara County Community College	‡ 2,354	1,125/—	536				750	650	650
Niagara University	13,032		500	5,388	300	650	1,500	500	650
North Country Community College	‡ 2,335	2,200/—	500				700	800	700
Nyack College	‡ 9,450		500	4,130	300	600		600	900
Ohr Somayach Tanenbaum Education Center	‡ 3,600		300	3,600	150	725	1,800	1,000	725
Olean Business Institute	5,380		500				1,600		
Onondaga Community College	‡ 2,326	4,460/2,030	540				1,647	750	450
Orange County Community College	‡ 2,085	2,000/—	525				2,340	535	465
Pace University	13,080		550	5,620	150	925	1,750	500	875
Parsons School of Design	17,585		1,200		800	1,200	1,800	600	1,200

†Figures are projected for 1996-97. ‡Figures are for 1995-96.

All aid		Need-based aid		Grants and scholarships								Financial aid deadlines		Inst aid form	Notes
				Need-based				Non-need-based							
Total freshmen	Percent receiving aid	Freshmen judged to have need	Percent offered aid	Acad	Music/ drama	Art	Athl	Acad	Music/ drama	Art	Athl	Priority	Closing		
2,019	80	1,437	100	X	X		X	X	X		X	3/1	none		
1,120	86			X				X				4/1	none	X	
37	68	17	100					X					3/1		
106	87			X	X			X	X				2/15	X	
													none		
													none		
202	95	191	100	X				X				3/1	none	X	
43	80	42	100	X									none		
414	95	310	100	X	X	X	X	X			X	2/15	4/15		
													none		
1,106	90			X	X	X	X	X	X	X	X		none		
686	77	438	86	X	X	X	X	X	X	X	X	2/1	5/15		
241	85			X				X		X	X		none	X	
													none		
617	91	432	100	X				X			X	2/15	4/15	X	
93	72	66	100	X	X			X	X			3/15	4/15	X	
								X	X	X				X	
25	90				X			X				5/15	none		
83	50											8/1	none		
844	77	605	100	X	X	X	X	X	X		X	3/15	none		
113	90	113	100	X		X	X	X	X	X	X	1/1	none	X	
271	93	148	100	X	X	X		X	X	X		2/15	4/1		
103	90	93	100	X			X	X			X	4/1	9/1		
90	74	65	100	X				X				5/1	none	X	
1,119	80							X			X		none		
1,326	85			X				X				4/15	none	X	
		130	100	X				X	X	X	X	4/15	none		
1,359	98	1,298	99										3/31		
4,263	70			X			X	X			X	5/1	none		
275	88	235	93	X				X				3/15	none	X	
				X	X	X		X	X	X		5/30	none	X	
304	89	250	100	X	X	X		X	X	X		3/1	none		
693	92							X			X	6/1	none		
29	40			X		X		X		X		7/1		X	
2,901	86	2,081	99	X				X	X				2/15		
1,598	65	1,452	100	X			X	X			X	4/1	none		
425	94	349	100	X	X		X	X	X		X	2/15	none	X	
346	85											5/30	none		
167	87			X	X		X	X				3/1	none		
													none		
													none		
2,104	80							X				2/15	none		
				X				X	X	X	X	5/1	none	X	
1,519	76	989	94	X	X		X	X	X		X	3/15	7/1		
387	73	266	98	X		X		X			X	4/1	none	X	

Institution	Tuition and fees	Add'l out-of-state/ district tuition	Books and supplies	Costs for campus residents			Costs for students at home		
				Room and board	Trans-portation	Other costs	Board only	Trans-portation	Other costs
Paul Smith's College	11,600		750	4,970	400	1,000	1,500	600	1,000
Phillips Beth Israel School of Nursing	† 8,200		1,000				4,170	950	1,300
Plaza Business Institute	5,225		600					900	1,800
Polytechnic University									
Brooklyn	18,030		479	4,700	1,200	1,307	2,430	705	1,245
Long Island Campus	18,030		457	4,700	1,200	1,286	1,315	705	1,245
Pratt Institute	16,400		2,000	7,385	500	650	1,966	500	650
Rabbinical Academy Mesivta Rabbi Chaim									
Berlin	4,750			2,900					
Rabbinical College Bobover Yeshiva									
B'nei Zion	3,600		400	3,000		500			500
Rabbinical College Ch'san Sofer of New									
York	‡ 4,000								
Rabbinical College of Long Island	‡ 6,300								
Rabbinical Seminary Adas Yereim	‡ 4,200								
Rabbinical Seminary of America	5,000			2,000					
Rensselaer Polytechnic Institute	19,652		1,305	6,375			1,500	1,175	
Roberts Wesleyan College	11,675		520	4,056	560	990	1,290	2,230	990
Rochester Business Institute	5,700		600				1,000	927	1,485
Rochester Institute of Technology	15,748		600	6,135	300	600	1,500	300	600
Rockland Community College	‡ 2,135	2,050/—	600				1,800	800	600
Russell Sage College	13,670		500	6,400	200	650	1,500	300	700
Sage Junior College of Albany	‡ 7,700		500	5,560	300	650	1,500	300	700
St. Bonaventure University	12,439		500	5,340	400	650	1,500	600	650
St. Francis College	‡ 6,910		500				2,250	450	1,125
St. John Fisher College	11,950		400	5,750	200	600	1,500	600	600
St. John's University 11,050	‡ 10,450		600				2,700	1,100	1,800
St. Joseph's College									
Brooklyn	8,116		600				1,600	1,000	600
Suffolk Campus	8,356		500				1,500	1,000	600
St. Joseph's Hospital Health Center									
School of Nursing	† 5,211		650		120	780	1,500	320	780
St. Lawrence University	20,685		650	6,130		1,000		300	1,000
St. Thomas Aquinas College	10,000		500	6,450	750	1,000	3,100	1,000	1,000
Sarah Lawrence College	21,976		600	7,830	350	725	2,300	200	
Schenectady County Community College	‡ 2,193	2,090/—	550				1,750	900	900
School of Visual Arts	13,220		1,435		735	1,815	2,525	735	1,815
Shor Yoshuv Rabbinical College	4,600			3,400					
Siena College	12,150		575	5,435	350	565	850	575	575
Skidmore College	20,895		545	6,110	250	700	2,695	250	700
State University of New York									
Albany	‡ 3,956	4,900/—	700	4,836	300	908	1,500	525	919
Binghamton	‡ 3,909	4,900/—	750	4,654	400	709	1,468	740	1,054
Buffalo	‡ 4,060	4,900/—	800	5,235	690	784	2,200	690	784
Oswego	‡ 3,746	4,900/—	500	5,230	600	900		600	900
Purchase	‡ 3,765	4,900/—	775	5,224	315	1,204	1,800	609	900
Stony Brook	‡ 3,759	4,099/—	750	5,166	600	1,120	1,500	1,922	1,120
College of Agriculture and Technology									
at Cobleskill	‡ 3,635	5,100/—	500	5,240	200	600	1,500	550	600
College of Agriculture and Technology									
at Morrisville	‡ 3,510	5,100/—	600	5,080	350	600	1,600	2,700	1,000
College at Brockport	‡ 3,795	4,900/—	600	4,660	290	950	1,702	1,125	950
College at Buffalo	‡ 3,720	4,900/—	670	4,660	675	775	1,800	675	775

†Figures are projected for 1996-97. ‡Figures are for 1995-96.

| All aid | | Need–based aid | | Grants and scholarships | | | | | | | | Financial aid deadlines | | Inst aid form | Notes |
| | | | | Need–based | | | | Non–need–based | | | | | | | |
Total freshmen	Percent receiving aid	Freshmen judged to have need	Percent offered aid	Acad	Music/drama	Art	Athl	Acad	Music/drama	Art	Athl	Priority	Closing		
417	85			X			X	X			X	2/28	none		
5	98	5	100	X				X					6/1	X	
188	95			X				X					none	X	
253	98			X				X				3/1	none	X	
92	98							X				3/1	none	X	
410	76	280	100	X		X		X		X		2/1		X	
													none		
963	85							X			X	2/15	none		
205	91				X	X	X	X	X	X	X	3/1		X	
													none		
1,647	80	1,315	87	X		X		X		X		3/15	none		
1,950	58			X				X				6/15	none		
156	90	129	100	X				X				3/1	none		
				X				X		X	X	3/15	4/15		
548	93	389	100	X				X	X		X	2/1		X	
344	88	223	100	X			X	X			X	2/15	none	X	
341	98	284	100	X				X				3/1	none		
2,296	82	1,636	100	X	X			X	X	X	X	4/1	none		
84	90			X				X				2/25	none	X	
176	78	138	100	X				X				2/25	none	X	
60	85	53	100					X				5/1	none		
572	76	392	100	X				X					2/15		
295	70			X		X		X		X	X	3/1	none		
230	63	161	100	X	X								2/1		
779	70			X			X	X				5/1	none		
385	74	358	100	X		X		X		X		3/1	none		
594	86	435	100	X			X	X			X		2/1	X	
610	39	233	92	X					X				2/1		
1,914	74	1,105	100	X			X	X				4/19	none		
1,790	92			X	X	X		X	X	X		3/1	none		
2,685	75	1,693	100	X	X	X		X	X	X	X	3/1	none		
1,350	80			X	X			X	X			3/1	none		
431	86	229	100	X	X	X		X	X	X		2/15	none	X	
1,763	53							X			X	3/1	none		
925	65			X				X				4/1	none		
1,501	85							X				3/1	none		
990	97	637	100					X	X	X		3/15	none	X	
1,240	68			X	X	X	X	X	X	X	X	3/15	none	X	

Institution	Tuition and fees	Add'l out-of-state/district tuition	Books and supplies	Costs for campus residents			Costs for students at home		
				Room and board	Trans-portation	Other costs	Board only	Trans-portation	Other costs
College at Cortland	‡ 3,842	4,900/—	650	5,050	400	845	1,575	700	520
College of Environmental Science and Forestry	‡ 3,714	4,900/—	700		200	450	3,150	600	450
College at Fredonia	‡ 3,919	4,900/—	620	4,670	671	800	1,920	981	800
College at Geneseo	‡ 3,859	4,900/—	600	4,500	650	650	1,690	650	650
College at Old Westbury	‡ 3,678	3,900/—	675	5,072	750	1,210	404	1,675	990
College at Oneonta	‡ 3,778	4,900/—	450	5,650	350	1,000	575	1,000	950
College at Plattsburgh	‡ 3,743	4,900/—	650	4,326	462	1,099	750	1,512	1,095
College at Potsdam	‡ 4,339	4,900/—	500	4,900	300	700	985	600	700
College of Technology at Alfred	‡ 3,537	5,100/—	600	4,684	448	700	700	858	700
College of Technology at Canton	‡ 3,617	5,100/—	600	4,800	400	700	1,660	1,500	700
College of Technology at Delhi	‡ 3,625	5,100/—	500	4,902	500	1,000	1,000	860	1,000
College of Technology at Farmingdale	‡ 3,621	5,100/—	600	5,491	600	800	2,100	1,200	800
Empire State College	‡ 3,846	4,900/—	600				2,730	405	1,500
Health Science Center at Brooklyn	‡ 3,634	4,900/—	685		330	820	1,155	520	820
Health Science Center at Syracuse	‡ 3,615	4,900/—	515		615	700	1,540	835	700
Health Sciences Center at Stony Brook	‡ 3,759	4,900/—	1,000	5,166	600	1,120	1,500	1,922	1,120
Institute of Technology at Utica/Rome	‡ 3,799	4,900/—	620	5,250	400	1,000	750	1,100	1,390
Maritime College	‡ 3,715	4,900/—	500	5,000	400	1,200			
New Paltz	‡ 3,751	4,900/—	600	4,898	600	900	1,500	900	900
Stenotype Academy	‡ 7,400		800					600	4,000
Suffolk County Community College									
Eastern Campus	‡ 2,228	2,100/—	550				975	1,248	1,048
Selden	‡ 2,228	2,100/—	550				975	1,248	1,048
Western Campus	‡ 2,228	2,100/—	550				975	1,248	1,048
Sullivan County Community College	‡ 2,356	2,000/—	600				700	650	700
Syracuse University	17,148		820	7,210	400	700	3,300	530	700
Talmudical Institute of Upstate New York	4,250			3,300					
Talmudical Seminary Oholei Torah	‡ 4,600			2,200					
Taylor Business Institute	‡ 6,250						1,053	385	
Technical Career Institutes	6,066		800				2,168	375	1,280
Tompkins-Cortland Community College	‡ 2,586	2,400/—	600				1,500	1,200	1,200
Torah Teminah Talmudical Seminary	5,625			3,000					
Trocaire College	‡ 5,800		700				1,500	700	600
Ulster County Community College	‡ 2,346	2,220/—	600				1,500	700	480
Union College	20,995		450	6,330	250	794	1,650	250	478
United States Merchant Marine Academy	4,900								
United States Military Academy	0		1,195			2,564			
University of Rochester	20,105		525	6,930	225	1,000	1,725	700	1,000
University of the State of New York: Regents College	‡ 565								
Utica College of Syracuse University	14,206		600	5,272	500	782	1,235	550	782
Utica School of Commerce	† 6,450		750						
Vassar College	21,150		650	6,310	300	600	2,600	150	600
Villa Maria College of Buffalo	‡ 6,480		637				1,700	650	650
Wadhams Hall Seminary-College	† 4,560		500	4,000	500	500	2,700	1,500	1,000
Wagner College	15,300		625	5,800	625	1,100	1,800	525	1,100
Webb Institute	0		750	5,800	2,000	600			
Wells College	17,400		600	5,900		500	1,300		500
Westchester Business Institute	10,494		675					2,052	1,339
Westchester Community College	‡ 2,282	2,050/—	600				2,000	900	500

†Figures are projected for 1996-97. ‡Figures are for 1995-96.

Total freshmen	Percent receiving aid	Freshmen judged to have need	Percent offered aid	Acad	Music/drama	Art	Athl	Acad	Music/drama	Art	Athl	Priority	Closing	Inst aid form	Notes
1,111	79			X				X	X	X		4/1	none		
76	85	70	100	X				X				3/1	none	X	
899	68	449	100	X	X								none		
1,210	50			X				X	X				2/15		
				X				X					4/26	X	
1,094	61	698	100	X			X	X				5/1	none		
950	66	568	99	X	X	X		X	X	X		4/15	none		
665	84	449	100					X	X				none		
1,574	75							X	X		X	5/1	none		
659	85			X				X				3/15	none	X	
829	60											3/1	none		
1,609	68			X				X				4/1	none	X	
				X									4/1		
													none		
				X				X							
				X				X				5/1	none	X	
183	90	183	100	X				X				4/15	none	X	
750	85	420	100									3/15	4/15		
													none		
													none		
2,409	75	1,383	100	X	X	X		X	X	X	X		2/15		
14	20												none		
													none		
													none		
				X									none		
551	80			X				X					none		
145	86	116	100	X				X				3/31	none		
1,429	80	346	100	X				X				6/1	none		
515	60	307	100									2/1		X	
260	30											1/15	3/15		
1,227	91	708	100	X	X	X		X	X	X		2/1	none		
				X				X				7/1	none	X	
323	89	252	100	X				X				2/15	none		
													none		
636	58												1/1		
76	80							X	X	X		5/1	none		
3	100	3	100					X					8/1		
377	91	235	100	X	X		X	X	X		X	4/1	5/1	X	
24	29	3	100	X				X					7/1		
100	95	79	100	X				X				2/15	5/1		
298	91							X				6/1	none		
2,725	30			X				X	X	X			none	X	

Institution	Tuition and fees	Add'l out-of-state/ district tuition	Books and supplies	Room and board	Trans-portation	Other costs	Board only	Trans-portation	Other costs
				Costs for campus residents			Costs for students at home		
Wood Tobe-Coburn School	9,030		1,165				4,200	1,200	2,110
Yeshiva Derech Chaim	4,000		400	1,500					
Yeshiva Gedolah Zichron Moshe	4,400		200	2,600	200	3,003	1,833	200	2,000
Yeshiva Shaar Hatorah	‡ 7,200 (comprehensive)								
Yeshiva University	13,980		550	6,550	750	800	2,660	750	720

North Carolina

Institution	Tuition and fees	Add'l out-of-state/ district tuition	Books and supplies	Room and board	Trans-portation	Other costs	Board only	Trans-portation	Other costs
Alamance Community College	‡ 578	3,959/—	600				1,900	750	800
Anson Community College	‡ 579	3,960/—	650				1,500	1,300	900
Appalachian State University	‡ 1,627	6,842/—	250	2,980	1,000	1,000	1,500	1,000	1,000
Asheville Buncombe Technical Community College	‡ 582	3,959/—	600				788	1,247	500
Barber-Scotia College	5,294		600	3,220	1,000	1,000	1,500	800	1,000
Barton College	8,984		850	4,066	1,150	1,100	1,200	1,350	1,100
Beaufort County Community College	‡ 575	3,959/—	600				1,500	3,023	2,197
Belmont Abbey College	10,896		500	5,346	900	1,280	2,500	1,600	960
Bennett College	7,290		750	3,334	1,500	1,000	2,300	400	1,500
Bladen Community College	‡ 588	3,959/—	300				500	800	1,550
Blue Ridge Community College	‡ 587	3,959/—	750				750	2,358	1,386
Brevard College	9,125		500	3,900	500	700	1,500	500	700
Brunswick Community College	† 581	3,959/—	390		1,184	660	1,500	1,184	660
Caldwell Community College and Technical Institute	‡ 578	3,959/—	475				2,300	1,000	1,305
Campbell University	9,533		700	3,550	550	2,112	2,525	1,630	1,677
Cape Fear Community College	‡ 575	3,959/—	460				1,000	1,200	770
Carteret Community College	‡ 582	3,959/—	500				1,100	900	200
Catawba College	10,726		600	4,250	660	1,200	2,000	990	1,200
Catawba Valley Community College	‡ 575	3,959/—	800					900	800
Cecils College	5,005		400				1,503	911	1,080
Central Carolina Community College	‡ 584	3,959/—	666				3,237	1,342	1,204
Central Piedmont Community College	‡ 572	3,960/—	800				2,400	2,400	1,500
Chowan College	9,650		500	3,780	490	1,000	1,800	1,250	3,500
Cleveland Community College	‡ 587	3,950/—	490				2,000	750	1,175
Coastal Carolina Community College	‡ 578	3,959/—	450				1,800	450	800
College of The Albemarle	† 624	4,241/—	500				3,150	783	1,000
Craven Community College	† 584	3,949/—	750					612	918
Davidson College	19,631		600	5,636		916	2,529		916
Davidson County Community College	‡ 579	3,959/—	800				1,500	1,237	463
Duke University	21,041		686	6,558	571	1,135	2,950	600	1,135
Durham Technical Community College	† 575	3,959/—	600				1,125	900	562
East Carolina University	‡ 1,673	6,842/—	550	3,620	600	1,007	1,700	600	1,007
East Coast Bible College	4,845		600	2,700					
Edgecombe Community College	‡ 578	3,959/—	700				2,550	925	1,800
Elizabeth City State University	‡ 1,410	6,040/—	220	3,232	700	945	2,000	900	945
Elon College	10,667		650	4,170	690	1,293	1,875	640	978
Fayetteville State University	‡ 1,334	6,842/—	350	2,850	190	750	1,500	185	750
Fayetteville Technical Community College	‡ 569	3,959/—	700				1,700	495	525
Forsyth Technical Community College	‡ 572	3,959/—	650				2,500	750	750
Gardner-Webb University	8,990		500	4,470	570	900		650	450
Gaston College	‡ 587	3,959/—	1,000					1,000	1,000
Greensboro College	9,550		600	4,040	815	1,000	1,500	650	820

†Figures are projected for 1996-97. ‡Figures are for 1995-96.

| All aid | | Need–based aid | | Grants and scholarships | | | | | | | | Financial aid deadlines | | Inst aid form | Notes |
| Total freshmen | Percent receiving aid | Freshmen judged to have need | Percent offered aid | Need–based | | | | Non–need–based | | | | | | | |
				Acad	Music/drama	Art	Athl	Acad	Music/drama	Art	Athl	Priority	Closing		
359	84							X					none		
													none		
670	75							X				4/15	5/1		
1,071	29	674	76	X				X				5/15	none	X	
													none		
2,206	44	850	100	X	X	X	X	X	X	X	X	2/1	none		
		392	100	X				X				3/1	none		
155	94							X			X	5/1	none		
285	88	192	100	X	X	X	X	X	X	X	X	5/1	none	X	
125	26			X				X				7/1	none		
139	70	89	100	X			X	X			X	3/1	none		
183	84			X				X	X				4/15	X	
													none		
695	15	394	100	X				X	X			6/30	none	X	
387	69	210	100					X	X	X	X	4/15	none		
312	35	189	92	X			X	X			X	6/30	none	X	
765	25	270	100	X				X				5/1	none		
529	85	476	100					X	X		X	3/15	none		
1,226	25			X				X				3/15	none		
290	60			X								8/1	none	X	
316	98	215	100					X	X		X	3/1	none	X	
1,287	12	500	75	X				X			X	7/1	none		
													none		
537	40	400	100	X								3/31	none		
				X								4/1	6/1		
294	98			X				X				4/1	none		
262	20			X				X					none		
850	75	500	100	X								5/15	none	X	
407	35			X	X			X	X	X		5/1	none	X	
438	35	237	88	X			X	X			X	4/1	none		
432	63			X				X	X	X	X		2/15		
303	35	165	100	X				X				5/30	none	X	
1,640	48	682	100	X				X	X	X	X	2/1	none		
1,306	50	700	100										none	X	
				X	X	X	X	X	X	X	X	4/15	none		
38	58	27	89					X	X	X		5/15	5/15	X	
754	40	100	88	X			X	X			X		7/15		
382	91							X	X		X	4/1	none		
907	59	412	100	X	X		X	X	X		X	4/1	none	X	
389	74			X	X		X	X	X		X	4/1	5/1		
3,279	50	1,351	100	X				X				6/1	8/1		
		386	100	X				X				5/1	8/1		
370	65			X	X		X	X	X		X	4/1	none		
													none		
200	86			X	X	X		X	X	X		3/1	none		

Institution	Tuition and fees	Add'l out-of-state/district tuition	Books and supplies	Costs for campus residents			Costs for students at home		
				Room and board	Transportation	Other costs	Board only	Transportation	Other costs
Guilford College	14,390		550	5,270	450	700	2,550	450	700
Guilford Technical Community College	‡ 585	3,959/—	650				1,500	1,000	1,000
Halifax Community College	‡ 576	3,959/—	377				1,500	1,031	896
Haywood Community College	‡ 577	3,959/—	450				2,358	1,326	1,305
High Point University	9,740		740	4,820	600	1,200	1,500	1,250	1,400
Isothermal Community College	‡ 588	3,959/—	450				1,500	402	783
James Sprunt Community College	‡ 581	3,959/—	600				1,800	1,350	800
John Wesley College	4,540		300		100	1,500	1,500	765	1,500
Johnson C. Smith University	7,452		755	3,253	950	1,260	1,500	618	773
Johnston Community College	‡ 578	3,959/—	450				1,500	900	900
Lees-McRae College	† 9,670		600	3,530		550	1,500	400	550
Lenoir Community College	‡ 584	3,959/—	500				1,500	680	540
Lenoir-Rhyne College	11,416		400	4,324	600	400	2,500	600	400
Livingstone College	6,090		650	3,450	850	1,000	2,000	1,000	1,000
Louisburg College	† 7,905		550	4,240	750	1,125	1,500	1,500	1,125
Mars Hill College	8,900		600	3,800	800	800	2,000	800	800
Martin Community College	‡ 575	3,959/—	400				3,024	990	400
Mayland Community College	‡ 587	3,959/—	750				980	893	1,087
McDowell Technical Community College	‡ 576	3,959/—	600				2,358	693	1,386
Meredith College	7,420		550	3,570	320	1,200	1,500	325	1,200
Methodist College	10,600		790	4,200	600	2,150	2,200	650	4,820
Mitchell Community College	‡ 582	3,959/—	550				1,860	800	1,575
Montgomery Community College	‡ 578	3,959/—	800				1,500	2,000	1,900
Montreat College	9,656		500	3,752	500	1,000		900	1,000
Mount Olive College	8,175		700	3,215	600	900	1,500	600	900
Nash Community College	‡ 578	3,959/—	750				1,200	1,200	800
North Carolina Agricultural and Technical State University	‡ 1,532	6,842/—	600	3,400	487	1,246	1,500	487	1,246
North Carolina Central University	‡ 1,512	6,842/—	530	3,154	465	1,40_	1,622	761	1,400
North Carolina School of the Arts	‡ 2,064	7,851/—	595	3,706		1,565	1,680		755
North Carolina State University	‡ 1,666	8,116/—	650	3,700	400	1,100	2,000	400	1,100
North Carolina Wesleyan College	7,150		750	4,500	432	863	2,000	757	938
Pamlico Community College	‡ 572	3,959/—	380				3,180	1,370	1,630
Peace College	6,640		600	5,020	900	1,350	1,500	900	1,350
Pembroke State University	‡ 1,325	6,440/—	598	2,800	606	900	1,800	898	700
Pfeiffer College	9,260		675	4,000	1,235	900	2,000	720	900
Piedmont Bible College	5,040		500	2,990	550	600	754	850	600
Piedmont Community College	‡ 584	3,959/—	500				2,000	1,200	750
Pitt Community College	‡ 585	3,959/—	600				3,600	3,200	400
Queens College	12,310		610	5,380	1,000	900	1,950	1,260	900
Randolph Community College	‡ 564	3,959/—	500				2,385	832	1,305
Richmond Community College	‡ 584	3,959/—	600				1,800	900	750
Roanoke Bible College	4,340		425	2,930	500	350	2,100	1,075	350
Roanoke-Chowan Community College	‡ 581	3,959/—	360				1,500	1,620	150
Robeson Community College	‡ 578	3,959/—	600				1,800	1,041	75
Rockingham Community College	‡ 584	3,959/—	450				2,500	1,040	1,000
Rowan-Cabarrus Community College	‡ 599	3,959/—	500				1,500	645	525
St. Andrews Presbyterian College	11,595		500	5,050	200	850		1,011	1,750
St. Augustine's College	5,982		475	3,708	1,166	1,300	2,088	980	1,300
St. Mary's College	7,880		300	6,500		1,000	1,300	600	1,000
Salem College	11,835		500	6,970	800	1,895	1,700	800	1,865
Sampson Community College	‡ 587	3,959/—	600				1,800	800	900

†Figures are projected for 1996-97. ‡Figures are for 1995-96.

Total freshmen	Percent receiving aid	Freshmen judged to have need	Percent offered aid	Acad	Music/drama	Art	Athl	Acad	Music/drama	Art	Athl	Priority	Closing	Inst aid form	Notes
	All aid		Need-based aid	Need-based				Non-need-based				Financial aid deadlines			
291	78	198	97	X	X	X		X	X	X			3/1		
3,814	13			X				X				5/31	none		
													none		
442	27			X				X				4/1	none	X	
486	56	320	88	X				X			X	3/1	none		
													none		
383	45			X				X				7/1	none	X	
4	65			X	X			X	X			5/1	none		
385	91			X				X	X		X	4/15	none		
													none	X	
147	85			X	X		X	X	X		X	3/15	5/1		
												6/1	7/15		
134	60			X	X		X	X	X		X	3/1	8/15	X	
158	95			X	X		X	X	X		X	5/1	5/15		
348	80			X	X		X	X	X		X	3/15	none	X	
308	80	268	100	X	X		X	X	X		X	4/15	none	X	
306	50			X				X				5/1	none	X	
													none	X	
													none		
420	40	215	100	X	X	X		X	X	X		2/15	none	X	
336	87	336	100	X				X	X				7/1		
				X	X	X		X	X	X		4/1	none	X	
62	52	189	100	X				X				7/15	none	X	
157	98			X			X	X			X	3/15	none		
142	100	108	100					X	X	X	X	3/1	none	X	
181	9			X				X					none	X	
		947	96	X	X	X		X	X	X	X	5/15	none		
553	69							X					3/31		
163	91				X	X		X	X	X		3/15	none		
3,528	43	1,201	100	X				X			X	3/1	none		
175	81	169	100	X				X				3/1	none		
													none		
188	72	96	100	X	X	X		X	X	X	X	4/1	none		
418	45			X	X	X	X	X	X	X	X	4/15	none		
146	95	105	99					X	X		X	5/1	none		
													none		
				X			X	X				3/15	8/24		
183	90	135	100	X	X	X	X	X	X	X	X	3/1	none		
164	15			X								5/1	none		
80	65			X				X				7/15	none	X	
49	100	41	100					X	X			4/1	5/1		
301	68			X				X					none		
													none		
466	25	148	100	X				X				4/15	none	X	
													none		
174	99	125	100	X	X	X	X	X	X	X	X	4/1	7/1		
550	80							X	X		X	4/30	7/1		
72	37	25	100	X				X	X	X		4/1	none	X	
148	93	94	100	X	X	X		X	X			3/1	none	X	
													none		

Institution	Tuition and fees	Add'l out-of-state/ district tuition	Books and supplies	Costs for campus residents			Costs for students at home		
				Room and board	Trans-portation	Other costs	Board only	Trans-portation	Other costs
Sandhills Community College	‡ 578	3,959/—	650				1,800	1,300	750
Shaw University	† 5,946		600	3,824	500	500		600	500
Southeastern Baptist Theological Seminary	2,200		500						
Southeastern Community College	‡ 589	3,959/—	425				1,500	1,300	900
Southwestern Community College	‡ 575	3,959/—	500				1,500	1,650	630
Stanly Community College	‡ 578	3,959/—	525				2,000	800	1,200
Surry Community College	‡ 578	3,959/—	600				1,500	1,238	660
Tri-County Community College	‡ 573	3,959/—	300				600	200	450
University of North Carolina									
Asheville	‡ 1,658	6,040/—	600	3,480	1,203	750	1,500	1,124	680
Chapel Hill ♪ 14,696	‡ 1,640	8,116/—	600	4,340	136	1,100	1,500	100	1,100
Charlotte	‡ 1,618	6,842/—	650	3,326	950	1,100	1,800	1,650	1,100
Greensboro	‡ 1,868	7,956/—	630	3,491	392	1,422	3,744	816	1,188
Wilmington	‡ 1,664	6,842/—	500	4,035	800	1,090	2,240	560	1,090
Vance-Granville Community College	‡ 584	3,959/—	475				1,500	900	400
Wake Forest University	18,500		600	5,200	350	950	1,600	350	950
Wake Technical Community College	‡ 566	3,959/—	600				2,500	1,100	1,050
Warren Wilson College	11,915		500	3,152	560	738	1,500	900	738
Wayne Community College	‡ 584	3,959/—	600				1,500	1,100	400
Western Carolina University	‡ 1,545	6,842/—	200	2,840	525	756	1,666	940	840
Western Piedmont Community College	‡ 579	3,959/—	525				1,500	825	1,200
Wilkes Community College	‡ 581	3,959/—	750				1,500	908	660
Wilson Technical Community College	‡ 578	3,959/—	800				2,200	800	2,500
Wingate University	11,050		600	3,850	700	950		700	900
Winston-Salem State University	‡ 1,351	6,040/—	600	3,225	551	2,100	1,100	476	2,100
North Dakota									
Bismarck State College	‡ 1,761	2,592/—	600	2,330	400	1,600	1,380	635	1,365
Dickinson State University	‡ 1,856	2,806/—	618	2,212	1,000	1,000	1,740	1,000	1,000
Fort Bethold Community College	1,820		400				3,800	600	800
Jamestown College	8,420		400	3,080	250	400	775	450	450
Little Hoop Community College	1,160		175					650	875
Mayville State University	‡ 1,920	2,806/420	600	2,572	600	2,000		600	2,000
Medcenter One College of Nursing	2,690		990		585	1,000	1,934	585	1,000
Minot State University	‡ 1,960	2,974/446	600	2,049	500	1,401	1,776	500	1,401
North Dakota State College of Science	‡ 1,701	2,592/—	400	2,090	500	1,255	1,500	500	500
North Dakota State University									
Bottineau	‡ 1,757	2,592/—	600	2,340	600	1,200	1,000	600	1,200
Fargo	‡ 2,310	3,524/—	600	2,854	270	2,000		500	2,000
Standing Rock College	‡ 1,870		500				1,350	1,000	1,125
Trinity Bible College	‡ 5,140		500	3,084	1,130	1,754	1,500	400	1,400
Turtle Mountain Community College	‡ 1,176		380				1,200	1,200	3,240
United Tribes Technical College	‡ 2,740		600	2,400	450	1,880	700	600	1,880
University of Mary	‡ 7,000		500	2,750	800	815		800	815
University of North Dakota									
Grand Forks	‡ 2,428	3,524/—	500	2,840	500	1,300	1,500	500	1,300
Lake Region	‡ 1,794	2,592/—	550	2,430	500	1,500	1,200	500	1,500
Williston	‡ 1,758	2,592/—	600	1,080	550	500	1,500	550	500
Valley City State University	‡ 1,893	2,806/420	600	2,400	641	1,359	500	641	1,359

†Figures are projected for 1996-97. ‡Figures are for 1995-96.

All aid		Need-based aid		Grants and scholarships								Financial aid deadlines		Inst aid form	Notes
				Need-based				Non-need-based							
Total freshmen	Percent receiving aid	Freshmen judged to have need	Percent offered aid	Acad	Music/drama	Art	Athl	Acad	Music/drama	Art	Athl	Priority	Closing		
492	40			X	X	X		X	X	X		6/1	none	X	
532	95	505	100	X	X	X	X					4/30	none	X	
				X				X			X	4/1	none		
													none		
				X				X					5/1	none		
408	50			X				X				6/1	none	X	
250	44			X				X				5/31	none		
397	69	157	100	X			X	X	X	X	X	3/1	none		
3,315	56	1,080	98	X				X	X		X	3/1	none		
1,686	47	995	100	X				X			X	4/1	none		
1,821	52	846	94	X	X	X	X	X	X		X	3/1	none	X	
1,412	52	629	99	X	X	X	X	X	X	X	X	3/15	none		
793	50			X				X				7/15	none		
966	69	275	100	X				X	X	X	X	3/1	none		
520	18			X				X				8/1	none	X	
194	59			X				X				3/15	4/1	X	
													none		
1,161	63	359	93	X	X	X	X	X	X	X	X	3/31	none	X	
155	35							X				5/15	none		
335	23	185	81	X	X	X		X	X	X		8/1	none	X	
469	30			X									none		
382	85	252	100	X				X	X	X	X	3/15	none	X	
456	77			X	X		X	X	X	X	X	5/15	none		
858	75							X	X		X	4/15	none		
340	82							X	X	X	X	2/1	none	X	
288	100			X	X		X	X	X		X	6/1	none		
78	100	55	100	X									8/20	X	
													none		
				X								5/1	none	X	
568	66			X	X	X	X	X	X		X	4/15	none		
919	80	500	100	X	X		X	X	X		X	4/14	none		
178	75			X	X		X	X			X	4/15	none		
1,619	66			X	X		X	X				3/15	4/15	X	
													none		
132	95			X				X	X			3/1	none		
				X									5/1	X	
													none	X	
													none		
1,649	50	841	100					X	X	X	X	4/15	none		
490	84	253	100	X		X		X			X	4/15	none		
466	60			X		X		X			X	4/15	none		
188	89	161	100	X	X	X	X	X	X	X	X	4/15	none		

Institution	Tuition and fees	Add'l out-of-state/district tuition	Books and supplies	Costs for campus residents			Costs for students at home		
				Room and board	Trans-portation	Other costs	Board only	Trans-portation	Other costs
Ohio									
Academy of Court Reporting	‡ 1,725								
Antioch College	† 17,832		400	3,796	400	700		400	700
Antonelli College	8,010		1,500		1,408			1,408	1,000
Art Academy of Cincinnati	10,625		1,200				2,000	1,140	590
Ashland University	12,900		600	5,001	399	1,333	1,500	1,387	1,333
Baldwin-Wallace College	12,765		500	4,740	250	250	1,700	250	250
Belmont Technical College	‡ 2,099	495/—	495				1,593	1,138	1,028
Bluffton College	11,250		500	4,641		700		700	800
Bohecker's Business College	‡ 4,200								
Bowling Green State University									
Bowling Green	‡ 3,954	4,558/—	618	3,622	460	1,320	2,232	1,200	1,320
Firelands College	‡ 3,014	4,558/—	600					720	1,511
Bradford School	7,320		900						
Bryant & Stratton Business Institute:									
Cleveland West	6,720		900						
Bryant & Stratton College	6,850		800						
Capital University	14,200		520	4,000	120	670	630	540	1,510
Case Western Reserve University	17,235		585	4,860		1,210			1,210
Cedarville College	8,586		648	4,716		1,110	1,500		450
Central Ohio Technical College	‡ 2,286	1,170/—	700				550	1,200	2,300
Central State University	‡ 2,895	3,537/—	604	4,575	1,452	1,929		1,739	
Chatfield College	‡ 4,605		488				760	580	1,460
Cincinnati Bible College and Seminary	5,680		500	3,450	500	1,600	1,536	1,200	1,600
Cincinnati College of Mortuary Science	8,330		750					750	375
Cincinnati State Technical and Community College	‡ 2,872	2,852/—	700				1,700	450	500
Circleville Bible College	5,340		400	3,802	450	910	1,800	450	910
Clark State Community College	‡ 2,304	2,284/—	585				1,500	630	750
Cleveland College of Jewish Studies	4,965		150						
Cleveland Institute of Art	12,675		1,100	4,650	520	800	1,700	1,575	800
Cleveland Institute of Music	16,178		700	5,056	750	750		750	750
Cleveland State University	‡ 3,386	3,332/—	600	4,176	410	1,222	1,500	525	1,192
College of Mount St. Joseph	‡ 10,600		600	4,750	400	600	1,830	650	600
College of Wooster	23,230 (comprehensive)		500		150	500			
Columbus College of Art and Design	11,520		1,800	5,700	350	800	3,500	400	800
Columbus State Community College	2,087	2,448/—	650				1,950	800	750
Cuyahoga Community College									
Eastern Campus	1,733	2,869/563	675				1,503	600	1,053
Metropolitan Campus	1,733	2,869/563	675				1,503	525	1,053
Western Campus	1,733	2,869/563	675				1,503	600	1,053
David N. Myers College	‡ 7,200		600					814	1,035
Davis College	‡ 6,000		700				1,995	900	1,800
Defiance College	12,950		500	3,780	400	1,140	1,730	1,300	1,140
Denison University	19,470		500	5,160		600	1,500		600
DeVry Institute of Technology: Columbus	6,560		560				1,926	2,035	1,894
Edison State Community College	‡ 2,010	1,740/—	744				3,500	809	500
Franciscan University of Steubenville	10,870		600	4,700	1,400	1,000	2,000	1,400	1,000
Franklin University	4,880		520				4,560	650	400
God's Bible School and College	3,910		400	3,050	800	800	800	1,100	1,275
Heidelberg College	15,140		530	4,840	500	500		500	500
Hiram College	16,090		400	4,936		900	1,860	500	900

†Figures are projected for 1996-97. ‡Figures are for 1995-96.

| All aid | | Need-based aid | | Grants and scholarships | | | | | | | | Financial aid deadlines | | Inst aid form | Notes |
| Total freshmen | Percent receiving aid | Freshmen judged to have need | Percent offered aid | Need-based | | | | Non-need-based | | | | | | | |
				Acad	Music/drama	Art	Athl	Acad	Music/drama	Art	Athl	Priority	Closing		
134	77	97	100	X				X				3/1	none	X	
85	80												none		
34	95							X		X		4/1	none		
702	98	355	100					X	X	X	X	3/15	none	X	
651	95	470	100					X	X	X		3/1	none	X	
								X					none		
243	100	197	100	X	X	X		X	X	X		5/1	none		
3,273	55			X				X	X	X	X	2/15	4/1		
								X	X			4/1	none	X	
165	85												none		
230	75	125	100					X					none		
120	80	101	100	X				X					none		
510	95	428	100	X	X			X	X			2/15	none		
732	94	519	100	X	X	X		X	X	X		2/1	none	X	
626	84	381	100	X				X	X		X	3/1	none	X	
422	50			X				X				4/15	none	X	
75	65	25	100	X								7/15	none	X	
200	95			X	X			X	X			5/1	none	X	
88	50	41	100									7/1	none		
				X				X			X	3/15	none		
29	95			X	X								none		
				X			X	X				7/15	none		
5	1	3	100										none	X	
99	74	78	100	X		X		X		X		3/15	none		
59	90	37	100	X	X			X	X			3/1	none	X	
1,071	52			X				X	X	X	X	4/15	none		
339	93	149	100					X	X	X		4/15	none		
522	97	325	100	X				X	X			2/15	none		
307	88										X	5/1	none	X	
4,739	36			X				X				4/1	none		
807	26			X	X	X	X	X					none		
				X	X	X	X	X	X	X	X		none		
1,182	45			X	X	X	X	X	X	X	X		none		
250	80			X				X				4/30	none		
67	71							X					none		
													none		
701	95	354	100	X	X	X		X	X	X		4/1	none		
								X					none		
								X			X	6/15	none		
248	85	168	100	X				X	X			3/15	none		
				X				X				3/30	none		
62	79			X	X			X	X			6/1	none		
241	95	195	100	X				X	X			3/1	none		
203	88	199	100	X	X	X		X	X	X		3/1	none	X	

Institution	Tuition and fees	Add'l out-of-state/district tuition	Books and supplies	Costs for campus residents			Costs for students at home		
				Room and board	Trans-portation	Other costs	Board only	Trans-portation	Other costs
Hocking Technical College	‡ 2,016	2,001/—	780		325	1,200	1,000	1,850	510
ITT Technical Institute: Youngstown	‡ 6,426		1,050				2,358	2,181	1,386
Jefferson Community College	‡ 1,710	690/150	600				1,500	496	400
John Carroll University	13,122		600	5,550	800	450	2,500	1,600	450
Kent State University									
East Liverpool Regional Campus	‡ 2,942	4,084/—	525				1,645	885	1,315
Kent	‡ 4,084	4,084/—	560	3,834	700	1,370		980	1,370
Salem Regional Campus	‡ 2,942	4,084/—	600				1,800	900	1,500
Stark Campus	‡ 2,942	4,084/—	560				1,745	940	1,370
Trumbull Campus	‡ 2,942	4,084/—	560				1,730	940	1,484
Tuscarawas Campus	‡ 2,942	4,084/—	580					980	1,385
Kenyon College	22,010		830	3,820	160	380			
Kettering College of Medical Arts	5,588		643		588		588	1,037	
Lake Erie College	12,950		500	4,815	1,390	1,900	1,500	1,390	1,900
Lakeland Community College	‡ 1,876	3,035/425	600				1,600	1,030	1,055
Lima Technical College	‡ 2,175	2,115/—	900				2,000	820	450
Lorain County Community College	‡ 2,174	3,195/450	580				1,500	500	950
Lourdes College	7,700		550				2,050	910	730
Malone College	10,765		450	4,300	400	800	1,000	640	640
Marietta College	15,490		450	4,410	460	390	430	460	
Marion Technical College	2,252	1,656/—	600				1,800	1,200	850
McGregor School of Antioch University	8,820		400					400	
Miami University									
Hamilton Campus	‡ 3,052	5,430/—	550				2,260	896	1,420
Middletown Campus	‡ 3,052	5,430/—	500				1,800	890	1,198
Oxford Campus	‡ 4,810	5,430/—	550	4,210	330	1,118	2,260	896	1,118
Miami-Jacobs College	6,675		700				2,000	1,000	2,500
Mount Union College	13,880		450	3,760	1,000	1,000	2,130	1,000	550
Mount Vernon Nazarene College	9,240		600	3,720	610	970	1,710	400	900
MTI Business College	5,095		799						
Muskingum Area Technical College	‡ 2,220	690/150	675						
Muskingum College	10,285		600	4,280	400	800		400	800
North Central Technical College	‡ 2,331	2,331/—	705				1,530	1,500	990
Northwest State Community College	‡ 2,670	2,340/—	660				750	1,230	450
Northwestern College	‡ 4,275		600		720	1,053		1,440	1,053
Notre Dame College of Ohio	11,130		650	4,095	550	700	1,890	850	700
Oberlin College	21,576		575	6,174		525	2,900		525
Ohio Dominican College	8,910		600	4,570	350	800	1,900	780	800
Ohio Institute of Photography and Technology	9,600		1,400						
Ohio Northern University	17,970		540	4,500	360	525	1,600	360	525
Ohio State University									
Agricultural Technical Institute	‡ 3,156	6,540/—	525		700	3,000	1,863	1,162	1,034
Columbus Campus	‡ 3,273	6,540/—	798	4,484	411	1,767	1,929	928	1,751
Lima Campus	‡ 3,156	6,540/—	525				1,991	810	400
Mansfield Campus	‡ 3,156	6,540/—	525				550	1,100	2,335
Marion Campus	‡ 3,156	6,540/—	525				1,040	1,135	2,600
Newark Campus	‡ 3,156	6,540/—	525				495	1,188	2,276
Ohio University									
Athens	‡ 3,861	4,239/—	615	4,260	456	1,152	2,166	1,848	1,206
Chillicothe Campus	‡ 2,880	4,140/—	615					1,848	
Eastern Campus	‡ 2,880	4,140/—	390					1,995	

†Figures are projected for 1996-97. ‡Figures are for 1995-96.

Total freshmen	Percent receiving aid	Freshmen judged to have need	Percent offered aid	Acad	Music/drama	Art	Athl	Acad	Music/drama	Art	Athl	Priority	Closing	Inst aid form	Notes
				Need-based				Non-need-based				Financial aid deadlines			
165	76			X				X				3/31	none		
												9/29	none		
532	42			X				X				6/1	none	X	
847	85	655	100	X				X				3/1	none		
121	68			X				X				2/15	none		
2,782	70			X				X	X	X	X	2/15	4/1		
								X				2/15	none		
700	45			X				X				2/15	none		
				X	X	X		X	X	X		3/15	none		
249	66			X				X				2/15	none		
441	60	178	93					X					2/15		
70	100	66	100	X				X				4/1	none	X	
				X	X	X		X	X	X		3/1	none	X	
				X	X	X	X	X	X	X	X	3/1	none		
509	53			X				X					none		
4,604	34	870	99		X			X				8/15	none		
78	50			X				X				3/1	none	X	
411	98	386	100	X	X		X	X	X		X	3/1	7/31	X	
317	94	267	100	X				X	X	X		3/1	none	X	
1,126	65	240	98	X				X				7/1	none	X	
													none		
454	54			X				X				2/15	none		
468	23			X		X		X				2/15	none		
3,244	54	1,107	98	X				X	X	X	X	2/15	none		
134	85			X									none		
533	90	407	100	X				X	X	X		4/1	none	X	
379	98	308	100	X	X		X	X	X		X	4/15	none	X	
													none		
507	78			X				X				5/1	7/15		
284	96	257	100	X				X	X	X		3/15	8/1	X	
436	53	240	75	X				X				4/1	none		
544	58							X				6/1	none	X	
910	75	675	100					X				4/1	none		
76	100	64	100	X				X					none		
668	75							X	X				2/1	X	
211	100	199	100					X			X	6/1	none		
													none		
737	92	570	100	X	X	X		X	X	X		5/1	7/31	X	
		130	100	X				X				5/1	none		
5,794	60			X	X	X		X	X	X	X	2/15	none		
352	60			X	X	X		X	X	X		4/1	none		
344	60			X	X			X	X	X		4/1	none		
248	62			X				X				4/1	none		
435	40			X				X				4/1	none		
3,413	79	1,415	100	X				X	X	X	X	2/15	4/1		
425	70			X				X					4/1	X	

Institution	Tuition and fees	Add'l out-of-state/ district tuition	Books and supplies	Costs for campus residents			Costs for students at home		
				Room and board	Trans- portation	Other costs	Board only	Trans- portation	Other costs
Lancaster Campus	‡ 2,880	4,140/—	500					400	
Southern Campus at Ironton	‡ 2,658	114/—	600				1,896	1,800	
Zanesville Campus	‡ 2,880	4,140/—	500					2,049	489
Ohio Valley Business College	3,085		550					450	
Ohio Wesleyan University	18,228		550	5,994		500	1,750		500
Otterbein College	14,358		400	4,569	210	720		1,250	550
Owens Technical College									
Findlay Campus	1,916	1,656/—	615				1,800	1,000	800
Toledo	‡ 1,808	1,548/—	615				1,800	1,000	800
Pontifical College Josephinum	6,495		350	4,220		2,500	550		2,150
Rabbinical College of Telshe	‡ 4,750			2,300	400	1,000			
RETS Tech Center	5,495		700				1,100	900	945
Shawnee State University	‡ 2,763	1,866/—	525		945	2,919	2,914	945	2,919
Sinclair Community College	1,395	2,025/720	774				1,854	465	2,000
Southeastern Business College	† 4,920		750					475	1,296
Southeastern Business College	† 5,240		900					2,064	3,000
Southeastern Business College	† 4,660		185						
Southern Ohio College	‡ 6,190		500				1,250	600	
Southern State Community College	† 2,574	2,164/—	600				1,500	750	
Southwestern College of Business	‡ 3,600								
Stark Technical College	‡ 2,393	900/—	740				1,500	770	798
Stautzenberger College	† 7,000		700					300	100
Terra Community College	‡ 2,088	2,982/—	675					928	400
Tiffin University	8,700		600	4,200	700	1,300	2,200	750	1,250
Union Institute	5,522		500					480	
University of Akron									
Akron	‡ 3,384	5,049/—	578	4,062	840	1,298	2,110	1,260	1,190
Wayne College	‡ 3,384	4,880/—	578				2,110	1,260	1,190
University of Cincinnati									
Access Colleges	‡ 3,918	5,955/—	678	4,881	123	2,823	2,157	462	2,694
Cincinnati *15,247*	‡ 3,918	5,955/—	678	4,698	123	2,823	2,157	462	2,694
Clermont College	‡ 2,961	4,284/—	520						
Raymond Walters College	‡ 3,339	5,082/—	660				2,095	450	2,616
University of Dayton	13,640		600	4,430	300	800	1,700	300	500
University of Findlay	13,112		550	5,210	400	650	1,000	300	
University of Rio Grande	‡ 2,976	4,296/—	700	4,221	400	1,500	2,000	2,025	1,500
University of Toledo	‡ 3,588	5,009/—	690	4,476	1,047	2,727	800	1,047	2,727
Urbana University	9,980		500	4,350	150	508	2,450	150	508
Ursuline College	10,920		450	4,330	450	950	3,000	850	850
Virginia Marti College of Fashion and Art	8,565		800				2,700	500	1,700
Walsh University	10,200		500	4,760	500	1,090		1,800	2,090
Washington State Community College	‡ 2,340	2,295/—	538				3,756	400	1,084
West Side Institute of Technology	5,200		750				2,043	1,008	1,386
Wilberforce University	‡ 7,350		550	3,900	970	1,490	1,760	970	1,800
Wilmington College	11,910		500	4,370	250	450	1,500	400	200
Wittenberg University	18,228		400	4,718		800			
Wright State University									
Dayton	‡ 3,429	3,429/—	650	4,356	600	1,000		1,310	1,000
Lake Campus	‡ 3,069	3,429/—	650					1,200	1,000
Xavier University *19,080*	12,950		650	5,480	600	650	1,700	600	650
Youngstown State University	3,366	3,636/1,620	500	4,200	375	950	1,800	900	950

†Figures are projected for 1996-97. ‡Figures are for 1995-96.

All aid		Need-based aid		Grants and scholarships								Financial aid deadlines		Inst aid form	Notes
				Need-based				Non-need-based							
Total freshmen	Percent receiving aid	Freshmen judged to have need	Percent offered aid	Acad	Music/drama	Art	Athl	Acad	Music/drama	Art	Athl	Priority	Closing		
													none		
													none		
								X				3/15	none		
92	80											4/15	8/1		
495	83	323	100	X	X	X		X	X	X		3/1	none	X	
395	90	348	100					X	X	X		3/1	none		
1,299	40											3/15	none		
2,907	40						X	X				3/15	none		
8	95							X				6/30	none		
													none	X	
546	85			X	X	X	X	X	X	X	X	6/15	none		
2,689	38	994	87	X	X	X		X	X	X	X	4/15	none	X	
														X	
														X	
													none		
													none		
								X	X	X	X	7/1	none		
277	46			X				X				5/1	none	X	
														X	
1,859	40							X				3/30	none	X	
232	94	173	100	X			X	X			X	3/31	none		
		13	92									9/1	none	X	
2,926	63	1,864	100	X				X	X	X	X	3/1	none	X	
				X				X				3/1	none	X	
2,026	27	739	93	X				X	X	X	X	3/1	none		
2,485	44	1,196	92	X	X			X	X	X	X	3/1	none		
				X	X			X	X	X		3/1	none		
491	40			X				X					none		
1,621	90	1,268	100	X				X	X	X	X	3/31	none	X	
568	95	400	94	X	X		X	X	X		X	4/1	8/1		
2,057	80			X	X	X	X	X	X		X	3/15	none		
2,922	80	1,735	98	X	X	X	X	X	X	X	X	3/15	none	X	
263	100			X				X	X		X	5/1	none		
				X		X		X				3/15	none		
													none		
313	82	276	100	X			X	X			X	3/1	8/1	X	
306	72			X				X					none		
													none		
376	95			X				X				4/30	6/1		
278	92			X	X			X	X			3/1	6/1	X	
587	91	394	100	X	X	X		X	X	X		3/15	none		
1,960	58			X				X	X	X	X	4/1	none		
190	45			X				X				3/1	none		
701	81							X	X	X	X	2/15	none		
2,045	65			X	X	X	X	X	X	X	X	3/1	none	X	

Institution	Tuition and fees	Add'l out-of-state/ district tuition	Books and supplies	Costs for campus residents			Costs for students at home		
				Room and board	Trans- portation	Other costs	Board only	Trans- portation	Other costs
Oklahoma									
Bacone College	3,590		600	3,270	500	500	3,500	1,000	1,000
Bartlesville Wesleyan College	7,600		650	3,700	1,000	1,000	2,600	1,000	1,000
Cameron University	‡ 1,620	2,205/—	690	2,430	950	900	1,500	950	900
Carl Albert State College	‡ 1,095	1,800/—	700		1,391	1,678		1,391	1,388
Connors State College	‡ 1,118	1,800/—	750	1,944	900	1,000	1,500	900	1,000
East Central University	‡ 1,607	2,205/—	400	2,068	653	1,148	1,548	930	1,148
Eastern Oklahoma State College	‡ 1,050	1,800/—	500	2,224	250	500	1,250	900	500
Langston University	‡ 1,653	2,205/—	450	2,560					
Mid-America Bible College	4,346		600	3,236	1,525	2,405	2,896	1,125	2,405
Murray State College	‡ 1,185	1,800/—	544	2,430	512	1,984	1,650	922	1,984
National Education Center: Spartan School of Aeronautics	9,000		660		648	1,330	2,000	639	1,260
Northeastern Oklahoma Agricultural and Mechanical College	‡ 1,095	1,800/—	400	2,214	300	675			675
Northeastern State University	‡ 1,575	2,205/—	350	3,144	540	625			625
Northern Oklahoma College	‡ 1,110	1,800/—	500	2,120	500	1,200	1,500	1,600	1,000
Northwestern Oklahoma State University	‡ 1,562	2,205/—	500	2,036	500	1,000	1,000	600	1,200
Oklahoma Baptist University	7,141		560	3,270	800	1,350	750	1,000	1,350
Oklahoma Christian University of Science and Arts	7,510		500	3,400	1,050	900	1,900	1,050	900
Oklahoma City Community College	‡ 1,128	1,800/—	675					900	600
Oklahoma City University	8,175		400	3,990	110	960	2,560	809	960
Oklahoma Panhandle State University	‡ 1,532	2,205/—	1,400	1,940	400	1,800	1,500	1,000	1,000
Oklahoma State University									
Oklahoma City	‡ 1,439	2,145/—	450				3,500	850	1,800
Stillwater	‡ 2,002	3,465/—	810	3,344	200		1,880	1,100	1,250
Okmulgee	‡ 1,350	2,145/—	517	2,258	800	800	400	800	800
Oral Roberts University	9,604		800	4,653	1,313	1,525	1,700	1,313	1,525
Phillips University	6,850		750	3,904			2,204	480	640
Redlands Community College	‡ 1,207	1,800/—	400					700	1,200
Rogers State College	‡ 1,204	1,800/—	600					1,000	1,200
Rose State College	‡ 1,065	1,800/—	625					225	125
St. Gregory's College	5,860		567	3,764	340	958	1,690	546	958
Seminole Junior College	‡ 1,035	1,800/—	324	1,880	90	175	1,500	510	855
Southeastern Oklahoma State University	‡ 1,554	2,205/—	600	2,612	850	1,124	1,752	971	1,355
Southern Nazarene University	7,670		400	3,998	400	1,200	2,400	800	1,200
Southwestern College of Christian Ministries	‡ 3,850		400	2,700	600	1,000	800	600	1,000
Southwestern Oklahoma State University	‡ 1,664	2,368/—	500	2,016	800	900	1,650	800	900
Tulsa Junior College	‡ 1,020	1,838/—	588				1,783	840	750
University of Central Oklahoma	‡ 1,545	2,205/—	500	2,391	600	1,400		600	1,400
University of Oklahoma									
Health Sciences Center	‡ 1,909	3,915/—	875				1,650	882	1,566
Norman	‡ 1,967	3,465/—	765	4,593	1,586	1,586	2,625	1,586	1,586
University of Science and Arts of Oklahoma	‡ 1,493	2,205/—	850	2,070	250	1,200		350	1,200
University of Tulsa	12,940		1,200	4,260	1,000	1,350	1,800	1,650	850
Western Oklahoma State College	‡ 1,035	1,800/—	450					900	400

20,750

†Figures are projected for 1996-97. ‡Figures are for 1995-96.

Total freshmen	Percent receiving aid	Freshmen judged to have need	Percent offered aid	Acad	Music/drama	Art	Athl	Acad	Music/drama	Art	Athl	Priority	Closing	Inst aid form	Notes
138	86			X		X	X				X	5/1	none		
111	90			X	X		X	X	X		X	3/1	none	X	
884	71	792	88	X	X	X	X	X	X	X	X	5/15	none	X	
													none		
499	60			X			X	X	X		X	2/28	5/1	X	
551	75			X	X	X	X	X	X	X	X	4/15	none	X	
1,331	70			X				X	X		X	3/1	none		
480	70							X	X		X	3/1	5/1		
87	95	73	99					X	X			5/1	none		
466	60			X	X	X	X	X	X	X	X	4/15	none		
													none		
850	80							X	X	X	X		3/1		
631	35			X	X	X	X	X	X	X	X	3/1	none		
													none		
435	74	352	100	X	X	X	X	X	X	X	X	3/1	none		
309	86	199	100					X	X	X	X	4/15	7/31	X	
2,028	50							X				7/1	none	X	
354	93	158	100	X	X	X	X	X	X	X	X	3/1	none		
206	73	187	100	X	X		X	X	X		X	8/25	none	X	
2,437	30			X				X				7/1	none		
2,470	62	1,105	100	X	X	X	X	X	X	X	X	3/1	none		
755	60			X								3/1	none	X	
668	85	440	100					X	X	X	X	4/1	none		
76	76			X	X		X	X	X	X	X	3/1	none		
533	64			X	X	X	X	X	X	X	X	3/30	none	X	
1,800	49	350	100	X				X	X	X		4/15	none		
5,786	30			X	X	X	X	X	X	X	X	5/1	none		
165	90			X	X	X	X	X	X	X	X	6/1	none		
													none		
537	60	300	100	X	X	X	X	X	X	X	X	4/1	11/1	X	
													none		
30	80							X	X			8/1	none		
850	52			X	X		X	X	X	X	X	3/1	none		
4,661	28			X				X				3/1	none		
1,482	30			X	X	X	X	X	X	X	X	6/1	none		
				X				X				3/1	none		
2,699	79	1,094	95	X				X	X	X	X	3/1	none		
267	87	151	100	X	X	X		X	X	X	X	3/15	none		
545	92	407	100					X	X	X	X	4/1	none	X	
754	60			X	X	X	X					3/30	none		

Institution	Tuition and fees	Add'l out-of-state/district tuition	Books and supplies	Costs for campus residents			Costs for students at home		
				Room and board	Transportation	Other costs	Board only	Transportation	Other costs
Oregon									
Bassist College	9,060		1,300	4,000	600	900	1,500	650	900
Blue Mountain Community College	1,152	2,304/—	450					600	900
Central Oregon Community College	‡ 1,580	4,050/450	750	3,900	900	800	1,800	900	800
Chemeketa Community College	1,530	5,400/—	1,200					840	840
Clackamas Community College	1,513	3,735/—	600				2,061	840	720
Clatsop Community College	1,260	2,340/—	780				3,560	1,200	1,000
Concordia University	11,030		500	3,500	400	900	1,500	400	900
Eastern Oregon State College	‡ 2,898		600	3,760	650	950	1,800	650	950
Eugene Bible College	4,767		600	2,904	1,000	600	1,800	750	1,000
George Fox College	14,520		400	4,620	350	800	2,100	350	800
Lane Community College	‡ 954	2,250/—	795				1,600	396	1,800
Lewis & Clark College	17,740		600	5,370	300	900	1,730		900
Linfield College	15,086		600	5,000	200	1,100	1,500	75	1,100
Linn-Benton Community College	1,530	3,915/—	900				1,665	1,104	831
Marylhurst College	‡ 9,000		500				1,760	600	1,688
Mount Angel Seminary	7,135		400	6,250	1,000	1,000			
Mount Hood Community College	‡ 1,485	4,995/—	621				1,038	816	540
Multnomah Bible College	7,100		440	3,390	700	900		900	900
Northwest Christian College	10,115		500	4,137		1,530	1,900		1,530
Oregon Health Sciences University	‡ 4,707	6,195/—	500		1,250	1,000	2,050	1,250	1,000
Oregon Institute of Technology	‡ 3,060	6,300/—	810	3,875	600	2,130	1,800	200	2,130
Oregon Polytechnic Institute	6,100		750				2,000	550	750
Oregon State University	‡ 2,898	6,804/—	780	3,760	470	2,388	2,056	300	1,746
Pacific Northwest College of Art	10,572		900					600	4,500
Pacific University	15,598		550	4,514	500	1,174	1,500	500	1,174
Portland Community College	1,641	4,050/—	855				1,845	855	795
Portland State University	‡ 3,183	6,633/—	750		657	1,098	1,800	657	846
Reed College	21,490		500	6,000	720	450	1,500		450
Rogue Community College	‡ 1,146	2,592/648	450				1,800	925	825
Southern Oregon State College	‡ 2,949	5,481/—	660	3,969	440	1,750	1,800	750	1,750
Southwestern Oregon Community College	1,554	3,060/—	600				1,800	840	510
Treasure Valley Community College	‡ 1,845	2,205/—	420	3,580	750	750		750	750
Umpqua Community College	1,530	2,970/—	600				1,125	900	1,170
University of Oregon									
Eugene	‡ 3,381	7,812/—	630	3,949	275	1,202	1,654	275	1,202
Robert Donald Clark Honors College	‡ 3,381	7,812/—	570	3,949	275	1,550	1,600	275	1,550
University of Portland	14,400		600	4,480	500	600	1,800	500	600
Warner Pacific College	9,642		450	3,750	370	1,250	1,600	370	1,250
Western Baptist College	10,740		600	4,550	800	1,100		1,100	1,100
Western Oregon State College	‡ 2,985	5,481/—	720	3,839	1,000	1,240	1,980	800	1,240
Willamette University	18,390		400	5,070	200	510	1,800	1,200	710
Pennsylvania									
Academy of the New Church	‡ 4,440			3,729		1,400			
Albright College	17,395		750	5,180	200	900	2,000	580	900
Allegheny College	18,720		600	4,670	460	550	1,500	460	500
Allentown College of St. Francis de Sales	11,110		500	5,260		800	2,210		800
Alvernia College	10,700		650	4,600	600	700	1,800	800	700
American Institute of Design	‡ 15,315		815						
Antonelli Institute of Art and Photography	8,125		1,500					1,500	1,400

†Figures are projected for 1996-97. ‡Figures are for 1995-96.

| All aid | | Need-based aid | | Grants and scholarships | | | | | | | | Financial aid deadlines | | Inst aid form | Notes |
| Total freshmen | Percent receiving aid | Freshmen judged to have need | Percent offered aid | Need-based | | | | Non-need-based | | | | Priority | Closing | | |
				Acad	Music/drama	Art	Athl	Acad	Music/drama	Art	Athl				
48	76	10	100	X				X				6/1	none	X	
					X		X		X		X	3/30	none		
730	33	301	100	X				X	X	X		2/28	none		
	60			X							X	4/1	9/4		
3,902	45			X	X	X	X	X	X	X	X	3/1	none		
				X				X	X	X		6/1	none		
85	95	80	100				X	X	X		X	5/1	none	X	
397	80	293	100	X	X			X	X			2/15	none		
107	79	70	100	X	X			X	X			5/1	none	X	
346	86	271	100					X	X			3/1	8/1		
								X	X		X	3/15	none		
458	74	251	100	X	X	X		X	X			3/1	none	X	
445	89	311	100	X	X	X		X	X			2/1	none	X	
737	50			X				X		X	X	4/1	none	X	
28	65			X	X	X			X	X		6/1	none	X	
4	75			X				X					none	X	
3,900	30			X	X	X	X	X	X	X	X	4/1	none	X	
220	90			X	X			X	X			3/1	none	X	
56	93			X				X				4/15	none		
												3/1	none		
256	80			X			X	X				3/1	none		
													none	X	
20	63	10	100					X		X		4/1	none		
243	87	227	87	X	X	X		X	X	X		2/15	none		
				X			X				X	3/1	none		
827	34			X				X	X	X	X	3/1	none		
355	45	188	84									2/1	3/1	X	
1,129	70			X				X				4/1		X	
824	70	530	100	X			X	X	X	X		3/1	none		
				X				X	X	X	X	2/8	none		
900	80			X				X	X	X	X	4/1	none		
649	60	525	100	X	X	X	X	X	X	X	X	3/1	none		
4,200	45			X				X	X	X	X	3/1	none		
				X				X	X	X	X		2/1		
412	88	261	100	X				X	X		X	3/1	none	X	
197	96			X	X			X	X		X	2/15	none		
643	73			X	X		X	X	X	X		3/1	none		
455	85	309	100	X	X	X		X	X	X		2/1	6/1		
312	96	264	100	X				X	X			3/1	5/1		
565	95	451	100	X	X	X		X	X	X		2/15	none		
270	90	191	100	X	X			X	X			2/1	none	X	
175	85	158	100					X				4/1	8/30		
													none		
120	84	75	100									8/1	none		

Institution	Tuition and fees	Add'l out-of-state/ district tuition	Books and supplies	Costs for campus residents			Costs for students at home		
				Room and board	Transportation	Other costs	Board only	Transportation	Other costs
Art Institute of Pittsburgh	‡ 9,740		490	6,240			2,315	360	1,220
Baptist Bible College of Pennsylvania	‡ 6,686		500	4,070	500	600	2,320	1,766	600
Beaver College	14,870		400	6,120	250	550	1,500	450	550
Berean Institute	‡ 3,800		400				1,500	600	500
Bloomsburg University of Pennsylvania	‡ 3,915	4,974/—	500	2,984	385	1,350	500	788	1,350
Bradley Academy for the Visual Arts	9,180		800						
Bryn Mawr College	20,610		550	7,370	300	800	2,900	450	800
Bucknell University	20,360		600	5,060	200	1,380	2,350	2,710	1,380
Bucks County Community College	‡ 1,998	6,540/4,260	500				750	2,100	1,350
Business Institute of Pennsylvania	4,625		900						
Butler County Community College	‡ 1,500	3,000/1,500	600				1,500	1,100	900
Cabrini College	12,155		690	6,695	315	1,150	1,650	2,300	1,150
California University of Pennsylvania	‡ 4,136	4,974/—	600	3,890	400	1,500	1,000	1,227	1,030
Cambria-Rowe Business College	4,800		600						
Carlow College	11,064		500	4,692		1,200	1,500	240	760
Carnegie Mellon University	19,500		450	5,850	700	1,000	2,140	500	1,840
Cedar Crest College	15,210		550	5,525	550	550	1,600	550	550
Central Pennsylvania Business School	6,290		900		700	800	1,650	950	800
Chatham College	‡ 14,196		400	5,440		850	952	582	850
Chestnut Hill College	‡ 11,825		700	5,445	450	350	1,600	700	350
Cheyney University of Pennsylvania	‡ 3,729	4,974/—	400	4,040	675	1,000	1,500	675	700
CHI Institute	7,515								
C.H.I/RETS Campus	6,975		375						
Churchman Business School	5,440		850					775	
Clarion University of Pennsylvania	‡ 4,054	4,974/—	575	2,974	660	834	1,450	660	850
College Misericordia	12,880		550	6,050	500	400	1,500	600	400
Community College of Allegheny County									
Allegheny Campus	‡ 2,111	3,840/1,920	500				1,500	722	950
Boyce Campus	‡ 1,906	3,584/1,792	600				1,550	700	1,000
North Campus	‡ 1,907	3,584/1,792	600				1,500	722	950
South Campus	‡ 1,906	3,584/1,792	600				1,500	722	950
Community College of Beaver County	1,980	4,475/2,280	600				1,500	900	1,000
Community College of Philadelphia	2,235	4,140/2,070	545				2,034	560	3,604
Computer Tech	16,550								
Consolidated School of Business	9,825		1,500						
Curtis Institute of Music	675		250				1,100	540	1,795
Dean Institute of Technology	9,720		515					1,000	
Delaware County Community College	1,920	5,580/1,740	400				1,000	800	1,200
Delaware Valley College	13,708		550	5,490	500	1,050	1,800	1,000	1,050
Dickinson College	20,410		600	5,560	250	1,000	1,650	250	1,000
Drexel University	14,472		500	7,348	350	1,500		780	1,500
DuBois Business College	5,425		500	4,800					
Duff's Business Institute	11,760		400		900	6,450		900	3,250
Duquesne University	13,396		400	5,803	550	450	1,500	550	450
East Stroudsburg University of Pennsylvania	‡ 4,017	4,974/—	600	3,448	350	1,100		1,000	1,700
Eastern College	12,220		400	5,230	200	970	1,400	900	800
Edinboro University of Pennsylvania	‡ 3,924	4,974/—	500	3,578	300	1,174		1,500	1,680
Electronic Institutes									
Middletown	† 5,750		225				2,400	1,554	1,280
Pittsburgh	8,070		700						
Elizabethtown College	16,040		500	4,700	150	600	1,500	350	600

†Figures are projected for 1996-97. ‡Figures are for 1995-96.

| All aid | | Need-based aid | | Grants and scholarships | | | | | | | | Financial aid deadlines | | Inst aid form | Notes |
| Total freshmen | Percent receiving aid | Freshmen judged to have need | Percent offered aid | Need-based | | | | Non-need-based | | | | Priority | Closing | | |
				Acad	Music/drama	Art	Athl	Acad	Music/drama	Art	Athl				
770	80			X				X		X			none	X	
202	85			X				X					4/1		
468	76	214	100	X				X	X	X	X	3/15	4/15		
													none		
1,066	80			X	X		X	X				3/15	5/1		
													none		
344	53	187	100										1/15	X	
910	60	445	100					X	X	X	X	1/1	1/11		
				X	X	X		X	X	X		5/1	none		
														X	
925	55			X			X	X				4/16	5/1		
225	74	187	100	X				X				4/1	none		
918	69			X				X	X		X	4/1	none		
83	95												8/1	X	
180	94			X			X	X		X	X	5/1	none	X	
1,237	74	849	98	X	X	X		X	X	X		2/15	none		
170	93	149	100					X				5/1	none	X	
298	47			X				X				5/1	none	X	
109	84	99	100					X	X			3/15	5/1	X	
115	70	81	100	X				X				3/15	none		
258	86	231	85	X				X	X		X	4/1	none		
325	88												9/20		
100	67	80	93	X				X					8/1		
1,333	76	1,187	85					X	X	X	X	3/15	5/1		
294	95	241	100	X				X				3/1	4/1	X	
1,100	24			X				X			X	5/1	none		
1,022	24	572	100	X				X	X	X	X	5/1	none		
													none		
1,102	24			X				X	X	X	X	5/1	none	X	
				X			X	X				5/1	none	X	
				X				X	X	X			5/1	X	
23	100							X					3/3	X	
3,304	30			X								5/1	none		
499	82	307	100	X				X				3/1	4/1		
534	67	334	100										2/15		
973	76							X	X	X	X	5/1	none		
101	80			X				X					8/1		
														X	
1,413	80	930	99	X				X	X		X		5/1		
855	75							X			X		3/15		
229	92	190	100					X	X				none	X	
1,361	83	1,105	100	X			X	X			X		5/1		
												8/1	none		
57	90											8/1	none		
453	93	343	100	X	X	X		X	X			3/1	4/1	X	

Institution	Tuition and fees	Add'l out-of-state/district tuition	Books and supplies	Costs for campus residents			Costs for students at home		
				Room and board	Transportation	Other costs	Board only	Transportation	Other costs
Erie Business Center	† 2.600		300	1,000		100			100
Franklin and Marshall College	26,400 (comprehensive)		590		200	880			2,680
Gannon University	12,384		700	4,710	750	600	1,800	700	600
Geneva College	10,864		600	4,600	750	1,150		850	1,150
Gettysburg College	21,616		300	4,760	200	500	1,900	500	300
Gratz College	6,450							370	
Grove City College	6,478		650	3,652	250	350	2,242	800	350
Gwynedd-Mercy College	11,794		500	6,000	250	600	900	600	600
Harcum College	‡ 8,615		400	4,884		1,500			1,500
Harrisburg Area Community College	† 1,654	3,005/1,502	600				1,800	884	790
Haverford College	21,030		750	6,810		1,070			
Holy Family College	10,050		675				2,400	1,248	1,500
Hussian School of Art	7,750		800				2,400	900	1,600
Immaculata College	11,580		550	5,855	650	1,050		2,250	800
Indiana University of Pennsylvania	‡ 3,891	4,974/—	500	3,138	500	1,500	1,200	500	900
Johnson Technical Institute	‡ 6,036		450		100	1,386	2,358	952	1,386
Juniata College	16,480		450	4,700	250	420	1,650	600	420
Keystone College	‡ 9,256		600	5,240	350	1,226	1,650	1,588	726
King's College	12,980		580	5,780	350	1,795	1,845	740	1,430
Kutztown University of Pennsylvania	‡ 3,940	4,974/—	734	3,250		1,750		900	1,750
La Roche College	9,912		600	5,198	100	1,000	1,500	300	1,000
La Salle University	14,090		500	6,720		1,000	1,000		2,000
Lackawanna Junior College	6,920		516				2,750	402	2,400
Lafayette College	20,390		600	6,335	100	925		750	850
Lancaster Bible College	8,220		500	3,650	550	1,510	1,850	860	1,510
Lansdale School of Business	6,000		425						
Laurel Business Institute	1,975		260						
Lebanon Valley College of Pennsylvania	15,360		450	4,940	100	770	1,500	800	770
Lehigh Carbon Community College	2,040	3,780/1,890	866				1,500	1,280	640
Lehigh University	20,500		750	6,020	150	1,130	3,060	450	1,130
Lincoln Technical Institute	9,600		750						
Lincoln University	4,715	2,310/—	350	4,060	500	915	750	500	900
Lock Haven University of Pennsylvania	‡ 3,822	4,974/—	450	3,856	200	1,000		400	1,000
Luzerne County Community College	1,590	2,880/1,440	400				725	500	625
Lycoming College	15,460		500	4,500	300	600	2,000	300	600
Manor Junior College	‡ 7,015		600	3,600	700	1,975	1,700	1,100	1,500
Mansfield University of Pennsylvania	‡ 3,904	4,974/—	650	3,432	800	800	1,700	800	800
Marywood College	13,140		600	5,200	300	700	750	600	700
McCann School of Business	‡ 5,880								
Median School of Allied Health Careers	7,265		590	5,200	765	7,416		765	3,987
Medical College of Pennsylvania and Hahnemann University	9,210		650		500	2,000	3,888	750	
Mercyhurst College	11,619		465	4,464	275	800		475	
Messiah College	11,888		475	5,400	400	800	1,000	400	800
Millersville University of Pennsylvania	‡ 4,100	4,974/—	500	4,038	300	960	1,230	600	990
Montgomery County Community College	‡ 2,040	4,140/2,070	590				1,748	1,086	1,040
Moore College of Art and Design	14,422		800	5,337	500	1,000	1,500	600	700
Moravian College	16,621		575	5,225	324	1,055	2,110	1,379	1,315
Mount Aloysius College	8,815		750	3,985		1,500			1,500
Muhlenberg College	18,050		560	4,920	150	800	2,060	150	800
Neumann College	‡ 11,090		650					800	500
New Castle School of Trades	7,200	7,200/—	1,000						

†Figures are projected for 1996-97. ‡Figures are for 1995-96.

188

| All aid | | Need–based aid | | Grants and scholarships | | | | | | | | Financial aid deadlines | | Inst aid form | Notes |
| Total freshmen | Percent receiving aid | Freshmen judged to have need | Percent offered aid | Need–based | | | | Non–need–based | | | | Priority | Closing | | |
				Acad	Music/ drama	Art	Athl	Acad	Music/ drama	Art	Athl				
														X	
509	60	260	100	X				X					2/1		
603	91	561	100	X			X	X			X	3/1	none	X	
267	91	211	100	X			X	X	X			4/15	none		
605	53	336	97	X	X			X					2/15		
16	38			X	X							9/15	none		
625	58	258	97	X	X			X				3/15	4/15	X	
50	93	48	100	X				X				3/15	none	X	
123	82			X				X				4/15	none	X	
				X		X		X		X		5/15	none		
306	45	129	100										1/31		
193	89	137	100	X			X	X			X	2/15	5/1	X	
													none		
91	98	72	100					X	X				3/1	X	
1,914	82	1,403	95										5/1		
232	80			X									8/1	X	
248	90			X	X	X		X	X	X		3/1	none		
401	85	221	99	X		X		X				5/1	none		
428	92	319	99	X				X				3/1	none	X	
1,232	85	980	72	X	X	X	X	X		X	X		3/15		
148	90	131	100					X				5/1	none	X	
742	87	602	100	X				X			X	2/15	none		
244	80			X			X	X			X	5/1	none		
526	57	265	99	X	X	X	X					2/15	none		
132	85	100	100					X	X			6/1	none		
														X	
299	96	244	100					X	X			3/1	none		
890	40			X				X				5/1	none		
1,046	56	560	100					X	X		X	2/15		X	
													none		
464	91			X	X			X	X			3/15	none		
646	90			X	X		X	X	X		X	4/15	5/1		
1,901	65	747	93									4/15	none		
369	87	305	100	X				X	X	X		4/15	5/1	X	
283	90			X			X	X			X	3/1	8/15	X	
874	75			X				X	X	X	X	3/15	4/1		
256	90			X	X	X		X	X	X		2/15	none	X	
50	70	9	100	X				X					none		
				X				X				5/1	5/31		
390	92	336	100	X	X			X	X	X	X	3/15	none	X	
673	88	605	100	X				X				4/1	none	X	
1,163	70	580	91	X			X	X	X	X	X		5/1		
2,804	12	1,175	100	X				X				5/1	none	X	
156	80					X		X		X		4/1	5/1		
321	92	266	100	X	X	X		X				2/15	3/15		
464	89			X	X		X	X	X		X	5/1	8/1		
487	62			X	X			X	X				2/15		
299	79	61	100	X				X					none		

Institution	Tuition and fees	Add'l out-of-state/ district tuition	Books and supplies	Costs for campus residents Room and board	Trans-portation	Other costs	Costs for students at home Board only	Trans-portation	Other costs
Newport Business Institute									
Lower Burrell	4,675		200						
Williamsport	5,890								
Northampton County Area Community									
College	2,100	3,660/1,830	630	3,980	400	1,050	1,040	400	1,050
Peirce College	7,174		650		550	3,200			
Penn State									
Allentown Campus	‡ 5,094	2,784/—	528				1,800	990	1,854
Altoona Campus	‡ 5,094	2,784/—	528	4,300	378	2,016	1,800	990	1,854
Beaver Campus # 12,706	‡ 5,094	2,784/—	528	4,300	378	2,016	1,800	990	1,854
Berks Campus	‡ 5,094	2,784/—	528	4,300	378	2,016	1,800	990	1,854
Delaware County Campus	‡ 5,094	2,784/—	528				1,800	990	1,854
Du Bois Campus	‡ 5,094	2,784/—	528				1,800	990	1,854
Erie Behrend College	‡ 5,258	6,052/—	528	4,300	378	2,016	1,800	990	1,854
Fayette Campus	‡ 5,094	2,784/—	528				1,800	990	1,854
Harrisburg Capital College	‡ 5,258	6,052/—	528	4,300	378	2,016	1,800	990	1,854
Hazleton Campus	‡ 5,094	2,784/—	528	4,300	378	2,016	1,800	990	1,854
McKeesport Campus	‡ 5,094	2,784/—	528	4,300	378	2,016	1,800	990	1,854
Mont Alto Campus	‡ 5,094	2,784/—	528	4,300	378	2,016	1,800	990	1,854
New Kensington Campus	‡ 5,094	2,784/—	528				1,800	990	1,854
Ogontz Campus	‡ 5,094	2,784/—	528				1,800	990	1,854
Schuylkill Campus	‡ 5,094	2,784/—	528	4,300	378	2,016	1,800	990	1,854
Shenango Campus	‡ 5,094	2,784/—	528				1,800	990	1,854
University Park Campus	‡ 5,258	6,052/—	528	4,300	378	2,016	1,800	990	1,854
Wilkes-Barre Campus	‡ 5,094	2,784/—	528				1,800	990	1,854
Worthington-Scranton Campus	‡ 5,094	2,784/—	528				1,800	990	1,854
York Campus	‡ 5,094	2,784/—	528				1,800	990	1,854
Penn Technical Institute	‡ 7,070		360					1,000	
Pennco Tech	‡ 7,435		800						
Pennsylvania College of Technology	† 6,400	1,200/—	800				1,800	150	1,950
Pennsylvania Institute of Culinary Arts	‡ 8,630			6,749					
Pennsylvania Institute of Technology	7,320		700						
Philadelphia College of Bible	8,556		640	4,630	600	900	2,490	1,050	1,050
Philadelphia College of Pharmacy and									
Science	12,660		540	5,300	400	800	2,000	1,060	800
Philadelphia College of Textiles and									
Science	12,762		500	5,874	500	1,038		700	1,038
Pittsburgh Institute of Mortuary									
Science	8,260		700						
Pittsburgh Technical Institute	‡ 9,610		800					675	1,386
Point Park College	10,816		400	5,072		450		350	200
Reading Area Community College	2,050	3,800/1,900	500					800	1,200
Remington Education Center: Vale Campus	6,395		850	2,861	540	1,109	1,814	540	1,109
Robert Morris College	7,740		500	4,744	400	600	1,500	400	600
Rosemont College	‡ 12,405		700	6,100	300	700		650	700
St. Charles Borromeo Seminary-Overbrook	† 6,205		1,000	4,020	1,100	3,000			
St. Francis College	13,238		500	5,650	450	800	1,500	450	800
St. Joseph's University	14,850		550	6,450	560	1,190	2,000	1,100	2,030
St. Vincent College	12,400		500	4,410		800	1,800		800
Sawyer School	3,410		1,355						
Schuylkill Business Institute	5,300		500						
Seton Hill College	12,210		550	4,570	500	1,500	1,600	1,300	1,900

†Figures are projected for 1996-97. ‡Figures are for 1995-96.

All aid		Need–based aid		Grants and scholarships									Financial aid deadlines		Inst aid form	Notes
Total freshmen	Percent receiving aid	Freshmen judged to have need	Percent offered aid	Need–based				Non–need–based								
				Acad	Music/drama	Art	Athl	Acad	Music/drama	Art	Athl	Priority	Closing		
1,728	65			X		X		X				3/31	none	X	
386	24			X				X				4/15	6/1		
				X	X	X		X	X	X		2/15	none		
				X	X	X		X	X	X		2/15	none		
				X	X	X		X	X	X		2/15	none		
				X	X	X		X	X	X		2/15	none		
				X	X	X		X	X	X		2/15	none		
				X	X	X		X	X	X		2/15	none		
726	67			X	X	X		X	X	X		3/15	none		
				X	X	X		X	X	X		2/15	none		
				X	X	X		X	X	X		2/15	none		
				X	X	X		X	X	X		2/15	none		
				X	X	X		X	X	X		2/15	none		
				X	X	X		X	X	X		2/15	none		
				X	X	X		X	X	X		2/15	none		
				X	X	X		X	X	X		2/15	none		
				X	X	X		X	X	X		2/15	none		
				X	X	X		X	X	X		2/15	none		
4,310	67			X	X	X	X	X	X	X	X	2/15	none		
				X	X	X		X	X	X		2/15	none		
				X	X	X		X	X	X		2/15	none		
				X	X	X		X	X	X		2/15	none		
													none		
													none		
1,330	75			X				X				3/1	none	X	
296	5	227	100										none	X	
150	92	77	100	X	X			X	X			5/1	none		
392	68	292	94	X				X			X	3/15	4/15		
501	91							X			X	4/15	none		
				X				X					none	X	
													none		
234	94							X	X	X	X	5/1	none		
470	45			X				X				7/15	none		
													none		
520	89	361	95	X			X	X			X	3/1	5/1		
117	70	94	100	X	X	X		X		X		2/15	none	X	
11	80	8	100										4/1		
334	94	288	100	X			X	X			X	5/1	none	X	
819	86	585	100	X				X			X		3/1		
261	95	214	100					X	X		X	3/1	5/1		
110	90	159	100	X	X	X	X	X	X	X	X	5/1	8/1	X	

Institution	Tuition and fees	Add'l out-of-state/district tuition	Books and supplies	Costs for campus residents			Costs for students at home		
				Room and board	Trans-portation	Other costs	Board only	Trans-portation	Other costs
Shippensburg University of Pennsylvania	‡ 4,010	4,974/—	400	3,600	200	1,100		800	1,300
Slippery Rock University of Pennsylvania	‡ 4,014	4,974/—	600	3,478	413	725		413	725
South Hills Business School	7,080		566				2,183	874	3,162
Susquehanna University	17,690		600	5,080	200	770	1,500	200	770
Swarthmore College	21,054		780	7,176	420	790	3,488	1,200	790
Talmudical Yeshiva of Philadelphia	5,080			4,200					
Temple University	‡ 5,514	4,782/—	600	5,282		1,000			2,953
Thaddeus Stevens State School of Technology	‡ 4,370		275	3,910	600	300	1,000	1,000	300
Thiel College	12,670		600	5,090		1,420	2,000	1,320	575
Thomas Jefferson University: College of Allied Health Sciences	14,924		1,250		900	600	2,380	1,500	600
Triangle Tech: Pittsburgh Campus	6,659		500	4,842			1,500	1,754	1,440
University of the Arts	14,350		1,700	6,000	500	1,245	800	800	1,830
University of Pennsylvania	21,130		570	7,500		1,290	1,390		1,290
University of Pittsburgh									
Bradford	‡ 5,594	6,086/—	500	4,240	600	500		1,200	500
Greensburg	‡ 5,600	6,086/—	550	3,830	550	900	1,900	1,100	900
Johnstown	‡ 5,656	6,086/—	600	2,500		1,500			1,500
Pittsburgh	‡ 5,638	6,086/—	400	4,834	400	900	1,650	600	900
Titusville	† 2,927	5,842/—	600	4,336	400	550	1,500	950	550
University of Scranton	15,000		675	6,376	365	950	2,000	840	950
Ursinus College	16,600		500	5,490	135	800	900	450	800
Valley Forge Christian College	‡ 5,680		450	3,280	350	1,200	300	1,600	1,200
Valley Forge Military College	14,000		450	4,800		250			
Villanova University	17,885		800	6,740		1,200	2,000	500	800
Washington and Jefferson College	17,470		200	4,205	145	500	1,500	1,100	500
Waynesburg College	‡ 9,600		600	3,895	350	850	1,930	1,035	1,000
Welder Training and Testing Institute	6,300		300						
West Chester University of Pennsylvania	‡ 3,874	4,974/—	450	4,232	514	1,000	1,200	870	1,000
Westminster College	14,085		450	4,120		685	1,980		685
Westmoreland County Community College	‡ 1,313	2,580/1,440	550				1,000	500	150
Widener University	13,650		500	6,280	500	900	1,500	900	900
Wilkes University	13,147		550	5,708	500	760	1,500	800	700
Williamson Free School of Mechanical Trades	358		414		450	400			
Wilson College	12,117		450	5,338	125	350	1,500	300	350
Yeshivath Beth Moshe	‡ 8,400 (comprehensive)		150						
York College of Pennsylvania	5,790		500	4,100	400	850		750	850
Yorktowne Business Institute	9,360		600				1,614	1,032	

Puerto Rico

Institution	Tuition and fees	Add'l out-of-state/district tuition	Books and supplies	Room and board	Trans-portation	Other costs	Board only	Trans-portation	Other costs
American University of Puerto Rico	3,070		400					780	
Bayamon Central University	† 3,114		500				1,600	554	1,020
Caribbean University	2,800		640				1,200	955	1,950
Colegio Universitario del Este	‡ 2,620		300				1,080	720	1,045
Columbia College	‡ 3,825		500						331
Conservatory of Music of Puerto Rico	‡ 560		400				2,268	650	450
Electronic Data Processing College of Puerto Rico	2,956		465				600	900	1,455
Escuela de Artes Plasticas de Puerto Rico	‡ 1,584		2,250				1,250	500	1,750

†Figures are projected for 1996-97. ‡Figures are for 1995-96.

Total freshmen	Percent receiving aid	Freshmen judged to have need	Percent offered aid	Acad	Music/drama	Art	Athl	Acad	Music/drama	Art	Athl	Priority	Closing	Inst aid form	Notes
	All aid		Need-based aid	Need-based				Non-need-based				Financial aid deadlines			
1,281	65	431	100	X			X	X			X	5/1	none	X	
1,288	75	900	90	X	X		X	X	X	X	X	5/1	none		
191	95			X									none		
449	85	325	100					X	X			3/1	5/1		
354	60	168	100					X					5/1	X	
													none		
2,575	63	1,769	95	X				X	X		X		3/31		
													none		
341	98	241	100	X				X				4/1	none		
				X				X					5/1		
													none	X	
302	95	268	100	X	X	X		X	X	X		2/15	none		
2,384	58	1,092	100									2/15	none	X	
301	60	224	100					X				3/1	none		
324	87	291	100	X				X				3/15	none	X	
700	81	596	96	X				X			X	4/1	none		
2,424	70	1,696	100	X				X			X	3/1	none		
113	87							X				5/1	none		
927	82	640	97	X				X				2/15	none	X	
317	76	272	100					X	X	X			2/15		
105	84	72	100	X				X	X			5/1	none	X	
120	80			X	X				X				4/15	X	
1,672	67			X			X	X			X	2/15	3/15	X	
281	80	264	85	X				X				3/15	none		
366	96	285	100	X				X				3/15	none	X	
1,393	83							X	X		X	3/1	none		
365	81			X	X		X	X	X		X	5/1	6/30		
1,283	56	440	100	X								5/1	none	X	
561	85	436	98	X	X			X	X			3/1	none	X	
517	90			X	X	X	X	X	X	X	X		none		
100	100														
78	84	58	100	X	X	X		X					4/30	X	
													none		
1,053	72	329	100					X	X	X		4/15	none	X	
												5/1	none		
926	72			X								5/31	6/30		
582	91			X			X	X			X	4/30	8/1	X	
576	87			X								7/30	none		
														X	
322	90												8/15	X	
													none		
													none		

Institution	Tuition and fees	Add'l out-of-state/ district tuition	Books and supplies	Costs for campus residents			Costs for students at home		
				Room and board	Trans-portation	Other costs	Board only	Trans-portation	Other costs
Huertas Junior College	‡ 3,235		600				500	600	600
Humacao Community College	‡ 2,190		500				213	900	
ICPR Junior College	† 2,775		528				2,376	1,152	1,190
Inter American University of Puerto Rico									
Aguadilla Campus	‡ 3,292		640				2,016	600	880
Arecibo Campus	‡ 3,188		640				1,200	540	880
Barranquitas Campus	‡ 3,213		640				800	540	880
Bayamon Campus	3,473								
Fajardo Campus	‡ 3,213		640				1,200	600	
Guayama Campus	‡ 3,213		640				540	880	
Metropolitan Campus	‡ 3,213		640				1,200	600	880
Ponce Campus	‡ 3,213								
San German Campus	‡ 3,213		700	2,060	100	800	1,000	500	1,000
Pontifical Catholic University of Puerto Rico	3,221		400	2,660	408	1,100	1,700	408	1,100
Technological College of the Municipality of San Juan	1,705		621				900	564	920
Turabo University	‡ 2,620		300				1,080	720	1,045
Universidad Adventista de las Antillas	3,250		500	1,790	500	500	1,400	500	500
Universidad Metropolitana	‡ 2,620		300				1,080	720	1,045
Universidad Politecnica de Puerto Rico	† 4,655		1,000				1,500	984	1,848
University of Puerto Rico									
Aguadilla	‡ 970		1,000				1,100	500	800
Arecibo Campus	‡ 970		1,000				1,100	1,000	3,200
Bayamon Technological University College	‡ 970		800				2,160	700	600
Carolina Regional College	‡ 970		1,000				2,400	1,000	800
Cayey University College	‡ 1,242		1,000				1,000		800
Humacao University College	‡ 970		1,000				2,400	1,000	800
La Montana Regional College	‡ 970		900				1,350	700	600
Mayaguez Campus	‡ 970		1,000					1,000	800
Medical Sciences Campus	‡ 970		350				1,800	700	663
Ponce Technological University College	‡ 970		1,000				2,160	1,000	800
Rio Piedras Campus	‡ 970		800	2,890	700	600	1,890	700	600
University of the Sacred Heart	3,640		560		1,350	1,350	1,350	1,400	1,400
Rhode Island									
Brown University	22,280		760	6,538		1,072	2,552	2,986	1,072
Bryant College	13,900		500	6,700	200	700	1,500	950	700
Community College of Rhode Island	‡ 1,726	3,020/—	600				2,700	704	1,000
Johnson & Wales University	11,457		500	5,157	750	500	1,800	750	500
New England Institute of Technology	‡ 9,735		600				2,317	1,008	1,872
Providence College	16,080		600	6,670		1,200	1,400	1,600	1,200
Rhode Island College	‡ 2,969	4,520/—	600	5,383	400	1,000	1,800	1,000	1,120
Rhode Island School of Design	18,630		1,300	6,618	470	1,100	2,750	2,485	1,100
Roger Williams University	15,280		600	7,000	720	735	1,500	720	735
Salve Regina University	15,190		500	6,900	600	900	2,250	800	1,100
University of Rhode Island	‡ 4,404	7,692/—	600	5,750	131	1,332	1,728	2,160	1,332
South Carolina									
Aiken Technical College	‡ 912	334/—	450				2,500	1,125	900
Allen University	‡ 4,950		500	3,910					
Anderson College	9,223		900	4,145	800	1,450	2,000	1,050	950

†Figures are projected for 1996-97. ‡Figures are for 1995-96.

All aid		Need-based aid		Grants and scholarships								Financial aid deadlines		Inst aid form	Notes
				Need-based				Non-need-based							
Total freshmen	Percent receiving aid	Freshmen judged to have need	Percent offered aid	Acad	Music/drama	Art	Athl	Acad	Music/drama	Art	Athl	Priority	Closing		
													none		
107	90			X								1/1	6/30	X	
766	90	738	100	X									4/15		
786	95	672	100	X							X		4/28		
822	87						X					4/29	none		
453	85	428	85									4/30	none	X	
791	98			X			X						4/29		
1,791	85			X	X						X		4/30	X	
1,146	90			X			X						4/28	X	
2,218	90			X			X		X	X	X	4/25	none	X	
1,183	80												none		
144	89	122	100	X				X					none		
				X									6/30		
		851	100	X				X				3/31	6/30	X	
938	61			X	X		X						6/16		
1,200	87	998	88	X				X				5/26	6/16		
1,411	65			X				X					6/15	X	
1,017	60							X	X		X		5/3		
1,023	80	782	100	X	X	X	X						6/15	X	
1,067	83	880	100	X									6/30	X	
493	86			X			X				X	5/31	none		
2,423	75	1,344	100					X	X		X		6/30		
				X				X				4/30	none		
1,221	80	1,057	100	X				X	X		X		6/2		
				X				X					5/30	X	
1,418	45	575	100										1/22	X	
692	72	380	100	X				X			X		2/15		
2,678	40											3/1	none	X	
2,347	76	1,733	99					X				3/1	none		
903	85											6/1	none		
962	80	625	100	X			X	X			X		2/1		
921	61	592	99	X				X	X	X		3/1		X	
380	57	121	60	X		X		X		X		2/15			
653	80	522	100	X				X				3/1	none	X	
375	76	267	100	X				X				3/1	none	X	
1,988	73			X	X	X	X	X	X		X	3/1	none		
499	39			X				X				5/1	none		
237	94			X	X	X	X	X	X	X	X	4/1	none		

195

Institution		Tuition and fees	Add'l out-of-state/ district tuition	Books and supplies	Costs for campus residents			Costs for students at home		
					Room and board	Trans- portation	Other costs	Board only	Trans- portation	Other costs
Benedict College		6,864		700	3,620	833	1,070		833	1,070
Central Carolina Technical College	‡	800	630/220	600				3,700	1,500	1,200
Charleston Southern University		8,724		750	3,360	1,000	1,125	2,000	1,260	1,000
Chesterfield-Marlboro Technical College	‡	826	362/52	600				2,000	1,694	1,884
The Citadel	‡	3,176	3,994/—	800	3,239		1,100			
Claflin College		5,166		700	2,845	1,100	1,125	900	1,100	1,125
Clemson University	†	3,170	5,308/—	820	3,888	1,135	1,673	1,895	2,054	1,217
Coastal Carolina University	‡	2,800	4,670/—	603	4,120	796	1,480	887	1,186	1,480
Coker College		12,411		1,000	4,516		500	750		500
College of Charleston		3,190	3,190/—	684	3,690			1,340	1,898	2,598
Columbia Bible College		7,425		800	3,970		1,800	2,170	2,210	1,800
Columbia College		11,535		700	4,160	850	1,600	2,100	1,050	1,500
Columbia Junior College of Business	‡	3,615		675					900	2,250
Converse College		13,800		500	4,025	300	700	750	400	750
Denmark Technical College	‡	1,220	1,080/—	500	2,674	1,200	1,200	1,500	1,200	1,600
Erskine College		13,087		475	4,490	500	784	656	650	2,204
Florence-Darlington Technical College		1,000	376/150	700				1,200		700
Francis Marion University	‡	3,100	3,010/—	400	3,138	1,500	890	1,500	1,500	860
Furman University		15,514		600	4,304	600	760		760	2,425
Greenville Technical College	‡	1,006	600/80	456				1,674	1,140	547
Horry-Georgetown Technical College	‡	1,000	1,208/—	400						
Lander University	‡	3,400	1,626/—	618	3,202	497	1,205	1,550	843	1,238
Limestone College		8,200		800	3,700	450	900		2,025	900
Medical University of South Carolina		3,379	6,116/—	825						250
Midlands Technical College	‡	1,020	990/248	400					772	676
Morris College	‡	5,105		850	2,691	1,050	1,050	2,500	1,550	1,300
Newberry College	‡	10,950		450	2,600	400	1,000		700	1,000
Nielsen Electronics Institute	‡	3,000								
North Greenville College		6,800		500	4,000	350	500	1,600	500	1,000
Orangeburg-Calhoun Technical College	‡	840	420/210	400				1,000	300	500
Piedmont Technical College	‡	1,144	536/236	600					800	800
Presbyterian College		14,121		650	4,402	500	1,350	2,380	500	1,350
South Carolina State University	‡	2,500	2,480/—	400	2,986	100	700		300	700
Southern Wesleyan University		9,615		800	3,380	750	500		800	600
Spartanburg Methodist College		6,500		500	3,950	700	500		700	500
Spartanburg Technical College		878	878/222	500					1,200	600
Technical College of the Lowcountry	‡	1,000	500/—	425					1,050	1,600
Tri-County Technical College	‡	972	756/—	504				1,575	947	1,014
Trident Technical College	‡	1,018	808/160	650					1,275	1,000
University of South Carolina										
Aiken	†	2,578	3,868/—	600		1,500	1,500	2,100	1,500	1,500
Beaufort	‡	1,786	2,694/—	485				1,665	1,176	975
Columbia	‡	3,280	5,044/—	495	3,589	735	2,206	1,500	2,207	2,206
Lancaster	‡	1,888	2,592/—	500				1,700	1,176	938
Salkehatchie Regional Campus	‡	1,786	2,694/—	450				1,665	1,176	950
Spartanburg	‡	2,578	3,868/—	450				1,665	1,176	950
Sumter	‡	1,786	2,694/—	500				1,700	1,176	938
Union	‡	1,786	2,694/—	450				1,665	1,176	950
Voorhees College		7,490		500	2,706	1,200	1,500	1,700	1,200	1,500
Williamsburg Technical College		1,023		545					1,600	
Winthrop University	†	3,865	3,100/—	633	3,628	850	1,480	2,506	850	1,480
Wofford College		14,675		625	4,185	530	970	2,015	700	970
York Technical College	‡	864	864/168	600					1,175	

†Figures are projected for 1996-97. ‡Figures are for 1995-96.

| All aid | | Need–based aid | | Grants and scholarships | | | | | | | | Financial aid deadlines | | Inst aid form | Notes |
| Total freshmen | Percent receiving aid | Freshmen judged to have need | Percent offered aid | Need–based | | | | Non–need–based | | | | | | | |
				Acad	Music/drama	Art	Athl	Acad	Music/drama	Art	Athl	Priority	Closing		
625	80			X	X		X	X			X	4/15	none		
													none		
					X			X		X	X	4/15	none		
215	53	100	100	X				X					none		
501	55			X				X			X	3/15	none		
303	93	278	100	X	X	X	X					4/16	6/1	X	
2,575	59	1,106	100	X				X	X		X	4/1	none		
773	52			X	X	X		X	X	X	X		4/1		
246	83			X	X	X	X	X	X	X	X	4/1	8/1		
1,427	64	1,018	94	X	X	X	X	X	X	X	X	3/15	none		
81	37			X	X			X	X			2/15	none		
272	93	180	100	X				X	X	X	X	4/1	none		
100	76			X				X				5/30	none		
185	98	118	100	X	X			X	X			5/1	none		
276	96			X				X				5/1	6/1		
142	95	110	100					X	X		X	3/15	none	X	
600	52											5/1	none		
				X	X	X	X	X	X	X	X	3/1			
703	63	339	100	X				X	X	X	X		2/1	X	
2,543	30			X				X		X		5/1	none	X	
				X				X				4/1	5/1		
494	45			X				X	X	X	X	4/15	none		
410	96	398	99	X	X	X	X	X	X	X	X	3/31	6/30	X	
													none		
1,889	30			X				X				5/31	none		
242	98	238	100	X	X		X	X				3/30	none	X	
339	95			X	X	X	X	X	X	X	X	6/1	6/30		
449	60							X					none		
493	70							X				5/1	none		
354	86	222	100	X	X		X	X	X		X	3/1	none	X	
				X				X	X		X	6/1	none		
71	94	60	100	X			X	X	X		X	4/1	none	X	
375	83	330	100	X	X		X	X	X		X	6/1	none		
616	38	202	100	X								2/28	5/1		
				X				X				6/1	none		
				X				X				5/1	none		
431	47	190	79	X				X	X	X	X	3/15	none	X	
550	80			X				X				4/15	none		
2,656	25	1,428	76	X				X	X	X	X	4/15	none	X	
218	45	77	87					X				4/15	none	X	
													none		
494	47	178	95	X			X	X	X		X	4/15	7/1		
705	71			X				X					4/15	X	
150	70							X				4/15	none		
													none		
122	32	37	100	X				X					5/1	X	
878	73	529	100					X	X	X	X	5/1	none		
286	85	163	99	X	X		X	X	X		X	3/15	none		
690	40			X				X				3/31	none		

Institution	Tuition and fees	Add'l out-of-state/district tuition	Books and supplies	Costs for campus residents			Costs for students at home		
				Room and board	Trans-portation	Other costs	Board only	Trans-portation	Other costs
South Dakota									
Augustana College	12,350		600	3,576	200	800		400	400
Black Hills State University	‡ 2,458	2,280/—	600	2,791	900	1,300	1,800	900	700
Dakota State University	‡ 2,629	2,280/—	600	2,842	320	3,280	750	420	2,480
Dakota Wesleyan University	† 8,475		600	3,045	480	1,054	1,825	480	1,054
Huron University	7,878		600	3,470	720		1,500	720	960
Kilian Community College	† 3,750		500				2,300	1,450	2,000
Lake Area Technical Institute	2,520		400				1,800	450	675
Mitchell Technical Institute	2,600		800				4,000	900	750
Mount Marty College	8,734		500	3,470	540	950	1,800	540	720
National College	† 7,970		828	3,480	897	1,053	1,800	1,092	
Nettleton Junior College	‡ 5,520		450						
Northern State University	‡ 2,320	2,280/—	550	2,600	735	1,100	1,800	735	1,100
Oglala Lakota College	1,620		260				945	320	450
Presentation College	7,445		800	3,046	950	600	1,500	950	600
Sinte Gleska University	1,528		500					900	500
Sisseton-Wahpeton Community College	2,620		440					480	
South Dakota School of Mines and Technology	‡ 2,637	2,640/—	500	2,786	555	1,152	1,140	642	1,152
South Dakota State University	‡ 2,554	2,640/—	500	2,708					
Southeast Technical Institute	2,110		500				1,800	900	1,350
University of Sioux Falls	10,120		600	3,420	800	950	2,100	675	650
University of South Dakota	‡ 2,665	2,655/—	700	2,757	685	1,187	900	605	867
Western Dakota Technical Institute	2,625		600				1,800	500	
Tennessee									
American Baptist College of ABT Seminary	2,250		440	2,512					
American Technical Institute	‡ 5,250								
Aquinas College	‡ 8,910		500				1,971	1,248	1,098
Austin Peay State University	‡ 1,946	2,466/—	735	3,050	760	1,575	1,500	1,382	1,575
Belmont University	9,550		750	3,840	1,000	1,200	2,140	1,000	1,200
Bethel College	7,240		500	3,660		1,000	650	700	
Bryan College	9,700		450	3,950	600	800	1,125	800	400
Carson-Newman College	9,480		500	3,500	1,000	700	1,710	1,200	750
Chattanooga State Technical Community College	‡ 1,042	1,932/—	450				1,900	1,600	1,700
Christian Brothers University	11,030		800	3,400					2,200
Cleveland State Community College	‡ 1,015	2,926/—	500				1,600	600	800
Columbia State Community College	‡ 1,034	1,932/—	450				1,200	820	625
Crichton College	5,880		664			2,170	1,500	300	2,170
Cumberland University	7,660		600	3,300					
David Lipscomb University	8,408		600	3,650	1,000	1,000	1,920	1,000	1,000
Draughons Junior College of Business: Nashville	‡ 3,340		500						
Dyersburg State Community College	‡ 1,040	1,932/—	450				1,500	1,250	500
East Tennessee State University	‡ 1,888	2,466/—	600	2,740	800	1,900		1,000	1,900
Electronic Computer Programming College	4,590		340						
Fisk University	7,443		700	4,062	1,100	1,700		950	1,700
Free Will Baptist Bible College	4,895		438	3,200	760	430	1,800	640	570
Freed-Hardeman University	7,120		700	3,780	725	1,075	1,940	1,150	1,100
Hiwassee College	5,380		460	3,510	300	900			
Jackson State Community College	‡ 1,040	1,932/—	600				1,900	1,123	653

†Figures are projected for 1996-97. ‡Figures are for 1995-96.

Total freshmen	Percent receiving aid	Freshmen judged to have need	Percent offered aid	Acad	Music/drama	Art	Athl	Acad	Music/drama	Art	Athl	Priority	Closing	Inst aid form	Notes
				Need-based				Non-need-based				Financial aid deadlines			
398	90			X			X	X	X	X	X	3/4	none		
469	58	296	100	X	X	X		X	X	X	X	4/1	none		
				X			X	X	X		X	3/1	none		
147	97	139	100	X	X	X	X	X	X	X	X	3/15	none	X	
80	97	66	100	X			X	X			X		none		
52	90	42	100	X				X					none	X	
586	80	300	100					X				4/15	none		
													none		
94	97	67	100	X	X		X	X	X		X	3/1	none		
													none	X	
598	79	440	100	X	X			X	X	X	X	3/1	none		
													none		
147	98			X				X				4/1	none		
													none		
														none		
376	52							X			X	4/1	none		
1,670	85							X	X	X	X	3/15	none		
955	65	450	100					X					none		
216	91	197	100	X	X		X	X	X		X	4/1	none		
1,205	81			X	X	X	X	X	X	X	X	3/1	none		
324	80											7/1	none		
													none		
													none		
928	65	605	100					X	X	X	X	4/1	none		
819	65	380	99	X				X	X		X	3/15	none	X	
207	90							X	X		X	5/1	none		
													none		
448	92	332	100	X	X	X	X	X	X	X	X	3/1	none	X	
				X	X	X	X	X	X	X	X	6/1	none		
329	95			X	X		X	X			X	4/1	none		
527	43	350	100	X			X	X				6/15	none		
													none	X	
													none		
188	70			X				X			X	3/1	none		
584	74	317	68	X				X	X	X	X	4/15	none		
													none		
433	75			X	X		X	X	X		X	3/15	none	X	
1,613	67							X	X	X	X	4/15	none		
															X	
205	82			X				X				4/20	none		
													none	X	
295	93	250	100	X				X	X	X	X	4/1	none		
165	80			X	X		X	X	X		X	5/1	none		
505	39							X			X	4/1	none	X	

Institution	Tuition and fees	Add'l out-of-state/ district tuition	Books and supplies	Costs for campus residents			Costs for students at home		
				Room and board	Trans-portation	Other costs	Board only	Trans-portation	Other costs
John A. Gupton College	6,856		650						
Johnson Bible College	4,600		700	3,200	600	1,000	1,800	1,100	1,400
King College	10,280		600	3,444	1,000	1,200	1,500	320	3,600
Knoxville Business College	6,025		750					1,200	1,200
Knoxville College	‡ 6,032		600	3,450	1,000	1,280	1,500	600	1,280
Lambuth University	5,882		600	3,750		1,200	1,872		1,000
Lane College	‡ 5,196		550	3,202	405	675	2,250	630	675
Lee College	5,372		550	3,540	908	900	1,125	1,050	448
LeMoyne-Owen College	‡ 6,000		425	3,790				515	1,000
Lincoln Memorial University	6,950		550	3,160	500	1,200	900	1,280	1,200
Martin Methodist College	6,350		400	2,950					
Maryville College	‡ 12,246		500	4,378	642	1,000	1,875	500	750
Memphis College of Art	10,300		875	4,275	700	1,000	1,350	1,350	1,000
Middle Tennessee State University	‡ 1,972	2,466/—	600	2,430	750	1,046	1,500	2,350	1,046
Milligan College	9,560		550	3,440	1,300	1,100	1,000	850	2,000
Motlow State Community College	‡ 1,046	1,932/—	600						3,200
Nashville State Technical Institute	‡ 1,010	1,932/—	550				1,800	1,157	500
Northeast State Technical Community College	‡ 1,038	1,932/—	500					750	890
O'More College of Design	‡ 7,300		750				1,500		
Pellissippi State Technical Community College	‡ 1,068	1,932/—	500				1,700	1,650	1,500
Rhodes College	16,550		600	5,110	600	900	2,072	500	900
Roane State Community College	‡ 1,042	1,932/—	500				1,500	1,440	750
Shelby State Community College	‡ 1,020	1,932/—	500				4,272	540	800
Southern College of Seventh-day Adventists	9,236		548	2,710	210	740		210	740
State Technical Institute at Memphis	‡ 1,044	1,932/—	600				1,918	792	675
Tennessee Institute of Electronics	4,178		450				2,000		1,200
Tennessee State University	‡ 1,846	2,466/—	500	2,720	450	700	1,500	450	700
Tennessee Technological University	‡ 1,840	2,466/—	700	3,360	700	700		700	700
Tennessee Temple University	6,270		600	4,750	880	850		765	680
Tennessee Wesleyan College	6,400		400	3,700	1,000	1,000	2,168	1,200	900
Trevecca Nazarene University	8,644		600	3,650	820	1,025	1,800	608	1,025
Tusculum College	9,750		450	3,600	600	600	2,000	600	600
Union University	7,084		600	2,940		500		500	500
University of Memphis	‡ 2,026	2,324/—	850	3,080	500	715	1,800	825	715
University of the South	16,965		500	4,460	325	810		325	810
University of Tennessee									
Chattanooga	‡ 1,937	4,130/—	550		500	900	1,457	1,200	900
Knoxville	‡ 2,164	4,130/—	760	3,364	494	1,432	1,650	1,760	1,432
Martin	‡ 1,958	4,130/—	750	3,008	465	1,545	975	575	1,545
Memphis	‡ 2,166	4,820/—	1,097	3,610	1,370	1,527		1,305	1,455
Vanderbilt University	19,132		600	7,088		600			600
Volunteer State Community College	‡ 1,014	1,932/—	500				1,500	1,500	400
Walters State Community College	‡ 1,034	1,932/—	500				1,500	1,200	900
Texas									
Abilene Christian University	8,520		500	3,700	960	1,350	1,600	960	1,350
Alvin Community College	567	780/—	550				1,751	800	1,200
Amarillo College	606	1,155/270	540	1,150			1,180	1,136	900
Ambassador University	4,250		600	3,200	500	800	1,000	300	800
Amber University	4,000		350						

†Figures are projected for 1996-97. ‡Figures are for 1995-96.

| All aid | | Need–based aid | | Grants and scholarships | | | | | | | | Financial aid deadlines | | Inst | |
| Total freshmen | Percent receiving aid | Freshmen judged to have need | Percent offered aid | Need–based | | | | Non–need–based | | | | | | aid | |
				Acad	Music/ drama	Art	Athl	Acad	Music/ drama	Art	Athl	Priority	Closing	form	Notes
													none		
97	93	90	100					X	X			7/1	none	X	
167	90	130	100	X	X	X	X	X	X		X	3/1	none	X	
91	95	50	100	X								5/31	none		
													none		
270	70	230	100	X	X	X	X	X	X	X	X	3/15	none	X	
612	90			X	X		X	X	X		X	4/15	none	X	
443	88											4/15	none		
323	70			X	X		X	X	X		X	4/1	4/1		
196	71			X	X	X	X	X	X	X	X	4/1	9/13		
217	87							X	X	X		3/1	none		
58	84					X		X		X		4/1	none		
2,157	60	1,236	100	X	X	X	X	X	X		X	3/15	5/15		
193	75	126	100	X	X	X	X	X	X	X	X	3/1	3/1	X	
742	62			X	X		X	X	X		X	5/1	none		
538	19			X				X				5/1	none	X	
1,875	36			X				X				8/1	none		
														X	
				X	X			X	X	X		5/1	none		
391	44	170	100	X	X	X		X	X	X		3/1		X	
814	35	480	100					X	X	X	X	5/1	none		
966	46			X	X		X	X	X	X	X	4/15	8/1	X	
357	86	106	100	X	X			X	X			3/1	none	X	
1,013	25			X				X				3/15	none		
													none		
1,081	82			X	X		X	X	X		X	4/1	none		
1,133	65	748	100	X				X	X		X	3/15	none		
													none		
106	85	77	100					X	X		X	3/1	none	X	
249	95	101	100	X	X		X					4/15	none		
158	92	106	100	X			X	X			X	4/1	none	X	
458	82	275	86					X	X	X	X	2/1	8/1		
1,920	50			X			X	X	X	X	X	4/1	none		
370	54	151	100	X				X				3/1	none		
1,095	65	693	97	X	X			X	X	X	X	4/1	none		
3,509	69	1,204	89	X	X	X	X	X	X	X	X	2/15	none		
1,141	65	711	97	X	X	X	X	X	X	X	X	3/1	none		
				X				X				2/15	none	X	
1,539	59	681	100	X	X			X	X		X	2/15	none		
				X				X			X	4/15	none		
917	50			X				X	X		X	3/31	6/30		
939	90	648	90					X	X	X	X	3/1	none	X	
													none		
1,898	38							X				6/1	none		
176	82	176	100	X				X	X		X	4/15	none		

Institution		Tuition and fees	Add'l out-of-state/ district tuition	Books and supplies	Costs for campus residents			Costs for students at home		
					Room and board	Trans-portation	Other costs	Board only	Trans-portation	Other costs
Angelina College	‡	588	300/158	600	2,600	300	600	900	1,400	600
Angelo State University	†	1,820	7,610/—	500	3,820	620	1,440	1,324	1,440	1,440
Arlington Baptist College		2,300		700		600	720	1,100	600	800
Austin College		12,800		400	4,975	200	700	2,710	200	700
Austin Community College	‡	878	2,828/532	452				1,851	968	1,273
Baptist Missionary Association Theological Seminary		1,775		500		600	1,200	4,000	600	1,200
Baylor College of Dentistry	‡	2,200		2,094				7,400		2,600
Baylor University		8,806		652	4,254	904	1,468	1,228	1,386	1,522
Bee County College		574	750/—	600	2,310	381	872	1,639	1,344	872
Blinn College		1,295	1,890/270	850	2,815	412	1,094		306	1,094
Brazosport College		470	1,650/150	540				2,090	720	880
Brookhaven College	‡	570	1,490/380	390					1,560	1,245
Cedar Valley College	‡	570	1,490/380	600				1,500	1,330	1,045
Central Texas College		810	1,350/—	1,980	3,200	714	1,912	2,554	657	1,652
Cisco Junior College	‡	750	426/120	600	2,200	250	650	850	600	850
Clarendon College	‡	730	80/60	400	1,760		150	1,060	400	800
College of the Mainland		521	923/473	450					1,225	1,035
Collin County Community College District		741	1,260/210	434				1,860	1,430	1,160
Commonwealth Institute of Funeral Service	‡	6,075		560				1,500	2,185	2,529
Concordia Lutheran College		8,680		500	4,200	775	1,050	1,500	650	1,050
Criswell College		3,064		600						
Dallas Baptist University		7,525		650	3,540	500	1,250	1,500	1,500	1,250
Dallas Christian College		4,000		850	2,790	250	1,000	2,500	800	1,000
Del Mar College	‡	750	780/240	500				1,500	630	810
DeVry Institute of Technology: Irving		6,560		560				1,965	2,097	1,979
East Texas Baptist University		6,490		545	4,260	530	1,015	1,800	575	960
East Texas State University										
Commerce	‡	2,036	5,760/—	600	3,600	990	1,080	1,500	990	1,080
Texarkana	‡	1,740	5,760/—	650				1,590	875	970
Eastfield College	‡	570	1,490/380	400				1,100	1,170	935
El Centro College	‡	570	1,490/380	675					400	600
El Paso Community College	‡	952	2,170/—	530				1,500	1,462	1,188
Frank Phillips College		670	270/210	475	2,000	600	900	2,000	1,150	865
Galveston College	‡	640	360/—	600				2,000	1,250	1,150
Grayson County College	‡	785	1,122/—	457	2,191	483	1,003	1,845	1,230	1,504
Hallmark Institute of Technology		10,000								
Hardin-Simmons University		7,415		730	3,050	850	1,245	1,350	990	1,245
Hill College		720	580/180	526	2,500	723	937		1,202	965
Houston Baptist University		12,038		525	3,489	1,260	1,400	1,700	1,260	1,370
Houston Community College		840	2,200/570	1,000				2,047	341	1,023
Howard College		1,100	400/164	400	2,600	800	1,175	750	800	1,175
Howard Payne University		6,450		460	3,650	638	1,250	1,500	765	1,085
Huston-Tillotson College		5,940		575	4,253	745	1,225	2,230	1,225	1,225
Incarnate Word College	‡	9,570		750	4,190	950	1,980	1,920	1,442	1,980
Institute for Christian Studies		910		400			1,540			600
Jacksonville College		3,410		500	2,628				600	
Jarvis Christian College		6,694		600	3,485	800	950		800	950
Kilgore College		600	480/—	575	2,200		1,200			1,200
Lamar University at Orange		1,710		500					1,200	1,000

†Figures are projected for 1996-97. ‡Figures are for 1995-96.

All aid		Need-based aid		Grants and scholarships								Financial aid deadlines		Inst aid form	Notes
Total fresh-men	Percent receiving aid	Freshmen judged to have need	Percent offered aid	Need-based				Non-need-based							
				Acad	Music/drama	Art	Athl	Acad	Music/drama	Art	Athl	Priority	Closing		
1,100	27			X	X	X	X	X	X	X	X	6/15	none	X	
				X				X				6/1	none	X	
94	52	23	100	X	X							8/15	none		
293	90	181	100	X				X	X	X		4/1	none	X	
1,790	30							X				2/15	4/1		
												8/1	8/16		
		21	100	X				X				4/1	none		
2,339	70	1,108	83	X	X	X	X	X	X	X	X	5/1	none		
930	36	445	100	X				X	X	X		4/1	none		
7,017	30			X	X		X	X	X		X	6/30	none	X	
2,000	21							X				8/1	none		
													none		
2,046	31			X	X	X		X	X	X		5/1	none		
1,924	31			X				X				7/1	8/1	X	
983	50							X	X		X	8/15	none		
180	80							X				8/1	none		
				X	X	X		X	X	X			none		
1,897	10	650	100	X	X	X	X	X	X	X	X	5/11	none	X	
134	59	52	100					X				7/15	none		
87	70			X	X		X	X			X	4/15	none		
25	80							X	X			7/1	none	X	
160	55	117	100	X	X	X	X	X	X	X	X	3/15	none	X	
30	73			X	X			X	X				4/15	X	
1,879	40			X	X	X		X	X	X		5/1	none		
								X					none		
								X	X		X	6/1	none		
				X	X	X	X	X	X	X	X	5/1	10/1	X	
												5/1	none		
2,936	24			X	X	X		X	X	X		5/1	none		
3,510	65							X					6/1		
250	48							X	X		X	7/1	none		
													none		
													none		
													none		
831	72	358	100	X				X	X	X		3/15	none	X	
													none		
191	70							X	X	X	X	4/1	none	X	
4,739	21	2,408	100	X				X				4/15	none		
751	60			X	X	X	X	X	X	X	X	4/1	none		
302	75			X				X	X	X		5/1	none	X	
140	95	120	83	X	X		X	X					5/1	X	
													none		
				X				X						X	
112	94			X	X		X	X	X		X	6/10	none		
251	95			X	X			X	X			7/30	none		
2,300	65							X				8/1	none		

Institution		Tuition and fees	Add'l out-of-state/district tuition	Books and supplies	Costs for campus residents			Costs for students at home		
					Room and board	Trans-portation	Other costs	Board only	Trans-portation	Other costs
Lamar University at Port Arthur		1,710		500					1,200	1,000
Lamar University—Beaumontt	‡	1,654	5,760/—	538	3,118	1,606	1,506	1,798	2,601	1,387
Laredo Community College		766	1,680/840	500					1,710	1,820
Lee College		470	624/336	600				2,150	800	1,100
LeTourneau University	‡	9,550		600	4,430	500	900	1,700	843	1,021
Lon Morris College		6,400		450	3,690	1,000	1,500	1,150	200	400
Lubbock Christian University		8,136		350	3,387	1,360	1,379	1,477	1,360	1,379
McLennan Community College		870	1,800/150	527				1,764	1,283	1,525
McMurry University		8,000		444	3,767	576	1,808	1,210	798	1,808
Microcomputer Technology Institute		14,500								
Midland College		760	292/48	605				1,179	1,077	1,314
Midwestern State University	‡	1,674	5,760/—	630	3,530	900	938	856	670	540
Miss Wade's Fashion Merchandising College		6,115		780		1,160	936	1,440	1,160	936
Mountain View College	‡	570	1,490/380	800				1,500	1,330	1,045
Navarro College		1,212	430/270	450	3,282	780	835	1,500	833	835
North Central Texas College		630	300/—	545	2,000	885	1,220	1,740	1,050	1,220
North Harris Montgomery Community College District		734	1,350/900	696				1,607	1,238	964
North Lake College	‡	570	1,490/380	600						
Northeast Texas Community College	‡	762	400/240	580	2,700	1,230	1,475	1,500	1,233	1,475
Northwood University: Texas Campus	‡	10,328		600	4,634	500	750	1,500	750	650
Odessa College		1,100	210/130	700	2,983	600	850	1,545	800	850
Our Lady of the Lake University of San Antonio		9,674		630	3,984	740	1,580	1,590	920	1,400
Palo Alto College	‡	830	1,950/630							
Panola College		570	490/240	650	2,080	920	1,150	1,650	920	1,100
Paris Junior College	‡	2,790	810/264	400	3,600					
Paul Quinn College	‡	4,110		800	3,015	700	500	1,500	400	350
Prairie View A&M University	‡	1,926	5,760/—	616	3,510	2,251	1,563	1,500	2,664	1,723
Ranger College	‡	830	140/40	450	2,515	1,000	810	1,834	1,200	810
Rice University		13,206		525	6,000	300	1,350	1,500	700	825
Richland College	‡	570	1,490/380	350						935
St. Edward's University		10,400		650	4,568	800	2,050	1,500	1,000	2,100
St. Mary's University		10,314		750	4,274	300	1,258	1,700	1,300	1,258
St. Philip's College		870	2,040/660							
Sam Houston State University	‡	2,007	5,760/—	498	3,160	1,176	1,282	1,370	2,482	1,214
San Antonio College		878	2,040/750	720				1,600	1,270	1,627
San Jacinto College										
Central Campus	‡	430	990/300	400					1,000	1,209
North	†	510	1,230/360	382				3,180	1,298	1,746
Schreiner College		9,695		500	6,380	372	1,116	1,500	478	1,066
South Plains College		1,016	480/270	400	2,340	700	1,100		700	1,100
Southern Methodist University		15,990		576	5,268	326	1,100	1,500	842	1,000
Southwest Institute of Merchandising & Design		3,800		750					1,400	
Southwest School of Electronics		15,594								
Southwest Texas Junior College	‡	818	1,380/240	350	1,980	634	411	900	430	773
Southwest Texas State University	‡	1,832	5,760/—	500	3,675	980	1,710	2,290	1,020	1,260
Southwestern Adventist College		8,092		430	3,926	923	728	1,500	671	874
Southwestern Assemblies of God College	‡	2,900		495	2,762	996	1,310		785	1,310
Southwestern Christian College		4,688		460	2,990	800	400	1,700	800	400

†Figures are projected for 1996-97. ‡Figures are for 1995-96.

Total freshmen	Percent receiving aid	Freshmen judged to have need	Percent offered aid	Acad	Music/ drama	Art	Athl	Acad	Music/ drama	Art	Athl	Priority	Closing	Inst aid form	Notes
All aid		*Need-based aid*		*Need-based*				*Non-need-based*				*Financial aid deadlines*			
1,468	31	610	100					X	X	X	X	4/1	none	X	
1,541	61			X	X		X	X	X		X	5/1	none		
				X	X	X		X	X	X	X	4/1	none	X	
													none		
													none	X	
546	90			X	X	X	X					7/1	8/1	X	
1,255	34			X	X		X	X			X	6/1	none		
262	92	230	100					X	X	X		3/15	8/26		
1,025	45							X	X	X	X		5/1		
796	44			X				X	X	X	X	4/1	none		
													none		
													none		
4,230	12	1,100	95	X								4/15	none		
				X				X				5/1	none		
													none		
													none		
1,288	35	501	100	X				X	X	X	X	5/1	none		
266	85	238	100	X				X	X	X		4/15	none		
520	65	290	81	X	X	X	X	X	X	X	X	6/1	none	X	
													none		
													none	X	
1,047	78	866	100	X				X	X	X		4/16	none	X	
696	75			X	X		X	X	X		X		2/2	X	
													none		
396	74	368	95					X	X		X	3/1	none		
460	85	369	100	X				X	X		X	3/31	none		
				X				X	X				6/1		
2,584	31	643	100					X	X	X	X	3/29	5/31	X	
2,500	40			X	X	X		X	X	X		5/1	none		
													none		
892	18	658	100	X	X	X	X	X	X	X	X	6/1	none	X	
193	65	87	100					X	X		X	4/1	none		
													none		
1,229	80	514	100	X	X	X	X	X	X	X	X	2/1	none	X	
2,513	45	1,096	94	X	X			X	X		X	4/1	none		
158	85			X				X	X			3/15	none		

Institution	Tuition and fees	Add'l out–of–state/ district tuition	Books and supplies	Costs for campus residents			Costs for students at home		
				Room and board	Trans-portation	Other costs	Board only	Trans-portation	Other costs
Southwestern University	13,400		600	5,024	200	850	1,550	630	800
Stephen F. Austin State University	‡ 1,908	5,760/—	515	3,808	1,197	1,150	1,984	1,197	1,150
Sul Ross State University	‡ 1,596	5,760/—	600	3,160	623	1,112	1,660	890	1,112
Tarleton State University	‡ 1,878	5,760/—	425	3,380	404	1,266	1,500	506	1,094
Tarrant County Junior College	‡ 558	3,294/270	578					1,590	1,266
Temple College	‡ 810	1,410/390	570	3,500	825	1,150	1,975	1,200	1,150
Texarkana College	‡ 950	500/—	750					750	1,200
Texas A&M International University	‡ 1,462	5,760/—	565				1,946	1,911	1,215
Texas A&M University									
College Station	‡ 1,736	5,760/—	616	3,550	750	1,460	1,500	1,000	1,460
Galveston	‡ 1,655	5,760/—	680	3,402	750	900	1,000	750	900
Texas A&M University-Corpus Christi	‡ 1,746	5,760/—	500	5,106	700	1,200	1,700	1,250	1,200
Texas A&M University-Kingsville	‡ 1,712	5,760/—	515	3,584	1,236	1,765	1,545	1,541	1,335
Texas Christian University	10,510		650	3,500	554	1,850	1,800	554	1,286
Texas College	‡ 4,485		400	2,430	586	1,095	2,500	674	1,095
Texas Lutheran College	9,450		500	3,612	750	1,000	1,300	900	1,000
Texas Southern University	‡ 1,453	5,760/—	500	3,380	1,400	1,700	1,500	1,400	1,700
Texas Southmost College	‡ 1,188	4,410/600	400				1,633	824	412
Texas State Technical College									
Amarillo	‡ 1,205	2,880/—	900	3,815	360	810	1,125	900	630
Harlingen	‡ 1,205	2,880/—	900	3,216	995	1,380	2,500	1,493	1,380
Sweetwater	‡ 1,205	2,880/—	924	2,490	1,380	650	825	1,380	650
Waco	‡ 1,205	2,880/—	560		664	1,122		1,196	1,156
Texas Tech University	‡ 2,200	5,760/—	600	3,963					
Texas Wesleyan University	7,600		468	3,484	672	1,240	1,700	672	1,240
Texas Woman's University	‡ 1,648	5,760/—	730	3,170	704	4,752	928	992	1,854
Trinity University	13,644		500	5,545	540	490	2,050		
Trinity Valley Community College	420	1,560/300	400	2,682	780	850	1,000	870	850
Tyler Junior College	800	750/450	600	2,300	1,944	1,274		1,944	1,274
University of Central Texas	3,990		554	3,879	888	878			
University of Dallas	12,690		600	4,918	700	600	1,500	500	600
University of Houston									
Clear Lake	‡ 1,674	5,760/—	750				1,638	2,021	2,678
Downtown	‡ 1,670	5,760/—	515				1,330	1,755	850
Houston	‡ 1,666	5,760/—	580	4,355	1,250	1,600	1,500	1,250	1,600
Victoria	‡ 1,758	5,760/—	600				1,900	1,175	1,600
University of Mary Hardin-Baylor	6,720		600	3,214	762	1,224	1,545	930	1,398
University of North Texas	‡ 1,713	5,760/—	600	3,659	600	1,100		1,000	1,200
University of St. Thomas	9,948		530	4,490	770	1,425	1,909	1,367	1,425
University of Texas									
Arlington	‡ 1,632	5,760/—	500	4,320	1,770	1,080	1,100	1,770	1,080
Austin	‡ 2,208	5,760/—	650	4,550	750	1,648	1,500	750	1,648
Brownsville	‡ 1,638	5,760/—	487				1,894	917	458
Dallas	‡ 2,033	5,760/—	664		1,626	1,442	1,716	1,626	588
El Paso	1,897	5,760/—	374	3,600	1,350	1,142	1,750	1,350	1,142
Health Science Center at San Antonio	‡ 1,271	5,760/—	830				4,260	1,025	1,050
Medical Branch at Galveston	‡ 1,438	5,760/—	2,665		2,508	4,488	6,168	2,964	7,728
Pan American	‡ 1,500	5,760/—	507	4,088	492	2,390	1,946	2,039	2,431
Permian Basin	‡ 1,792	5,760/—	555		1,452	1,375	1,000	1,452	1,375
San Antonio	‡ 1,766	5,760/—	452	5,538	2,080	1,700	1,844	2,080	1,652
Southwestern Medical Center at Dallas	‡ 1,288	5,760/—	576				3,355	1,501	4,156
Tyler	‡ 1,801	5,760/—	400				1,620	580	934

†Figures are projected for 1996-97. ‡Figures are for 1995-96.

| | All aid | | Need–based aid | | Grants and scholarships | | | | | | | | Financial aid deadlines | | Inst | |
| | | | | | Need–based | | | | Non–need–based | | | | | | aid | |
Total freshmen	Percent receiving aid	Freshmen judged to have need	Percent offered aid	Acad	Music/drama	Art	Athl	Acad	Music/drama	Art	Athl	Priority	Closing	form	Notes
328	78	210	100	X				X	X	X			3/1	X	
1,777	50	383	100					X	X		X	6/1	11/1		
													none		
													none		
4,706	14			X				X				4/15	none	X	
1,410	52			X	X	X	X	X	X		X	8/1	none		
				X				X				3/15	none	X	
6,072	45	2,413	94	X				X	X		X	4/1	none		
387	48			X				X				4/1	none		
								X	X	X			3/15		
870	85			X				X	X	X	X		4/15		
1,330	66	548	100	X				X	X	X	X	5/1	none		
													none		
227	85			X	X	X	X	X	X	X	X	5/1	none		
2,210	80	1,740	100	X	X		X					5/1	none		
													none		
723	80	570	95	X				X				4/26	none	X	
													none		
2,559	68			X				X				6/1	none	X	
3,350	41			X	X	X		X	X	X	X	4/1	none		
457	95	249	100	X				X	X	X	X	3/15	none		
412	47	246	100	X				X	X	X	X	4/1	none	X	
615	78			X	X	X		X	X	X		2/15			
													none		
2,584	16			X	X	X	X	X	X	X	X	6/1	none	X	
				X								7/1	9/1		
248	96	192	100					X	X	X		3/1	none		
				X	X	X		X	X	X		4/1	none	X	
913	53	763	100	X		X		X		X		6/1	none	X	
2,218	60			X	X	X		X	X	X	X	4/1	none	X	
				X				X				4/15	none		
													none		
3,622	42			X			X	X			X	6/1	none		
238	82	117	100	X	X			X	X			3/1	none	X	
1,370	46	551	80	X				X	X	X	X	6/1	none	X	
5,687	60	2,200	100	X	X	X	X	X	X	X	X	4/1	none		
390	71			X				X				3/1	11/1	X	
1,908	55			X	X		X	X	X		X	3/15	none		
													none		
				X				X				3/15	none	X	
													none		
1,673	46			X				X			X	3/31	none		
				X				X							

Institution	Tuition and fees	Add'l out-of-state/district tuition	Books and supplies	Costs for campus residents			Costs for students at home		
				Room and board	Transportation	Other costs	Board only	Transportation	Other costs
Houston Health Science Center	‡ 1,975	5,760/—	450		1,449	168	2,340	1,449	1,728
University of Texas Health Science Center at Houston	‡ 2,305	9,630/—							
Vernon Regional Junior College	‡ 780	500/196	600	1,999	2,500	3,000		2,500	3,000
Victoria College	‡ 743	1,950/—	425				2,500	485	1,170
Wayland Baptist University	6,404		480	3,218	672	1,030	1,772	688	925
Weatherford College	‡ 830	1,920/210	300	2,626	100	1,000	1,000	100	1,000
West Texas A&M University	‡ 1,646	5,760/—	500	3,261	580	1,040	1,550	1,760	770
Western Texas College	810	300/150	350	2,500	960	900	2,500	960	900
Wharton County Junior College	810	1,740/570	600	2,180	1,300	1,100	1,420	1,300	1,100
Wiley College	4,556		210	3,138	314	572	1,500	314	572
Utah									
Brigham Young University	2,530		950	3,930	1,190	1,330	3,880	1,190	1,330
College of Eastern Utah	‡ 1,248	3,069/—	652	3,000	1,162	1,393	1,276	724	1,325
Dixie College	‡ 1,332	3,507/—	675	2,649		450	1,600	225	450
LDS Business College	1,940		675		600	945	1,875	600	945
Phillips Junior College: Salt Lake City Campus	5,100								
Salt Lake Community College	‡ 1,446	3,060/—	1,035				1,590	495	1,275
Snow College	‡ 1,218	3,717/—	530	1,980	550	900	1,500	600	700
Southern Utah University	‡ 1,776	3,852/—	1,035	3,708	1,059	1,560		1,059	1,560
Stevens-Henager College of Business	‡ 12,890				960	2,046	2,844	769	2,123
University of Utah *12,632*	‡ 2,508	5,199/—	945	3,980	738	3,452	2,430	738	2,444
Utah State University *10,292*	‡ 1,992	4,050/—	715	3,525	1,050	1,490	2,100	1,055	1,530
Utah Valley State College	‡ 1,456	3,135/—	670				1,500	650	650
Weber State University *10,746*	‡ 1,854	3,687/—	630	4,575	1,005	2,073	1,800	1,005	2,073
Westminster College of Salt Lake City	10,270		600	4,358	950	1,650	1,500	675	1,070
Vermont									
Bennington College	25,800 (comprehensive)		500			600			4,100
Burlington College	‡ 7,950		750				2,115	1,150	2,475
Castleton State College	‡ 4,026	4,512/—	400	4,794	300	600	2,100	800	600
Champlain College	9,325		550	6,285		600	1,500	650	600
College of St. Joseph in Vermont	‡ 9,070		600	5,100	550	900	1,500	750	900
Community College of Vermont	‡ 2,898	2,712/—						650	
Goddard College	15,056		508	5,084	470	911	2,500	795	911
Green Mountain College	14,660		400	3,190	500	375	1,500	500	375
Johnson State College	‡ 4,036	4,512/—	500	4,804	350	650	750	350	650
Landmark College	‡ 24,600		500	5,400	1,200	1,500		300	1,500
Lyndon State College	‡ 4,036	4,512/—	500	4,854	300	600	1,000	300	600
Marlboro College	19,580		400	6,400	200	320	2,020	50	320
Middlebury College	28,240 (comprehensive)		550			1,000			
New England Culinary Institute	16,255		550	2,860	1,683	3,996		1,683	3,996
Norwich University	14,634		500	5,436		800			800
St. Michael's College	1,605		350	6,375	250	400	2,500	250	400
School for International Training	12,975		1,000	4,623	450	960	2,500	450	960
Southern Vermont College	10,750		500	4,790	600	550	1,000	600	550
Sterling College	18,532 (comprehensive)		600		350	350			
Trinity College of Vermont	† 12,415		550	5,988	250	500	200	500	500
University of Vermont	† 6,909	9,696/—	569	5,032	959	1,368	1,853	959	1,368
Vermont Technical College	‡ 4,760	4,152/—	700	4,854	350	650	2,050	600	650

†Figures are projected for 1996-97. ‡Figures are for 1995-96.

Total freshmen	Percent receiving aid	Freshmen judged to have need	Percent offered aid	Need Acad	Music/drama	Art	Athl	Non-need Acad	Music/drama	Art	Athl	Priority	Closing	Inst aid form	Notes
				X				X						X	
943	35	240	100	X	X		X	X	X	X	X	7/15	none	X	
1,199	35			X	X	X		X	X	X		4/15	none		
200	85			X	X	X	X					4/15	none		
1,631	20			X	X	X	X	X	X		X		6/1		
923	55	327	100	X				X	X	X	X	5/1	none	X	
304	70							X	X	X	X	7/1	none		
								X	X		X	6/1	none		
													none		
				X	X	X	X	X	X	X	X	6/1	none		
1,170	49	561	100	X				X	X	X	X	4/15	none	X	
1,160	64							X	X	X	X	5/15	none		
373	50							X					none		
120	85			X				X					none		
6,151	49			X				X		X	X	4/1	none		
1,733	59	962	47					X	X	X	X		7/15		
1,027	55	583	90					X	X		X		none	X	
													none		
2,728	56	2,156	100	X	X	X	X	X	X	X	X	2/15	5/30		
				X	X	X	X	X	X	X	X	2/10	5/15		
3,117	65							X			X	7/1	none		
2,173	67	2,150	100					X	X	X	X	4/1	none		
258	80	170	100	X				X	X	X			none		
78	92	53	100	X				X	X	X		3/1	none	X	
				X								6/1	none		
330	77	237	100	X	X	X		X	X			3/15	none		
727	88	485	100								X	5/1	none	X	
													none		
715	86							X					none	X	
												4/1	6/15		
167	80			X				X		X	X	3/1	none		
280	65							X	X	X		3/1	none		
		46	100	X								5/15	none	X	
407	60			X				X				3/15	none		
55	90	63	100	X	X	X		X	X	X		3/1	none		
580	51	292	100										none		
280	80												none		
				X				X				3/1	none	X	
538	60	352	100	X	X	X	X	X			X	3/15	none	X	
				X				X				4/1	none	X	
165	92	116	100	X								5/1	none		
60	70	41	10	X				X				3/15	none	X	
107	92	104	100	X				X				3/1	none	X	
1,889	53	1,241	100	X	X	X	X	X	X	X	X	3/1	none	X	
321	78			X				X				3/1	none	X	

Institution	Tuition and fees	Add'l out-of-state/district tuition	Books and supplies	Costs for campus residents			Costs for students at home		
				Room and board	Transportation	Other costs	Board only	Transportation	Other costs
Virginia									
Averett College	11,450		750	4,150	600	1,350		600	1,350
Blue Ridge Community College	‡ 1,412	3,281/—	600				1,750	1,050	500
Bluefield College	8,200		500	4,610	900	900	2,860	1,065	1,065
Bridgewater College	12,505		650	5,220	200	925	2,475	600	925
Central Virginia Community College	‡ 1,420	3,281/—	500				600	500	3,000
Christendom College	‡ 9,404		450	3,600	400	300	1,456		300
Christopher Newport University	3,366	4,620/—	564	4,650	710	1,710	910	1,710	1,048
Clinch Valley College of the University of Virginia	3,258	4,524/—	600	4,158	660	800	1,500	1,100	800
College of Health Sciences	4,500		750		900	2,100	2,400	1,900	2,100
College of William and Mary	4,906	10,010/—	600	4,470	150	800	1,800	600	800
Commonwealth College	‡ 6,292		750		350	300		350	300
Dabney S. Lancaster Community College	‡ 1,423	3,281/—	550				1,500	1,130	1,530
Danville Community College	‡ 1,410	3,281/—	500				1,984	900	2,176
Eastern Mennonite University	11,130		600	4,200	200	450	2,500	200	450
Eastern Shore Community College	‡ 1,445	3,281/—	450						2,790
ECPI College of Technology	6,224		720		420	1,120		630	1,120
Emory and Henry College	10,938		700	4,502	600	1,000	1,500	1,100	800
Ferrum College	10,200		500	4,700	400	1,200	2,100	600	1,000
George Mason University	‡ 4,212	7,392/—	660	5,100	1,135	1,390	3,000	1,384	1,390
Germanna Community College	‡ 1,433	3,281/—	300				1,000	1,440	1,274
Hampden-Sydney College	14,789		800	5,176		700	2,700		700
Hampton University	8,948		600	3,878	1,200	1,000	1,500	856	1,000
Hollins College	14,810		500	5,975	350	550		300	1,500
J. Sargeant Reynolds Community College	‡ 1,427	3,281/—	600				1,500	900	900
James Madison University	‡ 4,014	4,280/—	500	4,680	600	800	2,200	600	800
John Tyler Community College	1,450	3,280/—	500				1,500	900	900
Liberty University	7,680		650	4,800	825	825	1,600	1,050	825
Longwood College	4,370	5,472/—	550	4,222	1,000	1,200	4,080	1,000	1,200
Lord Fairfax Community College	‡ 1,426	3,281/—	450				1,500	1,152	990
Lynchburg College	14,720		500	4,400	430	440	1,500	390	
Mary Baldwin College	12,355		600	7,400	400	1,200	1,500	700	1,200
Mary Washington College	‡ 3,489	4,890/—	670	5,024	811	1,414	2,310	1,644	1,755
Marymount University	12,400		500	5,640	470	900	1,500	750	900
Mountain Empire Community College	‡ 1,418	3,281/—	400				500	1,000	
National Business College	4,170		500	7,092	960	500		1,060	500
New River Community College	‡ 1,418	3,281/—	350					1,200	950
Norfolk State University	2,865	3,662/—	600	4,096	700	1,300	1,700	1,300	1,300
Northern Virginia Community College	‡ 1,440	3,281/—	550				736	1,096	1,920
Old Dominion University	‡ 3,990	6,360/—	600	4,585	1,000	1,200	1,500	1,080	1,200
Patrick Henry Community College	‡ 1,410	3,281/—	425				1,600	1,040	840
Paul D. Camp Community College	‡ 1,400	3,281/—	450				1,500	900	900
Piedmont Virginia Community College	‡ 1,416	3,281/—	500				1,500	920	1,200
Radford University	† 3,200	4,711/—	550	4,250	400	1,000	1,500	600	1,000
Randolph-Macon College	15,630		400	3,985	400	550	750	650	550
Randolph-Macon Woman's College	15,740		400	6,520	265	600	1,500	225	
Rappahannock Community College	‡ 1,431	3,281/—	500				1,100	1,000	600
Richard Bland College	1,990	3,850/—	500				1,500	750	1,000
Roanoke College	14,750		450	4,850	600	600	1,500	600	600
St. Paul's College	6,760		400	4,040	360	500	1,500	500	500
Shenandoah University	13,700		450	5,000	900	900	1,500	900	900

†Figures are projected for 1996-97. ‡Figures are for 1995-96.

Total freshmen	Percent receiving aid	Freshmen judged to have need	Percent offered aid	Acad	Music/drama	Art	Athl	Acad	Music/drama	Art	Athl	Priority	Closing	Inst aid form	Notes
				Need-based				Non-need-based				Financial aid deadlines			
186	82	81	100	X	X	X		X	X	X		4/1	none	X	
635	15			X									none		
253	91	135	100	X	X	X	X	X	X	X	X	3/8	none	X	
305	99	258	100	X	X			X	X				3/1		
				X				X				5/1	none		
65	72							X				4/1	6/1		
554	37			X				X	X			4/1	none		
				X			X	X			X	4/1	none		
6	59			X				X				7/1	none		
1,371	60			X	X	X	X	X			X	2/15	2/15	X	
													none		
447	60	246	100	X				X				3/15	none	X	
				X									none		
208	98	153	100	X	X			X	X			5/1	none	X	
220	66							X				6/1	none		
														X	
238	95	172	100	X	X			X	X	X		2/15	4/1	X	
302	95	235	100	X	X			X	X			4/1	none	X	
1,926	47	968	100	X				X	X		X	3/1	none		
730	30			X				X				5/1	none		
285	82	139	100	X				X				3/1	none		
1,289	70							X	X		X	3/31	6/1		
226	79	116	100	X	X			X	X	X		2/15	3/1	X	
													none		
2,539	62			X	X	X		X	X	X	X	2/15	none		
				X				X				4/15	7/15		
1,868	80			X			X	X	X		X	4/15	none		
680	66	346	96	X				X	X	X	X	2/15	none		
													none		
262	78	180	99	X				X	X			3/1	none		
284	74			X				X				3/15	none		
766	55	357	100	X				X	X				3/1		
222	72	170	100	X		X		X				3/1	none	X	
1,570	81	555	97	X				X				4/15	none	X	
				X				X					none		
705	42			X				X				4/15	none	X	
1,275	85							X				3/15	none	X	
4,980	14			X				X				3/1	none	X	
1,571	75	801	100	X	X	X	X	X	X	X	X	2/15	6/30	X	
				X				X					none		
				X				X				7/30	8/16		
845	15											4/15	none		
1,390	66	607	99					X	X	X	X	3/1	none	X	
314	84	163	100	X				X				3/1	none	X	
189	99	128	100	X				X	X			3/15	none	X	
400	55			X				X				5/15	none	X	
397	48			X				X				4/1	5/1	X	
430	87	272	100	X	X	X		X	X	X		3/1	none		
130	85							X					none		
230	92	363	83	X	X			X	X			3/15	none	X	

Institution	Tuition and fees	Add'l out-of-state/district tuition	Books and supplies	Costs for campus residents			Costs for students at home		
				Room and board	Transportation	Other costs	Board only	Transportation	Other costs
Southside Virginia Community College	‡ 1,421	3,281/—	523				1,500	1,440	1,602
Southwest Virginia Community College	‡ 1,415	3,281/—	500				1,500	1,200	1,258
Sweet Briar College	15,115		600	6,510	500	750		500	750
Thomas Nelson Community College	‡ 1,413	3,281/—	500				1,550	700	650
Tidewater Community College	‡ 1,531	3,281/—	520				1,900	900	500
University of Richmond	16,778		800	3,595		1,175	1,500		810
University of Virginia	4,650	9,790/—	700	3,960	290	1,100		200	1,100
Virginia Commonwealth University	4,071	7,925/—	600	4,352	1,700	2,040	670	1,700	2,040
Virginia Highlands Community College	‡ 1,400	3,281/—	420				1,575	850	850
Virginia Intermont College	‡ 9,600		800	4,250	350	990	2,300	1,650	1,440
Virginia Military Institute	5,355	7,925/—	600	3,435	300	1,000			
Virginia Polytechnic Institute and State University	4,131	6,652/—	800	3,250	600	1,600	1,450	600	1,600
Virginia State University	‡ 3,256	4,009/—	500	4,845	500	500	1,350	600	525
Virginia Union University	8,559		500	3,780	450	1,000	1,866	450	1,000
Virginia Wesleyan College	12,700		650	5,550	1,250	1,500	750	1,550	1,500
Virginia Western Community College	‡ 1,404	3,281/—	550				1,600	800	1,200
Washington and Lee University	15,435		680	5,360	400	1,115		500	1,115
Wytheville Community College	‡ 1,430	3,281/—	550				1,500	1,665	1,050
Washington									
Antioch University Seattle	10,200		750					939	1,164
Art Institute of Seattle	† 9,980		993	5,410	1,873	1,383	2,461	1,078	1,383
Bastyr University	† 7,620		750						
Bellevue Community College	‡ 1,401	4,110/—	678				2,113	1,026	1,584
Big Bend Community College	1,401	4,110/—	600	3,628	1,026	1,692	2,113	1,026	1,584
Central Washington University	2,432	6,185/—	600	4,195	1,026	1,692		1,026	1,584
Centralia College	1,401	4,110/—	750					1,500	
City University	‡ 2,790		800				1,050	850	1,200
Clark College	1,401	—/4,110	702				2,040	1,044	
Columbia Basin College	1,401	4,110/—	678				974	1,008	714
Cornish College of the Arts	10,900		1,800				2,500	450	1,200
Eastern Washington University	2,432	6,185/—	600	4,294	1,026	1,692	2,113	1,026	1,584
Edmonds Community College	1,401	4,110/—	678				1,974	1,008	1,416
Everett Community College	‡ 1,350	3,968/—	500					900	1,000
Evergreen State College	2,432	6,185/—	732		990	1,584	2,112	990	1,584
Gonzaga University	14,900		600	4,670	590	1,060	1,000	500	900
Grays Harbor College	1,401	4,110/—	600				2,113	1,026	1,584
Green River Community College	‡ 1,350	3,968/—	677				1,975	1,012	714
Henry Cogswell College	8,520		550					100	
Heritage College	‡ 6,350		870				2,947	1,392	1,066
Highline Community College	1,401	4,110/—	600				2,113	1,026	1,584
Lake Washington Technical College	‡ 1,533		702				2,040	1,044	738
Lower Columbia College	1,401	4,110/—	720		900	1,470	1,020	900	735
Lutheran Bible Institute of Seattle	‡ 4,160		500	3,900	1,000	1,200		1,000	800
North Seattle Community College	1,401	4,110/—	500				1,570	800	1,000
Northwest College	8,415		600	3,990	200	1,692	2,114	1,026	1,584
Northwest College of Art	7,000		1,000					420	
Northwest Indian College	1,350	600/—	640				4,461	973	1,114
Olympic College	1,401	4,110/—	600				2,500	1,026	1,197
Pacific Lutheran University	14,560		600	4,690	550	1,692	3,051	1,026	1,584
Peninsula College	1,401	4,110/—	675	3,930	1,020	1,470	1,350	1,020	750

†Figures are projected for 1996-97. ‡Figures are for 1995-96.

All aid		Need-based aid		Grants and scholarships — Need-based				Grants and scholarships — Non-need-based				Financial aid deadlines		Inst aid form	Notes
Total freshmen	Percent receiving aid	Freshmen judged to have need	Percent offered aid	Acad	Music/drama	Art	Athl	Acad	Music/drama	Art	Athl	Priority	Closing		
				X				X				6/1	8/1	X	
								X				5/30	none		
171	67	130	85	X	X			X	X			3/1	none		
1,289	20	250	80	X				X				5/1	none		
												8/1	none	X	
797	60	279	100					X	X		X		2/25	X	
2,876	43	1,180	89								X	3/1	none	X	
1,690	71	1,028	100					X	X	X	X	4/15	none		
													none		
114	78	100	100	X			X	X			X	3/1	none	X	
409	62	140	96	X				X			X	3/1	4/1	X	
4,652	70			X				X	X	X	X	3/1	none		
738	85			X			X	X	X	X	X	3/31	5/1	X	
455	87	392						X	X		X	5/15	none		
267	95	196	100	X	X	X		X	X	X		3/1	none		
													none		
435	54	127	100	X				X				2/1	none		
534	50			X				X				4/1	none	X	
													none		
681	86			X		X							none		
								X				6/1	none	X	
4,822	26			X			X	X			X	4/14	none	X	
629	60							X	X		X	4/1	7/1	X	
993	37	575	99	X				X	X			3/1	none		
89	50							X	X		X	5/15	none	X	
1,700	25							X	X		X	5/1	none		
640	41							X	X	X	X	4/1	none		
214	94	194	100	X	X	X		X	X	X		2/15	none	X	
712	60	275	92	X			X	X	X	X	X	2/15	none		
3,473	22			X	X		X	X	X	X	X	5/1	none		
														X	
437	15	230	99					X	X	X	X	3/15	none	X	
626	88	394	100	X	X		X	X	X		X	2/1	none		
600	80			X	X	X	X	X	X	X	X	5/15	none	X	
													none		
				X				X					7/1	X	
													none		
3,000	60											4/4	none	X	
													none		
755	35	183	100	X	X	X	X	X	X	X	X	5/1	none		
													none	X	
				X	X	X		X	X	X		4/3	9/1		
171	93	156	100	X				X	X	X	X	3/1	none	X	
													none		
				X	X			X	X	X	X	4/30	4/1	X	
668	86			X	X	X	X	X	X	X		1/31	none		
866	60			X				X	X	X		6/1	none		

Institution	Tuition and fees	Add'l out-of-state/district tuition	Books and supplies	Costs for campus residents			Costs for students at home		
				Room and board	Transportation	Other costs	Board only	Transportation	Other costs
Pierce College	1,401	4,110/—	600				2,113	1,026	1,584
Puget Sound Christian College	5,790		750	3,870	360	2,250	2,400	924	1,800
Renton Technical College	‡ 1,635		702				2,040	1,044	738
St. Martin's College	12,740		678	4,590	1,050	1,505	1,920	1,050	1,620
Seattle Central Community College	‡ 1,350	3,968/—	594				1,908	978	690
Seattle Pacific University	13,680		618	5,019	321	1,296	1,752	321	763
Seattle University	14,265		702	5,283	1,044	1,464	2,040	1,044	1,464
Shoreline Community College	1,401	4,110/—	738				2,003	1,096	787
Skagit Valley College	‡ 1,350	3,968/—	690				1,005	1,050	1,500
South Puget Sound Community College	1,401	4,110/—	750				2,113	1,026	1,000
South Seattle Community College	† 1,401	4,110/—	600				2,070	945	1,185
Spokane Community College	1,401	4,110/—	654				1,650	840	510
Spokane Falls Community College	1,401	4,110/—	540				1,620	840	500
Tacoma Community College	‡ 1,401	4,110/—	750				2,040	1,044	738
University of Puget Sound	18,170		660	4,800	500	1,300	1,850	500	1,300
University of Washington	3,141	5,724/—	756	5,215	396	1,893	2,211	396	1,893
Walla Walla College	12,033		795	3,768	1,000		2,220	1,000	1,320
Walla Walla Community College	1,401	4,110/—	535				1,800	100	450
Washington State University $39 GB	3,142	5,724/—	763		866	1,256	2,464	918	1,256
Wenatchee Valley College	1,401	4,110/—	678	3,945	1,008	1,416	1,974	1,008	714
Western Washington University	2,432	6,185/—	639	4,308	978	1,407	1,920	978	714
Whatcom Community College	1,401	—/4,110	594				1,845	933	669
Whitman College	18,805		750	5,420		500		700	500
Whitworth College	14,324		600	5,100	1,026	1,692		1,026	1,534
Yakima Valley Community College	1,401	—/4,110	600	4,300	900	1,300	1,800	900	1,100
West Virginia									
Alderson-Broaddus College	11,750		690	3,766	650	1,250	1,500	850	1,250
Appalachian Bible College	5,030		550	2,880	750	750	1,500	1,000	650
Bethany College	17,177		400	5,660	700	900	2,000	1,200	1,000
Bluefield State College	‡ 1,916	2,660/—	500				1,700	850	1,500
College of West Virginia	‡ 3,240		550				550	1,000	900
Concord College	‡ 2,150	2,500/—	400	3,382	408	978	750	896	978
Davis and Elkins College	10,710		400	4,890			1,500		
Fairmont State College	‡ 1,858	2,470/—	500	3,300		500		600	500
Glenville State College	‡ 1,800	2,400/—	350	3,300	200	1,000		900	1,000
Huntington Junior College of Business	3,600								
Marshall University	‡ 2,050	3,646/2,801	630	4,120	525	1,050	1,575	491	212
National Education Center: National Institute of Technology Campus	11,750								
Ohio Valley College	6,574		425	3,580	400	800	1,500	800	600
Potomac State College of West Virginia University	‡ 1,812	3,832/—	450	3,636		1,120	1,300		1,120
Salem-Teikyo University	11,658		550	3,952	320	300	1,600	320	300
Shepherd College	‡ 2,064	2,630/—	700	3,960	270	925	1,600	1,210	925
Southern West Virginia Community and Technical College	‡ 1,030	2,010/—	450				1,500		900
University of Charleston	11,140		400	3,870	250	500			1,800
West Liberty State College	‡ 1,960	3,340/—	600	3,000	310	900	1,500	800	650
West Virginia Business College	12,000		475					2,000	
West Virginia Institute of Technology	‡ 2,226	3,372/—	500	3,660	400	700	1,200	700	700
West Virginia Northern Community College	‡ 1,438	2,448/—	450				1,610	896	1,114

†Figures are projected for 1996-97. ‡Figures are for 1995-96.

All aid		Need–based aid		Grants and scholarships								Financial aid deadlines		Inst aid form	Notes
				Need–based				Non–need–based							
Total freshmen	Percent receiving aid	Freshmen judged to have need	Percent offered aid	Acad	Music/drama	Art	Athl	Acad	Music/drama	Art	Athl	Priority	Closing		
2,857	18							X	X		X	4/15	none	X	
24	96	30	100	X				X	X				none	X	
				X				X					none		
72	66			X			X	X			X	3/1	none		
403	75	287	100	X	X	X		X	X	X	X	1/31	none		
432	81	295	100	X	X		X	X	X	X	X	2/1	none		
1,000	18							X			X	4/1	none	X	
													none		
1,704	45			X				X			X	5/1	none	X	
1,123	27	760	100	X				X	X			5/15	none	X	
1,756	52			X			X				X	2/28	none		
1,580	55			X			X				X	2/28	none		
				X				X	X	X	X	4/13	7/22	X	
658	79	407	100	X	X	X		X	X	X		2/1	none	X	
3,701	35	1,519	83	X	X		X	X			X	2/28	none		
				X				X	X			4/1	none	X	
				X				X	X		X	5/1	none		
2,537	54			X	X	X	X	X	X	X	X	3/1	none		
								X	X	X	X	4/1	4/1		
1,782	70	573	100	X	X	X	X	X	X	X	X	2/15	none		
								X				4/15	none		
366	88	218	100	X	X	X		X	X	X			2/15	X	
420	88			X	X	X	X	X	X	X		3/1	none	X	
				X	X		X					6/3	none		
154	94	145	100	X	X		X	X	X		X	5/1	none	X	
													none		
242	75	154	100	X				X	X			4/1	none	X	
606	72			X			X	X			X	3/1	none	X	
													none		
1,326	77	616	68	X	X	X	X	X	X	X	X	4/15	none		
170	68	160	100	X	X	X	X	X	X	X	X	3/1	none		
2,184	60	2,184	67	X	X	X	X	X	X	X	X		3/1	X	
543	79			X	X	X	X	X	X	X	X		3/1		
													none		
2,032	50							X	X	X	X	3/1	none		
													none		
163	93			X	X	X	X	X	X	X	X	6/1	none		
				X	X		X	X				3/1	none		
119	59			X			X	X			X	4/15	none		
660	22							X	X	X	X	3/1	none	X	
													none		
514	60	365	100	X	X	X	X	X	X	X	X	3/1	none		
529	80			X	X		X	X	X		X	1/31	4/1		
417	50			X				X				3/15	none		

Institution	Tuition and fees	Add'l out-of-state/district tuition	Books and supplies	Costs for campus residents			Costs for students at home		
				Room and board	Trans-portation	Other costs	Board only	Trans-portation	Other costs
West Virginia State College	‡ 1,960	3,340/—	500	3,450	375	940	1,400	940	1,000
West Virginia University									
Morgantown	‡ 2,192	4,592/—	560	4,310	310	1,190	1,595	1,045	1,195
Parkersburg	‡ 1,164	2,472/—	470				1,730	1,100	1,270
West Virginia Wesleyan College	15,175		450	3,975	750	1,100	2,500	750	1,100
Wheeling Jesuit College	13,000		600	4,870	500	600	750	500	750
Wisconsin									
Alverno College	9,288		550	3,890	200	1,800	1,200	500	1,280
Bellin College of Nursing	8,191		560				1,008	774	1,278
Beloit College	18,230		350	3,980	400	700	1,500	600	700
Blackhawk Technical College	‡ 1,603	9,668/—	475				1,900	625	1,025
Cardinal Stritch College	9,060		500	3,880	350	1,200	1,700	800	1,200
Carroll College	13,340		510	4,130	220	990		1,000	
Carthage College	14,600		500	4,195	900	1,300	810	900	1,300
Chippewa Valley Technical College	‡ 1,603	9,668/—	400				1,852	450	800
Columbia College of Nursing	13,590		490	3,960	210	960		970	810
Concordia University Wisconsin	10,760		620	3,700	130	1,300	2,080	570	1,300
Edgewood College	9,650		625	4,000	265	1,400	950	400	1,400
Fox Valley Technical College	‡ 1,603	9,668/—	670				1,852	673	800
Gateway Technical College	‡ 1,603	9,668/—	500				1,852	673	691
Herzing College of Technology	‡ 4,661		500						
Lac Courte Oreilles Ojibwa Community College	2,425		300		500				
Lakeland College	10,820		500	4,220	700	800	1,000	700	750
Lakeshore Technical College	‡ 1,603	9,668/—	704				1,945	715	1,195
Lawrence University	18,864		500	4,213	300	700			700
Madison Area Technical College	‡ 1,603	9,668/—	663				1,852	673	1,124
Madison Junior College of Business	‡ 5,940						1,200	260	1,160
Maranatha Baptist Bible College	‡ 5,300		560	3,250	850	1,100	1,330	1,000	5,645
Marian College of Fond du Lac	10,730		550	4,400	1,100	1,100	1,500	1,100	1,100
Marquette University	14,930		600	5,350	1,000	1,350	800	1,000	1,350
Mid-State Technical College	‡ 1,603	9,668/—	704				1,964	1,357	550
Milwaukee Area Technical College	‡ 1,603	9,668/—	663				1,852	673	1,124
Milwaukee Institute of Art & Design	† 12,900		1,300	5,800	800	1,250	2,550	800	1,250
Milwaukee School of Engineering	13,305		1,025	3,855	945	1,275	1,575	945	1,275
Moraine Park Technical College	1,645		684				1,909	694	1,159
Mount Mary College	10,230		550	3,488	400	1,289	1,920	800	1,289
Mount Senario College	8,980		600	3,250	580	1,350	1,825	530	1,350
Nicolet Area Technical College	‡ 1,603	9,668/—	663				1,852	673	1,124
Northcentral Technical College	‡ 1,603	9,668/—	740		700	4,164	1,882	700	1,200
Northeast Wisconsin Technical College	‡ 1,603	9,668/—	663				1,852	673	1,124
Northland College	11,610		450	4,060	600	1,000	2,190	500	1,000
Ripon College	17,000		350	4,400		650	2,330		650
St. Norbert College	13,900		425	4,845	350	750	900	450	750
Silver Lake College	9,400		530	4,054			1,854	1,000	1,053
Southwest Wisconsin Technical College	1,741		704		714	1,193	1,964	714	1,193
Stratton College	5,970		875				2,320	520	1,542
University of Wisconsin									
Eau Claire	‡ 2,339	5,135/—	175	2,800	780	1,260	1,060	915	965
Green Bay	‡ 2,425	5,135/—	500	2,502	405	1,377	990	747	594
La Crosse	‡ 2,422	5,135/—	160	2,630	350	1,800	920	159	1,600
Madison	‡ 2,879	6,755/—	600	3,799	340	1,290	1,500	310	1,290

†Figures are projected for 1996-97. ‡Figures are for 1995-96.

| All aid | | Need-based aid | | Grants and scholarships | | | | | | | | Financial aid deadlines | | Inst aid form | Notes |
| | | | | Need-based | | | | Non-need-based | | | | | | | |
Total fresh-men	Percent receiving aid	Freshmen judged to have need	Percent offered aid	Acad	Music/ drama	Art	Athl	Acad	Music/ drama	Art	Athl	Priority	Closing		
706	64			X	X	X	X	X	X	X	X	3/1	6/15		
3,006	57			X				X	X	X	X	2/1	3/1		
				X				X				5/1	none		
457	91	414	100	X	X	X	X	X	X	X	X	3/1	none		
268	89	218	100	X				X	X		X	3/1	none		
157	81			X	X	X		X	X	X		3/15	none		
												3/1	none		
299	84	202	100	X	X			X	X			4/15	none	X	
2,550	30											4/1	6/15		
371	82	128	100	X				X	X	X	X	4/1	none		
516	94	342	100	X	X	X		X	X	X		4/15	none		
405	97	361	100	X				X	X	X		2/15	none		
1,060	76			X				X				3/15	none		
43	94			X				X				3/15	none		
682	90							X	X		X	5/1	6/1	X	
316	85	163	100	X	X	X		X	X	X		3/15	none		
1,130	75			X				X					none		
													none	X	
140	65														
													none		
176	95			X	X		X	X				5/1	8/1		
													none		
327	88	235	100	X	X			X	X			3/15	none	X	
													none		
37	48							X					none	X	
220	68	196	97	X				X				3/1	none	X	
191	90			X	X	X		X	X	X		3/1	none	X	
1,639	92	1,066	100	X				X	X		X	3/1	none		
740	65			X			X	X					6/30	X	
10,000	70							X				3/15	none		
180	89	168	100	X		X		X		X		3/1	none	X	
607	85			X				X				3/15	none		
833	40	322	100					X				5/1	none	X	
108	98			X	X	X		X	X	X		3/15	none	X	
118	95	74	100	X				X				6/15	none		
560	75			X				X				4/15	none		
810	66											4/1	none		
													none		
254	92	205	100	X	X		X	X	X		X	5/1	7/1		
184	80	188	100	X	X			X	X			3/1	none		
525	93	403	100	X	X	X		X	X	X		3/1	none	X	
31	88			X	X	X	X	X	X	X		3/15	none		
700	88	579	100	X								4/15	none	X	
273	76							X					none		
2,035	50	1,040	100	X	X			X	X			4/15	none		
833	61			X			X	X	X	X	X	4/15	none		
1,743	48	750	100	X				X	X			3/15	none	X	
5,164	40	1,632	100	X	X	X	X	X	X	X	X		none	X	

Institution		Tuition and fees	Add'l out-of-state/district tuition	Books and supplies	Costs for campus residents			Costs for students at home		
					Room and board	Trans-portation	Other costs	Board only	Trans-portation	Other costs
Milwaukee	‡	2,946	6,451/—	570	3,050	826	4,194	1,751	826	1,154
Oshkosh	‡	2,299	5,135/—	518	2,400	360	1,530	1,000	920	1,390
Parkside	‡	2,405	5,135/—	600	3,512	700	1,150		700	1,000
Platteville	‡	2,400	5,135/—	300	2,743	400	1,100	1,780	690	930
River Falls	‡	2,364	5,135/—	210	2,856	500	1,590	2,010	1,500	1,590
Stevens Point	‡	2,411	5,135/—	300	3,062	360	1,190	1,500	280	1,190
Stout	‡	2,369	5,138/—	342	2,718	394	1,340		510	1,104
Superior	‡	2,334	5,135/—	575	3,016	575	1,385		575	1,385
Whitewater	‡	2,389	5,135/—	450	2,600	650	1,300	2,800	650	1,300
University of Wisconsin Center										
Baraboo/Sauk County	‡	1,817	4,272/—	455				1,315	705	810
Barron County	‡	1,817	4,272/—	455				1,315	705	2,645
Fond du Lac	‡	1,845	4,272/—	455				1,315	705	810
Fox Valley	‡	1,870	4,272/—	455				1,315	705	810
Manitowoc County	‡	1,794	4,272/—	455				1,315	705	810
Marathon County	‡	1,837	4,272/—	455	2,516	550	900	1,315	705	810
Marinette County	‡	1,791	4,272/—	455				1,315	705	810
Marshfield/Wood County	‡	1,823	4,272/—	455				1,315	705	810
Richland	‡	1,852	4,272/—	455		670	1,170	1,315	705	810
Rock County	‡	1,823	4,272/—	455				1,315	705	810
Sheboygan County	‡	1,825	4,272/—	470				1,360	730	900
Washington County	‡	1,846	4,272/—	455				1,315	705	810
Waukesha	‡	1,802	4,272/—	455				1,315	705	810
Viterbo College		10,630		600	3,930	640	1,500	1,500	640	1,000
Waukesha County Technical College	‡	1,603	9,668/—	663				1,852	673	1,124
Western Wisconsin Technical College	‡	1,603	9,668/—	663		673	1,124	1,852	673	1,124
Wisconsin Indianhead Technical College	‡	1,603	9,668/—	663				1,852	673	1,124
Wisconsin Lutheran College		11,000		500	4,100	300	1,265	1,500	600	1,130

Wyoming

Institution		Tuition and fees	Add'l out-of-state/district tuition	Books and supplies	Room and board	Trans-portation	Other costs	Board only	Trans-portation	Other costs
Casper College	‡	880	1,520/—	500	2,330	450	900	1,500	450	450
Central Wyoming College	‡	1,036	1,520/—	500	2,812	500	1,000	1,800	400	750
Eastern Wyoming College	‡	1,048	1,648/—	500	2,500	525	1,300	1,750	325	1,300
Laramie County Community College	‡	928	1,520/—	500	3,298	300	500		750	600
Northwest College	‡	944	1,400/—	500	2,690	866	1,000	1,500	600	800
Sheridan College	‡	940	1,520/—	500	2,730	540	800	1,600	540	800
University of Wyoming	‡	2,005	4,080/—	600	3,520	500	1,500	1,960	302	780
Western Wyoming Community College		1,022	1,648/—	500	2,773	500	950	1,522	250	950

†Figures are projected for 1996-97. ‡Figures are for 1995-96.

All aid		Need–based aid		Grants and scholarships									Financial aid deadlines		Inst aid form	Notes
				Need–based				Non–need–based								
Total fresh–men	Percent receiving aid	Freshmen judged to have need	Percent offered aid	Acad	Music/ drama	Art	Athl	Acad	Music/ drama	Art	Athl	Priority	Closing		
1,988	53	1,042	98	X			X	X	X	X	X	3/1	none		
1,536	55			X				X	X	X		3/15	none		
744	40			X	X	X	X	X	X	X	X	4/1	6/15	X	
322	75	449	100	X				X	X	X		3/15	none		
968	60	545	100					X	X	X		3/15	none	X	
1,502	68							X	X	X		3/15	7/15		
1,140	62	720	93	X				X	X	X		4/1	none		
295	67			X	X	X		X				4/15	5/1		
1,900	64			X	X			X	X			4/15	none		
160	48	90	100	X	X	X		X	X	X		4/15	none	X	
				X	X	X		X	X	X		3/1	none		
202	35			X	X			X	X			4/15	none	X	
				X				X				4/15	none		
160	30	80	100	X				X				3/1	none		
													none	X	
													none		
190	46			X				X				4/15	none	X	
275	65			X	X	X		X	X	X		4/15	8/1		
192	50			X	X			X	X			4/15	none	X	
204	25			X				X				4/15	none	X	
230	23			X	X		X	X	X			4/15	none	X	
512	16							X	X	X		3/1	none	X	
485	88							X	X	X		3/1	none		
1,300	19			X				X					none		
1,342	60												none	X	
1,627	75			X				X					none		
111	99	94	100	X				X	X			3/1	none	X	
													none		
350	85	130	85	X	X	X	X	X	X	X	X	3/15	none		
													none		
526	78							X	X	X	X		none		
311	40	725	100	X	X	X	X	X	X	X	X	3/1	none	X	
1,347	59			X				X	X	X	X	3/1	none	X	
700	50							X	X	X	X	4/1	none	X	

13. Sources of information about state grant programs

The major state scholarship and grant programs are described in the following list. Included in the description of each program are eligibility requirements, average awards, and the address of the administrative agency. **Unless otherwise indicated, funds are available to state residents who are enrolled for full-time study at eligible postsecondary institutions in their state of residence.** Unless otherwise noted, state grant programs are for the 1996-97 academic year. If 1996-97 program information was not available by time of publication, the 1995-96 program information is printed.

Alabama

Alabama Student Assistance Program—Variable grants at in-state postsecondary institutions.

Alabama Student Grant Program—Non-need-based grants of up to $1,200 at private nonprofit colleges and universities.

National Guard Educational Assistance Program—Available to members of the Alabama National Guard for college study. Pays for tuition, fees, books, and supplies up to $500 per term or $1,000 per year.

For more information, contact the Alabama Commission on Higher Education, P.O. Box 302000, Montgomery, AL 36130-2000.

Alaska

Alaska State Educational Incentive Grant—Need-based grants of up to $1,500 for use by Alaska residents at eligible in-state and out-of-state postsecondary institutions.

For more information, contact the Alaska Commission on Postsecondary Education, 3030 Vintage Boulevard, Juneau, AK 99801-7109.

Arizona

Arizona State Student Incentive Grant Program—Need-based grants of up to $1,500 for use by Arizona residents at eligible in-state postsecondary institutions.

For more information, contact the financial aid office at the institution you wish to attend.

Arkansas

Arkansas Student Assistance Grant Program—Need-based grants of $200 to $624 at colleges and universities.

Governor's Scholars Program—100 merit-based $4,000 scholarships for attendance at colleges and universities in Arkansas, renewable for four years, awarded to high school seniors.

Emergency Secondary Education Loan Program—Available to secondary school education majors in shortage areas. Must pursue secondary teacher certification in state. Loans up to $2,500.

For more information, contact the Department of Higher Education, 114 East Capitol, Little Rock, AR 72201.

California

As of June 1995: Three state student aid programs: Cal Grant A—Grants of $700 to $5,250 at independent colleges, $700 to $3,799 at the University of California, and $700 to $1,584 at California State University. Cal Grant B—Subsistence grants of $700 to $1,410 and in some cases tuition. Cal Grant C—Grants of up to $2,360 for tuition plus $530 for training-related expenses at vocational and technical schools.

For more information, contact the California Student Aid Commission, P.O. Box 510845, Sacramento, CA 94245-0845.

Colorado

Student Grant—Need-based grants of up to $5,000 at eligible postsecondary institutions.

Colorado Diversity Grant—Available as part of a statewide effort to increase participation of underrepresented groups in the Colorado public higher education system.

Colorado Nursing Scholarship—Designed to provide assistance to individuals seeking nursing education who agree to practice in Colorado.

Colorado Part-time Grant—Need-based grants for less than full-time students attending eligible Colorado institutions.

Colorado Student Incentive Grant (CSIG)—Available to qualified undergraduates with substantial financial need.

Colorado Work-Study—Part-time employment program designed to assit students with financial need or work experience.

Undergraduate Merit—Available to students who demonstrate superior scholarship or talent as defined by the college or university they attend.

Colorado Graduate Grant—Available to graduate students with financial need.

Colorado Graduate Fellowship—Merit-based awards to graduate students.

Dependent Tuition Assistance Program—Tuition for dependents of Colorado law enforcement officers, fire or national guard personnel killed or disabled in the line of duty, and for dependents of prisoners of war or service personnel listed as missing in action. Dependents of disabled personnel must have demonstrated financial need for the assistance.

For more information, contact the financial aid office at the institution you wish to attend.

Connecticut

State Scholastic Achievement Grant Program—Grants of up to $2,000 may be taken to Connecticut colleges. Grants of up to $500 may be taken to colleges located in reciprocal states. Based on academic performance and financial need. February 15 application deadline.

For more information, contact the Department of Higher Education, 61 Woodland Street, Hartford, CT 06105.

Delaware

Scholarship Incentive Program—Need-based grants of $600 and above at approved Delaware or Pennsylvania colleges and at colleges in other states if the program of study is not offered at Delaware tax-supported colleges.

For more information, contact the Delaware Higher Education Commission, 820 North French Street, Fourth Floor, Wilmington, DE 19801.

Florida

Florida Student Assistance Grant Program—Grants of $200 to $1,500 at eligible Florida colleges. One-year state residency required.

Florida Resident Access Grant—Non-need grants of up to $2,000 at eligible private Florida colleges and universities. One-year state residency required.

Florida Undergraduate Scholars' Fund—Academic-based scholarships of up to $2,500 at eligible Florida colleges and universities. Recipient must have a Florida high school diploma or equivalent.

Scholarship for Children of Deceased or Disabled Veteran of Children of Servicemen Classified as Prisoners of War or Missing in Action—Grants of the cost of tuition and fees at Florida public postsecondary institutions for students who are dependents of deceased or 100 percent disabled Florida veterans or servicemen, or Florida servicemen classified as prisoners of war or missing in action during one of the wars, conflicts, or events as specified.

Florida Teacher Scholarship and Forgivable Loan Program—Assistance program created to attract capable students to teaching careers in critical teacher shortage subjects in Florida public elementary and secondary schools. Program consists of a scholarship of $1,500 per year to be used during freshman and sophomore undergraduate study and a loan of up to $4,000 per year to be used during junior and senior undergraduate study. The loan portion can be repaid through teaching in designated subjects or schools.

Florida Work Experience Program—Need-based program providing eligible Florida students with the opportunity to secure work experiences that are complimentary to and reinforce the students' educational program and career goals.

José Marti Scholarship Challenge Grant Fund—Grant of $2,000 per year for Hispanic-American high school seniors and graduate students who meet scholastic requirements, demonstrate financial need, and enroll for undergraduate or graduate study at an approved Florida university.

Mary McLeod Bethune Scholarship—Scholarships of $3,000 per year to undergraduate students who meet scholastic requirements, demonstrate financial need, and attend Bethune-Cookman College, Edward Waters College, Florida A&M University, or Florida Memorial College.

Nicaraguan and Haitian Scholarship Program—Scholarships averaging between $4,000 and $5,000, based on legislative appropriations, for one Nicaraguan and one Haitian student in Florida to attend a state university system institution.

Robert C. Byrd Honors Scholarship Program—Scholarships of $1,500 per year offered to outstanding high school graduates who show promise of continued academic achievement.

Rosewood Family Scholarship—Annual scholarship of $4,000 or the cost of tuition and fees, whichever is less, for eligible minority students to attend a state university, public community college, or public postsecondary vocational-technical school.

Seminole and Miccosukee Indian Scholarships Program—Scholarships up to the cost of education for Florida Seminole or Miccosukee Indian students who are enrolled as undergraduate or graduate students and demonstrate financial need.

Vocational Gold Seal Endorsement Scholarship Program—Annual scholarships up to $2,000 to recipients of the Vocational Gold Deal Endorsement to be used at a postsecondary institution or certification program.

For more information, contact the Florida Department of Education, Office of Student Financial Assistance, 1344 Florida Education Center, Tallahassee, FL 32399-0400.

Georgia

Georgia Student Incentive Grant Program—Grants of $300 to $5,000 at nonprofit postsecondary institutions.

Georgia Tuition Equalization Grant Program—Grants of $1,000 at private colleges. Does not require financial need.

Law Enforcement Personnel Dependents Grant—$2,000 a year for dependents of Georgia Law Enforcement Personnel who have been killed or rendered disabled in the line of duty.

For more information, contact the Georgia Student Finance Authority, 2082 East Exchange Place, Suite 200, Tucker, GA 30084

Hawaii †

Tuition Waivers and Pacific-Asian Scholarships—provide for tuition expenses at campuses of the University of Hawaii.

Hawaii Student Incentive Grant Program—Grants covering tuition expenses at nonprofit postsecondary institutions.

For more information, contact the financial aid office at the institution you wish to attend.

† Information is for 1995-96.

Idaho

State of Idaho Scholarship—Grants of up to $2,700 per year at Idaho public and private postsecondary institutions. Based on academic ability.

Paul L. Fowler Scholarship Program—Memorial one-time grant of $3,000 to Idaho high school graduates. Based on academic ability.

For more information, contact the Office of the State Board of Education, P.O. Box 83720, Boise, ID 83720-0037.

Illinois

General Assembly Scholarships—Waivers of tuition and fees at public postsecondary institutions. Selection by general assembly members from residents of their districts. For more information on this program contact your district legislator directly.

Illinois Monetary Award Program—Need-based grants of up to $3,900 at approved Illinois postsecondary institutions for at least half-time (6 hours minimum) enrollment.

Illinois Merit Recognition Scholarship—$1,000 scholarships to Illinois students who rank in the top 5 percent of their high school class at the end of the seventh semester. Financial need is not a factor. Not renewable.

For more information, contact the Illinois Student Assistance Commission, 1755 Lake Cook Road, Deerfield, IL 60015, or call 1-800-899-ISAC [4722].

Indiana

Byrd Scholarship Program—Federally funded grants of $1,500 to promote student excellence and achievement. One scholarship per congressional district awarded to the highest scoring graduates of GED programs.

Higher Education Awards—Grants of $200 to $2,600 for full-time students at private, nonprofit in-state postsecondary institutions and of $200 to $5,100 at state-supported universities. Based on need. Awarded to Indiana residents working on their first undergraduate degree.

Hoosier Scholar Awards—One-time grants of $500 to residents in the top 20 percent of their graduating class who are nominated by their high schools. Financial need is not considered.

Minority Teacher Scholarship—Grants of up to $4,000 for black or Hispanic students who want to be teachers. Renewable for up to four out of six years. Obligation to teach in Indiana for three out of five years following certification.

Special Education Services Scholarship—Grants of up to $1,000 for students who desire to teach in the field of special education. Renewable for up to four out of six years at eligible nonprofit and public postsecondary institutions. Obligation to teach in Indiana for three out of five years after certification.

Nursing Scholarship—Need-based grants for tuition of up to $5,000 for students who attend eligible nonprofit and public postsecondary institutions with nursing programs. Award is renewable.

State Work-Study Program—Summer work available to students who receive the Higher Education Grant or Lilly Grant during the preceding academic year. Funds awarded statewide to employers to reimburse 50 percent of student earnings.

For more information, contact the State Student Assistance Commission of Indiana, 150 W. Market Street, Suite 500, Indianapolis, IN 46204.

Iowa

Iowa Grants—Grants of $1,000 based on financial need for Iowa residents attending Iowa public, independent, and community colleges. Grants may be prorated for less than full-time study.

Iowa Tuition Grant Program—Grants of up to $2,900 at private institutions (including nursing and business schools) for part-time and full-time study.

Iowa Vocational-Technical Tuition Grant Program—Grants of up to $600 at two-year public vocational and technical institutions for full-time study.

State of Iowa Scholarship Program—Grants of $410 to Iowa residents who rank in the top 15 percent of senior class. Based on academic ability. Award to freshmen only.

Robert C. Byrd Honors Scholarship Program—Federally funded grants to promote student excellence and achievement and to recognize exceptionally able students who show promise of continued excellence. Applicants must be Iowa residents and accepted at an approved postsecondary school. Award is renewable for up to four years.

For more information, contact the Iowa College Student Aid Commission, 200 Tenth Street, Fourth Floor, Des Moines, IA 50309-3609.

Kansas

Kansas Tuition Grant Program—Grants for Kansas residents of up to $1,700 at private, nonprofit postsecondary institutions.

State Scholarship Program—Stipends of up to $1,000 for Kansas residents. Based on academic ability and financial need.

Kansas Minority Scholarship—Stipends of up to $1,500 a year for Kansas resident minority students attending in-state two- or four-year colleges. Based on academic ability and need.

Kansas Teacher Scholarship—Up to $5,000 a year for Kansas residents who will teach in Kansas one year for each year of funding.

Regents Supplemental Grant Program—Grants of up to $900 at Regents institutions for Kansas Residents.

Kansas Nursing Scholarship—Up to $2,500 a year for Kansas residents pursuing LPN degrees; $3,500 a year for those pursuing RPN degrees.

For more information, contact the Board of Regents, 700 SW Harrison, Suite 1410, Topeka, KS 66603-3760.

Kentucky

College Access Program Grant—Need-based grants of $1,000 per year for full-time undergraduates who attend public and private colleges and universities, and $600 for those attending proprietary schools and vocational-technical schools. Smaller awards for half-time students.

Kentucky Tuition Grant Program—Need-based grants of up to $1,500 per year at eligible private, nonprofit postsecondary institutions.

Teacher Scholarship Program—Need-based awards up to $5,000 per year to Kentucky residents who intend to become teachers. One year of teaching in a Kentucky-accredited school required for each year of award or one semester of teaching in a critical shortage area required for every two semesters of award.

KHEAA Work-Study Program—Career-related job opportunities for eligibile Kentucky resident students attending approved in-state postsecondary institutions. Must be enrolled at least half time.

For more information, contact KHEAA Student Aid Program, 1050 U.S. 127 South, Frankfort, KY 40601.

Louisiana

State Student Incentive Grant Program—Grants of $200 to $2,000 to Louisiana residents at eligible postsecondary institutions in Louisiana.

Louisiana Honors Scholarship Program—Tuition waivers for students who graduate in top 5 percent of graduating class from Louisiana public or state-approved nonpublic high schools. Must be enrolled as full-time undergraduates in a Louisiana college.

Louisiana Tuition Assistance Plan—Tuition exemption for Louisiana residents who attend public colleges full time and meet specific academic and financial need criteria.

T.H. Harris State Academic Scholarship—Awards based on academic achievement for Louisiana high school graduates attending public colleges within the state. 3.0 GPA required. $400 per year with 5-year maximum of $2,000.

Rockefeller Scholarship for Wildlife Programs—Up to $1,000 per year for students in forestry, wildlife management, fisheries, and marine science programs. A 2.5 overall grade-point average is required. Does not require financial need.

For more information, contact the Office of Student Financial Assistance for Louisiana, Scholarship/Grant Division, P.O. Box 91202, Baton Rouge, LA 70821-9202.

Maine

Maine Student Incentive Scholarship Program—Need-based grants of $500 to $1,000 for Maine Students attending eligible postsecondary institutions in New England and states with signed reciprocity agreements.

For more information, contact the Finance Authority of Maine, Maine Education Assistance Division, 119 State House Station, Augusta ME 04333.

Maryland

Educational Assistance Grant Program—Grants of $200 to $3,000 at public or private postsecondary institutions. Undergraduate awards based on need.

Delegates Scholarship Program—Variable amounts, $200 minimum, to assist with tuition and fees at public and private postsecondary institutions for half-time and full-time study. Undergraduate and graduate students eligible.

Senatorial Scholarship Program—Grants of $200 to $2,000 at postsecondary institutions for half-time and full-time study. Undergraduate, graduate, and non-degree seeking students eligible.

Distinguished Scholar Program—$3,000 undergraduate annual awards based on merit or artistic talent for students nominated by their high schools or who are Merit/Achievement finalists.

For more information, contact the Maryland Higher Education

Commission/State Scholarship Administration, 16 Francis Street, Annapolis, MD 21401-1781.

Massachusetts

Massachusetts Grant—Grants of $200 to $2,500 for Massachusetts residents attending eligible in-state (and reciprocal state) postsecondary institutions on a full-time basis.

Tuition-Waiver Program—Up to the full cost of tuition waived for students attending a state-supported college or university. Amount of waiver determined by the financial aid office.

For more information, contact the Higher Education Coordinating Council, Office of Student Financial Assistance, 330 Stuart Street, Boston, MA 02116

Michigan

Tuition Grant Program—Need-based grants of up to $2,250 at independent nonprofit colleges and universities.

Competitive Scholarship Program—Awards based on ACT scores and financial need.

For more information, contact Michigan Higher Education Assistance Authority, Office of Scholarships and Grants, P.O. Box 30462, Lansing, MI 48909.

Minnesota

Minnesota State Grant Program—Grants from $300 to $5,932.

Interstate Tuition Reciprocity Programs—Under these programs Minnesota residents pay a tuition rate that is less than the normal out-of-state charge at public college and vocational institutions in Wisconsin, North Dakota, South Dakota, some Iowa institutions, and the Canadian province of Manitoba.

For more information, contact the Minnesota Higher Education Services Office, 550 Cedar Street, Suite 400, St. Paul, MN 55101.

Mississippi

State Student Incentive Grant—Grants of $100 to $1,500.

For more information, contact your college financial aid office or the Mississippi Postsecondary Education Financial Assistance Board, 3825 Ridgewood Road, Jackson, MS 39211-6453.

Missouri

Student Grant Program—Grants of up to $1,500 (averaging $1,200) for study at undergraduate nonprofit Missouri postsecondary institutions. Divinity, theology, or religion majors are not eligible. Based on need; renewable.

Missouri Higher Education Academic Scholarship Program—Grants of up to $2,000 for full-time undergraduate students at eligible Missouri institutions. Students must have ACT composite scores or SAT combined scores in top 3 percent of all Missouri students taking those tests. Theology or divinity majors are not eligible. State residency required.

For more information, contact the Missouri Coordinating Board for Higher Education, P.O. Box 6730, Jefferson City, MO 65102.

Montana

Montana Student Incentive Grant Program—Grants of up to $900 at public postsecondary institutions and the three private colleges.

Honor Scholarships—Tuition and fee waivers at public postsecondary institutions for high school graduates.

For more information, contact the Montana University System, 2500 East Broadway, Helena, MT 59620-3101.

Nebraska

For information about the Scholarship Assistance Program and State Scholarship Award Program, contact a Nebraska postsecondary education institution.

Nevada

Nevada Student Incentive Grant Program—Grants of up to $5,000 for half-time and full-time study.

For more information, contact Nevada Department of Education, Financial Aid, 700 East 5th Street, Capitol Complex, Carson City, NV 89710.

New Hampshire

New Hampshire Incentive Program—Need-based grants of $225 to $1,000 for undergraduate, full-time day students. Grants portable by New Hampshire residents to five other New England states. 2.0 college average required of those with sophomore standing and above.

For more information, contact the New Hampshire Postsecondary Education Commission, 2 Industrial Park Drive, Concord, NH 03301-8512.

New Jersey

Tuition Aid Grant Program—Need-based grants of $600 to $5,210 at in-state colleges only, for full-time students.

Educational Opportunity Fund Grant Program—Need-based grants of $200 to $2,100 at in-state colleges only, for full-time students.

Edward J. Bloustein Distinguished Scholars Program—Grants of $1,000 per year at in-state colleges only. Based on academic ability.

Garden State Scholar Program—Grants of $500 per year at in-state colleges only. Based on academic ability.

For more information, contact the New Jersey Office of Student Assistance, CN 540, Trenton, NJ 08625.

New Mexico

New Mexico Scholars Program—Scholarships provide tuition, required student fees, and books for an academic year for outstanding high school students attending eligible postsecondary institutions as full-time students. Renewable up to four times. Student must have combined family income below $30,000.

New Mexico Student Choice Grant Program—For undergraduates attending an eligible private postsecondary institution who are enrolled at least half-time.

New Mexico Student Incentive Grant Program—Need-based grants of $200 to $2,500 per year at public and private postsecondary institutions.

New Mexico Vietnam Veterans' Scholarship Program—Tuition grants for undergraduate and graduate students attending postsecondary institutions.

For more information, contact the Commission on Higher Education, 1068 Cerillos Road, Santa Fe, New Mexico 87501-4295.

New York

New York Tuition Assistance Program—Grants of $100 to $3,900 depending on type of institution and need. Annual; available to undergraduate or graduate students.

Vietnam Veterans Tuition Awards—Grants of up to $1,000 per semester for full-time study and $500 per semester for part-time study for eligible applicants who served in the U.S. Armed Forces between December 22, 1961, and May 7, 1975.

For more information, contact the Higher Education Services Corporation, Student Information, 99 Washington Avenue, 14th Floor, Albany, NY 12255.

North Carolina

North Carolina Legislative Tuition Grant Program—Grants of up to $1,250 annually for North Carolina residents enrolled full-time at private colleges and universities in North Carolina. Does not require financial need.

North Carolina Student Incentive Grant Program—Need-based grants of up to $1,500 or one-half of unmet need, whichever is less, at colleges, universities, and technical and vocational schools.

North Carolina Student Loan Program for Health, Science, and Mathematics—Scholarships/loans ranging from $3,000 to $8,500 annually depending on degree level, to be repaid through practice/service in the state. Available to legal residents in accredited associate, baccalaureate, master's or doctoral programs.

North Carolina Teaching Fellows Program—Grants of up to $5,000 for North Carolina residents to encourage entry into the elementary and secondary teaching profession. May be used to attend 14 designated institutions in North Carolina (12 public, 2 private). Does not require financial need. Must repay by teaching in the public schools in North Carolina or by cash at 10 percent interest.

State Contractual Scholarship Fund—Grants for North Carolina residents at eligible North Carolina private colleges and universities, based on need.

For more information, contact the North Carolina State Education Assistance Authority, Box 2688, Chapel Hill, NC 27515-2688.

North Dakota

Student Financial Assistance Program—Grants of up to $600 for attendance at public and nonprofit postsecondary institutions.

North Dakota Scholars Program—Tuition scholarships available to students who score at the 95th percentile or above on the ACT, and who rank in the top 20 percent of their graduating class.

For more information, contact the Student Financial Assistance Program, State Capitol, Tenth Floor, 600 East Boulevard, Bismarck, ND 58505.

Ohio

Ohio Instructional Grant Program—Grants of up to $3,750 at Ohio and Pennsylvania approved private postsecondary institutions, and up to $1,512 at Ohio and Pennsylvania approved public postsecondary institutions, and up to $2,284 at Ohio and Pennsylvania approved proprietary institutions. For full-time undergraduates enrolled in eligible associate or bachelor's degree or nursing diploma programs.

Ohio Academic Scholarship Program—Scholarships of $2,000 per year at eligible public, private, and proprietary postsecondary Ohio institutions. Based on high school academic ability and ACT scores.

Ohio Student Choice Grant Program—Grants in varying amounts at eligible private postsecondary Ohio institutions. For full-time undergraduates enrolled in a bachelor's degree program who did not attend any institution full time before July 1, 1984.

For more information, contact the Ohio Student Aid Commission, P.O. Box 16610, Columbus, OH 43216-6610.

Oklahoma

Tuition Aid Grant Program—Grants of up to $1,000 or 75 percent of tuition and fees, whichever is less, at eligible colleges, universities, and vocational-technical schools. Based on financial need. Available to undergraduate and graduate students, full time and part time.

For more information, contact the Oklahoma State Regents for Higher Education, Tuition Aid Grant Program, P.O. Box 3020, Oklahoma City, OK 73101-3020.

Oregon

Need Grant Program—Need-based grants of up to $1,518 at accredited nonprofit postsecondary institutions.

For more information, contact the Oregon State Scholarship Commission, Valley River Office Park, 1500 Valley River Drive, Suite 100, Eugene, OR 97401.

Pennsylvania

State Higher Education Grant Program—Grants of up to $2,632 pending passage of state budget, or 80 percent of tuition and fees, whichever is less, at in-state postsecondary institutions; up to $600 at approved out-of-state postsecondary institutions.

POW/MIA Grant Program—Grants of $100 to $1,200 for dependents of U.S. Armed Forces veterans who were taken prisoner or declared missing-in-action; for use at in-state postsecondary institutions. Lower limits at eligible out-of-state institutions.

Veterans Grant Program—Grants of up to $2,632 or 80 percent of tuition and fees, whichever is less, at in-state postsecondary institutions; up to $800 at approved out-of-state postsecondary institutions for applicants who served in the U.S. Armed Forces.

For more information, contact the Pennsylvania Higher Education Assistance Agency, 1200 N. Seventh St., Harrisburg, PA 17102.

Puerto Rico

Legislative Scholarship Program—Grants for attendance at the University of Puerto Rico.

Supplemental Aid Program—University of Puerto Rico institutional program for supplemental aid that provides additional aid to needy students.

Legislative Scholarship Program—Grants for attendance at private accredited institutions of higher education.

Educational Fund—Grants for attendance at private accredited institutions of higher education.

Robert C. Byrd Honor Scholarship program—Scholarships to promote student excellence and to recognize exceptionally able students. Grants are $1,500 for one academic year.

Rosa A. Axtmayer Scholarship Program—Grants to needy students for attendance at the University of Puerto Rico.

For more information, contact the Council on Higher Education, Box 23305-UPR Station, Rio Piedras, PR 00931.

Rhode Island

State Grant or Scholarship Program—Scholarships and grants of up to $700 at eligible in-state and out-of-state postsecondary institutions. Scholarships based on SAT scores and financial need; grants based on financial need.

For more information, contact the Rhode Island Higher Education Assistance Authority, 560 Jefferson Boulevard, Warwick, RI 02886.

South Carolina

Tuition Grants Program—Need-based grants of up to $4,060 at in-state private postsecondary institutions.

For more information, contact the South Carolina Tuition Grants Commission, 1310 Lady Street, Suite 811, P.O. Box 12159, Columbia, SC 29211.

South Dakota

South Dakota Student Incentive Grant Program—Grants of up to $600 for South Dakota residents at participating South Dakota postsecondary institutions.

South Dakota Tuition Equalization Grant—Grants for South Dakota residents of up to $300 at participating South Dakota private colleges.

National Guard Tuition—Members of the Army or Air National Guard of the state of South Dakota attending any undergraduate-level institution under the control of the Board of Regents or a state vocational institution are entitled to a 50 percent reduction of tuition charges. There is a four-year limit.

Robert C. Byrd Honors Scholarship Program—$1,500 scholarships for South Dakota residents to promote student excellence and achievement and to recognize exceptionally able students who show promise of continued excellence.

For more information, contact the Department of Education and Cultural Affairs, Office of the Secretary, 700 Governors Drive, Pierre, SD 57501-2291.

Tennessee

Tennessee Student Assistance Award Program—Maximum grants of $1,482.

Dependent Children Scholarship—For dependent children of a law enforcement officer, firefighter, or emergency medical service technician in Tennessee who was killed or totally and permanently disabled while performing duties within the scope of his or her employment.

Ned McWherter Scholars Program—Awards of up to $6,000 per academic year for academically superior high school graduates.

Robert C. Byrd Honors Scholarship—Federal scholarships to promote student excellence through awards of $1,500 per academic year.

For more information, contact the Tennessee Student Assistance Corporation, Suite 1950, Parkway Towers, 404 James Robertson Parkway, Nashville, TN 37243-0820.

Texas

Texas Tuition Equalization Grant Program—Grants of up to $2,640 at private, nonprofit postsecondary institutions.

Texas Public Grant Program—Grants of up to $2,500 at public postsecondary institutions.

State Scholarship for Ethnic Recruitment—Scholarships up to $2,000 for eligible minority students attending general academic teaching institutions.

Robert C. Byrd Honors Scholarship Program—Scholarships to promote student excellence and achievement and to recognize exceptionally able students who show promise of continued excellence. Grants are $1,121 for one academic year.

For more information, contact the financial aid office at the institution you wish to attend.

Utah

State Student Incentive Grant Program—Grants of up to $2,500 based on need.

Utah Educational Career Teaching Scholarship—Available to students who plan a career teaching in the public educational institutions of Utah. Tuition and fees waived, with additional stipends in some instances awarded on merit. Recipient must teach in the public educational institutions of Utah one year for each year they received the scholarship, for a maximum of five years. This must begin no later than two years after certification.

Robert C. Byrd Honors Scholarship Program—Scholarships of $1,200 to promote student excellence and achievement and to recognize exceptionally able students who show promise of continued excellence. Available for graduating high school seniors and renwable for four years based on continued academic achievement.

National Guard State Tuition Assistance—Members of the National Guard may receive up to $1,000 per year, not to exceed a $4,000 maximum. Extended service period required.

For more information, contact the financial aid office at the institution you wish to attend.

Vermont

Vermont Incentive Grant Program—Grants of $500 to $5,200 at in-state postsecondary institutions, and grants of $500 to $4,000 at out-of-state postsecondary institutions.

Part-Time Student Grant Program—Grants of $250 to $3,900 for students going less than full time to in-state postsecondary institutions, and grants of $250 to $3,000 for study at out-of-state postsecondary institutions.

For more information, contact the Vermont Student Assistance Corporation, Champlain Mill, P.O. Box 2000, Winooski, VT 05404-2601.

Virginia

College Scholarship Assistance Program—Need-based grants of $400 to $5,000 for Virginia residents enrolled at least half-time at Virginia's public and private colleges.

Virginia Tuition Assistance Grant Program—Non-need-based grants of up to $1,750 for Virginia residents who attend private colleges in Virginia.

Virginia Transfer Grant Program—Grants up to full tuition and mandatory fees or remaining need, whichever is lower, awarded to minority transfer students who enroll in a historically white public institution or any transfer student who enrolls in a historically black public college or university in Virginia. Applicants must meet minimum merit criteria and be first-time transfer students.

Last Dollar Program—Need-based grants of $400 to the cost of full-time tuition and fees for minority undergraduates enrolled for the first time in a public college or university.

Virginia Student Financial Assistance Program—For undergraduate students who have financial need, are enrolled at least half-time, and are domiciliary residents of Virginia. Also open to some graduate students; however, they do not have to demonstrate financial need. The award amount may be up to tuition and required fees. An additional merit component aids students who demonstrate academic achievement in high school.

Robert C. Byrd Scholarship Program—Merit-based scholarships to high school senior based on demonstrated academic achievement.

Medical Scholarship Program—Scholarships of $10,000 per year to medical students studying to become primary care physicians who agree to practice in a medically underserved area or become employed with the State of Virginia in an approved department. One year of service is required for each year of scholarship receipt.

Regional Contract Programs—Tuition assistance for Virginia residents to study library science, optometry, forensic science, and paper and pulp technology at specific out-of-state institutions.

Virginia Army National Guard—Grants of varying amounts based on enlistment to members of the Virginia Army National Guard.

Virginia Assistance for the Visually Handicapped—Financial assistance to visually handicapped students who attend postsecondary institutions. Eligibility determined by the Virginia Department for the Visually Handicapped. Funding available only if financial need remains after federal, state, and other private funding sources have been utilized.

Lee-Jackson Foundation Scholarship—Awards of $1,000 based on essays from high school juniors and seniors who plan to ateend Virginia public or private institutions.

For more information, contact the Virginia Council of Higher Education, James Monroe Building, 101 North 14th Street, Richmond, VA 23219.

Washington

State Need Grant Program—Variable grants for low-income state residents attending in-state postsecondary institutions.

Educational Opportunity Grant—Grants of $2,500 to needy state residents entering as juniors or seniors into four-year Washington colleges and universities with existing unused capacity.

Washington Scholars Program—Grants of variable amounts, approximately $3,000, to three graduating high school seniors from each Washington State legislative district. Principals nominate from top 1 percent of class.

Health Professional Scholarship Program—Renewable conditional loans of up to $15,000. Recipients agree to provide primary care services in state-defined shortage areas for a minimum of three years to qualify for a 100 percent loan forgiveness.

For more information, contact the Higher Education Coordinating Board, 917 Lakeridge Way, P.O. Box 43430, Olympia WA 98504-3430.

West Virginia

Higher Education Grant Program—Grants of up to $2,136 at approved in-state higher education institutions, and of up to $600 at approved Pennsylvania institutions for full-time students.

Robert C. Byrd Honors Scholarship Program—Merit scholarships of $1,500 awarded for study at a degree-granting institution of higher education.

Underwood-Smith Teacher Scholarship Program—Grants of up to $5,000 for state residents who graduated in the top 10 percent of their high school class or scored in the top 10 percent statewide of those students taking the ACT, who are enrolled in a West Virginia state college or university in a course of study leading to certification as a teacher, and who agree to teach in the state's public school system for two years for each year of scholarship assistance.

For more information, contact the State Colleges and University Systems of West Virginia Central Office, Higher Education Grant Program, P.O. Box 4007, Charleston, WV 25364.

Wisconsin

Wisconsin Higher Education Grants Program—Grants of up to $1,800 at eligible public postsecondary institutions for half-time and full-time study.

Tuition Grant Program—Grants of up to $2,172 at eligible private colleges, universities, and nursing schools for half-time and full-time study.

Interstate Program (Minnesota-Wisconsin)—A reciprocal arrangement paying for Wisconsin resident tuition at public colleges and vocational institutions in Minnesota.

Wisconsin Indian Student Grant Program—Grants of up to $1,100 at any eligible public or private institution of higher education in Wisconsin for half-time or full-time students who are of at least 25 percent Native American heritage.

For more information, contact the Wisconsin Higher Educational Aids Board, P.O. Box 7885, Madison WI 53707.

Wyoming

State Student Incentive Grants Program—Grants at public non-profit postsecondary institutions averaging $300.

Douvas Memorial Scholarship—Scholarship of $500 to be used at a Wyoming public, nonprofit, postsecondary institution. Applicants must be a first-generation American.

Robert C. Byrd Honors Scholarship Program—Scholarships of

$1,121 to promote student excellence and achievement and to recognize exceptionally able students who show promise of continued excellence. Available for graduating high school seniors; renewable for four-years based on continued academic achievement.

For more information, contact the college you plan to attend.

Guam

Government-sponsored scholarships for Teaching and Nursing programs for attendance at the University of Guam. Program covers tuition, fees, book allowance, and monthly stipends ranging from $200 to $500.

Government-sponsored loan programs for undergraduate and graduate students for attendance at the University of Guam and off-island U.S. accredited institutions if the degree programs are not offered at the University of Guam. Programs range from $3,000 to $12,000 per academic year.

Government-sponsored Merit Program for graduating high school seniors from Guam for attendance at the University of Guam. Program covers tuition, fees, and monthly stipends of approximately $600.

For more information, contact the Student Financial Aid Office, UOG Station, Mangilao, GU 96923.

Virgin Islands

Student Incentive Grant Program—Grants of up to $5,000 at accredited, eligible institutions.

Territorial Scholarship Program—Grants of $500 to $3,000 and loans of $1,000 to $4,000 for students at the College of the Virgin Islands and United States nonprofit accredited postsecondary institutions.

For more information, contact the Financial Aid Office, Virgin Islands Board of Education, P.O. Box 11900, St. Thomas, VI 00801.

14. Sources of information about the Federal Stafford Loan Program

Alabama

Alabama Commission on
    Higher Education
P.O. Box 302000
Montgomery, AL 36130-2000
(334) 242-1998

Alaska

United Student Aid Funds, Inc.
Loan Information Services, M372
P.O. Box 6180
Indianapolis, IN 46206
(317) 849-6510
(800) LOAN USA (562-6872)

Arizona

Arizona Education Loan Program
25 S. Arizona Place, Suite 530
Chandler, AZ 85225
(800) 352-3033

Arkansas

Student Loan Guarantee
    Foundation of Arkansas
219 South Victory
Little Rock, AR 72201
(501) 372-1491
(800) 622-3446

California

California Student Aid Commission
P.O. Box 510845
Sacramento, CA 94245-0845
(916) 445-0880

Colorado

Colorado Student Loan Program
Denver Place
999 Eighteenth Street, Suite 425

Denver, CO 80202-2440
(303) 294-5050

Connecticut

Connecticut Student Loan
    Foundation
P.O. Box 1009
Rocky Hill, CT 06067
(203) 257-4001

Delaware

Delaware Higher Education
    Commission
820 North French Street
Wilmington, DE 19801
(302) 577-6055

Florida

Office of Student Financial Assistance
Federal Programs
1344 Florida Education Center
Florida Department of Education
Tallahassee, FL 32399-0400
(904) 488-4095

Georgia

Georgia Higher Education Assistance
    Corporation
2082 East Exchange Place, Suite 200
Tucker, GA 30084
(770) 414-3000

Hawaii

Hawaii Education Loan Program
United Student Aid Funds, Inc.
P.O. Box 22187
Honolulu, HI 96823-2187
(808) 593-2262

Idaho

Student Loan Fund of Idaho, Inc.
6905 Highway 95
P.O. Box 730
Fruitland, ID 83619-0730
(208) 452-4058

Illinois

Illinois Student Assistance Commission
1755 Lake Cook Road
Deerfield, IL 60015
(800) 899-ISAC [4722]

Indiana

United Student Aid Funds, Inc.
P.O. Box 6180
Indianapolis, IN 46206
(317) 849-6510
(800) LOAN USA [562-6872]

Iowa

Iowa College Student Aid Commission
200 Tenth Street, Fourth Floor
Des Moines, IA 50309-3609
(515) 281-4890

Kansas

USA Group
120 Southwest 6th Street
3 Townsite Plaza, Suite 22D
Topeka, KS 66608
(913)234-0072

Kentucky

Kentucky Higher Education Assistance
    Authority
1050 U.S. 127 South
Frankfort, KY 40601-4323
(502) 564-7990

Louisiana

Office of Student Financial Assistance
for Louisiana Student Financial
Assistance Commission
P.O. Box 91202
Baton Rouge, LA 70821-9202
(800) 259-5626

Maine

Maine Education Assistance Division
Finance Authority of Maine
119 State House Station
Augusta, ME 04333
(207) 287-2183

Maryland

Maryland Higher Education
Loan Corporation
Jeffrey Building
16 Francis Street
Annapolis, MD 21401-1781
(410) 974-2971

Massachusetts

American Student Assistance
330 Stuart Street
Boston, MA 02116
(617) 426-9434

Michigan

Michigan Higher Education
Assistance Authority
Michigan Guaranty Agency
P.O. Box 30047
Lansing, MI 48909
(517) 373-0760
(800) 642-5626

Minnesota

Northstar Guarantee Inc.
444 Cedar Street, Suite 1910
St. Paul, MN 55101-2133
(612) 290-8795

Mississippi

Mississippi Guarantee Student Loan
Agency
3825 Ridgewood Road
Jackson, MS 39211-6453
(601) 982-6663

Missouri

Missouri Coordinating Board
for Higher Education
P.O. Box 6730
Jefferson City, MO 65102
(573) 751-3940

Montana

Montana Guaranteed Student
Loan Program
2500 Broadway, P.O. Box 203101
Helena, MT 59620-3101
(406) 444-6594

Nebraska

Nebraska Student Loan Program
1300 O Street
P.O. Box 82507
Lincoln, NE 68501-2507
(402) 475-8686

Nevada

United Student Aid Funds, Inc.
Western Regional Center
25 South Arizona Place, Suite 530
Chandler, AZ 85225
(800) 824-7044

New Hampshire

New Hampshire Higher Education
Assistance Foundation
44 Warren Street
P.O. Box 877
Concord, NH 03302
(603) 225-6612
(800) 525-2577

New Jersey

New Jersey Higher Education
Assistance Authority
4 Quaker Bridge Plaza
CN 543
Trenton, NJ 08625
(609) 588-3200
(800) 356-5562

New Mexico

New Mexico Student Loan Guarantee
Corporation
P.O. Box 27020
Albuquerque, NM 87125-7020
(505) 345-8821

New York

Higher Education
Services Corporation
99 Washington Avenue
Albany, NY 12255
(518) 473-7087

North Carolina

North Carolina State Education
Assistance Authority
P.O. Box 2688
Chapel Hill, NC 27515-2688
(919) 549-8614
or
College Foundation Inc.
P.O. Box 12100
Raleigh, NC 27605-2100
(919) 821-4771

North Dakota

Student Loans of North Dakota
—Guarantor
Box 5524
Bismarck, ND 58506-5524
(701) 328-5753
(800) 472-2166

Ohio

Ohio Student Aid Commission
309 South Fourth Street
P.O. Box 16610
Columbus, OH 43216-0610
(614) 644-8892

Oklahoma

Oklahoma State Regents for
Higher Education
P.O. Box 3000
Oklahoma City, OK 73101-3000
(405) 552-4300
(800) 442-8642

Oregon

Oregon State Scholarship
Commission
Valley River Office Park
1500 Valley River Drive, Suite 100
Eugene, OR 97401
(541) 687-7400

Pennsylvania

Pennsylvania Higher Education
Assistance Agency
1200 N. Seventh Street
Harrisburg, PA 17102
(717) 257-2860
(800) 692-7392 (Pennsylvania)

Puerto Rico

Puerto Rico Council on Higher Education
P.O. Box 19900
San Juan, Puerto Rico 00910-1900

Rhode Island

Rhode Island Higher Education
    Assistance Authority
560 Jefferson Boulevard
Warwick, RI 02886
(401) 736-1170

South Carolina

South Carolina Student Loan Corporation
Interstate Center, Suite 210
P.O. Box 21487
Columbia, SC 29221
(803) 798-0916

South Dakota

Education Assistance Corporation
115 First Avenue, S.W.
Aberdeen, SD 57401-4174
(605) 225-6423

Tennessee

Tennessee Student Assistance Corporation
404 James Robertson Parkway
Parkway Towers, Suite 1950
Nashville, TN 37243-0820
(615) 741-1346

Texas

Texas Guaranteed Student Loan
    Corporation
P.O. Box 201725
Austin, TX 78720-1725
(800) 252-9743

Utah

EduServe
P.O. Box 30802
Salt Lake City, UT 84130
(801) 975-2200

Vermont

Vermont Student Assistance
    Corporation
Champlain Mill
P.O. Box 2000
Winooski, VT 05404-2601
(802) 655-9602
(800) 642-3177 (Vermont)

Virginia

State Education Assistance Authority
411 East Franklin Street, suite 300
Richmond, VA 23219-2243
(804) 775-4000
(800) 792-LOAN

Washington

Northwest Education Loan Association
500 Colman Building
811 First Avenue
Seattle, WA 98104
(206) 461-5300

West Virginia

West Virginia Education Loan Services
PHEAA Regional Office
20 Kenton Drive
Charleston, WV 25311
(304) 345-7211
(800) 437-3692

Wisconsin

Great Lakes Higher Education
    Corporation
2401 International Lane
Madison, WI 53704
(608) 246-1800

Wyoming

United Student Aid Funds
1912 Capitol Avenue, Suite 320
Cheyenne, WY 82001
(307) 635-3259

Virgin Islands

Virgin Islands Board of Education
P.O. Box 11900
Charlotte Amalie
St. Thomas, VI 00801
(809) 774-4546

Guam, American Samoa, Northern Marianas, Palau

Hawaii Education Loan Program
United Student Aid Funds, Inc.
P.O. Box 22187
Honolulu, HI 96823-2187
(808) 593-2262

United Student Aid Funds, Inc.

United Student Aid Funds, Inc.
Loan Information Services, M372
P.O. Box 6180
Indianapolis, IN 46206
(800) LOAN USA [562-6872]
(317) 849-6510

Part III. College indexes

15. Colleges that offer academic, music or drama, and art scholarships

Academic scholarships

Alabama

Alabama Agricultural and Mechanical University
Alabama Aviation and Technical College
Alabama State University
Athens State College
Auburn University
    Auburn
    Montgomery
Bessemer State Technical College
Bevill State Community College
Birmingham-Southern College
Bishop State Community College
Calhoun Community College
Central Alabama Community College
Chattahoochee Valley Community College
Douglas MacArthur State Technical College
Enterprise State Junior College
Faulkner University
Gadsden State Community College
George C. Wallace State Community College at Selma
Huntingdon College
J. F. Drake State Technical College
Jacksonville State University
James H. Faulkner State Community College
Jefferson State Community College
John M. Patterson State Technical College
Lurleen B. Wallace State Junior College
Marion Military Institute
Miles College
Northeast Alabama Community College
Northwest-Shoals Community College
Oakwood College
Samford University
Snead State Community College
Southeastern Bible College
Southern Christian University
Sparks State Technical College
Spring Hill College
Stillman College
Talladega College
Troy State University
    Dothan
    Troy
Tuskegee University

University of Alabama
    Birmingham
    Huntsville
    Tuscaloosa
University of Alabama at Birmingham: Walker College
University of Mobile
University of Montevallo
University of North Alabama
University of West Alabama
Wallace State College at Hanceville

Alaska

Alaska Bible College
Alaska Pacific University
Prince William Sound Community College
University of Alaska
    Anchorage
    Southeast

Arizona

American Indian College of the Assemblies of God
Arizona College of the Bible
Arizona State University
Arizona Western College
Cochise College
DeVry Institute of Technology: Phoenix
Embry-Riddle Aeronautical University: Prescott Campus
Gateway Community College
Glendale Community College
Mesa Community College
Mohave Community College
Navajo Community College
Northern Arizona University
Northland Pioneer College
Paradise Valley Community College
Pima Community College
Prescott College
Scottsdale Community College
South Mountain Community College
University of Arizona
Yavapai College

Arkansas

Arkansas State University
    Beebe Branch
    Jonesboro
Arkansas Tech University
Central Baptist College
Garland County Community College
Harding University
Henderson State University
Hendrix College
John Brown University

Lyon College
Mississippi County Community College
North Arkansas Community/Technical College
Ouachita Baptist University
Philander Smith College
Phillips County Community College
Rich Mountain Community College
South Arkansas Community College
Southern Arkansas University
    Magnolia
    Tech
University of Arkansas
    Fayetteville
    Little Rock
    Monticello
University of Central Arkansas
University of the Ozarks
Westark Community College
Williams Baptist College

California

Academy of Art College
Allan Hancock College
American Academy of Dramatic Arts: West
American River College
Antelope Valley College
Art Institute of Southern California
Azusa Pacific University
Bakersfield College
Bethany College
Biola University
Brooks Institute of Photography
California Baptist College
California College of Arts and Crafts
California Institute of Technology
California Lutheran University
California Maritime Academy
California Polytechnic State University: San Luis Obispo
California State Polytechnic University: Pomona
California State University
    Bakersfield
    Chico
    Dominguez Hills
    Fresno
    Fullerton
    Hayward
    Long Beach
    Los Angeles
    Northridge
    Sacramento
    San Bernardino
    San Marcos
    Stanislaus
Cerro Coso Community College

Chaffey Community College
Chapman University
Charles R. Drew University: College of Allied Health
Christian Heritage College
Citrus College
City College of San Francisco
Claremont McKenna College
Cogswell Polytechnical College
Coleman College
College of the Desert
College of Notre Dame
College of the Redwoods
College of the Sequoias
College of the Siskiyous
Columbia College
Concordia University
Cosumnes River College
Crafton Hills College
Cuesta College
De Anza College
DeVry Institute of Technology: Pomona
Diablo Valley College
Dominican College of San Rafael
El Camino College
Evergreen Valley College
Feather River College
Foothill College
Fresno City College
Fresno Pacific College
Fullerton College
Gavilan Community College
Golden Gate University
Golden West College
Heald College: Sacramento
Holy Names College
Humboldt State University
Humphreys College
Imperial Valley College
John F. Kennedy University
Kings River Community College
La Sierra University
Las Positas College
LIFE Bible College
Long Beach City College
Los Angeles Harbor College
Los Angeles Mission College
Los Angeles Pierce College
Los Angeles Southwest College
Los Medanos College
Loyola Marymount University
Marymount College
Menlo College
Merced College
Mills College
Modesto Junior College
Monterey Institute of International Studies
Monterey Peninsula College

Mount St. Mary's College
Mount San Jacinto College
Napa Valley College
New School of Architecture
Occidental College
Ohlone College
Orange Coast College
Pacific Christian College
Pacific Oaks College
Pacific Union College
Palomar College
Pasadena City College
Patten College
Pepperdine University
Point Loma Nazarene College
Porterville College
Rio Hondo College
Riverside Community College
Saddleback College
St. Mary's College of California
Samuel Merritt College
San Diego Mesa College
San Diego State University
San Francisco State University
San Joaquin Delta College
San Jose Christian College
Santa Barbara City College
Santa Clara University
Santa Monica College
Santa Rosa Junior College
Scripps College
Shasta College
Sierra College
Simpson College
Sonoma State University
Southern California College
Southern California Institute of
    Architecture
Southwestern College
Taft College
United States International
    University
University of California
    Berkeley
    Davis
    Irvine
    Los Angeles
    Riverside
    San Diego
    San Francisco
    Santa Barbara
    Santa Cruz
University of Judaism
University of La Verne
University of the Pacific
University of Redlands
University of San Diego
University of San Francisco
University of Southern California
Victor Valley College
Westmont College
Whittier College
Woodbury University
Yuba College

Colorado

Adams State College
Aims Community College
Arapahoe Community College
Bel-Rea Institute of Animal
    Technology
Colorado Christian University
Colorado College
Colorado Institute of Art
Colorado Mountain College
    Alpine Campus
    Spring Valley Campus
    Timberline Campus
Colorado Northwestern Community
    College
Colorado School of Mines
Colorado State University

Colorado Technical University
Fort Lewis College
Front Range Community College
Lamar Community College
Mesa State College
Metropolitan State College of
    Denver
Naropa Institute
Nazarene Bible College
Northeastern Junior College
Pikes Peak Community College
Pueblo Community College
Red Rocks Community College
Regis University
Rocky Mountain College of Art &
    Design
Trinidad State Junior College
University of Colorado
    Boulder
    Colorado Springs
    Denver
    Health Sciences Center
University of Denver
University of Northern Colorado
University of Southern Colorado
Western State College of Colorado

Connecticut

Albertus Magnus College
Briarwood College
Capital Community-Technical
    College
Central Connecticut State
    University
Eastern Connecticut State
    University
Fairfield University
Gateway Community-Technical
    College
Manchester Community-Technical
    College
Mitchell College
Naugatuck Valley Community-
    Technical College
Northwestern Connecticut
    Community-Technical College
Norwalk Community-Technical
    College
Quinebaug Valley Community-
    Technical College
Quinnipiac College
Sacred Heart University
St. Joseph College
Southern Connecticut State
    University
Teikyo-Post University
Tunxis Community-Technical
    College
University of Bridgeport
University of Connecticut
University of Hartford
University of New Haven
Western Connecticut State
    University

Delaware

Delaware State University
Delaware Technical and
    Community College
    Owens Campus
    Stanton/Wilmington Campus
    Terry Campus
Goldey-Beacom College
University of Delaware
Wesley College
Wilmington College

District of Columbia

American University
Catholic University of America
Corcoran School of Art
George Washington University

Howard University
Mount Vernon College
Southeastern University
Strayer College
Trinity College
University of the District of
    Columbia

Florida

Barry University
Bethune-Cookman College
Brevard Community College
Broward Community College
Central Florida Community College
Chipola Junior College
Daytona Beach Community College
Eckerd College
Edison Community College
Embry-Riddle Aeronautical
    University
Flagler College
Florida Agricultural and Mechanical
    University
Florida Atlantic University
Florida Bible College
Florida Christian College
Florida College
Florida Community College at
    Jacksonville
Florida Institute of Technology
Florida International University
Florida Keys Community College
Florida Memorial College
Florida Southern College
Florida State University
Gulf Coast Community College
Hillsborough Community College
Hobe Sound Bible College
Indian River Community College
Jacksonville University
Lake City Community College
Lake-Sumter Community College
Lynn University
Manatee Community College
Miami-Dade Community College
New College of the University of
    South Florida
North Florida Junior College
Nova Southeastern University
Okaloosa-Walton Community
    College
Palm Beach Atlantic College
Palm Beach Community College
Pasco-Hernando Community
    College
Pensacola Junior College
Polk Community College
Rollins College
St. Johns River Community College
St. Leo College
St. Petersburg Junior College
St. Thomas University
Santa Fe Community College
Schiller International University
Seminole Community College
South Florida Community College
Southeastern College of the
    Assemblies of God
Stetson University
Tallahassee Community College
Tampa College
Trinity International University
University of Central Florida
University of Florida
University of Miami
University of North Florida
University of South Florida
University of Tampa
University of West Florida
Valencia Community College
Warner Southern College
Webber College

Georgia

Abraham Baldwin Agricultural
    College
Agnes Scott College
Albany State College
American College: Atlanta
Andrew College
Armstrong State College
Atlanta College of Art
Augusta College
Augusta Technical Institute
Bainbridge College
Berry College
Brenau University
Brewton-Parker College
Brunswick College
Chattahoochee Technical Institute
Clark Atlanta University
Clayton State College
Columbus College
Covenant College
Dalton College
Darton College
DeKalb Technical Institute
DeVry Institute of Technology:
    Atlanta
East Georgia College
Emmanuel College
Emory University
Floyd College
Fort Valley State College
Gainesville College
Georgia Baptist College of Nursing
Georgia College
Georgia Institute of Technology
Georgia Southern University
Georgia Southwestern College
Georgia State University
Gordon College
Gwinnett Technical Institute
Kennesaw State College
LaGrange College
Macon College
Medical College of Georgia
Mercer University
    Atlanta
    Macon
Middle Georgia College
Morehouse College
Morris Brown College
North Georgia College
Oglethorpe University
Oxford College of Emory University
Paine College
Piedmont College
Reinhardt College
Savannah State College
Shorter College
South College
Southern College of Technology
Spelman College
Thomas College
University of Georgia
Valdosta State University
Wesleyan College
West Georgia College
Young Harris College

Hawaii

Brigham Young University-Hawaii
Chaminade University of Honolulu
Hawaii Pacific University
University of Hawaii
    Hilo
    Kapiolani Community College
    Kauai Community College
    Manoa
    West Oahu
    Windward Community College

Idaho

Albertson College

Boise Bible College
Boise State University
College of Southern Idaho
Eastern Idaho Technical College
Idaho State University
Lewis-Clark State College
North Idaho College
Northwest Nazarene College
Ricks College
University of Idaho

Illinois

Augustana College
Aurora University
Belleville Area College
Benedictine University
Black Hawk College
Blackburn College
Blessing-Reiman College of Nursing
Bradley University
Carl Sandburg College
Chicago College of Commerce
Chicago State University
City Colleges of Chicago
    Kennedy-King College
    Malcolm X College
    Olive-Harvey College
    Wright College
College of DuPage
College of Lake County
Columbia College
Concordia University
Danville Area Community College
De Paul University
DeVry Institute of Technology
    Addison
    Chicago
Eastern Illinois University
East-West University
Elgin Community College
Elmhurst College
Eureka College
Governors State University
Greenville College
Highland Community College
Illinois College
Illinois Eastern Community
    Colleges
    Frontier Community College
    Lincoln Trail College
    Olney Central College
    Wabash Valley College
Illinois Institute of Technology
Illinois State University
Illinois Valley Community College
Illinois Wesleyan University
International Academy of
    Merchandising and Design
John A. Logan College
Joliet Junior College
Kaskaskia College
Kendall College
Kishwaukee College
Knox College
Lake Forest College
Lake Land College
Lewis and Clark Community
    College
Lewis University
Lexington College
Lincoln Christian College and
    Seminary
Lincoln College
Lincoln Land Community College
Loyola University of Chicago
MacCormac Junior College
MacMurray College
McHenry County College
McKendree College
Mennonite College of Nursing
Millikin University
Monmouth College

Moraine Valley Community College
Morrison Institute of Technology
Morton College
National-Louis University
North Central College
North Park College
Northeastern Illinois University
Northern Illinois University
Northwestern Business College
Oakton Community College
Olivet Nazarene University
Parkland College
Principia College
Quincy University
Rend Lake College
Richland Community College
Robert Morris College: Chicago
Rock Valley College
Rockford College
Rosary College
Rush University
St. Francis Medical Center College
    of Nursing
St. Xavier University
Southeastern Illinois College
Southern Illinois University
    Carbondale
    Edwardsville
Spoon River College
Trinity Christian College
Trinity International University
Triton College
University of Chicago
University of Illinois
    Chicago
    Springfield
    Urbana-Champaign
Western Illinois University
Wheaton College
William Rainey Harper College

Indiana

Ancilla College
Anderson University
Ball State University
Bethel College
Butler University
Calumet College of St. Joseph
DePauw University
Earlham College
Franklin College
Goshen College
Grace College
Hanover College
Huntington College
Indiana Institute of Technology
Indiana State University
Indiana University
    Bloomington
    East
    Kokomo
    Northwest
    South Bend
    Southeast
Indiana University—Purdue
    University
    Fort Wayne
    Indianapolis
Indiana Wesleyan University

Ivy Tech State College
    Central Indiana
    Columbus
    Eastcentral
    Kokomo
    Lafayette
    Northcentral
    Northeast
    Northwest
    Southcentral
    Southeast
    Southwest
    Wabash Valley
    Whitewater
Lutheran College of Health
    Professions
Manchester College
Marian College
Oakland City University
Purdue University
    Calumet
    North Central Campus
    West Lafayette
Rose-Hulman Institute of
    Technology
St. Francis College
St. Joseph's College
St. Mary-of-the-Woods College
St. Meinrad College
Saint Mary's College
Taylor University
Tri-State University
University of Evansville
University of Indianapolis
University of Southern Indiana
Valparaiso University
Vincennes University
Wabash College

Iowa

American Institute of Business
Briar Cliff College
Buena Vista University
Central College
Clarke College
Clinton Community College
Coe College
Cornell College
Des Moines Area Community
    College
Dordt College
Drake University
Ellsworth Community College
Faith Baptist Bible College and
    Theological Seminary
Graceland College
Grand View College
Grinnell College
Hawkeye Community College
Indian Hills Community College
Iowa Central Community College
Iowa Lakes Community College
Iowa State University
Iowa Wesleyan College
Iowa Western Community College
Loras College
Luther College
Maharishi University of
    Management
Morningside College
Mount Mercy College
Muscatine Community College
North Iowa Area Community
    College
Northeast Iowa Community College
Northwest Iowa Community
    College
Northwestern College
St. Ambrose University
Scott Community College
Simpson College

Southeastern Community College
    North Campus
    South Campus
Southwestern Community College
Teikyo Marycrest University
University of Dubuque
University of Iowa
University of Northern Iowa
Upper Iowa University
Waldorf College
Wartburg College
Westmar University

Kansas

Baker University
Barclay College
Barton County Community College
Benedictine College
Bethany College
Bethel College
Butler County Community College
Colby Community College
Donnelly College
Emporia State University
Fort Hays State University
Friends University
Garden City Community College
Hesston College
Hutchinson Community College
Independence Community College
Kansas City Kansas Community
    College
Kansas Newman College
Kansas State University
Manhattan Christian College
MidAmerica Nazarene College
Neosho County Community College
Ottawa University
Pittsburg State University
Pratt Community College
St. Mary College
Southwestern College
Tabor College
University of Kansas
    Lawrence
    Medical Center
Washburn University of Topeka
Wichita State University

Kentucky

Asbury College
Ashland Community College
Bellarmine College
Brescia College
Centre College
Clear Creek Baptist Bible College
Cumberland College
Eastern Kentucky University
Elizabethtown Community College
Georgetown College
Hazard Community College
Hopkinsville Community College
Kentucky Christian College
Kentucky State University
Kentucky Wesleyan College
Lexington Community College
Lindsey Wilson College
Madisonville Community College
Maysville Community College
Mid-Continent Baptist Bible College
Morehead State University
Murray State University
Northern Kentucky University
Paducah Community College
Pikeville College
Prestonsburg Community College
Somerset Community College
Southeast Community College
Spalding University
Sue Bennett College
Sullivan College
Transylvania University

Colleges that offer academic, music or drama, or art scholarships

Union College
University of Kentucky
University of Louisville
Western Kentucky University

Louisiana

Bossier Parish Community College
Centenary College of Louisiana
Dillard University
Grambling State University
Louisiana College
Louisiana State University
    Agricultural and Mechanical
        College
    Alexandria
    Eunice
    Shreveport
Louisiana Tech University
Loyola University New Orleans
McNeese State University
Nicholls State University
Northeast Louisiana University
Northwestern State University
Nunez Community College
Our Lady of Holy Cross College
St. Joseph Seminary College
Southeastern Louisiana University
Tulane University
University of New Orleans
University of Southwestern
    Louisiana
Xavier University of Louisiana

Maine

Andover College
College of the Atlantic
Husson College
Maine College of Art
Maine Maritime Academy
St. Joseph's College
Thomas College
Unity College
University of Maine
    Augusta
    Farmington
    Fort Kent
    Orono
    Presque Isle
University of New England
University of Southern Maine

Maryland

Allegany College
Anne Arundel Community College
Baltimore International Culinary
    College
Bowie State University
Capitol College
Carroll Community College
Catonsville Community College
Cecil Community College
Charles County Community College
Chesapeake College
Columbia Union College
Dundalk Community College
Essex Community College
Frederick Community College
Frostburg State University
Goucher College
Hagerstown Business College
Hagerstown Junior College
Harford Community College
Hood College
Johns Hopkins University
Loyola College in Maryland
Maryland College of Art and
    Design
Maryland Institute College of Art
Morgan State University
Mount St. Mary's College
Prince George's Community College
St. Mary's College of Maryland

Salisbury State University
Towson State University
University of Baltimore
University of Maryland
    Baltimore County
    College Park
    Eastern Shore
    University College
Villa Julie College
Washington Bible College
Washington College
Western Maryland College
Wor-Wic Community College

Massachusetts

American International College
Anna Maria College
Aquinas College at Milton
Aquinas College at Newton
Atlantic Union College
Babson College
Bay Path College
Bay State College
Becker College
    Leicester Campus
    Worcester Campus
Bentley College
Berklee College of Music
Boston Architectural Center
Boston College
Boston University
Bradford College
Brandeis University
Bridgewater State College
Clark University
College of the Holy Cross
Dean College
Eastern Nazarene College
Elms College
Emerson College
Emmanuel College
Fisher College
Fitchburg State College
Forsyth School for Dental
    Hygienists
Framingham State College
Gordon College
Hampshire College
Hellenic College
Holyoke Community College
Katharine Gibbs School
Laboure College
Lasell College
Lesley College
Massachusetts Bay Community
    College
Massachusetts College of Pharmacy
    and Allied Health Sciences
Massachusetts Maritime Academy
Massasoit Community College
Merrimack College
Montserrat College of Art
Newbury College
Nichols College
North Adams State College
Northeastern University
Pine Manor College
Quincy College
Quinsigamond Community College
Regis College
St. Hyacinth College and Seminary
Salem State College
Simmons College
Simon's Rock College of Bard
Stonehill College
Suffolk University
Tufts University
University of Massachusetts
    Amherst
    Boston
    Dartmouth
Wentworth Institute of Technology

Westfield State College
Worcester Polytechnic Institute
Worcester State College

Michigan

Adrian College
Albion College
Alma College
Alpena Community College
Andrews University
Aquinas College
Baker College
    Auburn Hills
    Cadillac
    Flint
    Mount Clemens
    Muskegon
    Owosso
    Port Huron
Bay de Noc Community College
Calvin College
Central Michigan University
Cleary College
Concordia College
Cornerstone College and Grand
    Rapids Baptist Seminary
Davenport College of Business
Delta College
Detroit College of Business
Eastern Michigan University
Ferris State University
Glen Oaks Community College
GMI Engineering & Management
    Institute
Gogebic Community College
Grace Bible College
Grand Rapids Community College
Grand Valley State University
Great Lakes Christian College
Great Lakes Junior College of
    Business
Henry Ford Community College
Hillsdale College
Hope College
Jackson Community College
Kalamazoo College
Kalamazoo Valley Community
    College
Kellogg Community College
Kendall College of Art and Design
Lake Superior State University
Lansing Community College
Lawrence Technological University
Macomb Community College
Madonna University
Michigan Christian College
Michigan State University
Michigan Technological University
Mid Michigan Community College
Monroe County Community
    College
Montcalm Community College
Mott Community College
Muskegon Community College
North Central Michigan College
Northern Michigan University
Northwestern Michigan College
Northwood University
Oakland Community College
Oakland University
Olivet College
Reformed Bible College
Saginaw Valley State University
St. Clair County Community
    College
St. Mary's College
Schoolcraft College
Siena Heights College
Spring Arbor College
Suomi College

University of Michigan
    Ann Arbor
    Flint
Walsh College of Accountancy and
    Business Administration
Washtenaw Community College
Wayne State University
West Shore Community College
Western Michigan University
William Tyndale College

Minnesota

Alexandria Technical College
Anoka-Ramsey Community College
Augsburg College
Austin Community College
Bemidji State University
Bethany Lutheran College
Bethel College
Carleton College
Central Lakes College
College of St. Benedict
College of St. Catherine: St.
    Catherine Campus
College of St. Catherine-
    Minneapolis
College of St. Scholastica
College of Visual Arts
Concordia College: Moorhead
Concordia College: St. Paul
Crown College
Fergus Falls Community College
Gustavus Adolphus College
Hamline University
Hibbing Community College
Itasca Community College:
    Arrowhead Region
Lakewood Community College
Macalester College
Mankato State University
Martin Luther College
Mesabi Community College:
    Arrowhead Region
Minneapolis College of Art and
    Design
Minneapolis Community College
Minnesota Bible College
Moorhead State University
National College
NEI College of Technology
North Central Bible College
Northland Community & Technical
    College
Northwestern College
Pillsbury Baptist Bible College
Rainy River Community College
Rochester Community College
St. Cloud State University
St. John's University
St. Mary's University of Minnesota
St. Olaf College
Southwest State University
University of Minnesota
    Crookston
    Duluth
    Morris
    Twin Cities
University of St. Thomas
Vermilion Community College
Willmar Community College
Winona State University

Mississippi

Alcorn State University
Belhaven College
Blue Mountain College
Copiah-Lincoln Community College
Delta State University
East Central Community College
East Mississippi Community College
Hinds Community College
Holmes Community College

Itawamba Community College
Jackson State University
Jones County Junior College
Magnolia Bible College
Meridian Community College
Millsaps College
Mississippi College
Mississippi Delta Community
  College
Mississippi Gulf Coast Community
  College
    Jackson County Campus
    Jefferson Davis Campus
    Perkinston
Mississippi State University
Mississippi University for Women
Mississippi Valley State University
Northeast Mississippi Community
  College
Pearl River Community College
Rust College
Tougaloo College
University of Mississippi
  Medical Center
  University
University of Southern Mississippi
Wesley College
William Carey College

Missouri

Avila College
Baptist Bible College
Calvary Bible College
Central Bible College
Central Christian College of the
  Bible
Central Methodist College
Central Missouri State University
College of the Ozarks
Columbia College
Cottey College
Crowder College
Culver-Stockton College
Deaconess College of Nursing
DeVry Institute of Technology:
  Kansas City
Drury College
East Central College
Evangel College
Fontbonne College
Hannibal-LaGrange College
Harris Stowe State College
Jefferson College
Kansas City Art Institute
Lincoln University
Lindenwood College
Longview Community College
Maple Woods Community College
Maryville University of Saint Louis
Mineral Area College
Missouri Baptist College
Missouri Southern State College
Missouri Technical School
Missouri Valley College
Missouri Western State College
Moberly Area Community College
National College
North Central Missouri College
Northwest Missouri State
  University
Ozark Christian College
Park College
Penn Valley Community College
Ranken Technical College
Research College of Nursing
Rockhurst College
St. Charles County Community
  College
St. Louis Christian College
St. Louis College of Pharmacy

St. Louis Community College
  Florissant Valley
  Forest Park
  Meramec
St. Louis University
Southeast Missouri State University
Southwest Baptist University
Southwest Missouri State University
State Fair Community College
Stephens College
Three Rivers Community College
Truman State University
University of Missouri
  Columbia
  Kansas City
  Rolla
  St. Louis
Washington University
Webster University
Wentworth Military Academy
Westminster College
William Jewell College
William Woods University

Montana

Carroll College
Dawson Community College
Flathead Valley Community College
Helena College of Technology of
  the University of Montana
Little Big Horn College
Miles Community College
Montana State University
  Billings
  Bozeman
  Northern
Montana Tech of The University of
  Montana
Montana Tech of the University of
  Montana: College of Technology
Stone Child College
University of Great Falls
University of Montana-Missoula
University of Montana College of
  Technology
Western Montana College of the
  University of Montana

Nebraska

Bellevue University
Central Community College
Chadron State College
College of St. Mary
Concordia College
Creighton University
Dana College
Doane College/Lincoln Campus
Grace University
Hastings College
Lincoln School of Commerce
McCook Community College
Metropolitan Community College
Mid Plains Community College
Midland Lutheran College
Nebraska Christian College
Nebraska College of Technical
  Agriculture
Nebraska Methodist College of
  Nursing and Allied Health
Nebraska Wesleyan University
Northeast Community College
Peru State College
Southeast Community College
  Beatrice Campus
  Lincoln Campus
  Milford Campus
Union College
University of Nebraska
  Medical Center
  Kearney
  Lincoln
  Omaha

Wayne State College
Western Nebraska Community
  College
York College

Nevada

Great Basin College
Morrison College: Reno
Sierra Nevada College
University of Nevada
  Las Vegas
  Reno
Western Nevada Community
  College

New Hampshire

Castle College
Colby-Sawyer College
Daniel Webster College
Franklin Pierce College
Hesser College
Keene State College
McIntosh College
New England College
New Hampshire College
Notre Dame College
Plymouth State College of the
  University System of New
  Hampshire
Rivier College
St. Anselm College
University of New Hampshire
  Durham
  Manchester
White Pines College

New Jersey

Bergen Community College
Berkeley College of Business
Bloomfield College
Brookdale Community College
Burlington County College
Caldwell College
Camden County College
Centenary College
College of St. Elizabeth
County College of Morris
DeVry Technical Institute
Drew University
Essex County College
Fairleigh Dickinson University
  Edward Williams College
  Teaneck
Georgian Court College
Jersey City State College
Mercer County Community College
Middlesex County College
Monmouth University
Montclair State University
New Jersey Institute of Technology
Ocean County College
Ramapo College of New Jersey
Richard Stockton College of New
  Jersey
Rider University
Rowan College of New Jersey
Rutgers, The State University of
  New Jersey
    Camden College of Arts and
      Sciences
    College of Engineering
    College of Nursing
    College of Pharmacy
    Cook College
    Douglass College
    Livingston College
    Mason Gross School of the
      Arts
    Newark College of Arts and
      Sciences
    Rutgers College
St. Peter's College

Salem Community College
Seton Hall University
Stevens Institute of Technology
Trenton State College
Union County College
Warren County Community College
William Paterson College of New
  Jersey

New Mexico

Clovis Community College
College of Santa Fe
College of the Southwest
Eastern New Mexico University
  Portales
  Roswell Campus
National College
New Mexico Highlands University
New Mexico Institute of Mining
  and Technology
New Mexico Junior College
New Mexico Military Institute
New Mexico State University
  Carlsbad
  Las Cruces
Parks College
San Juan College
Santa Fe Community College
University of New Mexico

New York

Adelphi University
Adirondack Community College
Alfred University
American Academy McAllister
  Institute of Funeral Service
Bard College
Berkeley College
Bramson ORT Technical Institute
Briarcliffe: The College for Business
  and Technology
Broome Community College
Bryant & Stratton Business Institute
  Albany
  Syracuse
Canisius College
Cayuga County Community College
Cazenovia College
City University of New York
  Baruch College
  Brooklyn College
  City College
  Hostos Community College
  Hunter College
  John Jay College of Criminal
    Justice
  Lehman College
  Queens College
  Queensborough Community
    College
Clarkson University
Clinton Community College
College of Aeronautics
College of Insurance
College of Mount St. Vincent
College of New Rochelle
College of St. Rose
Columbia University: School of
  Nursing
Columbia-Greene Community
  College
Concordia College
Cooper Union
Cornell University
Corning Community College
Culinary Institute of America
Daemen College
Dominican College of Blauvelt
Dowling College
Dutchess Community College
D'Youville College

Eastman School of Music of the
University of Rochester
Elmira College
Eugene Lang College/New School
for Social Research
Fashion Institute of Technology
Finger Lakes Community College
Fordham University
Fulton-Montgomery Community
College
Genesee Community College
Hartwick College
Helene Fuld College of Nursing
Herkimer County Community
College
Hilbert College
Hobart and William Smith Colleges
Hofstra University
Houghton College
Iona College
Ithaca College
Jamestown Business College
Jamestown Community College
Jefferson Community College
Jewish Theological Seminary of
America
Juilliard School
Keuka College
Le Moyne College
Long Island University
Brooklyn Campus
C. W. Post Campus
Southampton College
Manhattan College
Manhattan School of Music
Manhattanville College
Marist College
Marymount College
Marymount Manhattan College
Mater Dei College
Medaille College
Mercy College
Mohawk Valley Community College
Molloy College
Monroe Community College
Mount St. Mary College
Nassau Community College
Nazareth College of Rochester
New York Institute of Technology
New York School of Interior
Design
New York University
Niagara County Community College
Niagara University
Nyack College
Onondaga Community College
Orange County Community College
Pace University
Paul Smith's College
Phillips Beth Israel School of
Nursing
Plaza Business Institute
Polytechnic University
Brooklyn
Long Island Campus
Pratt Institute
Rensselaer Polytechnic Institute
Roberts Wesleyan College
Rochester Institute of Technology
Rockland Community College
Russell Sage College
Sage Junior College of Albany
St. Bonaventure University
St. Francis College
St. John Fisher College
St. John's University
St. Joseph's College
Brooklyn
Suffolk Campus
St. Joseph's Hospital Health Center
School of Nursing
St. Lawrence University

St. Thomas Aquinas College
Schenectady County Community
College
School of Visual Arts
Siena College
State University of New York
Albany
Binghamton
Buffalo
Oswego
Purchase
Stony Brook
College of Agriculture and
Technology at Cobleskill
College of Agriculture and
Technology at Morrisville
College at Brockport
College at Buffalo
College at Cortland
College of Environmental
Science and Forestry
College at Geneseo
College at Old Westbury
College at Oneonta
College at Plattsburgh
College at Potsdam
College of Technology at
Alfred
College of Technology at
Canton
College of Technology at
Farmingdale
Health Sciences Center at
Stony Brook
Institute of Technology at
Utica/Rome
Maritime College
Syracuse University
Tompkins-Cortland Community
College
Trocaire College
Ulster County Community College
University of Rochester
University of the State of New
York: Regents College
Utica College of Syracuse
University
Villa Maria College of Buffalo
Wadhams Hall Seminary-College
Wagner College
Webb Institute
Wells College
Westchester Business Institute
Westchester Community College
Wood Tobe-Coburn School
Yeshiva University

North Carolina
Alamance Community College
Appalachian State University
Asheville Buncombe Technical
Community College
Barber-Scotia College
Barton College
Beaufort County Community
College
Belmont Abbey College
Bennett College
Blue Ridge Community College
Brevard College
Brunswick Community College
Caldwell Community College and
Technical Institute
Campbell University
Cape Fear Community College
Catawba College
Catawba Valley Community College
Chowan College
Cleveland Community College
College of The Albemarle
Craven Community College
Davidson College

Davidson County Community
College
Duke University
East Carolina University
East Coast Bible College
Edgecombe Community College
Elizabeth City State University
Elon College
Fayetteville State University
Fayetteville Technical Community
College
Forsyth Technical Community
College
Gardner-Webb University
Greensboro College
Guilford College
Guilford Technical Community
College
Haywood Community College
High Point University
James Sprunt Community College
John Wesley College
Johnson C. Smith University
Lees-McRae College
Lenoir-Rhyne College
Livingstone College
Louisburg College
Mars Hill College
Martin Community College
Meredith College
Methodist College
Mitchell Community College
Montgomery Community College
Montreat College
Mount Olive College
Nash Community College
North Carolina Agricultural and
Technical State University
North Carolina Central University
North Carolina School of the Arts
North Carolina State University
North Carolina Wesleyan College
Peace College
Pembroke State University
Pfeiffer College
Pitt Community College
Queens College
Richmond Community College
Roanoke Bible College
Roanoke-Chowan Community
College
Rockingham Community College
St. Andrews Presbyterian College
St. Augustine's College
St. Mary's College
Salem College
Sandhills Community College
Southeastern Community College
Stanly Community College
Surry Community College
Tri-County Community College
University of North Carolina
Asheville
Chapel Hill
Charlotte
Greensboro
Wilmington
Vance-Granville Community
College
Wake Forest University
Wake Technical Community
College
Warren Wilson College
Western Carolina University
Western Piedmont Community
College
Wilkes Community College
Wingate University
Winston-Salem State University

North Dakota
Bismarck State College

Dickinson State University
Jamestown College
Minot State University
North Dakota State College of
Science
North Dakota State University
Bottineau
Fargo
Trinity Bible College
University of North Dakota
Grand Forks
Lake Region
Williston
Valley City State University

Ohio
Antioch College
Art Academy of Cincinnati
Ashland University
Baldwin-Wallace College
Belmont Technical College
Bluffton College
Bowling Green State University
Bowling Green
Firelands College
Bryant & Stratton Business
Institute: Cleveland West
Bryant & Stratton College
Capital University
Case Western Reserve University
Cedarville College
Central Ohio Technical College
Cincinnati Bible College and
Seminary
Cincinnati State Technical and
Community College
Clark State Community College
Cleveland Institute of Art
Cleveland Institute of Music
Cleveland State University
College of Mount St. Joseph
College of Wooster
Columbus State Community College
Cuyahoga Community College
Eastern Campus
Metropolitan Campus
Western Campus
David N. Myers College
Davis College
Denison University
DeVry Institute of Technology:
Columbus
Edison State Community College
Franciscan University of
Steubenville
Franklin University
God's Bible School and College
Heidelberg College
Hiram College
Hocking Technical College
Jefferson Community College
John Carroll University
Kent State University
East Liverpool Regional
Campus
Kent
Salem Regional Campus
Stark Campus
Trumbull Campus
Tuscarawas Campus
Kenyon College
Kettering College of Medical Arts
Lake Erie College
Lakeland Community College
Lima Technical College
Lorain County Community College
Lourdes College
Malone College
Marietta College
Marion Technical College

Miami University
  Hamilton Campus
  Middletown Campus
  Oxford Campus
Mount Union College
Mount Vernon Nazarene College
Muskingum Area Technical College
Muskingum College
North Central Technical College
Northwest State Community
  College
Northwestern College
Notre Dame College of Ohio
Oberlin College
Ohio Dominican College
Ohio Northern University
Ohio State University
  Agricultural Technical Institute
  Columbus Campus
  Lima Campus
  Mansfield Campus
  Marion Campus
  Newark Campus
Ohio University
  Athens
  Chillicothe Campus
  Zanesville Campus
Ohio Wesleyan University
Otterbein College
Owens Community College: Toledo
Pontifical College Josephinum
Shawnee State University
Sinclair Community College
Southern State Community College
Stark Technical College
Terra Community College
Tiffin University
University of Akron
  Akron
  Wayne College
University of Cincinnati
  Access Colleges
  Cincinnati
  Clermont College
  Raymond Walters College
University of Dayton
University of Findlay
University of Rio Grande
University of Toledo
Urbana University
Ursuline College
Walsh University
Washington State Community
  College
Wilberforce University
Wilmington College
Wittenberg University
Wright State University
  Dayton
  Lake Campus
Xavier University
Youngstown State University

Oklahoma

Bartlesville Wesleyan College
Cameron University
Connors State College
East Central University
Eastern Oklahoma State College
Langston University
Mid-America Bible College
Murray State College
Northeastern Oklahoma
  Agricultural and Mechanical
  College
Northern Oklahoma College
Oklahoma Baptist University
Oklahoma Christian University of
  Science and Arts
Oklahoma City Community College
Oklahoma City University

Oklahoma Panhandle State
  University
Oklahoma State University
  Oklahoma City
  Stillwater
Oral Roberts University
Phillips University
Redlands Community College
Rogers State College
Rose State College
St. Gregory's College
Southeastern Oklahoma State
  University
Southwestern College of Christian
  Ministries
Southwestern Oklahoma State
  University
Tulsa Junior College
University of Central Oklahoma
University of Oklahoma
  Health Sciences Center
  Norman
University of Science and Arts of
  Oklahoma
University of Tulsa

Oregon

Bassist College
Central Oregon Community College
Clackamas Community College
Clatsop Community College
Concordia University
Eastern Oregon State College
Eugene Bible College
George Fox College
Lane Community College
Lewis & Clark College
Linfield College
Linn-Benton Community College
Mount Angel Seminary
Mount Hood Community College
Multnomah Bible College
Northwest Christian College
Oregon Institute of Technology
Pacific Northwest College of Art
Pacific University
Portland State University
Rogue Community College
Southern Oregon State College
Southwestern Oregon Community
  College
Treasure Valley Community College
Umpqua Community College
University of Oregon
  Eugene
  Robert Donald Clark Honors
    College
University of Portland
Western Baptist College
Western Oregon State College
Willamette University

Pennsylvania

Albright College
Allegheny College
Allentown College of St. Francis de
  Sales
Alvernia College
Art Institute of Pittsburgh
Baptist Bible College of
  Pennsylvania
Beaver College
Bloomsburg University of
  Pennsylvania
Bucknell University
Bucks County Community College
Butler County Community College
Cabrini College
California University of
  Pennsylvania
Carlow College
Carnegie Mellon University

Cedar Crest College
Central Pennsylvania Business
  School
Chatham College
Chestnut Hill College
Cheyney University of Pennsylvania
Clarion University of Pennsylvania
College Misericordia
Community College of Allegheny
  County
  Allegheny Campus
  Boyce Campus
  South Campus
Community College of Beaver
  County
Community College of Philadelphia
Delaware Valley College
Drexel University
DuBois Business College
Duquesne University
East Stroudsburg University of
  Pennsylvania
Eastern College
Edinboro University of
  Pennsylvania
Elizabethtown College
Franklin and Marshall College
Gannon University
Geneva College
Gettysburg College
Grove City College
Gwynedd-Mercy College
Harcum College
Harrisburg Area Community
  College
Holy Family College
Immaculata College
Juniata College
Keystone College
King's College
Kutztown University of
  Pennsylvania
La Roche College
La Salle University
Lackawanna Junior College
Lancaster Bible College
Lebanon Valley College of
  Pennsylvania
Lehigh Carbon Community College
Lehigh University
Lincoln University
Lock Haven University of
  Pennsylvania
Lycoming College
Manor Junior College
Mansfield University of
  Pennsylvania
Marywood College
McCann School of Business
Medical College of Pennsylvania
  and Hahnemann University
Mercyhurst College
Messiah College
Millersville University of
  Pennsylvania
Montgomery County Community
  College
Moore College of Art and Design
Moravian College
Mount Aloysius College
Muhlenberg College
Neumann College
Northampton County Area
  Community College
Peirce College

Penn State
  Allentown Campus
  Altoona Campus
  Beaver Campus
  Berks Campus
  Delaware County Campus
  Du Bois Campus
  Erie Behrend College
  Fayette Campus
  Harrisburg Capital College
  Hazleton Campus
  McKeesport Campus
  Mont Alto Campus
  New Kensington Campus
  Ogontz Campus
  Schuylkill Campus
  Shenango Campus
  University Park Campus
  Wilkes-Barre Campus
  Worthington-Scranton Campus
  York Campus
Pennsylvania College of Technology
Philadelphia College of Bible
Philadelphia College of Pharmacy
  and Science
Philadelphia College of Textiles and
  Science
Pittsburgh Institute of Mortuary
  Science
Point Park College
Reading Area Community College
Robert Morris College
Rosemont College
St. Francis College
St. Joseph's University
St. Vincent College
Seton Hill College
Shippensburg University of
  Pennsylvania
Slippery Rock University of
  Pennsylvania
Susquehanna University
Swarthmore College
Temple University
Thiel College
Thomas Jefferson University:
  College of Allied Health Sciences
University of the Arts
University of Pittsburgh
  Bradford
  Greensburg
  Johnstown
  Pittsburgh
  Titusville
University of Scranton
Ursinus College
Valley Forge Christian College
Villanova University
Washington and Jefferson College
Waynesburg College
West Chester University of
  Pennsylvania
Westminster College
Widener University
Wilkes University
Wilson College
York College of Pennsylvania

Puerto Rico

Bayamon Central University
Universidad Adventista de las
  Antillas
Universidad Politecnica de Puerto
  Rico

239

Colleges that offer academic, music or drama, or art scholarships

University of Puerto Rico
    Arecibo Campus
    Bayamon Technological
        University College
    Carolina Regional College
    Mayaguez Campus
    Medical Sciences Campus
    Ponce Technological
        University College
University of the Sacred Heart

Rhode Island

Bryant College
Johnson & Wales University
Providence College
Rhode Island College
Rhode Island School of Design
Roger Williams University
Salve Regina University
University of Rhode Island

South Carolina

Aiken Technical College
Anderson College
Benedict College
Charleston Southern University
Chesterfield-Marlboro Technical
    College
The Citadel
Clemson University
Coastal Carolina University
Coker College
College of Charleston
Columbia Bible College
Columbia College
Columbia Junior College of Business
Converse College
Denmark Technical College
Erskine College
Francis Marion University
Furman University
Greenville Technical College
Horry-Georgetown Technical
    College
Lander University
Limestone College
Midlands Technical College
Morris College
North Greenville College
Orangeburg-Calhoun Technical
    College
Piedmont Technical College
Presbyterian College
South Carolina State University
Southern Wesleyan University
Spartanburg Methodist College
Tri-County Technical College
Trident Technical College
University of South Carolina
    Aiken
    Beaufort
    Columbia
    Lancaster
    Spartanburg
    Sumter
    Union
Williamsburg Technical College
Winthrop University
Wofford College
York Technical College

South Dakota

Augustana College
Black Hills State University
Dakota State University
Dakota Wesleyan University
Huron University
Kilian Community College
Lake Area Technical Institute
Mount Marty College
Northern State University
Presentation College

South Dakota School of Mines and
    Technology
South Dakota State University
Southeast Technical Institute
University of Sioux Falls
University of South Dakota

Tennessee

Austin Peay State University
Belmont University
Bethel College
Carson-Newman College
Chattanooga State Technical
    Community College
Christian Brothers University
Cleveland State Community College
Cumberland University
David Lipscomb University
Dyersburg State Community
    College
East Tennessee State University
Fisk University
Freed-Hardeman University
Hiwassee College
Jackson State Community College
Johnson Bible College
King College
Lambuth University
Lee College
Lincoln Memorial University
Martin Methodist College
Maryville College
Memphis College of Art
Middle Tennessee State University
Milligan College
Motlow State Community College
Nashville State Technical Institute
Northeast State Technical
    Community College
Pellissippi State Technical
    Community College
Rhodes College
Roane State Community College
Shelby State Community College
Southern College of Seventh-day
    Adventists
State Technical Institute at
    Memphis
Tennessee State University
Tennessee Technological University
Tennessee Wesleyan College
Tusculum College
Union University
University of Memphis
University of the South
University of Tennessee
    Chattanooga
    Knoxville
    Martin
    Memphis
Vanderbilt University
Volunteer State Community College
Walters State Community College

Texas

Abilene Christian University
Amarillo College
Ambassador University
Angelina College
Angelo State University
Austin College
Austin Community College
Baylor College of Dentistry
Baylor University
Bee County College
Blinn College
Brazosport College
Cedar Valley College
Central Texas College
Cisco Junior College
College of the Mainland

Collin County Community College
    District
Commonwealth Institute of Funeral
    Service
Concordia Lutheran College
Criswell College
Dallas Baptist University
Dallas Christian College
Del Mar College
DeVry Institute of Technology:
    Irving
East Texas Baptist University
East Texas State University
El Centro College
El Paso Community College
Frank Phillips College
Hardin-Simmons University
Houston Baptist University
Houston Community College
Howard College
Howard Payne University
Huston-Tillotson College
Institute for Christian Studies
Jacksonville College
Jarvis Christian College
Kilgore College
Lamar University—Beaumont
Laredo Community College
Lee College
McLennan Community College
McMurry University
Midland College
Midwestern State University
North Lake College
Odessa College
Our Lady of the Lake University of
    San Antonio
Panola College
Prairie View A&M University
Rice University
St. Edward's University
St. Mary's University
St. Philip's College
Sam Houston State University
San Antonio College
San Jacinto College: North
Schreiner College
Southern Methodist University
Southwest Texas State University
Southwestern Adventist College
Southwestern University
Stephen F. Austin State University
Tarrant County Junior College
Temple College
Texas A&M International
    University
Texas A&M University
    College Station
    Galveston
Texas A&M University-Corpus
    Christi
Texas A&M University-Kingsville
Texas Christian University
Texas Lutheran College
Texas State Technical College
    Harlingen
    Waco
Texas Tech University
Texas Wesleyan University
Texas Woman's University
Trinity University
Tyler Junior College
University of Dallas
University of Houston
    Clear Lake
    Downtown
    Houston
    Victoria
University of North Texas
University of St. Thomas

University of Texas
    Arlington
    Austin
    Dallas
    El Paso
    Medical Branch at Galveston
    San Antonio
    Southwestern Medical Center
        at Dallas
    Houston Health Science
        Center
Vernon Regional Junior College
Victoria College
Weatherford College
West Texas A&M University
Western Texas College
Wharton County Junior College

Utah

Brigham Young University
College of Eastern Utah
Dixie College
LDS Business College
Phillips Junior College: Salt Lake
    City Campus
Salt Lake Community College
Snow College
Southern Utah University
University of Utah
Utah State University
Utah Valley State College
Weber State University
Westminster College of Salt Lake
    City

Vermont

Bennington College
Castleton State College
Community College of Vermont
Green Mountain College
Johnson State College
Lyndon State College
Marlboro College
Norwich University
St. Michael's College
School for International Training
Sterling College
Trinity College of Vermont
University of Vermont
Vermont Technical College

Virginia

Averett College
Bluefield College
Bridgewater College
Central Virginia Community College
Christendom College
Christopher Newport University
Clinch Valley College of the
    University of Virginia
College of Health Sciences
College of William and Mary
Dabney S. Lancaster Community
    College
Eastern Mennonite University
Eastern Shore Community College
Emory and Henry College
Ferrum College
George Mason University
Germanna Community College
Hampden-Sydney College
Hampton University
Hollins College
James Madison University
John Tyler Community College
Liberty University
Longwood College
Lynchburg College
Mary Baldwin College
Mary Washington College
Marymount University

Mountain Empire Community
College
National Business College
New River Community College
Norfolk State University
Northern Virginia Community
College
Old Dominion University
Patrick Henry Community College
Paul D. Camp Community College
Radford University
Randolph-Macon College
Randolph-Macon Woman's College
Rappahannock Community College
Richard Bland College
Roanoke College
St. Paul's College
Shenandoah University
Southside Virginia Community
College
Southwest Virginia Community
College
Sweet Briar College
Thomas Nelson Community College
University of Richmond
Virginia Commonwealth University
Virginia Intermont College
Virginia Military Institute
Virginia Polytechnic Institute and
State University
Virginia State University
Virginia Union University
Virginia Wesleyan College
Washington and Lee University
Wytheville Community College

Washington

Bastyr University
Bellevue Community College
Big Bend Community College
Central Washington University
Centralia College
Clark College
Columbia Basin College
Cornish College of the Arts
Eastern Washington University
Edmonds Community College
Evergreen State College
Gonzaga University
Grays Harbor College
Henry Cogswell College
Lower Columbia College
North Seattle Community College
Northwest College
Olympic College
Pacific Lutheran University
Peninsula College
Pierce College
Puget Sound Christian College
Renton Technical College
St. Martin's College
Seattle Pacific University
Seattle University
Shoreline Community College
South Puget Sound Community
College
South Seattle Community College
Tacoma Community College
University of Puget Sound
University of Washington
Walla Walla College
Walla Walla Community College
Washington State University
Wenatchee Valley College
Western Washington University
Whatcom Community College
Whitman College
Whitworth College

West Virginia

Alderson-Broaddus College
Bethany College

Bluefield State College
Concord College
Davis and Elkins College
Fairmont State College
Glenville State College
Marshall University
Ohio Valley College
Potomac State College of West
Virginia University
Salem-Teikyo University
Shepherd College
West Liberty State College
West Virginia Institute of
Technology
West Virginia Northern Community
College
West Virginia State College
West Virginia University
Morgantown
Parkersburg
West Virginia Wesleyan College
Wheeling Jesuit College

Wisconsin

Alverno College
Beloit College
Cardinal Stritch College
Carroll College
Carthage College
Chippewa Valley Technical College
Columbia College of Nursing
Concordia University Wisconsin
Edgewood College
Fox Valley Technical College
Lakeland College
Lawrence University
Madison Junior College of Business
Maranatha Baptist Bible College
Marian College of Fond du Lac
Marquette University
Mid-State Technical College
Milwaukee Area Technical College
Milwaukee Institute of Art &
Design
Milwaukee School of Engineering
Moraine Park Technical College
Mount Mary College
Mount Senario College
Nicolet Area Technical College
Northland College
Ripon College
St. Norbert College
Silver Lake College
Stratton College
University of Wisconsin
Eau Claire
Green Bay
La Crosse
Madison
Milwaukee
Oshkosh
Parkside
Platteville
River Falls
Stevens Point
Stout
Superior
Whitewater
University of Wisconsin Center
Baraboo/Sauk County
Barron County
Fond du Lac
Fox Valley
Manitowoc County
Marshfield/Wood County
Richland
Rock County
Sheboygan County
Washington County
Waukesha
Viterbo College

Waukesha County Technical
College
Wisconsin Indianhead Technical
College
Wisconsin Lutheran College

Wyoming

Eastern Wyoming College
Northwest College
Sheridan College
University of Wyoming
Western Wyoming Community
College

Music or drama
scholarships

Alabama

Alabama Agricultural and
Mechanical University
Alabama State University
Athens State College
Auburn University
Auburn
Montgomery
Bevill State Community College
Birmingham-Southern College
Bishop State Community College
Calhoun Community College
Central Alabama Community
College
Chattahoochee Valley Community
College
Enterprise State Junior College
Gadsden State Community College
George C. Wallace State
Community College at Selma
Huntingdon College
Jacksonville State University
James H. Faulkner State
Community College
Jefferson State Community College
Lurleen B. Wallace State Junior
College
Marion Military Institute
Northeast Alabama Community
College
Northwest-Shoals Community
College
Samford University
Snead State Community College
Southeastern Bible College
Stillman College
Troy State University
Tuskegee University
University of Alabama
Birmingham
Huntsville
Tuscaloosa
University of Mobile
University of Montevallo
University of North Alabama
University of West Alabama
Wallace State College at Hanceville

Alaska

Alaska Bible College
University of Alaska
Anchorage
Fairbanks

Arizona

Arizona College of the Bible
Arizona State University
Arizona Western College
Glendale Community College
Mesa Community College
Mohave Community College
Northern Arizona University

Northland Pioneer College
Scottsdale Community College
South Mountain Community
College
University of Arizona
Yavapai College

Arkansas

Arkansas State University
Beebe Branch
Jonesboro
Arkansas Tech University
Central Baptist College
Garland County Community
College
Harding University
Henderson State University
Hendrix College
John Brown University
Lyon College
Mississippi County Community
College
North Arkansas Community/
Technical College
Ouachita Baptist University
Phillips County Community College
South Arkansas Community College
Southern Arkansas University
Magnolia
Tech
University of Arkansas
Fayetteville
Little Rock
Monticello
University of Central Arkansas
University of the Ozarks
Williams Baptist College

California

Allan Hancock College
American Academy of Dramatic
Arts: West
Antelope Valley College
Azusa Pacific University
Bethany College
Biola University
California Baptist College
California Institute of the Arts
California Lutheran University
California Polytechnic State
University: San Luis Obispo
California State University
Bakersfield
Dominguez Hills
Fresno
Fullerton
Long Beach
Los Angeles
Northridge
Sacramento
Stanislaus
Cerro Coso Community College
Chapman University
Christian Heritage College
Citrus College
College of the Desert
College of Notre Dame
Columbia College
Concordia University
De Anza College
Dominican College of San Rafael
El Camino College
Evergreen Valley College
Foothill College
Fresno City College
Fresno Pacific College
Fullerton College
Gavilan Community College
Holy Names College
Humboldt State University
Imperial Valley College
Kings River Community College

Colleges that offer academic, music or drama, or art scholarships

La Sierra University
Las Positas College
LIFE Bible College
Long Beach City College
Los Medanos College
Loyola Marymount University
Mills College
Modesto Junior College
Monterey Peninsula College
Mount San Jacinto College
Napa Valley College
Occidental College
Ohlone College
Orange Coast College
Pacific Christian College
Pacific Union College
Pasadena City College
Patten College
Pepperdine University
Point Loma Nazarene College
Rio Hondo College
Riverside Community College
Saddleback College
San Diego State University
San Francisco Conservatory of
  Music
San Francisco State University
San Joaquin Delta College
San Jose Christian College
Santa Clara University
Santa Monica College
Santa Rosa Junior College
Shasta College
Sierra College
Simpson College
Sonoma State University
Southwestern College
University of California
  Berkeley
  Irvine
  Los Angeles
  Riverside
  Santa Barbara
  Santa Cruz
University of the Pacific
University of Redlands
University of San Diego
University of Southern California
Westmont College
Whittier College

Colorado

Adams State College
Colorado Christian University
Colorado Institute of Art
Colorado School of Mines
Colorado State University
Fort Lewis College
Mesa State College
Metropolitan State College of
  Denver
Northeastern Junior College
Trinidad State Junior College
University of Colorado
  Boulder
  Denver
University of Denver
University of Northern Colorado
University of Southern Colorado
Western State College of Colorado

Connecticut

Fairfield University
University of Bridgeport
University of Connecticut
University of Hartford

Delaware

Delaware State University
University of Delaware

District of Columbia

Catholic University of America
George Washington University
Howard University
University of the District of
  Columbia

Florida

Barry University
Bethune-Cookman College
Brevard Community College
Broward Community College
Central Florida Community College
Chipola Junior College
Daytona Beach Community College
Eckerd College
Edison Community College
Flagler College
Florida Agricultural and Mechanical
  University
Florida Atlantic University
Florida Bible College
Florida Christian College
Florida College
Florida Community College at
  Jacksonville
Florida International University
Florida Memorial College
Florida Southern College
Florida State University
Gulf Coast Community College
Hillsborough Community College
Indian River Community College
Jacksonville University
Lake-Sumter Community College
Manatee Community College
Miami-Dade Community College
North Florida Junior College
Okaloosa-Walton Community
  College
Palm Beach Atlantic College
Palm Beach Community College
Pensacola Junior College
Polk Community College
Rollins College
St. Johns River Community College
St. Petersburg Junior College
Santa Fe Community College
Seminole Community College
South Florida Community College
Southeastern College of the
  Assemblies of God
Stetson University
Tallahassee Community College
University of Central Florida
University of Florida
University of Miami
University of North Florida
University of South Florida
University of Tampa
University of West Florida
Valencia Community College

Georgia

Abraham Baldwin Agricultural
  College
Agnes Scott College
Andrew College
Armstrong State College
Augusta College
Berry College
Brenau University
Brewton-Parker College
Clark Atlanta University
Clayton State College
Columbus College
Covenant College
Darton College
Emmanuel College
Emory University
Fort Valley State College
Gainesville College

Georgia College
Georgia Southern University
Georgia Southwestern College
Georgia State University
Gordon College
Kennesaw State College
LaGrange College
Macon College
Mercer University
Middle Georgia College
Morehouse College
Morris Brown College
North Georgia College
Oglethorpe University
Paine College
Piedmont College
Reinhardt College
Savannah State College
Shorter College
Spelman College
University of Georgia
Valdosta State University
Wesleyan College
West Georgia College
Young Harris College

Hawaii

Brigham Young University-Hawaii
Hawaii Pacific University
University of Hawaii
  Hilo
  Kauai Community College
  Manoa
  West Oahu

Idaho

Albertson College
Boise State University
College of Southern Idaho
Idaho State University
Lewis-Clark State College
North Idaho College
Northwest Nazarene College
Ricks College
University of Idaho

Illinois

American Conservatory of Music
Augustana College
Belleville Area College
Benedictine University
Black Hawk College
Bradley University
Carl Sandburg College
Chicago State University
College of DuPage
College of Lake County
Concordia University
De Paul University
Eastern Illinois University
Elgin Community College
Elmhurst College
Eureka College
Governors State University
Greenville College
Highland Community College
Illinois College
Illinois State University
Illinois Valley Community College
Illinois Wesleyan University
John A. Logan College
Joliet Junior College
Kaskaskia College
Knox College
Lake Forest College
Lake Land College
Lewis and Clark Community
  College
Lewis University
Lincoln College
Lincoln Land Community College
Loyola University of Chicago

MacMurray College
McHenry County College
McKendree College
Millikin University
Monmouth College
Morton College
National-Louis University
North Central College
North Park College
Northeastern Illinois University
Northern Illinois University
Northwestern University
Oakton Community College
Olivet Nazarene University
Parkland College
Quincy University
Rock Valley College
St. Xavier University
Southeastern Illinois College
Southern Illinois University
  Carbondale
  Edwardsville
Spoon River College
Trinity Christian College
Trinity International University
University of Chicago
University of Illinois
  Chicago
  Urbana-Champaign
Western Illinois University
Wheaton College
William Rainey Harper College

Indiana

Anderson University
Ball State University
Bethel College
Butler University
DePauw University
Franklin College
Goshen College
Grace College
Huntington College
Indiana State University
Indiana University
  Bloomington
  South Bend
  Southeast
Indiana University-Purdue
  University Fort Wayne
Indiana Wesleyan University
Manchester College
Marian College
Oakland City University
St. Joseph's College
St. Mary-of-the-Woods College
Saint Mary's College
Taylor University
University of Evansville
University of Indianapolis
University of Southern Indiana
Valparaiso University
Vincennes University
Wabash College

Iowa

Briar Cliff College
Buena Vista University
Central College
Clarke College
Coe College
Cornell College
Dordt College
Drake University
Ellsworth Community College
Graceland College
Grand View College
Indian Hills Community College
Iowa Central Community College
Iowa Lakes Community College
Iowa State University
Iowa Wesleyan College

Loras College
Luther College
Morningside College
Mount Mercy College
Muscatine Community College
North Iowa Area Community
   College
Northwestern College
St. Ambrose University
Simpson College
Southwestern Community College
University of Dubuque
University of Iowa
University of Northern Iowa
Upper Iowa University
Waldorf College
Wartburg College
Westmar University

Kansas

Baker University
Barclay College
Barton County Community College
Benedictine College
Bethany College
Bethel College
Butler County Community College
Colby Community College
Emporia State University
Fort Hays State University
Friends University
Garden City Community College
Hutchinson Community College
Independence Community College
Kansas City Kansas Community
   College
Kansas Newman College
Kansas State University
MidAmerica Nazarene College
Neosho County Community College
Ottawa University
Pittsburg State University
Pratt Community College
St. Mary College
Southwestern College
Tabor College
University of Kansas
Washburn University of Topeka
Wichita State University

Kentucky

Asbury College
Bellarmine College
Brescia College
Clear Creek Baptist Bible College
Cumberland College
Eastern Kentucky University
Georgetown College
Kentucky Christian College
Kentucky State University
Kentucky Wesleyan College
Lindsey Wilson College
Morehead State University
Murray State University
Northern Kentucky University
Somerset Community College
Spalding University
Transylvania University
Union College
University of Kentucky
University of Louisville
Western Kentucky University

Louisiana

Bossier Parish Community College
Centenary College of Louisiana
Grambling State University
Louisiana College
Louisiana State University and
   Agricultural and Mechanical
   College
Louisiana Tech University

Loyola University New Orleans
McNeese State University
Nicholls State University
Northeast Louisiana University
Northwestern State University
Southeastern Louisiana University
University of New Orleans
University of Southwestern
   Louisiana
Xavier University of Louisiana

Maine

University of Maine
   Augusta
   Orono
   Presque Isle
University of New England
University of Southern Maine

Maryland

Bowie State University
Cecil Community College
Charles County Community College
Columbia Union College
Essex Community College
Frederick Community College
Frostburg State University
Goucher College
Harford Community College
Johns Hopkins University
Johns Hopkins University: Peabody
   Conservatory of Music
Mount St. Mary's College
Prince George's Community College
St. Mary's College of Maryland
Towson State University
University of Maryland
   Baltimore County
   College Park
   Eastern Shore
Washington Bible College
Washington College
Western Maryland College

Massachusetts

Anna Maria College
Atlantic Union College
Bay Path College
Berklee College of Music
Boston Conservatory
Boston University
Eastern Nazarene College
Emerson College
Fitchburg State College
Gordon College
Holyoke Community College
New England Conservatory of
   Music
Quinsigamond Community College
Salem State College
Stonehill College
University of Massachusetts
   Amherst

Michigan

Adrian College
Albion College
Alma College
Andrews University
Aquinas College
Calvin College
Central Michigan University
Concordia College
Cornerstone College and Grand
   Rapids Baptist Seminary
Eastern Michigan University
Ferris State University
Glen Oaks Community College
Grace Bible College
Grand Rapids Community College
Grand Valley State University
Great Lakes Christian College

Henry Ford Community College
Hillsdale College
Hope College
Jackson Community College
Kalamazoo College
Kellogg Community College
Lansing Community College
Macomb Community College
Madonna University
Michigan Christian College
Michigan State University
Monroe County Community
   College
Montcalm Community College
Mott Community College
Muskegon Community College
Northern Michigan University
Northwestern Michigan College
Oakland University
Olivet College
Saginaw Valley State University
St. Clair County Community
   College
Schoolcraft College
Siena Heights College
Spring Arbor College
Suomi College
University of Michigan
   Ann Arbor
   Flint
Wayne State University
West Shore Community College
Western Michigan University
William Tyndale College

Minnesota

Augsburg College
Austin Community College
Bemidji State University
Bethany Lutheran College
Bethel College
Central Lakes College
College of St. Benedict
College of St. Catherine: St.
   Catherine Campus
College of St. Scholastica
Concordia College: Moorhead
Concordia College: St. Paul
Crown College
Fergus Falls Community College
Gustavus Adolphus College
Hibbing Community College
Mankato State University
Martin Luther College
Minnesota Bible College
Moorhead State University
North Central Bible College
North Hennepin Community
   College
Northland Community & Technical
   College
Northwestern College
Oak Hills Bible College
Pillsbury Baptist Bible College
Rainy River Community College
St. Cloud State University
St. John's University
St. Mary's University of Minnesota
St. Olaf College
Southwest State University
University of Minnesota
   Duluth
   Morris
   Twin Cities
University of St. Thomas
Willmar Community College
Winona State University

Mississippi

Alcorn State University
Belhaven College
Blue Mountain College

Copiah-Lincoln Community College
Delta State University
East Central Community College
East Mississippi Community College
Hinds Community College
Holmes Community College
Itawamba Community College
Jackson State University
Jones County Junior College
Meridian Community College
Millsaps College
Mississippi College
Mississippi Delta Community
   College
Mississippi Gulf Coast Community
   College
   Jackson County Campus
   Jefferson Davis Campus
   Perkinston
Mississippi State University
Mississippi University for Women
Mississippi Valley State University
Northeast Mississippi Community
   College
Pearl River Community College
Rust College
Tougaloo College
University of Mississippi
University of Southern Mississippi
Wesley College
William Carey College

Missouri

Avila College
Central Bible College
Central Christian College of the
   Bible
Central Methodist College
Central Missouri State University
College of the Ozarks
Columbia College
Cottey College
Crowder College
Culver-Stockton College
Drury College
East Central College
Evangel College
Fontbonne College
Hannibal-LaGrange College
Harris Stowe State College
Jefferson College
Lincoln University
Lindenwood College
Longview Community College
Maple Woods Community College
Mineral Area College
Missouri Baptist College
Missouri Southern State College
Missouri Valley College
Missouri Western State College
Moberly Area Community College
Northwest Missouri State
   University
Ozark Christian College
Park College
Research College of Nursing
Rockhurst College
St. Charles County Community
   College
St. Louis Christian College
St. Louis Community College
   Florissant Valley
   Forest Park
   Meramec
St. Louis University
Southeast Missouri State University
Southwest Baptist University
Southwest Missouri State University
State Fair Community College
Stephens College
Three Rivers Community College
Truman State University

Colleges that offer academic, music or drama, or art scholarships

University of Missouri
  Columbia
  Kansas City
  Rolla
Webster University
Westminster College
William Jewell College
William Woods University

Montana

Carroll College
Dawson Community College
Miles Community College
Montana State University
  Billings
  Bozeman
  Northern
University of Montana-Missoula
Western Montana College of the
  University of Montana

Nebraska

Central Community College
Chadron State College
College of St. Mary
Concordia College
Dana College
Doane College/Lincoln Campus
Grace University
Hastings College
McCook Community College
Mid Plains Community College
Midland Lutheran College
Nebraska Wesleyan University
Northeast Community College
Peru State College
Southeast Community College:
  Beatrice Campus
Union College
University of Nebraska
  Kearney
  Lincoln
  Omaha
Wayne State College
Western Nebraska Community
  College
York College

Nevada

Sierra Nevada College
University of Nevada
  Las Vegas
  Reno

New Hampshire

Colby-Sawyer College
Keene State College
Plymouth State College of the
  University System of New
  Hampshire
University of New Hampshire

New Jersey

Georgian Court College
Jersey City State College
Mercer County Community College
Richard Stockton College of New
  Jersey
Rider University
Rowan College of New Jersey
Rutgers, The State University of
  New Jersey
  Douglass College
  Livingston College
  Mason Gross School of the
    Arts
  Rutgers College
Trenton State College
William Paterson College of New
  Jersey

New Mexico

College of Santa Fe
College of the Southwest
Eastern New Mexico University
New Mexico Highlands University
New Mexico Junior College
New Mexico Military Institute
New Mexico State University
San Juan College
Santa Fe Community College
University of New Mexico

New York

Adelphi University
Bard College
City University of New York:
  Brooklyn College
Clarkson University
College of New Rochelle
College of St. Rose
Concordia College
Dowling College
Eastman School of Music of the
  University of Rochester
Elmira College
Finger Lakes Community College
Fordham University
Genesee Community College
Hartwick College
Hofstra University
Houghton College
Ithaca College
Jamestown Community College
Juilliard School
Long Island University
  Brooklyn Campus
  C. W. Post Campus
Manhattan School of Music
Manhattanville College
Mannes College of Music
Marist College
Marymount College
Marymount Manhattan College
Molloy College
Nassau Community College
Nazareth College of Rochester
New York University
Niagara University
Orange County Community College
Pace University
Roberts Wesleyan College
St. Bonaventure University
St. John's University
Skidmore College
State University of New York
  Binghamton
  Buffalo
  Oswego
  Purchase
  College at Brockport
  College at Buffalo
  College at Cortland
  College at Geneseo
  College at Plattsburgh
  College at Potsdam
  College of Technology at
    Alfred
Syracuse University
University of Rochester
Villa Maria College of Buffalo
Wagner College
Westchester Community College

North Carolina

Appalachian State University
Barton College
Bennett College
Blue Ridge Community College
Brevard College
Campbell University
Catawba College
College of The Albemarle

Davidson College
Duke University
East Carolina University
East Coast Bible College
Elizabeth City State University
Elon College
Fayetteville State University
Gardner-Webb University
Greensboro College
Guilford College
John Wesley College
Johnson C. Smith University
Lees-McRae College
Lenoir-Rhyne College
Livingstone College
Louisburg College
Mars Hill College
Meredith College
Methodist College
Mitchell Community College
Mount Olive College
North Carolina Agricultural and
  Technical State University
North Carolina School of the Arts
Peace College
Pembroke State University
Pfeiffer College
Queens College
Roanoke Bible College
St. Andrews Presbyterian College
St. Augustine's College
St. Mary's College
Salem College
Sandhills Community College
University of North Carolina
  Asheville
  Chapel Hill
  Greensboro
  Wilmington
Wake Forest University
Western Carolina University
Wilkes Community College
Wingate University
Winston-Salem State University

North Dakota

Bismarck State College
Dickinson State University
Jamestown College
Minot State University
North Dakota State College of
  Science
Trinity Bible College
University of North Dakota
Valley City State University

Ohio

Ashland University
Baldwin-Wallace College
Bluffton College
Bowling Green State University
  Bowling Green
  Firelands College
Capital University
Case Western Reserve University
Cedarville College
Cincinnati Bible College and
  Seminary
Cleveland Institute of Music
Cleveland State University
College of Mount St. Joseph
College of Wooster
Cuyahoga Community College
  Metropolitan Campus
  Western Campus
Denison University
Franciscan University of
  Steubenville
God's Bible School and College
Heidelberg College
Hiram College

Kent State University
  Kent
  Trumbull Campus
Lake Erie College
Lakeland Community College
Malone College
Marietta College
Miami University: Oxford Campus
Mount Union College
Mount Vernon Nazarene College
Muskingum College
Oberlin College
Ohio Northern University
Ohio State University
  Columbus Campus
  Lima Campus
  Mansfield Campus
Ohio University
Ohio Wesleyan University
Otterbein College
Shawnee State University
Sinclair Community College
Southern State Community College
University of Akron
University of Cincinnati
  Access Colleges
  Cincinnati
  Clermont College
University of Dayton
University of Findlay
University of Rio Grande
University of Toledo
Urbana University
Wilmington College
Wittenberg University
Wright State University
Xavier University
Youngstown State University

Oklahoma

Bartlesville Wesleyan College
Cameron University
Connors State College
East Central University
Eastern Oklahoma State College
Langston University
Mid-America Bible College
Murray State College
Northeastern Oklahoma
  Agricultural and Mechanical
  College
Northern Oklahoma College
Oklahoma Baptist University
Oklahoma Christian University of
  Science and Arts
Oklahoma City University
Oklahoma Panhandle State
  University
Oklahoma State University
Oral Roberts University
Phillips University
Redlands Community College
Rogers State College
Rose State College
St. Gregory's College
Southeastern Oklahoma State
  University
Southwestern College of Christian
  Ministries
Southwestern Oklahoma State
  University
University of Central Oklahoma
University of Oklahoma
University of Science and Arts of
  Oklahoma
University of Tulsa

Oregon

Blue Mountain Community College
Central Oregon Community College
Clackamas Community College
Clatsop Community College

Concordia University
Eastern Oregon State College
Eugene Bible College
George Fox College
Lane Community College
Lewis & Clark College
Linfield College
Linn-Benton Community College
Marylhurst College
Mount Hood Community College
Multnomah Bible College
Pacific University
Portland State University
Southern Oregon State College
Southwestern Oregon Community
  College
Treasure Valley Community College
Umpqua Community College
University of Oregon
  Eugene
  Robert Donald Clark Honors
    College
University of Portland
Western Baptist College
Western Oregon State College
Willamette University

Pennsylvania

Albright College
Allegheny College
Allentown College of St. Francis de
  Sales
Beaver College
Bucknell University
Bucks County Community College
California University of
  Pennsylvania
Carnegie Mellon University
Chatham College
Cheyney University of Pennsylvania
Clarion University of Pennsylvania
Community College of Allegheny
  County
    Boyce Campus
    South Campus
Community College of Philadelphia
Curtis Institute of Music
Drexel University
Duquesne University
Eastern College
Elizabethtown College
Geneva College
Immaculata College
Juniata College
Lancaster Bible College
Lebanon Valley College of
  Pennsylvania
Lehigh University
Lincoln University
Lock Haven University of
  Pennsylvania
Lycoming College
Mansfield University of
  Pennsylvania
Marywood College
Mercyhurst College
Millersville University of
  Pennsylvania
Mount Aloysius College
Muhlenberg College

Penn State
  Allentown Campus
  Altoona Campus
  Beaver Campus
  Berks Campus
  Delaware County Campus
  Du Bois Campus
  Erie Behrend College
  Fayette Campus
  Harrisburg Capital College
  Hazleton Campus
  McKeesport Campus
  Mont Alto Campus
  New Kensington Campus
  Ogontz Campus
  Schuylkill Campus
  Shenango Campus
  University Park Campus
  Wilkes-Barre Campus
  Worthington-Scranton Campus
  York Campus
Philadelphia College of Bible
Point Park College
St. Vincent College
Seton Hill College
Slippery Rock University of
  Pennsylvania
Susquehanna University
Temple University
University of the Arts
Ursinus College
Valley Forge Christian College
Valley Forge Military College
West Chester University of
  Pennsylvania
Westminster College
Widener University
Wilkes University
York College of Pennsylvania

Puerto Rico

Pontifical Catholic University of
  Puerto Rico
University of Puerto Rico
    Carolina Regional College
    La Montana Regional College
    Mayaguez Campus
    Ponce Technological
      University College

Rhode Island

Rhode Island College
University of Rhode Island

South Carolina

Anderson College
Clemson University
Coastal Carolina University
Coker College
College of Charleston
Columbia Bible College
Columbia College
Converse College
Erskine College
Francis Marion University
Furman University
Lander University
Limestone College
North Greenville College
Presbyterian College
South Carolina State University
Southern Wesleyan University
Spartanburg Methodist College
University of South Carolina
    Aiken
    Columbia
    Spartanburg
Winthrop University
Wofford College

South Dakota

Augustana College

Black Hills State University
Dakota State University
Dakota Wesleyan University
Mount Marty College
Northern State University
South Dakota State University
University of Sioux Falls
University of South Dakota

Tennessee

Austin Peay State University
Belmont University
Bethel College
Carson-Newman College
Chattanooga State Technical
  Community College
Christian Brothers University
David Lipscomb University
Dyersburg State Community
  College
East Tennessee State University
Freed-Hardeman University
Hiwassee College
Johnson Bible College
King College
Lambuth University
Lee College
Lincoln Memorial University
Martin Methodist College
Maryville College
Middle Tennessee State University
Milligan College
Motlow State Community College
Pellissippi State Technical
  Community College
Rhodes College
Roane State Community College
Shelby State Community College
Southern College of Seventh-day
  Adventists
Tennessee State University
Tennessee Technological University
Tennessee Wesleyan College
Union University
University of Memphis
University of Tennessee
  Chattanooga
  Knoxville
  Martin
Vanderbilt University
Walters State Community College

Texas

Abilene Christian University
Ambassador University
Angelina College
Austin College
Baylor University
Bee County College
Blinn College
Cedar Valley College
Cisco Junior College
College of the Mainland
Collin County Community College
  District
Concordia Lutheran College
Criswell College
Dallas Baptist University
Dallas Christian College
Del Mar College
East Texas Baptist University
East Texas State University
El Centro College
Frank Phillips College
Hardin-Simmons University
Houston Baptist University
Howard College
Howard Payne University
Jacksonville College
Jarvis Christian College
Lamar University—Beaumont
Laredo Community College

Lee College
McMurry University
Midland College
Midwestern State University
Odessa College
Our Lady of the Lake University of
  San Antonio
Panola College
Prairie View A&M University
Rice University
St. Edward's University
St. Mary's University
St. Philip's College
Sam Houston State University
San Antonio College
San Jacinto College: North
Schreiner College
Southern Methodist University
Southwest Texas State University
Southwestern Adventist College
Southwestern University
Stephen F. Austin State University
Temple College
Texas A&M University
Texas A&M University-Corpus
  Christi
Texas A&M University-Kingsville
Texas Christian University
Texas Lutheran College
Texas Tech University
Texas Wesleyan University
Texas Woman's University
Trinity University
Tyler Junior College
University of Dallas
University of Houston
  Clear Lake
  Houston
University of St. Thomas
University of Texas
  Arlington
  Austin
  El Paso
Vernon Regional Junior College
Victoria College
Weatherford College
West Texas A&M University
Western Texas College
Wharton County Junior College

Utah

Brigham Young University
College of Eastern Utah
Dixie College
Snow College
Southern Utah University
University of Utah
Utah State University
Weber State University
Westminster College of Salt Lake
  City

Vermont

Bennington College
Castleton State College
Johnson State College
Marlboro College
University of Vermont

Virginia

Averett College
Bluefield College
Bridgewater College
Christopher Newport University
Eastern Mennonite University
Emory and Henry College
Ferrum College
George Mason University
Hampton University
Hollins College
James Madison University
Liberty University

Colleges that offer academic, music or drama, or art scholarships

Longwood College
Lynchburg College
Mary Washington College
Old Dominion University
Radford University
Randolph-Macon Woman's College
Roanoke College
Shenandoah University
Sweet Briar College
University of Richmond
Virginia Commonwealth University
Virginia Polytechnic Institute and
State University
Virginia State University
Virginia Union University
Virginia Wesleyan College

Washington

Big Bend Community College
Central Washington University
Centralia College
Clark College
Columbia Basin College
Cornish College of the Arts
Eastern Washington University
Edmonds Community College
Evergreen State College
Gonzaga University
Grays Harbor College
Lower Columbia College
North Seattle Community College
Northwest College
Olympic College
Pacific Lutheran University
Peninsula College
Pierce College
Puget Sound Christian College
Seattle Pacific University
Seattle University
South Seattle Community College
Tacoma Community College
University of Puget Sound
Walla Walla College
Walla Walla Community College
Washington State University
Wenatchee Valley College
Western Washington University
Whitman College
Whitworth College

West Virginia

Alderson-Broaddus College
Bethany College
Concord College
Davis and Elkins College
Fairmont State College
Glenville State College
Marshall University
Ohio Valley College
Shepherd College
West Liberty State College
West Virginia Institute of
Technology
West Virginia State College
West Virginia University
West Virginia Wesleyan College
Wheeling Jesuit College

Wisconsin

Alverno College
Beloit College
Cardinal Stritch College
Carroll College
Carthage College
Concordia University Wisconsin
Edgewood College
Lawrence University
Marian College of Fond du Lac
Marquette University
Mount Mary College
Northland College
Ripon College

St. Norbert College
Silver Lake College
University of Wisconsin
Eau Claire
Green Bay
La Crosse
Madison
Milwaukee
Oshkosh
Parkside
Platteville
River Falls
Stevens Point
Stout
Whitewater
University of Wisconsin Center
Baraboo/Sauk County
Barron County
Fond du Lac
Richland
Rock County
Washington County
Waukesha
Viterbo College
Wisconsin Lutheran College

Wyoming

Eastern Wyoming College
Northwest College
Sheridan College
University of Wyoming
Western Wyoming Community
College

Art scholarships

Alabama

Alabama State University
Athens State College
Auburn University
Birmingham-Southern College
Calhoun Community College
Central Alabama Community
College
Chattahoochee Valley Community
College
Enterprise State Junior College
Huntingdon College
Jacksonville State University
James H. Faulkner State
Community College
Lawson State Community College
Lurleen B. Wallace State Junior
College
Northeast Alabama Community
College
Northwest-Shoals Community
College
Samford University
Snead State Community College
Troy State University
University of Alabama
Birmingham
Huntsville
Tuscaloosa
University of Alabama at
Birmingham: Walker College
University of Mobile
University of North Alabama
University of West Alabama
Wallace State College at Hanceville

Alaska

University of Alaska
Anchorage
Fairbanks

Arizona

Arizona State University

Arizona Western College
Glendale Community College
Mesa Community College
Mohave Community College
Northern Arizona University
Northland Pioneer College
Scottsdale Community College
South Mountain Community
College
University of Arizona
Yavapai College

Arkansas

Arkansas State University
Garland County Community
College
Harding University
Henderson State University
Hendrix College
John Brown University
Lyon College
Mississippi County Community
College
North Arkansas Community/
Technical College
Southern Arkansas University Tech
University of Arkansas
Fayetteville
Little Rock
University of Central Arkansas
Williams Baptist College

California

Academy of Art College
Allan Hancock College
Antelope Valley College
Art Institute of Southern California
Bethany College
Biola University
Brooks Institute of Photography
California College of Arts and
Crafts
California Institute of the Arts
California Lutheran University
California Polytechnic State
University: San Luis Obispo
California State University
Bakersfield
Dominguez Hills
Fresno
Fullerton
Long Beach
Los Angeles
Northridge
Sacramento
Stanislaus
Cerro Coso Community College
Chapman University
Citrus College
College of the Desert
College of Notre Dame
College of the Redwoods
Columbia College
De Anza College
Dominican College of San Rafael
El Camino College
Evergreen Valley College
Foothill College
Fresno City College
Fresno Pacific College
Fullerton College
Gavilan Community College
Golden West College
Holy Names College
Humboldt State University
Imperial Valley College
La Sierra University
Las Positas College
LIFE Bible College
Long Beach City College
Mills College
Modesto Junior College

Monterey Peninsula College
Mount San Jacinto College
Napa Valley College
New School of Architecture
Ohlone College
Pasadena City College
Pepperdine University
Point Loma Nazarene College
Rio Hondo College
Riverside Community College
Saddleback College
San Diego State University
San Francisco Art Institute
San Joaquin Delta College
Santa Monica College
Santa Rosa Junior College
Shasta College
Sierra College
Southern California Institute of
Architecture
Southwestern College
University of California
Berkeley
Irvine
Los Angeles
Riverside
Santa Barbara
Santa Cruz
University of the Pacific
University of Redlands
University of Southern California
Westmont College
Whittier College

Colorado

Adams State College
Colorado Institute of Art
Colorado State University
Fort Lewis College
Lamar Community College
Mesa State College
Northeastern Junior College
Rocky Mountain College of Art &
Design
Trinidad State Junior College
University of Colorado
Boulder
Denver
University of Denver
University of Northern Colorado
University of Southern Colorado
Western State College of Colorado

Connecticut

Quinebaug Valley Community-
Technical College
Sacred Heart University
University of Connecticut
University of Hartford

Delaware

University of Delaware

District of Columbia

Corcoran School of Art
George Washington University
Howard University

Florida

Brevard Community College
Broward Community College
Central Florida Community College
Chipola Junior College
Daytona Beach Community College
Eckerd College
Edison Community College
Flagler College
Florida Atlantic University
Florida Community College at
Jacksonville
Florida International University
Florida Keys Community College

Florida Southern College
Florida State University
Gulf Coast Community College
Hillsborough Community College
Indian River Community College
Jacksonville University
Lake-Sumter Community College
Manatee Community College
Miami-Dade Community College
North Florida Junior College
Okaloosa-Walton Community
   College
Pensacola Junior College
Polk Community College
Ringling School of Art and Design
Rollins College
St. Johns River Community College
St. Petersburg Junior College
Santa Fe Community College
Seminole Community College
University of Central Florida
University of South Florida
University of Tampa
University of West Florida
Valencia Community College

Georgia

Abraham Baldwin Agricultural
   College
Andrew College
Armstrong State College
Atlanta College of Art
Augusta College
Berry College
Brenau University
Brewton-Parker College
Clayton State College
Columbus College
Darton College
Gainesville College
Georgia Southwestern College
Georgia State University
Gordon College
Kennesaw State College
LaGrange College
Macon College
Mercer University
Morris Brown College
North Georgia College
Piedmont College
Reinhardt College
Shorter College
Valdosta State University
Wesleyan College
West Georgia College
Young Harris College

Hawaii

Brigham Young University-Hawaii
University of Hawaii
   Hilo
   West Oahu

Idaho

Albertson College
Boise State University
College of Southern Idaho
Idaho State University
North Idaho College
Northwest Nazarene College
Ricks College
University of Idaho

Illinois

American Academy of Art
Augustana College
Belleville Area College
Benedictine University
Black Hawk College
Bradley University
Carl Sandburg College
Chicago State University

College of DuPage
College of Lake County
Concordia University
De Paul University
Eastern Illinois University
Elgin Community College
Eureka College
Governors State University
Highland Community College
Illinois State University
Illinois Valley Community College
Illinois Wesleyan University
John A. Logan College
Joliet Junior College
Knox College
Lake Land College
Lewis and Clark Community
   College
Lewis University
Lincoln College
Lincoln Land Community College
Loyola University of Chicago
MacMurray College
McHenry County College
McKendree College
Millikin University
Monmouth College
Morton College
North Central College
North Park College
Northeastern Illinois University
Northern Illinois University
Oakton Community College
Olivet Nazarene University
Parkland College
Quincy University
School of the Art Institute of
   Chicago
Southeastern Illinois College
Southern Illinois University
   Carbondale
   Edwardsville
Spoon River College
Trinity Christian College
University of Chicago
University of Illinois at Urbana-
   Champaign
Western Illinois University
William Rainey Harper College

Indiana

Anderson University
Bethel College
DePauw University
Franklin College
Grace College
Huntington College
Indiana State University
Indiana University
   Bloomington
   South Bend
   Southeast
Indiana University—Purdue
   University
   Fort Wayne
   Indianapolis
Indiana Wesleyan University
Manchester College
Marian College
Oakland City University
St. Francis College
St. Mary-of-the-Woods College
Taylor University
University of Evansville
University of Indianapolis
University of Southern Indiana
Valparaiso University
Vincennes University
Wabash College

Iowa

Briar Cliff College

Buena Vista University
Central College
Clarke College
Clinton Community College
Coe College
Cornell College
Dordt College
Drake University
Graceland College
Grand View College
Indian Hills Community College
Iowa Lakes Community College
Iowa State University
Iowa Wesleyan College
Loras College
Luther College
Morningside College
Mount Mercy College
North Iowa Area Community
   College
Northwestern College
St. Ambrose University
Simpson College
Teikyo Marycrest University
University of Iowa
University of Northern Iowa
Upper Iowa University
Waldorf College
Wartburg College

Kansas

Baker University
Barton County Community College
Bethany College
Bethel College
Butler County Community College
Colby Community College
Emporia State University
Fort Hays State University
Friends University
Garden City Community College
Hutchinson Community College
Independence Community College
Kansas State University
Neosho County Community College
Ottawa University
Pittsburg State University
Pratt Community College
St. Mary College
Southwestern College
University of Kansas
Washburn University of Topeka
Wichita State University

Kentucky

Asbury College
Bellarmine College
Brescia College
Cumberland College
Eastern Kentucky University
Georgetown College
Kentucky Wesleyan College
Lindsey Wilson College
Morehead State University
Murray State University
Northern Kentucky University
Spalding University
Transylvania University
University of Kentucky
University of Louisville
Western Kentucky University

Louisiana

Centenary College of Louisiana
Louisiana State University
   Agricultural and Mechanical
      College
   Alexandria
Louisiana Tech University
Loyola University New Orleans
McNeese State University
Northeast Louisiana University

Northwestern State University
University of Southwestern
   Louisiana
Xavier University of Louisiana

Maine

Maine College of Art
University of Maine
   Augusta
   Orono
   Presque Isle
University of New England

Maryland

Cecil Community College
Charles County Community College
Frederick Community College
Frostburg State University
Goucher College
Maryland College of Art and
   Design
Maryland Institute College of Art
Mount St. Mary's College
Towson State University
University of Maryland
   Baltimore County
   College Park
   Eastern Shore
Washington College
Western Maryland College

Massachusetts

Boston Architectural Center
Boston University
Bradford College
Fitchburg State College
Holyoke Community College
Montserrat College of Art
Mount Ida College
Quinsigamond Community College
Salem State College
University of Massachusetts
   Amherst

Michigan

Adrian College
Albion College
Alma College
Aquinas College
Calvin College
Center for Creative Studies: College
   of Art and Design
Central Michigan University
Concordia College
Eastern Michigan University
Glen Oaks Community College
Grand Rapids Community College
Grand Valley State University
Henry Ford Community College
Hillsdale College
Hope College
Kalamazoo College
Kellogg Community College
Kendall College of Art and Design
Lansing Community College
Madonna University
Michigan State University
Monroe County Community
   College
Mott Community College
Muskegon Community College
Northern Michigan University
Northwestern Michigan College
Olivet College
Saginaw Valley State University
St. Clair County Community
   College
Schoolcraft College
Siena Heights College
Spring Arbor College
Suomi College
University of Michigan

Colleges that offer academic, music or drama, or art scholarships

Washtenaw Community College
Wayne State University
Western Michigan University

Minnesota

Bemidji State University
Bethany Lutheran College
Bethel College
Central Lakes College
College of St. Benedict
College of Visual Arts
Fergus Falls Community College
Mankato State University
Minneapolis College of Art and
 Design
Moorhead State University
North Central Bible College
North Hennepin Community
 College
Northland Community & Technical
 College
Northwestern College
Rainy River Community College
St. Cloud State University
St. John's University
St. Mary's University of Minnesota
University of Minnesota
 Duluth
 Twin Cities
Willmar Community College
Winona State University

Mississippi

Belhaven College
Copiah-Lincoln Community College
Delta State University
East Central Community College
Hinds Community College
Holmes Community College
Itawamba Community College
Jackson State University
Jones County Junior College
Meridian Community College
Millsaps College
Mississippi College
Mississippi Delta Community
 College
Mississippi Gulf Coast Community
 College: Perkinston
Mississippi University for Women
Northeast Mississippi Community
 College
University of Mississippi
University of Southern Mississippi

Missouri

Avila College
Central Missouri State University
College of the Ozarks
Columbia College
Cottey College
Crowder College
Culver-Stockton College
Drury College
East Central College
Evangel College
Fontbonne College
Hannibal-LaGrange College
Jefferson College
Kansas City Art Institute
Lincoln University
Lindenwood College
Longview Community College
Maple Woods Community College
Maryville University of Saint Louis
Mineral Area College
Missouri Southern State College
Missouri Valley College
Northwest Missouri State
 University
Park College

St. Louis Community College
 Florissant Valley
 Forest Park
 Meramec
St. Louis University
Southeast Missouri State University
Southwest Baptist University
Southwest Missouri State University
State Fair Community College
Three Rivers Community College
Truman State University
University of Missouri
 Columbia
 Kansas City
Washington University
Webster University
Westminster College
William Jewell College
William Woods University

Montana

Dawson Community College
Montana State University
 Billings
 Bozeman
University of Montana-Missoula
Western Montana College of the
 University of Montana

Nebraska

Central Community College
Chadron State College
College of St. Mary
Concordia College
Dana College
Doane College/Lincoln Campus
Hastings College
McCook Community College
Mid Plains Community College
Midland Lutheran College
Nebraska Wesleyan University
Northeast Community College
Peru State College
Southeast Community College:
 Beatrice Campus
University of Nebraska
 Kearney
 Omaha
Wayne State College
Western Nebraska Community
 College

Nevada

Sierra Nevada College
University of Nevada
 Las Vegas
 Reno

New Hampshire

Colby-Sawyer College
Keene State College
Notre Dame College
University of New Hampshire
White Pines College

New Jersey

Caldwell College
College of St. Elizabeth
Georgian Court College
Jersey City State College
Richard Stockton College of New
 Jersey
Rowan College of New Jersey
Rutgers, The State University of
 New Jersey: Mason Gross School
 of the Arts
Union County College

New Mexico

College of Santa Fe
Eastern New Mexico University
New Mexico Highlands University

New York

Adelphi University
Alfred University
Bard College
Cazenovia College
City University of New York:
 Brooklyn College
Clarkson University
College of New Rochelle
College of St. Rose
Elmira College
Finger Lakes Community College
Fordham University
Genesee Community College
Hofstra University
Houghton College
Iona College
Long Island University
 Brooklyn Campus
 C. W. Post Campus
 Southampton College
Manhattanville College
Marymount College
Marymount Manhattan College
Molloy College
Nassau Community College
Nazareth College of Rochester
New York School of Interior
 Design
Orange County Community College
Parsons School of Design
Pratt Institute
Roberts Wesleyan College
Rochester Institute of Technology
Sage Junior College of Albany
St. John's University
St. Thomas Aquinas College
School of Visual Arts
State University of New York
 Binghamton
 Buffalo
 Purchase
 College at Brockport
 College at Buffalo
 College at Cortland
 College at Plattsburgh
Syracuse University
University of Rochester
Villa Maria College of Buffalo
Westchester Community College

North Carolina

Appalachian State University
Barton College
Brevard College
College of The Albemarle
Davidson College
Duke University
East Carolina University
East Coast Bible College
Greensboro College
Guilford College
Meredith College
Mitchell Community College
Mount Olive College
North Carolina Agricultural and
 Technical State University
North Carolina School of the Arts
Peace College
Pembroke State University
Queens College
St. Andrews Presbyterian College
St. Mary's College
Sandhills Community College
University of North Carolina
 Asheville
 Wilmington
Wake Forest University
Western Carolina University
Wilkes Community College
Wingate University
Winston-Salem State University

North Dakota

Dickinson State University
University of North Dakota
Valley City State University

Ohio

Art Academy of Cincinnati
Ashland University
Baldwin-Wallace College
Bluffton College
Bowling Green State University
Case Western Reserve University
Cleveland Institute of Art
Cleveland State University
College of Mount St. Joseph
Columbus College of Art and
 Design
Cuyahoga Community College
 Metropolitan Campus
 Western Campus
Denison University
Hiram College
Kent State University
 Kent
 Trumbull Campus
Lake Erie College
Lakeland Community College
Marietta College
Miami University: Oxford Campus
Mount Union College
Muskingum College
Ohio Northern University
Ohio State University
 Columbus Campus
 Lima Campus
 Mansfield Campus
Ohio University
Ohio Wesleyan University
Otterbein College
Shawnee State University
Sinclair Community College
Southern State Community College
University of Akron
University of Cincinnati
 Access Colleges
 Cincinnati
 Clermont College
University of Dayton
University of Toledo
Wittenberg University
Wright State University
Xavier University
Youngstown State University

Oklahoma

Cameron University
East Central University
Murray State College
Northeastern Oklahoma
 Agricultural and Mechanical
 College
Northern Oklahoma College
Oklahoma Baptist University
Oklahoma Christian University of
 Science and Arts
Oklahoma City University
Oklahoma State University
Oral Roberts University
Phillips University
Redlands Community College
Rogers State College
Rose State College
St. Gregory's College
Southeastern Oklahoma State
 University
Southwestern Oklahoma State
 University
University of Central Oklahoma
University of Oklahoma
University of Science and Arts of
 Oklahoma
University of Tulsa

Oregon
Central Oregon Community College
Clackamas Community College
Clatsop Community College
Linn-Benton Community College
Marylhurst College
Mount Hood Community College
Pacific Northwest College of Art
Pacific University
Portland State University
Southern Oregon State College
Southwestern Oregon Community
College
Treasure Valley Community College
Umpqua Community College
University of Oregon
Eugene
Robert Donald Clark Honors
College
Western Oregon State College
Willamette University

Pennsylvania
Allegheny College
Art Institute of Pittsburgh
Beaver College
Bucknell University
Bucks County Community College
Carlow College
Carnegie Mellon University
Clarion University of Pennsylvania
Community College of Allegheny
County
Boyce Campus
South Campus
Community College of Philadelphia
Drexel University
Harrisburg Area Community
College
Juniata College
Kutztown University of
Pennsylvania
Lycoming College
Mansfield University of
Pennsylvania
Marywood College
Mercyhurst College
Millersville University of
Pennsylvania
Moore College of Art and Design
Penn State
Allentown Campus
Altoona Campus
Beaver Campus
Berks Campus
Delaware County Campus
Du Bois Campus
Erie Behrend College
Fayette Campus
Harrisburg Capital College
Hazleton Campus
McKeesport Campus
Mont Alto Campus
New Kensington Campus
Ogontz Campus
Schuylkill Campus
Shenango Campus
University Park Campus
Wilkes-Barre Campus
Worthington-Scranton Campus
York Campus
Point Park College
Rosemont College
Seton Hill College
Slippery Rock University of
Pennsylvania
University of the Arts
Ursinus College
Wilkes University
York College of Pennsylvania

Puerto Rico
Pontifical Catholic University of
Puerto Rico

Rhode Island
Rhode Island College
Rhode Island School of Design

South Carolina
Anderson College
Charleston Southern University
Coastal Carolina University
Coker College
College of Charleston
Columbia College
Francis Marion University
Furman University
Greenville Technical College
Lander University
Limestone College
North Greenville College
University of South Carolina
Aiken
Columbia
Winthrop University

South Dakota
Augustana College
Black Hills State University
Dakota Wesleyan University
Northern State University
South Dakota State University
University of South Dakota

Tennessee
Austin Peay State University
Carson-Newman College
Chattanooga State Technical
Community College
David Lipscomb University
East Tennessee State University
Freed-Hardeman University
Lambuth University
Martin Methodist College
Maryville College
Memphis College of Art
Milligan College
Pellissippi State Technical
Community College
Rhodes College
Roane State Community College
Shelby State Community College
Union University
University of Memphis
University of Tennessee
Chattanooga
Knoxville
Martin

Texas
Abilene Christian University
Angelina College
Austin College
Baylor University
Bee County College
Cedar Valley College
College of the Mainland
Collin County Community College
District
Dallas Baptist University
Del Mar College
East Texas State University
El Centro College
Hardin-Simmons University
Houston Baptist University
Howard College
Howard Payne University
Lamar University—Beaumont
Lee College
McMurry University
Midland College
Midwestern State University

Odessa College
Our Lady of the Lake University of
San Antonio
Panola College
Prairie View A&M University
Sam Houston State University
San Antonio College
San Jacinto College: North
Southern Methodist University
Southwestern University
Texas A&M University-Corpus
Christi
Texas A&M University-Kingsville
Texas Christian University
Texas Lutheran College
Texas Tech University
Texas Wesleyan University
Texas Woman's University
Trinity University
Tyler Junior College
University of Dallas
University of Houston
Clear Lake
Downtown
Houston
University of Texas
Arlington
Austin
Vernon Regional Junior College
Victoria College
West Texas A&M University
Western Texas College

Utah
Brigham Young University
College of Eastern Utah
Dixie College
Salt Lake Community College
Snow College
University of Utah
Utah State University
Weber State University
Westminster College of Salt Lake
City

Vermont
Bennington College
Green Mountain College
Johnson State College
Marlboro College
University of Vermont

Virginia
Averett College
Bluefield College
Emory and Henry College
Hollins College
James Madison University
Longwood College
Old Dominion University
Radford University
Roanoke College
Virginia Commonwealth University
Virginia Polytechnic Institute and
State University
Virginia State University
Virginia Wesleyan College

Washington
Columbia Basin College
Cornish College of the Arts
Eastern Washington University
Edmonds Community College
Evergreen State College
Grays Harbor College
Lower Columbia College
North Seattle Community College
Northwest College
Olympic College
Pacific Lutheran University
Peninsula College
Seattle Pacific University

Seattle University
Tacoma Community College
University of Puget Sound
Washington State University
Wenatchee Valley College
Western Washington University
Whitman College
Whitworth College

West Virginia
Concord College
Davis and Elkins College
Fairmont State College
Glenville State College
Marshall University
Ohio Valley College
Shepherd College
West Liberty State College
West Virginia State College
West Virginia University
West Virginia Wesleyan College

Wisconsin
Alverno College
Cardinal Stritch College
Carroll College
Carthage College
Edgewood College
Marian College of Fond du Lac
Milwaukee Institute of Art &
Design
Mount Mary College
St. Norbert College
Silver Lake College
University of Wisconsin
Green Bay
Madison
Milwaukee
Oshkosh
Parkside
Platteville
River Falls
Stevens Point
Stout
University of Wisconsin Center
Baraboo/Sauk County
Barron County
Richland
Waukesha
Viterbo College

Wyoming
Eastern Wyoming College
Northwest College
Sheridan College
University of Wyoming
Western Wyoming Community
College

16. Colleges that offer athletic scholarships

Archery

Arizona
Glendale Community College W
Navajo Community College M, W

Badminton

Texas
University of Texas at Austin M

Baseball

Alabama
Alabama Agricultural and
  Mechanical University M
Alabama State University M
Auburn University M
Bevill State Community College M
Birmingham-Southern College M
Central Alabama Community
  College M
Chattahoochee Valley Community
  College M
Enterprise State Junior College M
Gadsden State Community College
  M
George C. Wallace State
  Community College at Selma M
Huntingdon College M
Jacksonville State University M
James H. Faulkner State
  Community College M
Jefferson State Community College
  M
Lurleen B. Wallace State Junior
  College M
Miles College M
Northwest-Shoals Community
  College M
Samford University M
Snead State Community College M
Spring Hill College M
Troy State University M
Tuskegee University M
University of Alabama
  Birmingham M
  Huntsville M
  Tuscaloosa M
University of Mobile M
University of Montevallo M
University of North Alabama M

University of West Alabama M
Wallace State College at Hanceville
  M

Arizona
Arizona State University M
Arizona Western College M
Cochise College M
Glendale Community College M
Pima Community College M
Scottsdale Community College M
South Mountain Community
  College M
University of Arizona M
Yavapai College M

Arkansas
Arkansas State University M
Harding University M
University of Arkansas
  Fayetteville M
  Little Rock M

California
Azusa Pacific University M
Biola University M
California Baptist College M
California Polytechnic State
  University: San Luis Obispo M
California State Polytechnic
  University: Pomona M
California State University
  Fresno M
  Fullerton M
  Long Beach M
  Los Angeles M
  Northridge M
  Sacramento M
  San Bernardino M
Concordia University M
Loyola Marymount University M
Pepperdine University M
Point Loma Nazarene College M
St. Mary's College of California M
San Diego State University M
San Jose State University M
Santa Clara University M
Southern California College M
Stanford University M
University of California
  Berkeley M
  Los Angeles M
  Riverside M
  Santa Barbara M
University of the Pacific M
University of San Diego M
University of San Francisco M
University of Southern California M
Westmont College M

Colorado
Colorado Northwestern Community
  College M
Colorado School of Mines M
Lamar Community College M
Mesa State College M
Metropolitan State College of
  Denver M
Otero Junior College M
Regis University M
Trinidad State Junior College M
University of Denver M
University of Northern Colorado M

Connecticut
Central Connecticut State
  University M
Fairfield University M
Quinnipiac College M
Teikyo-Post University M
University of Bridgeport M
University of Connecticut M
University of Hartford M
University of New Haven M

Delaware
Delaware State University M
Delaware Technical and
  Community College
  Owens Campus M
  Stanton/Wilmington Campus
  M
University of Delaware M

District of Columbia
George Washington University M
Howard University M

Florida
Bethune-Cookman College M
Brevard Community College M
Central Florida Community College
  M
Chipola Junior College M
Eckerd College M
Embry-Riddle Aeronautical
  University M
Flagler College M
Florida Atlantic University M
Florida Community College at
  Jacksonville M
Florida Institute of Technology M
Florida International University M
Florida Memorial College M
Florida Southern College M
Florida State University M
Gulf Coast Community College M
Hillsborough Community College M
Lake City Community College M
Lynn University M

Manatee Community College M
North Florida Junior College M
Nova Southeastern University M
Okaloosa-Walton Community
  College M
Palm Beach Atlantic College M
Palm Beach Community College M
Pasco-Hernando Community
  College M
Rollins College M
St. Johns River Community College
  M
St. Leo College M
St. Petersburg Junior College M
St. Thomas University M
Stetson University M
Tallahassee Community College M
University of Central Florida M
University of Florida M
University of Miami M
University of North Florida M
University of South Florida M
University of Tampa M
University of West Florida M
Valencia Community College M
Warner Southern College M
Webber College M

Georgia
Abraham Baldwin Agricultural
  College M
Andrew College M
Augusta College M
Berry College M
Brewton-Parker College M
Columbus College M
Darton College M
Emmanuel College M
Georgia College M
Georgia Institute of Technology M
Georgia Southern University M
Georgia Southwestern College M
Gordon College M
Kennesaw State College M
Mercer University M
Middle Georgia College M
Paine College M
Piedmont College M
Savannah State College M
Shorter College M
Southern College of Technology M
Thomas College M
University of Georgia M
Valdosta State University M
West Georgia College M
Young Harris College M

Hawaii
Hawaii Pacific University M
University of Hawaii at Manoa M

Idaho

Albertson College M
College of Southern Idaho M
Lewis-Clark State College M
North Idaho College M
Northwest Nazarene College M
Ricks College M

Illinois

Belleville Area College M
Bradley University M
Carl Sandburg College M
Chicago State University M
Danville Area Community College
  M
Eastern Illinois University M
Elgin Community College M
Highland Community College M
Illinois Eastern Community
  Colleges
    Olney Central College M
    Wabash Valley College M
Illinois Institute of Technology M
Illinois State University M
John A. Logan College M
Kaskaskia College M
Kishwaukee College M
Lake Land College M
Lewis and Clark Community
  College M
Lewis University M
Lincoln College M
McHenry County College M
McKendree College M
Moraine Valley Community College
  M
Morton College M
Northeastern Illinois University M
Northwestern University M
Olivet Nazarene University M
Quincy University M
Rend Lake College M, W
Rosary College M
St. Xavier University M
Southeastern Illinois College M
Southern Illinois University
    Carbondale M
    Edwardsville M
Trinity International University M
University of Illinois
    Chicago M
    Urbana-Champaign M
Western Illinois University M

Indiana

Ball State University M
Bethel College M
Butler University M
Goshen College M
Grace College M
Huntington College M
Indiana Institute of Technology M
Indiana State University M
Indiana University
    Bloomington M
    Southeast M
Indiana University-Purdue
    University Indianapolis M
Indiana Wesleyan University M
Marian College M
Oakland City University M
Purdue University M
St. Francis College M
St. Joseph's College M
Taylor University M
Tri-State University M
University of Evansville M
University of Indianapolis M
University of Notre Dame M
University of Southern Indiana M
Valparaiso University M
Vincennes University M

Iowa

Briar Cliff College M
Ellsworth Community College M
Graceland College M
Grand View College M
Indian Hills Community College M
Iowa Central Community College
  M
Iowa Lakes Community College M
Iowa State University M
Iowa Wesleyan College M
Morningside College M
Muscatine Community College M
North Iowa Area Community
  College M
Northwestern College M
St. Ambrose University M
Teikyo Marycrest University M
University of Iowa M
University of Northern Iowa M
Waldorf College M
Westmar University M

Kansas

Baker University M
Benedictine College M
Bethany College M
Butler County Community College
  M
Colby Community College M
Emporia State University M
Fort Scott Community College M
Friends University M
Garden City Community College M
Hesston College M
Hutchinson Community College M
Independence Community College
  M
Kansas City Kansas Community
  College M
Kansas Newman College M
Kansas State University M
MidAmerica Nazarene College M
Neosho County Community College
  M
Ottawa University M
Pratt Community College M
University of Kansas M
Wichita State University M

Kentucky

Bellarmine College M
Cumberland College M
Eastern Kentucky University M
Kentucky State University M
Kentucky Wesleyan College M
Lindsey Wilson College M
Morehead State University M
Murray State University M
Northern Kentucky University M
Pikeville College M
Sue Bennett College M
Transylvania University M
Union College M
University of Kentucky M
University of Louisville M
Western Kentucky University M

Louisiana

Bossier Parish Community College
  M
Centenary College of Louisiana M
Grambling State University M
Louisiana College M
Louisiana State University and
  Agricultural and Mechanical
  College M
Louisiana Tech University M
Nicholls State University M
Northeast Louisiana University M
Northwestern State University M

Southeastern Louisiana University
  M
Tulane University M
University of New Orleans M
University of Southwestern
  Louisiana M

Maine

Husson College M
University of Maine M

Maryland

Bowie State University M
Charles County Community College
  M
Chesapeake College M
Columbia Union College M
Dundalk Community College M
Hagerstown Junior College M
Mount St. Mary's College M
Towson State University M
University of Maryland
    Baltimore County M
    College Park M
    Eastern Shore M

Massachusetts

American International College M
Becker College: Leicester Campus
  M
Dean College M
Northeastern University M
University of Massachusetts
  Amherst M

Michigan

Aquinas College M
Central Michigan University M
Concordia College M
Cornerstone College and Grand
  Rapids Baptist Seminary M
Eastern Michigan University M
Glen Oaks Community College M
Henry Ford Community College M
Highland Park Community College
  M
Hillsdale College M
Kellogg Community College M
Macomb Community College M
Michigan Christian College M
Michigan State University M
Northwood University M
Oakland University M
Saginaw Valley State University M
University of Michigan M
Wayne State University M

Minnesota

Mankato State University M
St. Cloud State University M
Southwest State University M
University of Minnesota
    Crookston M
    Duluth M
    Twin Cities M
Winona State University M

Mississippi

Alcorn State University M
Belhaven College M
Copiah-Lincoln Community College
  M
Delta State University M
Hinds Community College M
Holmes Community College M
Meridian Community College M
Mississippi State University M
Mississippi Valley State University
  M
Southwest Mississippi Community
  College M
University of Mississippi M

University of Southern Mississippi
  M
William Carey College M

Missouri

Avila College M
Central Methodist College M
Central Missouri State University M
College of the Ozarks M
Crowder College M
Culver-Stockton College M
Hannibal-LaGrange College M
Harris Stowe State College M
Jefferson College M
Lincoln University M
Lindenwood College M
Longview Community College M
Maple Woods Community College
  M
Mineral Area College M
Missouri Southern State College M
Missouri Western State College M
North Central Missouri College M
Research College of Nursing M
Rockhurst College M
St. Louis Community College at
  Forest Park M
St. Louis University M
Southeast Missouri State University
  M
Southwest Baptist University M
Southwest Missouri State University
  M
Truman State University M
University of Missouri
    Columbia M
    Rolla M
    St. Louis M
William Jewell College M

Nebraska

Bellevue University M
Concordia College M
Creighton University M
Dana College M
Doane College/Lincoln Campus M
Hastings College M
Midland Lutheran College M
Peru State College M
University of Nebraska
    Kearney M
    Lincoln M
    Omaha M
Wayne State College M
York College M

Nevada

University of Nevada
    Las Vegas M
    Reno M

New Hampshire

Franklin Pierce College M
University of New Hampshire M

New Jersey

Bloomfield College M
Burlington County College M
Caldwell College M
Fairleigh Dickinson University
    Edward Williams College M
    Teaneck M
Monmouth University M
Rider University M

Rutgers, The State University of
New Jersey
   College of Engineering M
   College of Pharmacy M
   Cook College M
   Livingston College M
   Mason Gross School of the
     Arts M
   Rutgers College M
St. Peter's College M
Salem Community College M
Seton Hall University M

New Mexico

College of the Southwest M
Eastern New Mexico University M
New Mexico Highlands University
M
New Mexico Junior College M
New Mexico Military Institute M
New Mexico State University M
University of New Mexico M

New York

Adelphi University M
Briarcliffe: The College for Business
  and Technology M
Canisius College M
College of St. Rose M
Concordia College M
Dominican College of Blauvelt M
Dowling College M
Fordham University M
Genesee Community College M
Hofstra University M
Iona College M
Le Moyne College M
Long Island University
   Brooklyn Campus M
   C. W. Post Campus M
Manhattan College M
Marist College M
Mercy College M
Molloy College M
Monroe Community College M
New York Institute of Technology
M
Niagara University M
Onondaga Community College M
Pace University M
St. Bonaventure University M
St. Francis College M
St. John's University M
St. Thomas Aquinas College M
Siena College M
State University of New York at
  Albany M
Wagner College M

North Carolina

Appalachian State University M
Barton College M
Belmont Abbey College M
Brevard College M
Campbell University M
Catawba College M
Davidson College M
Duke University M
East Carolina University M
Elon College M
Gardner-Webb University M
High Point University M
Lees-McRae College M
Lenoir-Rhyne College M
Louisburg College M
Mars Hill College M
Montreat College M
Mount Olive College M
North Carolina Agricultural and
  Technical State University M
North Carolina State University M
Pembroke State University M

Pfeiffer College M
Pitt Community College M
St. Andrews Presbyterian College M
St. Augustine's College M
Southeastern Community College M
University of North Carolina
   Asheville M
   Chapel Hill M
   Charlotte M
   Greensboro M
   Wilmington M
Wake Forest University M
Western Carolina University M
Wingate University M

North Dakota

Dickinson State University M
North Dakota State University
   Bottineau M
   Fargo M
University of North Dakota
   Grand Forks M
   Williston M

Ohio

Ashland University M
Bowling Green State University M
Cedarville College M
Cleveland State University M
Cuyahoga Community College:
  Western Campus M
Kent State University M
Malone College M
Miami University: Oxford Campus
M
Mount Vernon Nazarene College M
Ohio Dominican College M
Ohio State University: Columbus
  Campus M
Ohio University M
Shawnee State University M
Sinclair Community College M
Tiffin University M
University of Akron M
University of Cincinnati M
University of Dayton M
University of Findlay M
University of Rio Grande M
University of Toledo M
Urbana University M
Walsh University M
Wright State University M
Xavier University M
Youngstown State University M

Oklahoma

Bacone College M
Cameron University M
Eastern Oklahoma State College M
Northeastern Oklahoma
  Agricultural and Mechanical
  College M
Oklahoma Baptist University M
Oklahoma Christian University of
  Science and Arts M
Oklahoma City University M
Oral Roberts University M
Redlands Community College M
Rose State College M
Southwestern Oklahoma State
  University M
University of Central Oklahoma M
University of Oklahoma M
Western Oklahoma State College M

Oregon

Blue Mountain Community College
M
Chemeketa Community College M
Clackamas Community College M
Concordia University M
Linn-Benton Community College M

Mount Hood Community College
M
Portland State University M
Treasure Valley Community College
M
University of Portland M
Western Baptist College M

Pennsylvania

California University of
  Pennsylvania M
Drexel University M
Duquesne University M
East Stroudsburg University of
  Pennsylvania M
Edinboro University of
  Pennsylvania M
Gannon University M
Geneva College M
Kutztown University of
  Pennsylvania M
La Salle University M
Lock Haven University of
  Pennsylvania M
Mercyhurst College M
Millersville University of
  Pennsylvania M
Penn State University Park Campus
M
Philadelphia College of Pharmacy
  and Science M
Point Park College M
St. Joseph's University M
St. Vincent College M
Shippensburg University of
  Pennsylvania M
Temple University M
University of Pittsburgh M
Villanova University M
West Chester University of
  Pennsylvania M

Puerto Rico

Inter American University of Puerto
  Rico
   Metropolitan Campus M, W
   San German Campus M
University of Puerto Rico:
  Mayaguez Campus M

Rhode Island

Providence College M
University of Rhode Island M

South Carolina

Anderson College M
Charleston Southern University M
Clemson University M
Coastal Carolina University M
Coker College M
College of Charleston M
Erskine College M
Francis Marion University M
Furman University M
Limestone College M
Morris College M
North Greenville College M
Presbyterian College M
Southern Wesleyan University M
Spartanburg Methodist College M
University of South Carolina
   Aiken M
   Columbia M
   Spartanburg M
Winthrop University M
Wofford College M

South Dakota

Dakota Wesleyan University M
Huron University M
Mount Marty College M
South Dakota State University M

University of Sioux Falls M
University of South Dakota M

Tennessee

Austin Peay State University M
Belmont University M
Bethel College M
Carson-Newman College M
Chattanooga State Technical
  Community College M
Christian Brothers University M
Cleveland State Community College
M
David Lipscomb University M
Dyersburg State Community
  College M
East Tennessee State University M
Freed-Hardeman University M
Jackson State Community College
M
King College M
Lambuth University M
Lincoln Memorial University M
Middle Tennessee State University
M
Milligan College M
Roane State Community College M
Shelby State Community College M
Tennessee Technological University
M
Tennessee Wesleyan College M
Trevecca Nazarene University M
Tusculum College M
Union University M
University of Memphis M
University of Tennessee
   Knoxville M
   Martin M
Vanderbilt University M
Volunteer State Community College
M

Texas

Abilene Christian University M
Angelina College M
Baylor University M
Blinn College M
Concordia Lutheran College M
Dallas Baptist University M
East Texas Baptist University M
El Paso Community College M
Frank Phillips College M
Houston Baptist University M
Lamar University—Beaumont M
Laredo Community College M
Lee College M
McLennan Community College M
Odessa College M
Rice University M
St. Edward's University M
St. Mary's University M
San Jacinto College: North M
Schreiner College M
Southwest Texas State University M
Texas A&M University M
Texas Christian University M
Texas Lutheran College M
Texas Tech University M
Texas Wesleyan University M
University of Houston M
University of Texas
   Arlington M
   Austin M
Vernon Regional Junior College M
West Texas A&M University M
Wharton County Junior College M

Utah

Brigham Young University M
College of Eastern Utah M
Dixie College M
Snow College M

University of Utah M
Utah Valley State College M

Vermont

University of Vermont M

Virginia

Bluefield College M
Clinch Valley College of the
University of Virginia M
College of William and Mary M
George Mason University M
James Madison University M
Liberty University M
Longwood College M
Norfolk State University M
Old Dominion University M
Radford University M
St. Paul's College M
University of Richmond M
University of Virginia M
Virginia Commonwealth University
M
Virginia Intermont College M
Virginia Military Institute M
Virginia Polytechnic Institute and
State University M

Washington

Big Bend Community College M
Central Washington University M
Centralia College M
Edmonds Community College M
Gonzaga University M
Lower Columbia College M
Olympic College M
Pierce College M
Shoreline Community College M
Spokane Community College M
Spokane Falls Community College
M
Tacoma Community College M
University of Washington M
Walla Walla Community College M
Washington State University M
Wenatchee Valley College M
Yakima Valley Community College
M

West Virginia

Alderson-Broaddus College M
Bluefield State College M
Concord College M
Davis and Elkins College M
Marshall University M
Ohio Valley College M
Potomac State College of West
Virginia University M
Salem-Teikyo University M
West Liberty State College M
West Virginia Institute of
Technology M
West Virginia State College M
West Virginia University M
West Virginia Wesleyan College M

Wyoming

University of Wyoming M

Basketball

Alabama

Alabama Agricultural and
Mechanical University M, W
Alabama State University M, W
Athens State College M
Auburn University M, W
Bevill State Community College M,
W

Birmingham-Southern College M
Calhoun Community College M, W
Chattahoochee Valley Community
College M, W
Enterprise State Junior College M
Faulkner University M
Gadsden State Community College
M, W
George C. Wallace State
Community College at Selma M,
W
Jacksonville State University M, W
James H. Faulkner State
Community College M, W
Lawson State Community College
M, W
Lurleen B. Wallace State Junior
College M, W
Miles College M, W
Northwest-Shoals Community
College M, W
Samford University M
Snead State Community College M,
W
Spring Hill College M, W
Talladega College M, W
Troy State University M, W
Tuskegee University M, W
University of Alabama
Birmingham M, W
Huntsville M, W
Tuscaloosa M, W
University of Alabama at
Birmingham: Walker College M
University of Mobile M, W
University of Montevallo M, W
University of North Alabama M, W
University of West Alabama M, W
Wallace State College at Hanceville
M, W

Alaska

University of Alaska
Anchorage M, W
Fairbanks M, W

Arizona

Arizona State University M, W
Arizona Western College M
Cochise College M, W
Glendale Community College M, W
Mesa Community College M, W
Northern Arizona University M, W
Pima Community College M, W
Scottsdale Community College M,
W
South Mountain Community
College M, W
University of Arizona M, W
Yavapai College M, W

Arkansas

Arkansas State University M, W
Harding University M, W
Henderson State University M, W
John Brown University M, W
Lyon College M, W
North Arkansas Community/
Technical College M, W
Ouachita Baptist University M, W
Philander Smith College M, W
Shorter College W
University of Arkansas
Fayetteville M, W
Little Rock M
Pine Bluff M, W
University of Central Arkansas M,
W
Williams Baptist College M, W

California

Azusa Pacific University M, W

Biola University M, W
California Baptist College M, W
California Polytechnic State
University: San Luis Obispo M,
W
California State Polytechnic
University: Pomona M, W
California State University
Bakersfield M
Fresno M, W
Fullerton M, W
Long Beach M, W
Los Angeles M, W
Northridge M, W
Sacramento M, W
San Bernardino M, W
Christian Heritage College M, W
Concordia University M, W
Dominican College of San Rafael
M, W
Fresno Pacific College M, W
Holy Names College M, W
Loyola Marymount University M,
W
Patten College M
Pepperdine University M, W
Point Loma Nazarene College M,
W
St. Mary's College of California M,
W
San Diego State University M, W
San Jose State University M, W
Santa Clara University M, W
Southern California College M, W
Stanford University M, W
University of California
Berkeley M, W
Irvine M, W
Los Angeles M, W
Riverside M, W
Santa Barbara M, W
University of the Pacific M, W
University of San Diego M, W
University of San Francisco M, W
University of Southern California
M, W
Westmont College M

Colorado

Adams State College M, W
Colorado Christian University M,
W
Colorado Northwestern Community
College M, W
Colorado School of Mines M, W
Colorado State University M, W
Fort Lewis College M, W
Lamar Community College M
Mesa State College M, W
Metropolitan State College of
Denver M, W
Northeastern Junior College M, W
Otero Junior College M, W
Regis University M, W
Trinidad State Junior College M
University of Colorado
Boulder M, W
Colorado Springs M, W
University of Denver M, W
University of Northern Colorado M,
W
University of Southern Colorado M,
W
Western State College of Colorado
M, W

Connecticut

Central Connecticut State
University M, W
Fairfield University M, W
Mitchell College M, W
Quinnipiac College M, W

Teikyo-Post University M, W
University of Bridgeport M, W
University of Connecticut M, W
University of Hartford M, W
University of New Haven M, W

Delaware

Delaware State University M, W
Delaware Technical and
Community College: Stanton/
Wilmington Campus M, W
University of Delaware M, W

District of Columbia

American University M, W
George Washington University M,
W
Georgetown University M, W
Howard University M, W
University of the District of
Columbia M, W

Florida

Bethune-Cookman College M, W
Brevard Community College M, W
Central Florida Community College
M
Chipola Junior College M, W
Daytona Beach Community College
M
Eckerd College M, W
Embry-Riddle Aeronautical
University M
Flagler College M, W
Florida Agricultural and Mechanical
University M
Florida Atlantic University M, W
Florida College M
Florida Community College at
Jacksonville M, W
Florida Institute of Technology M,
W
Florida International University M,
W
Florida Memorial College M, W
Florida Southern College M, W
Florida State University M, W
Gulf Coast Community College M
Hillsborough Community College
M, W
Lake City Community College M,
W
Lynn University M, W
Manatee Community College M, W
North Florida Junior College M, W
Nova Southeastern University M
Okaloosa-Walton Community
College M, W
Palm Beach Atlantic College M
Palm Beach Community College M,
W
Pasco-Hernando Community
College M
Rollins College M, W
St. Johns River Community College
M
St. Leo College M, W
St. Petersburg Junior College M, W
St. Thomas University M
Stetson University M, W
Tallahassee Community College M,
W
University of Central Florida M, W
University of Florida M, W
University of Miami M, W
University of North Florida M, W
University of South Florida M, W
University of Tampa M, W
University of West Florida M, W
Valencia Community College M, W
Warner Southern College M, W
Webber College M, W

Georgia

Abraham Baldwin Agricultural
College M
Augusta College M, W
Berry College M, W
Brewton-Parker College M, W
Clark Atlanta University M, W
Clayton State College M, W
Columbus College M, W
Covenant College M, W
Darton College W
Emmanuel College M, W
Fort Valley State College M, W
Georgia College M, W
Georgia Institute of Technology M,
W
Georgia Southern University M, W
Georgia Southwestern College M,
W
Kennesaw State College M, W
Macon College M
Mercer University M, W
Middle Georgia College M
Morehouse College M
North Georgia College M, W
Paine College M, W
Piedmont College M, W
Reinhardt College M, W
Savannah State College M, W
Shorter College M, W
Southern College of Technology M
University of Georgia M, W
Valdosta State University M, W
West Georgia College M, W

Hawaii

Hawaii Pacific University M
University of Hawaii
Hilo M
Manoa M, W

Idaho

Albertson College M, W
Boise State University M, W
College of Southern Idaho M, W
Idaho State University M, W
Lewis-Clark State College M, W
North Idaho College M, W
Northwest Nazarene College M, W
Ricks College M, W
University of Idaho M, W

Illinois

Belleville Area College M, W
Bradley University M, W
Carl Sandburg College M, W
Chicago State University M, W
City Colleges of Chicago: Kennedy-
King College M
Danville Area Community College
M, W
De Paul University M, W
Eastern Illinois University M, W
Elgin Community College M, W
Highland Community College M, W
Illinois Eastern Community
Colleges
Lincoln Trail College M, W
Olney Central College M, W
Wabash Valley College M, W
Illinois Institute of Technology M,
W
Illinois State University M, W
John A. Logan College M, W
Kaskaskia College M, W
Kishwaukee College M, W
Lake Land College M, W
Lewis and Clark Community
College M, W
Lewis University M, W
Lincoln College M, W

Lincoln Land Community College
M, W
Loyola University of Chicago M, W
McHenry County College M, W
McKendree College M, W
Moraine Valley Community College
M, W
Morton College M, W
Northeastern Illinois University M,
W
Northwestern University M, W
Olivet Nazarene University M, W
Quincy University M, W
Rend Lake College M, W
Rosary College M, W
St. Xavier University M
Southeastern Illinois College M, W
Southern Illinois University
Carbondale M, W
Edwardsville M, W
Trinity International University M,
W
University of Illinois
Chicago M, W
Urbana-Champaign M, W
Western Illinois University M, W

Indiana

Ancilla College M
Ball State University M, W
Bethel College M, W
Butler University M, W
Goshen College M, W
Grace College M, W
Huntington College M, W
Indiana Institute of Technology M,
W
Indiana State University M, W
Indiana University
Bloomington M, W
Southeast M, W
Indiana University-Purdue
University Indianapolis M, W
Indiana Wesleyan University M, W
Marian College M, W
Oakland City University M, W
Purdue University M, W
St. Francis College M, W
St. Joseph's College M, W
St. Mary-of-the-Woods College W
Taylor University M, W
Tri-State University M, W
University of Evansville M, W
University of Indianapolis M, W
University of Notre Dame M, W
University of Southern Indiana M,
W
Valparaiso University M, W
Vincennes University M, W

Iowa

Briar Cliff College M, W
Clinton Community College M
Drake University M, W
Ellsworth Community College M,
W
Graceland College M, W
Grand View College M, W
Indian Hills Community College M
Iowa Central Community College
M, W
Iowa Lakes Community College M,
W
Iowa State University M, W
Iowa Wesleyan College M, W
Morningside College M, W
North Iowa Area Community
College M, W
Northwestern College M, W
St. Ambrose University M, W
Teikyo Marycrest University M, W
University of Iowa M, W

University of Northern Iowa M, W
Waldorf College M, W
Westmar University M, W

Kansas

Baker University M, W
Barton County Community College
M
Benedictine College M, W
Bethany College M, W
Bethel College M, W
Butler County Community College
M, W
Colby Community College M, W
Emporia State University M, W
Fort Hays State University M
Fort Scott Community College M,
W
Friends University M, W
Garden City Community College
M, W
Hesston College M, W
Hutchinson Community College M,
W
Independence Community College
M
Kansas City Kansas Community
College M, W
Kansas Newman College W
Kansas State University M, W
MidAmerica Nazarene College M,
W
Neosho County Community College
M, W
Ottawa University M, W
Pratt Community College M, W
St. Mary College M, W
Southwestern College M, W
University of Kansas M, W
Wichita State University M, W

Kentucky

Bellarmine College M, W
Brescia College M, W
Cumberland College M, W
Eastern Kentucky University M, W
Georgetown College M, W
Kentucky State University M, W
Kentucky Wesleyan College M, W
Lindsey Wilson College M, W
Morehead State University M, W
Murray State University M, W
Northern Kentucky University M,
W
Pikeville College M, W
Spalding University M, W
Sue Bennett College M, W
Transylvania University M, W
Union College M, W
University of Kentucky M, W
University of Louisville M, W
Western Kentucky University M, W

Louisiana

Bossier Parish Community College
M
Centenary College of Louisiana M
Dillard University M, W
Grambling State University M, W
Louisiana State University and
Agricultural and Mechanical
College M, W
Louisiana Tech University M, W
Nicholls State University M, W
Northeast Louisiana University M,
W
Northwestern State University M,
W
Southeastern Louisiana University
M, W
Tulane University M, W
University of New Orleans M, W

University of Southwestern
Louisiana M, W
Xavier University of Louisiana M,
W

Maine

Husson College M, W
Unity College M
University of Maine M, W

Maryland

Bowie State University M, W
Charles County Community College
M
Chesapeake College M, W
Columbia Union College M, W
Dundalk Community College M, W
Hagerstown Junior College M, W
Loyola College in Maryland M, W
Morgan State University M, W
Mount St. Mary's College M, W
Prince George's Community College
M, W
Towson State University M, W
University of Maryland
Baltimore County M, W
College Park M, W
Eastern Shore M, W

Massachusetts

American International College M,
W
Assumption College M, W
Becker College
Leicester Campus M
Worcester Campus M
Bentley College M, W
Boston College M, W
Boston University M, W
Dean College M
Merrimack College M, W
Mount Ida College M
Newbury College M, W
North Shore Community College M
Northeastern University M, W
Roxbury Community College M
Stonehill College M, W
University of Massachusetts
Amherst M, W
Lowell M, W

Michigan

Alpena Community College M, W
Aquinas College M, W
Central Michigan University M, W
Concordia College M, W
Cornerstone College and Grand
Rapids Baptist Seminary M, W
Delta College M, W
Eastern Michigan University M, W
Glen Oaks Community College M,
W
Gogebic Community College M, W
Grand Valley State University M,
W
Henry Ford Community College M,
W
Highland Park Community College
M, W
Hillsdale College M, W
Kellogg Community College M, W
Lake Superior State University M,
W
Lansing Community College M, W
Macomb Community College M, W
Michigan Christian College M, W
Michigan State University M, W
Michigan Technological University
M, W
Mott Community College M, W
Northern Michigan University M,
W

Northwood University M, W
Oakland University M, W
Saginaw Valley State University M, W
Spring Arbor College M, W
University of Michigan M, W
Wayne State University M, W
Western Michigan University M, W

Minnesota

Bemidji State University M, W
Mankato State University M, W
Moorhead State University M, W
St. Cloud State University M, W
Southwest State University M, W
University of Minnesota
    Crookston M, W
    Duluth M, W
    Twin Cities M, W
Winona State University M, W

Mississippi

Alcorn State University M, W
Belhaven College M, W
Copiah-Lincoln Community College M, W
Delta State University M, W
East Central Community College M, W
Hinds Community College M, W
Holmes Community College M, W
Itawamba Community College M, W
Mary Holmes College M, W
Meridian Community College M, W
Mississippi State University M, W
Mississippi University for Women W
Southwest Mississippi Community College M, W
University of Mississippi M, W
University of Southern Mississippi M, W
William Carey College M, W

Missouri

Avila College M, W
Central Methodist College M, W
Central Missouri State University M, W
College of the Ozarks M, W
Columbia College M
Crowder College W
Culver-Stockton College M, W
Drury College M
Hannibal-LaGrange College M, W
Harris Stowe State College M, W
Jefferson College W
Lincoln University M, W
Lindenwood College M, W
Mineral Area College M, W
Missouri Southern State College M, W
Missouri Western State College M, W
Park College M, W
Penn Valley Community College M
Research College of Nursing M, W
Rockhurst College M, W
St. Louis Community College
    Forest Park M, W
    Meramec M, W
St. Louis University M, W
Southeast Missouri State University M, W
Southwest Baptist University M, W
Southwest Missouri State University M, W
State Fair Community College M, W
Truman State University M, W

University of Missouri
    Columbia M, W
    Kansas City M, W
    Rolla M, W
    St. Louis M, W
William Jewell College M, W
William Woods University W

Montana

Carroll College M, W
Dawson Community College M, W
Miles Community College M, W
Montana State University
    Billings M, W
    Bozeman M, W
    Northern M, W
Montana Tech of The University of Montana M, W
Rocky Mountain College M, W
University of Montana-Missoula M, W
Western Montana College of the University of Montana M, W

Nebraska

Bellevue University M
Central Community College M, W
Chadron State College M, W
Concordia College M, W
Creighton University M, W
Dana College M, W
Doane College/Lincoln Campus M, W
Hastings College M, W
McCook Community College M, W
Mid Plains Community College M, W
Midland Lutheran College M, W
Northeast Community College M, W
Peru State College M, W
Southeast Community College:
    Beatrice Campus M, W
University of Nebraska
    Kearney M, W
    Lincoln M, W
    Omaha M, W
Wayne State College M, W
Western Nebraska Community College M, W
York College M, W

Nevada

Sierra Nevada College M
University of Nevada
    Las Vegas M, W
    Reno M, W

New Hampshire

Franklin Pierce College M, W
Hesser College M, W
New Hampshire College M, W
Notre Dame College M, W
St. Anselm College M, W
University of New Hampshire M, W

New Jersey

Bloomfield College M, W
Burlington County College M
Caldwell College M, W
Essex County College M, W
Fairleigh Dickinson University
    Edward Williams College M, W
    Teaneck M, W
Georgian Court College W
Monmouth University M, W
Rider University M, W

Rutgers, The State University of
New Jersey
    College of Engineering M, W
    College of Pharmacy M, W
    Cook College M, W
    Douglass College W
    Livingston College M, W
    Mason Gross School of the Arts M, W
    Rutgers College M, W
St. Peter's College M, W
Salem Community College W
Seton Hall University M, W
Union County College W

New Mexico

Eastern New Mexico University M, W
New Mexico Highlands University M, W
New Mexico Junior College M, W
New Mexico Military Institute M
New Mexico State University M, W
University of New Mexico M, W

New York

Adelphi University M, W
Canisius College M, W
Cazenovia College M, W
City University of New York:
    Queens College M, W
College of St. Rose M, W
Concordia College M, W
Daemen College M, W
Dominican College of Blauvelt M, W
Dowling College M
D'Youville College M, W
Fordham University M, W
Genesee Community College M, W
Hofstra University M, W
Houghton College M, W
Iona College M, W
Le Moyne College M, W
Long Island University
    Brooklyn Campus M, W
    C. W. Post Campus M, W
    Southampton College M, W
Manhattan College M, W
Marist College M, W
Mater Dei College W
Mercy College M, W
Molloy College M, W
Monroe Community College M
New York Institute of Technology M, W
Niagara County Community College M
Niagara University M, W
Nyack College M, W
Pace University M, W
Paul Smith's College M, W
Roberts Wesleyan College M, W
Sage Junior College of Albany M
St. Bonaventure University M, W
St. Francis College M, W
St. John's University M, W
St. Thomas Aquinas College M, W
Siena College M, W
State University of New York
    Albany M, W
    Buffalo M, W
    Stony Brook M, W
    College of Technology at Alfred M, W
Syracuse University M, W
Wagner College M, W

North Carolina

Appalachian State University M, W
Barber-Scotia College M, W
Barton College M, W

Belmont Abbey College M, W
Brevard College M, W
Campbell University M, W
Catawba College M, W
Craven Community College M
Davidson College M, W
Duke University M, W
East Carolina University M, W
Elizabeth City State University M, W
Elon College M, W
Fayetteville State University M, W
Gardner-Webb University M, W
High Point University M, W
Johnson C. Smith University M, W
Lees-McRae College M, W
Lenoir-Rhyne College M, W
Livingstone College M, W
Louisburg College M, W
Mars Hill College M, W
Montreat College M, W
Mount Olive College M, W
North Carolina Agricultural and Technical State University M, W
North Carolina Central University M, W
North Carolina State University M, W
Pembroke State University M, W
Pfeiffer College M, W
Queens College M, W
St. Andrews Presbyterian College M, W
St. Augustine's College M, W
University of North Carolina
    Asheville M, W
    Chapel Hill M, W
    Charlotte M, W
    Greensboro M, W
    Wilmington M, W
Wake Forest University M, W
Western Carolina University M, W
Wingate University M, W
Winston-Salem State University M, W

North Dakota

Dickinson State University M, W
Minot State University M, W
North Dakota State College of Science M, W
North Dakota State University
    Bottineau M, W
    Fargo M, W
University of North Dakota
    Grand Forks M, W
    Lake Region M, W
    Williston M, W

Ohio

Ashland University M
Bowling Green State University M, W
Cedarville College M, W
Cincinnati State Technical and Community College M, W
Clark State Community College M, W
Cleveland State University M, W
Edison State Community College M, W
Kent State University M, W
Malone College M, W
Miami University: Oxford Campus M, W
Mount Vernon Nazarene College M, W
Ohio Dominican College M, W
Ohio State University: Columbus Campus M, W
Ohio University M, W

Owens Technical College
Findlay Campus M, W
Toledo M, W
Shawnee State University M, W
Sinclair Community College M, W
Tiffin University M, W
University of Akron M, W
University of Cincinnati M, W
University of Dayton M, W
University of Findlay M, W
University of Rio Grande M, W
University of Toledo M, W
Urbana University M, W
Walsh University M, W
Wright State University M, W
Xavier University M, W
Youngstown State University M, W

Oklahoma

Bacone College M, W
Bartlesville Wesleyan College M, W
Cameron University M, W
East Central University M, W
Eastern Oklahoma State College M, W
Northeastern Oklahoma
Agricultural and Mechanical
College M, W
Northern Oklahoma College M, W
Oklahoma Baptist University M, W
Oklahoma Christian University of
Science and Arts M, W
Oklahoma City University M, W
Oklahoma Panhandle State
University M, W
Oral Roberts University M, W
Phillips University M, W
Redlands Community College M, W
Rose State College M, W
St. Gregory's College M, W
Southwestern Oklahoma State
University M, W
University of Central Oklahoma M, W
University of Oklahoma M, W
University of Tulsa M, W
Western Oklahoma State College M, W

Oregon

Blue Mountain Community College M, W
Chemeketa Community College M, W
Clackamas Community College M, W
Concordia University M, W
Linn-Benton Community College M, W
Mount Hood Community College M, W
Oregon Institute of Technology M
Portland State University W
Treasure Valley Community College M, W
University of Oregon M, W
University of Portland M, W
Western Baptist College M, W

Pennsylvania

Bloomsburg University of
Pennsylvania M, W
California University of
Pennsylvania M, W
Carlow College W
Cheyney University of Pennsylvania M, W
Community College of Beaver
County M
Drexel University M, W
Duquesne University M, W

East Stroudsburg University of
Pennsylvania M, W
Edinboro University of
Pennsylvania M, W
Gannon University M, W
Geneva College M, W
Indiana University of Pennsylvania M, W
Kutztown University of
Pennsylvania M, W
La Salle University M, W
Lock Haven University of
Pennsylvania M, W
Manor Junior College M, W
Mercyhurst College M, W
Millersville University of
Pennsylvania M, W
Mount Aloysius College M, W
Penn State University Park Campus M, W
Philadelphia College of Pharmacy
and Science M, W
Point Park College M, W
Robert Morris College M, W
St. Francis College M, W
St. Joseph's University M, W
St. Vincent College M, W
Seton Hill College W
Shippensburg University of
Pennsylvania M, W
Temple University M, W
University of Pittsburgh
Johnstown M, W
Pittsburgh M, W
Villanova University M, W
West Chester University of
Pennsylvania M, W
Westminster College M, W

Puerto Rico

Inter American University of Puerto
Rico
Fajardo Campus M
Guayama Campus M, W
Metropolitan Campus M, W
San German Campus M, W
University of Puerto Rico
Bayamon Technological
University College M, W
La Montana Regional College M, W
Mayaguez Campus M, W
University of the Sacred Heart M

Rhode Island

Bryant College M, W
Providence College M, W
University of Rhode Island M, W

South Carolina

Anderson College M, W
Charleston Southern University M, W
Claflin College M, W
Clemson University M, W
Coastal Carolina University M, W
Coker College M, W
College of Charleston M, W
Erskine College M, W
Francis Marion University M, W
Furman University M, W
Lander University M, W
Limestone College M, W
Morris College M, W
North Greenville College M, W
Presbyterian College M, W
South Carolina State University M, W
Southern Wesleyan University M, W
Spartanburg Methodist College M, W

University of South Carolina
Aiken M, W
Columbia M, W
Spartanburg M, W
Winthrop University M, W
Wofford College M, W

South Dakota

Augustana College M, W
Black Hills State University M, W
Dakota State University M, W
Dakota Wesleyan University M, W
Huron University M, W
Mount Marty College M, W
Northern State University M, W
South Dakota State University M, W
University of Sioux Falls M, W
University of South Dakota M, W

Tennessee

Austin Peay State University M, W
Belmont University M, W
Bethel College M, W
Carson-Newman College M, W
Chattanooga State Technical
Community College M, W
Christian Brothers University M, W
Cleveland State Community College M, W
David Lipscomb University M, W
Dyersburg State Community
College M, W
East Tennessee State University M, W
Freed-Hardeman University M, W
Jackson State Community College M, W
King College M, W
Lambuth University M, W
Lee College M, W
LeMoyne-Owen College M, W
Lincoln Memorial University M, W
Martin Methodist College M, W
Middle Tennessee State University M, W
Milligan College M, W
Roane State Community College M, W
Shelby State Community College M, W
Tennessee Technological University M, W
Tennessee Wesleyan College M, W
Trevecca Nazarene University M
Tusculum College M, W
Union University M, W
University of Memphis M, W
University of Tennessee
Chattanooga M, W
Knoxville M, W
Martin M, W
Vanderbilt University M, W
Volunteer State Community College M, W

Texas

Abilene Christian University M, W
Ambassador University M, W
Angelina College M, W
Angelo State University M, W
Baylor University M, W
Blinn College M, W
Clarendon College M, W
Concordia Lutheran College M, W
East Texas Baptist University M, W
East Texas State University M, W
Frank Phillips College M, W
Houston Baptist University M
Jacksonville College M
Kilgore College M, W
Lamar University—Beaumont M, W

Lee College M
McLennan Community College M, W
Midland College M, W
Odessa College M, W
Rice University M, W
St. Edward's University M, W
St. Mary's University M, W
Sam Houston State University M, W
San Jacinto College: North W
Schreiner College M, W
Southern Methodist University M, W
Southwest Texas State University M, W
Stephen F. Austin State University M, W
Texas A&M University M, W
Texas A&M University-Kingsville M, W
Texas Christian University M, W
Texas Lutheran College M, W
Texas Tech University M, W
Texas Wesleyan University M, W
Texas Woman's University W
University of Houston M, W
University of North Texas M, W
University of Texas
Arlington M, W
Austin M, W
San Antonio M, W
Wayland Baptist University M, W
Weatherford College M, W
West Texas A&M University M, W
Western Texas College W

Utah

Brigham Young University M, W
College of Eastern Utah M, W
Dixie College M, W
Salt Lake Community College M, W
Snow College M, W
Southern Utah University M, W
University of Utah M, W
Utah State University M
Utah Valley State College M, W
Weber State University M, W

Vermont

Champlain College M
Green Mountain College M, W
St. Michael's College M, W
University of Vermont M, W

Virginia

Bluefield College M, W
Clinch Valley College of the
University of Virginia M, W
College of William and Mary M, W
George Mason University M, W
Hampton University M, W
James Madison University M, W
Liberty University M, W
Longwood College M, W
Norfolk State University M, W
Old Dominion University M, W
Radford University M, W
St. Paul's College M, W
University of Richmond M, W
University of Virginia M, W
Virginia Commonwealth University M, W
Virginia Intermont College M, W
Virginia Military Institute M
Virginia Polytechnic Institute and
State University M, W
Virginia State University M, W
Virginia Union University M, W

256

Washington

Big Bend Community College M, W
Central Washington University M, W
Centralia College M, W
Eastern Washington University M, W
Edmonds Community College M, W
Gonzaga University M, W
Highline Community College M, W
Lower Columbia College M, W
Northwest College M, W
Olympic College M, W
Pierce College M, W
St. Martin's College M, W
Seattle Pacific University M, W
Seattle University M, W
Shoreline Community College M, W
Spokane Community College M, W
Spokane Falls Community College M, W
Tacoma Community College M, W
University of Washington M, W
Walla Walla Community College M, W
Washington State University M, W
Wenatchee Valley College M, W
Western Washington University M, W
Yakima Valley Community College M, W

West Virginia

Alderson-Broaddus College M, W
Bluefield State College M, W
Concord College M, W
Davis and Elkins College M, W
Fairmont State College M, W
Marshall University M, W
Ohio Valley College M, W
Potomac State College of West Virginia University M, W
Salem-Teikyo University M, W
Shepherd College M, W
West Liberty State College M, W
West Virginia Institute of Technology M, W
West Virginia State College M, W
West Virginia University M, W
West Virginia Wesleyan College M, W
Wheeling Jesuit College M, W

Wisconsin

Marquette University M, W
Mid-State Technical College M
Northland College M, W
University of Wisconsin
  Green Bay M, W
  Madison M, W

Wyoming

Eastern Wyoming College M
Northwest College M, W
Sheridan College M, W
University of Wyoming M, W
Western Wyoming Community College M, W

Bowling

Florida

Florida Agricultural and Mechanical University M, W

Indiana

Vincennes University M, W

Kansas

Fort Hays State University M, W

Maryland

Dundalk Community College M, W
Prince George's Community College M, W

Michigan

Aquinas College M, W
Saginaw Valley State University M

Mississippi

Mississippi Valley State University M, W

New York

Niagara County Community College M, W

North Carolina

North Carolina Central University M, W

Pennsylvania

Community College of Beaver County M

Utah

Weber State University W

Cross-country

Alabama

Alabama Agricultural and Mechanical University M, W
Alabama State University M, W
Auburn University M, W
Jacksonville State University M, W
Lurleen B. Wallace State Junior College M, W
Miles College M, W
Northwest-Shoals Community College M, W
Samford University M, W
Spring Hill College W
Troy State University M, W
University of Alabama
  Birmingham M, W
  Huntsville M, W
  Tuscaloosa M, W
University of Mobile M, W
University of North Alabama M, W
Wallace State College at Hanceville M, W

Alaska

University of Alaska
  Anchorage M
  Fairbanks M, W

Arizona

Arizona State University M, W
Glendale Community College M, W
Mesa Community College M, W
Navajo Community College M, W
Northern Arizona University M, W
Pima Community College M, W
Scottsdale Community College M, W
South Mountain Community College M, W
University of Arizona M, W
Yavapai College M, W

Arkansas

Arkansas State University M, W
Harding University M, W
Henderson State University W

Lyon College M, W

University of Arkansas
  Fayetteville M, W
  Little Rock M, W

California

Azusa Pacific University M, W
Biola University M, W
California Baptist College M, W
California Polytechnic State University: San Luis Obispo M, W
California State Polytechnic University: Pomona M, W
California State University
  Bakersfield M, W
  Fresno M
  Fullerton M, W
  Long Beach M, W
  Los Angeles M, W
  Northridge M, W
  Sacramento M, W
Concordia University M, W
Dominican College of San Rafael M, W
Fresno Pacific College M, W
Point Loma Nazarene College M, W
St. Mary's College of California M, W
San Jose State University W
Southern California College M, W
Stanford University M
University of California
  Berkeley M, W
  Irvine M, W
  Los Angeles M, W
  Riverside M, W
  Santa Barbara M, W
University of San Diego M, W
University of San Francisco M, W
Westmont College M, W

Colorado

Adams State College M, W
Colorado School of Mines M, W
Colorado State University M, W
Fort Lewis College M, W
Mesa State College W
University of Colorado
  Boulder M, W
  Colorado Springs M, W
University of Northern Colorado W
Western State College of Colorado M, W

Connecticut

Central Connecticut State University M, W
Fairfield University M, W
Quinnipiac College M, W
Teikyo-Post University M, W
University of Connecticut M, W
University of Hartford M, W
University of New Haven M

District of Columbia

American University M, W
George Washington University M, W
Howard University M, W

Florida

Bethune-Cookman College M, W
Brevard Community College M, W
Eckerd College W
Flagler College M, W
Florida Atlantic University M, W
Florida Community College at Jacksonville M, W
Florida Southern College M, W
Florida State University M, W

Nova Southeastern University M, W

Palm Beach Atlantic College M, W
Stetson University M, W
University of Central Florida M, W
University of Florida M, W
University of Miami M, W
University of Tampa M, W
Warner Southern College M, W
Webber College M, W

Georgia

Andrew College M, W
Augusta College M, W
Berry College M, W
Brenau University W
Clayton State College M, W
Columbus College M, W
Covenant College M, W
Georgia College M, W
Georgia Institute of Technology M, W
Georgia Southwestern College M, W
Kennesaw State College M, W
Mercer University M, W
Morehouse College M
Paine College M, W
Piedmont College M, W
Savannah State College W
Shorter College M, W
University of Georgia M, W
Valdosta State University M, W
West Georgia College M, W

Hawaii

Hawaii Pacific University M, W
University of Hawaii
  Hilo M, W
  Manoa W

Idaho

Boise State University M, W
College of Southern Idaho M, W
Idaho State University M, W
North Idaho College M, W
University of Idaho M, W

Illinois

Bradley University M, W
Chicago State University M, W
Danville Area Community College M, W
De Paul University M, W
Eastern Illinois University M, W
Illinois Institute of Technology M, W
Illinois State University M, W
Lewis University M, W
Loyola University of Chicago M, W
Morton College M, W
Northeastern Illinois University M, W
Olivet Nazarene University M, W
St. Xavier University W
Southern Illinois University
  Carbondale M, W
  Edwardsville M, W
University of Illinois
  Chicago M, W
  Urbana-Champaign M, W
Western Illinois University M, W

Indiana

Ancilla College M, W
Ball State University M, W
Bethel College M, W
Butler University M, W
Goshen College M, W
Huntington College M, W
Indiana State University M, W

Colleges that offer athletic scholarships

Indiana

Indiana University Bloomington M, W
Indiana Wesleyan University M, W
Marian College M, W
Oakland City University M, W
Purdue University M, W
St. Francis College M, W
St. Joseph's College M, W
Taylor University M, W
Tri-State University M, W
University of Evansville M, W
University of Indianapolis M, W
University of Notre Dame M, W
University of Southern Indiana M, W
Valparaiso University M, W
Vincennes University M, W

Iowa

Drake University M, W
Graceland College M, W
Iowa State University M, W
Iowa Wesleyan College M, W
Morningside College M, W
Northwestern College M, W
St. Ambrose University M, W
University of Iowa M, W
University of Northern Iowa M, W

Kansas

Baker University M, W
Barton County Community College M
Benedictine College M, W
Bethany College M, W
Butler County Community College M, W
Colby Community College M, W
Emporia State University M, W
Fort Hays State University M, W
Garden City Community College M, W
Hutchinson Community College M, W
Independence Community College M, W
Kansas City Kansas Community College M, W
Kansas State University M, W
Neosho County Community College M, W
Ottawa University M, W
Pratt Community College M, W
Southwestern College M, W
University of Kansas M, W
Wichita State University M, W

Kentucky

Bellarmine College M, W
Cumberland College M, W
Eastern Kentucky University M, W
Georgetown College M, W
Kentucky State University M, W
Lindsey Wilson College M
Murray State University M, W
Northern Kentucky University M, W
Transylvania University M, W
University of Kentucky M, W
University of Louisville M, W
Western Kentucky University M, W

Louisiana

Centenary College of Louisiana M, W
Louisiana State University and Agricultural and Mechanical College M, W
Louisiana Tech University M, W
Nicholls State University M, W
Northeast Louisiana University M, W

Northwestern State University M, W
Southeastern Louisiana University M, W
Tulane University M, W
University of New Orleans M, W
University of Southwestern Louisiana M, W

Maine

Unity College M, W
University of Maine M, W

Maryland

Bowie State University M, W
Columbia Union College M, W
Hagerstown Junior College M, W
Morgan State University M, W
Mount St. Mary's College M, W
Towson State University M, W
University of Maryland
Baltimore County M, W
College Park M, W
Eastern Shore M, W

Massachusetts

Boston College W
Boston University M, W
Northeastern University M, W
University of Massachusetts
Amherst M, W
Lowell M, W

Michigan

Aquinas College M, W
Central Michigan University M, W
Concordia College M, W
Cornerstone College and Grand Rapids Baptist Seminary M, W
Eastern Michigan University M, W
Highland Park Community College M, W
Hillsdale College M, W
Lake Superior State University M, W
Lansing Community College M, W
Macomb Community College M, W
Michigan Christian College M, W
Michigan State University M, W
Northern Michigan University W
Northwood University M, W
Saginaw Valley State University M, W
Spring Arbor College M, W
University of Michigan M, W
Wayne State University M
Western Michigan University M, W

Minnesota

Mankato State University M, W
Moorhead State University M, W
St. Cloud State University M, W
University of Minnesota
Duluth M, W
Twin Cities M, W
Winona State University W

Mississippi

Alcorn State University M, W
Delta State University W
Meridian Community College M, W
Mississippi State University M, W
Mississippi Valley State University M, W
University of Southern Mississippi M, W

Missouri

Central Methodist College M, W
Central Missouri State University M, W
Lindenwood College M, W

Missouri Southern State College M, W
Park College M, W
St. Louis University M, W
Southeast Missouri State University M, W
Southwest Baptist University M, W
Southwest Missouri State University M, W
Truman State University M, W
University of Missouri
Columbia M, W
Kansas City M, W
Rolla M, W
William Jewell College M, W

Montana

Montana State University
Billings M, W
Bozeman M, W
University of Montana-Missoula M, W

Nebraska

Concordia College M, W
Creighton University M, W
Dana College M, W
Doane College/Lincoln Campus M, W
Hastings College M, W
Midland Lutheran College M, W
University of Nebraska
Kearney M, W
Lincoln M, W
Omaha W
Wayne State College M, W

Nevada

University of Nevada
Las Vegas W
Reno W

New Hampshire

University of New Hampshire W

New Jersey

Fairleigh Dickinson University
Edward Williams College M, W
Teaneck M, W
Georgian Court College W
Monmouth University M, W
Rider University M, W
Rutgers, The State University of New Jersey
College of Engineering M, W
College of Pharmacy M, W
Cook College M, W
Douglass College W
Livingston College M, W
Mason Gross School of the Arts M, W
Rutgers College M, W
St. Peter's College M, W
Seton Hall University M, W

New Mexico

Eastern New Mexico University M, W
New Mexico Highlands University M, W
New Mexico State University M, W
University of New Mexico M, W

New York

Adelphi University M, W
Canisius College M, W
College of St. Rose M, W
Concordia College M, W
Fordham University M, W
Hofstra University M, W
Houghton College M, W

Iona College M
Le Moyne College M, W
Long Island University: C. W. Post Campus M, W
Manhattan College M, W
Marist College M, W
Mercy College M, W
New York Institute of Technology M, W
Niagara University M, W
Pace University M, W
Roberts Wesleyan College M, W
St. Bonaventure University M, W
St. Francis College M, W
St. John's University M, W
St. Thomas Aquinas College M, W
State University of New York
Albany M, W
Buffalo M, W
College of Technology at Alfred M, W
Syracuse University M, W

North Carolina

Appalachian State University M, W
Brevard College M, W
Campbell University W
Davidson College W
East Carolina University M, W
Elon College M, W
Fayetteville State University M, W
High Point University M, W
Johnson C. Smith University M, W
Lees-McRae College M, W
Lenoir-Rhyne College M, W
Livingstone College M, W
Mars Hill College M, W
North Carolina Agricultural and Technical State University M, W
North Carolina Central University M, W
North Carolina State University M, W
Pembroke State University M, W
Pfeiffer College M, W
St. Andrews Presbyterian College M, W
St. Augustine's College M, W
University of North Carolina
Asheville M, W
Chapel Hill M, W
Charlotte M, W
Greensboro M
Wilmington M, W
Wake Forest University M, W
Western Carolina University M, W
Wingate University M, W
Winston-Salem State University M, W

North Dakota

Dickinson State University M, W
Minot State University M, W
North Dakota State College of Science M, W
North Dakota State University M, W

Ohio

Ashland University M, W
Bowling Green State University M, W
Cedarville College M, W
Cleveland State University W
Kent State University M, W
Malone College M, W
Miami University: Oxford Campus M, W
Ohio State University: Columbus Campus M, W
Ohio University M, W
Tiffin University M, W

258

University of Akron M, W
University of Dayton M, W
University of Findlay M, W
University of Rio Grande M, W
University of Toledo M, W
Walsh University M, W
Wright State University M, W
Xavier University M, W
Youngstown State University M, W

Oklahoma

Oklahoma Baptist University M, W
Oklahoma Christian University of
Science and Arts M, W
Oral Roberts University M, W
University of Central Oklahoma M,
W
University of Oklahoma M, W
University of Tulsa M, W

Oregon

Chemeketa Community College M,
W
Clackamas Community College M,
W
Mount Hood Community College
M, W
Oregon Institute of Technology M,
W
Portland State University M, W
University of Portland M, W

Pennsylvania

Bloomsburg University of
Pennsylvania W
Carlow College W
Cheyney University of Pennsylvania
M, W
Drexel University M
Duquesne University M, W
Edinboro University of
Pennsylvania M, W
Gannon University M, W
Geneva College M, W
Indiana University of Pennsylvania
M, W
Kutztown University of
Pennsylvania M, W
La Salle University M, W
Lock Haven University of
Pennsylvania M, W
Mercyhurst College M, W
Millersville University of
Pennsylvania M, W
Penn State University Park Campus
M, W
Robert Morris College M, W
St. Francis College M, W
St. Joseph's University M, W
St. Vincent College M, W
Seton Hill College W
Shippensburg University of
Pennsylvania M, W
University of Pittsburgh M, W
Villanova University M, W
Westminster College W

Puerto Rico

Inter American University of Puerto
Rico
Guayama Campus M, W
San German Campus M, W
University of Puerto Rico
La Montana Regional College
M, W
Mayaguez Campus M, W
University of the Sacred Heart M,
W

Rhode Island

Providence College M, W
University of Rhode Island M, W

South Carolina

Anderson College M, W
Charleston Southern University M,
W
Claflin College M, W
Clemson University M, W
Coastal Carolina University M, W
College of Charleston M, W
Erskine College M, W
Francis Marion University M, W
Furman University M, W
Lander University M, W
South Carolina State University M,
W
Southern Wesleyan University M,
W
University of South Carolina
Aiken M, W
Columbia M, W
Spartanburg M
Winthrop University M, W
Wofford College M, W

South Dakota

Augustana College M, W
Black Hills State University M, W
Dakota State University M, W
Dakota Wesleyan University M, W
Mount Marty College M, W
South Dakota State University M,
W
University of Sioux Falls M, W
University of South Dakota M, W

Tennessee

Austin Peay State University M, W
Belmont University M, W
Carson-Newman College M, W
Christian Brothers University M, W
David Lipscomb University M, W
East Tennessee State University M,
W
Lincoln Memorial University M, W
Middle Tennessee State University
M, W
Tennessee Technological University
M, W
University of Memphis M
University of Tennessee
Chattanooga M, W
Knoxville M, W
Martin M, W
Vanderbilt University W

Texas

Abilene Christian University M, W
Ambassador University M, W
Angelo State University M, W
Baylor University M, W
East Texas State University M, W
Lamar University—Beaumont M, W
Prairie View A&M University W
Rice University M, W
Sam Houston State University M,
W
Southern Methodist University M,
W
Southwest Texas State University
M, W
Stephen F. Austin State University
M, W
Texas A&M University M, W
Texas Christian University M, W
Texas Tech University M, W
University of Houston M, W
University of North Texas M, W
University of Texas
Arlington M, W
Austin M, W
San Antonio M, W
Wayland Baptist University M, W

Utah

Brigham Young University M, W
University of Utah M, W
Utah State University M, W
Weber State University M, W

Virginia

George Mason University M, W
Hampton University M, W
James Madison University M, W
Liberty University M, W
Norfolk State University M, W
Old Dominion University W
Radford University M, W
St. Paul's College M, W
University of Virginia M, W
Virginia Commonwealth University
M, W
Virginia Military Institute M
Virginia Polytechnic Institute and
State University M, W
Virginia State University M, W

Washington

Central Washington University M,
W
Eastern Washington University M,
W
Gonzaga University M, W
Highline Community College M, W
Lower Columbia College M, W
Northwest College M, W
Seattle Pacific University M, W
Seattle University M, W
Spokane Community College M, W
Spokane Falls Community College
M, W
University of Washington M, W
Washington State University M, W
Western Washington University M,
W

West Virginia

Alderson-Broaddus College M, W
Bluefield State College M, W
Concord College M, W
Davis and Elkins College M, W
West Virginia University M, W
West Virginia Wesleyan College M,
W
Wheeling Jesuit College M, W

Wisconsin

Marquette University M, W
University of Wisconsin
Green Bay M, W
Madison M, W

Wyoming

University of Wyoming M, W

Diving

Alabama

Auburn University M, W
University of Alabama M, W

Arizona

Arizona State University M, W
Northern Arizona University M, W
University of Arizona M, W

Arkansas

University of Arkansas M, W

California

California State University:
Northridge M, W
Pepperdine University W

San Diego State University W
Stanford University M, W
University of California
Irvine M, W
Santa Barbara M, W
University of San Diego W
University of Southern California
M, W

Colorado

Colorado State University W
University of Denver M, W

Connecticut

Central Connecticut State
University M, W
University of Connecticut M, W

District of Columbia

American University M, W
George Washington University M,
W
Howard University M, W

Florida

Florida State University M, W
University of Florida M, W
University of Miami M, W

Georgia

University of Georgia M, W

Hawaii

University of Hawaii at Manoa M,
W

Illinois

Bradley University M
Illinois Institute of Technology M,
W
Illinois State University W
Lincoln College M, W
Northeastern Illinois University M,
W
Northwestern University M, W
Southern Illinois University at
Carbondale M, W
University of Illinois
Chicago M, W
Urbana-Champaign W
Western Illinois University M, W

Indiana

Ball State University M, W
Butler University M, W
Indiana University Bloomington M,
W
Purdue University M, W
University of Evansville M, W
University of Indianapolis M, W
University of Notre Dame M, W
Valparaiso University M, W

Iowa

Iowa State University M, W
University of Iowa M, W

Kansas

University of Kansas M, W

Kentucky

Transylvania University M, W
Union College M, W
University of Kentucky M, W
University of Louisville M, W
Western Kentucky University M, W

Maine

University of Maine M, W

Maryland

Towson State University M, W

University of Maryland: Baltimore
County M, W

Massachusetts
Boston College W
Boston University M, W
Northeastern University M, W
University of Massachusetts
Amherst M, W

Michigan
Eastern Michigan University M, W
Hillsdale College W
Northern Michigan University W
Oakland University M, W
University of Michigan M, W
Wayne State University M, W

Minnesota
Mankato State University M, W
St. Cloud State University M, W
University of Minnesota: Twin
Cities M, W

Mississippi
Delta State University M, W

Missouri
Drury College M, W
St. Louis University M, W
Southwest Missouri State University
M
Truman State University W
University of Missouri: Columbia
M, W

Nebraska
University of Nebraska
Kearney W
Lincoln M, W

Nevada
University of Nevada: Reno W

New Jersey
Rider University M, W
Rutgers, The State University of
New Jersey
College of Engineering M, W
College of Pharmacy M, W
Cook College M, W
Douglass College W
Livingston College M, W
Mason Gross School of the
Arts M, W
Rutgers College M, W
St. Peter's College M, W

New Mexico
University of New Mexico M, W

New York
Canisius College M, W
Fordham University M, W
Iona College M, W
Marist College M, W
Niagara University M, W
St. Bonaventure University M, W
St. John's University M, W
State University of New York at
Buffalo M, W
Syracuse University M, W

North Carolina
Davidson College M, W
East Carolina University M, W
North Carolina State University M,
W
University of North Carolina at
Wilmington M, W

Ohio
Bowling Green State University M,
W
Cleveland State University M, W
Miami University: Oxford Campus
M, W
Ohio State University: Columbus
Campus M, W
Ohio University M, W
University of Toledo M, W
Wright State University M, W
Xavier University M, W

Pennsylvania
Duquesne University M, W
Gannon University M, W
Indiana University of Pennsylvania
M, W
La Salle University M, W
Lock Haven University of
Pennsylvania W
University of Pittsburgh M, W
Villanova University M, W

Rhode Island
University of Rhode Island M, W

South Carolina
Clemson University M, W
College of Charleston M, W

South Dakota
South Dakota State University M,
W
University of South Dakota M, W

Tennessee
University of Tennessee: Knoxville
M, W

Texas
Southern Methodist University M,
W
Texas A&M University M, W
Texas Christian University M, W
University of Houston W
University of Texas at Austin M, W

Utah
Brigham Young University M, W
University of Utah M, W

Virginia
James Madison University M, W
Old Dominion University M, W
University of Virginia M, W
Virginia Military Institute M
Virginia Polytechnic Institute and
State University M, W

Wisconsin
University of Wisconsin
Green Bay M, W
Madison M, W

Fencing

California
California State University:
Fullerton M, W
Stanford University M, W

Illinois
Northwestern University W

Indiana
Tri-State University M, W
University of Notre Dame M, W

Kansas
Pratt Community College W

Michigan
Wayne State University M, W

New Jersey
Fairleigh Dickinson University
Edward Williams College W
Teaneck W
Rutgers, The State University of
New Jersey
College of Engineering M, W
College of Pharmacy M, W
Cook College M, W
Douglass College W
Livingston College M, W
Mason Gross School of the
Arts M, W
Rutgers College M, W

New York
St. John's University M, W

North Carolina
North Carolina State University M,
W
University of North Carolina at
Chapel Hill M, W

Ohio
Cleveland State University M, W
Ohio State University: Columbus
Campus W

Oklahoma
St. Gregory's College M, W

Pennsylvania
Penn State University Park Campus
M, W
Temple University W

Field hockey

California
Stanford University W
University of California: Berkeley W
University of the Pacific W

Connecticut
Fairfield University W
Mitchell College W
Quinnipiac College W
University of Connecticut W

Delaware
University of Delaware W

District of Columbia
American University W

Illinois
Northwestern University W

Indiana
Ball State University W

Iowa
University of Iowa W

Kentucky
Bellarmine College W
Transylvania University W
University of Louisville W

Maine
University of Maine W

Maryland
Towson State University W
University of Maryland: College
Park W

Massachusetts
American International College W
Becker College
Leicester Campus W
Worcester Campus W
Boston College W
Boston University W
Dean College W
Northeastern University W
University of Massachusetts
Amherst W

Michigan
Central Michigan University W
Michigan State University W
University of Michigan W

Missouri
St. Louis University W
Southwest Missouri State University
W

New Hampshire
University of New Hampshire W

New Jersey
Rider University W
Rutgers, The State University of
New Jersey
College of Engineering W
College of Pharmacy W
Cook College W
Douglass College W
Livingston College W
Mason Gross School of the
Arts W
Rutgers College W

New Mexico
New Mexico State University W

New York
Hofstra University W
Houghton College W
Long Island University: C. W. Post
Campus W
State University of New York at
Albany W
Syracuse University W

North Carolina
Appalachian State University W
Catawba College W
Davidson College W
Duke University W
University of North Carolina at
Chapel Hill W

Ohio
Kent State University W
Ohio State University: Columbus
Campus W
Ohio University W

Pennsylvania
Bloomsburg University of
Pennsylvania W
Drexel University W
East Stroudsburg University of
Pennsylvania W
Indiana University of Pennsylvania
W
Kutztown University of
Pennsylvania W
La Salle University W
Lock Haven University of
Pennsylvania W

Millersville University of
  Pennsylvania W
Penn State University Park Campus
  W
Shippensburg University of
  Pennsylvania W
Temple University W
Villanova University W
West Chester University of
  Pennsylvania W

Rhode Island
Providence College W
University of Rhode Island W

Virginia
College of William and Mary W
James Madison University W
Longwood College W
Radford University W
University of Richmond W
University of Virginia W
Virginia Commonwealth University
  W

West Virginia
Davis and Elkins College W

Football (tackle)

Alabama
Alabama State University M
Auburn University M
Jacksonville State University M
Miles College M
Samford University M
Troy State University M
Tuskegee University M
University of Alabama
      Birmingham M
      Tuscaloosa M
University of North Alabama M
University of West Alabama M

Arizona
Arizona State University M
Arizona Western College M
Glendale Community College M
Mesa Community College M
Northern Arizona University M
Scottsdale Community College M
University of Arizona M

Arkansas
Arkansas State University M
Harding University M
Henderson State University M
Ouachita Baptist University M
University of Arkansas at Pine Bluff
  M
University of Central Arkansas M

California
Azusa Pacific University M
California Polytechnic State
  University: San Luis Obispo M
California State University
      Fresno M
      Northridge M
      Sacramento M
St. Mary's College of California M
San Diego State University M
San Jose State University M
Stanford University M
University of California: Los
  Angeles M
University of the Pacific M
University of Southern California M

Colorado
Adams State College M
Colorado School of Mines M
Colorado State University M
Fort Lewis College M
Mesa State College M
University of Northern Colorado M
Western State College of Colorado
  M

Connecticut
Central Connecticut State
  University M
University of Connecticut M
University of New Haven M

Delaware
Delaware State University M
University of Delaware M

District of Columbia
Howard University M

Florida
Bethune-Cookman College M
Florida Agricultural and Mechanical
  University M
Florida State University M
University of Central Florida M
University of Florida M
University of Miami M
University of South Florida M

Georgia
Clark Atlanta University M
Fort Valley State College M
Georgia Institute of Technology M
Georgia Southern University M
Middle Georgia College M
Morehouse College M
Savannah State College M
University of Georgia M
Valdosta State University M
West Georgia College M

Hawaii
University of Hawaii at Manoa M

Idaho
Boise State University M
Idaho State University M
Ricks College M
University of Idaho M

Illinois
Eastern Illinois University M
Illinois State University M
Northwestern University M
Olivet Nazarene University M
St. Xavier University M
Southern Illinois University at
  Carbondale M
Trinity International University M
University of Illinois at Urbana-
  Champaign M

Indiana
Ball State University M
Butler University M
Indiana State University M
Indiana University Bloomington M
Purdue University M, W
St. Joseph's College M
Taylor University M
Tri-State University M
University of Indianapolis M
University of Notre Dame M
Valparaiso University M

Iowa
Ellsworth Community College M
Graceland College M

Iowa Central Community College
  M
Iowa Lakes Community College M
Iowa State University M
Iowa Wesleyan College M
Morningside College M
North Iowa Area Community
  College M
Northwestern College M
St. Ambrose University M
University of Iowa M
University of Northern Iowa M
Waldorf College M
Westmar University M

Kansas
Baker University M
Benedictine College M
Bethany College M, W
Bethel College M
Butler County Community College
  M
Emporia State University M
Fort Hays State University M
Fort Scott Community College M
Friends University M
Garden City Community College M
Hutchinson Community College M
Kansas State University M
MidAmerica Nazarene College M
Ottawa University M
Southwestern College M
University of Kansas M

Kentucky
Cumberland College M
Eastern Kentucky University M
Kentucky State University M
Morehead State University M
Murray State University M
Sue Bennett College M
Union College M
University of Kentucky M
University of Louisville M
Western Kentucky University M

Louisiana
Grambling State University M
Louisiana State University and
  Agricultural and Mechanical
  College M
Louisiana Tech University M
Nicholls State University M
Northeast Louisiana University M
Northwestern State University M
Tulane University M
University of Southwestern
  Louisiana M

Maine
University of Maine M

Maryland
Bowie State University M
Morgan State University M
Towson State University M
University of Maryland: College
  Park M

Massachusetts
American International College M
Boston College M
Boston University M
Dean College M
Northeastern University M
University of Massachusetts
  Amherst M

Michigan
Central Michigan University M
Eastern Michigan University M
Grand Valley State University M

Hillsdale College M
Michigan State University M
Michigan Technological University
  M
Northern Michigan University M
Northwood University M
Saginaw Valley State University M
University of Michigan M
Wayne State University M
Western Michigan University M

Minnesota
Bemidji State University M
Mankato State University M
Moorhead State University M
St. Cloud State University M
Southwest State University M
University of Minnesota
      Crookston M
      Duluth M
      Twin Cities M
Winona State University M

Mississippi
Alcorn State University M
Copiah-Lincoln Community College
  M
Delta State University M
East Central Community College M
Hinds Community College M
Holmes Community College M
Itawamba Community College M
Mississippi College M
Mississippi State University M
Mississippi Valley State University
  M
University of Mississippi M
University of Southern Mississippi
  M

Missouri
Central Methodist College M
Central Missouri State University M
Culver-Stockton College M
Lindenwood College M
Missouri Southern State College M
Missouri Western State College M
Southeast Missouri State University
  M
Southwest Baptist University M
Southwest Missouri State University
  M
Truman State University M
University of Missouri
      Columbia M
      Rolla M
      St. Louis M
William Jewell College M

Montana
Carroll College M
Montana State University-Bozeman
  M
Montana Tech of The University of
  Montana M
Rocky Mountain College M
Western Montana College of the
  University of Montana M

Nebraska
Chadron State College M
Concordia College M
Dana College M
Doane College/Lincoln Campus M
Hastings College M
McCook Community College M
Midland Lutheran College M
Peru State College M
University of Nebraska
      Kearney M
      Omaha M
Wayne State College M

Nevada

University of Nevada
Las Vegas M
Reno M

New Hampshire

University of New Hampshire M

New Jersey

Monmouth University M
Rutgers, The State University of
New Jersey
College of Engineering M
College of Pharmacy M
Cook College M
Livingston College M
Mason Gross School of the
Arts M
Rutgers College M

New Mexico

Eastern New Mexico University M
New Mexico Highlands University
M
New Mexico Military Institute M
New Mexico State University M
University of New Mexico M

New York

Fordham University M
Hofstra University M
State University of New York
Buffalo M
College of Technology at
Alfred M
Syracuse University M

North Carolina

Appalachian State University M
Catawba College M
Duke University M
East Carolina University M
Elizabeth City State University M
Elon College M
Fayetteville State University M
Gardner-Webb University M
Johnson C. Smith University M
Lenoir-Rhyne College M
Livingstone College M
Mars Hill College M
North Carolina Agricultural and
Technical State University M
North Carolina Central University
M
North Carolina State University M
University of North Carolina at
Chapel Hill M
Wake Forest University M
Western Carolina University M
Wingate University M
Winston-Salem State University M

North Dakota

Dickinson State University M
Minot State University M
North Dakota State College of
Science M
North Dakota State University M
University of North Dakota M

Ohio

Ashland University M
Bowling Green State University M
Kent State University M
Malone College M
Miami University: Oxford Campus
M
Ohio State University: Columbus
Campus M
Ohio University M
Tiffin University M
University of Akron M

University of Cincinnati M
University of Findlay M
University of Toledo M
Urbana University M
Walsh University M
Youngstown State University M

Oklahoma

East Central University M
Northeastern Oklahoma
Agricultural and Mechanical
College M
Oklahoma Panhandle State
University M
Southwestern Oklahoma State
University M
University of Central Oklahoma M
University of Oklahoma M
University of Tulsa M

Oregon

Portland State University M
University of Oregon M

Pennsylvania

Bloomsburg University of
Pennsylvania M
California University of
Pennsylvania M
Cheyney University of Pennsylvania
M
Duquesne University M
East Stroudsburg University of
Pennsylvania M
Edinboro University of
Pennsylvania M
Geneva College M
Indiana University of Pennsylvania
M
Kutztown University of
Pennsylvania M
Lock Haven University of
Pennsylvania M
Millersville University of
Pennsylvania M
Penn State University Park Campus
M
Shippensburg University of
Pennsylvania M
Temple University M
University of Pittsburgh M
Villanova University M
West Chester University of
Pennsylvania M
Westminster College M

Rhode Island

University of Rhode Island M

South Carolina

Charleston Southern University M
Clemson University M
Francis Marion University M
Furman University M
North Greenville College M
Presbyterian College M
South Carolina State University M
University of South Carolina M
Wofford College M

South Dakota

Augustana College M
Black Hills State University M
Dakota State University M
Dakota Wesleyan University M
Huron University M
Northern State University M
South Dakota State University M
University of Sioux Falls M
University of South Dakota M

Tennessee

Austin Peay State University M
Carson-Newman College M
East Tennessee State University M
Lambuth University M
Tennessee Technological University
M
Tusculum College M
University of Memphis M
University of Tennessee
Chattanooga M
Knoxville M
Martin M
Vanderbilt University M

Texas

Abilene Christian University M
Angelo State University M
Baylor University M
Blinn College M
East Texas State University M
Kilgore College M
Prairie View A&M University M
Rice University M
Sam Houston State University M
Southern Methodist University M
Southwest Texas State University M
Stephen F. Austin State University
M
Texas A&M University M
Texas A&M University-Kingsville
M
Texas Christian University M
Texas Tech University M
University of Houston M
University of North Texas M
University of Texas at Austin M
West Texas A&M University M

Utah

Brigham Young University M
Dixie College M
Snow College M
Southern Utah University M
University of Utah M
Utah State University M
Weber State University M

Virginia

College of William and Mary M
Hampton University M
James Madison University M
Liberty University M
Norfolk State University M
University of Richmond M
University of Virginia M
Virginia Military Institute M
Virginia Polytechnic Institute and
State University M
Virginia State University M
Virginia Union University M

Washington

Central Washington University M
Eastern Washington University M
Pacific Lutheran University M
University of Puget Sound M
University of Washington M
Walla Walla Community College M
Washington State University M
Western Washington University M

West Virginia

Concord College M
Fairmont State College M
Marshall University M
Potomac State College of West
Virginia University M
Shepherd College M
West Liberty State College M
West Virginia Institute of
Technology M

West Virginia State College M
West Virginia University M
West Virginia Wesleyan College M

Wisconsin

University of Wisconsin-Madison M

Wyoming

University of Wyoming M

Golf

Alabama

Alabama State University M, W
Auburn University M, W
Central Alabama Community
College M
Enterprise State Junior College M
Gadsden State Community College
M
Huntingdon College M
Jacksonville State University M, W
James H. Faulkner State
Community College M, W
Northwest-Shoals Community
College M, W
Samford University M, W
Snead State Community College M
Spring Hill College M, W
Talladega College M, W
Troy State University M, W
University of Alabama
Birmingham M, W
Tuscaloosa M, W
University of Mobile M, W
University of Montevallo M, W
University of North Alabama M
Wallace State College at Hanceville
M

Arizona

Arizona State University M, W
Glendale Community College M
Mesa Community College M
Northern Arizona University W
Pima Community College M
Scottsdale Community College M
University of Arizona M, W

Arkansas

Arkansas State University M, W
Lyon College M
University of Arkansas
Fayetteville M, W
Little Rock M, W

California

California Baptist College M
California State University
Fresno M
Long Beach M, W
Northridge M
Sacramento M
San Bernardino M
Loyola Marymount University M
Pepperdine University M, W
Point Loma Nazarene College M
St. Mary's College of California M
San Diego State University M, W
San Jose State University M, W
Stanford University M, W
University of California
Berkeley M, W
Irvine M
Los Angeles M, W
Santa Barbara M
University of the Pacific M
University of San Diego M
University of San Francisco M, W

University of Southern California
M, W

Colorado

Colorado Christian University M,
W
Colorado School of Mines M
Colorado State University W
Fort Lewis College M
Mesa State College W
Northeastern Junior College M
Regis University M
University of Colorado
Boulder M, W
Colorado Springs M
University of Northern Colorado M,
W
University of Southern Colorado M

Connecticut

Central Connecticut State
University M
Fairfield University M
Quinnipiac College M
University of Connecticut M
University of Hartford M, W

District of Columbia

American University M
George Washington University M
Georgetown University M

Florida

Bethune-Cookman College M, W
Brevard Community College M
Eckerd College M
Flagler College M
Florida Atlantic University M, W
Florida Community College at
Jacksonville M
Florida International University M,
W
Florida Southern College M, W
Florida State University M, W
Lynn University M, W
Manatee Community College M
Nova Southeastern University M
Palm Beach Atlantic College M
Palm Beach Community College W
Rollins College M, W
St. Petersburg Junior College W
St. Thomas University M, W
Stetson University M, W
University of Central Florida M, W
University of Florida M, W
University of Miami W
University of North Florida M, W
University of South Florida M, W
University of West Florida M, W
Webber College M

Georgia

Abraham Baldwin Agricultural
College M
Augusta College M
Augusta Technical Institute M
Berry College M
Brewton-Parker College M
Clayton State College M
Columbus College M
Darton College M, W
Georgia College M, W
Georgia Institute of Technology M
Georgia Southern University M
Georgia Southwestern College M
Kennesaw State College M
Mercer University M
Piedmont College M, W
Reinhardt College M
Shorter College M
Thomas College M
University of Georgia M, W

Valdosta State University M

Hawaii

University of Hawaii
Hilo M
Manoa M, W

Idaho

Albertson College M, W
Boise State University M, W
University of Idaho M, W

Illinois

Bradley University M, W
Danville Area Community College
M, W
De Paul University M
Elgin Community College M
Highland Community College M, W
Illinois State University M, W
John A. Logan College M
Kishwaukee College M, W
Lewis and Clark Community
College M
Lewis University M, W
Lincoln College M, W
Loyola University of Chicago M, W
McKendree College M, W
Moraine Valley Community College
M
Morton College M, W
Northeastern Illinois University M,
W
Northwestern University M, W
Olivet Nazarene University M
Rend Lake College M
Southern Illinois University at
Carbondale M, W
Trinity International University M
University of Illinois at Urbana-
Champaign M, W
Western Illinois University M

Indiana

Ancilla College M, W
Bethel College M
Butler University M
Goshen College M
Grace College M
Huntington College M, W
Indiana University Bloomington M,
W
Indiana Wesleyan University M
Marian College M, W
Oakland City University M, W
Purdue University M, W
St. Francis College M
St. Joseph's College M, W
Taylor University M
Tri-State University M, W
University of Evansville M
University of Indianapolis M, W
University of Notre Dame M, W
University of Southern Indiana M
Vincennes University M, W

Iowa

Briar Cliff College M, W
Drake University M
Grand View College W
Indian Hills Community College M
Iowa Central Community College
M, W
Iowa Lakes Community College M,
W
Iowa State University M, W
Iowa Wesleyan College M, W
North Iowa Area Community
College M
Northwestern College M, W
St. Ambrose University M, W
University of Iowa M, W

University of Northern Iowa W
Waldorf College M
Westmar University M, W

Kansas

Baker University M
Benedictine College M, W
Bethany College M
Butler County Community College
M
Friends University M
Hutchinson Community College M
Kansas Newman College M
Kansas State University M, W
Ottawa University M
Southwestern College M
University of Kansas M, W
Wichita State University M, W

Kentucky

Bellarmine College M, W
Brescia College M
Cumberland College M, W
Eastern Kentucky University M
Georgetown College M
Kentucky State University M
Kentucky Wesleyan College M
Lindsey Wilson College M
Morehead State University M
Murray State University M, W
Northern Kentucky University M
Transylvania University M
Union College M
University of Kentucky M, W
University of Louisville M
Western Kentucky University M, W

Louisiana

Centenary College of Louisiana M
Grambling State University M
Louisiana State University and
Agricultural and Mechanical
College M, W
Louisiana Tech University M
Nicholls State University M
Northeast Louisiana University M
Northwestern State University M
Southeastern Louisiana University
M
Tulane University M, W
University of New Orleans M
University of Southwestern
Louisiana M

Maryland

Charles County Community College
M, W
Loyola College in Maryland M
University of Maryland
Baltimore County M
College Park M

Michigan

Aquinas College M
Cornerstone College and Grand
Rapids Baptist Seminary M
Eastern Michigan University M
Glen Oaks Community College M
Kellogg Community College W
Lansing Community College M
Michigan State University M, W
Mott Community College M
Northern Michigan University M
Northwood University M
Oakland University M, W
Saginaw Valley State University M
Spring Arbor College M
University of Michigan M, W
Wayne State University M

Minnesota

Mankato State University M, W

Moorhead State University W
St. Cloud State University M, W
University of Minnesota: Twin
Cities M, W
Winona State University M, W

Mississippi

Alcorn State University M, W
Belhaven College M
Delta State University M
Itawamba Community College M
Mississippi State University M, W
Mississippi Valley State University
M, W
University of Mississippi M, W
University of Southern Mississippi
M, W

Missouri

Central Methodist College M, W
Culver-Stockton College M
Drury College M
Lincoln University M
Lindenwood College M, W
Missouri Southern State College M
Missouri Western State College M
Penn Valley Community College M
St. Louis University M
Southeast Missouri State University
M
Southwest Baptist University M
Southwest Missouri State University
M, W
Truman State University W
University of Missouri
Columbia M, W
Kansas City M, W
Rolla M
St. Louis M
William Jewell College M

Montana

Montana State University-Bozeman
W

Nebraska

Central Community College W
Chadron State College M
College of St. Mary W
Concordia College M, W
Creighton University M, W
Hastings College M, W
McCook Community College M, W
Midland Lutheran College M, W
Northeast Community College M,
W
Southeast Community College:
Beatrice Campus M
University of Nebraska
Kearney M, W
Lincoln M
Wayne State College M, W
Western Nebraska Community
College M

Nevada

University of Nevada
Las Vegas M
Reno M

New Jersey

Caldwell College M, W
Fairleigh Dickinson University
Edward Williams College M
Teaneck M

263

Rutgers, The State University of
New Jersey
    College of Engineering M, W
    College of Pharmacy M, W
    Cook College M, W
    Douglass College W
    Livingston College M, W
    Mason Gross School of the
        Arts M, W
    Rutgers College M, W
Seton Hall University M

New Mexico
New Mexico Junior College M
New Mexico Military Institute M
New Mexico State University M, W
University of New Mexico M, W

New York
Adelphi University M
Canisius College M, W
Dominican College of Blauvelt M
Fordham University M
Hofstra University M
Iona College M
Le Moyne College M
Long Island University: Brooklyn
    Campus M
Manhattan College M
Mercy College M
Monroe Community College M
Niagara University M
St. Bonaventure University M
St. John's University M
St. Thomas Aquinas College M
Wagner College M, W

North Carolina
Appalachian State University M, W
Barton College M
Belmont Abbey College M
Brevard College M
Campbell University M, W
Catawba Valley Community College
    M
Craven Community College M, W
Davidson College M
Duke University M, W
East Carolina University M
Edgecombe Community College M
Elon College M
Fayetteville State University M
Gardner-Webb University M
High Point University M
Johnson C. Smith University M
Lees-McRae College M
Lenoir-Rhyne College M
Livingstone College M
Louisburg College M
Mars Hill College M
Mount Olive College M
North Carolina State University M,
    W
Pembroke State University M
Pfeiffer College M
Queens College M
St. Andrews Presbyterian College
    M, W
St. Augustine's College M, W
University of North Carolina
    Chapel Hill M, W
    Charlotte M
    Greensboro M, W
    Wilmington M, W
Wake Forest University M, W
Western Carolina University M, W
Wingate University M

North Dakota
Dickinson State University M

Ohio
Bowling Green State University M,
    W
Cedarville College M
Clark State Community College M
Cleveland State University M
Kent State University M
Malone College M
Miami University: Oxford Campus
    M
Mount Vernon Nazarene College M
Ohio State University: Columbus
    Campus M, W
Ohio University M
Shawnee State University M
Sinclair Community College M
Southern State Community College
    M
Tiffin University M
University of Akron M
University of Dayton M, W
University of Findlay M, W
University of Toledo M, W
Urbana University M, W
Walsh University M
Wright State University M
Xavier University M, W
Youngstown State University M

Oklahoma
Cameron University M
Oklahoma City University M
Oklahoma Panhandle State
    University M
Oral Roberts University M, W
Phillips University M
St. Gregory's College M, W
Southwestern Oklahoma State
    University M
University of Central Oklahoma M
University of Oklahoma M, W
University of Tulsa M, W

Oregon
Portland State University M
University of Oregon M, W
University of Portland M

Pennsylvania
Duquesne University M
Edinboro University of
    Pennsylvania M
Gannon University M
Indiana University of Pennsylvania
    M
La Salle University M, W
Mercyhurst College M, W
Millersville University of
    Pennsylvania M
Penn State University Park Campus
    M, W
Robert Morris College M
St. Francis College M, W
St. Joseph's University M
Temple University M
Villanova University M
West Chester University of
    Pennsylvania M

Rhode Island
University of Rhode Island M

South Carolina
Anderson College M
Charleston Southern University M,
    W
Clemson University M
Coastal Carolina University M, W
Coker College M
College of Charleston M, W
Erskine College M
Francis Marion University M

Furman University M, W
Limestone College M
North Greenville College M
Presbyterian College M, W
South Carolina State University M
Southern Wesleyan University M
Spartanburg Methodist College M
University of South Carolina at
    Aiken M
Winthrop University M, W
Wofford College M, W

South Dakota
Northern State University W
South Dakota State University M,
    W

Tennessee
Austin Peay State University M
Bethel College M
Carson-Newman College M
Christian Brothers University M
David Lipscomb University M
East Tennessee State University M
Freed-Hardeman University M
King College M
Lambuth University M
Lee College M
Lincoln Memorial University M
Martin Methodist College M
Middle Tennessee State University
    M
Shelby State Community College M
Tennessee Technological University
    M, W
Tennessee Wesleyan College M
Tusculum College M
Union University M
University of Memphis M, W
University of Tennessee
    Knoxville M, W
    Martin M, W
Vanderbilt University M, W

Texas
Abilene Christian University M
Baylor University M, W
Concordia Lutheran College M
East Texas State University M
Lamar University—Beaumont M, W
McLennan Community College M
Midland College M
Odessa College M
St. Edward's University M
St. Mary's University M
Sam Houston State University M
San Jacinto College: North M
Southern Methodist University M
Southwest Texas State University M
Stephen F. Austin State University
    M
Texas A&M University M, W
Texas Christian University M, W
Texas Lutheran College M
Texas Tech University M, W
Texas Wesleyan University M
University of Houston M
University of North Texas M, W
University of Texas
    Arlington M
    Austin M, W
    San Antonio M
Weatherford College M
Western Texas College M

Utah
Brigham Young University M, W
Southern Utah University M
University of Utah M
Utah State University M
Weber State University M, W

Virginia
Bluefield College M
George Mason University M
Hampton University M
James Madison University M, W
Liberty University M
Longwood College M, W
Old Dominion University M
Radford University M, W
St. Paul's College M
University of Richmond M
University of Virginia M
Virginia Commonwealth University
    M, W
Virginia Military Institute M
Virginia Polytechnic Institute and
    State University M
Virginia Union University M, W

Washington
Eastern Washington University M,
    W
Edmonds Community College M,
    W
Gonzaga University M, W
Lower Columbia College M, W
St. Martin's College M, W
Spokane Community College M, W
Spokane Falls Community College
    M, W
Tacoma Community College M, W
University of Puget Sound W
University of Washington M, W
Walla Walla Community College M,
    W
Washington State University M, W
Western Washington University M

West Virginia
Bluefield State College M
Concord College M
Davis and Elkins College M
Marshall University M
West Liberty State College M
West Virginia Institute of
    Technology M
West Virginia Wesleyan College M

Wisconsin
Mid-State Technical College M
University of Wisconsin
    Green Bay M
    Madison M, W

Wyoming
Eastern Wyoming College M, W
University of Wyoming M, W

Gymnastics

Alabama
Auburn University W
University of Alabama W

Alaska
University of Alaska Anchorage W

Arizona
Arizona State University W
University of Arizona W

California
California Polytechnic State
    University: San Luis Obispo W
California State University:
    Fullerton W
San Jose State University M, W

University of California
Berkeley M, W
Los Angeles W
Santa Barbara W

Colorado
University of Denver W

Connecticut
University of Bridgeport W

District of Columbia
George Washington University W
Howard University M, W

Florida
University of Florida W

Georgia
University of Georgia W

Idaho
Boise State University W

Illinois
Illinois State University W
University of Illinois
Chicago M, W
Urbana-Champaign M, W

Indiana
Ball State University W

Iowa
Iowa State University W
University of Iowa M, W

Kansas
Fort Hays State University M

Louisiana
Centenary College of Louisiana W
Louisiana State University and
Agricultural and Mechanical
College W

Maryland
Columbia Union College M, W
Towson State University W
University of Maryland: College
Park W

Massachusetts
University of Massachusetts
Amherst M, W

Michigan
Eastern Michigan University W
Michigan State University M, W
University of Michigan M, W
Western Michigan University M, W

Minnesota
University of Minnesota: Twin
Cities M, W
Winona State University W

Missouri
Southeast Missouri State University
W
University of Missouri: Columbia W

Nebraska
University of Nebraska—Lincoln M,
W

New Hampshire
University of New Hampshire W

New Jersey
Rutgers, The State University of
New Jersey
College of Engineering W
College of Pharmacy W
Cook College W
Douglass College W
Livingston College W
Mason Gross School of the
Arts W
Rutgers College W

New Mexico
University of New Mexico M

New York
Syracuse University M

North Carolina
North Carolina State University M,
W
University of North Carolina at
Chapel Hill W

Ohio
Bowling Green State University W
Kent State University M, W
Ohio State University: Columbus
Campus M, W

Oklahoma
University of Oklahoma M, W

Pennsylvania
Indiana University of Pennsylvania
W
Penn State University Park Campus
M, W
Temple University M, W
University of Pittsburgh W
West Chester University of
Pennsylvania W

Puerto Rico
University of Puerto Rico: La
Montana Regional College M

Rhode Island
University of Rhode Island W

Tennessee
Southern College of Seventh-day
Adventists M, W

Texas
Texas Woman's University W

Utah
Brigham Young University M, W
Southern Utah University W
University of Utah W
Utah State University W

Virginia
College of William and Mary M, W
James Madison University M, W
Radford University M, W

Washington
Seattle Pacific University W

West Virginia
West Virginia University W

Horseback riding

Kentucky
Murray State University M, W

Massachusetts
Mount Ida College M, W

Michigan
Hillsdale College M

Missouri
William Woods University W

New York
Cazenovia College M, W
Molloy College M, W

North Carolina
St. Andrews Presbyterian College
M, W

Virginia
Virginia Intermont College M, W

Ice hockey

Alabama
University of Alabama in Huntsville
M

Alaska
University of Alaska
Anchorage M
Fairbanks M

Colorado
Colorado College M
University of Denver M

Connecticut
Fairfield University M
University of Connecticut M

Illinois
University of Illinois at Chicago M

Indiana
University of Notre Dame M

Maine
University of Maine M

Massachusetts
Boston College M
Boston University M
Merrimack College M
Northeastern University M
University of Massachusetts Lowell
M

Michigan
Lake Superior State University M
Michigan State University M
Michigan Technological University
M
Northern Michigan University M
University of Michigan M

Minnesota
Mankato State University M
St. Cloud State University M
University of Minnesota
Duluth M
Twin Cities M, W

New Hampshire
University of New Hampshire M

New York
Canisius College M
Clarkson University M
Niagara University M, W
Rensselaer Polytechnic Institute M

St. John's University M

North Dakota
North Dakota State University:
Bottineau M
University of North Dakota M

Ohio
Bowling Green State University M
Kent State University M
Ohio State University: Columbus
Campus M

Pennsylvania
Villanova University M

Rhode Island
Providence College M, W

Vermont
University of Vermont M

Wisconsin
University of Wisconsin-Madison M

Lacrosse

California
Stanford University W

Connecticut
Fairfield University M
Mitchell College M
University of Hartford M

Delaware
University of Delaware M, W

District of Columbia
Georgetown University M

Indiana
Butler University M

Louisiana
Bossier Parish Community College
W

Maryland
Johns Hopkins University M
Loyola College in Maryland M, W
Mount St. Mary's College M
Towson State University M, W
University of Maryland
Baltimore County M, W
College Park M, W

Massachusetts
American International College W
Boston College W
Boston University W
Dean College M
Mount Ida College M
University of Massachusetts
Amherst M, W
Lowell M

Michigan
Michigan State University M
Northwood University M

New Jersey
Monmouth University W

Rutgers, The State University of
New Jersey
  College of Engineering M, W
  College of Pharmacy M, W
  Cook College M, W
  Douglass College W
  Livingston College M, W
  Mason Gross School of the
    Arts M, W
  Rutgers College M, W

New York
Adelphi University M
Canisius College M
Dowling College M
Hofstra University M, W
Long Island University
  C. W. Post Campus M
  Southampton College M
Manhattan College M
New York Institute of Technology
  M
Niagara University M, W
State University of New York
  Albany M
  Stony Brook M
Syracuse University M, W
Wagner College W

North Carolina
Davidson College W
Duke University M
Lees-McRae College M
St. Andrews Presbyterian College M
University of North Carolina at
  Chapel Hill M
Wingate University M

Ohio
Ohio State University: Columbus
  Campus W

Pennsylvania
Drexel University M
East Stroudsburg University of
  Pennsylvania W
Gannon University W
Lock Haven University of
  Pennsylvania W
Mercyhurst College M, W
Millersville University of
  Pennsylvania W
Penn State University Park Campus
  M, W
St. Joseph's University M, W
St. Vincent College M
Shippensburg University of
  Pennsylvania W
Temple University W
Villanova University M, W
West Chester University of
  Pennsylvania M, W

South Carolina
Limestone College M, W

Tennessee
Vanderbilt University W

Virginia
College of William and Mary W
James Madison University W
Old Dominion University W
Radford University M
University of Richmond W
University of Virginia M, W
Virginia Military Institute M
Virginia Polytechnic Institute and
  State University W

Wisconsin
University of Wisconsin-Madison W

Racquetball

Illinois
Principia College M

Rifle

Alabama
Jacksonville State University M, W
University of North Alabama M

Alaska
University of Alaska Fairbanks M,
  W

California
University of San Francisco M, W

Georgia
Mercer University M, W
North Georgia College M, W

Illinois
De Paul University M, W

Kentucky
Murray State University M, W

Louisiana
Centenary College of Louisiana M,
  W

Missouri
University of Missouri: Kansas City
  M, W

Nevada
University of Nevada: Reno M, W

New Mexico
Eastern New Mexico University M,
  W

New York
Canisius College M, W

Ohio
University of Akron M, W
Xavier University M, W

Pennsylvania
Duquesne University M, W

Tennessee
Austin Peay State University W
University of Memphis M
University of Tennessee: Martin M

Virginia
George Mason University M, W
Virginia Military Institute M

West Virginia
West Virginia University M, W

Wyoming
University of Wyoming M, W

Rowing (crew)

California
California State University:
  Sacramento M, W

District of Columbia
George Washington University M,
  W

Florida
Florida Institute of Technology M,
  W
Stetson University M, W

Georgia
Brenau University W

Iowa
University of Iowa W

Kansas
University of Kansas W

Massachusetts
Boston University M, W
Northeastern University M, W

Michigan
University of Michigan W

Nebraska
Creighton University M, W

New Jersey
Rutgers, The State University of
New Jersey
  College of Engineering M, W
  College of Pharmacy M, W
  Cook College M, W
  Douglass College W
  Livingston College M, W
  Mason Gross School of the
    Arts M, W
  Rutgers College M, W

New York
Syracuse University M, W

Ohio
Ohio State University: Columbus
  Campus W

Oklahoma
University of Tulsa W

Pennsylvania
Drexel University M
Mercyhurst College M, W
Temple University M, W

Tennessee
University of Tennessee: Knoxville
  W

Virginia
University of Virginia W

Washington
Washington State University W

Wisconsin
University of Wisconsin-Madison
  M, W

Sailing

Virginia
Old Dominion University M, W

Skiing

Alaska
University of Alaska
  Anchorage M, W
  Fairbanks M, W

Colorado
University of Colorado at Boulder
  M, W
University of Denver M, W
Western State College of Colorado
  M, W

Idaho
Albertson College M, W

Massachusetts
University of Massachusetts
  Amherst M, W

Michigan
Northern Michigan University M,
  W

Minnesota
University of Minnesota: Twin
  Cities M, W

Montana
Montana State University-Bozeman
  W
Rocky Mountain College M, W

Nevada
Sierra Nevada College M, W
University of Nevada: Reno M, W

New Hampshire
University of New Hampshire M,
  W

New Mexico
University of New Mexico M, W

New York
Paul Smith's College M, W

North Carolina
Lees-McRae College M, W

Utah
Brigham Young University M, W
University of Utah M, W

Vermont
Green Mountain College M, W
University of Vermont M, W

Washington
Seattle University M, W

Soccer

Alabama
Alabama Agricultural and
  Mechanical University M
Auburn University W
Birmingham-Southern College M,
  W
Huntingdon College M, W
Spring Hill College M
University of Alabama
  Birmingham M, W
  Huntsville M
  Tuscaloosa W
University of Mobile M, W

University of Montevallo M, W
Wallace State College at Hanceville
   M

Arizona

Arizona Western College M
Glendale Community College M
Mesa Community College M
Pima Community College M
Scottsdale Community College M
South Mountain Community
   College M
University of Arizona W
Yavapai College M

Arkansas

John Brown University M
University of Arkansas
   Fayetteville W
   Little Rock M, W

California

Azusa Pacific University M, W
Biola University M
California Baptist College M, W
California Polytechnic State
   University: San Luis Obispo M
California State Polytechnic
   University: Pomona M, W
California State University
   Bakersfield M
   Fresno M
   Fullerton M, W
   Los Angeles M, W
   Northridge M
   Sacramento M, W
   San Bernardino M, W
Christian Heritage College M
Concordia University M
Dominican College of San Rafael
   M, W
Fresno Pacific College M
Loyola Marymount University M,
   W
Pepperdine University W
Point Loma Nazarene College M
St. Mary's College of California M,
   W
San Diego State University M, W
San Jose State University M
Santa Clara University M, W
Southern California College M
Stanford University M, W
United States International
   University M, W
University of California
   Berkeley M, W
   Los Angeles M, W
   Santa Barbara M, W
University of the Pacific W
University of San Diego M, W
University of San Francisco M, W
University of Southern California W
Westmont College M, W

Colorado

Colorado Christian University M,
   W
Colorado College W
Colorado School of Mines M
Fort Lewis College M, W
Mesa State College W
Metropolitan State College of
   Denver M, W
Regis University M, W
University of Colorado at Colorado
   Springs M
University of Denver M, W
University of Northern Colorado W
University of Southern Colorado M,
   W

Connecticut

Central Connecticut State
   University M, W
Fairfield University M, W
Mitchell College M, W
Quinnipiac College M, W
Teikyo-Post University M, W
University of Bridgeport M, W
University of Connecticut M, W
University of Hartford M, W
University of New Haven M, W

Delaware

Goldey-Beacom College M
University of Delaware M, W

District of Columbia

American University M, W
George Washington University M,
   W
Howard University M

Florida

Eckerd College M, W
Embry-Riddle Aeronautical
   University M
Flagler College M
Florida Atlantic University M, W
Florida Institute of Technology M,
   W
Florida International University M,
   W
Florida Southern College M
Florida State University W
Lynn University M, W
Nova Southeastern University M,
   W
Palm Beach Atlantic College M, W
Rollins College M
St. Leo College M
St. Thomas University M, W
Stetson University M, W
University of Central Florida M, W
University of North Florida M, W
University of South Florida M, W
University of Tampa M
University of West Florida M, W
Warner Southern College M
Webber College M, W

Georgia

Andrew College M, W
Augusta College M
Berry College M, W
Brenau University W
Brewton-Parker College M, W
Clayton State College M, W
Covenant College M, W
Georgia Southern University M, W
Mercer University M, W
North Georgia College M, W
Piedmont College M, W
Reinhardt College M
Thomas College M
Young Harris College M

Hawaii

Hawaii Pacific University M, W
University of Hawaii at Manoa W

Idaho

Albertson College M, W
Northwest Nazarene College M

Illinois

Belleville Area College M
Bradley University M
De Paul University M
Eastern Illinois University M, W
Elgin Community College M, W
Illinois State University W
Kishwaukee College M

Lewis and Clark Community
   College M, W
Lewis University M, W
Lincoln College M, W
Lincoln Land Community College
   M
Loyola University of Chicago M, W
McHenry County College M
McKendree College M, W
Moraine Valley Community College
   M, W
Northeastern Illinois University M
Northwestern University W
Olivet Nazarene University M
Quincy University M, W
Rosary College M
St. Xavier University M
Southern Illinois University at
   Edwardsville M, W
Trinity International University M,
   W
University of Illinois at Chicago M
Western Illinois University M

Indiana

Ancilla College M, W
Bethel College M
Butler University M, W
Goshen College M, W
Grace College M, W
Huntington College M
Indiana Institute of Technology M,
   W
Indiana University Bloomington M,
   W
Indiana University-Purdue
   University Indianapolis M
Indiana Wesleyan University M, W
Marian College M
St. Francis College M, W
St. Joseph's College M, W
Tri-State University M, W
University of Evansville M, W
University of Indianapolis M, W
University of Notre Dame M, W
University of Southern Indiana M
Valparaiso University M, W

Iowa

Briar Cliff College M, W
Drake University M
Graceland College M, W
Grand View College M
Iowa State University W
Iowa Wesleyan College W
St. Ambrose University M, W
Teikyo Marycrest University M, W
Waldorf College M
Westmar University M, W

Kansas

Baker University M, W
Benedictine College M, W
Bethany College M, W
Bethel College M, W
Friends University M, W
Hesston College M
Kansas Newman College M, W
Ottawa University M, W
St. Mary College M, W
University of Kansas W

Kentucky

Bellarmine College M, W
Cumberland College M, W
Georgetown College M
Kentucky Wesleyan College M, W
Lindsey Wilson College M, W
Northern Kentucky University M
Spalding University M, W
Sue Bennett College M
Transylvania University M, W

Union College M, W
University of Kentucky M, W
University of Louisville M, W

Louisiana

Centenary College of Louisiana M,
   W
Louisiana State University and
   Agricultural and Mechanical
   College W
Tulane University W

Maine

Husson College M, W
Unity College M
University of Maine M, W

Maryland

Charles County Community College
   M
Chesapeake College M
Columbia Union College M
Dundalk Community College M, W
Hagerstown Junior College M
Loyola College in Maryland M, W
Mount St. Mary's College M, W
Towson State University M, W
University of Maryland
   Baltimore County M, W
   College Park M, W
   Eastern Shore M

Massachusetts

American International College W
Becker College
   Leicester Campus M, W
   Worcester Campus M, W
Boston College M, W
Boston University M, W
Dean College M, W
Mount Ida College M, W
Northeastern University M, W
University of Massachusetts
   Amherst M, W
   Lowell M, W

Michigan

Aquinas College M, W
Concordia College M, W
Cornerstone College and Grand
   Rapids Baptist Seminary M, W
Eastern Michigan University M, W
Grand Valley State University W
Michigan Christian College M
Michigan State University M, W
Northern Michigan University W
Northwood University W
Oakland University M, W
Saginaw Valley State University M,
   W
Spring Arbor College M, W
University of Michigan W
Western Michigan University M

Minnesota

Mankato State University W
Moorhead State University W
St. Cloud State University W
University of Minnesota
   Duluth W
   Twin Cities W
Winona State University W

Mississippi

Belhaven College M
Hinds Community College M
Mary Holmes College M
Meridian Community College M
Mississippi State University W
William Carey College M, W

Missouri

Avila College M, W
Central Methodist College M, W
Columbia College M
Culver-Stockton College M
Drury College M, W
Harris Stowe State College M, W
Lincoln University M
Lindenwood College M, W
Missouri Southern State College M
Park College M, W
Research College of Nursing M, W
Rockhurst College M, W
St. Louis Community College
    Forest Park M
    Meramec M, W
St. Louis University M, W
Southwest Baptist University M, W
Southwest Missouri State University
    M, W
State Fair Community College M
Truman State University M, W
University of Missouri
    Columbia W
    Kansas City M
    Rolla M, W
    St. Louis M, W
William Woods University W

Montana

University of Montana-Missoula W

Nebraska

Central Community College M
College of St. Mary W
Concordia College M, W
Creighton University M, W
Dana College W
York College M, W

Nevada

University of Nevada: Las Vegas M

New Hampshire

Franklin Pierce College M, W
Hesser College M, W
New Hampshire College M, W
Notre Dame College M, W
University of New Hampshire M,
    W

New Jersey

Bloomfield College M
Burlington County College M, W
Caldwell College M
Essex County College M
Fairleigh Dickinson University
    Edward Williams College M
    Teaneck M
Georgian Court College W
Monmouth University M, W
Rider University M
Rutgers, The State University of
    New Jersey
    College of Engineering M, W
    College of Pharmacy M, W
    Cook College M, W
    Douglass College W
    Livingston College M, W
    Mason Gross School of the
      Arts M, W
    Rutgers College M, W
St. Peter's College M, W
Seton Hall University M, W

New Mexico

College of the Southwest W
University of New Mexico M, W

New York

Adelphi University M, W
Canisius College M, W

Cazenovia College M, W
City University of New York:
    Queens College M
College of St. Rose M, W
Concordia College M, W
Dominican College of Blauvelt M,
    W
Dowling College M
Fordham University M, W
Genesee Community College M, W
Hartwick College M
Hofstra University M, W
Houghton College M, W
Iona College M
Le Moyne College M, W
Long Island University
    Brooklyn Campus M
    C. W. Post Campus M, W
    Southampton College M, W
Manhattan College M, W
Marist College M, W
Mercy College M
Monroe Community College M, W
New York Institute of Technology
    M, W
Niagara County Community College
    M, W
Niagara University M, W
Nyack College M, W
Paul Smith's College M, W
Roberts Wesleyan College M, W
St. Bonaventure University M, W
St. Francis College M
St. John's University M, W
Siena College M, W
State University of New York
    Albany M, W
    Buffalo M, W
    Stony Brook M, W
Syracuse University M, W
Wagner College W

North Carolina

Appalachian State University M
Barton College M, W
Belmont Abbey College M
Brevard College M, W
Campbell University M, W
Catawba College M, W
Davidson College M, W
Duke University M, W
East Carolina University M, W
Elon College M, W
Gardner-Webb University M
High Point University M, W
Lees-McRae College M, W
Lenoir-Rhyne College M, W
Louisburg College M, W
Mars Hill College M, W
Montreat College M, W
Mount Olive College M
North Carolina State University M,
    W
Pembroke State University M
Pfeiffer College M, W
Queens College M, W
St. Andrews Presbyterian College
    M, W
University of North Carolina
    Asheville M, W
    Chapel Hill M, W
    Charlotte M, W
    Greensboro M, W
    Wilmington M, W
Wake Forest University M, W
Wingate University M, W

North Dakota

North Dakota State University W

Ohio

Bowling Green State University M

Cedarville College M
Cleveland State University M
Malone College M
Mount Vernon Nazarene College M
Ohio Dominican College M
Ohio State University: Columbus
    Campus M, W
Shawnee State University M
Southern State Community College
    M
Tiffin University M, W
University of Akron M
University of Dayton M, W
University of Findlay M, W
University of Rio Grande M
University of Toledo W
Walsh University M, W
Wright State University M, W
Xavier University M, W

Oklahoma

Bartlesville Wesleyan College M, W
Oklahoma Christian University of
    Science and Arts M, W
Oklahoma City University M, W
Oral Roberts University M, W
Phillips University M
St. Gregory's College M, W
University of Tulsa M, W

Oregon

Concordia University M, W
Portland State University W
University of Portland M, W
Western Baptist College M, W

Pennsylvania

Bloomsburg University of
    Pennsylvania M, W
California University of
    Pennsylvania M, W
Drexel University M
Duquesne University M, W
East Stroudsburg University of
    Pennsylvania M, W
Gannon University M, W
Geneva College M, W
Kutztown University of
    Pennsylvania M, W
La Salle University M, W
Lock Haven University of
    Pennsylvania M, W
Manor Junior College M, W
Mercyhurst College M, W
Millersville University of
    Pennsylvania M, W
Penn State University Park Campus
    M, W
Point Park College M
Robert Morris College M, W
St. Francis College M, W
St. Joseph's University M
St. Vincent College M, W
Seton Hill College W
Shippensburg University of
    Pennsylvania M, W
Temple University M, W
University of Pittsburgh M
Villanova University M, W
West Chester University of
    Pennsylvania M, W

Puerto Rico

Inter American University of Puerto
    Rico
    Guayama Campus M
    San German Campus M
University of Puerto Rico:
    Mayaguez Campus M

Rhode Island

Providence College M, W

University of Rhode Island M, W

South Carolina

Anderson College M, W
Charleston Southern University M,
    W
Clemson University M, W
Coastal Carolina University M
Coker College M, W
College of Charleston M, W
Erskine College M, W
Francis Marion University M, W
Furman University M, W
Lander University M
Limestone College M, W
Presbyterian College M, W
Southern Wesleyan University M
Spartanburg Methodist College M,
    W
University of South Carolina
    Aiken M
    Spartanburg M
Winthrop University M
Wofford College M, W

South Dakota

Dakota Wesleyan University W
University of Sioux Falls M, W

Tennessee

Belmont University M
Carson-Newman College M, W
Christian Brothers University W
David Lipscomb University M
King College M
Lambuth University M, W
Lee College M, W
Lincoln Memorial University M, W
Martin Methodist College M, W
Middle Tennessee State University
    W
Milligan College M
Tennessee Wesleyan College M, W
Tusculum College M, W
University of Memphis M
University of Tennessee: Martin M
Vanderbilt University M, W

Texas

Ambassador University M
Angelo State University W
Baylor University W
Dallas Baptist University W
East Texas State University W
St. Edward's University M, W
St. Mary's University M, W
Schreiner College M
Southern Methodist University M,
    W
Stephen F. Austin State University
    W
Texas A&M University W
Texas Lutheran College M, W
Texas Tech University W
Texas Wesleyan University M
University of North Texas W
University of Texas at Austin W
West Texas A&M University M, W

Vermont

Champlain College M, W
Green Mountain College M, W
University of Vermont M

Virginia

Bluefield College M
College of William and Mary M, W
George Mason University M, W
James Madison University M, W
Liberty University M, W
Longwood College M
Old Dominion University M, W

Radford University M, W
University of Richmond M, W
University of Virginia M, W
Virginia Commonwealth University M
Virginia Military Institute M
Virginia Polytechnic Institute and State University M, W

Washington

Central Washington University M, W
Edmonds Community College M, W
Evergreen State College M, W
Gonzaga University M, W
Northwest College M
Pierce College M
Seattle Pacific University M
Seattle University M, W
Shoreline Community College M
Spokane Community College M, W
Spokane Falls Community College M, W
Tacoma Community College M
University of Washington M, W
Washington State University W
Western Washington University M, W

West Virginia

Alderson-Broaddus College M
Davis and Elkins College M
Marshall University M
Salem-Teikyo University M
West Virginia University M, W
West Virginia Wesleyan College M, W
Wheeling Jesuit College M, W

Wisconsin

Marquette University M, W
Northland College M
University of Wisconsin
    Green Bay M, W
    Madison M, W

Softball

Alabama

Athens State College W
Auburn University W
Bevill State Community College W
Calhoun Community College W
Central Alabama Community College W
Chattahoochee Valley Community College W
Enterprise State Junior College W
Faulkner University W
Gadsden State Community College W
George C. Wallace State Community College at Selma W
Huntingdon College W
Jacksonville State University W
James H. Faulkner State Community College W
Lurleen B. Wallace State Junior College W
Miles College W
Northwest-Shoals Community College W
Samford University W
Snead State Community College W
Troy State University W
University of Alabama in Huntsville W

University of Alabama at Birmingham: Walker College W
University of Mobile W
University of West Alabama W
Wallace State College at Hanceville W

Arizona

Arizona State University W
Arizona Western College W
Glendale Community College W
Mesa Community College W
Pima Community College W
Scottsdale Community College W
South Mountain Community College W
University of Arizona W

Arkansas

University of Arkansas W

California

Azusa Pacific University W
California Baptist College W
California Polytechnic State University: San Luis Obispo W
California State University
    Bakersfield W
    Fresno W
    Fullerton W
    Long Beach W
    Northridge W
    San Bernardino W
Concordia University W
Point Loma Nazarene College W
St. Mary's College of California W
San Diego State University W
San Jose State University W
Southern California College W
Stanford University W
University of California
    Berkeley W
    Los Angeles W
    Riverside W
    Santa Barbara W
University of the Pacific W

Colorado

Adams State College W
Colorado Northwestern Community College W
Colorado School of Mines W
Fort Lewis College W
Mesa State College W
Northeastern Junior College W
Regis University W
University of Colorado at Colorado Springs W

Connecticut

Central Connecticut State University W
Fairfield University W
Mitchell College W
Quinnipiac College W
Teikyo-Post University W
University of Bridgeport W
University of Connecticut W
University of New Haven W

Delaware

Goldey-Beacom College W
University of Delaware W

Florida

Bethune-Cookman College W
Brevard Community College W
Central Florida Community College W
Chipola Junior College W
Daytona Beach Community College W

Eckerd College W
Florida Atlantic University W
Florida Community College at Jacksonville W
Florida Institute of Technology W
Florida Southern College W
Florida State University W
Gulf Coast Community College W
Hillsborough Community College W
Lake City Community College W
Manatee Community College W
Nova Southeastern University W
Okaloosa-Walton Community College W
Palm Beach Community College W
Pasco-Hernando Community College W
Rollins College W
St. Johns River Community College W
St. Leo College W
St. Petersburg Junior College W
St. Thomas University W
Stetson University W
Tallahassee Community College W
University of North Florida W
University of South Florida W
University of Tampa W
Valencia Community College W
Webber College W

Georgia

Abraham Baldwin Agricultural College W
Andrew College W
Augusta College W
Brewton-Parker College W
Columbus College W
Darton College W
Emmanuel College W
Georgia College W
Georgia Southern University W
Georgia Southwestern College W
Gordon College W
Kennesaw State College W
Macon College W
Mercer University W
Middle Georgia College W
Paine College W
Piedmont College W
Reinhardt College W
Shorter College W
Thomas College W
Valdosta State University W
West Georgia College W
Young Harris College W

Hawaii

Hawaii Pacific University W
University of Hawaii
    Hilo W
    Manoa W

Illinois

Belleville Area College W
Bradley University W
Carl Sandburg College W
Danville Area Community College W
De Paul University W
Eastern Illinois University W
Elgin Community College W
Highland Community College W
Illinois Eastern Community Colleges
    Lincoln Trail College M, W
    Olney Central College W
    Wabash Valley College W
Illinois Institute of Technology W
Illinois State University W
John A. Logan College W
Kaskaskia College W

Kishwaukee College W
Lake Land College W
Lewis University W
Lincoln College M, W
Lincoln Land Community College W
Loyola University of Chicago M, W
McHenry County College W
McKendree College W
Moraine Valley Community College W
Morton College W
Northeastern Illinois University W
Northwestern University W
Olivet Nazarene University W
Quincy University W
Rend Lake College W
St. Xavier University W
Southeastern Illinois College W
Southern Illinois University
    Carbondale W
    Edwardsville W
Trinity International University W
University of Illinois at Chicago W
Western Illinois University W

Indiana

Ball State University W
Bethel College W
Butler University W
Goshen College W
Grace College W
Huntington College W
Indiana Institute of Technology W
Indiana State University W
Indiana University Bloomington W
Indiana University-Purdue University Indianapolis W
Indiana Wesleyan University W
Marian College W
Oakland City University M, W
Purdue University W
St. Francis College W
St. Joseph's College W
St. Mary-of-the-Woods College W
Tri-State University W
University of Evansville W
University of Indianapolis W
University of Notre Dame W
University of Southern Indiana W
Valparaiso University W

Iowa

Briar Cliff College W
Drake University W
Ellsworth Community College W
Graceland College W
Grand View College W
Indian Hills Community College W
Iowa Central Community College W
Iowa Lakes Community College W
Iowa State University W
Iowa Wesleyan College W
Morningside College W
Muscatine Community College W
North Iowa Area Community College W
Northwestern College W
St. Ambrose University W
Teikyo Marycrest University W
University of Iowa W
University of Northern Iowa W
Waldorf College W
Westmar University W

Kansas

Baker University W
Benedictine College W
Bethany College W
Butler County Community College W

269

Colby Community College W
Emporia State University W
Fort Scott Community College W
Friends University W
Garden City Community College W
Hutchinson Community College W
Kansas City Kansas Community
    College W
Kansas Newman College W
Neosho County Community College
    W
Ottawa University W
Pratt Community College W
St. Mary College W
University of Kansas W
Wichita State University W

Kentucky

Bellarmine College W
Brescia College M, W
Cumberland College W
Eastern Kentucky University W
Georgetown College W
Kentucky State University W
Kentucky Wesleyan College W
Northern Kentucky University W
Pikeville College W
Sue Bennett College W
Transylvania University W
Union College W

Louisiana

Bossier Parish Community College
    W
Centenary College of Louisiana W
Louisiana Tech University W
Nicholls State University W
Northeast Louisiana University W
Northwestern State University W
Southeastern Louisiana University
    W
University of Southwestern
    Louisiana W

Maine

Husson College W
University of Maine W

Maryland

Bowie State University W
Charles County Community College
    W
Chesapeake College W
Columbia Union College W
Dundalk Community College W
Hagerstown Junior College W
Mount St. Mary's College W
Prince George's Community College
    W
Towson State University W
University of Maryland
    Baltimore County W
    College Park W
    Eastern Shore W

Massachusetts

American International College W
Becker College
    Leicester Campus W
    Worcester Campus W
Boston College W
Boston University W
Dean College W
Mount Ida College W
Northeastern University W
University of Massachusetts
    Amherst W

Michigan

Aquinas College W
Central Michigan University W
Concordia College W

Cornerstone College and Grand
    Rapids Baptist Seminary W
Eastern Michigan University W
Grand Valley State University W
Henry Ford Community College W
Hillsdale College W
Kellogg Community College W
Lake Superior State University W
Michigan Christian College W
Michigan State University W
Northwood University W
Saginaw Valley State University W
Spring Arbor College W
University of Michigan W
Wayne State University W
Western Michigan University W

Minnesota

Mankato State University W
Moorhead State University W
St. Cloud State University W
Southwest State University W
University of Minnesota
    Crookston W
    Duluth W
Winona State University W

Mississippi

Delta State University W
East Central Community College W
Hinds Community College W
Mary Holmes College W
Meridian Community College W
Mississippi State University W
Mississippi University for Women
    W
Southwest Mississippi Community
    College W

Missouri

Avila College W
Central Methodist College W
Central Missouri State University W
Columbia College W
Culver-Stockton College W
Hannibal-LaGrange College W
Lincoln University W
Lindenwood College W
Missouri Southern State College W
Missouri Western State College W
North Central Missouri College W
Park College W
St. Louis Community College
    Forest Park W
    Meramec W
St. Louis University W
Southeast Missouri State University
    W
Southwest Baptist University W
Southwest Missouri State University
    W
Truman State University W
University of Missouri
    Columbia W
    Kansas City W
    Rolla W
    St. Louis W
William Jewell College W
William Woods University W

Nebraska

College of St. Mary W
Concordia College W
Creighton University W
Dana College W
Doane College/Lincoln Campus W
Hastings College W
Midland Lutheran College W
Peru State College W

University of Nebraska
    Kearney W
    Lincoln W
    Omaha W
Wayne State College W

Nevada

University of Nevada: Las Vegas W

New Hampshire

Franklin Pierce College W
Hesser College W

New Jersey

Bloomfield College W
Burlington County College W
Caldwell College W
Georgian Court College W
Monmouth University W
Rider University W
Rutgers, The State University of
    New Jersey
    College of Engineering W
    College of Pharmacy W
    Cook College W
    Douglass College W
    Livingston College W
    Mason Gross School of the
        Arts W
    Rutgers College W
St. Peter's College W
Seton Hall University W

New Mexico

Eastern New Mexico University W
New Mexico Highlands University
    W
New Mexico State University W
University of New Mexico W

New York

Adelphi University W
Canisius College W
Cazenovia College W
City University of New York:
    Queens College W
College of St. Rose W
Concordia College W
Dominican College of Blauvelt W
Fordham University W
Genesee Community College W
Hofstra University W
Iona College W
Le Moyne College W
Long Island University
    Brooklyn Campus W
    C. W. Post Campus W
    Southampton College W
Manhattan College W
Marist College W
Mercy College W
Molloy College W
Monroe Community College W
New York Institute of Technology
    W
Niagara County Community College
    W
Niagara University W
Pace University W
St. Bonaventure University W
St. Francis College W
St. John's University W
St. Thomas Aquinas College W
Siena College W
State University of New York at
    Albany W
Wagner College W

North Carolina

Barber-Scotia College W
Barton College W
Campbell University W

East Carolina University W
Elon College W
Fayetteville State University W
Gardner-Webb University W
Johnson C. Smith University W
Lees-McRae College W
Lenoir-Rhyne College W
Livingstone College W
Louisburg College W
Mars Hill College W
Montreat College W
Mount Olive College W
North Carolina Central University
    W
Pembroke State University W
Pfeiffer College W
Queens College W
St. Andrews Presbyterian College W
St. Augustine's College W
University of North Carolina
    Chapel Hill W
    Charlotte W
    Greensboro W
    Wilmington W
Wingate University W
Winston-Salem State University W

North Dakota

Dickinson State University M, W
North Dakota State University W
University of North Dakota W

Ohio

Ashland University W
Bowling Green State University W
Cedarville College W
Cleveland State University W
Kent State University W
Malone College W
Miami University: Oxford Campus
    W
Mount Vernon Nazarene College W
Ohio Dominican College W
Ohio State University: Columbus
    Campus W
Ohio University W
Shawnee State University W
Southern State Community College
    W
Tiffin University W
University of Akron W
University of Dayton W
University of Findlay W
University of Rio Grande W
University of Toledo W
Urbana University W
Walsh University W
Wright State University W
Youngstown State University W

Oklahoma

Bacone College W
Cameron University M
Eastern Oklahoma State College W
Northeastern Oklahoma
    Agricultural and Mechanical
    College W
Oklahoma Baptist University W
Oklahoma Christian University of
    Science and Arts W
Oklahoma City University W
University of Central Oklahoma W
University of Oklahoma W
University of Tulsa W

Oregon

Clackamas Community College W
Concordia University W
Oregon Institute of Technology W
Portland State University W
University of Oregon W

Pennsylvania
Bloomsburg University of
  Pennsylvania W
California University of
  Pennsylvania W
Community College of Beaver
  County W
Drexel University W
East Stroudsburg University of
  Pennsylvania W
Edinboro University of
  Pennsylvania W
Gannon University W
Geneva College W
Indiana University of Pennsylvania
  W
Kutztown University of
  Pennsylvania W
Lock Haven University of
  Pennsylvania W
Mercyhurst College W
Millersville University of
  Pennsylvania W
Penn State University Park Campus
  W
Philadelphia College of Pharmacy
  and Science W
Point Park College W
Robert Morris College W
St. Francis College W
St. Joseph's University W
St. Vincent College W
Seton Hill College W
Shippensburg University of
  Pennsylvania W
Temple University W
Villanova University W
West Chester University of
  Pennsylvania W
Westminster College W

Puerto Rico
Inter American University of Puerto
  Rico: Guayama Campus M, W
University of Puerto Rico:
  Mayaguez Campus W

Rhode Island
Providence College W
University of Rhode Island W

South Carolina
Anderson College W
Charleston Southern University W
Claflin College W
Coastal Carolina University W
Coker College W
College of Charleston W
Erskine College W
Francis Marion University W
Furman University W
Lander University W
Limestone College W
Morris College W
North Greenville College W
South Carolina State University W
Southern Wesleyan University W
Spartanburg Methodist College W
University of South Carolina
      Aiken W
      Spartanburg W
Winthrop University W

South Dakota
Augustana College W
Dakota Wesleyan University W
Northern State University W
South Dakota State University W
University of Sioux Falls W
University of South Dakota W

Tennessee
Austin Peay State University W
Belmont University W
Bethel College W
Carson-Newman College W
Christian Brothers University W
Cleveland State Community College
  W
Freed-Hardeman University W
Jackson State Community College
  W
King College W
Lambuth University W
Lincoln Memorial University W
Martin Methodist College W
Middle Tennessee State University
  W
Milligan College W
Roane State Community College W
Tennessee Technological University
  W
Tennessee Wesleyan College W
Trevecca Nazarene University W
Tusculum College W
Union University W
University of Tennessee
      Chattanooga W
      Knoxville W
      Martin W

Texas
Abilene Christian University W
Baylor University W
Blinn College M
Houston Baptist University W
St. Edward's University W
St. Mary's University W
Southwest Texas State University W
Stephen F. Austin State University
  W
Texas A&M University W
Texas Lutheran College W
Texas Tech University W
Texas Wesleyan University W
University of Texas
      Arlington W
      Austin W
Vernon Regional Junior College W

Utah
College of Eastern Utah W
Dixie College W
Snow College W
Southern Utah University W
University of Utah W
Utah State University W
Utah Valley State College W

Vermont
Green Mountain College W

Virginia
Bluefield College W
George Mason University W
Hampton University W
Longwood College W
Norfolk State University W
Radford University W
St. Paul's College W
University of Virginia W
Virginia Polytechnic Institute and
  State University W
Virginia Union University W

Washington
Central Washington University W
Edmonds Community College W
Lower Columbia College W
Olympic College W
Pierce College W
St. Martin's College W
Shoreline Community College W

Spokane Community College W
Spokane Falls Community College
  W
University of Washington W
Walla Walla Community College W
Wenatchee Valley College W
Western Washington University W
Yakima Valley Community College
  W

West Virginia
Alderson-Broaddus College W
Bluefield State College W
Concord College W
Davis and Elkins College W
Marshall University W
Salem-Teikyo University W
Shepherd College W
West Liberty State College W
West Virginia Institute of
  Technology W
West Virginia State College W
West Virginia Wesleyan College W

Wisconsin
University of Wisconsin
  Green Bay W
  Madison W

Squash

New York
Nyack College M, W

Swimming

Alabama
Auburn University M, W
University of Alabama M, W

Alaska
University of Alaska Anchorage M

Arizona
Arizona State University M, W
Northern Arizona University M, W
University of Arizona M, W

Arkansas
Henderson State University M, W
John Brown University M, W
University of Arkansas
      Fayetteville M, W
      Little Rock M, W

California
California State University
      Bakersfield M, W
      Fresno M
      Northridge M, W
      San Bernardino M, W
Pepperdine University W
San Diego State University W
San Jose State University W
Stanford University M, W
University of California
      Berkeley M, W
      Irvine M, W
      Los Angeles W
      Santa Barbara M, W
University of the Pacific M, W
University of San Diego W
University of Southern California
  M, W

Colorado
Colorado School of Mines M, W
Colorado State University W
Metropolitan State College of
  Denver M, W
University of Denver M, W
University of Northern Colorado W

Connecticut
Central Connecticut State
  University M, W
Fairfield University M, W
University of Connecticut M, W

District of Columbia
American University M, W
George Washington University M,
  W
Howard University M, W

Florida
Brevard Community College M, W
Eckerd College M, W
Florida Atlantic University M, W
Florida State University M, W
University of Florida M, W
University of Miami M, W
University of Tampa M, W

Georgia
Darton College M, W
Georgia Institute of Technology M
Georgia Southern University M, W
Mercer University M, W
Morehouse College M
University of Georgia M, W

Hawaii
University of Hawaii at Manoa M,
  W

Illinois
Bradley University M, W
Illinois Institute of Technology M,
  W
Lincoln College M, W
Loyola University of Chicago M
Northeastern Illinois University M,
  W
Northwestern University M, W
Southern Illinois University at
  Carbondale M, W
University of Illinois
      Chicago M, W
      Urbana-Champaign W
Western Illinois University M, W

Indiana
Ball State University M, W
Butler University M, W
Indiana University Bloomington M,
  W
Purdue University M, W
University of Evansville M, W
University of Indianapolis M, W
University of Notre Dame M, W
Valparaiso University M, W
Vincennes University M, W

Iowa
Iowa State University M, W
University of Iowa M, W
University of Northern Iowa W

Kansas
University of Kansas M, W

Kentucky
Cumberland College M
Transylvania University M, W
Union College M, W
University of Kentucky M, W

271

University of Louisville M, W
Western Kentucky University M

Louisiana
Louisiana State University and
   Agricultural and Mechanical
   College M, W
Northeast Louisiana University M,
   W

Maine
University of Maine M, W

Maryland
Towson State University M, W
University of Maryland
      Baltimore County M, W
      College Park M, W

Massachusetts
Boston College W
Boston University M, W
Northeastern University W
University of Massachusetts
      Amherst M, W
      Lowell M

Michigan
Eastern Michigan University M, W
Grand Valley State University W
Hillsdale College W
Michigan State University M, W
Northern Michigan University W
Oakland University M, W
University of Michigan M, W
Wayne State University M, W

Minnesota
Mankato State University M, W
St. Cloud State University M, W
University of Minnesota: Twin
      Cities M, W

Mississippi
Delta State University M, W

Missouri
Drury College M, W
Lindenwood College M, W
St. Louis University M, W
Southwest Missouri State University
   M
University of Missouri
      Columbia M, W
      Rolla M
      St. Louis M, W
William Woods University W

Nebraska
University of Nebraska
      Kearney W
      Lincoln M, W

Nevada
University of Nevada
      Las Vegas M, W
      Reno W

New Hampshire
University of New Hampshire W

New Jersey
Rider University M, W

Rutgers, The State University of
   New Jersey
      College of Engineering M, W
      College of Pharmacy M, W
      Cook College M, W
      Douglass College W
      Livingston College M, W
      Mason Gross School of the
         Arts M, W
      Rutgers College M, W
St. Peter's College M, W
Seton Hall University M, W

New Mexico
New Mexico State University M, W
University of New Mexico M, W

New York
Adelphi University M, W
Canisius College M, W
City University of New York:
      Queens College M, W
College of St. Rose M, W
Fordham University M, W
Iona College M
Manhattan College W
Marist College M, W
Monroe Community College M, W
Niagara University M, W
St. Bonaventure University M, W
St. Francis College M, W
St. John's University M, W
State University of New York at
      Buffalo M, W
Syracuse University M, W

North Carolina
Davidson College M, W
East Carolina University M, W
North Carolina State University M,
   W
Pfeiffer College W
University of North Carolina
      Chapel Hill M, W
      Wilmington M, W

North Dakota
University of North Dakota M, W

Ohio
Ashland University M, W
Bowling Green State University M,
   W
Cleveland State University M, W
Miami University: Oxford Campus
   M, W
Ohio State University: Columbus
   Campus M, W
Ohio University M, W
University of Findlay M, W
University of Toledo M, W
Walsh University W
Wright State University M, W
Xavier University M, W

Pennsylvania
Bloomsburg University of
   Pennsylvania M, W
Drexel University M, W
Duquesne University M, W
Edinboro University of
   Pennsylvania M, W
Gannon University M, W
Indiana University of Pennsylvania
   M, W
Kutztown University of
   Pennsylvania M, W
La Salle University M, W
Lock Haven University of
   Pennsylvania W
Millersville University of
   Pennsylvania W

Penn State University Park Campus
   M, W
St. Francis College W
Shippensburg University of
   Pennsylvania M, W
University of Pittsburgh M, W
Villanova University M, W
West Chester University of
   Pennsylvania M, W
Westminster College W

Puerto Rico
University of Puerto Rico
      La Montana Regional College
      M, W
      Mayaguez Campus M, W
University of the Sacred Heart M,
   W

Rhode Island
Providence College M, W
University of Rhode Island M, W

South Carolina
Clemson University M, W
College of Charleston M, W

South Dakota
South Dakota State University M,
   W
University of South Dakota M, W

Tennessee
University of Tennessee: Knoxville
   M, W

Texas
Rice University W
Southern Methodist University M,
   W
Texas A&M University M, W
Texas Christian University M, W
University of Houston W
University of Texas at Austin M, W

Utah
Brigham Young University M, W
University of Utah M, W

Virginia
James Madison University M, W
Old Dominion University M, W
University of Richmond W
University of Virginia M, W
Virginia Military Institute M
Virginia Polytechnic Institute and
   State University M, W

Washington
Central Washington University M,
   W
Evergreen State College M, W
University of Washington M, W
Washington State University W

West Virginia
Salem-Teikyo University M, W
West Virginia University M, W
West Virginia Wesleyan College M,
   W
Wheeling Jesuit College M, W

Wisconsin
University of Wisconsin
      Green Bay M, W
      Madison M, W

Wyoming
University of Wyoming M, W

Table tennis

Arizona
South Mountain Community
   College M, W

Maryland
Chesapeake College M

Ohio
Ohio State University: Columbus
   Campus M, W

Pennsylvania
La Salle University M, W

Puerto Rico
Inter American University of Puerto
   Rico: Metropolitan Campus M,
   W
University of Puerto Rico:
   Mayaguez Campus M, W

South Carolina
Anderson College M, W
South Carolina State University M

Texas
Rice University M, W

Washington
Central Washington University M,
   W

Tennis

Alabama
Alabama Agricultural and
   Mechanical University M
Auburn University M, W
Birmingham-Southern College M,
   W
Central Alabama Community
   College M, W
Chattahoochee Valley Community
   College M, W
Enterprise State Junior College M,
   W
George C. Wallace State
   Community College at Selma M,
   W
Huntingdon College M, W
Jacksonville State University M, W
James H. Faulkner State
   Community College M, W
Jefferson State Community College
   M, W
Lurleen B. Wallace State Junior
   College M
Miles College M, W
Northwest-Shoals Community
   College M, W
Samford University M, W
Snead State Community College W
Spring Hill College M, W
Troy State University M, W
University of Alabama
      Birmingham M, W
      Huntsville M, W
      Tuscaloosa M, W
University of Mobile M, W
University of Montevallo W
University of North Alabama M, W
University of West Alabama M, W
Wallace State College at Hanceville
   M, W

Arizona

Arizona State University M, W
Glendale Community College M, W
Northern Arizona University M, W
Pima Community College M, W
Scottsdale Community College M, W
South Mountain Community College M, W
University of Arizona M, W

Arkansas

Arkansas State University W
Harding University M, W
Henderson State University W
John Brown University M, W
Lyon College M, W
University of Arkansas
    Fayetteville M, W
    Little Rock M, W

California

Azusa Pacific University M
Biola University W
California Baptist College M
California Polytechnic State University: San Luis Obispo M, W
California State Polytechnic University: Pomona M, W
California State University
    Bakersfield M, W
    Fresno M
    Fullerton W
    Long Beach W
    Los Angeles M, W
    Northridge W
    Sacramento M, W
Dominican College of San Rafael M, W
Loyola Marymount University W
Marymount College M, W
Pepperdine University M, W
Point Loma Nazarene College M, W
St. Mary's College of California M, W
San Diego State University M, W
San Jose State University M, W
Southern California College M, W
Stanford University M, W
United States International University M, W
University of California
    Berkeley M, W
    Irvine M, W
    Los Angeles M, W
    Riverside M, W
    Santa Barbara M, W
University of the Pacific M, W
University of San Diego M, W
University of San Francisco M, W
University of Southern California M, W
Westmont College M, W

Colorado

Colorado School of Mines M
Colorado State University M, W
Mesa State College M, W
Metropolitan State College of Denver M, W
Northeastern Junior College M, W
Regis University M, W
University of Colorado
    Boulder M, W
    Colorado Springs M, W
University of Denver M, W
University of Northern Colorado M, W
University of Southern Colorado M, W

Connecticut

Central Connecticut State University M, W
Fairfield University M, W
Quinnipiac College M, W
University of Connecticut M, W
University of Hartford M, W
University of New Haven M

Delaware

Delaware State University M, W

District of Columbia

American University M, W
George Washington University M, W
Georgetown University W
Howard University M, W

Florida

Bethune-Cookman College M, W
Eckerd College M, W
Embry-Riddle Aeronautical University M
Flagler College M, W
Florida Atlantic University M, W
Florida Community College at Jacksonville W
Florida Institute of Technology M
Florida International University M, W
Florida Southern College M, W
Florida State University M, W
Hillsborough Community College W
Lynn University M, W
Nova Southeastern University W
Palm Beach Atlantic College M, W
Palm Beach Community College M, W
Rollins College M, W
St. Leo College M, W
St. Thomas University M, W
Stetson University M, W
University of Central Florida M, W
University of Florida M, W
University of Miami M, W
University of North Florida M, W
University of South Florida M, W
University of Tampa M, W
University of West Florida M, W
Webber College M, W

Georgia

Abraham Baldwin Agricultural College M, W
Andrew College M, W
Augusta College M, W
Berry College M, W
Brenau University W
Brewton-Parker College M, W
Clark Atlanta University M, W
Clayton State College W
Columbus College M, W
Darton College M, W
Fort Valley State College M, W
Georgia College M, W
Georgia Southern University M, W
Georgia Southwestern College M, W
Gordon College W
Kennesaw State College W
Mercer University M, W
Middle Georgia College W
Morehouse College M
North Georgia College M, W
Piedmont College M, W
Savannah State College W
Shorter College M, W
Southern College of Technology M
Thomas College M, W
University of Georgia M, W
Valdosta State University M, W

West Georgia College M, W
Young Harris College W

Hawaii

Hawaii Pacific University M, W
University of Hawaii
    Hilo M, W
    Manoa M, W

Idaho

Albertson College W
Boise State University M, W
Idaho State University M, W
Lewis-Clark State College M, W
Northwest Nazarene College W
University of Idaho M, W

Illinois

Belleville Area College M, W
Bradley University M, W
Chicago State University M, W
De Paul University M, W
Elgin Community College M, W
Illinois Eastern Community Colleges: Olney Central College M
Illinois State University M, W
John A. Logan College M, W
Lake Land College M
Lewis and Clark Community College M, W
Lewis University M, W
McHenry County College M, W
McKendree College M, W
Moraine Valley Community College W
Northeastern Illinois University M, W
Northwestern University M, W
Olivet Nazarene University M, W
Quincy University W
Rosary College W
Southern Illinois University
    Carbondale M, W
    Edwardsville M, W
Trinity International University M, W
University of Illinois
    Chicago M, W
    Urbana-Champaign M, W
Western Illinois University M, W

Indiana

Ancilla College M, W
Ball State University M, W
Bethel College M, W
Butler University M, W
Goshen College M, W
Grace College M
Huntington College M, W
Indiana State University M, W
Indiana University Bloomington M, W
Indiana University-Purdue University Indianapolis M, W
Indiana Wesleyan University M, W
Marian College M, W
Purdue University M, W
St. Francis College W
Tri-State University M, W
University of Evansville M, W
University of Indianapolis M, W
University of Notre Dame M, W
University of Southern Indiana M, W
Valparaiso University M, W
Vincennes University M, W

Iowa

Drake University M, W
Graceland College M, W
Iowa State University W

Northwestern College M, W
St. Ambrose University M, W
University of Iowa M, W
University of Northern Iowa W
Westmar University M, W

Kansas

Baker University M, W
Barton County Community College M, W
Benedictine College M, W
Bethany College M, W
Bethel College M, W
Butler County Community College M, W
Emporia State University M, W
Fort Hays State University W
Friends University M, W
Hesston College M, W
Hutchinson Community College M, W
Independence Community College M, W
Kansas State University W
Ottawa University M, W
Pratt Community College M, W
Southwestern College M, W
University of Kansas M, W
Wichita State University M, W

Kentucky

Bellarmine College M, W
Brescia College M, W
Cumberland College M, W
Eastern Kentucky University M, W
Georgetown College M, W
Kentucky State University M, W
Kentucky Wesleyan College M, W
Morehead State University M, W
Murray State University M, W
Northern Kentucky University M, W
Transylvania University M, W
Union College M, W
University of Kentucky M, W
University of Louisville M, W
Western Kentucky University M, W

Louisiana

Bossier Parish Community College M, W
Centenary College of Louisiana M, W
Grambling State University M, W
Louisiana College W
Louisiana State University and Agricultural and Mechanical College M, W
Louisiana Tech University W
Nicholls State University W
Northeast Louisiana University M, W
Northwestern State University W
Southeastern Louisiana University M, W
Tulane University M, W
University of New Orleans M, W
University of Southwestern Louisiana M, W

Maryland

Charles County Community College M, W
Dundalk Community College M, W
Morgan State University M, W
Mount St. Mary's College M, W
Towson State University M, W
University of Maryland
    Baltimore County M, W
    College Park M, W
    Eastern Shore M, W

Massachusetts
Becker College
  Leicester Campus M
  Worcester Campus M
Boston College W
Boston University W
Dean College M
University of Massachusetts
  Amherst M, W
  Lowell M, W

Michigan
Aquinas College M, W
Cornerstone College and Grand
  Rapids Baptist Seminary M
Eastern Michigan University M, W
Grand Valley State University W
Henry Ford Community College M,
  W
Hillsdale College M, W
Lake Superior State University M,
  W
Michigan State University M, W
Michigan Technological University
  W
Northern Michigan University W
Northwood University M, W
Oakland University W
Saginaw Valley State University W
Spring Arbor College M, W
University of Michigan M, W
Wayne State University M, W
Western Michigan University M, W

Minnesota
Bemidji State University W
Mankato State University M, W
Moorhead State University W
St. Cloud State University M, W
Southwest State University W
University of Minnesota
  Duluth M, W
  Twin Cities M, W
Winona State University M, W

Mississippi
Alcorn State University M, W
Belhaven College M, W
Blue Mountain College W
Delta State University M, W
Hinds Community College M, W
Holmes Community College M, W
Meridian Community College M, W
Mississippi State University M, W
Mississippi University for Women
  W
Southwest Mississippi Community
  College M
University of Mississippi M, W
University of Southern Mississippi
  M, W
William Carey College M, W

Missouri
Central Methodist College M, W
Drury College M, W
Jefferson College M
Lincoln University W
Missouri Southern State College W
Missouri Western State College W
Research College of Nursing M, W
Rockhurst College M, W
St. Louis Community College at
  Forest Park M
St. Louis University M, W
Southeast Missouri State University
  W
Southwest Baptist University M, W
Southwest Missouri State University
  M, W
Truman State University M, W

University of Missouri
  Kansas City M, W
  St. Louis M, W
William Woods University W

Montana
Montana State University
  Billings M, W
  Bozeman M, W
University of Montana-Missoula M,
  W

Nebraska
College of St. Mary W
Concordia College M, W
Creighton University M, W
Hastings College M, W
Midland Lutheran College M, W
University of Nebraska
  Kearney M, W
  Lincoln M, W
York College M, W

Nevada
University of Nevada
  Las Vegas M, W
  Reno M, W

New Hampshire
Franklin Pierce College M, W

New Jersey
Burlington County College M, W
Caldwell College M, W
Fairleigh Dickinson University
  Edward Williams College M,
    W
  Teaneck M, W
Monmouth University M, W
Rider University M, W
Rutgers, The State University of
  New Jersey
  College of Engineering M, W
  College of Pharmacy M, W
  Cook College M, W
  Douglass College W
  Livingston College M, W
  Mason Gross School of the
    Arts M, W
  Rutgers College M, W
St. Peter's College M, W
Seton Hall University M, W

New Mexico
Eastern New Mexico University W
New Mexico Military Institute M
New Mexico State University M, W
University of New Mexico M, W

New York
Adelphi University M, W
Canisius College M, W
Cazenovia College M, W
City University of New York:
  Queens College M, W
College of St. Rose M, W
Concordia College M, W
Dowling College M, W
Fordham University M, W
Hofstra University M, W
Iona College M, W
Le Moyne College M, W
Manhattan College M, W
Marist College M, W
Mercy College M
Molloy College W
Monroe Community College M, W
Niagara University M, W
Pace University M, W
St. Bonaventure University M, W
St. Francis College M, W
St. John's University M, W

State University of New York at
  Buffalo M, W
Syracuse University W
Wagner College M, W

North Carolina
Appalachian State University M, W
Barber-Scotia College M, W
Barton College M, W
Belmont Abbey College M, W
Campbell University M, W
Catawba College M, W
Craven Community College M, W
Davidson College W
Duke University M, W
East Carolina University M, W
Elon College M, W
Fayetteville State University W
Gardner-Webb University M, W
High Point University M, W
Johnson C. Smith University M
Lees-McRae College M, W
Lenoir-Rhyne College M, W
Livingstone College M
Louisburg College M, W
Mars Hill College M, W
Mount Olive College M, W
North Carolina Central University
  M, W
North Carolina State University M,
  W
Peace College W
Pfeiffer College M, W
Queens College M, W
St. Andrews Presbyterian College
  M, W
St. Augustine's College M
University of North Carolina
  Asheville M, W
  Chapel Hill M, W
  Charlotte M, W
  Greensboro M, W
  Wilmington M, W
Wake Forest University M, W
Western Carolina University W
Wingate University M, W
Winston-Salem State University M,
  W

North Dakota
Dickinson State University M, W

Ohio
Bowling Green State University M,
  W
Cedarville College M, W
Cleveland State University W
Lake Erie College W
Malone College M, W
Miami University: Oxford Campus
  M, W
Mount Vernon Nazarene College
  M, W
Ohio State University: Columbus
  Campus M, W
Shawnee State University W
Sinclair Community College M, W
Tiffin University M, W
University of Akron M, W
University of Dayton M, W
University of Findlay M, W
University of Toledo M, W
Walsh University M, W
Wright State University M, W
Xavier University M, W
Youngstown State University M, W

Oklahoma
Cameron University M
East Central University W
Oklahoma Baptist University M

Oklahoma Christian University of
  Science and Arts M, W
Oklahoma City University M, W
Oral Roberts University M, W
St. Gregory's College M, W
Southwestern Oklahoma State
  University M, W
University of Central Oklahoma M,
  W
University of Oklahoma M, W
University of Tulsa M, W

Oregon
Portland State University W
University of Oregon M, W
University of Portland M, W

Pennsylvania
Bloomsburg University of
  Pennsylvania W
California University of
  Pennsylvania W
Carlow College W
Cheyney University of Pennsylvania
  M, W
Drexel University M
Duquesne University M, W
Edinboro University of
  Pennsylvania M, W
Gannon University M, W
Geneva College M, W
Indiana University of Pennsylvania
  W
Kutztown University of
  Pennsylvania M, W
La Salle University M, W
Mercyhurst College M, W
Millersville University of
  Pennsylvania M, W
Penn State University Park Campus
  M, W
Robert Morris College M, W
St. Francis College M, W
St. Joseph's University M, W
St. Vincent College M
Seton Hill College W
Shippensburg University of
  Pennsylvania W
Temple University M, W
University of Pittsburgh W
Villanova University M, W
West Chester University of
  Pennsylvania M, W
Westminster College W

Puerto Rico
Inter American University of Puerto
  Rico: San German Campus M, W
University of Puerto Rico
  Bayamon Technological
    University College M, W
  Mayaguez Campus M, W
University of the Sacred Heart M,
  W

Rhode Island
Providence College M, W

South Carolina
Anderson College M, W
Charleston Southern University M,
  W
Clemson University M, W
Coastal Carolina University M, W
Coker College M, W
College of Charleston M, W
Erskine College M, W
Francis Marion University M, W
Furman University M, W
Lander University M, W
Limestone College M, W
North Greenville College M

Presbyterian College M, W
South Carolina State University M, W
Spartanburg Methodist College W
University of South Carolina
    Aiken M
    Columbia M, W
    Spartanburg M, W
Winthrop University M, W
Wofford College M, W

South Dakota

Northern State University W
University of Sioux Falls W
University of South Dakota M, W

Tennessee

Austin Peay State University M, W
Belmont University M, W
Bethel College W
Carson-Newman College M, W
Christian Brothers University M, W
David Lipscomb University M, W
East Tennessee State University M, W
Freed-Hardeman University M, W
Lambuth University M, W
Lee College M, W
Lincoln Memorial University M, W
Martin Methodist College M, W
Middle Tennessee State University M, W
Milligan College M, W
Tennessee Technological University M, W
Tennessee Wesleyan College W
Union University M, W
University of Memphis M, W
University of Tennessee
    Chattanooga M, W
    Knoxville M, W
    Martin M, W
Vanderbilt University M, W

Texas

Abilene Christian University M, W
Ambassador University M, W
Baylor University M, W
Collin County Community College District M
Concordia Lutheran College M, W
Lamar University—Beaumont M, W
Laredo Community College M, W
Lee College W
McLennan Community College W
Rice University M, W
St. Edward's University M, W
St. Mary's University M, W
Sam Houston State University W
Schreiner College M, W
Southern Methodist University M, W
Southwest Texas State University M, W
Stephen F. Austin State University W
Texas A&M University M, W
Texas A&M University-Kingsville M, W
Texas Christian University M, W
Texas Lutheran College M, W
Texas Tech University M, W
Texas Wesleyan University M, W
Texas Woman's University W
University of Houston M, W
University of North Texas M, W
University of Texas
    Arlington M, W
    Austin M, W
    San Antonio M, W
Weatherford College M
West Texas A&M University M, W

Utah

Brigham Young University M, W
Southern Utah University W
University of Utah M, W
Utah State University M, W
Weber State University M, W

Virginia

Bluefield College M, W
Clinch Valley College of the University of Virginia M, W
College of William and Mary M, W
George Mason University M, W
Hampton University M
James Madison University M, W
Liberty University M
Longwood College W
Old Dominion University M, W
Radford University M, W
St. Paul's College M, W
University of Richmond M, W
University of Virginia M, W
Virginia Commonwealth University M, W
Virginia Intermont College M, W
Virginia Military Institute M
Virginia Polytechnic Institute and State University M, W
Virginia Union University M, W

Washington

Eastern Washington University M, W
Gonzaga University M, W
Lower Columbia College W
Seattle University M, W
Shoreline Community College M, W
Spokane Community College M, W
Spokane Falls Community College M, W
University of Washington M, W
Walla Walla Community College M, W
Washington State University M, W
Yakima Valley Community College M, W

West Virginia

Bluefield State College M, W
Concord College M, W
Davis and Elkins College M, W
Marshall University W
West Liberty State College M, W
West Virginia Institute of Technology M, W
West Virginia University M, W
West Virginia Wesleyan College M, W

Wisconsin

Marquette University M, W
University of Wisconsin
    Green Bay M, W
    Madison M, W

Track and field

Alabama

Alabama Agricultural and Mechanical University M, W
Alabama State University M, W
Auburn University M, W
Chattahoochee Valley Community College M, W
Gadsden State Community College M, W
Lawson State Community College M

Miles College M, W
Troy State University M, W
University of Alabama
    Birmingham M, W
    Tuscaloosa M, W
Wallace State College at Hanceville M, W

Arizona

Arizona State University M, W
Glendale Community College M, W
Mesa Community College M, W
Northern Arizona University M, W
Pima Community College M, W
Scottsdale Community College M, W
South Mountain Community College W
University of Arizona M, W

Arkansas

Arkansas State University M, W
University of Arkansas
    Fayetteville M, W
    Little Rock M, W
    Pine Bluff M, W

California

Azusa Pacific University M, W
Biola University M, W
California Baptist College M, W
California Polytechnic State University: San Luis Obispo M, W
California State Polytechnic University: Pomona M, W
California State University
    Bakersfield M, W
    Fresno M
    Fullerton M, W
    Long Beach M, W
    Los Angeles M, W
    Northridge M, W
    Sacramento M, W
Fresno Pacific College M, W
Point Loma Nazarene College M, W
San Diego State University W
Southern California College M, W
Stanford University M, W
University of California
    Berkeley M, W
    Irvine M, W
    Los Angeles M, W
    Riverside M, W
    Santa Barbara M, W
University of Southern California M, W
Westmont College M, W

Colorado

Adams State College M, W
Colorado School of Mines M, W
Colorado State University W
University of Colorado at Boulder M, W
University of Northern Colorado M, W
Western State College of Colorado M, W

Connecticut

Central Connecticut State University M, W
University of Connecticut M, W
University of New Haven M

Delaware

Delaware State University M, W

District of Columbia

Georgetown University M, W

Howard University M, W

Florida

Bethune-Cookman College M, W
Brevard Community College M, W
Florida Agricultural and Mechanical University M, W
Florida Community College at Jacksonville M, W
Florida International University M, W
Florida Memorial College M
Florida State University M, W
University of Central Florida M, W
University of Florida M, W
University of Miami M, W

Georgia

Fort Valley State College M, W
Georgia Institute of Technology M, W
Morehouse College M
Paine College M, W
Savannah State College M, W
Shorter College M
University of Georgia M, W

Idaho

Boise State University M, W
College of Southern Idaho M, W
Idaho State University M, W
North Idaho College M, W
Northwest Nazarene College M, W
Ricks College M, W
University of Idaho M, W

Illinois

Chicago State University M, W
Danville Area Community College M, W
De Paul University M, W
Eastern Illinois University M, W
Illinois State University M, W
Lewis University M, W
Loyola University of Chicago M, W
Olivet Nazarene University M, W
Southern Illinois University
    Carbondale M, W
    Edwardsville M, W
University of Illinois at Urbana-Champaign M, W
Western Illinois University M, W

Indiana

Ball State University M, W
Butler University M, W
Goshen College M, W
Grace College M, W
Huntington College M, W
Indiana State University M, W
Indiana University Bloomington M, W
Indiana Wesleyan University M, W
Marian College M, W
Purdue University M, W
St. Joseph's College M, W
Tri-State University M, W
University of Indianapolis M, W
University of Notre Dame M, W
Valparaiso University M, W
Vincennes University M, W

Iowa

Drake University M, W
Graceland College M, W
Iowa State University M, W
Iowa Wesleyan College M, W
Morningside College M, W
Northwestern College M, W
St. Ambrose University M, W
University of Iowa M, W
University of Northern Iowa M, W

Westmar University M, W

Kansas

Baker University M, W
Barton County Community College M, W
Benedictine College M, W
Bethany College M, W
Bethel College M, W
Butler County Community College M, W
Colby Community College M, W
Emporia State University M, W
Fort Hays State University M, W
Garden City Community College M, W
Hutchinson Community College M, W
Kansas City Kansas Community College W
Kansas State University W
MidAmerica Nazarene College M, W
Neosho County Community College M, W
Ottawa University M, W
Pratt Community College M, W
Southwestern College M, W
University of Kansas M, W
Wichita State University M, W

Kentucky

Cumberland College M, W
Eastern Kentucky University M, W
Kentucky State University M, W
Murray State University M, W
University of Louisville M, W
Western Kentucky University M, W

Louisiana

Grambling State University M, W
Louisiana State University and Agricultural and Mechanical College M, W
Louisiana Tech University M, W
Nicholls State University M, W
Northeast Louisiana University M, W
Northwestern State University M, W
Southeastern Louisiana University M, W
Tulane University M, W
University of New Orleans M, W
University of Southwestern Louisiana M, W

Maine

University of Maine M, W

Maryland

Bowie State University M, W
Columbia Union College M, W
Hagerstown Junior College M, W
Morgan State University M, W
Mount St. Mary's College M, W
Towson State University M, W
University of Maryland
    Baltimore County M, W
    College Park M, W
    Eastern Shore M, W

Massachusetts

Boston College M, W
Boston University M, W
Northeastern University M, W
University of Massachusetts
    Amherst M, W
    Lowell M, W

Michigan

Aquinas College M, W

Central Michigan University M, W
Eastern Michigan University M, W
Hillsdale College M, W
Lake Superior State University M, W
Macomb Community College M, W
Michigan Christian College M, W
Michigan State University M, W
Northwood University M, W
Saginaw Valley State University M, W
University of Michigan M, W
Western Michigan University M, W

Minnesota

Bemidji State University M, W
Mankato State University M, W
Moorhead State University M, W
St. Cloud State University M, W
University of Minnesota
    Duluth M, W
    Twin Cities M, W
Winona State University W

Mississippi

Alcorn State University M, W
Hinds Community College M
Meridian Community College M, W
Mississippi State University M, W
University of Mississippi M, W
University of Southern Mississippi M, W

Missouri

Central Methodist College M, W
Central Missouri State University M, W
Harris Stowe State College W
Lincoln University M, W
Lindenwood College M, W
Missouri Southern State College M, W
Park College M, W
Southeast Missouri State University M, W
Southwest Baptist University M, W
Southwest Missouri State University M, W
Truman State University M, W
University of Missouri
    Columbia M, W
    Kansas City M, W
    Rolla M, W
William Jewell College M, W

Montana

Montana State University-Bozeman M, W
University of Montana-Missoula M, W

Nebraska

Chadron State College M, W
Concordia College M, W
Dana College M, W
Doane College/Lincoln Campus M, W
Hastings College M, W
Midland Lutheran College M, W
University of Nebraska
    Kearney M, W
    Lincoln M, W
Wayne State College M, W

Nevada

University of Nevada
    Las Vegas W
    Reno W

New Jersey

Essex County College M, W

Fairleigh Dickinson University
    Edward Williams College M, W
    Teaneck M, W
Monmouth University M, W
Rider University M, W
Rutgers, The State University of New Jersey
    College of Engineering M, W
    College of Pharmacy M, W
    Cook College M, W
    Douglass College W
    Livingston College M, W
    Mason Gross School of the Arts M, W
    Rutgers College M, W
St. Peter's College M, W
Seton Hall University M, W

New Mexico

New Mexico Military Institute M
New Mexico State University M, W
University of New Mexico M, W

New York

Canisius College M, W
City University of New York: Queens College M, W
College of St. Rose M
Fordham University M, W
Houghton College M, W
Iona College M
Long Island University
    Brooklyn Campus M, W
    C. W. Post Campus M, W
Manhattan College M, W
Marist College M, W
New York Institute of Technology M, W
Roberts Wesleyan College M, W
St. Francis College M, W
St. John's University M, W
State University of New York
    Albany M, W
    Buffalo M, W
    College of Technology at Alfred M, W
Syracuse University M, W
Wagner College M, W

North Carolina

Appalachian State University M, W
Barber-Scotia College M, W
Brevard College M, W
Campbell University M, W
Davidson College W
East Carolina University M, W
Elon College M
Fayetteville State University W
High Point University M
Johnson C. Smith University M, W
Lees-McRae College W
Livingstone College M, W
North Carolina Agricultural and Technical State University M, W
North Carolina Central University M, W
North Carolina State University M, W
Pembroke State University M
St. Augustine's College M, W
University of North Carolina
    Chapel Hill M, W
    Charlotte M, W
    Wilmington M
Wake Forest University M, W
Western Carolina University M, W
Winston-Salem State University M, W

North Dakota

Dickinson State University M, W

Minot State University M, W
North Dakota State College of Science M, W
North Dakota State University M, W
University of North Dakota M, W

Ohio

Ashland University M, W
Bowling Green State University M, W
Cedarville College M, W
Kent State University M, W
Malone College M, W
Miami University: Oxford Campus M, W
Ohio State University: Columbus Campus M, W
Ohio University M, W
University of Akron M, W
University of Dayton W
University of Findlay M, W
University of Rio Grande M, W
University of Toledo M, W
Urbana University M, W
Walsh University M, W
Youngstown State University M, W

Oklahoma

Oklahoma Baptist University M, W
Oklahoma Christian University of Science and Arts M, W
Oral Roberts University M, W
Southwestern Oklahoma State University M, W
University of Central Oklahoma M, W
University of Oklahoma M, W
University of Tulsa M, W

Oregon

Chemeketa Community College M, W
Clackamas Community College M, W
Linn-Benton Community College M, W
Mount Hood Community College M, W
Oregon Institute of Technology M, W
Portland State University M, W
University of Oregon M, W
University of Portland M, W

Pennsylvania

Cheyney University of Pennsylvania M, W
Drexel University M
Duquesne University M, W
East Stroudsburg University of Pennsylvania M, W
Edinboro University of Pennsylvania M, W
Geneva College M, W
Indiana University of Pennsylvania M, W
Kutztown University of Pennsylvania M, W
La Salle University M, W
Lock Haven University of Pennsylvania M, W
Millersville University of Pennsylvania M, W
Penn State University Park Campus M, W
Robert Morris College M, W
St. Francis College M, W
St. Joseph's University M, W
Shippensburg University of Pennsylvania M, W
Temple University M, W

University of Pittsburgh M, W
Villanova University M, W
West Chester University of
  Pennsylvania M, W

Puerto Rico

Inter American University of Puerto Rico
  Fajardo Campus M, W
  Metropolitan Campus M, W
  San German Campus M, W
University of Puerto Rico
  Bayamon Technological University College M, W
  La Montana Regional College M, W
  Mayaguez Campus M, W
University of the Sacred Heart M, W

Rhode Island

Providence College M, W
University of Rhode Island M, W

South Carolina

Anderson College M, W
Charleston Southern University M, W
Claflin College M, W
Clemson University M, W
Coastal Carolina University M, W
Francis Marion University M, W
Furman University M, W
Morris College M, W
South Carolina State University M, W
Winthrop University M, W
Wofford College W

South Dakota

Augustana College M, W
Black Hills State University M, W
Dakota State University M, W
Dakota Wesleyan University M, W
Huron University M, W
Mount Marty College M, W
Northern State University M, W
South Dakota State University M, W
University of Sioux Falls M, W
University of South Dakota M, W

Tennessee

Austin Peay State University M, W
Belmont University M, W
David Lipscomb University M
East Tennessee State University M, W
Martin Methodist College M, W
Middle Tennessee State University M, W
University of Tennessee
  Chattanooga M, W
  Knoxville M, W
  Martin M, W
Vanderbilt University W

Texas

Abilene Christian University M, W
Ambassador University M, W
Angelo State University M, W
Baylor University M, W
East Texas State University M, W
Lamar University—Beaumont M, W
Odessa College W
Prairie View A&M University W
Rice University M, W
Sam Houston State University M, W
Southern Methodist University M, W

Southwest Texas State University M, W
Stephen F. Austin State University M, W
Texas A&M University M, W
Texas Christian University M, W
Texas Tech University M, W
University of Houston M, W
University of North Texas M, W
University of Texas
  Arlington M, W
  Austin M, W
  San Antonio M, W
Wayland Baptist University M, W

Utah

Brigham Young University M, W
Southern Utah University M, W
University of Utah M, W
Utah State University M, W
Weber State University M, W

Virginia

College of William and Mary M, W
George Mason University M, W
Hampton University M, W
James Madison University M, W
Liberty University M, W
Norfolk State University M, W
St. Paul's College M, W
University of Virginia M, W
Virginia Commonwealth University M, W
Virginia Military Institute M
Virginia Polytechnic Institute and State University M, W
Virginia Union University M, W

Washington

Central Washington University M, W
Eastern Washington University M, W
Highline Community College M, W
Lower Columbia College W
Northwest College M, W
Seattle Pacific University M, W
Spokane Community College M, W
Spokane Falls Community College M, W
University of Puget Sound M, W
University of Washington M, W
Washington State University M, W
Western Washington University M, W
Yakima Valley Community College M, W

West Virginia

Marshall University M, W
West Virginia State College M, W
West Virginia University M, W
West Virginia Wesleyan College M, W
Wheeling Jesuit College M, W

Wisconsin

Marquette University M, W
University of Wisconsin-Madison M, W

Wyoming

University of Wyoming M, W

Volleyball

Alabama

Alabama Agricultural and Mechanical University

Alabama State University W
Auburn University W
Bevill State Community College W
Central Alabama Community College W
Enterprise State Junior College W
Gadsden State Community College W
Huntingdon College W
Jacksonville State University W
James H. Faulkner State Community College M, W
Lawson State Community College W
Miles College W
Northwest-Shoals Community College W
Samford University W
Snead State Community College W
Tuskegee University W
University of Alabama
  Birmingham W
  Huntsville W
  Tuscaloosa W
University of Montevallo W
University of North Alabama W
University of West Alabama W
Wallace State College at Hanceville W

Alaska

University of Alaska
  Anchorage M, W
  Fairbanks W

Arizona

Arizona State University W
Arizona Western College W
Glendale Community College W
Northern Arizona University W
Pima Community College W
Scottsdale Community College W
University of Arizona W
Yavapai College W

Arkansas

Arkansas State University W
Harding University W
Henderson State University W
John Brown University W
Lyon College W
Ouachita Baptist University W
University of Arkansas
  Fayetteville W
  Little Rock W
University of Central Arkansas W
Williams Baptist College W

California

Azusa Pacific University W
California Baptist College W
California Polytechnic State University: San Luis Obispo W
California State Polytechnic University: Pomona W
California State University
  Bakersfield W
  Fresno W
  Fullerton W
  Long Beach M, W
  Los Angeles W
  Northridge M, W
  Sacramento W
  San Bernardino W
Christian Heritage College W
Concordia University W
Dominican College of San Rafael M, W
Fresno Pacific College W
Holy Names College W
Loyola Marymount University M, W

Pepperdine University M, W
Point Loma Nazarene College W
St. Mary's College of California W
San Diego State University M, W
San Jose State University W
Santa Clara University W
Southern California College W
Stanford University M, W
University of California
  Berkeley W
  Irvine W
  Los Angeles M, W
  Riverside W
  Santa Barbara M, W
University of the Pacific M, W
University of San Diego W
University of San Francisco W
University of Southern California M, W
Westmont College W

Colorado

Adams State College W
Colorado Christian University W
Colorado Northwestern Community College W
Colorado School of Mines W
Colorado State University W
Fort Lewis College W
Lamar Community College W
Mesa State College W
Metropolitan State College of Denver W
Northeastern Junior College W
Otero Junior College W
Regis University W
Trinidad State Junior College W
University of Colorado
  Boulder W
  Colorado Springs W
University of Denver W
University of Northern Colorado W
University of Southern Colorado W
Western State College of Colorado W

Connecticut

Central Connecticut State University W
Fairfield University M, W
Mitchell College W
Quinnipiac College W
University of Connecticut W
University of Hartford W
University of New Haven W

Delaware

Delaware State University W
University of Delaware W

District of Columbia

American University W
George Washington University W
Georgetown University W
Howard University W

Florida

Bethune-Cookman College W
Brevard Community College W
Eckerd College M, W
Embry-Riddle Aeronautical University M
Flagler College W
Florida Agricultural and Mechanical University M
Florida Atlantic University W
Florida Community College at Jacksonville W
Florida Institute of Technology W
Florida International University W
Florida Memorial College W
Florida Southern College W

Florida State University W
Hillsborough Community College W
Manatee Community College W
Nova Southeastern University W
Palm Beach Atlantic College W
Pasco-Hernando Community
    College W
Rollins College W
St. Leo College W
St. Thomas University W
Stetson University W
University of Central Florida W
University of Florida W
University of North Florida W
University of South Florida W
University of Tampa W
Warner Southern College W
Webber College M, W

Georgia

Abraham Baldwin Agricultural
    College W
Augusta College W
Brenau University W
Covenant College W
Fort Valley State College W
Georgia Institute of Technology W
Georgia Southern University W
Georgia Southwestern College M,
    W
Mercer University W
Paine College W
University of Georgia W
Valdosta State University W
West Georgia College W

Hawaii

Hawaii Pacific University W
University of Hawaii
    Hilo W
    Manoa M, W

Idaho

Albertson College W
Boise State University W
College of Southern Idaho W
Idaho State University W
Lewis-Clark State College W
North Idaho College W
Northwest Nazarene College W
Ricks College W
University of Idaho W

Illinois

Belleville Area College W
Bradley University W
Carl Sandburg College W
Chicago State University W
Danville Area Community College
    W
De Paul University W
Eastern Illinois University W
Elgin Community College W
Highland Community College W
Illinois Eastern Community
    Colleges
        Lincoln Trail College W
        Olney Central College W
        Wabash Valley College W
Illinois Institute of Technology M,
    W
Illinois State University W
John A. Logan College W
Kaskaskia College W
Kishwaukee College W
Lake Land College W
Lewis and Clark Community
    College W
Lewis University M, W
Lincoln College W
Loyola University of Chicago M, W
McHenry County College W

McKendree College W
Moraine Valley Community College
    W
Morton College W
Northeastern Illinois University W
Northwestern University W
Olivet Nazarene University W
Quincy University M, W
Rosary College W
St. Xavier University W
Southern Illinois University
    Carbondale W
    Edwardsville W
Trinity International University M,
    W
University of Illinois
    Chicago W
    Urbana-Champaign W
Western Illinois University W

Indiana

Ball State University M, W
Bethel College W
Butler University W
Goshen College W
Grace College M
Huntington College W
Indiana State University W
Indiana University
    Bloomington W
    Southeast W
Indiana University-Purdue
    University Indianapolis W
Indiana Wesleyan University W
Marian College W
Oakland City University M
Purdue University W
St. Francis College W
St. Joseph's College M, W
Tri-State University M, W
University of Evansville W
University of Indianapolis W
University of Notre Dame W
University of Southern Indiana W
Valparaiso University W
Vincennes University M, W

Iowa

Briar Cliff College W
Clinton Community College W
Drake University W
Ellsworth Community College W
Graceland College M, W
Grand View College W
Iowa Central Community College
    W
Iowa Lakes Community College M,
    W
Iowa State University W
Iowa Wesleyan College W
Morningside College W
North Iowa Area Community
    College W
Northwestern College W
St. Ambrose University W
Teikyo Marycrest University M, W
University of Iowa W
University of Northern Iowa W
Waldorf College W
Westmar University W

Kansas

Baker University W
Barton County Community College
    W
Benedictine College W
Bethany College W
Bethel College W
Butler County Community College
    W
Colby Community College W
Emporia State University W

Fort Scott Community College W
Friends University W
Garden City Community College W
Hutchinson Community College W
Independence Community College
    W
Kansas City Kansas Community
    College W
Kansas Newman College W
Kansas State University W
MidAmerica Nazarene College W
Neosho County Community College
    W
Ottawa University W
Pratt Community College W
St. Mary College W
Southwestern College W
University of Kansas W
Wichita State University W

Kentucky

Bellarmine College W
Brescia College W
Cumberland College W
Eastern Kentucky University W
Georgetown College W
Kentucky State University W
Kentucky Wesleyan College W
Morehead State University W
Murray State University W
Northern Kentucky University W
Spalding University W
Sue Bennett College W
Union College W
University of Kentucky W
University of Louisville W
Western Kentucky University W

Louisiana

Centenary College of Louisiana W
Louisiana State University and
    Agricultural and Mechanical
    College W
Louisiana Tech University W
Nicholls State University W
Northeast Louisiana University W
Northwestern State University W
Southeastern Louisiana University
    W
Tulane University W
University of New Orleans W

Maine

Unity College W

Maryland

Bowie State University W
Charles County Community College
    W
Chesapeake College W
Columbia Union College M, W
Dundalk Community College W
Hagerstown Junior College W
Loyola College in Maryland W
Morgan State University W
Prince George's Community College
    W
Towson State University M, W
University of Maryland
    Baltimore County W
    College Park W
    Eastern Shore W

Massachusetts

American International College W
Becker College
    Leicester Campus W
    Worcester Campus W
Boston College W
Dean College W
Mount Ida College M
Northeastern University W

University of Massachusetts
    Amherst W
    Lowell W

Michigan

Aquinas College W
Central Michigan University M, W
Concordia College W
Cornerstone College and Grand
    Rapids Baptist Seminary W
Eastern Michigan University W
Glen Oaks Community College W
Grand Valley State University W
Hillsdale College W
Kellogg Community College W
Lake Superior State University W
Lansing Community College W
Macomb Community College W
Michigan Christian College W
Michigan State University W
Michigan Technological University
    W
Mott Community College W
Northwood University W
Oakland University W
Saginaw Valley State University W
Spring Arbor College W
University of Michigan W
Wayne State University W
Western Michigan University W

Minnesota

Bemidji State University W
Mankato State University W
Moorhead State University W
St. Cloud State University W
Southwest State University W
University of Minnesota
    Crookston W
    Duluth W
    Twin Cities W
Winona State University W

Mississippi

Alcorn State University W
Mississippi State University W
Mississippi University for Women
    W
Mississippi Valley State University
    W
University of Mississippi W
University of Southern Mississippi
    W

Missouri

Avila College W
Central Methodist College W
Central Missouri State University W
College of the Ozarks W
Columbia College M, W
Culver-Stockton College W
Drury College W
Hannibal-LaGrange College W
Harris Stowe State College W
Jefferson College W
Lindenwood College M, W
Longview Community College W
Mineral Area College W
Missouri Southern State College W
Missouri Western State College W
Park College M, W
Research College of Nursing W
Rockhurst College M, W
St. Louis Community College at
    Forest Park W
St. Louis University W
Southeast Missouri State University
    W
Southwest Baptist University W
Southwest Missouri State University
    W
Truman State University W

University of Missouri
  Columbia W
  Kansas City W
  St. Louis W
William Jewell College W
William Woods University W

Montana

Carroll College W
Montana State University
  Billings M, W
  Bozeman W
  Northern W
Montana Tech of The University of
  Montana W
Rocky Mountain College W
University of Montana-Missoula W
Western Montana College of the
  University of Montana W

Nebraska

Bellevue University W
Central Community College W
Chadron State College W
College of St. Mary W
Concordia College W
Creighton University W
Dana College W
Doane College/Lincoln Campus M,
  W
Hastings College W
McCook Community College W
Mid Plains Community College W
Midland Lutheran College W
Northeast Community College W
Peru State College W
Southeast Community College:
  Beatrice Campus W
University of Nebraska
  Kearney W
  Lincoln W
  Omaha W
Wayne State College W
Western Nebraska Community
  College W
York College W

Nevada

Sierra Nevada College M
University of Nevada
  Las Vegas W
  Reno W

New Hampshire

Franklin Pierce College W
Hesser College M, W
University of New Hampshire W

New Jersey

Bloomfield College W
Fairleigh Dickinson University
  Edward Williams College W
  Teaneck W
Rider University W
Rutgers, The State University of
  New Jersey
  College of Engineering W
  College of Nursing M
  College of Pharmacy W
  Cook College W
  Douglass College W
  Livingston College W
  Mason Gross School of the
    Arts W
  Newark College of Arts and
    Sciences M
  Rutgers College W
St. Peter's College W
Seton Hall University W

New Mexico

College of the Southwest W

Eastern New Mexico University W
New Mexico Highlands University
  W
New Mexico State University W
University of New Mexico W

New York

Adelphi University W
Canisius College W
Cazenovia College W
City University of New York:
  Queens College W
College of St. Rose W
Concordia College M, W
Dominican College of Blauvelt W
D'Youville College M
Fordham University W
Genesee Community College M, W
Hofstra University W
Houghton College W
Iona College W
Le Moyne College W
Long Island University
  Brooklyn Campus W
  C. W. Post Campus W
  Southampton College M, W
Manhattan College W
Marist College M, W
Mercy College W
Molloy College W
New York Institute of Technology
  W
Niagara County Community College
  W
Niagara University W
Nyack College W
Pace University W
Roberts Wesleyan College M, W
Sage Junior College of Albany W
St. Bonaventure University W
St. Francis College W
St. John's University W
St. Thomas Aquinas College W
Siena College W
State University of New York
  Albany W
  Buffalo W
  Stony Brook W
Syracuse University W
Wagner College W

North Carolina

Appalachian State University W
Barber-Scotia College W
Barton College W
Belmont Abbey College W
Campbell University W
Catawba College W
Davidson College W
Duke University W
East Carolina University W
Elon College W
Fayetteville State University W
Gardner-Webb University W
High Point University W
Johnson C. Smith University W
Lees-McRae College W
Lenoir-Rhyne College W
Livingstone College W
Mars Hill College W
Montreat College W
Mount Olive College W
North Carolina Agricultural and
  Technical State University W
North Carolina Central University
  W
North Carolina State University W
Pembroke State University W
Pfeiffer College W
Queens College W
St. Andrews Presbyterian College W
St. Augustine's College W

University of North Carolina
  Asheville W
  Chapel Hill W
  Charlotte W
  Greensboro W
  Wilmington W
Wake Forest University W
Western Carolina University W
Wingate University W
Winston-Salem State University W

North Dakota

Dickinson State University W
Minot State University W
North Dakota State College of
  Science W
North Dakota State University
  Bottineau W
  Fargo W
University of North Dakota
  Grand Forks W
  Lake Region W
  Williston W

Ohio

Ashland University W
Bowling Green State University W
Cedarville College W
Clark State Community College W
Cleveland State University W
Kent State University W
Malone College W
Miami University: Oxford Campus
  W
Mount Vernon Nazarene College W
Ohio Dominican College W
Ohio State University: Columbus
  Campus M, W
Ohio University W
Shawnee State University W
Sinclair Community College W
Southern State Community College
  W
Tiffin University W
University of Akron W
University of Dayton W
University of Findlay W
University of Rio Grande W
University of Toledo W
Urbana University W
Walsh University W
Wright State University W
Xavier University W
Youngstown State University W

Oklahoma

Bartlesville Wesleyan College W
Cameron University M
Northeastern Oklahoma
  Agricultural and Mechanical
  College W
Oral Roberts University W
University of Central Oklahoma W
University of Oklahoma W
University of Tulsa W

Oregon

Blue Mountain Community College
  W
Chemeketa Community College W
Clackamas Community College W
Concordia University W
Linn-Benton Community College W
Mount Hood Community College
  W
Portland State University W
Treasure Valley Community College
  W
University of Oregon W
University of Portland W
Western Baptist College W

Pennsylvania

California University of
  Pennsylvania W
Carlow College W
Cheyney University of Pennsylvania
  W
Community College of Beaver
  County W
Duquesne University W
Edinboro University of
  Pennsylvania W
Gannon University W
Geneva College W
Indiana University of Pennsylvania
  W
Kutztown University of
  Pennsylvania W
La Salle University W
Lock Haven University of
  Pennsylvania W
Manor Junior College W
Mercyhurst College M, W
Millersville University of
  Pennsylvania W
Penn State University Park Campus
  M, W
Point Park College W
Robert Morris College W
St. Francis College M, W
St. Vincent College W
Seton Hill College W
Shippensburg University of
  Pennsylvania W
University of Pittsburgh W
Villanova University W
West Chester University of
  Pennsylvania W
Westminster College W

Puerto Rico

Inter American University of Puerto
  Rico
  Metropolitan Campus M, W
  San German Campus M, W
University of Puerto Rico
  Bayamon Technological
    University College M, W
  La Montana Regional College
    M, W
  Mayaguez Campus M, W
University of the Sacred Heart M,
  W

Rhode Island

Providence College W
University of Rhode Island W

South Carolina

Anderson College W
Charleston Southern University W
Claflin College M, W
Clemson University W
Coastal Carolina University W
Coker College W
College of Charleston W
Erskine College W
Francis Marion University W
Furman University W
Limestone College W
North Greenville College W
Presbyterian College W
South Carolina State University W
Southern Wesleyan University W
Spartanburg Methodist College W
University of South Carolina
  Aiken W
  Spartanburg W
Winthrop University W
Wofford College W

South Dakota

Augustana College W

279

Black Hills State University W
Dakota State University W
Dakota Wesleyan University W
Huron University W
Mount Marty College W
South Dakota State University W
University of Sioux Falls W
University of South Dakota W

Tennessee

Austin Peay State University W
Belmont University W
Carson-Newman College W
Christian Brothers University W
David Lipscomb University W
East Tennessee State University W
Freed-Hardeman University W
King College W
Lambuth University M, W
Lee College W
Lincoln Memorial University W
Martin Methodist College W
Middle Tennessee State University
  W
Milligan College W
Tennessee Technological University
  W
Trevecca Nazarene University W
Tusculum College W
University of Memphis M
University of Tennessee
  Chattanooga W
  Knoxville W
  Martin M, W

Texas

Abilene Christian University W
Ambassador University W
Angelo State University W
Baylor University W
Blinn College W
Concordia Lutheran College W
Dallas Baptist University W
East Texas State University W
Frank Phillips College W
Houston Baptist University W
Jacksonville College W
Lamar University—Beaumont W
Laredo Community College W
Lee College W
Rice University W
St. Edward's University W
St. Mary's University W
Schreiner College W
Southern Methodist University W
Southwest Texas State University W
Stephen F. Austin State University
  W
Texas A&M University W
Texas A&M University-Kingsville
  W
Texas Lutheran College W
Texas Tech University W
Texas Wesleyan University W
Texas Woman's University W
University of Houston W
University of North Texas W
University of Texas
  Arlington W
  Austin W
  San Antonio W
Vernon Regional Junior College W
West Texas A&M University W
Wharton County Junior College W

Utah

Brigham Young University M, W
College of Eastern Utah W
Dixie College W
Snow College W
University of Utah W
Utah State University W

Utah Valley State College W
Weber State University W

Virginia

Bluefield College W
Clinch Valley College of the
  University of Virginia W
College of William and Mary W
George Mason University M, W
Hampton University W
James Madison University W
Liberty University W
Norfolk State University W
Radford University W
St. Paul's College W
University of Virginia W
Virginia Commonwealth University
  W
Virginia Polytechnic Institute and
  State University W
Virginia Union University W

Washington

Big Bend Community College W
Central Washington University W
Centralia College W
Eastern Washington University W
Edmonds Community College W
Gonzaga University W
Highline Community College W
Lower Columbia College W
Northwest College W
Olympic College W
Pierce College W
St. Martin's College W
Seattle Pacific University W
Shoreline Community College W
Spokane Community College W
Spokane Falls Community College
  W
Tacoma Community College W
University of Washington W
Walla Walla Community College W
Washington State University W
Western Washington University W
Yakima Valley Community College
  W

West Virginia

Alderson-Broaddus College W
Concord College W
Marshall University W
Ohio Valley College W
Potomac State College of West
  Virginia University W
Salem-Teikyo University W
Shepherd College W
West Virginia Institute of
  Technology W
West Virginia University W
West Virginia Wesleyan College W
Wheeling Jesuit College W

Wisconsin

Marquette University W
Northland College W
University of Wisconsin
  Green Bay W
  Madison W

Wyoming

Eastern Wyoming College W
Northwest College W
Sheridan College W
University of Wyoming W

Water polo

California

California State University: Long
  Beach M
Pepperdine University M
Stanford University M, W
University of California
  Berkeley M
  Irvine M
  Los Angeles M
University of the Pacific M, W
University of Southern California M

District of Columbia

George Washington University M

Kansas

Wichita State University W

Massachusetts

University of Massachusetts
  Amherst M, W

Nebraska

University of Nebraska—Kearney
  W

New York

City University of New York:
  Queens College M
Fordham University M
Manhattan College M
St. Francis College M

Ohio

Bowling Green State University W

Pennsylvania

Villanova University M

Puerto Rico

University of Puerto Rico:
  Mayaguez Campus M

Washington

Central Washington University W

Wyoming

Western Wyoming Community
  College M

Wrestling

Arizona

Arizona State University M
Embry-Riddle Aeronautical
  University: Prescott Campus M

California

California Polytechnic State
  University: San Luis Obispo M
California State University
  Bakersfield M
  Fresno M
  Fullerton M
Stanford University M

Colorado

Adams State College M
Colorado Northwestern Community
  College M
Colorado School of Mines M
Fort Lewis College M
University of Northern Colorado M
University of Southern Colorado M

Western State College of Colorado
  M

Connecticut

Central Connecticut State
  University M

Delaware

Delaware State University M

District of Columbia

American University M
Howard University M

Idaho

Boise State University M
North Idaho College M
Ricks College M

Illinois

Belleville Area College M
Chicago State University M
Lincoln College M
Northwestern University M
Southern Illinois University at
  Edwardsville M
University of Illinois at Urbana-
  Champaign M

Indiana

Indiana University Bloomington M
Purdue University M
University of Indianapolis M
Valparaiso University M

Iowa

Ellsworth Community College M
Iowa Central Community College
  M
Iowa State University M
Northwestern College M
University of Iowa M
University of Northern Iowa M
Waldorf College M
Westmar University M

Kansas

Colby Community College M
Fort Hays State University M

Maryland

Morgan State University M
University of Maryland: College
  Park M

Massachusetts

Boston University M
University of Massachusetts Lowell
  M

Michigan

Central Michigan University M
Eastern Michigan University M
Michigan State University M
University of Michigan M

Minnesota

Mankato State University M
Moorhead State University M
St. Cloud State University M
Southwest State University M
University of Minnesota
  Duluth M
  Twin Cities M

Missouri

Central Missouri State University M
Lindenwood College M
St. Louis Community College at
  Meramec M
University of Missouri: Columbia M

Montana

Montana State University-Northern
M

Nebraska

Chadron State College M
Dana College M
University of Nebraska
    Kearney M
    Lincoln M
    Omaha M

New Jersey

Rider University M
Rutgers, The State University of
New Jersey
    College of Engineering M
    College of Pharmacy M
    Cook College M
    Livingston College M
    Mason Gross School of the
        Arts M
    Rutgers College M
Seton Hall University M

New Mexico

University of New Mexico M

New York

Hofstra University M
Niagara County Community College
M
State University of New York at
    Buffalo M
Syracuse University M
Wagner College M

North Carolina

Appalachian State University M
Campbell University M
Davidson College M
Duke University M
Gardner-Webb University M
North Carolina State University M
Pembroke State University M
University of North Carolina at
    Chapel Hill M

North Dakota

Dickinson State University M
North Dakota State College of
    Science M
North Dakota State University M
University of North Dakota M

Ohio

Ashland University M
Cleveland State University M
Cuyahoga Community College:
    Western Campus M
Kent State University M
Miami University: Oxford Campus
M
Ohio State University: Columbus
    Campus M
Ohio University M
University of Findlay M

Oklahoma

University of Central Oklahoma M
University of Oklahoma M

Oregon

Clackamas Community College M
Portland State University M
University of Oregon M

Pennsylvania

Bloomsburg University of
    Pennsylvania M
California University of
    Pennsylvania M

Cheyney University of Pennsylvania
M
Drexel University M
Duquesne University M
East Stroudsburg University of
    Pennsylvania M
Edinboro University of
    Pennsylvania M
Gannon University M
Kutztown University of
    Pennsylvania M
Lehigh University M
Lock Haven University of
    Pennsylvania M
Millersville University of
    Pennsylvania M
Penn State University Park Campus
M
Shippensburg University of
    Pennsylvania M
University of Pittsburgh
    Johnstown M
    Pittsburgh M
Wilkes University M

Puerto Rico

University of Puerto Rico
    Bayamon Technological
        University College M
    Mayaguez Campus M

South Carolina

Anderson College M
Clemson University M

South Dakota

Augustana College M
Dakota Wesleyan University M
Northern State University M
South Dakota State University M

Tennessee

Carson-Newman College M
University of Tennessee:
    Chattanooga M

Utah

Brigham Young University M

Virginia

George Mason University M
James Madison University M
Liberty University M
Longwood College M
Norfolk State University M
Old Dominion University M
University of Virginia M
Virginia Military Institute M
Virginia Polytechnic Institute and
    State University M

Washington

Central Washington University M
Highline Community College M
Yakima Valley Community College
M

West Virginia

West Liberty State College M
West Virginia University M

Wisconsin

Marquette University M
University of Wisconsin-Madison M

Wyoming

Northwest College M
University of Wyoming M

17. Colleges that offer tuition and/or fee waivers and special tuition payment plans

Tuition and/or fee waiver for adult students

Alabama
Community College of the Air Force
Faulkner University

Arizona
Northern Arizona University

Arkansas
John Brown University
Southern Arkansas University Tech

California
California State University: Dominguez Hills
City College of San Francisco
Contra Costa College
Cosumnes River College
Feather River College
Fresno City College
Fullerton College
Napa Valley College
Orange Coast College
Riverside Community College
Saddleback College

Colorado
Aims Community College
Northeastern Junior College
Regis University

Connecticut
Trinity College

Florida
Palm Beach Atlantic College
Webber College

Georgia
Berry College
Emmanuel College
Wesleyan College

Idaho
Albertson College

Illinois
Lewis University
Northeastern Illinois University

Indiana
Anderson University
Bethel College
St. Francis College

Iowa
Coe College
Northwestern College
Simpson College

Kansas
Fort Hays State University
Kansas Newman College
Tabor College

Kentucky
Brescia College
Kentucky State University
University of Kentucky

Louisiana
University of New Orleans

Maryland
Harford Community College
Western Maryland College

Massachusetts
Atlantic Union College
Bay Path College
Berkshire Community College
Marian Court College
Massasoit Community College
Middlesex Community College
Pine Manor College
Simmons College

Michigan
Aquinas College
Mid Michigan Community College

Minnesota
Fergus Falls Community College
North Hennepin Community College
St. Olaf College
University of Minnesota: Crookston
Willmar Community College

Mississippi
Millsaps College
Mississippi College
Rust College

Missouri
Culver-Stockton College
North Central Missouri College
St. Louis University
William Jewell College

Montana
Montana State University
    College of Technology-Great
    Falls
    Northern

Nebraska
Chadron State College
Hastings College
Nebraska Wesleyan University

New Mexico
College of Santa Fe

New York
Medaille College
Nyack College

North Carolina
Barton College
Campbell University
Salem College

North Dakota
University of North Dakota: Lake Region

Ohio
Cleveland College of Jewish Studies
Denison University
Otterbein College

Oklahoma
Northern Oklahoma College
Oklahoma State University: Oklahoma City
Redlands Community College
Southeastern Oklahoma State University

Oregon
Central Oregon Community College
Concordia University
Southwestern Oregon Community College

Pennsylvania
Immaculata College
Juniata College
Keystone College
Mercyhurst College
Rosemont College
St. Francis College
Seton Hill College
Thiel College

South Carolina
Anderson College
Coker College
Spartanburg Methodist College

South Dakota
South Dakota School of Mines and Technology

Tennessee
Carson-Newman College
Hiwassee College
Jackson State Community College
Lambuth University

Texas
Concordia Lutheran College
Dallas Baptist University
Texas Christian University

Utah
Utah State University

Virginia
Bluefield College
Lynchburg College
Randolph-Macon Woman's College

Washington
Grays Harbor College
Lower Columbia College

West Virginia
Fairmont State College

Wisconsin
Beloit College
Blackhawk Technical College
Viterbo College

Wyoming
Eastern Wyoming College

Tuition and/or fee waiver for children of alumni

Alabama
Lawson State Community College

Alaska
University of Alaska Fairbanks

Arizona
Arizona College of the Bible

Arkansas
Arkansas State University
Southern Arkansas University

California
LIFE Bible College
Mount St. Mary's College
Patten College
Saddleback College
Santa Clara University

282

Colorado
Colorado Christian University

Connecticut
Paier College of Art

District of Columbia
Trinity College

Florida
Florida Bible College
Florida Southern College
Webber College

Georgia
Oglethorpe University
Paine College
Wesleyan College

Idaho
Albertson College

Illinois
Augustana College
Aurora University
Benedictine University
Chicago State University
Eureka College
Lewis University
MacCormac Junior College
MacMurray College
Quincy University

Indiana
Goshen College
Indiana State University
Manchester College
Marian College
St. Francis College
St. Joseph's College
St. Mary-of-the-Woods College
University of Evansville

Iowa
American Institute of Business
Clarke College
Dordt College
Iowa Wesleyan College
Loras College
Morningside College
Northwestern College
St. Ambrose University
Teikyo Marycrest University
Upper Iowa University

Kansas
Kansas Newman College
Tabor College

Kentucky
Asbury College
Brescia College
Cumberland College
Morehead State University
Sue Bennett College
Union College
Western Kentucky University

Louisiana
Grambling State University
Louisiana State University
 Agricultural and Mechanical
  College
 Shreveport
Louisiana Tech University
McNeese State University
University of New Orleans

Massachusetts
Anna Maria College
Bay Path College
Boston University

Curry College
Eastern Nazarene College
Hellenic College
Pine Manor College
Springfield College

Michigan
Aquinas College
Detroit College of Business
Lake Superior State University
Michigan Christian College
Michigan Technological University
Northwood University
Wayne State University

Mississippi
Delta State University
Millsaps College
Mississippi State University
Mississippi University for Women
University of Mississippi
University of Southern Mississippi

Missouri
Avila College
Central Christian College of the
 Bible
Columbia College
Culver-Stockton College
Missouri Baptist College
Missouri Valley College
Northwest Missouri State
 University
Research College of Nursing
Rockhurst College
University of Missouri: Rolla
Westminster College
William Jewell College
William Woods University

Nebraska
Dana College
Grace University
York College

Nevada
University of Nevada
 Las Vegas
 Reno

New Hampshire
Notre Dame College
Rivier College

New Jersey
Bloomfield College

New Mexico
College of the Southwest

New York
Adelphi University
Daemen College
Dowling College
Hartwick College
Iona College
Long Island University: Brooklyn
 Campus
Manhattan College
Plaza Business Institute
St. Joseph's College
Trocaire College
University of Rochester

North Carolina
Montreat College

Ohio
Ashland University
Cedarville College
Kent State University
Malone College

Mount Union College
Muskingum College
Ohio Wesleyan University
Otterbein College
University of Findlay
Walsh University

Oklahoma
Bartlesville Wesleyan College
Oklahoma Baptist University
Oklahoma Christian University of
 Science and Arts
Oklahoma State University
Oral Roberts University
Southwestern Oklahoma State
 University
University of Oklahoma
 Health Sciences Center
 Norman

Oregon
Bassist College

Pennsylvania
Albright College
Baptist Bible College of
 Pennsylvania
Cabrini College
Chatham College
Keystone College
Lancaster Bible College
McCann School of Business
Mercyhurst College
Peirce College
Philadelphia College of Bible
Point Park College
University of the Arts
Wilkes University
Wilson College

Puerto Rico
ICPR Junior College

South Carolina
Anderson College
Coker College
Erskine College
North Greenville College
Spartanburg Methodist College

South Dakota
Augustana College
Northern State University
South Dakota School of Mines and
 Technology

Tennessee
Christian Brothers University
Tennessee Wesleyan College

Texas
Dallas Baptist University
University of St. Thomas

Utah
Utah State University

Virginia
Marymount University

Washington
Pacific Lutheran University
Seattle Pacific University

West Virginia
Bethany College
Fairmont State College

Wisconsin
Blackhawk Technical College
Carroll College
Concordia University Wisconsin

Viterbo College

Wyoming
Eastern Wyoming College
University of Wyoming

Tuition and/or fee waiver for senior citizens

Alabama
Alabama Aviation and Technical
 College
Athens State College
Bessemer State Technical College
Bevill State Community College
Bishop State Community College
Calhoun Community College
Central Alabama Community
 College
Chattahoochee Valley Community
 College
Douglas MacArthur State Technical
 College
Enterprise State Junior College
Faulkner University
Gadsden State Community College
George C. Wallace State
 Community College at Selma
J. F. Drake State Technical College
James H. Faulkner State
 Community College
Jefferson State Community College
John M. Patterson State Technical
 College
Lawson State Community College
Lurleen B. Wallace State Junior
 College
Northeast Alabama Community
 College
Northwest-Shoals Community
 College
Reid State Technical College
Snead State Community College
Sparks State Technical College
University of Montevallo
Wallace State College at Hanceville

Alaska
Alaska Pacific University
Prince William Sound Community
 College
University of Alaska
 Anchorage
 Fairbanks
 Southeast

Arizona
Arizona Western College
Cochise College
Mohave Community College
Southwestern College
Yavapai College

Arkansas
Arkansas State University
 Beebe Branch
 Jonesboro
Arkansas Tech University
East Arkansas Community College
Garland County Community
 College
Harding University
Henderson State University
John Brown University
Mississippi County Community
 College
North Arkansas Community/
 Technical College

Phillips County Community College
Rich Mountain Community College
South Arkansas Community College
Southern Arkansas University
    Magnolia
    Tech
University of Arkansas
    Fayetteville
    Little Rock
    Monticello
    Pine Bluff
University of Central Arkansas
Westark Community College

California

Azusa Pacific University
California Polytechnic State
    University: San Luis Obispo
California State Polytechnic
    University: Pomona
California State University
    Bakersfield
    Chico
    Dominguez Hills
    Fresno
    Fullerton
    Hayward
    Long Beach
    Los Angeles
    Northridge
    Sacramento
    San Bernardino
    San Marcos
    Stanislaus
Citrus College
City College of San Francisco
College of the Desert
College of Notre Dame
Foothill College
Fullerton College
Humboldt State University
Los Angeles Harbor College
Pacific Christian College
Point Loma Nazarene College
Porterville College
Saddleback College
San Diego State University
San Francisco State University
San Jose State University

Colorado

Adams State College
Arapahoe Community College
Colorado Mountain College
    Alpine Campus
    Spring Valley Campus
    Timberline Campus
Colorado Northwestern Community
    College
Front Range Community College
Lamar Community College
Mesa State College
Metropolitan State College of
    Denver
Naropa Institute
Northeastern Junior College
Pikes Peak Community College
Pueblo Community College
Red Rocks Community College
University of Colorado
    Boulder
    Denver
University of Northern Colorado
University of Southern Colorado
Western State College of Colorado

Connecticut

Asnuntuck Community-Technical
    College
Capital Community-Technical
    College

Central Connecticut State
    University
Eastern Connecticut State
    University
Gateway Community-Technical
    College
Housatonic Community-Technical
    College
Manchester Community-Technical
    College
Middlesex Community-Technical
    College
Naugatuck Valley Community-
    Technical College
Northwestern Connecticut
    Community-Technical College
Norwalk Community-Technical
    College
Quinebaug Valley Community-
    Technical College
Quinnipiac College
Southern Connecticut State
    University
Teikyo-Post University
Three Rivers Community-Technical
    College
Tunxis Community-Technical
    College
University of Connecticut
University of New Haven
Western Connecticut State
    University

Delaware

Delaware State University
Delaware Technical and
    Community College
    Owens Campus
    Stanton/Wilmington Campus
    Terry Campus
University of Delaware

Florida

Brevard Community College
Broward Community College
Daytona Beach Community College
Edison Community College
Florida Agricultural and Mechanical
    University
Florida Atlantic University
Florida Institute of Technology
Florida International University
Florida State University
Hillsborough Community College
Lake-Sumter Community College
North Florida Junior College
Palm Beach Atlantic College
Pensacola Junior College
St. Petersburg Junior College
Santa Fe Community College
Seminole Community College
Tallahassee Community College
University of Central Florida
University of Florida
University of North Florida
University of South Florida
Valencia Community College
Webber College

Georgia

Abraham Baldwin Agricultural
    College
Albany State College
Armstrong State College
Atlanta Metropolitan College
Augusta College
Bainbridge College
Berry College
Brunswick College
Chattahoochee Technical Institute
Clayton State College
Columbus College

Columbus Technical Institute
Darton College
DeKalb College
DeKalb Technical Institute
Emmanuel College
Floyd College
Fort Valley State College
Gainesville College
Georgia College
Georgia Southern University
Georgia Southwestern College
Georgia State University
Gordon College
Kennesaw State College
Macon College
Middle Georgia College
North Georgia College
Savannah State College
Shorter College
Southern College of Technology
Thomas College
University of Georgia
Valdosta State University
Wesleyan College
West Georgia College

Hawaii

University of Hawaii
    Hilo
    Kapiolani Community College
    West Oahu
    Windward Community College

Idaho

Albertson College
Boise State University
College of Southern Idaho
Idaho State University
Lewis-Clark State College
North Idaho College
Northwest Nazarene College

Illinois

Aurora University
Belleville Area College
Black Hawk College
Bradley University
Carl Sandburg College
Chicago State University
City Colleges of Chicago
    Kennedy-King College
    Malcolm X College
    Olive-Harvey College
    Richard J. Daley College
    Wright College
College of DuPage
College of Lake County
Danville Area Community College
Eastern Illinois University
Elgin Community College
Elmhurst College
Governors State University
Greenville College
Highland Community College
Illinois College
Illinois Eastern Community
    Colleges
    Frontier Community College
    Lincoln Trail College
    Olney Central College
    Wabash Valley College
Illinois State University
Illinois Valley Community College
John A. Logan College
Joliet Junior College
Kaskaskia College
Kendall College
Kishwaukee College
Lake Land College
Lewis and Clark Community
    College
Lincoln Land Community College

Loyola University of Chicago
MacMurray College
McHenry County College
Moraine Valley Community College
Morton College
Northeastern Illinois University
Oakton Community College
Parkland College
Rend Lake College
Richland Community College
Rock Valley College
St. Xavier University
Southeastern Illinois College
Southern Illinois University
    Carbondale
    Edwardsville
Spoon River College
State Community College
Trinity Christian College
Triton College
University of Illinois
    Chicago
    Springfield
    Urbana-Champaign
Western Illinois University
William Rainey Harper College

Indiana

Anderson University
Ball State University
Calumet College of St. Joseph
Franklin College
Huntington College
Indiana State University
Indiana University
    Bloomington
    Kokomo
    Southeast
Indiana University-Purdue
    University Fort Wayne
Indiana Wesleyan University
Ivy Tech State College: Northwest
Marian College
Oakland City University
Purdue University: North Central
    Campus
St. Francis College
Taylor University
University of Evansville
University of Indianapolis
University of Southern Indiana
Vincennes University

Iowa

Briar Cliff College
Clarke College
Clinton Community College
Des Moines Area Community
    College
Drake University
Graceland College
Grand View College
Indian Hills Community College
Iowa Wesleyan College
Iowa Western Community College
Kirkwood Community College
Morningside College
Muscatine Community College
St. Ambrose University
Scott Community College
Simpson College
Southeastern Community College
    North Campus
    South Campus
Westmar University

Kansas

Baker University
Barton County Community College
Butler County Community College
Donnelly College
Emporia State University

Garden City Community College
Hesston College
Hutchinson Community College
Independence Community College
Kansas Newman College
Labette Community College
Manhattan Christian College
MidAmerica Nazarene College
Neosho County Community College
Pittsburg State University
Pratt Community College
St. Mary College
Southwestern College
Tabor College
Washburn University of Topeka
Wichita State University

Kentucky

Asbury College
Ashland Community College
Bellarmine College
Brescia College
Cumberland College
Eastern Kentucky University
Elizabethtown Community College
Hazard Community College
Hopkinsville Community College
Kentucky State University
Kentucky Wesleyan College
Lexington Community College
Madisonville Community College
Maysville Community College
Mid-Continent Baptist Bible College
Morehead State University
Murray State University
Northern Kentucky University
Paducah Community College
Pikeville College
Prestonsburg Community College
Somerset Community College
Southeast Community College
Spalding University
Sue Bennett College
Union College
University of Kentucky
University of Louisville
Western Kentucky University

Louisiana

Bossier Parish Community College
Grambling State University
Louisiana College
Louisiana State University
    Agricultural and Mechanical
      College
    Alexandria
    Eunice
    Shreveport
Louisiana Tech University
McNeese State University
Nicholls State University
Northeast Louisiana University
Northwestern State University
Nunez Community College
Our Lady of Holy Cross College
Southeastern Louisiana University
University of New Orleans
University of Southwestern
   Louisiana
Xavier University of Louisiana

Maine

Colby College
Husson College
Unity College
University of Maine
    Augusta
    Farmington
    Fort Kent
    Machias
    Orono
    Presque Isle

University of Southern Maine

Maryland

Allegany College
Anne Arundel Community College
Baltimore Hebrew University
Bowie State University
Carroll Community College
Catonsville Community College
Cecil Community College
Charles County Community College
Chesapeake College
Dundalk Community College
Essex Community College
Frederick Community College
Frostburg State University
Hagerstown Junior College
Harford Community College
Hood College
Howard Community College
Maryland Institute College of Art
Montgomery College
    Germantown Campus
    Rockville Campus
    Takoma Park Campus
Morgan State University
Prince George's Community College
St. Mary's College of Maryland
Salisbury State University
Towson State University
University of Baltimore
University of Maryland
    Baltimore County
    College Park
    Eastern Shore
    University College
Wor-Wic Community College

Massachusetts

American International College
Anna Maria College
Atlantic Union College
Bay Path College
Becker College
    Leicester Campus
    Worcester Campus
Bentley College
Berkshire Community College
Boston University
Bridgewater State College
Bunker Hill Community College
Cape Cod Community College
Eastern Nazarene College
Elms College
Fitchburg State College
Framingham State College
Greenfield Community College
Holyoke Community College
Marian Court College
Massachusetts Bay Community
   College
Massachusetts College of Art
Massasoit Community College
Merrimack College
Middlesex Community College
Mount Wachusett Community
   College
Nichols College
North Adams State College
North Shore Community College
Northeastern University
Northern Essex Community College
Quincy College
Quinsigamond Community College
Roxbury Community College
Salem State College
Springfield Technical Community
   College
Stonehill College
Suffolk University

University of Massachusetts
    Amherst
    Boston
    Dartmouth
    Lowell
Western New England College
Westfield State College
Worcester State College

Michigan

Alpena Community College
Andrews University
Aquinas College
Bay de Noc Community College
Delta College
Glen Oaks Community College
Gogebic Community College
Great Lakes Junior College of
   Business
Henry Ford Community College
Highland Park Community College
Jackson Community College
Kalamazoo Valley Community
   College
Kellogg Community College
Lake Superior State University
Madonna University
Michigan Christian College
Michigan Technological University
Mid Michigan Community College
Monroe County Community
   College
Montcalm Community College
Mott Community College
Muskegon Community College
North Central Michigan College
Northern Michigan University
Reformed Bible College
St. Clair County Community
   College
Schoolcraft College
University of Michigan: Flint
Washtenaw Community College
Wayne State University
West Shore Community College
Western Michigan University
William Tyndale College

Minnesota

Alexandria Technical College
Anoka-Ramsey Community College
Augsburg College
Austin Community College
Bemidji State University
Bethel College
Central Lakes College
College of St. Catherine: St.
   Catherine Campus
College of St. Scholastica
Concordia College: St. Paul
Fergus Falls Community College
Gustavus Adolphus College
Itasca Community College:
   Arrowhead Region
Lakewood Community College
Mankato State University
Mesabi Community College:
   Arrowhead Region
Metropolitan State University
Minneapolis Community College
Minnesota Bible College
Moorhead State University
Normandale Community College
North Central Bible College
North Hennepin Community
   College
Northwestern College
Rainy River Community College
Rochester Community College
St. Cloud State University
St. Cloud Technical College
St. Olaf College

St. Paul Technical College
Southwest State University
University of Minnesota
    Crookston
    Duluth
University of St. Thomas
Willmar Community College
Willmar Technical College
Winona State University

Mississippi

Belhaven College
Copiah-Lincoln Community College
Delta State University
East Central Community College
Hinds Community College
Holmes Community College
Itawamba Community College
Jones County Junior College
Meridian Community College
Millsaps College
Mississippi Gulf Coast Community
   College
    Jackson County Campus
    Jefferson Davis Campus
    Perkinston
Mississippi State University
Mississippi University for Women
Northeast Mississippi Community
   College
Northwest Mississippi Community
   College
Pearl River Community College
Southeastern Baptist College
Southwest Mississippi Community
   College
University of Mississippi
University of Southern Mississippi

Missouri

Avila College
Calvary Bible College
Central Methodist College
Columbia College
Crowder College
Culver-Stockton College
Drury College
East Central College
Fontbonne College
Hannibal-LaGrange College
Lincoln University
Lindenwood College
Longview Community College
Maple Woods Community College
Maryville University of Saint Louis
Missouri Baptist College
Missouri Southern State College
Missouri Valley College
Missouri Western State College
Moberly Area Community College
North Central Missouri College
Northwest Missouri State
   University
Ozark Christian College
Park College
Penn Valley Community College
Rockhurst College
St. Charles County Community
   College
St. Louis Community College
    Forest Park
    Meramec
Southeast Missouri State University
Southwest Missouri State University
State Fair Community College
Three Rivers Community College
Truman State University
William Jewell College

Montana

Carroll College
Dawson Community College

285

Flathead Valley Community College
Helena College of Technology of
the University of Montana
Little Big Horn College
Miles Community College
Montana State University
Billings
Bozeman
Northern
Montana Tech of The University of
Montana
Stone Child College
University of Great Falls
University of Montana-Missoula
University of Montana College of
Technology
Western Montana College of the
University of Montana

Nebraska

Doane College/Lincoln Campus
Grace University
Hastings College
McCook Community College
Metropolitan Community College
Mid Plains Community College
Midland Lutheran College
Nebraska Indian Community
College
Nebraska Wesleyan University
Southeast Community College:
Lincoln Campus
Western Nebraska Community
College

Nevada

Community College of Southern
Nevada
Great Basin College
Truckee Meadows Community
College
University of Nevada
Las Vegas
Reno
Western Nevada Community
College

New Hampshire

Franklin Pierce College
Keene State College
New Hampshire Technical College
Berlin
Manchester
Notre Dame College
Plymouth State College of the
University System of New
Hampshire
Rivier College
St. Anselm College
University of New Hampshire
Durham
Manchester

New Jersey

Atlantic Community College
Bergen Community College
Bloomfield College
Brookdale Community College
Burlington County College
Caldwell College
Camden County College
Centenary College
College of St. Elizabeth
County College of Morris
Cumberland County College
Drew University
Essex County College
Fairleigh Dickinson University
Edward Williams College
Teaneck
Georgian Court College
Jersey City State College

Mercer County Community College
Monmouth University
Montclair State University
Ocean County College
Ramapo College of New Jersey
Raritan Valley Community College
Richard Stockton College of New
Jersey
Rutgers, The State University of
New Jersey
Camden College of Arts and
Sciences
College of Engineering
College of Nursing
College of Pharmacy
Cook College
Douglass College
Livingston College
Mason Gross School of the
Arts
Newark College of Arts and
Sciences
Rutgers College
Salem Community College
Seton Hall University
Sussex County Community College
Trenton State College
Union County College
Warren County Community College
William Paterson College of New
Jersey

New Mexico

Clovis Community College
College of Santa Fe
Dona Ana Branch Community
College of New Mexico State
University
Eastern New Mexico University:
Roswell Campus
National College
New Mexico Institute of Mining
and Technology
New Mexico State University
Carlsbad
Las Cruces
San Juan College
Santa Fe Community College

New York

Adelphi University
Adirondack Community College
Broome Community College
Cayuga County Community College
City University of New York
Baruch College
Borough of Manhattan
Community College
Brooklyn College
City College
College of Staten Island
Hostos Community College
Hunter College
John Jay College of Criminal
Justice
Lehman College
Medgar Evers College
New York City Technical
College
Queens College
York College
Clinton Community College
College of Mount St. Vincent
College of St. Rose
Columbia-Greene Community
College
Concordia College
Daemen College
Dominican College of Blauvelt
Dowling College
Dutchess Community College
D'Youville College

Erie Community College
North Campus
South Campus
Finger Lakes Community College
Fordham University
Fulton-Montgomery Community
College
Hofstra University
Houghton College
Iona College
Jamestown Community College
Jefferson Community College
Jewish Theological Seminary of
America
Maria College
Mercy College
Mohawk Valley Community College
New York Institute of Technology
Niagara County Community College
North Country Community College
Nyack College
Orange County Community College
Pace University
Roberts Wesleyan College
Rockland Community College
Russell Sage College
Sage Junior College of Albany
St. Bonaventure University
St. John Fisher College
St. John's University
St. Joseph's College: Suffolk
Campus
St. Thomas Aquinas College
Schenectady County Community
College
State University of New York
Albany
Purchase
College of Agriculture and
Technology at Cobleskill
College at Cortland
College at Old Westbury
Institute of Technology at
Utica/Rome
Tompkins-Cortland Community
College
Trocaire College
Ulster County Community College
Utica College of Syracuse
University
Villa Maria College of Buffalo
Wagner College
Wells College
Westchester Business Institute

North Carolina

Alamance Community College
Appalachian State University
Asheville Buncombe Technical
Community College
Beaufort County Community
College
Blue Ridge Community College
Brunswick Community College
Caldwell Community College and
Technical Institute
Cape Fear Community College
Carteret Community College
Catawba Valley Community College
Central Carolina Community
College
Central Piedmont Community
College
Chowan College
Cleveland Community College
Coastal Carolina Community
College
College of The Albemarle
Craven Community College
Davidson County Community
College

Durham Technical Community
College
East Carolina University
Edgecombe Community College
Fayetteville State University
Fayetteville Technical Community
College
Forsyth Technical Community
College
Guilford Technical Community
College
Haywood Community College
Lenoir Community College
Lenoir-Rhyne College
Martin Community College
Methodist College
Mitchell Community College
Montgomery Community College
Montreat College
Nash Community College
North Carolina Agricultural and
Technical State University
North Carolina State University
Pembroke State University
Pitt Community College
Randolph Community College
Richmond Community College
Roanoke Bible College
Roanoke-Chowan Community
College
Rockingham Community College
Sandhills Community College
Southeastern Community College
Stanly Community College
Surry Community College
Tri-County Community College
University of North Carolina
Asheville
Chapel Hill
Charlotte
Greensboro
Wilmington
Vance-Granville Community
College
Wake Technical Community
College
Western Carolina University
Western Piedmont Community
College
Wilkes Community College
Wilson Technical Community
College
Winston-Salem State University

North Dakota

Dickinson State University
North Dakota State University:
Bottineau
University of North Dakota
Grand Forks
Lake Region
Williston
Valley City State University

Ohio

Belmont Technical College
Bowling Green State University
Bowling Green
Firelands College
Cedarville College
Central Ohio Technical College
Chatfield College
Cincinnati Bible College and
Seminary
Cincinnati State Technical and
Community College
Clark State Community College
Cleveland College of Jewish Studies
Cleveland State University
Columbus College of Art and
Design
Columbus State Community College

Cuyahoga Community College
  Eastern Campus
  Metropolitan Campus
  Western Campus
Denison University
Edison State Community College
Hocking Technical College
Jefferson Community College
Kent State University
  East Liverpool Regional
    Campus
  Trumbull Campus
  Tuscarawas Campus
Lake Erie College
Lakeland Community College
Lima Technical College
Lourdes College
Malone College
Marion Technical College
Miami University: Hamilton
  Campus
Mount Union College
Mount Vernon Nazarene College
Muskingum Area Technical College
North Central Technical College
Northwest State Community
  College
Ohio Dominican College
Ohio University
  Athens
  Chillicothe Campus
  Zanesville Campus
Owens Technical College
  Findlay Campus
  Toledo
Shawnee State University
Sinclair Community College
Southern State Community College
Stark Technical College
Terra Community College
Tiffin University
University of Akron
University of Cincinnati: Raymond
  Walters College
University of Dayton
University of Findlay
University of Rio Grande
University of Toledo
Urbana University
Walsh University
Washington State Community
  College
Wittenberg University
Wright State University
  Dayton
  Lake Campus
Xavier University
Youngstown State University

Oklahoma

Bartlesville Wesleyan College
Cameron University
Connors State College
East Central University
Murray State College
Northeastern Oklahoma
  Agricultural and Mechanical
  College
Oklahoma Baptist University
Oklahoma City Community College
Oklahoma City University
Oklahoma Panhandle State
  University
Oklahoma State University
  Oklahoma City
  Stillwater
Phillips University
Redlands Community College
Rogers State College
Rose State College
Southeastern Oklahoma State
  University

Southwestern Oklahoma State
  University
Tulsa Junior College
University of Oklahoma
  Health Sciences Center
  Norman
University of Science and Arts of
  Oklahoma
Western Oklahoma State College

Oregon

Blue Mountain Community College
Central Oregon Community College
Chemeketa Community College
Clackamas Community College
Clatsop Community College
Concordia University
George Fox College
Lane Community College
Linfield College
Linn-Benton Community College
Portland Community College
Portland State University
Southwestern Oregon Community
  College
Treasure Valley Community College
Umpqua Community College
Western Oregon State College

Pennsylvania

Albright College
Alvernia College
Beaver College
Bryn Mawr College
Bucks County Community College
Butler County Community College
California University of
  Pennsylvania
Chestnut Hill College
Clarion University of Pennsylvania
College Misericordia
Community College of Beaver
  County
Community College of Philadelphia
Delaware County Community
  College
Delaware Valley College
Duquesne University
East Stroudsburg University of
  Pennsylvania
Edinboro University of
  Pennsylvania
Gannon University
Gratz College
Gwynedd-Mercy College
Holy Family College
Immaculata College
Indiana University of Pennsylvania
Juniata College
Keystone College
King's College
Lackawanna Junior College
Lancaster Bible College
Lehigh Carbon Community College
Lock Haven University of
  Pennsylvania
Luzerne County Community
  College
Manor Junior College
Marywood College
Messiah College
Millersville University of
  Pennsylvania
Montgomery County Community
  College
Northampton County Area
  Community College

Penn State
  Allentown Campus
  Altoona Campus
  Beaver Campus
  Berks Campus
  Delaware County Campus
  Du Bois Campus
  Erie Behrend College
  Fayette Campus
  Harrisburg Capital College
  Hazleton Campus
  McKeesport Campus
  Mont Alto Campus
  New Kensington Campus
  Ogontz Campus
  Schuylkill Campus
  Shenango Campus
  University Park Campus
  Wilkes-Barre Campus
  Worthington-Scranton Campus
  York Campus
Point Park College
Reading Area Community College
Rosemont College
Seton Hill College
Shippensburg University of
  Pennsylvania
Temple University
University of Pittsburgh
  Bradford
  Greensburg
University of Scranton
Ursinus College
Villanova University
West Chester University of
  Pennsylvania
Westmoreland County Community
  College
Wilkes University

Puerto Rico

Inter American University of Puerto
  Rico: Fajardo Campus

Rhode Island

Community College of Rhode
  Island
Rhode Island College
University of Rhode Island

South Carolina

Aiken Technical College
Anderson College
Benedict College
Chesterfield-Marlboro Technical
  College
The Citadel
Clemson University
Coastal Carolina University
College of Charleston
Denmark Technical College
Florence-Darlington Technical
  College
Francis Marion University
Greenville Technical College
Horry-Georgetown Technical
  College
Lander University
Limestone College
Medical University of South
  Carolina
Midlands Technical College
Orangeburg-Calhoun Technical
  College
Piedmont Technical College
South Carolina State University
Southern Wesleyan University
Spartanburg Methodist College
Spartanburg Technical College
Tri-County Technical College
Trident Technical College

University of South Carolina
  Aiken
  Beaufort
  Columbia
  Lancaster
  Spartanburg
  Sumter
  Union
Williamsburg Technical College
Winthrop University
York Technical College

South Dakota

Augustana College
Black Hills State University
Dakota State University
Dakota Wesleyan University
Kilian Community College
Mount Marty College
Northern State University
South Dakota School of Mines and
  Technology
South Dakota State University
University of Sioux Falls

Tennessee

Austin Peay State University
Belmont University
Bethel College
Carson-Newman College
Chattanooga State Technical
  Community College
Cleveland State Community College
Dyersburg State Community
  College
East Tennessee State University
Freed-Hardeman University
Hiwassee College
Jackson State Community College
King College
Lambuth University
Lee College
Lincoln Memorial University
Middle Tennessee State University
Motlow State Community College
Nashville State Technical Institute
Pellissippi State Technical
  Community College
Roane State Community College
Shelby State Community College
Southern College of Seventh-day
  Adventists
State Technical Institute at
  Memphis
Tennessee State University
Tennessee Technological University
University of Memphis
University of Tennessee
  Chattanooga
  Knoxville
  Martin
Volunteer State Community College
Walters State Community College

Texas

Angelina College
Bee County College
Central Texas College
College of the Mainland
Collin County Community College
  District
Del Mar College
East Texas State University
El Paso Community College
Hardin-Simmons University
Houston Baptist University
Houston Community College
Howard College
Howard Payne University
Laredo Community College
Lee College
McMurry University

St. Philip's College
Southwestern Adventist College
Temple College
Texas A&M University
Texas A&M University-Corpus
  Christi
Texas A&M University-Kingsville
Texas State Technical College:
  Harlingen
Texas Woman's University
University of Houston
    Downtown
    Houston
    Victoria
University of Texas Medical Branch
  at Galveston
Vernon Regional Junior College
Wayland Baptist University
Weatherford College
Western Texas College

Utah

College of Eastern Utah
Dixie College
Salt Lake Community College
University of Utah
Utah Valley State College
Weber State University

Vermont

Burlington College
Castleton State College
Champlain College
Community College of Vermont
Johnson State College
Lyndon State College
Southern Vermont College
Trinity College of Vermont
University of Vermont

Virginia

Averett College
Blue Ridge Community College
Bluefield College
Bridgewater College
Central Virginia Community College
Christopher Newport University
Clinch Valley College of the
  University of Virginia
College of William and Mary
Dabney S. Lancaster Community
  College
Danville Community College
Eastern Shore Community College
Ferrum College
George Mason University
Germanna Community College
John Tyler Community College
Longwood College
Mary Washington College
Marymount University
Mountain Empire Community
  College
New River Community College
Norfolk State University
Northern Virginia Community
  College
Old Dominion University
Patrick Henry Community College
Paul D. Camp Community College
Piedmont Virginia Community
  College
Radford University
Rappahannock Community College
Richard Bland College
Roanoke College
Southside Virginia Community
  College
Southwest Virginia Community
  College
Thomas Nelson Community College
Tidewater Community College

University of Virginia
Virginia Commonwealth University
Wytheville Community College

Washington

Big Bend Community College
Central Washington University
Centralia College
Clark College
Columbia Basin College
Edmonds Community College
Gonzaga University
Grays Harbor College
Highline Community College
Lower Columbia College
North Seattle Community College
Northwest College
Olympic College
Peninsula College
Pierce College
Puget Sound Christian College
Seattle Pacific University
Shoreline Community College
South Seattle Community College
Spokane Falls Community College
Tacoma Community College
University of Washington
Walla Walla College
Walla Walla Community College
Washington State University
Western Washington University
Whatcom Community College
Whitworth College
Yakima Valley Community College

West Virginia

Fairmont State College
Wheeling Jesuit College

Wisconsin

Blackhawk Technical College
Lakeland College
Marian College of Fond du Lac
Milwaukee Area Technical College
Mount Mary College
Mount Senario College
Northland College
Silver Lake College
University of Wisconsin
    Eau Claire
    Green Bay
    La Crosse
    Milwaukee
    River Falls
    Stout
    Whitewater
University of Wisconsin Center
    Fond du Lac
    Fox Valley
Viterbo College

Wyoming

Eastern Wyoming College
Northwest College
Sheridan College
University of Wyoming
Western Wyoming Community
  College

Tuition and/or fee waiver for minority students

Alabama

Alabama State University
Faulkner University

Alaska

Prince William Sound Community
  College

Arizona

Arizona State University
Northern Arizona University
University of Arizona

California

American River College
Antioch Southern California at Los
  Angeles
College of the Desert
Fresno City College
Fullerton College
Napa Valley College
Orange Coast College
Porterville College
Saddleback College
Westmont College

Colorado

Colorado Technical University
Fort Lewis College
Northeastern Junior College
Red Rocks Community College

Connecticut

Albertus Magnus College
Sacred Heart University
University of Hartford

Florida

Brevard Community College
Broward Community College
Central Florida Community College
Florida Atlantic University
Florida International University
Lake City Community College
Okaloosa-Walton Community
  College
Santa Fe Community College
University of Florida

Georgia

Columbus College

Hawaii

University of Hawaii
    Manoa
    Windward Community College

Idaho

University of Idaho

Illinois

Benedictine University
Eureka College
Governors State University
Northern Illinois University
Parkland College

Indiana

Anderson University
Indiana Wesleyan University
Oakland City University
Purdue University: North Central
  Campus
St. Joseph's College
St. Mary-of-the-Woods College

Iowa

American Institute of Business
Iowa Wesleyan College
St. Ambrose University

Kansas

Kansas Newman College
Labette Community College
Ottawa University
Pittsburg State University

Kentucky

Asbury College
Cumberland College
Madisonville Community College
Murray State University
Transylvania University
University of Kentucky

Louisiana

Bossier Parish Community College
Grambling State University
Louisiana State University and
  Agricultural and Mechanical
  College

Maine

Central Maine Technical College
University of Maine
    Augusta
    Farmington
    Machias
    Orono
    Presque Isle

Maryland

Morgan State University
University of Maryland: Eastern
  Shore

Massachusetts

Eastern Nazarene College
Greenfield Community College
Hellenic College
St. John's Seminary College
Stonehill College
University of Massachusetts Boston

Michigan

Michigan Technological University
Northern Michigan University
Northwestern Michigan College

Minnesota

Bemidji State University
University of Minnesota
    Crookston
    Morris
    Twin Cities

Mississippi

Mississippi University for Women
University of Mississippi

Missouri

North Central Missouri College
Northwest Missouri State
  University
St. Louis University
University of Missouri: Rolla
Westminster College

Montana

Little Big Horn College
Montana State University
    College of Technology-Great
      Falls
    Billings
    Bozeman
    Northern
Montana Tech of The University of
  Montana
University of Montana-Missoula
University of Montana College of
  Technology
Western Montana College of the
  University of Montana

Nebraska

Chadron State College
College of St. Mary
Midland Lutheran College

New Hampshire

St. Anselm College

New York

Canisius College
Iona College
Parsons School of Design
St. Bonaventure University
State University of New York
    College at Buffalo
    College at Potsdam

North Carolina

Lenoir-Rhyne College
Queens College
Western Carolina University

North Dakota

Bismarck State College
Dickinson State University
Minot State University
North Dakota State College of
    Science
North Dakota State University:
    Bottineau
University of North Dakota
    Lake Region
    Williston

Ohio

Northwestern College
Otterbein College
Walsh University

Oklahoma

Northeastern Oklahoma
    Agricultural and Mechanical
    College
Northern Oklahoma College
Oklahoma State University
    Oklahoma City
    Stillwater
Southeastern Oklahoma State
    University
University of Central Oklahoma
University of Oklahoma Health
    Sciences Center

Oregon

Eastern Oregon State College
George Fox College
Oregon Health Sciences University
Oregon Institute of Technology
Portland State University
Southern Oregon State College
University of Oregon
    Eugene
    Robert Donald Clark Honors
      College
Western Oregon State College

Pennsylvania

Albright College
Bloomsburg University of
    Pennsylvania
California University of
    Pennsylvania
Cheyney University of Pennsylvania
Clarion University of Pennsylvania
Edinboro University of
    Pennsylvania
King's College
Kutztown University of
    Pennsylvania
Lock Haven University of
    Pennsylvania
Lycoming College
Manor Junior College
Mansfield University of
    Pennsylvania
Millersville University of
    Pennsylvania

St. Charles Borromeo Seminary-
    Overbrook
West Chester University of
    Pennsylvania

Puerto Rico

American University of Puerto Rico
Caribbean University

Rhode Island

Providence College

South Carolina

Spartanburg Methodist College
University of South Carolina at
    Lancaster

Tennessee

Carson-Newman College
Hiwassee College
Jackson State Community College
Northeast State Technical
    Community College
Shelby State Community College
Tennessee Wesleyan College
University of Tennessee: Memphis
Volunteer State Community College
Walters State Community College

Texas

Dallas Baptist University
El Centro College
McMurry University
Texas Southern University

Utah

Utah State University

Virginia

Blue Ridge Community College
Norfolk State University
Randolph-Macon Woman's College
St. Paul's College
Virginia State University

Washington

Edmonds Community College
Grays Harbor College

West Virginia

Bethany College
Fairmont State College
West Virginia University

Wisconsin

Blackhawk Technical College
University of Wisconsin-Superior

Tuition and/or fee waiver for family members enrolled simultaneously

Alabama

International Bible College
Marion Military Institute
Spring Hill College
Tuskegee University

Arizona

Arizona College of the Bible

Arkansas

Philander Smith College

California

Azusa Pacific University
California Lutheran University
La Sierra University

LIFE Bible College
New School of Architecture
Pacific Christian College
Patten College
Riverside Community College
St. Mary's College of California
San Jose Christian College
Santa Clara University
Solano Community College
University of San Francisco
Yeshiva Ohr Elchonon Chabad/
    West Coast Talmudical Seminary

Colorado

Colorado Christian University

Connecticut

Albertus Magnus College
Briarwood College
Fairfield University
Sacred Heart University
St. Joseph College
Teikyo-Post University
University of Bridgeport
University of Hartford
University of New Haven

Delaware

Goldey-Beacom College

District of Columbia

Catholic University of America
George Washington University
Trinity College

Florida

Barry University
Florida Christian College
Florida Southern College
Jacksonville University
Palm Beach Atlantic College
St. Leo College
Santa Fe Community College
Schiller International University
Trinity International University
Warner Southern College

Georgia

Berry College
Brenau University
Mercer University
Morris Brown College
Oglethorpe University
Paine College
Shorter College
Wesleyan College

Hawaii

Chaminade University of Honolulu

Idaho

Northwest Nazarene College

Illinois

Augustana College
Benedictine University
Eureka College
Kendall College
Lincoln Christian College and
    Seminary
MacCormac Junior College
Monmouth College
Olivet Nazarene University
Quincy University
Rosary College

Indiana

Bethel College
Huntington College
Indiana Institute of Technology
Indiana State University
Indiana Wesleyan University

Manchester College
Marian College
St. Francis College
St. Joseph's College
Saint Mary's College
University of Evansville
Vincennes University

Iowa

American Institute of Business
Clarke College
Loras College
Northwestern College
Simpson College
Teikyo Marycrest University
University of Dubuque
Upper Iowa University

Kansas

Colby Community College
Kansas Newman College
St. Mary College
Tabor College

Kentucky

Asbury College
Cumberland College
Morehead State University
Spalding University
Sue Bennett College

Louisiana

Xavier University of Louisiana

Maine

St. Joseph's College

Maryland

Hood College
Loyola College in Maryland
Mount St. Mary's College
Western Maryland College

Massachusetts

American International College
Anna Maria College
Assumption College
Atlantic Union College
Bay Path College
Becker College
    Leicester Campus
    Worcester Campus
Curry College
Eastern Nazarene College
Elms College
Lasell College
Merrimack College
Nichols College
Pine Manor College
Springfield College
Stonehill College
Suffolk University
Western New England College

Michigan

Andrews University
Great Lakes Christian College
Michigan Christian College
Northwood University
Reformed Bible College
Saginaw Valley State University
Siena Heights College
Yeshiva Beth Yehuda-Yeshiva
    Gedolah of Greater Detroit

Minnesota

Minnesota Bible College
North Central Bible College
Northwestern College
Oak Hills Bible College
University of St. Thomas

Tuition and/or fee waivers: family members enrolled simultaneously

Mississippi
Blue Mountain College
Holmes Community College
Magnolia Bible College
Rust College
University of Mississippi

Missouri
Avila College
Calvary Bible College
Central Bible College
Central Christian College of the Bible
Central Methodist College
Columbia College
Fontbonne College
Maryville University of Saint Louis
Missouri Baptist College
Missouri Valley College
National College
Research College of Nursing
Rockhurst College
St. Louis University
Stephens College
Wentworth Military Academy
William Woods University

Montana
Carroll College
University of Great Falls

Nebraska
College of St. Mary
Creighton University
Dana College
Grace University
Hastings College
Midland Lutheran College
Nebraska Christian College

Nevada
Sierra Nevada College
Western Nevada Community College

New Hampshire
Franklin Pierce College
Hesser College
McIntosh College
New England College
New Hampshire College
Notre Dame College
Rivier College
St. Anselm College

New Jersey
Bloomfield College
Burlington County College
Caldwell College
Centenary College
College of St. Elizabeth
Fairleigh Dickinson University
 Edward Williams College
 Teaneck
Georgian Court College
Mercer County Community College
Monmouth University
Seton Hall University

New York
Canisius College
College of Mount St. Vincent
College of New Rochelle
 New Rochelle
 School of New Resources
College of St. Rose
Daemen College
D'Youville College
Elmira College
Hartwick College
Houghton College
Iona College

Long Island University: Brooklyn Campus
Marymount College
Molloy College
Nazareth College of Rochester
Nyack College
Plaza Business Institute
Russell Sage College
Sage Junior College of Albany
St. Bonaventure University
St. John's University
St. Joseph's College
 Brooklyn
 Suffolk Campus
St. Thomas Aquinas College
Villa Maria College of Buffalo
Wagner College

North Carolina
Alamance Community College
Belmont Abbey College
East Coast Bible College
John Wesley College
Lenoir-Rhyne College
Livingstone College
Peace College
Pfeiffer College
Queens College
Roanoke Bible College

North Dakota
Trinity Bible College

Ohio
Antioch College
Ashland University
Capital University
Cincinnati Bible College and Seminary
Franciscan University of Steubenville
Lake Erie College
Malone College
Mount Union College
Mount Vernon Nazarene College
Muskingum College
Ohio Northern University
Otterbein College
Terra Community College
University of Dayton
University of Findlay
Ursuline College
Walsh University
Wilmington College
Xavier University

Oklahoma
Bartlesville Wesleyan College
Northeastern Oklahoma Agricultural and Mechanical College
Oklahoma Christian University of Science and Arts
Oral Roberts University

Oregon
Bassist College
Clatsop Community College
Eugene Bible College
George Fox College
Lewis & Clark College
Linn-Benton Community College
Multnomah Bible College
Southwestern Oregon Community College

Pennsylvania
Albright College
Allentown College of St. Francis de Sales
Baptist Bible College of Pennsylvania

Cabrini College
Carlow College
Cedar Crest College
Elizabethtown College
Gratz College
Immaculata College
King's College
La Roche College
Lackawanna Junior College
Lancaster Bible College
Lycoming College
Marywood College
Mercyhurst College
Messiah College
Moore College of Art and Design
Peirce College
Philadelphia College of Bible
Rosemont College
St. Francis College
Seton Hill College
Thiel College
University of the Arts
University of Scranton
Ursinus College
Valley Forge Christian College
Valley Forge Military College
Waynesburg College
Wilkes University

Puerto Rico
Caribbean University
ICPR Junior College
Universidad Adventista de las Antillas

Rhode Island
Bryant College
Johnson & Wales University
Providence College

South Carolina
Erskine College
Limestone College
North Greenville College
Southern Wesleyan University
Spartanburg Methodist College

South Dakota
Augustana College
Huron University
Mount Marty College

Tennessee
Belmont University
Carson-Newman College
Hiwassee College
Johnson Bible College
Lee College
Southern College of Seventh-day Adventists
Tennessee Wesleyan College
Union University

Texas
Arlington Baptist College
Dallas Baptist University
Southwestern Adventist College
Stephen F. Austin State University
University of Dallas

Utah
College of Eastern Utah
Westminster College of Salt Lake City

Vermont
Champlain College
Green Mountain College
Johnson State College
Lyndon State College
St. Michael's College

Virginia
Averett College
Christendom College
Ferrum College
Mary Baldwin College
Marymount University
Randolph-Macon College
Virginia Intermont College

Washington
Gonzaga University
Northwest College
Puget Sound Christian College
St. Martin's College

West Virginia
Alderson-Broaddus College

Wisconsin
Alverno College
Beloit College
Blackhawk Technical College
Cardinal Stritch College
Carroll College
Marian College of Fond du Lac
Marquette University
Mount Mary College
Viterbo College
Wisconsin Lutheran College

Wyoming
Northwest College

Tuition and/or fee waiver for unemployed or children of unemployed workers

Alabama
Faulkner University

Arizona
Mohave Community College

Arkansas
Southern Arkansas University Tech

California
City College of San Francisco
Coastline Community College
College of the Desert
Contra Costa College
Feather River College
Fresno City College
Fullerton College
La Sierra University
Laney College
Las Positas College
Long Beach City College
Merritt College
Orange Coast College
Palo Verde College
Pasadena City College
Porterville College
Queen of the Holy Rosary College
Riverside Community College
Saddleback College
San Diego Miramar College
Santa Barbara City College
Santa Monica College
Sierra College
West Hills Community College

Georgia
Brewton-Parker College

Hawaii
University of Hawaii: Kauai
 Community College

Idaho
Northwest Nazarene College

Iowa
Drake University

Kansas
Butler County Community College
Labette Community College
Neosho County Community College

Kentucky
Cumberland College

Massachusetts
Atlantic Union College
Berkshire Community College
Bridgewater State College
Massachusetts Bay Community
 College
Massachusetts College of Art
Massasoit Community College
Mount Wachusett Community
 College
North Adams State College
Salem State College

Michigan
Olivet College
St. Mary's College
Wayne State University

Minnesota
Rainy River Community College

Missouri
Calvary Bible College
St. Louis University

Montana
Montana State University College
 of Technology-Great Falls

Nebraska
Western Nebraska Community
 College

Nevada
Western Nevada Community
 College

New Jersey
Brookdale Community College
Camden County College
County College of Morris
Cumberland County College
Essex County College
Mercer County Community College
Ocean County College
Raritan Valley Community College
Rutgers, The State University of
 New Jersey
 Camden College of Arts and
  Sciences
 College of Engineering
 College of Nursing
 College of Pharmacy
 Cook College
 Douglass College
 Livingston College
 Mason Gross School of the
  Arts
 Newark College of Arts and
  Sciences
 Rutgers College
Sussex County Community College
Trenton State College
Warren County Community College

William Paterson College of New
 Jersey

New York
Bramson ORT Technical Institute
Herkimer County Community
 College
Mannes College of Music
New York Institute of Technology
Orange County Community College
Plaza Business Institute
Villa Maria College of Buffalo
Wagner College

Ohio
Belmont Technical College

Oklahoma
Northern Oklahoma College

Oregon
Linn-Benton Community College
Marylhurst College
Rogue Community College
Southwestern Oregon Community
 College

Pennsylvania
Bucks County Community College
Gratz College
King's College
Manor Junior College
Mercyhurst College
Point Park College
St. Charles Borromeo Seminary-
 Overbrook
University of the Arts

Rhode Island
Rhode Island College
Roger Williams University
University of Rhode Island

South Carolina
Greenville Technical College
Spartanburg Methodist College
York Technical College

Tennessee
Shelby State Community College

Texas
El Centro College

Utah
Utah State University

Washington
Big Bend Community College
Centralia College
Columbia Basin College
Edmonds Community College
Grays Harbor College
Lower Columbia College
North Seattle Community College
Peninsula College
Pierce College
South Puget Sound Community
 College
South Seattle Community College
Tacoma Community College
Walla Walla Community College
Whatcom Community College
Yakima Valley Community College

Wisconsin
Blackhawk Technical College

Tuition payment by credit card

Alabama
Alabama Agricultural and
 Mechanical University
Alabama State University
Athens State College
Bessemer State Technical College
Bevill State Community College
Birmingham-Southern College
Bishop State Community College
Calhoun Community College
Central Alabama Community
 College
Draughons Junior College
Enterprise State Junior College
Faulkner University
Gadsden State Community College
Huntingdon College
International Bible College
J. F. Drake State Technical College
Jacksonville State University
Jefferson State Community College
John M. Patterson State Technical
 College
Lawson State Community College
Lurleen B. Wallace State Junior
 College
Northwest-Shoals Community
 College
Oakwood College
Reid State Technical College
Samford University
Southeastern Bible College
Southern Christian University
Talladega College
Troy State University
 Dothan
 Montgomery
 Troy
University of Alabama
 Birmingham
 Huntsville
 Tuscaloosa
University of Alabama at
 Birmingham: Walker College
University of Mobile
University of Montevallo
Wallace State College at Hanceville

Alaska
Alaska Pacific University
Prince William Sound Community
 College
University of Alaska
 Anchorage
 Fairbanks
 Southeast

Arizona
Arizona College of the Bible
Arizona State University
Arizona Western College
Cochise College
DeVry Institute of Technology:
 Phoenix
Embry-Riddle Aeronautical
 University: Prescott Campus
Gateway Community College
Glendale Community College
Mesa Community College
Mohave Community College
Northern Arizona University
Paradise Valley Community College
Pima Community College
Prescott College
Rio Salado Community College
Scottsdale Community College

South Mountain Community
 College
University of Arizona
University of Phoenix
Western International University
Yavapai College

Arkansas
Arkansas Tech University
East Arkansas Community College
Garland County Community
 College
Harding University
Henderson State University
Mississippi County Community
 College
North Arkansas Community/
 Technical College
Ouachita Baptist University
South Arkansas Community College
Southern Arkansas University
 Magnolia
 Tech
University of Arkansas
 Fayetteville
 Little Rock
 Monticello
 Pine Bluff
University of Central Arkansas
Westark Community College
Williams Baptist College

California
Academy of Art College
American College: Los Angeles
Antioch Southern California at Los
 Angeles
Armstrong University
Art Center College of Design
Art Institute of Southern California
Azusa Pacific University
Bethany College
Biola University
Brooks Institute of Photography
Cabrillo College
California Baptist College
California College of Arts and
 Crafts
California Institute of the Arts
California Lutheran University
California State University
 Bakersfield
 Dominguez Hills
 Fresno
 Hayward
 Long Beach
 Los Angeles
 Sacramento
 San Bernardino
 San Marcos
 Stanislaus
Chapman University
Christian Heritage College
Citrus College
Claremont McKenna College
Coastline Community College
Cogswell Polytechnical College
Coleman College
College of Alameda
College of Notre Dame
College of San Mateo
College of the Sequoias
Columbia College: Hollywood
Contra Costa College
Cosumnes River College
Crafton Hills College
De Anza College
DeVry Institute of Technology:
 Pomona
Diablo Valley College
Dominican College of San Rafael
Evergreen Valley College

Fashion Institute of Design and
  Merchandising
Foothill College
Fresno City College
Fresno Pacific College
Gavilan Community College
Golden Gate University
Golden West College
Holy Names College
Humboldt State University
Humphreys College
John F. Kennedy University
Kings River Community College
La Sierra University
Long Beach City College
Los Angeles Pierce College
Los Medanos College
Marymount College
Menlo College
Merced College
Modesto Junior College
Monterey Institute of International
  Studies
Mount St. Mary's College
National University
New School of Architecture
Occidental College
Otis College of Art and Design
Pacific Christian College
Pacific Oaks College
Patten College
Pepperdine University
Point Loma Nazarene College
Queen of the Holy Rosary College
Riverside Community College
Sacramento City College
Saddleback College
St. Mary's College of California
Samuel Merritt College
San Diego Mesa College
San Diego Miramar College
San Francisco Conservatory of
  Music
San Francisco State University
San Jose City College
Santa Clara University
Santa Monica College
Santa Rosa Junior College
Scripps College
Shasta College
Simpson College
Skyline College
Solano Community College
Sonoma State University
Southern California College
Southern California Institute of
  Architecture
Southwestern College
Taft College
University of California: Los
  Angeles
University of Judaism
University of La Verne
University of the Pacific
University of Redlands
University of San Francisco
University of Southern California
University of West Los Angeles
Victor Valley College
Whittier College
Woodbury University
Yeshiva Ohr Elchonon Chabad/
  West Coast Talmudical Seminary

Colorado

Adams State College
Aims Community College
Arapahoe Community College
Beth-El College of Nursing
Colorado Christian University
Colorado Institute of Art

Colorado Mountain College
  Alpine Campus
  Spring Valley Campus
  Timberline Campus
Colorado Northwestern Community
  College
Colorado School of Mines
Colorado State University
Colorado Technical University
Fort Lewis College
Front Range Community College
Lamar Community College
Mesa State College
Metropolitan State College of
  Denver
Naropa Institute
Northeastern Junior College
Otero Junior College
Pikes Peak Community College
Pueblo Community College
Red Rocks Community College
Regis University
Rocky Mountain College of Art &
  Design
Technical Trades Institute
Trinidad State Junior College
University of Colorado
  Colorado Springs
  Denver
University of Denver
University of Northern Colorado
University of Southern Colorado
Western State College of Colorado

Connecticut

Albertus Magnus College
Asnuntuck Community-Technical
  College
Briarwood College
Capital Community-Technical
  College
Central Connecticut State
  University
Eastern Connecticut State
  University
Gateway Community-Technical
  College
Housatonic Community-Technical
  College
Manchester Community-Technical
  College
Middlesex Community-Technical
  College
Mitchell College
Naugatuck Valley Community-
  Technical College
Northwestern Connecticut
  Community-Technical College
Norwalk Community-Technical
  College
Paier College of Art
Quinebaug Valley Community-
  Technical College
Quinnipiac College
Sacred Heart University
St. Joseph College
Southern Connecticut State
  University
Teikyo-Post University
Three Rivers Community-Technical
  College
Tunxis Community-Technical
  College
University of Bridgeport
University of Hartford
University of New Haven
Western Connecticut State
  University
Yale University

Delaware

Delaware State University
Delaware Technical and
  Community College
  Owens Campus
  Stanton/Wilmington Campus
  Terry Campus
Goldey-Beacom College
Wesley College
Wilmington College

District of Columbia

American University
Catholic University of America
Corcoran School of Art
Howard University
Mount Vernon College
Southeastern University
Strayer College
Trinity College
University of the District of
  Columbia

Florida

Barry University
Bethune-Cookman College
Brevard Community College
Broward Community College
Central Florida Community College
Chipola Junior College
Daytona Beach Community College
Eckerd College
Edison Community College
Embry-Riddle Aeronautical
  University
Florida Agricultural and Mechanical
  University
Florida College
Florida Community College at
  Jacksonville
Florida Institute of Technology
Florida Keys Community College
Florida Memorial College
Florida Southern College
Gulf Coast Community College
Hillsborough Community College
Hobe Sound Bible College
Indian River Community College
Jacksonville University
Lake-Sumter Community College
Lynn University
Manatee Community College
Miami-Dade Community College
Nova Southeastern University
Okaloosa-Walton Community
  College
Palm Beach Atlantic College
Palm Beach Community College
Pensacola Junior College
Polk Community College
Ringling School of Art and Design
Rollins College
St. Johns River Community College
St. Leo College
St. Petersburg Junior College
St. Thomas University
Santa Fe Community College
Seminole Community College
South Florida Community College
Southeastern College of the
  Assemblies of God
Southern College
Tallahassee Community College
Tampa College
Trinity International University
University of Central Florida
University of Miami
University of North Florida
University of Tampa
University of West Florida
Valencia Community College
Warner Southern College

Webber College

Georgia

Abraham Baldwin Agricultural
  College
Albany State College
American College: Atlanta
Andrew College
Armstrong State College
Augusta College
Augusta Technical Institute
Berry College
Brenau University
Brunswick College
Chattahoochee Technical Institute
Clark Atlanta University
Clayton State College
Columbus College
Columbus Technical Institute
Covenant College
Darton College
DeKalb College
DeKalb Technical Institute
DeVry Institute of Technology:
  Atlanta
Emmanuel College
Floyd College
Fort Valley State College
Gainesville College
Georgia College
Georgia Institute of Technology
Georgia Southern University
Georgia Southwestern College
Georgia State University
Gordon College
Gwinnett Technical Institute
Kennesaw State College
LaGrange College
Macon College
Mercer University
  Atlanta
  Macon
Middle Georgia College
Morris Brown College
North Georgia College
Oglethorpe University
Piedmont College
Shorter College
South College
Southern College of Technology
Thomas College
Valdosta State University
Wesleyan College
West Georgia College

Hawaii

Chaminade University of Honolulu
Hawaii Pacific University
University of Hawaii
  Hilo
  Kapiolani Community College
  Kauai Community College
  Manoa
  West Oahu
  Windward Community College

Idaho

Albertson College
Boise Bible College
Boise State University
College of Southern Idaho
Eastern Idaho Technical College
Lewis-Clark State College
North Idaho College
Ricks College

Illinois

American Academy of Art
American Conservatory of Music
Aurora University
Belleville Area College
Benedictine University

Black Hawk College
Blackburn College
Bradley University
Carl Sandburg College
Chicago College of Commerce
Chicago State University
City Colleges of Chicago
    Kennedy-King College
    Malcolm X College
    Olive-Harvey College
    Richard J. Daley College
    Wright College
College of DuPage
College of Lake County
Columbia College
Concordia University
Danville Area Community College
De Paul University
DeVry Institute of Technology
    Addison
    Chicago
East-West University
Elgin Community College
Elmhurst College
Eureka College
Governors State University
Greenville College
Harrington Institute of Interior
    Design
Highland Community College
Illinois Institute of Technology
Illinois Wesleyan University
International Academy of
    Merchandising and Design
ITT Technical Institute: Hoffman
    Estates
Joliet Junior College
Kendall College
Kishwaukee College
Lake Land College
Lewis and Clark Community
    College
Lewis University
Lincoln Land Community College
Loyola University of Chicago
MacCormac Junior College
MacMurray College
McHenry County College
McKendree College
Millikin University
Moraine Valley Community College
Morrison Institute of Technology
Morton College
National-Louis University
North Central College
North Park College
Northeastern Illinois University
Northwestern Business College
Oakton Community College
Olivet Nazarene University
Parkland College
Principia College
Quincy University
Richland Community College
Rock Valley College
Rockford College
Rosary College
St. Xavier University
School of the Art Institute of
    Chicago
Southern Illinois University at
    Edwardsville
Spoon River College
Trinity International University
Triton College
University of Chicago
University of Illinois: Springfield
William Rainey Harper College

Indiana

Butler University
Calumet College of St. Joseph

Goshen College
Huntington College
Indiana Institute of Technology
Indiana State University
Indiana University
    Bloomington
    East
    Kokomo
    Northwest
    South Bend
    Southeast
Indiana University—Purdue
    University
    Fort Wayne
    Indianapolis
Indiana Wesleyan University
Ivy Tech State College
    Central Indiana
    Columbus
    Eastcentral
    Kokomo
    Lafayette
    Northcentral
    Northeast
    Northwest
    Southcentral
    Southeast
    Southwest
    Wabash Valley
    Whitewater
Lutheran College of Health
    Professions
Marian College
Oakland City University
Purdue University
    Calumet
    North Central Campus
Rose-Hulman Institute of
    Technology
St. Francis College
St. Mary-of-the-Woods College
St. Meinrad College
Tri-State University
University of Evansville
University of Indianapolis
University of Southern Indiana
Valparaiso University
Vincennes University

Iowa

American Institute of Business
American Institute of Commerce
Briar Cliff College
Buena Vista University
Central College
Clarke College
Clinton Community College
Coe College
Des Moines Area Community
    College
Drake University
Ellsworth Community College
Faith Baptist Bible College and
    Theological Seminary
Graceland College
Grand View College
Hawkeye Community College
Indian Hills Community College
Iowa Lakes Community College
Iowa Wesleyan College
Iowa Western Community College
Kirkwood Community College
Maharishi University of
    Management
Morningside College
Muscatine Community College
North Iowa Area Community
    College
Northeast Iowa Community College
Northwest Iowa Community
    College
St. Ambrose University

Scott Community College
Simpson College
Southeastern Community College:
    North Campus
Southwestern Community College
Teikyo Marycrest University
University of Dubuque
University of Osteopathic Medicine
    and Health Sciences
Westmar University

Kansas

Baker University
Barton County Community College
Benedictine College
Bethany College
Bethel College
Butler County Community College
Colby Community College
Emporia State University
Fort Hays State University
Fort Scott Community College
Friends University
Garden City Community College
Hutchinson Community College
Independence Community College
Kansas City Kansas Community
    College
Kansas Newman College
Labette Community College
MidAmerica Nazarene College
Neosho County Community College
Ottawa University
Pittsburg State University
Pratt Community College
St. Mary College
Southwestern College
Tabor College
University of Kansas
    Lawrence
    Medical Center
Washburn University of Topeka
Wichita State University

Kentucky

Ashland Community College
Bellarmine College
Centre College
Eastern Kentucky University
Elizabethtown Community College
Georgetown College
Hopkinsville Community College
Kentucky Christian College
Kentucky State University
Kentucky Wesleyan College
Lexington Community College
Madisonville Community College
Maysville Community College
Morehead State University
Murray State University
Northern Kentucky University
Paducah Community College
Pikeville College
Prestonsburg Community College
Southeast Community College
Spalding University
Sullivan College
Union College
University of Louisville
Western Kentucky University

Louisiana

Bossier Parish Community College
Dillard University
Grambling State University
Louisiana State University in
    Shreveport
Louisiana Tech University
Loyola University New Orleans
McNeese State University
Nicholls State University
Northeast Louisiana University

Nunez Community College
Our Lady of Holy Cross College
Southeastern Louisiana University
University of New Orleans
University of Southwestern
    Louisiana
Xavier University of Louisiana

Maine

Andover College
Casco Bay College
Central Maine Technical College
Husson College
Maine College of Art
St. Joseph's College
Southern Maine Technical College
Thomas College
Unity College
University of Maine
    Augusta
    Farmington
    Fort Kent
    Machias
    Orono
    Presque Isle
University of New England
University of Southern Maine
Westbrook College

Maryland

Allegany College
Anne Arundel Community College
Baltimore Hebrew University
Baltimore International Culinary
    College
Bowie State University
Capitol College
Carroll Community College
Catonsville Community College
Cecil Community College
Charles County Community College
Chesapeake College
Dundalk Community College
Essex Community College
Frederick Community College
Frostburg State University
Hagerstown Business College
Hagerstown Junior College
Harford Community College
Hood College
Howard Community College
Johns Hopkins University: Peabody
    Conservatory of Music
Loyola College in Maryland
Maryland College of Art and
    Design
Maryland Institute College of Art
Montgomery College
    Germantown Campus
    Rockville Campus
    Takoma Park Campus
Morgan State University
Mount St. Mary's College
Prince George's Community College
St. Mary's College of Maryland
Towson State University
University of Baltimore
University of Maryland
    Baltimore
    Baltimore County
    College Park
    Eastern Shore
    University College
Villa Julie College
Washington College
Western Maryland College
Wor-Wic Community College

Massachusetts

American International College
Anna Maria College
Atlantic Union College

Babson College
Bay Path College
Bentley College
Berklee College of Music
Berkshire Community College
Boston Architectural Center
Boston University
Bradford College
Brandeis University
Bridgewater State College
Bunker Hill Community College
Cape Cod Community College
Clark University
Curry College
Eastern Nazarene College
Elms College
Emerson College
Emmanuel College
Endicott College
Essex Agricultural and Technical
    Institute
Fisher College
Forsyth School for Dental
    Hygienists
Framingham State College
Franklin Institute of Boston
Gordon College
Greenfield Community College
Hebrew College
Hellenic College
Holyoke Community College
Lasell College
Marian Court College
Massachusetts Bay Community
    College
Massasoit Community College
Merrimack College
Middlesex Community College
Montserrat College of Art
Mount Holyoke College
Mount Ida College
Mount Wachusett Community
    College
New England Conservatory of
    Music
Newbury College
Nichols College
North Adams State College
North Shore Community College
Northeastern University
Northern Essex Community College
Pine Manor College
Quincy College
Quinsigamond Community College
Roxbury Community College
School of the Museum of Fine Arts
Springfield College
Springfield Technical Community
    College
Suffolk University
Tufts University
University of Massachusetts
    Amherst
    Dartmouth
Wentworth Institute of Technology
Western New England College
Westfield State College
Worcester State College

Michigan

Adrian College
Alma College
Alpena Community College
Andrews University
Aquinas College

Baker College
    Auburn Hills
    Cadillac
    Flint
    Mount Clemens
    Muskegon
    Owosso
    Port Huron
Center for Creative Studies: College
    of Art and Design
Central Michigan University
Cleary College
Concordia College
Cornerstone College and Grand
    Rapids Baptist Seminary
Davenport College of Business
Delta College
Detroit College of Business
Eastern Michigan University
Glen Oaks Community College
GMI Engineering & Management
    Institute
Grace Bible College
Grand Rapids Community College
Grand Valley State University
Great Lakes Junior College of
    Business
Henry Ford Community College
Highland Park Community College
Jackson Community College
Kalamazoo Valley Community
    College
Kellogg Community College
Kendall College of Art and Design
Macomb Community College
Madonna University
Michigan Christian College
Michigan Technological University
Mid Michigan Community College
Monroe County Community
    College
Montcalm Community College
Mott Community College
Muskegon Community College
Northwestern Michigan College
Oakland Community College
Oakland University
Olivet College
Reformed Bible College
Sacred Heart Major Seminary
Saginaw Valley State University
St. Clair County Community
    College
St. Mary's College
Schoolcraft College
Spring Arbor College
Suomi College
University of Michigan: Flint
Walsh College of Accountancy and
    Business Administration
Washtenaw Community College
Wayne State University
West Shore Community College
Western Michigan University

Minnesota

Anoka-Ramsey Community College
Augsburg College
Austin Community College
Bethany Lutheran College
Bethel College
College of St. Benedict
College of St. Catherine: St.
    Catherine Campus
College of St. Catherine-
    Minneapolis
College of St. Scholastica
Concordia College: St. Paul
Hamline University
Inver Hills Community College
Lakewood Community College
Mankato State University

Mesabi Community College:
    Arrowhead Region
Metropolitan State University
Minneapolis Community College
Moorhead State University
National College
Normandale Community College
North Central Bible College
North Hennepin Community
    College
Northwestern College
Pillsbury Baptist Bible College
Rainy River Community College
Rochester Community College
St. Cloud Technical College
St. Paul Technical College
Willmar Technical College

Mississippi

Alcorn State University
Belhaven College
Blue Mountain College
Delta State University
Hinds Community College
Jackson State University
Jones County Junior College
Magnolia Bible College
Mary Holmes College
Meridian Community College
Millsaps College
Mississippi Gulf Coast Community
    College
    Jackson County Campus
    Jefferson Davis Campus
    Perkinston
Mississippi State University
Mississippi University for Women
Northeast Mississippi Community
    College
Northwest Mississippi Community
    College
Pearl River Community College
Rust College
Tougaloo College
University of Mississippi
University of Southern Mississippi
William Carey College

Missouri

Avila College
Baptist Bible College
Calvary Bible College
Central Methodist College
Central Missouri State University
Columbia College
Cottey College
Crowder College
DeVry Institute of Technology:
    Kansas City
East Central College
Evangel College
Fontbonne College
Hannibal-LaGrange College
Harris Stowe State College
Jefferson College
Kansas City Art Institute
Lincoln University
Lindenwood College
Longview Community College
Maple Woods Community College
Maryville University of Saint Louis
Missouri Baptist College
Missouri Southern State College
Missouri Valley College
Missouri Western State College
Moberly Area Community College
National College
North Central Missouri College
Northwest Missouri State
    University
Ozark Christian College
Park College

Penn Valley Community College
Ranken Technical College
Research College of Nursing
Rockhurst College
St. Charles County Community
    College
St. Louis Christian College
St. Louis Community College
    Florissant Valley
    Forest Park
    Meramec
St. Louis University
Southeast Missouri State University
Southwest Baptist University
Southwest Missouri State University
State Fair Community College
Stephens College
Three Rivers Community College
Truman State University
University of Missouri
    Columbia
    Kansas City
    Rolla
    St. Louis
Webster University
Westminster College
William Jewell College
William Woods University

Montana

Flathead Valley Community College
Montana State University
    College of Technology-Great
        Falls
    Bozeman
    Northern
Rocky Mountain College
University of Great Falls
University of Montana-Missoula
University of Montana College of
    Technology
Western Montana College of the
    University of Montana

Nebraska

Bellevue University
Central Community College
Chadron State College
Clarkson College
College of St. Mary
Concordia College
Creighton University
Dana College
Doane College/Lincoln Campus
Grace University
Lincoln School of Commerce
Metropolitan Community College
Midland Lutheran College
Nebraska Christian College
Nebraska Methodist College of
    Nursing and Allied Health
Nebraska Wesleyan University
Northeast Community College
Peru State College
Southeast Community College
    Beatrice Campus
    Lincoln Campus
    Milford Campus
Union College
University of Nebraska Medical
    Center
Wayne State College
Western Nebraska Community
    College
York College

Nevada

Community College of Southern
    Nevada
Great Basin College
Morrison College: Reno
Sierra Nevada College

Truckee Meadows Community
College
University of Nevada
Las Vegas
Reno
Western Nevada Community
College

New Hampshire
Colby-Sawyer College
Daniel Webster College
Franklin Pierce College
Hesser College
Keene State College
McIntosh College
New England College
New Hampshire College
New Hampshire Technical College
Berlin
Manchester
Nashua
Notre Dame College
Rivier College
University of New Hampshire at
Manchester

New Jersey
Atlantic Community College
Bergen Community College
Berkeley College of Business
Bloomfield College
Brookdale Community College
Burlington County College
Caldwell College
Camden County College
Centenary College
Cumberland County College
DeVry Technical Institute
Drew University
Essex County College
Fairleigh Dickinson University
Edward Williams College
Teaneck
Georgian Court College
Mercer County Community College
Middlesex County College
Monmouth University
Montclair State University
New Jersey Institute of Technology
Ocean County College
Ramapo College of New Jersey
Raritan Valley Community College
Richard Stockton College of New
Jersey
Rider University
Rowan College of New Jersey
St. Peter's College
Salem Community College
Seton Hall University
Stevens Institute of Technology
Sussex County Community College
Union County College
William Paterson College of New
Jersey

New Mexico
Albuquerque Technical-Vocational
Institute
Clovis Community College
College of Santa Fe
College of the Southwest
Dona Ana Branch Community
College of New Mexico State
University
Eastern New Mexico University
Portales
Roswell Campus
National College
New Mexico Highlands University
New Mexico Institute of Mining
and Technology
New Mexico Military Institute

New Mexico State University
Parks College
San Juan College
Santa Fe Community College
University of New Mexico

New York
Adelphi University
Adirondack Community College
American Academy of Dramatic
Arts
Audrey Cohen College
Barnard College
Berkeley College
Briarcliffe: The College for Business
and Technology
Broome Community College
Bryant & Stratton Business Institute
Albany
Syracuse
Canisius College
Cayuga County Community College
Cazenovia College
City University of New York
Brooklyn College
City College
Hunter College
John Jay College of Criminal
Justice
Queens College
Queensborough Community
College
Clarkson University
Clinton Community College
College of Aeronautics
College of Insurance
College of Mount St. Vincent
College of New Rochelle
New Rochelle
School of New Resources
College of St. Rose
Columbia University
Columbia College
School of Engineering and
Applied Science
School of General Studies
School of Nursing
Columbia-Greene Community
College
Corning Community College
Daemen College
Dominican College of Blauvelt
Dowling College
Dutchess Community College
D'Youville College
Eastman School of Music of the
University of Rochester
Elmira College
Erie Community College
North Campus
South Campus
Eugene Lang College/New School
for Social Research
Fashion Institute of Technology
Finger Lakes Community College
Fordham University
Fulton-Montgomery Community
College
Genesee Community College
Herkimer County Community
College
Hilbert College
Hofstra University
Hudson Valley Community College
Interboro Institute
Iona College
Ithaca College
Jamestown Community College
Jefferson Community College
Keuka College
Le Moyne College

Long Island University
Brooklyn Campus
C. W. Post Campus
Southampton College
Manhattan College
Manhattanville College
Maria College
Marist College
Marymount College
Marymount Manhattan College
Mater Dei College
Medaille College
Mercy College
Mohawk Valley Community College
Molloy College
Monroe Community College
Mount St. Mary College
Nazareth College of Rochester
New York Institute of Technology
New York School of Interior
Design
New York University
Niagara County Community College
Niagara University
North Country Community College
Nyack College
Onondaga Community College
Orange County Community College
Pace University
Parsons School of Design
Paul Smith's College
Phillips Beth Israel School of
Nursing
Plaza Business Institute
Polytechnic University
Brooklyn
Long Island Campus
Pratt Institute
Rensselaer Polytechnic Institute
Roberts Wesleyan College
Rochester Institute of Technology
Rockland Community College
Russell Sage College
Sage Junior College of Albany
St. Francis College
St. John Fisher College
St. John's University
St. Joseph's College
Brooklyn
Suffolk Campus
St. Joseph's Hospital Health Center
School of Nursing
St. Thomas Aquinas College
Schenectady County Community
College
School of Visual Arts
Siena College

State University of New York
Albany
Binghamton
Buffalo
Oswego
Purchase
Stony Brook
College of Agriculture and
Technology at Cobleskill
College of Agriculture and
Technology at Morrisville
College at Brockport
College at Buffalo
College at Cortland
College at Fredonia
College at Geneseo
College at Old Westbury
College at Oneonta
College at Plattsburgh
College at Potsdam
College of Technology at
Alfred
College of Technology at
Canton
College of Technology at Delhi
College of Technology at
Farmingdale
Institute of Technology at
Utica/Rome
New Paltz
Tompkins-Cortland Community
College
Trocaire College
Ulster County Community College
University of the State of New
York: Regents College
Utica College of Syracuse
University
Villa Maria College of Buffalo
Wagner College
Wells College
Westchester Business Institute
Westchester Community College
Wood Tobe-Coburn School

North Carolina
Alamance Community College
Appalachian State University
Barton College
Belmont Abbey College
Bennett College
Brevard College
Brunswick Community College
Caldwell Community College and
Technical Institute
Campbell University
Cape Fear Community College
Carteret Community College
Catawba College
Catawba Valley Community College
Central Piedmont Community
College
Craven Community College
Davidson County Community
College
East Carolina University
East Coast Bible College
Elon College
Fayetteville State University
Fayetteville Technical Community
College
Forsyth Technical Community
College
Gardner-Webb University
Greensboro College
Guilford College
James Sprunt Community College
John Wesley College
Johnson C. Smith University
Lees-McRae College
Lenoir-Rhyne College
Louisburg College

Martin Community College
Methodist College
Montgomery Community College
Montreat College
Mount Olive College
Nash Community College
North Carolina Agricultural and
 Technical State University
North Carolina Central University
Pembroke State University
Pfeiffer College
Pitt Community College
Queens College
Randolph Community College
Roanoke-Chowan Community
 College
Sandhills Community College
Shaw University
Surry Community College
University of North Carolina
 Chapel Hill
 Charlotte
 Greensboro
 Wilmington
Warren Wilson College

North Dakota

North Dakota State University
Trinity Bible College
University of North Dakota

Ohio

Antioch College
Antonelli College
Art Academy of Cincinnati
Ashland University
Baldwin-Wallace College
Belmont Technical College
Bluffton College
Bowling Green State University
 Bowling Green
 Firelands College
Bradford School
Bryant & Stratton Business
 Institute: Cleveland West
Bryant & Stratton College
Capital University
Central Ohio Technical College
Chatfield College
Cincinnati Bible College and
 Seminary
Cincinnati State Technical and
 Community College
Circleville Bible College
Clark State Community College
Cleveland College of Jewish Studies
Cleveland Institute of Art
Cleveland Institute of Music
Cleveland State University
College of Mount St. Joseph
Columbus College of Art and
 Design
Columbus State Community College
Cuyahoga Community College
 Eastern Campus
 Metropolitan Campus
 Western Campus
David N. Myers College
Davis College
DeVry Institute of Technology:
 Columbus
Edison State Community College
Franklin University
God's Bible School and College
Heidelberg College
Hiram College
Hocking Technical College
ITT Technical Institute:
 Youngstown
Jefferson Community College
John Carroll University

Kent State University
 East Liverpool Regional
 Campus
 Kent
 Salem Regional Campus
 Stark Campus
 Trumbull Campus
 Tuscarawas Campus
Kenyon College
Kettering College of Medical Arts
Lake Erie College
Lakeland Community College
Lima Technical College
Lorain County Community College
Lourdes College
Malone College
Marietta College
Marion Technical College
Miami University
 Hamilton Campus
 Middletown Campus
Miami-Jacobs College
Mount Union College
Muskingum Area Technical College
Muskingum College
North Central Technical College
Northwest State Community
 College
Northwestern College
Notre Dame College of Ohio
Ohio Dominican College
Ohio Northern University
Ohio University
 Athens
 Chillicothe Campus
 Southern Campus at Ironton
 Zanesville Campus
Ohio Valley Business College
Ohio Wesleyan University
Otterbein College
Owens Technical College
 Findlay Campus
 Toledo
Shawnee State University
Sinclair Community College
Southern State Community College
Stark Technical College
Stautzenberger College
Terra Community College
Tiffin University
Union Institute
University of Akron
University of Cincinnati
 Access Colleges
 Cincinnati
 Clermont College
 Raymond Walters College
University of Dayton
University of Toledo
Urbana University
Ursuline College
Washington State Community
 College
Wilberforce University
Wilmington College
Wright State University
 Dayton
 Lake Campus
Xavier University
Youngstown State University

Oklahoma

Bacone College
Bartlesville Wesleyan College
Cameron University
Connors State College
East Central University
Langston University
Northeastern Oklahoma
 Agricultural and Mechanical
 College
Northern Oklahoma College

Oklahoma Baptist University
Oklahoma Christian University of
 Science and Arts
Oklahoma City Community College
Oklahoma City University
Oklahoma Panhandle State
 University
Oklahoma State University
 Oklahoma City
 Stillwater
Oral Roberts University
Phillips University
Redlands Community College
Rogers State College
Rose State College
St. Gregory's College
Southeastern Oklahoma State
 University
Southwestern Oklahoma State
 University
Tulsa Junior College
University of Central Oklahoma
University of Oklahoma
 Health Sciences Center
 Norman
University of Science and Arts of
 Oklahoma
University of Tulsa
Western Oklahoma State College

Oregon

Bassist College
Central Oregon Community College
Chemeketa Community College
Clackamas Community College
Clatsop Community College
Concordia University
Eastern Oregon State College
Lane Community College
Lewis & Clark College
Linfield College
Linn-Benton Community College
Marylhurst College
Multnomah Bible College
Oregon Health Sciences University
Oregon Institute of Technology
Pacific Northwest College of Art
Portland Community College
Portland State University
Rogue Community College
Southern Oregon State College
Southwestern Oregon Community
 College
Treasure Valley Community College
University of Portland
Western Baptist College
Willamette University

Pennsylvania

Albright College
Allentown College of St. Francis de
 Sales
Alvernia College
Antonelli Institute of Art and
 Photography
Art Institute of Pittsburgh
Baptist Bible College of
 Pennsylvania
Beaver College
Bryn Mawr College
Bucks County Community College
Butler County Community College
Cabrini College
Carlow College
Cedar Crest College
Central Pennsylvania Business
 School
Chatham College
Chestnut Hill College
Cheyney University of Pennsylvania
CHI Institute
Clarion University of Pennsylvania

College Misericordia
Community College of Allegheny
 County
 Allegheny Campus
 Boyce Campus
 South Campus
Community College of Beaver
 County
Community College of Philadelphia
Delaware County Community
 College
Delaware Valley College
Drexel University
Duquesne University
East Stroudsburg University of
 Pennsylvania
Eastern College
Elizabethtown College
Gannon University
Gratz College
Gwynedd-Mercy College
Harcum College
Harrisburg Area Community
 College
Holy Family College
Indiana University of Pennsylvania
Johnson Technical Institute
King's College
Kutztown University of
 Pennsylvania
La Roche College
La Salle University
Lackawanna Junior College
Lebanon Valley College of
 Pennsylvania
Lehigh Carbon Community College
Lincoln University
Luzerne County Community
 College
Manor Junior College
Mansfield University of
 Pennsylvania
Marywood College
Mercyhurst College
Millersville University of
 Pennsylvania
Montgomery County Community
 College
Moore College of Art and Design
Mount Aloysius College
Neumann College
Northampton County Area
 Community College
Peirce College
Pennsylvania Institute of Culinary
 Arts
Philadelphia College of Textiles and
 Science
Pittsburgh Institute of Mortuary
 Science
Point Park College
Reading Area Community College
Remington Education Center: Vale
 Campus
Robert Morris College
Rosemont College
St. Joseph's University
St. Vincent College
Seton Hill College
Slippery Rock University of
 Pennsylvania
Temple University
Thiel College
Thomas Jefferson University:
 College of Allied Health Sciences
University of the Arts
University of Pittsburgh
 Bradford
 Greensburg
 Pittsburgh
University of Scranton
Valley Forge Christian College

Villanova University
Waynesburg College
West Chester University of
Pennsylvania
Westmoreland County Community
College
Widener University
Wilkes University
Wilson College

Puerto Rico

American University of Puerto Rico
Caribbean University
Columbia College
Inter American University of Puerto
Rico
Aguadilla Campus
Arecibo Campus
Fajardo Campus
Guayama Campus
San German Campus
Pontifical Catholic University of
Puerto Rico
Turabo University
Universidad Metropolitana
Universidad Politecnica de Puerto
Rico
University of Puerto Rico: Ponce
Technological University College
University of the Sacred Heart

Rhode Island

Bryant College
Community College of Rhode
Island
Johnson & Wales University
New England Institute of
Technology
Rhode Island College
Rhode Island School of Design
Roger Williams University
Salve Regina University

South Carolina

Aiken Technical College
Chesterfield-Marlboro Technical
College
The Citadel
Claflin College
Clemson University
Coastal Carolina University
Coker College
College of Charleston
Columbia Bible College
Columbia Junior College of Business
Converse College
Florence-Darlington Technical
College
Francis Marion University
Greenville Technical College
Horry-Georgetown Technical
College
Lander University
Limestone College
Medical University of South
Carolina
Midlands Technical College
North Greenville College
Orangeburg-Calhoun Technical
College
Piedmont Technical College
Presbyterian College
Southern Wesleyan University
Spartanburg Technical College
Tri-County Technical College
Trident Technical College

University of South Carolina
Aiken
Beaufort
Columbia
Lancaster
Spartanburg
Sumter
Union
Winthrop University
York Technical College

South Dakota

Augustana College
Black Hills State University
Dakota State University
Dakota Wesleyan University
Huron University
Kilian Community College
Mount Marty College
Northern State University
Presentation College
South Dakota School of Mines and
Technology
South Dakota State University
University of Sioux Falls
University of South Dakota

Tennessee

Austin Peay State University
Belmont University
Carson-Newman College
Chattanooga State Technical
Community College
Christian Brothers University
Cleveland State Community College
Dyersburg State Community
College
East Tennessee State University
Fisk University
Freed-Hardeman University
Hiwassee College
Jackson State Community College
King College
Lee College
LeMoyne-Owen College
Lincoln Memorial University
Maryville College
Memphis College of Art
Middle Tennessee State University
Milligan College
Nashville State Technical Institute
Northeast State Technical
Community College
Pellissippi State Technical
Community College
Rhodes College
Roane State Community College
Shelby State Community College
Southern College of Seventh-day
Adventists
State Technical Institute at
Memphis
Tennessee State University
Tennessee Technological University
Tennessee Wesleyan College
Tusculum College
University of Memphis
University of the South
University of Tennessee
Chattanooga
Knoxville
Martin
Memphis
Volunteer State Community College
Walters State Community College

Texas

Abilene Christian University
Amarillo College
Ambassador University
Angelina College
Arlington Baptist College

Austin Community College
Bee County College
Blinn College
Brazosport College
Cedar Valley College
Central Texas College
Cisco Junior College
Collin County Community College
District
Concordia Lutheran College
Dallas Baptist University
Dallas Christian College
Del Mar College
DeVry Institute of Technology:
Irving
East Texas Baptist University
East Texas State University
Eastfield College
El Centro College
El Paso Community College
Frank Phillips College
Hardin-Simmons University
Houston Baptist University
Houston Community College
Howard College
Howard Payne University
Huston-Tillotson College
Jarvis Christian College
Lamar University—Beaumont
Lee College
Lubbock Christian University
McLennan Community College
McMurry University
Midland College
Midwestern State University
North Harris Montgomery
Community College District
North Lake College
Odessa College
Our Lady of the Lake University of
San Antonio
Panola College
Prairie View A&M University
St. Edward's University
St. Mary's University
St. Philip's College
Sam Houston State University
San Antonio College
San Jacinto College: North
Southwest Texas State University
Tarrant County Junior College
Temple College
Texas A&M International
University
Texas A&M University-Corpus
Christi
Texas A&M University-Kingsville
Texas Southern University
Texas State Technical College
Harlingen
Waco
Texas Tech University
Texas Wesleyan University
Texas Woman's University
Tyler Junior College
University of Dallas
University of Houston
Downtown
Victoria
University of North Texas
University of St. Thomas
University of Texas
Arlington
Austin
Dallas
El Paso
Medical Branch at Galveston
San Antonio
Wayland Baptist University
Weatherford College
West Texas A&M University
Western Texas College

Utah

College of Eastern Utah
Dixie College
LDS Business College
Salt Lake Community College
Snow College
Southern Utah University
University of Utah
Utah State University
Utah Valley State College
Weber State University

Vermont

Burlington College
Castleton State College
Champlain College
Community College of Vermont
Goddard College
Johnson State College
Lyndon State College
Marlboro College
Norwich University
St. Michael's College
School for International Training
Southern Vermont College
Sterling College
Trinity College of Vermont
University of Vermont

Virginia

Averett College
Blue Ridge Community College
Bluefield College
Central Virginia Community College
Christopher Newport University
Clinch Valley College of the
University of Virginia
College of Health Sciences
Dabney S. Lancaster Community
College
Danville Community College
Eastern Mennonite University
Eastern Shore Community College
Ferrum College
George Mason University
Germanna Community College
Hampton University
James Madison University
John Tyler Community College
Liberty University
Longwood College
Lynchburg College
Mary Baldwin College
Mary Washington College
Marymount University
Mountain Empire Community
College
New River Community College
Norfolk State University
Northern Virginia Community
College
Old Dominion University
Patrick Henry Community College
Paul D. Camp Community College
Piedmont Virginia Community
College
Randolph-Macon College
Rappahannock Community College
Richard Bland College
St. Paul's College
Shenandoah University
Southside Virginia Community
College
Southwest Virginia Community
College
Thomas Nelson Community College
Tidewater Community College
Virginia Commonwealth University
Virginia Intermont College
Virginia Polytechnic Institute and
State University
Virginia State University

297

Virginia Union University
Virginia Wesleyan College
Wytheville Community College

Washington

Art Institute of Seattle
Bellevue Community College
Big Bend Community College
Central Washington University
Centralia College
City University
Clark College
Columbia Basin College
Cornish College of the Arts
Eastern Washington University
Edmonds Community College
Evergreen State College
Gonzaga University
Grays Harbor College
Henry Cogswell College
Highline Community College
Lower Columbia College
North Seattle Community College
Northwest College
Olympic College
Pacific Lutheran University
Peninsula College
Pierce College
Puget Sound Christian College
Renton Technical College
St. Martin's College
Seattle Pacific University
Seattle University
Shoreline Community College
South Puget Sound Community
  College
South Seattle Community College
Spokane Falls Community College
Tacoma Community College
Walla Walla College
Walla Walla Community College
Wenatchee Valley College
Western Washington University
Whatcom Community College
Whitworth College
Yakima Valley Community College

West Virginia

Alderson-Broaddus College
Bluefield State College
Davis and Elkins College
Fairmont State College
Glenville State College
Shepherd College
West Liberty State College
West Virginia Northern Community
  College
West Virginia State College
West Virginia University
Wheeling Jesuit College

Wisconsin

Alverno College
Carroll College
Concordia University Wisconsin
Fox Valley Technical College
Lakeland College
Madison Junior College of Business
Marian College of Fond du Lac
Marquette University
Mid-State Technical College
Milwaukee Area Technical College
Moraine Park Technical College
Mount Senario College
Nicolet Area Technical College
Northcentral Technical College
Northland College
St. Norbert College
Stratton College
University of Wisconsin Center-
  Waukesha
Viterbo College

Waukesha County Technical
  College
Western Wisconsin Technical
  College
Wisconsin Lutheran College

Wyoming

Eastern Wyoming College
Northwest College

Tuition payment by installments

Alabama

Alabama State University
Birmingham-Southern College
Draughons Junior College
Faulkner University
Huntingdon College
Lawson State Community College
Marion Military Institute
Miles College
Stillman College
Talladega College
Tuskegee University
University of Alabama
University of Alabama at
  Birmingham: Walker College
University of Mobile
University of Montevallo
University of West Alabama

Alaska

Alaska Bible College
Alaska Pacific University
University of Alaska
  Fairbanks
  Southeast

Arizona

American Indian College of the
  Assemblies of God
Arizona College of the Bible
DeVry Institute of Technology:
  Phoenix
Embry-Riddle Aeronautical
  University: Prescott Campus
Gateway Community College
Navajo Community College
Northland Pioneer College
Prescott College
South Mountain Community
  College
Southwestern College
Western International University

Arkansas

Arkansas State University
Arkansas Tech University
Central Baptist College
Garland County Community
  College
Harding University
Hendrix College
John Brown University
Lyon College
Mississippi County Community
  College
North Arkansas Community/
  Technical College
Philander Smith College
Phillips County Community College
Rich Mountain Community College
Shorter College
South Arkansas Community College
Southern Arkansas University
  Magnolia
  Tech

University of Arkansas
  Fayetteville
  Little Rock
  Pine Bluff
University of the Ozarks
Westark Community College
Williams Baptist College

California

Academy of Art College
Allan Hancock College
American College: Los Angeles
Antelope Valley College
Antioch Southern California
  Los Angeles
  Santa Barbara
Armstrong University
Art Center College of Design
Art Institute of Southern California
Azusa Pacific University
Bethany College
Biola University
Brooks Institute of Photography
California Baptist College
California College of Arts and
  Crafts
California Institute of the Arts
California Institute of Technology
California Lutheran University
California Polytechnic State
  University: San Luis Obispo
California State Polytechnic
  University: Pomona
California State University
  Bakersfield
  Chico
  Fullerton
  Hayward
  Long Beach
  Sacramento
  Stanislaus
Cerro Coso Community College
Chapman University
Charles R. Drew University: College
  of Allied Health
Christian Heritage College
Claremont McKenna College
Cogswell Polytechnical College
College of Alameda
College of the Desert
College of Notre Dame
College of San Mateo
College of the Sequoias
Columbia College: Hollywood
Cosumnes River College
De Anza College
DeVry Institute of Technology:
  Pomona
Dominican College of San Rafael
Dominican School of Philosophy
  and Theology
Fashion Institute of Design and
  Merchandising
Feather River College
Fresno Pacific College
Golden Gate University
Harvey Mudd College
Heald Business College: Fresno
Heald College: Sacramento
Hebrew Union College: Jewish
  Institute of Religion
Holy Names College
Humphreys College
John F. Kennedy University
Kings River Community College
La Sierra University
LIFE Bible College
Loyola Marymount University
Marymount College
Menlo College
Mills College
Monterey Peninsula College

Mount St. Mary's College
Mount San Jacinto College
Napa Valley College
New College of California
New School of Architecture
Occidental College
Otis College of Art and Design
Pacific Christian College
Pacific Oaks College
Pacific Union College
Palo Verde College
Patten College
Pepperdine University
Pitzer College
Point Loma Nazarene College
Pomona College
Porterville College
Sacramento City College
St. John's Seminary College
St. Mary's College of California
Samuel Merritt College
San Diego State University
San Francisco Art Institute
San Francisco Conservatory of
  Music
San Francisco State University
San Jose Christian College
San Jose State University
Santa Clara University
Santa Rosa Junior College
Scripps College
Sierra College
Simpson College
Skyline College
Southern California College
Stanford University
Taft College
Thomas Aquinas College
United States International
  University
University of California
  Berkeley
  Riverside
  Santa Cruz
University of Judaism
University of La Verne
University of the Pacific
University of Redlands
University of San Diego
University of San Francisco
University of Southern California
University of West Los Angeles
Victor Valley College
Westmont College
Whittier College
Woodbury University
Yeshiva Ohr Elchonon Chabad/
  West Coast Talmudical Seminary
Yuba College

Colorado

Adams State College
Arapahoe Community College
Bel-Rea Institute of Animal
  Technology
Beth-El College of Nursing
Colorado College
Colorado Institute of Art
Colorado Northwestern Community
  College
Colorado School of Mines
Colorado State University
Colorado Technical University
Fort Lewis College
Lamar Community College
Northeastern Junior College
Otero Junior College
Pikes Peak Community College
Red Rocks Community College
Regis University
Rocky Mountain College of Art &
  Design

Technical Trades Institute
Trinidad State Junior College
University of Colorado
    Colorado Springs
    Denver
University of Denver
University of Northern Colorado
University of Southern Colorado
Western State College of Colorado

Connecticut

Albertus Magnus College
Briarwood College
Connecticut College
Eastern Connecticut State
    University
Fairfield University
Mitchell College
Paier College of Art
Quinnipiac College
Sacred Heart University
St. Joseph College
Teikyo-Post University
Trinity College
University of Bridgeport
University of Hartford
University of New Haven
Wesleyan University
Yale University

Delaware

Delaware State University
Delaware Technical and
    Community College
    Owens Campus
    Stanton/Wilmington Campus
    Terry Campus
Goldey-Beacom College
University of Delaware
Wesley College
Wilmington College

District of Columbia

American University
Catholic University of America
Corcoran School of Art
George Washington University
Georgetown University
Mount Vernon College
Southeastern University
Strayer College
Trinity College
University of the District of
    Columbia

Florida

Barry University
Brevard Community College
Embry-Riddle Aeronautical
    University
Florida Atlantic University
Florida Baptist Theological College
Florida Bible College
Florida Christian College
Florida College
Florida Memorial College
Florida Southern College
Florida State University
Hobe Sound Bible College
Jacksonville University
North Florida Junior College
Nova Southeastern University
Okaloosa-Walton Community
    College
Palm Beach Atlantic College
Rollins College
St. John Vianney College Seminary
Southeastern College of the
    Assemblies of God
Southern College
Stetson University
Tampa College

Trinity International University
University of Miami
University of South Florida
University of Tampa
University of West Florida
Warner Southern College
Webber College

Georgia

Agnes Scott College
American College: Atlanta
Andrew College
Atlanta College of Art
Augusta Technical Institute
Berry College
Brenau University
Brewton-Parker College
Clark Atlanta University
Covenant College
DeVry Institute of Technology:
    Atlanta
Emory University
Georgia Institute of Technology
Georgia Southwestern College
LaGrange College
Mercer University
Morris Brown College
Oglethorpe University
Paine College
Piedmont College
Reinhardt College
Shorter College
South College
Thomas College
Wesleyan College
Young Harris College

Hawaii

Chaminade University of Honolulu
Hawaii Pacific University

Idaho

Albertson College
Boise Bible College

Illinois

American Academy of Art
American Conservatory of Music
Augustana College
Aurora University
Belleville Area College
Benedictine University
Black Hawk College
Blackburn College
Blessing-Reiman College of Nursing
Bradley University
Carl Sandburg College
Chicago College of Commerce
City Colleges of Chicago
    Kennedy-King College
    Malcolm X College
    Wright College
College of DuPage
College of Lake County
Columbia College
Concordia University
Danville Area Community College
De Paul University
DeVry Institute of Technology
    Addison
    Chicago
Eastern Illinois University
East-West University
Elgin Community College
Elmhurst College
Governors State University
Greenville College
Harrington Institute of Interior
    Design
Illinois College
Illinois Institute of Technology
Illinois State University

Illinois Wesleyan University
International Academy of
    Merchandising and Design
ITT Technical Institute: Hoffman
    Estates
Kaskaskia College
Kendall College
Kishwaukee College
Knox College
Lake Forest College
Lakeview College of Nursing
Lewis and Clark Community
    College
Lewis University
Lexington College
Lincoln Christian College and
    Seminary
Lincoln College
Loyola University of Chicago
MacCormac Junior College
MacMurray College
McHenry County College
Millikin University
Monmouth College
Moraine Valley Community College
Morrison Institute of Technology
National-Louis University
North Central College
North Park College
Northeastern Illinois University
Northern Illinois University
Northwestern Business College
Northwestern University
Olivet Nazarene University
Parkland College
Principia College
Quincy University
Richland Community College
Robert Morris College: Chicago
Rockford College
Rosary College
St. Francis Medical Center College
    of Nursing
St. Xavier University
School of the Art Institute of
    Chicago
Southeastern Illinois College
Southern Illinois University
    Carbondale
    Edwardsville
Spoon River College
State Community College
Trinity Christian College
Trinity International University
Triton College
University of Chicago
University of Illinois
    Chicago
    Springfield
    Urbana-Champaign
Western Illinois University
Wheaton College
William Rainey Harper College

Indiana

Anderson University
Ball State University
Bethel College
Butler University
Calumet College of St. Joseph
Earlham College
Franklin College
Goshen College
Grace College
Hanover College
Huntington College
Indiana Institute of Technology
Indiana University at Kokomo
Indiana University-Purdue
    University Indianapolis
Indiana Wesleyan University

Ivy Tech State College
    Central Indiana
    Columbus
    Eastcentral
    Kokomo
    Lafayette
    Northcentral
    Northeast
    Southcentral
    Southeast
    Southwest
    Wabash Valley
    Whitewater
Lutheran College of Health
    Professions
Manchester College
Marian College
Oakland City University
Purdue University
    Calumet
    West Lafayette
St. Francis College
St. Mary-of-the-Woods College
St. Meinrad College
Sawyer College, Inc.
Taylor University
University of Evansville
University of Indianapolis
University of Notre Dame
University of Southern Indiana
Valparaiso University
Vincennes University
Wabash College

Iowa

American Institute of Business
American Institute of Commerce
Briar Cliff College
Buena Vista University
Central College
Clarke College
Coe College
Cornell College
Des Moines Area Community
    College
Drake University
Ellsworth Community College
Faith Baptist Bible College and
    Theological Seminary
Graceland College
Grand View College
Grinnell College
Hamilton Technical College
Hawkeye Community College
Indian Hills Community College
Iowa Central Community College
Iowa Lakes Community College
Iowa State University
Iowa Western Community College
Kirkwood Community College
Loras College
Luther College
Maharishi University of
    Management
Morningside College
Mount Mercy College
North Iowa Area Community
    College
Northeast Iowa Community College
Northwestern College
St. Ambrose University
Simpson College
Southeastern Community College:
    South Campus
Teikyo Marycrest University
University of Dubuque
University of Iowa
University of Northern Iowa
Upper Iowa University
Waldorf College
Wartburg College
Westmar University

299

Kansas

Baker University
Barclay College
Barton County Community College
Benedictine College
Bethany College
Bethel College
Butler County Community College
Donnelly College
Emporia State University
Fort Scott Community College
Friends University
Garden City Community College
Hesston College
Independence Community College
Kansas Newman College
Kansas State University
Manhattan Christian College
MidAmerica Nazarene College
Neosho County Community College
Pratt Community College
St. Mary College
Southwestern College
Tabor College
University of Kansas
Washburn University of Topeka
Wichita State University

Kentucky

Asbury College
Bellarmine College
Brescia College
Centre College
Clear Creek Baptist Bible College
Cumberland College
Eastern Kentucky University
Georgetown College
Kentucky Christian College
Kentucky State University
Kentucky Wesleyan College
Lindsey Wilson College
Morehead State University
Murray State University
Pikeville College
Southeast Community College
Spalding University
Sullivan College
Transylvania University
Union College
University of Louisville

Louisiana

Centenary College of Louisiana
Dillard University
Louisiana College
Louisiana State University and
  Agricultural and Mechanical
  College
McNeese State University
Northwestern State University
Nunez Community College
St. Joseph Seminary College
Southeastern Louisiana University
Xavier University of Louisiana

Maine

Bowdoin College
Casco Bay College
Central Maine Technical College
Colby College
College of the Atlantic
Husson College
Maine College of Art
Maine Maritime Academy
Southern Maine Technical College
Thomas College
Unity College

University of Maine
  Augusta
  Farmington
  Fort Kent
  Machias
  Orono
  Presque Isle
University of New England
University of Southern Maine

Maryland

Baltimore Hebrew University
Baltimore International Culinary
  College
Bowie State University
Capitol College
Cecil Community College
Columbia Union College
Dundalk Community College
Goucher College
Hagerstown Business College
Hood College
Howard Community College
Johns Hopkins University
Maryland Institute College of Art
Montgomery College
  Germantown Campus
  Rockville Campus
  Takoma Park Campus
Morgan State University
Mount St. Mary's College
St. John's College
University of Maryland
  Baltimore
  Baltimore County
  College Park
Villa Julie College
Washington Bible College
Washington College
Western Maryland College

Massachusetts

American International College
Anna Maria College
Aquinas College at Newton
Assumption College
Atlantic Union College
Babson College
Bay Path College
Bay State College
Bentley College
Berklee College of Music
Berkshire Community College
Boston Architectural Center
Boston College
Boston Conservatory
Boston University
Brandeis University
Bridgewater State College
Clark University
Dean College
Elms College
Emerson College
Emmanuel College
Endicott College
Essex Agricultural and Technical
  Institute
Fisher College
Forsyth School for Dental
  Hygienists
Framingham State College
Franklin Institute of Boston
Gordon College
Hampshire College
Harvard and Radcliffe Colleges
Hebrew College
Hellenic College
Katharine Gibbs School
Laboure College
Marian Court College
Massachusetts Institute of
  Technology

Massasoit Community College
Merrimack College
Middlesex Community College
Montserrat College of Art
Mount Holyoke College
Mount Ida College
Mount Wachusett Community
  College
Newbury College
Nichols College
North Adams State College
Northeastern University
Northern Essex Community College
Pine Manor College
Quinsigamond Community College
Regis College
St. Hyacinth College and Seminary
Salem State College
School of the Museum of Fine Arts
Simon's Rock College of Bard
Smith College
Springfield College
Suffolk University
Tufts University
University of Massachusetts
  Amherst
  Dartmouth
  Lowell
Wellesley College
Wentworth Institute of Technology
Western New England College
Westfield State College
Wheaton College
Williams College
Worcester Polytechnic Institute

Michigan

Adrian College
Albion College
Alma College
Andrews University
Aquinas College
Baker College
  Auburn Hills
  Cadillac
  Flint
  Mount Clemens
  Muskegon
  Owosso
  Port Huron
Calvin College
Center for Creative Studies: College
  of Art and Design
Cleary College
Concordia College
Cornerstone College and Grand
  Rapids Baptist Seminary
Davenport College of Business
Detroit College of Business
Eastern Michigan University
GMI Engineering & Management
  Institute
Grace Bible College
Grand Valley State University
Great Lakes Christian College
Great Lakes Junior College of
  Business
Highland Park Community College
Hillsdale College
Hope College
Kalamazoo College
Kellogg Community College
Kendall College of Art and Design
Lawrence Technological University
Madonna University
Michigan Christian College
Michigan Technological University
Mid Michigan Community College
Montcalm Community College
Northern Michigan University
Oakland University
Olivet College

Reformed Bible College
Sacred Heart Major Seminary
Saginaw Valley State University
St. Mary's College
Siena Heights College
Spring Arbor College
Suomi College
University of Michigan
  Ann Arbor
  Flint
Walsh College of Accountancy and
  Business Administration
William Tyndale College

Minnesota

Augsburg College
Bemidji State University
Bethany Lutheran College
Bethel College
Carleton College
College of St. Benedict
College of St. Catherine: St.
  Catherine Campus
College of St. Catherine-
  Minneapolis
College of St. Scholastica
Concordia College: Moorhead
Concordia College: St. Paul
Gustavus Adolphus College
Hamline University
Macalester College
Martin Luther College
Minneapolis College of Art and
  Design
Minnesota Bible College
National College
NEI College of Technology
North Central Bible College
Northwest Technical Institute
Northwestern College
Oak Hills Bible College
Pillsbury Baptist Bible College
St. John's University
St. Mary's University of Minnesota
St. Olaf College
Southwest State University
University of Minnesota
  Crookston
  Duluth
  Morris
  Twin Cities
University of St. Thomas

Mississippi

Blue Mountain College
Delta State University
East Mississippi Community College
Itawamba Community College
Jackson State University
Magnolia Bible College
Mary Holmes College
Millsaps College
Mississippi College
Mississippi Gulf Coast Community
  College: Perkinston
Mississippi State University
Mississippi University for Women
Mississippi Valley State University
Northeast Mississippi Community
  College
Northwest Mississippi Community
  College
Pearl River Community College
Rust College
Southeastern Baptist College
Tougaloo College
University of Mississippi
  Medical Center
  University
University of Southern Mississippi
Wesley College

Missouri

Avila College
Baptist Bible College
Calvary Bible College
Central Bible College
Central Christian College of the
  Bible
Central Methodist College
Central Missouri State University
Columbia College
Crowder College
Culver-Stockton College
DeVry Institute of Technology:
  Kansas City
Drury College
East Central College
Evangel College
Fontbonne College
Hannibal-LaGrange College
Harris Stowe State College
Jefferson College
Kansas City Art Institute
Lincoln University
Lindenwood College
Longview Community College
Maple Woods Community College
Maryville University of Saint Louis
Missouri Baptist College
Missouri Southern State College
Missouri Valley College
Missouri Western State College
Moberly Area Community College
National College
North Central Missouri College
Northwest Missouri State
  University
Ozark Christian College
Park College
Penn Valley Community College
Ranken Technical College
Research College of Nursing
Rockhurst College
St. Louis Christian College
St. Louis College of Pharmacy
St. Louis University
Southeast Missouri State University
Stephens College
Three Rivers Community College
Truman State University
University of Missouri
  Columbia
  Rolla
  St. Louis
Washington University
Webster University
Wentworth Military Academy
Westminster College
William Jewell College
William Woods University

Montana

Carroll College
Dawson Community College
Flathead Valley Community College
Little Big Horn College
Miles Community College
Montana State University
  Billings
  Bozeman
  Northern
Rocky Mountain College
Stone Child College
University of Great Falls
University of Montana-Missoula
Western Montana College of the
  University of Montana

Nebraska

Bellevue University
Central Community College
Chadron State College
Clarkson College

College of St. Mary
Concordia College
Creighton University
Dana College
Doane College/Lincoln Campus
Hastings College
Lincoln School of Commerce
McCook Community College
Mid Plains Community College
Midland Lutheran College
Nebraska Christian College
Nebraska Indian Community
  College
Nebraska Methodist College of
  Nursing and Allied Health
Nebraska Wesleyan University
Southeast Community College:
  Beatrice Campus
Union College
Wayne State College
Western Nebraska Community
  College
York College

Nevada

Community College of Southern
  Nevada
Morrison College: Reno
University of Nevada
  Las Vegas
  Reno

New Hampshire

Castle College
Daniel Webster College
Dartmouth College
Franklin Pierce College
Hesser College
McIntosh College
New England College
New Hampshire College
New Hampshire Technical College
  Berlin
  Manchester
  Nashua
Notre Dame College
White Pines College

New Jersey

Assumption College for Sisters
Berkeley College of Business
Bloomfield College
Burlington County College
Caldwell College
Camden County College
Centenary College
College of St. Elizabeth
DeVry Technical Institute
Drew University
Essex County College
Fairleigh Dickinson University
  Edward Williams College
  Teaneck
Georgian Court College
Jersey City State College
Middlesex County College
Monmouth University
Montclair State University
New Jersey Institute of Technology
Princeton University
Ramapo College of New Jersey
Richard Stockton College of New
  Jersey
Rider University
Rowan College of New Jersey

Rutgers, The State University of
  New Jersey
  Camden College of Arts and
    Sciences
  College of Engineering
  College of Nursing
  College of Pharmacy
  Cook College
  Douglass College
  Livingston College
  Mason Gross School of the
    Arts
  Newark College of Arts and
    Sciences
  Rutgers College
St. Peter's College
Salem Community College
Seton Hall University
Stevens Institute of Technology
Sussex County Community College
Trenton State College
William Paterson College of New
  Jersey

New Mexico

College of Santa Fe
College of the Southwest
Dona Ana Branch Community
  College of New Mexico State
  University
Eastern New Mexico University
National College
New Mexico Highlands University
New Mexico Institute of Mining
  and Technology
New Mexico Junior College
New Mexico State University
Parks College
St. John's College

New York

Adelphi University
Adirondack Community College
Albany College of Pharmacy
Alfred University
American Academy of Dramatic
  Arts
Audrey Cohen College
Bard College
Barnard College
Berkeley College
Bramson ORT Technical Institute
Briarcliffe: The College for Business
  and Technology
Bryant & Stratton Business Institute
  Albany
  Syracuse
Canisius College
Catholic Medical Center of
  Brooklyn and Queens School of
  Nursing
Cazenovia College
City University of New York
  Borough of Manhattan
    Community College
  Brooklyn College
  Hostos Community College
  John Jay College of Criminal
    Justice
Clarkson University
Colgate University
College of Aeronautics
College of Insurance
College of Mount St. Vincent
College of New Rochelle
  New Rochelle
  School of New Resources
College of St. Rose
Columbia University
  Columbia College
  School of Engineering and
    Applied Science

Columbia-Greene Community
  College
Concordia College
Cornell University
Daemen College
Dominican College of Blauvelt
Dowling College
Dutchess Community College
D'Youville College
Eastman School of Music of the
  University of Rochester
Elmira College
Eugene Lang College/New School
  for Social Research
Fashion Institute of Technology
Fordham University
Hamilton College
Hartwick College
Helene Fuld College of Nursing
Herkimer County Community
  College
Hilbert College
Hobart and William Smith Colleges
Houghton College
Hudson Valley Community College
Interboro Institute
Iona College
Ithaca College
Jamestown Community College
Jefferson Community College
Jewish Theological Seminary of
  America
Juilliard School
Keuka College
Laboratory Institute of
  Merchandising
Le Moyne College
Long Island University
  Brooklyn Campus
  C. W. Post Campus
  Southampton College
Manhattan College
Manhattan School of Music
Manhattanville College
Mannes College of Music
Marist College
Marymount College
Marymount Manhattan College
Mater Dei College
Medaille College
Mercy College
Molloy College
Monroe College
Monroe Community College
Nassau Community College
Nazareth College of Rochester
New York Institute of Technology
New York School of Interior
  Design
New York University
Niagara University
Orange County Community College
Pace University
Parsons School of Design
Paul Smith's College
Phillips Beth Israel School of
  Nursing
Plaza Business Institute
Polytechnic University
Pratt Institute
Rensselaer Polytechnic Institute
Roberts Wesleyan College
Rochester Institute of Technology
Sage Junior College of Albany
St. John Fisher College
St. John's University
St. Joseph's College
  Brooklyn
  Suffolk Campus
St. Lawrence University
St. Thomas Aquinas College
Sarah Lawrence College

301

School of Visual Arts
Skidmore College
State University of New York
   Albany
   Binghamton
   Buffalo
   Oswego
   Purchase
   Stony Brook
   College at Brockport
   College at Buffalo
   College at Cortland
   College at Fredonia
   College at Geneseo
   College at Oneonta
   College at Plattsburgh
   College at Potsdam
   College of Technology at
     Alfred
   College of Technology at Delhi
   College of Technology at
     Farmingdale
   Institute of Technology at
     Utica/Rome
   New Paltz
Syracuse University
Talmudical Institute of Upstate New
   York
Tompkins-Cortland Community
   College
Trocaire College
Ulster County Community College
University of Rochester
University of the State of New
   York: Regents College
Utica College of Syracuse
   University
Vassar College
Villa Maria College of Buffalo
Wadhams Hall Seminary-College
Wagner College
Wells College
Westchester Business Institute
Wood Tobe-Coburn School
Yeshiva University

North Carolina

Barber-Scotia College
Barton College
Belmont Abbey College
Bennett College
Campbell University
Catawba College
Chowan College
Davidson College
Duke University
East Carolina University
Elon College
Fayetteville State University
Gardner-Webb University
Greensboro College
Guilford College
High Point University
John Wesley College
Johnson C. Smith University
Lees-McRae College
Lenoir-Rhyne College
Livingstone College
Louisburg College
Mars Hill College
Meredith College
Methodist College
Montreat College
Mount Olive College
North Carolina Agricultural and
   Technical State University
North Carolina Wesleyan College
Peace College
Pembroke State University
Pfeiffer College
Queens College
Roanoke Bible College

St. Andrews Presbyterian College
St. Augustine's College
St. Mary's College
Salem College
Shaw University
University of North Carolina at
   Wilmington
Wake Forest University
Warren Wilson College
Wingate University
Winston-Salem State University

North Dakota

Bismarck State College
Jamestown College
Little Hoop Community College
North Dakota State University
Turtle Mountain Community
   College

Ohio

Antioch College
Antonelli College
Art Academy of Cincinnati
Ashland University
Baldwin-Wallace College
Belmont Technical College
Bluffton College
Bowling Green State University
   Bowling Green
   Firelands College
Bradford School
Bryant & Stratton Business
   Institute: Cleveland West
Bryant & Stratton College
Capital University
Case Western Reserve University
Cedarville College
Chatfield College
Cincinnati Bible College and
   Seminary
Cincinnati State Technical and
   Community College
Circleville Bible College
Cleveland College of Jewish Studies
Cleveland Institute of Art
Cleveland State University
College of Mount St. Joseph
College of Wooster
Columbus College of Art and
   Design
David N. Myers College
Davis College
Denison University
DeVry Institute of Technology:
   Columbus
Edison State Community College
Franciscan University of
   Steubenville
Franklin University
God's Bible School and College
Heidelberg College
Hiram College
Hocking Technical College
ITT Technical Institute:
   Youngstown
Jefferson Community College
John Carroll University
Kent State University
   East Liverpool Regional
     Campus
   Kent
   Salem Regional Campus
   Stark Campus
   Trumbull Campus
   Tuscarawas Campus
Kettering College of Medical Arts
Lake Erie College
Lakeland Community College
Lourdes College
Malone College
Marion Technical College

Miami University
   Hamilton Campus
   Middletown Campus
   Oxford Campus
Miami-Jacobs College
Mount Union College
Mount Vernon Nazarene College
Muskingum College
North Central Technical College
Northwestern College
Notre Dame College of Ohio
Oberlin College
Ohio Dominican College
Ohio Northern University
Ohio State University
   Agricultural Technical Institute
   Columbus Campus
   Mansfield Campus
   Marion Campus
   Newark Campus
Ohio University
   Athens
   Zanesville Campus
Ohio Valley Business College
Ohio Wesleyan University
Otterbein College
Owens Technical College
   Findlay Campus
   Toledo
Pontifical College Josephinum
Shawnee State University
Stark Technical College
Stautzenberger College
Terra Community College
Tiffin University
Union Institute
University of Akron
University of Cincinnati
   Cincinnati
   Clermont College
   Raymond Walters College
University of Findlay
University of Rio Grande
University of Toledo
Urbana University
Ursuline College
Walsh University
Washington State Community
   College
Wilmington College
Wittenberg University
Wright State University
   Dayton
   Lake Campus
Xavier University
Youngstown State University

Oklahoma

Bacone College
Bartlesville Wesleyan College
Connors State College
Mid-America Bible College
Northeastern Oklahoma
   Agricultural and Mechanical
   College
Oklahoma Baptist University
Oklahoma Christian University of
   Science and Arts
Oklahoma City Community College
Oklahoma City University
Oklahoma Panhandle State
   University
Oklahoma State University
   Oklahoma City
   Stillwater
Oral Roberts University
Phillips University
Redlands Community College
Rogers State College
Rose State College
St. Gregory's College

Southwestern College of Christian
   Ministries
Southwestern Oklahoma State
   University
University of Oklahoma
University of Tulsa

Oregon

Bassist College
Central Oregon Community College
Clackamas Community College
Clatsop Community College
Concordia University
Eastern Oregon State College
George Fox College
Lane Community College
Linfield College
Linn-Benton Community College
Multnomah Bible College
Northwest Christian College
Oregon Institute of Technology
Pacific Northwest College of Art
Pacific University
Portland Community College
Portland State University
Reed College
Southern Oregon State College
Southwestern Oregon Community
   College
University of Oregon
   Eugene
   Robert Donald Clark Honors
     College
University of Portland
Western Baptist College
Western Oregon State College
Willamette University

Pennsylvania

Albright College
Allegheny College
Allentown College of St. Francis de
   Sales
Alvernia College
Antonelli Institute of Art and
   Photography
Art Institute of Pittsburgh
Baptist Bible College of
   Pennsylvania
Beaver College
Bryn Mawr College
Bucknell University
Bucks County Community College
Cabrini College
Cambria-Rowe Business College
Carlow College
Carnegie Mellon University
Cedar Crest College
Central Pennsylvania Business
   School
Chatham College
Cheyney University of Pennsylvania
CHI Institute
Churchman Business School
Clarion University of Pennsylvania
College Misericordia
Community College of Beaver
   County
Delaware Valley College
Dickinson College
Drexel University
DuBois Business College
East Stroudsburg University of
   Pennsylvania
Eastern College
Edinboro University of
   Pennsylvania
Elizabethtown College
Franklin and Marshall College
Gannon University
Geneva College
Gettysburg College

Gratz College
Gwynedd-Mercy College
Harcum College
Harrisburg Area Community
College
Haverford College
Holy Family College
Immaculata College
Indiana University of Pennsylvania
Johnson Technical Institute
Juniata College
Keystone College
King's College
Kutztown University of
Pennsylvania
La Roche College
La Salle University
Lackawanna Junior College
Lafayette College
Lancaster Bible College
Lebanon Valley College of
Pennsylvania
Lehigh University
Lincoln University
Lock Haven University of
Pennsylvania
Manor Junior College
Mansfield University of
Pennsylvania
Marywood College.
McCann School of Business
Medical College of Pennsylvania
and Hahnemann University
Mercyhurst College
Messiah College
Millersville University of
Pennsylvania
Moore College of Art and Design
Neumann College
Northampton County Area
Community College
Peirce College
Pennsylvania Institute of Culinary
Arts
Philadelphia College of Bible
Philadelphia College of Pharmacy
and Science
Philadelphia College of Textiles and
Science
Pittsburgh Institute of Mortuary
Science
Point Park College
Reading Area Community College
Remington Education Center: Vale
Campus
Robert Morris College
St. Charles Borromeo Seminary-
Overbrook
St. Francis College
St. Joseph's University
St. Vincent College
Seton Hill College
Shippensburg University of
Pennsylvania
Slippery Rock University of
Pennsylvania
South Hills Business School
Swarthmore College
Temple University
Thiel College
Thomas Jefferson University:
College of Allied Health Sciences
University of the Arts
University of Pennsylvania
University of Pittsburgh
Bradford
Greensburg
Pittsburgh
Titusville
Ursinus College
Valley Forge Christian College
Valley Forge Military College

Waynesburg College
West Chester University of
Pennsylvania
Widener University
Wilkes University
Wilson College

Puerto Rico

American University of Puerto Rico
Caribbean University
Humacao Community College
ICPR Junior College
Inter American University of Puerto
Rico
Aguadilla Campus
San German Campus
Pontifical Catholic University of
Puerto Rico
Turabo University
Universidad Adventista de las
Antillas
Universidad Politecnica de Puerto
Rico
University of Puerto Rico
Cayey University College
Mayaguez Campus
Ponce Technological
University College

Rhode Island

Brown University
Bryant College
Johnson & Wales University
New England Institute of
Technology
Providence College
Rhode Island College
Rhode Island School of Design

South Carolina

Anderson College
Benedict College
Charleston Southern University
Claflin College
Coastal Carolina University
Coker College
College of Charleston
Columbia College
Columbia Junior College of Business
Erskine College
Furman University
Lander University
Limestone College
Morris College
North Greenville College
Presbyterian College
Southern Wesleyan University
Spartanburg Methodist College
University of South Carolina
Spartanburg
Union

South Dakota

Augustana College
Black Hills State University
Dakota Wesleyan University
Huron University
Kilian Community College
Mount Marty College
Oglala Lakota College
Presentation College
South Dakota School of Mines and
Technology
University of South Dakota

Tennessee

Bethel College
Carson-Newman College
Christian Brothers University
David Lipscomb University
Freed-Hardeman University
Hiwassee College

King College
Knoxville Business College
Lambuth University
Lee College
LeMoyne-Owen College
Lincoln Memorial University
Maryville College
Memphis College of Art
Milligan College
Rhodes College
Tennessee Wesleyan College
Trevecca Nazarene University
Tusculum College
Union University
University of the South
University of Tennessee
Chattanooga
Knoxville
Memphis
Vanderbilt University

Texas

Ambassador University
Angelo State University
Arlington Baptist College
Austin College
Austin Community College
Baptist Missionary Association
Theological Seminary
Blinn College
Central Texas College
Cisco Junior College
Commonwealth Institute of Funeral
Service
Concordia Lutheran College
Criswell College
Dallas Baptist University
Dallas Christian College
DeVry Institute of Technology:
Irving
East Texas Baptist University
East Texas State University
Hallmark Institute of Technology
Hardin-Simmons University
Houston Baptist University
Howard Payne University
Huston-Tillotson College
Institute for Christian Studies
Jacksonville College
Jarvis Christian College
Lamar University—Beaumont
Lubbock Christian University
McMurry University
Midwestern State University
North Harris Montgomery
Community College District
Our Lady of the Lake University of
San Antonio
Prairie View A&M University
Rice University
St. Edward's University
St. Mary's University
Sam Houston State University
Schreiner College
Southern Methodist University
Southwest Texas State University
Southwestern Adventist College
Southwestern University
Stephen F. Austin State University
Texas A&M International
University
Texas A&M University
College Station
Galveston
Texas A&M University-Corpus
Christi
Texas A&M University-Kingsville
Texas Christian University
Texas Lutheran College
Texas Southern University

Texas State Technical College
Harlingen
Waco
Texas Tech University
Texas Wesleyan University
Texas Woman's University
University of Central Texas
University of Dallas
University of Houston
Clear Lake
Downtown
Houston
Victoria
University of North Texas
University of St. Thomas
University of Texas
Arlington
Dallas
El Paso
Medical Branch at Galveston
San Antonio
Southwestern Medical Center
at Dallas
Houston Health Science
Center
Wayland Baptist University
West Texas A&M University

Utah

LDS Business College
Phillips Junior College: Salt Lake
City Campus
Salt Lake Community College
Westminster College of Salt Lake
City

Vermont

Bennington College
Burlington College
Castleton State College
Champlain College
Green Mountain College
Middlebury College
New England Culinary Institute
Norwich University
Southern Vermont College
Sterling College
Trinity College of Vermont
University of Vermont
Vermont Technical College

Virginia

Averett College
Bluefield College
Christendom College
Christopher Newport University
College of William and Mary
Emory and Henry College
Ferrum College
George Mason University
Hampden-Sydney College
Hollins College
James Madison University
Liberty University
Longwood College
Lynchburg College
Mary Baldwin College
Mary Washington College
Norfolk State University
Old Dominion University
Radford University
Randolph-Macon College
Randolph-Macon Woman's College
Roanoke College
St. Paul's College
Shenandoah University
Sweet Briar College
University of Virginia
Virginia Commonwealth University
Virginia Intermont College
Virginia Military Institute

Virginia Polytechnic Institute and
  State University
Virginia State University
Virginia Union University
Virginia Wesleyan College

Washington
Antioch University Seattle
Art Institute of Seattle
Cornish College of the Arts
Eastern Washington University
Evergreen State College
Gonzaga University
Henry Cogswell College
Northwest College
Pacific Lutheran University
Puget Sound Christian College
St. Martin's College
Seattle Pacific University
Seattle University
University of Puget Sound
Walla Walla College
Whitman College
Whitworth College

West Virginia
Bethany College
Bluefield State College
Davis and Elkins College
Fairmont State College
Glenville State College
Marshall University
Ohio Valley College
Shepherd College
West Liberty State College
West Virginia Institute of
  Technology
West Virginia Northern Community
  College
West Virginia University
West Virginia Wesleyan College
Wheeling Jesuit College

Wisconsin
Alverno College
Bellin College of Nursing
Beloit College
Cardinal Stritch College
Carroll College
Carthage College
Concordia University Wisconsin
Edgewood College
Lakeland College
Lawrence University
Maranatha Baptist Bible College
Marian College of Fond du Lac
Marquette University
Mid-State Technical College
Milwaukee Institute of Art &
  Design
Milwaukee School of Engineering
Mount Mary College
Mount Senario College
Northland College
Ripon College
St. Norbert College
Silver Lake College
Southwest Wisconsin Technical
  College
Stratton College

University of Wisconsin
  Eau Claire
  Green Bay
  La Crosse
  Milwaukee
  Oshkosh
  Parkside
  Platteville
  River Falls
  Stevens Point
  Stout
  Superior
  Whitewater
University of Wisconsin Center
  Baraboo/Sauk County
  Barron County
  Fond du Lac
  Fox Valley
  Manitowoc County
  Marshfield/Wood County
  Richland
  Rock County
  Sheboygan County
  Washington County
  Waukesha
Viterbo College
Wisconsin Lutheran College

Wyoming
Eastern Wyoming College
Sheridan College

Tuition discount for prepayment

Alabama
Faulkner University

Arizona
Arizona College of the Bible

California
American College: Los Angeles
Azusa Pacific University
Biola University
California Maritime Academy
Christian Heritage College
Fashion Institute of Design and
  Merchandising
La Sierra University
LIFE Bible College
New School of Architecture
Pacific Christian College
Pacific Union College
St. Mary's College of California
Southern California College
Thomas Aquinas College
University of Redlands
University of San Diego
University of San Francisco
University of Southern California
Westmont College
Yeshiva Ohr Elchonon Chabad/
  West Coast Talmudical Seminary

Colorado
Bel-Rea Institute of Animal
  Technology
Colorado Technical University

Connecticut
Albertus Magnus College

District of Columbia
Mount Vernon College
Southeastern University

Florida
Hobe Sound Bible College
Lynn University
New College of the University of
  South Florida
University of Miami
Webber College

Georgia
American College: Atlanta
Augusta Technical Institute
Oglethorpe University
Shorter College
Spelman College

Hawaii
Chaminade University of Honolulu

Idaho
Boise Bible College

Illinois
Chicago College of Commerce
Columbia College
National-Louis University
State Community College
Trinity International University

Indiana
Anderson University
Butler University
Goshen College
Huntington College
Ivy Tech State College: Northwest

Iowa
Coe College
Luther College

Kansas
Hesston College

Kentucky
Kentucky Christian College

Maine
Unity College

Maryland
Johns Hopkins University
Mount St. Mary's College
Washington Bible College

Massachusetts
American International College
Atlantic Union College
Boston College
Boston University
Gordon College
Marian Court College
Pine Manor College

Michigan
Alma College
Andrews University
Center for Creative Studies: College
  of Art and Design
Cleary College
Ferris State University
Great Lakes Junior College of
  Business
Kendall College of Art and Design

Minnesota
Bethel College
College of St. Benedict
Concordia College: Moorhead
Gustavus Adolphus College
Hamline University
Martin Luther College
North Central Bible College
Northwest Technical Institute

**St. John's University
St. Olaf College

Mississippi
Rust College
Tougaloo College

Missouri
Central Bible College
Evangel College
Lindenwood College
Research College of Nursing
Washington University
Wentworth Military Academy

Montana
Rocky Mountain College

Nebraska
Union College

New Hampshire
Colby-Sawyer College
Franklin Pierce College
New England College
Notre Dame College

New Jersey
Berkeley College of Business
Sussex County Community College

New Mexico
College of Santa Fe
St. John's College

New York
Alfred University
American Academy of Dramatic
  Arts
Barnard College
Berkeley College
Colgate University
Columbia University
  Columbia College
  School of Engineering and
    Applied Science
Hobart and William Smith Colleges
Medaille College
New York Institute of Technology
New York University
Nyack College
Rochester Institute of Technology
Wells College

North Carolina
Duke University
Pfeiffer College
Roanoke Bible College

North Dakota
Trinity Bible College

Ohio
Cedarville College
Cincinnati Bible College and
  Seminary
Circleville Bible College
God's Bible School and College
Heidelberg College
Hiram College
Kent State University: Trumbull
  Campus
Lake Erie College
Malone College
Ohio Northern University
Ohio Wesleyan University
Wittenberg University

Oklahoma
Mid-America Bible College
Oklahoma Christian University of
  Science and Arts

Oregon

Bassist College
Clatsop Community College
Eugene Bible College
Linfield College
Pacific University
Western Baptist College

Pennsylvania

Allegheny College
Baptist Bible College of
  Pennsylvania
Gettysburg College
Indiana University of Pennsylvania
Lafayette College
Mercyhurst College
Muhlenberg College
Philadelphia College of Bible
Susquehanna University
Thomas Jefferson University:
  College of Allied Health Sciences
University of Pennsylvania

Rhode Island

Brown University

South Carolina

Midlands Technical College

South Dakota

Dakota Wesleyan University
University of Sioux Falls

Tennessee

Milligan College
Southern College of Seventh-day
  Adventists

Texas

Austin Community College
Criswell College
Huston-Tillotson College
St. Mary's University
Schreiner College
Southwestern Adventist College

Vermont

Champlain College
Lyndon State College
Middlebury College
Norwich University
Southern Vermont College

Virginia

Christendom College
Clinch Valley College of the
  University of Virginia
Liberty University
Lynchburg College
Marymount University

Washington

City University
Pacific Lutheran University

Wisconsin

Carthage College
Lakeland College
Lawrence University

Tuition payment by deferred payments

Alabama

Alabama Agricultural and
  Mechanical University
Alabama State University
Birmingham-Southern College

Bishop State Community College
Draughons Junior College
Huntingdon College
Marion Military Institute
Spring Hill College
Troy State University
  Montgomery
  Troy
University of Alabama
  Huntsville
  Tuscaloosa
University of Alabama at
  Birmingham: Walker College
University of Mobile
University of West Alabama

Alaska

Prince William Sound Community
  College
University of Alaska
  Fairbanks
  Southeast

Arizona

DeVry Institute of Technology:
  Phoenix
Embry-Riddle Aeronautical
  University: Prescott Campus
Gateway Community College
Mohave Community College
Navajo Community College
Northern Arizona University
Paradise Valley Community College
Rio Salado Community College
Southwestern College
University of Arizona
Western International University

Arkansas

Garland County Community
  College
Mississippi County Community
  College
Shorter College
University of the Ozarks
Westark Community College

California

Academy of Art College
Allan Hancock College
American Academy of Dramatic
  Arts: West
Antelope Valley College
Antioch Southern California at Los
  Angeles
Armstrong University
Bakersfield College
Biola University
California Baptist College
California College of Arts and
  Crafts
California Lutheran University
California State University
  Chico
  Northridge
Charles R. Drew University: College
  of Allied Health
Christian Heritage College
Cogswell Polytechnical College
College of Alameda
College of the Desert
College of Notre Dame
College of San Mateo
Columbia College: Hollywood
Cosumnes River College
De Anza College
DeVry Institute of Technology:
  Pomona
Dominican College of San Rafael
Evergreen Valley College
Fashion Institute of Design and
  Merchandising

Feather River College
Glendale Community College
Golden Gate University
Holy Names College
Kings River Community College
Long Beach City College
Los Angeles Harbor College
Los Angeles Mission College
Los Angeles Southwest College
Los Angeles Trade and Technical
  College
Los Medanos College
Loyola Marymount University
Merced College
Mills College
Modesto Junior College
Monterey Peninsula College
Mount St. Mary's College
Napa Valley College
New College of California
Occidental College
Ohlone College
Orange Coast College
Pacific Christian College
Pacific Union College
Palo Verde College
Pasadena City College
Patten College
Pepperdine University
Riverside Community College
Sacramento City College
Samuel Merritt College
San Jose City College
Santa Barbara City College
Santa Clara University
Santa Monica College
Santa Rosa Junior College
Scripps College
Sierra College
Skyline College
Sonoma State University
Stanford University
Taft College
United States International
  University
University of California
  San Diego
  Santa Barbara
  Santa Cruz
University of Judaism
University of La Verne
University of San Francisco
University of Southern California
Victor Valley College
West Hills Community College
Woodbury University
Yuba College

Colorado

Adams State College
Aims Community College
Beth-El College of Nursing
Colorado Institute of Art
Colorado Mountain College
  Alpine Campus
  Spring Valley Campus
  Timberline Campus
Colorado School of Mines
Fort Lewis College
Mesa State College
Metropolitan State College of
  Denver
Naropa Institute
Northeastern Junior College
Pueblo Community College
Red Rocks Community College
Regis University
Trinidad State Junior College
University of Colorado at Boulder
University of Denver
University of Southern Colorado
Western State College of Colorado

Connecticut

Capital Community-Technical
  College
Central Connecticut State
  University
Connecticut College
Fairfield University
Manchester Community-Technical
  College
Quinebaug Valley Community-
  Technical College
Quinnipiac College
Sacred Heart University
Tunxis Community-Technical
  College
University of Bridgeport
Wesleyan University

Delaware

Delaware State University
Delaware Technical and
  Community College
  Owens Campus
  Stanton/Wilmington Campus
  Terry Campus
Goldey-Beacom College

District of Columbia

American University
George Washington University
Georgetown University
Howard University
Strayer College
Trinity College
University of the District of
  Columbia

Florida

Barry University
Bethune-Cookman College
Brevard Community College
Broward Community College
Central Florida Community College
Chipola Junior College
Embry-Riddle Aeronautical
  University
Florida Atlantic University
Florida Christian College
Florida Community College at
  Jacksonville
Florida International University
Florida State University
Jacksonville University
Lake City Community College
Lake-Sumter Community College
Nova Southeastern University
Okaloosa-Walton Community
  College
Pasco-Hernando Community
  College
St. John Vianney College Seminary
St. Thomas University
Schiller International University
Tallahassee Community College
Tampa College
University of Florida
University of Miami
University of North Florida
Warner Southern College
Webber College

Georgia

Andrew College
Clark Atlanta University
Covenant College
DeKalb Technical Institute
DeVry Institute of Technology:
  Atlanta
Emmanuel College
Fort Valley State College
Georgia Institute of Technology
Georgia Southern University

Gwinnett Technical Institute
LaGrange College
Morris Brown College
Oglethorpe University
Reinhardt College
South College
Spelman College
Thomas College

Idaho

Boise State University
College of Southern Idaho
Idaho State University
Lewis-Clark State College
Ricks College
University of Idaho

Illinois

Aurora University
Belleville Area College
Black Hawk College
Blackburn College
Bradley University
Carl Sandburg College
Chicago State University
City Colleges of Chicago
    Malcolm X College
    Olive-Harvey College
    Richard J. Daley College
College of DuPage.
College of Lake County
Danville Area Community College
De Paul University
DeVry Institute of Technology
    Addison
    Chicago
East-West University
Elgin Community College
Finch University of Health
    Sciences/The Chicago Medical
    School
Governors State University
Greenville College
International Academy of
    Merchandising and Design
Joliet Junior College
Kaskaskia College
Kishwaukee College
Knox College
Lake Land College
Lakeview College of Nursing
Lewis and Clark Community
    College
Lewis University
Lincoln Christian College and
    Seminary
Lincoln College
Lincoln Land Community College
MacMurray College
Moody Bible Institute
Moraine Valley Community College
Morton College
National-Louis University
Olivet Nazarene University
Rend Lake College
Richland Community College
Rockford College
Rush University
St. Xavier University
Southeastern Illinois College
Southern Illinois University at
    Edwardsville
State Community College
Trinity Christian College
Trinity International University
University of Illinois: Springfield
Western Illinois University
Wheaton College
William Rainey Harper College

Indiana

Ancilla College
Anderson University
Bethel College
DePauw University
Earlham College
Goshen College
Indiana Institute of Technology
Indiana State University
Indiana University
    Bloomington
    East
    Northwest
    South Bend
    Southeast
Indiana University-Purdue
    University Indianapolis
Indiana Wesleyan University
Ivy Tech State College
    Central Indiana
    Columbus
    Eastcentral
    Kokomo
    Lafayette
    Northcentral
    Northeast
    Northwest
    Southcentral
    Southeast
    Southwest
    Wabash Valley
    Whitewater
Manchester College
Oakland City University
Purdue University
    Calumet
    West Lafayette
St. Mary-of-the-Woods College
St. Meinrad College
University of Indianapolis

Iowa

Briar Cliff College
Cornell College
Drake University
Ellsworth Community College
Grand View College
Indian Hills Community College
Iowa Western Community College
Morningside College
North Iowa Area Community
    College
Northeast Iowa Community College
St. Ambrose University
Southeastern Community College
    North Campus
    South Campus
Teikyo Marycrest University
University of Dubuque
University of Iowa
University of Northern Iowa
Waldorf College
Wartburg College

Kansas

Bethel College
Butler County Community College
Colby Community College
Emporia State University
Fort Hays State University
Fort Scott Community College
Garden City Community College
Kansas City Kansas Community
    College
Manhattan Christian College
Neosho County Community College
Pittsburg State University
Pratt Community College
St. Mary College
University of Kansas
Washburn University of Topeka
Wichita State University

Kentucky

Asbury College
Brescia College
Clear Creek Baptist Bible College
Cumberland College
Eastern Kentucky University
Georgetown College
Kentucky State University
Kentucky Wesleyan College
Lindsey Wilson College
Madisonville Community College
Maysville Community College
Mid-Continent Baptist Bible College
Morehead State University
Murray State University
Northern Kentucky University
Paducah Community College
Somerset Community College
Southeast Community College
Sullivan College
Transylvania University

Louisiana

Bossier Parish Community College
Dillard University
Grambling State University
Louisiana State University
    Agricultural and Mechanical
    College
    Alexandria
    Eunice
    Shreveport
McNeese State University
Northwestern State University
Nunez Community College
Southeastern Louisiana University
University of New Orleans
Xavier University of Louisiana

Maine

Bowdoin College
Casco Bay College
Central Maine Medical Center
    School of Nursing
Unity College
University of Maine
    Augusta
    Fort Kent
University of Southern Maine

Maryland

Allegany College
Anne Arundel Community College
Bowie State University
Capitol College
Catonsville Community College
Cecil Community College
Dundalk Community College
Essex Community College
Frederick Community College
Frostburg State University
Hagerstown Junior College
Hood College
Johns Hopkins University
Maryland College of Art and
    Design
Montgomery College
    Germantown Campus
    Rockville Campus
    Takoma Park Campus
Morgan State University
Mount St. Mary's College
Prince George's Community College
University of Baltimore
University of Maryland
    Baltimore County
    College Park
Wor-Wic Community College

Massachusetts

Anna Maria College
Atlantic Union College

Boston Conservatory
Boston University
Cape Cod Community College
Elms College
Emerson College
Forsyth School for Dental
    Hygienists
Hampshire College
Massachusetts Bay Community
    College
Merrimack College
Middlesex Community College
Mount Holyoke College
School of the Museum of Fine Arts
Smith College
Springfield Technical Community
    College
Suffolk University
Wellesley College
Western New England College

Michigan

Albion College
Alma College
Aquinas College
Center for Creative Studies: College
    of Art and Design
Concordia College
Detroit College of Business
Eastern Michigan University
Ferris State University
Glen Oaks Community College
Grand Valley State University
Great Lakes Junior College of
    Business
Highland Park Community College
Jackson Community College
Kalamazoo College
Kalamazoo Valley Community
    College
Kellogg Community College
Kendall College of Art and Design
Lawrence Technological University
Michigan State University
Mid Michigan Community College
Monroe County Community
    College
Mott Community College
North Central Michigan College
Northwestern Michigan College
Sacred Heart Major Seminary
St. Clair County Community
    College
St. Mary's College
Siena Heights College
Spring Arbor College
Suomi College
Walsh College of Accountancy and
    Business Administration
Washtenaw Community College
Wayne State University
West Shore Community College
William Tyndale College

Minnesota

Anoka-Ramsey Community College
Bemidji State University
Central Lakes College
College of St. Catherine: St.
    Catherine Campus
Hibbing Community College
Inver Hills Community College
Lakewood Community College
NEI College of Technology
Normandale Community College
Rainy River Community College
Southwest State University
University of St. Thomas
Vermilion Community College
Willmar Community College
Willmar Technical College

Mississippi

Belhaven College
Blue Mountain College
Copiah-Lincoln Community College
East Central Community College
Hinds Community College
Itawamba Community College
Jackson State University
Jones County Junior College
Magnolia Bible College
Mary Holmes College
Meridian Community College
Millsaps College
Mississippi College
Mississippi Gulf Coast Community
  College
    Jackson County Campus
    Jefferson Davis Campus
    Perkinston
Mississippi State University
Mississippi University for Women
Mississippi Valley State University
Northwest Mississippi Community
  College
Pearl River Community College
Tougaloo College
University of Mississippi
    Medical Center
    University
University of Southern Mississippi
William Carey College

Missouri

Avila College
Central Christian College of the
  Bible
Columbia College
Deaconess College of Nursing
DeVry Institute of Technology:
  Kansas City
Drury College
East Central College
Fontbonne College
Hannibal-LaGrange College
Harris Stowe State College
Jefferson College
Lincoln University
Lindenwood College
Maryville University of Saint Louis
Missouri Baptist College
Missouri Western State College
Research College of Nursing
Rockhurst College
St. Louis University
Southwest Baptist University
Southwest Missouri State University
University of Missouri
    Columbia
    Rolla
Washington University
Webster University
Wentworth Military Academy

Montana

Dawson Community College
Flathead Valley Community College
Miles Community College
Montana State University
    College of Technology-Great
      Falls
    Billings
    Bozeman
    Northern
Montana Tech of The University of
  Montana
Montana Tech of the University of
  Montana: College of Technology
University of Great Falls
University of Montana College of
  Technology
Western Montana College of the
  University of Montana

Nebraska

Bellevue University
Central Community College
Chadron State College
College of St. Mary
Dana College
Grace University
Hastings College
Midland Lutheran College
Nebraska Christian College
Nebraska College of Technical
  Agriculture
Nebraska Indian Community
  College
Nebraska Methodist College of
  Nursing and Allied Health
Nebraska Wesleyan University
University of Nebraska—Omaha
Western Nebraska Community
  College
York College

Nevada

Community College of Southern
  Nevada
Great Basin College
Truckee Meadows Community
  College
University of Nevada
    Las Vegas
    Reno
Western Nevada Community
  College

New Hampshire

Dartmouth College
Franklin Pierce College
McIntosh College
New Hampshire College
New Hampshire Technical College
    Berlin
    Manchester
    Nashua
Rivier College

New Jersey

Bloomfield College
Burlington County College
Camden County College
DeVry Technical Institute
Essex County College
Fairleigh Dickinson University
    Edward Williams College
    Teaneck
Jersey City State College
Monmouth University
Princeton University
Raritan Valley Community College
Richard Stockton College of New
  Jersey
Rutgers, The State University of
  New Jersey
    Camden College of Arts and
      Sciences
    College of Engineering
    College of Nursing
    College of Pharmacy
    Cook College
    Douglass College
    Livingston College
    Mason Gross School of the
      Arts
    Newark College of Arts and
      Sciences
    Rutgers College
St. Peter's College
Salem Community College
Seton Hall University
Sussex County Community College
Trenton State College
Union County College

William Paterson College of New
  Jersey

New Mexico

Albuquerque Technical-Vocational
  Institute
Clovis Community College
College of the Southwest
Dona Ana Branch Community
  College of New Mexico State
  University
Eastern New Mexico University:
  Roswell Campus
National College
New Mexico Highlands University
New Mexico Military Institute
New Mexico State University
    Carlsbad
    Las Cruces
Santa Fe Community College

New York

Adelphi University
Adirondack Community College
Albany College of Pharmacy
American Academy of Dramatic
  Arts
Audrey Cohen College
Barnard College
Bramson ORT Technical Institute
Broome Community College
Canisius College
Catholic Medical Center of
  Brooklyn and Queens School of
  Nursing
Cazenovia College
City University of New York
    Baruch College
    Brooklyn College
    City College
    College of Staten Island
    Hostos Community College
    Hunter College
    John Jay College of Criminal
      Justice
    Lehman College
    Medgar Evers College
    Queensborough Community
      College
    York College
Clinton Community College
College of Insurance
College of Mount St. Vincent
College of New Rochelle
    New Rochelle
    School of New Resources
College of St. Rose
Columbia University
    Columbia College
    School of Engineering and
      Applied Science
Columbia-Greene Community
  College
Concordia College
Dominican College of Blauvelt
Dowling College
Dutchess Community College
D'Youville College
Elmira College
Erie Community College: North
  Campus
Eugene Lang College/New School
  for Social Research
Finger Lakes Community College
Fordham University
Fulton-Montgomery Community
  College
Genesee Community College
Hofstra University
Hudson Valley Community College
Ithaca College

Long Island University
    Brooklyn Campus
    C. W. Post Campus
    Southampton College
Manhattan College
Mannes College of Music
Marymount Manhattan College
Mater Dei College
Medaille College
Mercy College
Molloy College
Monroe College
Monroe Community College
Mount St. Mary College
New York Institute of Technology
New York School of Interior
  Design
New York University
Niagara County Community College
Niagara University
Onondaga Community College
Orange County Community College
Pace University
Paul Smith's College
Plaza Business Institute
Polytechnic University
    Brooklyn
    Long Island Campus
Pratt Institute
Rochester Institute of Technology
Sage Junior College of Albany
St. Bonaventure University
St. John Fisher College
St. John's University
School of Visual Arts
State University of New York
    Albany
    College at Brockport
    College at Cortland
    College of Environmental
      Science and Forestry
    College at Old Westbury
    College at Potsdam
    College of Technology at
      Alfred
    College of Technology at
      Canton
    College of Technology at Delhi
    New Paltz
Tompkins-Cortland Community
  College
Trocaire College
Ulster County Community College
Utica College of Syracuse
  University
Vassar College
Wadhams Hall Seminary-College
Westchester Business Institute
Westchester Community College
Yeshiva University

North Carolina

Alamance Community College
Asheville Buncombe Technical
  Community College
Chowan College
East Coast Bible College
Guilford College
Methodist College
North Carolina Agricultural and
  Technical State University
Peace College
Pfeiffer College
Richmond Community College
Roanoke Bible College
St. Andrews Presbyterian College
University of North Carolina at
  Asheville
Western Piedmont Community
  College
Wilson Technical Community
  College

North Dakota

North Dakota State University

Ohio

Art Academy of Cincinnati
Belmont Technical College
Bluffton College
Case Western Reserve University
Cedarville College
Central Ohio Technical College
Chatfield College
Circleville Bible College
Clark State Community College
Cleveland State University
Cuyahoga Community College
    Eastern Campus
    Metropolitan Campus
    Western Campus
Denison University
DeVry Institute of Technology:
    Columbus
Edison State Community College
Franklin University
God's Bible School and College
Hiram College
Kent State University
    East Liverpool Regional
      Campus
    Salem Regional Campus
    Stark Campus.
    Trumbull Campus
    Tuscarawas Campus
Lorain County Community College
Lourdes College
Malone College
Marietta College
Marion Technical College
Miami-Jacobs College
Mount Vernon Nazarene College
Muskingum Area Technical College
Muskingum College
North Central Technical College
Northwest State Community
    College
Oberlin College
Ohio Dominican College
Southern State Community College
Stautzenberger College
Terra Community College
Tiffin University
Union Institute
University of Cincinnati
    Cincinnati
    Clermont College
    Raymond Walters College
University of Dayton
University of Toledo
Urbana University
Walsh University
Wilberforce University
Wilmington College
Xavier University
Youngstown State University

Oklahoma

Bartlesville Wesleyan College
Oklahoma Christian University of
    Science and Arts
Oklahoma City Community College
Oklahoma City University
Oklahoma Panhandle State
    University
Oklahoma State University:
    Oklahoma City
Rogers State College
Southeastern Oklahoma State
    University
Southwestern Oklahoma State
    University
University of Central Oklahoma

Oregon

Bassist College
Central Oregon Community College
Chemeketa Community College
Clackamas Community College
Clatsop Community College
Concordia University
George Fox College
Lane Community College
Linfield College
Marylhurst College
Northwest Christian College
Oregon Health Sciences University
Oregon Institute of Technology
Pacific Northwest College of Art
Pacific University
Portland Community College
Southwestern Oregon Community
    College
Treasure Valley Community College
University of Portland
Western Baptist College
Western Oregon State College
Willamette University

Pennsylvania

Albright College
Allentown College of St. Francis de
    Sales
Art Institute of Pittsburgh
Baptist Bible College of
    Pennsylvania
Bryn Mawr College
Bucks County Community College
California University of
    Pennsylvania
Carnegie Mellon University
Central Pennsylvania Business
    School
Chestnut Hill College
Churchman Business School
Clarion University of Pennsylvania
College Misericordia
Community College of Allegheny
    County
    Allegheny Campus
    Boyce Campus
    South Campus
Community College of Beaver
    County
Delaware County Community
    College
Delaware Valley College
Drexel University
Duquesne University
East Stroudsburg University of
    Pennsylvania
Elizabethtown College
Gettysburg College
Gratz College
Harcum College
Haverford College
Holy Family College
Immaculata College
Kutztown University of
    Pennsylvania
La Roche College
La Salle University
Lackawanna Junior College
Lafayette College
Lancaster Bible College
Manor Junior College
Mansfield University of
    Pennsylvania
Marywood College
Moravian College
Neumann College
Peirce College

Penn State

    Allentown Campus
    Altoona Campus
    Beaver Campus
    Berks Campus
    Delaware County Campus
    Du Bois Campus
    Erie Behrend College
    Fayette Campus
    Harrisburg Capital College
    Hazleton Campus
    McKeesport Campus
    Mont Alto Campus
    New Kensington Campus
    Ogontz Campus
    Schuylkill Campus
    Shenango Campus
    University Park Campus
    Wilkes-Barre Campus
    Worthington-Scranton Campus
    York Campus
Pennsylvania College of Technology
Point Park College
Reading Area Community College
Robert Morris College
St. Charles Borromeo Seminary-
    Overbrook
Temple University
University of the Arts
University of Pennsylvania
University of Pittsburgh
Ursinus College
Valley Forge Military College
Wilkes University
York College of Pennsylvania

Puerto Rico

Bayamon Central University
Caribbean University
Columbia College
Humacao Community College
ICPR Junior College
Inter American University of Puerto
    Rico
    Aguadilla Campus
    Arecibo Campus
    Fajardo Campus
    Guayama Campus
    San German Campus
Pontifical Catholic University of
    Puerto Rico
Turabo University
Universidad Metropolitana
Universidad Politecnica de Puerto
    Rico
University of Puerto Rico
    Aguadilla
    Arecibo Campus
    Bayamon Technological
      University College
    Humacao University College
    La Montana Regional College
    Mayaguez Campus
    Ponce Technological
      University College
University of the Sacred Heart

Rhode Island

Rhode Island School of Design

South Carolina

The Citadel
Coastal Carolina University
Columbia Bible College
Columbia College
Columbia Junior College of Business
Southern Wesleyan University
University of South Carolina
    Aiken
    Columbia
    Spartanburg
    Union

Winthrop University

South Dakota

Black Hills State University
Dakota State University
Dakota Wesleyan University
Huron University
Northern State University
Presentation College
South Dakota School of Mines and
    Technology
Western Dakota Technical Institute

Tennessee

Carson-Newman College
Christian Brothers University
Johnson Bible College
Knoxville Business College
Lee College
Lincoln Memorial University
Memphis College of Art
Middle Tennessee State University
Tennessee Wesleyan College
Trevecca Nazarene University
Union University
University of Tennessee
    Chattanooga
    Knoxville
    Martin
Vanderbilt University

Texas

Abilene Christian University
Ambassador University
Arlington Baptist College
Austin Community College
Concordia Lutheran College
Dallas Baptist University
Dallas Christian College
DeVry Institute of Technology:
    Irving
East Texas State University
Huston-Tillotson College
Jarvis Christian College
Lee College
Midwestern State University
North Lake College
Odessa College
Prairie View A&M University
St. Edward's University
St. Mary's University
Southern Methodist University
Southwestern University
Texas A&M University-Corpus
    Christi
Texas Southern University
Texas Wesleyan University
University of Houston: Downtown
University of Texas
    El Paso
    Medical Branch at Galveston
    Houston Health Science
      Center

Utah

LDS Business College
Snow College
University of Utah
Utah State University
Utah Valley State College

Vermont

Champlain College
Goddard College
Southern Vermont College
Trinity College of Vermont
University of Vermont
Vermont Technical College

Virginia

George Mason University
Hampton University

Marymount University
Norfolk State University
Old Dominion University
Randolph-Macon Woman's College
Shenandoah University
Tidewater Community College
Virginia State University
Virginia Union University

Washington

Antioch University Seattle
Art Institute of Seattle
Centralia College
Cornish College of the Arts
Eastern Washington University
Gonzaga University
Henry Cogswell College
Lower Columbia College
Northwest College
Peninsula College
Pierce College
Puget Sound Christian College
St. Martin's College
Spokane Community College
Spokane Falls Community College
Tacoma Community College
University of Puget Sound

West Virginia

West Virginia State College
West Virginia University

Wisconsin

Alverno College
Blackhawk Technical College
Carroll College
Fox Valley Technical College
Marquette University
Mid-State Technical College
Milwaukee Area Technical College
Milwaukee Institute of Art &
    Design
Moraine Park Technical College
Nicolet Area Technical College
Northcentral Technical College
St. Norbert College
Silver Lake College
Southwest Wisconsin Technical
    College
University of Wisconsin Center
        Baraboo/Sauk County
        Barron County
        Fond du Lac
        Fox Valley
        Manitowoc County
        Marshfield/Wood County
        Rock County
        Sheboygan County
        Washington County
        Waukesha
Waukesha County Technical
    College
Western Wisconsin Technical
    College

Wyoming

Sheridan College
Western Wyoming Community
    College

18. Alphabetical list of colleges

Abilene Christian University, Abilene, TX 79699-6000
Abraham Baldwin Agricultural College, Tifton, GA 31794-2693
Academy of Art College, San Francisco, CA 94115-3410
Academy of Business College, Phoenix, AZ 85051
Academy of Court Reporting, Cleveland, OH 44113
Academy of the New Church, Bryn Athyn, PA 19009
Adams State College, Alamosa, CO 81102
Adelphi University, Garden City, NY 11530
Adirondack Community College, Queensbury, NY 12804-1498
Adrian College, Adrian, MI 49221-2575
Agnes Scott College, Decatur, GA 30030-3797
Aiken Technical College, Aiken, SC 29802-0696
Aims Community College, Greeley, CO 80632-0069
Al Collins Graphic Design School, Tempe, AZ 85281
Alabama Agricultural and Mechanical University, Normal, AL 35762
Alabama Aviation and Technical College, Ozark, AL 36361-1209
Alabama Southern Community College, Monroeville, AL 36461-2000
Alabama State University, Montgomery, AL 36101-0271
Alamance Community College, Graham, NC 27253
Alaska Bible College, Glennallen, AK 99588-0289
Alaska Pacific University, Anchorage, AK 99508-4672
Albany College of Pharmacy, Albany, NY 12208
Albany State College, Albany, GA 31705-2796
Albertson College, Caldwell, ID 83605
Albertus Magnus College, New Haven, CT 06511-1189
Albion College, Albion, MI 49224
Albright College, Reading, PA 19612-5234
Albuquerque Technical-Vocational Institute, Albuquerque, NM 87106
Alcorn State University, Lorman, MS 39096
Alderson-Broaddus College, Philippi, WV 26416
Alexandria Technical College, Alexandria, MN 56308-3799
Alfred University, Alfred, NY 14802-1205
Alice Lloyd College, Pippa Passes, KY 41844
Allan Hancock College, Santa Maria, CA 93454-6399
Allegany College, Cumberland, MD 21502
Allegheny College, Meadville, PA 16335-3902
Allen County Community College, Iola, KS 66749
Allen University, Columbia, SC 29204
Allentown College of St. Francis de Sales, Center Valley, PA 18034-9568
Alma College, Alma, MI 48801-1599
Alpena Community College, Alpena, MI 49707
Alvernia College, Reading, PA 19607-1799
Alverno College, Milwaukee, WI 53234-3922
Alvin Community College, Alvin, TX 77511-4898
Amarillo College, Amarillo, TX 79178
Ambassador University, Big Sandy, TX 75755
Amber University, Garland, TX 75041-5595
American Academy of Art, Chicago, IL 60604-4302
American Academy of Dramatic Arts
    New York, New York, NY 10016
    West, Pasadena, CA 91107
American Academy McAllister Institute of Funeral Service, New York, NY 10019-3602
American Baptist College of ABT Seminary, Nashville, TN 37207
American College
    Atlanta, Atlanta, GA 30326
    Los Angeles, Los Angeles, CA 90024-5603
American Conservatory of Music, Chicago, IL 60602-4792
American Indian College of the Assemblies of God, Phoenix, AZ 85021-2199

American Institute of Business, Des Moines, IA 50321
American Institute of Commerce, Davenport, IA 52807-2095
American Institute of Design, Philadelphia, PA 19124
American International College, Springfield, MA 01109-3184
American River College, Sacramento, CA 95841
American Technical Institute, Brunswick, TN 38014
American University, Washington, DC 20016-8001
American University of Puerto Rico, Bayamon, PR 00960-2037
Amherst College, Amherst, MA 01002
Ancilla College, Donaldson, IN 46513
Anderson College, Anderson, SC 29621
Anderson University, Anderson, IN 46012-3462
Andover College, Portland, ME 04103
Andrew College, Cuthbert, GA 31740-1395
Andrews University, Berrien Springs, MI 49104
Angelina College, Lufkin, TX 75902-1768
Angelo State University, San Angelo, TX 76909
Anna Maria College, Paxton, MA 01612-1198
Anne Arundel Community College, Arnold, MD 21012-1895
Anoka-Ramsey Community College, Coon Rapids, MN 55433
Anson Community College, Polkton, NC 28135
Antelope Valley College, Lancaster, CA 93536-5426
Antioch College, Yellow Springs, OH 45387
Antioch Southern California
    Los Angeles, Marina Del Rey, CA 90292-7090
    Santa Barbara, Santa Barbara, CA 93101
Antioch University Seattle, Seattle, WA 98121
Antonelli College, Cincinnati, OH 45202
Antonelli Institute of Art and Photography, Plymouth Meeting, PA 19462-0570
Appalachian Bible College, Bradley, WV 25818-1353
Appalachian State University, Boone, NC 28608
Aquinas College, Grand Rapids, MI 49506-1799
Aquinas College, Nashville, TN 37205
Aquinas College at Milton, Milton, MA 02186
Aquinas College at Newton, Newton, MA 02158-9990
Arapahoe Community College, Littleton, CO 80160-9002
Arizona College of the Bible, Phoenix, AZ 85021-5197
Arizona State University, Tempe, AZ 85287-0112
Arizona Western College, Yuma, AZ 85366-0929
Arkansas Baptist College, Little Rock, AR 72202
Arkansas State University
    Beebe Branch, Beebe, AR 72012-1008
    Jonesboro, Jonesboro, AR 72467-1630
Arkansas Tech University, Russellville, AR 72801-2222
Arlington Baptist College, Arlington, TX 76012-3425
Armstrong State College, Savannah, GA 31419-1997
Armstrong University, Berkeley, CA 94704
Art Academy of Cincinnati, Cincinnati, OH 45202-1700
Art Center College of Design, Pasadena, CA 91103
Art Institute of Atlanta, Atlanta, GA 30326
Art Institute of Fort Lauderdale, Fort Lauderdale, FL 33316-3000
Art Institute of Pittsburgh, Pittsburgh, PA 15222
Art Institute of Seattle, Seattle, WA 98121
Art Institute of Southern California, Laguna Beach, CA 92651
Asbury College, Wilmore, KY 40390-1198
Asheville Buncombe Technical Community College, Asheville, NC 28801-4897
Ashland Community College, Ashland, KY 41101-3683
Ashland University, Ashland, OH 44805-9981

Asnuntuck Community-Technical College, Enfield, CT 06082
Assumption College, Worcester, MA 01615-0005
Assumption College for Sisters, Mendham, NJ 07945-0800
Athens Area Technical Institute, Athens, GA 30610-0399
Athens State College, Athens, AL 35611
Atlanta Christian College, East Point, GA 30344
Atlanta College of Art, Atlanta, GA 30309
Atlanta Metropolitan College, Atlanta, GA 30310-4498
Atlantic Community College, Mays Landing, NJ 08330-2699
Atlantic Union College, South Lancaster, MA 01561
Auburn University
    Auburn, Auburn, AL 36849-5145
    Montgomery, Montgomery, AL 36117-3596
Audrey Cohen College, New York, NY 10013-1919
Augsburg College, Minneapolis, MN 55454
Augusta College, Augusta, GA 30904-2200
Augusta Technical Institute, Augusta, GA 30906
Augustana College, Rock Island, IL 61201-2296
Augustana College, Sioux Falls, SD 57197-9990
Aurora University, Aurora, IL 60506-4892
Austin College, Sherman, TX 75090-4440
Austin Community College, Austin, MN 55912-1407
Austin Community College, Austin, TX 78752-4390
Austin Peay State University, Clarksville, TN 37044
Averett College, Danville, VA 24541
Avila College, Kansas City, MO 64145-1698
Azusa Pacific University, Azusa, CA 91702-7000
Babson College, Babson Park, MA 02157-0310
Bacone College, Muskogee, OK 74403-1597
Bainbridge College, Bainbridge, GA 31717-0953
Baker College
    Auburn Hills, Auburn Hills, MI 48326
    Cadillac, Cadillac, MI 49601-9169
    Flint, Flint, MI 48507-5508
    Jackson, Jackson, MI 49201-2328
    Mount Clemens, Clinton Township, MI 48035-4701
    Muskegon, Muskegon, MI 49442
    Owosso, Owosso, MI 48867
    Port Huron, Port Huron, MI 48060-2597
Baker University, Baldwin City, KS 66006
Bakersfield College, Bakersfield, CA 93305
Baldwin-Wallace College, Berea, OH 44017-2088
Ball State University, Muncie, IN 47306-0855
Baltimore City Community College, Baltimore, MD 21215
Baltimore Hebrew University, Baltimore, MD 21215-3996
Baltimore International Culinary College, Baltimore, MD 21202-3230
Baptist Bible College, Springfield, MO 65803
Baptist Bible College of Pennsylvania, Clarks Summit, PA 18411
Baptist Missionary Association Theological Seminary, Jacksonville, TX 75766-5414
Barat College, Lake Forest, IL 60045
Barber-Scotia College, Concord, NC 28025
Barclay College, Haviland, KS 67059
Bard College, Annandale-on-Hudson, NY 12504-5000
Barnard College, New York, NY 10027-6598
Barry University, Miami Shores, FL 33161
Barstow College, Barstow, CA 92311-9984
Bartlesville Wesleyan College, Bartlesville, OK 74006
Barton College, Wilson, NC 27893
Barton County Community College, Great Bend, KS 67530-9283
Bassist College, Portland, OR 97201
Bastyr University, Bothell, WA 98011
Bates College, Lewiston, ME 04240-9917
Bauder College, Atlanta, GA 30326-9975
Bay de Noc Community College, Escanaba, MI 49829
Bay Mills Community College, Brimley, MI 49715
Bay Path College, Longmeadow, MA 01106
Bay State College, Boston, MA 02116
Bayamon Central University, Bayamon, PR 00960-1725
Baylor College of Dentistry, Dallas, TX 75266-0677
Baylor University, Waco, TX 76798-7056
Beal College, Bangor, ME 04401
Beaufort County Community College, Washington, NC 27889
Beaver College, Glenside, PA 19038-3295
Becker College
    Leicester Campus, Leicester, MA 01524-1197
    Worcester Campus, Worcester, MA 01615-0071
Bee County College, Beeville, TX 78102
Belhaven College, Jackson, MS 39202-1789
Bellarmine College, Louisville, KY 40205-0671
Belleville Area College, Belleville, IL 62221-9989
Bellevue Community College, Bellevue, WA 98007-6484

Bellevue University, Bellevue, NE 68005-3098
Bellin College of Nursing, Green Bay, WI 54305-3400
Belmont Abbey College, Belmont, NC 28012-2795
Belmont Technical College, St. Clairsville, OH 43950
Belmont University, Nashville, TN 37212-3757
Beloit College, Beloit, WI 53511-5595
Bel-Rea Institute of Animal Technology, Denver, CO 80231
Bemidji State University, Bemidji, MN 56601
Benedict College, Columbia, SC 29204
Benedictine College, Atchison, KS 66002-1499
Benedictine University, Lisle, IL 60532-0900
Bennett College, Greensboro, NC 27401-3239
Bennington College, Bennington, VT 05201
Bentley College, Waltham, MA 02154-4705
Berea College, Berea, KY 40404
Berean College, Springfield, MO 65802
Berean Institute, Philadelphia, PA 19130
Bergen Community College, Paramus, NJ 07652-1595
Berkeley College, White Plains, NY 10604
Berkeley College of Business, West Paterson, NJ 07424-0440
Berkeley College of New York City, New York, NY 10017
Berklee College of Music, Boston, MA 02215
Berkshire Community College, Pittsfield, MA 01201-5786
Berry College, Mount Berry, GA 30149
Bessemer State Technical College, Bessemer, AL 35021
Beth Hamedrash Shaarei Yosher Institute, Brooklyn, NY 11204
Beth Medrash Govoha, Lakewood, NJ 08701
Bethany College, Scotts Valley, CA 95066-2898
Bethany College, Bethany, WV 26032-0417
Bethany College, Lindsborg, KS 67456-1897
Bethany Lutheran College, Mankato, MN 56001-4490
Bethel College, McKenzie, TN 38201
Bethel College, Mishawaka, IN 46545
Bethel College, North Newton, KS 67117-9899
Bethel College, St. Paul, MN 55112
Beth-El College of Nursing, Colorado Springs, CO 80917-5338
Bethune-Cookman College, Daytona Beach, FL 32114-3099
Bevill State Community College, Sumiton, AL 35148
Big Bend Community College, Moses Lake, WA 98837-3299
Biola University, La Mirada, CA 90639-0001
Birmingham-Southern College, Birmingham, AL 35254
Bishop State Community College, Mobile, AL 36603-5898
Bismarck State College, Bismarck, ND 58501
Black Hawk College
    East Campus, Kewanee, IL 61443-0630
    Moline, Moline, IL 61265
Black Hills State University, Spearfish, SD 57799-9502
Blackburn College, Carlinville, IL 62626
Blackfeet Community College, Browning, MT 59417
Blackhawk Technical College, Janesville, WI 53547
Bladen Community College, Dublin, NC 28332
Blair Junior College, Colorado Springs, CO 80915
Blessing-Reiman College of Nursing, Quincy, IL 62301-7005
Blinn College, Brenham, TX 77833
Bloomfield College, Bloomfield, NJ 07003
Bloomsburg University of Pennsylvania, Bloomsburg, PA 17815
Blue Mountain College, Blue Mountain, MS 38610
Blue Mountain Community College, Pendleton, OR 97801
Blue Ridge Community College, Flat Rock, NC 28731-9624
Blue Ridge Community College, Weyers Cave, VA 24486-9989
Bluefield College, Bluefield, VA 24605-1799
Bluefield State College, Bluefield, WV 24701
Bluffton College, Bluffton, OH 45817-1196
Bohecker's Business College, Ravenna, OH 44266
Boise Bible College, Boise, ID 83714-1220
Boise State University, Boise, ID 83725
Boricua College, New York, NY 10032
Bossier Parish Community College, Bossier City, LA 71111
Boston Architectural Center, Boston, MA 02115-2795
Boston College, Chestnut Hill, MA 02167-3809
Boston Conservatory, Boston, MA 02215
Boston University, Boston, MA 02215
Bowdoin College, Brunswick, ME 04011-2595
Bowie State University, Bowie, MD 20715
Bowling Green State University
    Bowling Green, Bowling Green, OH 43403-0085
    Firelands College, Huron, OH 44839-9791
Bradford College, Bradford, MA 01835-7393
Bradford School, Columbus, OH 43209
Bradley Academy for the Visual Arts, York, PA 17403
Bradley University, Peoria, IL 61625
Bramson ORT Technical Institute, Forest Hills, NY 11375

Brandeis University, Waltham, MA 02254-9110
Brazosport College, Lake Jackson, TX 77566
Brenau University, Gainesville, GA 30501-3697
Brescia College, Owensboro, KY 42301-3023
Brevard College, Brevard, NC 28712
Brevard Community College, Cocoa, FL 32922-9987
Brewton-Parker College, Mount Vernon, GA 30445
Briar Cliff College, Sioux City, IA 51104-2100
Briarcliffe: The College for Business and Technology, Woodbury, NY 11797
Briarwood College, Southington, CT 06489-1057
Bridgewater College, Bridgewater, VA 22812-1599
Bridgewater State College, Bridgewater, MA 02325
Brigham Young University
    Provo, Provo, UT 84602
    Hawaii, Laie, HI 96762-1294
Brookdale Community College, Lincroft, NJ 07738
Brookhaven College, Farmers Branch, TX 75244
Brooks College, Long Beach, CA 90804
Brooks Institute of Photography, Santa Barbara, CA 93108
Broome Community College, Binghamton, NY 13902
Broward Community College, Fort Lauderdale, FL 33301
Brown Mackie College, Salina, KS 67402-1787
Brown University, Providence, RI 02912
Brunswick College, Brunswick, GA 31523
Brunswick Community College, Supply, NC 28462
Bryan College, Dayton, TN 37321-7000
Bryant College, Smithfield, RI 02917-1285
Bryant & Stratton Business Institute
    Albany, Albany, NY 12205
    Buffalo, Buffalo, NY 14202
    Cleveland West, Parma, OH 44130-1013
    Rochester, Rochester, NY 14604-1381
    Syracuse, Syracuse, NY 13203-2502
Bryant & Stratton College, Cleveland, OH 44114-3203
Bryn Mawr College, Bryn Mawr, PA 19010-2899
Bucknell University, Lewisburg, PA 17837-9988
Bucks County Community College, Newtown, PA 18940
Buena Vista University, Storm Lake, IA 50588-1798
Bunker Hill Community College, Boston, MA 02129-2991
Burlington College, Burlington, VT 05401
Burlington County College, Pemberton, NJ 08068-1599
Business Institute of Pennsylvania, Sharon, PA 16146
Butler County Community College, Butler, PA 16003-1203
Butler County Community College, Eldorado, KS 67042-3280
Butler University, Indianapolis, IN 46208
Butte College, Oroville, CA 95965
Cabrillo College, Aptos, CA 95003
Cabrini College, Radnor, PA 19087-3698
CAD Institute, Phoenix, AZ 85040
Caldwell College, Caldwell, NJ 07006-6195
Caldwell Community College and Technical Institute, Hudson, NC 28638-2397
Calhoun Community College, Decatur, AL 35609-2216
California Baptist College, Riverside, CA 92504-3297
California College of Arts and Crafts, Oakland, CA 94618-1487
California Culinary Academy, San Francisco, CA 94102
California Institute of the Arts, Valencia, CA 91355
California Institute of Technology, Pasadena, CA 91125
California Lutheran University, Thousand Oaks, CA 91360-2787
California Maritime Academy, Vallejo, CA 94590-0644
California Polytechnic State University: San Luis Obispo, San Luis Obispo, CA 93407
California State Polytechnic University: Pomona, Pomona, CA 91768-4019
California State University
    Bakersfield, Bakersfield, CA 93311-1099
    Chico, Chico, CA 95929-0722
    Dominguez Hills, Carson, CA 90747-9960
    Fresno, Fresno, CA 93740-0057
    Fullerton, Fullerton, CA 92634-9480
    Hayward, Hayward, CA 94542-3035
    Long Beach, Long Beach, CA 90840-0106
    Los Angeles, Los Angeles, CA 90032-8530
    Northridge, Northridge, CA 91328-1286
    Sacramento, Sacramento, CA 95819-6048
    San Bernardino, San Bernardino, CA 92407-2397
    San Marcos, San Marcos, CA 92096-0001
    Stanislaus, Turlock, CA 95382-0283
California University of Pennsylvania, California, PA 15419-1394
Calumet College of St. Joseph, Hammond, IN 46394-2195
Calvary Bible College, Kansas City, MO 64147-1341
Calvin College, Grand Rapids, MI 49546-4388
Cambria-Rowe Business College, Johnstown, PA 15902

Camden County College, Blackwood, NJ 08012
Cameron University, Lawton, OK 73505-6377
Campbell University, Buies Creek, NC 27506
Campbellsville College, Campbellsville, KY 42718-2799
Canada College, Redwood City, CA 94061
Canisius College, Buffalo, NY 14208-9989
Cape Cod Community College, West Barnstable, MA 02668-1599
Cape Fear Community College, Wilmington, NC 28401-3993
Capital Community-Technical College, Hartford, CT 06105-2354
Capital University, Columbus, OH 43209-2394
Capitol College, Laurel, MD 20708
Cardinal Stritch College, Milwaukee, WI 53217-3985
Caribbean Center for Advanced Studies: Miami Institute of Psychology, Miami, FL 33166
Caribbean University, Bayamon, PR 00960-0493
Carl Albert State College, Poteau, OK 74953-5208
Carl Sandburg College, Galesburg, IL 61401
Carleton College, Northfield, MN 55057
Carlow College, Pittsburgh, PA 15213-3165
Carnegie Mellon University, Pittsburgh, PA 15213-3890
Carroll College, Waukesha, WI 53186
Carroll College, Helena, MT 59625
Carroll Community College, Westminster, MD 21157
Carson-Newman College, Jefferson City, TN 37760
Carteret Community College, Morehead City, NC 28557-2989
Carthage College, Kenosha, WI 53140-1994
Casco Bay College, Portland, ME 04101-3483
Case Western Reserve University, Cleveland, OH 44106-7055
Casper College, Casper, WY 82601
Castle College, Windham, NH 03087-1297
Castleton State College, Castleton, VT 05735-9987
Catawba College, Salisbury, NC 28144-2488
Catawba Valley Community College, Hickory, NC 28602
Catholic Medical Center of Brooklyn and Queens School of Nursing, Woodhaven, NY 11421
Catholic University of America, Washington, DC 20064
Catonsville Community College, Catonsville, MD 21228
Cayuga County Community College, Auburn, NY 13021-3099
Cazenovia College, Cazenovia, NY 13035-9989
Cecil Community College, North East, MD 21901-1999
Cecils College, Asheville, NC 28816
Cedar Crest College, Allentown, PA 18104-6196
Cedar Valley College, Lancaster, TX 75134
Cedarville College, Cedarville, OH 45314-0601
Centenary College, Hackettstown, NJ 07840-9989
Centenary College of Louisiana, Shreveport, LA 71134-1188
Center for Creative Studies: College of Art and Design, Detroit, MI 48202-4034
Central Alabama Community College, Alexander City, AL 35011
Central Arizona College, Coolidge, AZ 85228
Central Baptist College, Conway, AR 72032
Central Bible College, Springfield, MO 65803-1069
Central Carolina Community College, Sanford, NC 27330
Central Carolina Technical College, Sumter, SC 29150
Central Christian College of the Bible, Moberly, MO 65270-1997
Central City Business Institute, Syracuse, NY 13202
Central College, Pella, IA 50219-1999
Central College, McPherson, KS 67460-5740
Central Community College, Grand Island, NE 68802-4903
Central Connecticut State University, New Britain, CT 06050
Central Florida Community College, Ocala, FL 34478
Central Lakes College, Brainerd, MN 56401
Central Maine Medical Center School of Nursing, Lewiston, ME 04240-9986
Central Maine Technical College, Auburn, ME 04210-6498
Central Methodist College, Fayette, MO 65248-1198
Central Michigan University, Mount Pleasant, MI 48859
Central Missouri State University, Warrensburg, MO 64093
Central Ohio Technical College, Newark, OH 43055
Central Oregon Community College, Bend, OR 97701-5998
Central Pennsylvania Business School, Summerdale, PA 17093-0309
Central Piedmont Community College, Charlotte, NC 28235-5009
Central State University, Wilberforce, OH 45384-3002
Central Texas College, Killeen, TX 76540-9990
Central Virginia Community College, Lynchburg, VA 24502-2498
Central Washington University, Ellensburg, WA 98926-7463
Central Wyoming College, Riverton, WY 82501
Central Yeshiva Tomchei Tmimim-Lubavitch, Brooklyn, NY 11230
Centralia College, Centralia, WA 98531
Centre College, Danville, KY 40422
Cerritos Community College, Norwalk, CA 90650
Cerro Coso Community College, Ridgecrest, CA 93555-7777

Chabot College, Hayward, CA 94545
Chadron State College, Chadron, NE 69337
Chaffey Community College, Rancho Cucamonga, CA 91701-3002
Chaminade University of Honolulu, Honolulu, HI 96816-1578
Champlain College, Burlington, VT 05402-0670
Chapman University, Orange, CA 92666-1099
Charles County Community College, La Plata, MD 20646
Charles R. Drew University: College of Allied Health, Los Angeles, CA 90059
Charleston Southern University, Charleston, SC 29411
Chatfield College, St. Martin, OH 45118-9705
Chatham College, Pittsburgh, PA 15232-9987
Chattahoochee Technical Institute, Marietta, GA 30060
Chattahoochee Valley Community College, Phenix City, AL 36869
Chattanooga State Technical Community College, Chattanooga, TN 37406
Chemeketa Community College, Salem, OR 97309-7070
Chesapeake College, Wye Mills, MD 21679-0008
Chesterfield-Marlboro Technical College, Cheraw, SC 29520
Chestnut Hill College, Philadelphia, PA 19118-2695
Cheyney University of Pennsylvania, Cheyney, PA 19319-0019
CHI Institute, Southampton, PA 18966
Chicago College of Commerce, Chicago, IL 60603-6301
Chicago State University, Chicago, IL 60628
Chipola Junior College, Marianna, FL 32446
Chippewa Valley Technical College, Eau Claire, WI 54701
C.H.I/RETS Campus, Broomall, PA 19008
Chowan College, Murfreesboro, NC 27855-9901
Christendom College, Front Royal, VA 22630
Christian Brothers University, Memphis, TN 38104-5581
Christian Heritage College, El Cajon, CA 92019-1157
Christopher Newport University, Newport News, VA 23606-2998
Churchman Business School, Easton, PA 18042
Cincinnati Bible College and Seminary, Cincinnati, OH 45204-3200
Cincinnati College of Mortuary Science, Cincinnati, OH 45224-1428
Cincinnati State Technical and Community College, Cincinnati, OH 45223-2690
Circleville Bible College, Circleville, OH 43113
Cisco Junior College, Cisco, TX 76437
The Citadel, Charleston, SC 29409
Citrus College, Glendora, CA 91740-1899
City College of San Francisco, San Francisco, CA 94112
City Colleges of Chicago
    Harold Washington College, Chicago, IL 60601
    Harry S. Truman College, Chicago, IL 60640
    Kennedy-King College, Chicago, IL 60621
    Malcolm X College, Chicago, IL 60612
    Olive-Harvey College, Chicago, IL 60628
    Richard J. Daley College, Chicago, IL 60652
    Wright College, Chicago, IL 60634-4276
City University, Bellevue, WA 98055
City University of New York
    Baruch College, New York, NY 10010-5585
    Borough of Manhattan Community College, New York, NY 10007-1097
    Bronx Community College, New York, NY 10453
    Brooklyn College, Brooklyn, NY 11210
    City College, New York, NY 10031-9198
    College of Staten Island, Staten Island, NY 10314
    Hostos Community College, Bronx, NY 10451
    Hunter College, New York, NY 10021
    John Jay College of Criminal Justice, New York, NY 10019
    Kingsborough Community College, Brooklyn, NY 11235
    La Guardia Community College, Long Island City, NY 11101
    Lehman College, Bronx, NY 10468
    Medgar Evers College, Brooklyn, NY 11225-2201
    New York City Technical College, Brooklyn, NY 11201-2983
    Queens College, Flushing, NY 11367
    Queensborough Community College, Bayside, NY 11364-1497
    York College, Jamaica, NY 11451-9989
Clackamas Community College, Oregon City, OR 97045
Claflin College, Orangeburg, SC 29115
Claremont McKenna College, Claremont, CA 91711-6420
Clarendon College, Clarendon, TX 79226
Clarion University of Pennsylvania, Clarion, PA 16214
Clark Atlanta University, Atlanta, GA 30314
Clark College, Vancouver, WA 98663
Clark State Community College, Springfield, OH 45501
Clark University, Worcester, MA 01610-1477
Clarke College, Dubuque, IA 52001-3198
Clarkson College, Omaha, NE 68131-2739
Clarkson University, Potsdam, NY 13699
Clatsop Community College, Astoria, OR 97103

Clayton State College, Morrow, GA 30260
Clear Creek Baptist Bible College, Pineville, KY 40977
Clearwater Christian College, Clearwater, FL 34619-9997
Cleary College, Ypsilanti, MI 48197
Clemson University, Clemson, SC 29634-5124
Cleveland College of Jewish Studies, Beachwood, OH 44122
Cleveland Community College, Shelby, NC 28152
Cleveland Institute of Art, Cleveland, OH 44106
Cleveland Institute of Music, Cleveland, OH 44106
Cleveland State Community College, Cleveland, TN 37320-3570
Cleveland State University, Cleveland, OH 44115-2403
Clinch Valley College of the University of Virginia, Wise, VA 24293
Clinton Community College, Plattsburgh, NY 12901-4297
Clinton Community College, Clinton, IA 52732-6299
Cloud County Community College, Concordia, KS 66901-1002
Clovis Community College, Clovis, NM 88101-8345
Coahoma Community College, Clarksdale, MS 38614-9799
Coastal Carolina Community College, Jacksonville, NC 28540-6877
Coastal Carolina University, Conway, SC 29526
Coastline Community College, Fountain Valley, CA 92708
Cochise College, Douglas, AZ 85607-9724
Cochran School of Nursing-St. John's Riverside Hospital, Yonkers, NY 10701
Coe College, Cedar Rapids, IA 52402-9983
Coffeyville Community College, Coffeyville, KS 67337
Cogswell Polytechnical College, Sunnyvale, CA 94089-1299
Coker College, Hartsville, SC 29550
Colby College, Waterville, ME 04901-8848
Colby Community College, Colby, KS 67701
Colby-Sawyer College, New London, NH 03257-4648
Colegio Universitario del Este, Carolina, PR 00983-2010
Coleman College, La Mesa, CA 91942-1500
Colgate University, Hamilton, NY 13346-1383
College of Aeronautics, Flushing, NY 11371
College of Alameda, Alameda, CA 94501
College of The Albemarle, Elizabeth City, NC 27906-2327
College of the Atlantic, Bar Harbor, ME 04609
College of the Canyons, Valencia, CA 91355
College of Charleston, Charleston, SC 29424
College of the Desert, Palm Desert, CA 92260
College of DuPage, Glen Ellyn, IL 60137-6599
College of Eastern Utah, Price, UT 84501
College of Health Sciences, Roanoke, VA 24031-3186
College of the Holy Cross, Worcester, MA 01610-2395
College of Insurance, New York, NY 10007-2132
College of Lake County, Grayslake, IL 60030-1198
College for Lifelong Learning, Concord, NH 03301
College of the Mainland, Texas City, TX 77591
College of Marin: Kentfield, Kentfield, CA 94904
College Misericordia, Dallas, PA 18612-9984
College of Mount St. Joseph, Cincinnati, OH 45233-1672
College of Mount St. Vincent, Riverdale, NY 10471-1093
College of New Rochelle
    New Rochelle, New Rochelle, NY 10805-2308
    School of New Resources, New Rochelle, NY 10805-2339
College of Notre Dame, Belmont, CA 94002-1997
College of Notre Dame of Maryland, Baltimore, MD 21210-2476
College of Oceaneering, Wilmington, CA 90744
College of the Ozarks, Point Lookout, MO 65726-0017
College of the Redwoods, Eureka, CA 95501-9300
College of St. Benedict, St. Joseph, MN 56374-2099
College of St. Catherine: St. Catherine Campus, St. Paul, MN 55105
College of St. Catherine-Minneapolis, Minneapolis, MN 55454
College of St. Elizabeth, Morristown, NJ 07960-6989
College of St. Francis, Joliet, IL 60435-6188
College of St. Joseph in Vermont, Rutland, VT 05701-3899
College of St. Mary, Omaha, NE 68124
College of St. Rose, Albany, NY 12203
College of St. Scholastica, Duluth, MN 55811-4199
College of San Mateo, San Mateo, CA 94402-3784
College of Santa Fe, Santa Fe, NM 87501-5634
College of the Sequoias, Visalia, CA 93277
College of the Siskiyous, Weed, CA 96094
College of Southern Idaho, Twin Falls, ID 83303-1238
College of the Southwest, Hobbs, NM 88240-9987
College of Visual Arts, St. Paul, MN 55102-2199
College of West Virginia, Beckley, WV 25802-2830
College of William and Mary, Williamsburg, VA 23187-8795
College of Wooster, Wooster, OH 44691-2363
Collin County Community College District, McKinney, TX 75070-2906
Colorado Christian University, Lakewood, CO 80226-7499
Colorado College, Colorado Springs, CO 80903-9854

Colorado Institute of Art, Denver, CO 80203
Colorado Mountain College
    Alpine Campus, Steamboat Springs, CO 80477
    Spring Valley Campus, Glenwood Springs, CO 81601
    Timberline Campus, Leadville, CO 80461
Colorado Northwestern Community College, Rangely, CO 81648-9988
Colorado School of Mines, Golden, CO 80401-1873
Colorado State University, Fort Collins, CO 80523-0015
Colorado Technical University, Colorado Springs, CO 80907-3896
Columbia Basin College, Pasco, WA 99301
Columbia Bible College, Columbia, SC 29230-3122
Columbia College, Chicago, IL 60605-1996
Columbia College, Columbia, CA 95310
Columbia College, Columbia, SC 29203-5998
Columbia College, Columbia, MO 65216
Columbia College, Caguas, PR 00726
Columbia College: Hollywood, Los Angeles, CA 90038
Columbia College of Nursing, Milwaukee, WI 53186
Columbia Junior College of Business, Columbia, SC 29203
Columbia State Community College, Columbia, TN 38401
Columbia Union College, Takoma Park, MD 20912
Columbia University
    Columbia College, New York, NY 10027
    School of Engineering and Applied Science, New York, NY 10027
    School of General Studies, New York, NY 10027
    School of Nursing, New York, NY 10032
Columbia-Greene Community College, Hudson, NY 12534
Columbus College, Columbus, GA 31907-5645
Columbus College of Art and Design, Columbus, OH 43215-3875
Columbus State Community College, Columbus, OH 43216-1609
Columbus Technical Institute, Columbus, GA 31904-6572
Commonwealth College, Virginia Beach, VA 23462-4417
Commonwealth Institute of Funeral Service, Houston, TX 77090-5913
Community College of Allegheny County
    Allegheny Campus, Pittsburgh, PA 15212
    Boyce Campus, Monroeville, PA 15146
    North Campus, Pittsburgh, PA 15237
    South Campus, West Mifflin, PA 15122
Community College of Aurora, Aurora, CO 80011
Community College of Beaver County, Monaca, PA 15061
Community College of Denver, Denver, CO 80217-3363
Community College of Philadelphia, Philadelphia, PA 19130-3991
Community College of Rhode Island, Warwick, RI 02886-1807
Community College of Southern Nevada, North Las Vegas, NV 89030
Community College of Vermont, Waterbury, VT 05676
Compton Community College, Compton, CA 90221
Computer Tech, Pittsburgh, PA 15222
Conception Seminary College, Conception, MO 64433
Concord College, Athens, WV 24712
Concordia College, Ann Arbor, MI 48105
Concordia College, Bronxville, NY 10708
Concordia College, Seward, NE 68434-9989
Concordia College: Moorhead, Moorhead, MN 56562-9981
Concordia College: St. Paul, St. Paul, MN 55104-5494
Concordia Lutheran College, Austin, TX 78705-2799
Concordia University, River Forest, IL 60305-1499
Concordia University, Irvine, CA 92715-3299
Concordia University, Portland, OR 97211-6099
Concordia University Wisconsin, Mequon, WI 53097-9650
Connecticut College, New London, CT 06320
Connors State College, Warner, OK 74469-9700
Conservatory of Music of Puerto Rico, Santurce, PR 00940
Consolidated School of Business, Lancaster, PA 17603
Contra Costa College, San Pablo, CA 94806
Converse College, Spartanburg, SC 29302-0006
Cooper Union, New York, NY 10003-7183
Copiah-Lincoln Community College, Wesson, MS 39191
Coppin State College, Baltimore, MD 21216
Corcoran School of Art, Washington, DC 20006
Cornell College, Mount Vernon, IA 52314-1098
Cornell University, Ithaca, NY 14850-2488
Cornerstone College and Grand Rapids Baptist Seminary, Grand Rapids, MI 49505
Corning Community College, Corning, NY 14830
Cornish College of the Arts, Seattle, WA 98102
Cosumnes River College, Sacramento, CA 95823-5799
Cottey College, Nevada, MO 64772
County College of Morris, Randolph, NJ 07869-2086
Covenant College, Lookout Mountain, GA 30750
Cowley County Community College, Arkansas City, KS 67005
Crafton Hills College, Yucaipa, CA 92399-1799
Craven Community College, New Bern, NC 28562

Creighton University, Omaha, NE 68178
Crichton College, Memphis, TN 38175-7830
Criswell College, Dallas, TX 75246-1537
Crowder College, Neosho, MO 64850
Crown College, St. Bonifacius, MN 55375-9001
Cuesta College, San Luis Obispo, CA 93403-8106
Culinary Institute of America, Hyde Park, NY 12538-1499
Culver-Stockton College, Canton, MO 63435-1299
Cumberland College, Williamsburg, KY 40769-6178
Cumberland County College, Vineland, NJ 08360
Cumberland University, Lebanon, TN 37087
Curry College, Milton, MA 02186-9984
Curtis Institute of Music, Philadelphia, PA 19103-6187
Cuyahoga Community College
    Eastern Campus, Highland Hills, OH 44122
    Metropolitan Campus, Cleveland, OH 44115-2878
    Western Campus, Parma, OH 44130
Cuyamaca College, El Cajon, CA 92019-4304
Cypress College, Cypress, CA 90630-5897
Dabney S. Lancaster Community College, Clifton Forge, VA 24422-1000
Daemen College, Amherst, NY 14226-3592
Dakota State University, Madison, SD 57042
Dakota Wesleyan University, Mitchell, SD 57301-4398
Dallas Baptist University, Dallas, TX 75211-9299
Dallas Christian College, Dallas, TX 75234-7299
Dalton College, Dalton, GA 30720
Dana College, Blair, NE 68008-1099
Daniel Webster College, Nashua, NH 03063-1300
Danville Area Community College, Danville, IL 61832
Danville Community College, Danville, VA 24541
Darkei Noam Rabbinical College, Brooklyn, NY 11210
Dartmouth College, Hanover, NH 03755
Darton College, Albany, GA 31707-3098
Davenport College of Business, Grand Rapids, MI 49503-4499
David Lipscomb University, Nashville, TN 37204-3951
David N. Myers College, Cleveland, OH 44115-1096
Davidson College, Davidson, NC 28036
Davidson County Community College, Lexington, NC 27293-1287
Davis College, Toledo, OH 43623
Davis and Elkins College, Elkins, WV 26241
Dawson Community College, Glendive, MT 59330
Daytona Beach Community College, Daytona Beach, FL 32120-2811
De Anza College, Cupertino, CA 95014
De Paul University, Chicago, IL 60604-2287
Deaconess College of Nursing, St. Louis, MO 63139
Dean College, Franklin, MA 02038-1994
Dean Institute of Technology, Pittsburgh, PA 15226
Defiance College, Defiance, OH 43512-1695
DeKalb College, Decatur, GA 30021-2396
DeKalb Technical Institute, Clarkston, GA 30021-2397
Del Mar College, Corpus Christi, TX 78404-3897
Delaware County Community College, Media, PA 19063-1094
Delaware State University, Dover, DE 19901
Delaware Technical and Community College
    Owens Campus, Georgetown, DE 19947
    Stanton/Wilmington Campus, Newark, DE 19713
    Terry Campus, Dover, DE 19904
Delaware Valley College, Doylestown, PA 18901-2697
Delgado Community College, New Orleans, LA 70119-4399
Delta College, University Center, MI 48710
Delta School of Business & Technology, Lake Charles, LA 70601
Delta State University, Cleveland, MS 38733
Denison University, Granville, OH 43023
Denmark Technical College, Denmark, SC 29042-0327
DePauw University, Greencastle, IN 46135-1611
Des Moines Area Community College, Ankeny, IA 50021
Detroit College of Business, Dearborn, MI 48126-3799
DeVry Institute of Technology
    Addison, Addison, IL 60101-6106
    Atlanta, Decatur, GA 30030-2198
    Chicago, Chicago, IL 60618-5994
    Columbus, Columbus, OH 43209-2705
    Irving, Irving, TX 75063-2440
    Kansas City, Kansas City, MO 64131-3626
    Phoenix, Phoenix, AZ 85021-2995
    Pomona, Pomona, CA 91768-2642
DeVry Technical Institute, Woodbridge, NJ 07095
Diablo Valley College, Pleasant Hill, CA 94523
Dickinson College, Carlisle, PA 17013-2896
Dickinson State University, Dickinson, ND 58601-4896
Dillard University, New Orleans, LA 70122-3097
Divine Word College, Epworth, IA 52045

Dixie College, St. George, UT 84770
Doane College/Lincoln Campus, Crete, NE 68333
Dodge City Community College, Dodge City, KS 67801-2399
Dominican College of Blauvelt, Orangeburg, NY 10962
Dominican College of San Rafael, San Rafael, CA 94901-2298
Dominican School of Philosophy and Theology, Berkeley, CA 94709-1295
Don Bosco Technical Institute, Rosemead, CA 91770-4299
Dona Ana Branch Community College of New Mexico State University, Las
  Cruces, NM 88003-0001
Donnelly College, Kansas City, KS 66102-4210
Dordt College, Sioux Center, IA 51250
Douglas MacArthur State Technical College, Opp, AL 36467
Dowling College, Oakdale, NY 11769-1999
D-Q University, Davis, CA 95617
Drake University, Des Moines, IA 50311-4505
Draughons Junior College, Montgomery, AL 36104
Draughons Junior College of Business: Nashville, Nashville, TN 37217
Drew University, Madison, NJ 07940
Drexel University, Philadelphia, PA 19104-2875
Drury College, Springfield, MO 65802-9977
DuBois Business College, DuBois, PA 15801
Duff's Business Institute, Pittsburgh, PA 15222
Duke University, Durham, NC 27706
Dull Knife Memorial College, Lame Deer, MT 59043
Dundalk Community College, Baltimore, MD 21222-4692
Dunwoody Industrial Institute, Minneapolis, MN 55403-1192
Duquesne University, Pittsburgh, PA 15282-0201
Durham Technical Community College, Durham, NC 27703
Dutchess Community College, Poughkeepsie, NY 12601-1595
Dyersburg State Community College, Dyersburg, TN 38024
D'Youville College, Buffalo, NY 14201-1084
Earlham College, Richmond, IN 47374
East Arkansas Community College, Forrest City, AR 72335-9598
East Carolina University, Greenville, NC 27858-4353
East Central College, Union, MO 63084-0529
East Central Community College, Decatur, MS 39327
East Central University, Ada, OK 74820-6899
East Coast Bible College, Charlotte, NC 28214
East Georgia College, Swainsboro, GA 30401-2699
East Los Angeles College, Monterey Park, CA 91754
East Mississippi Community College, Scooba, MS 39358
East Stroudsburg University of Pennsylvania, East Stroudsburg, PA 18301-
  2999
East Tennessee State University, Johnson City, TN 37614-0002
East Texas Baptist University, Marshall, TX 75670-1498
East Texas State University
    Commerce, Commerce, TX 75429-3011
    Texarkana, Texarkana, TX 75505-5518
Eastern Arizona College, Thatcher, AZ 85552-0769
Eastern College, St. Davids, PA 19087-3696
Eastern Connecticut State University, Willimantic, CT 06226-2295
Eastern Idaho Technical College, Idaho Falls, ID 83404
Eastern Illinois University, Charleston, IL 61920-3099
Eastern Kentucky University, Richmond, KY 40475-3101
Eastern Maine Technical College, Bangor, ME 04401
Eastern Mennonite University, Harrisonburg, VA 22801-2462
Eastern Michigan University, Ypsilanti, MI 48197-2260
Eastern Nazarene College, Quincy, MA 02170-2999
Eastern New Mexico University
    Portales, Portales, NM 88130
    Roswell Campus, Roswell, NM 88202-6000
Eastern Oklahoma State College, Wilburton, OK 74578-4999
Eastern Oregon State College, LaGrande, OR 97850-2899
Eastern Shore Community College, Melfa, VA 23410-9755
Eastern Washington University, Cheney, WA 99004-2431
Eastern Wyoming College, Torrington, WY 82240
Eastfield College, Mesquite, TX 75150-1212
Eastman School of Music of the University of Rochester, Rochester, NY
  14604-2599
East-West University, Chicago, IL 60605
Eckerd College, St. Petersburg, FL 33711-4700
ECPI College of Technology, Virginia Beach, VA 23462-6542
Edgecombe Community College, Tarboro, NC 27886
Edgewood College, Madison, WI 53711
Edinboro University of Pennsylvania, Edinboro, PA 16444
Edison Community College, Fort Myers, FL 33906-6210
Edison State Community College, Piqua, OH 45356-9253
Edmonds Community College, Lynnwood, WA 98036
Edward Waters College, Jacksonville, FL 32209
El Camino College, Torrance, CA 90506
El Centro College, Dallas, TX 75202
El Paso Community College, El Paso, TX 79998

Electronic Computer Programming College, Chattanooga, TN 37411-3798
Electronic Data Processing College of Puerto Rico, Hato Rey, PR 00918
Electronic Institutes
    Middletown, Middletown, PA 17057-4851
    Pittsburgh, Pittsburgh, PA 15217
Electronics Institute, Kansas City, MO 64147-1212
Elgin Community College, Elgin, IL 60123-7193
Elizabeth City State University, Elizabeth City, NC 27909
Elizabethtown College, Elizabethtown, PA 17022-2298
Elizabethtown Community College, Elizabethtown, KY 42701
Ellsworth Community College, Iowa Falls, IA 50126
Elmhurst College, Elmhurst, IL 60126-3296
Elmira College, Elmira, NY 14901-2345
Elms College, Chicopee, MA 01013-2839
Elon College, Elon College, NC 27244-2010
Embry-Riddle Aeronautical University
    Daytona Beach, Daytona Beach, FL 32114-3900
    Prescott Campus, Prescott, AZ 86301-3720
Emerson College, Boston, MA 02116-1596
Emmanuel College, Boston, MA 02115
Emmanuel College, Franklin Springs, GA 30639-0129
Emmaus Bible College, Dubuque, IA 52001
Emory and Henry College, Emory, VA 24327-0947
Emory University, Atlanta, GA 30322
Empire College, Santa Rosa, CA 95403
Emporia State University, Emporia, KS 66801-5087
Endicott College, Beverly, MA 01915-9985
Enterprise State Junior College, Enterprise, AL 36331
Erie Business Center, Erie, PA 16501
Erie Community College
    City Campus, Buffalo, NY 14203-2601
    North Campus, Williamsville, NY 14221
    South Campus, Orchard Park, NY 14127-2199
Erskine College, Due West, SC 29639-0176
Escuela de Artes Plasticas de Puerto Rico, San Juan, PR 00902-1112
Essex Agricultural and Technical Institute, Hathorne, MA 01937
Essex Community College, Baltimore, MD 21237-3899
Essex County College, Newark, NJ 07102
Eugene Bible College, Eugene, OR 97405
Eugene Lang College/New School for Social Research, New York, NY
  10011-8693
Eureka College, Eureka, IL 61530
Evangel College, Springfield, MO 65802
Everett Community College, Everett, WA 98201
Evergreen State College, Olympia, WA 98505
Evergreen Valley College, San Jose, CA 95135
Fairfield University, Fairfield, CT 06430-5195
Fairleigh Dickinson University
    Edward Williams College, Hackensack, NJ 07666-1914
    Teaneck, Teaneck, NJ 07666-1996
Fairmont State College, Fairmont, WV 26554-2491
Faith Baptist Bible College and Theological Seminary, Ankeny, IA 50021
Fashion Institute of Design and Merchandising
    Los Angeles, Los Angeles, CA 90015
    San Francisco, San Francisco, CA 94108-5805
Fashion Institute of Technology, New York, NY 10001-5992
Faulkner University, Montgomery, AL 36109-3398
Fayetteville State University, Fayetteville, NC 28301-4298
Fayetteville Technical Community College, Fayetteville, NC 28303-0236
Feather River College, Quincy, CA 95971
Felician College, Lodi, NJ 07644-2198
Fergus Falls Community College, Fergus Falls, MN 56537-1000
Ferris State University, Big Rapids, MI 49307-2020
Ferrum College, Ferrum, VA 24088
Finch University of Health Sciences/The Chicago Medical School, North
  Chicago, IL 60064
Finger Lakes Community College, Canandaigua, NY 14424-8399
Fisher College, Boston, MA 02116
Fisk University, Nashville, TN 37208
Fitchburg State College, Fitchburg, MA 01420-2697
Five Towns College, Dix Hills, NY 11746-6055
Flagler College, St. Augustine, FL 32084
Flathead Valley Community College, Kalispell, MT 59901
Florence-Darlington Technical College, Florence, SC 29501-0548
Florida Agricultural and Mechanical University, Tallahassee, FL 32307
Florida Atlantic University, Boca Raton, FL 33431-0991
Florida Baptist Theological College, Graceville, FL 32440-1830
Florida Bible College, Miramar, FL 33025
Florida Christian College, Kissimmee, FL 34744-4402
Florida College, Temple Terrace, FL 33617
Florida Community College at Jacksonville, Jacksonville, FL 32256
Florida Institute of Technology, Melbourne, FL 32901-6975

Florida International University, Miami, FL 33199
Florida Keys Community College, Key West, FL 33040
Florida Memorial College, Miami, FL 33054
Florida National College, Hialeah, FL 49715
Florida Southern College, Lakeland, FL 33801-5698
Florida State University, Tallahassee, FL 32306-1009
Floyd College, Rome, GA 30162-1864
Fontbonne College, St. Louis, MO 63105
Foothill College, Los Altos Hills, CA 94022-4599
Fordham University, Bronx, NY 10458
Forsyth School for Dental Hygienists, Boston, MA 02115
Forsyth Technical Community College, Winston-Salem, NC 27103
Fort Belknap College, Harlem, MT 59526-0159
Fort Bethold Community College, New Town, ND 58763
Fort Hays State University, Hays, KS 67601-4099
Fort Lauderdale College, Fort Lauderdale, FL 33304
Fort Lewis College, Durango, CO 81301-3999
Fort Peck Community College, Poplar, MT 59255-0398
Fort Scott Community College, Fort Scott, KS 66701
Fort Valley State College, Fort Valley, GA 31030
Fox Valley Technical College, Appleton, WI 54913-2277
Framingham State College, Framingham, MA 01701-9101
Francis Marion University, Florence, SC 29501-0547
Franciscan University of Steubenville, Steubenville, OH 43952-6701
Frank Phillips College, Borger, TX 79008-5118
Franklin College, Franklin, IN 46131-2598
Franklin Institute of Boston, Boston, MA 02116
Franklin and Marshall College, Lancaster, PA 17604-3003
Franklin Pierce College, Rindge, NH 03461-0060
Franklin University, Columbus, OH 43215-5399
Frederick Community College, Frederick, MD 21702
Free Will Baptist Bible College, Nashville, TN 37205-0117
Freed-Hardeman University, Henderson, TN 38340
Fresno City College, Fresno, CA 93741
Fresno Pacific College, Fresno, CA 93702-4709
Friends University, Wichita, KS 67213
Front Range Community College, Westminster, CO 80030
Frostburg State University, Frostburg, MD 21532-1099
Fullerton College, Fullerton, CA 92632-2095
Fulton-Montgomery Community College, Johnstown, NY 12095-9609
Furman University, Greenville, SC 29613-0645
Gadsden State Community College, Gadsden, AL 35902-0227
Gainesville College, Gainesville, GA 30503
Gallaudet University, Washington, DC 20002
Galveston College, Galveston, TX 77550
Gannon University, Erie, PA 16541-0001
Garden City Community College, Garden City, KS 67846
Gardner-Webb University, Boiling Springs, NC 28017-9980
Garland County Community College, Hot Springs, AR 71914
Garrett Community College, McHenry, MD 21541
Gaston College, Dallas, NC 28034-1499
Gateway Community College, Phoenix, AZ 85034-1795
Gateway Community-Technical College, New Haven, CT 06511-5970
Gateway Electronics Institute, Omaha, NE 68114
Gateway Technical College, Kenosha, WI 53144-1690
Gavilan Community College, Gilroy, CA 95020
Gem City College, Quincy, IL 62306
Genesee Community College, Batavia, NY 14020-9704
Geneva College, Beaver Falls, PA 15010-3599
George C. Wallace State Community College
    Dothan, Dothan, AL 36303-9234
    Selma, Selma, AL 36702-1049
George Fox College, Newberg, OR 97132-2697
George Mason University, Fairfax, VA 22030-4444
George Washington University, Washington, DC 20052
Georgetown College, Georgetown, KY 40324-1696
Georgetown University, Washington, DC 20057
Georgia Baptist College of Nursing, Atlanta, GA 30312
Georgia College, Milledgeville, GA 31061-0490
Georgia Institute of Technology, Atlanta, GA 30332-0320
Georgia Military College, Milledgeville, GA 31061
Georgia Southern University, Statesboro, GA 30460-8024
Georgia Southwestern College, Americus, GA 31709-4693
Georgia State University, Atlanta, GA 30303-3083
Georgian Court College, Lakewood, NJ 08701-2697
Germanna Community College, Locust Grove, VA 22508
Gettysburg College, Gettysburg, PA 17325-1484
Glen Oaks Community College, Centreville, MI 49032
Glendale Community College, Glendale, CA 91208
Glendale Community College, Glendale, AZ 85302-3090
Glenville State College, Glenville, WV 26351-1292
Gloucester County College, Sewell, NJ 08080

GMI Engineering & Management Institute, Flint, MI 48504-4898
Goddard College, Plainfield, VT 05667
God's Bible School and College, Cincinnati, OH 45210
Gogebic Community College, Ironwood, MI 49938
Golden Gate University, San Francisco, CA 94105-2968
Golden West College, Huntington Beach, CA 92647-2748
Goldey-Beacom College, Wilmington, DE 19808
Gonzaga University, Spokane, WA 99258-0001
Gordon College, Wenham, MA 01984-1899
Gordon College, Barnesville, GA 30204
Goshen College, Goshen, IN 46526-9988
Goucher College, Baltimore, MD 21204
Governors State University, University Park, IL 60466
Grace Bible College, Grand Rapids, MI 49509-0910
Grace College, Winona Lake, IN 46590
Grace University, Omaha, NE 68108
Graceland College, Lamoni, IA 50140
Grambling State University, Grambling, LA 71245
Grand Canyon University, Phoenix, AZ 85061-1097
Grand Rapids Community College, Grand Rapids, MI 49503
Grand Valley State University, Allendale, MI 49401-9403
Grand View College, Des Moines, IA 50316-1599
Gratz College, Melrose Park, PA 19027
Grays Harbor College, Aberdeen, WA 98520-7599
Grayson County College, Denison, TX 75020
Great Basin College, Elko, NV 89801
Great Lakes Christian College, Lansing, MI 48917
Great Lakes Junior College of Business, Saginaw, MI 48607-1184
Green Mountain College, Poultney, VT 05764
Green River Community College, Auburn, WA 98092
Greenfield Community College, Greenfield, MA 01301
Greensboro College, Greensboro, NC 27401-1875
Greenville College, Greenville, IL 62246-0159
Greenville Technical College, Greenville, SC 29606-5616
Grinnell College, Grinnell, IA 50112-0807
Grossmont Community College, El Cajon, CA 92020
Grove City College, Grove City, PA 16127-2104
Guilford College, Greensboro, NC 27410-4171
Guilford Technical Community College, Jamestown, NC 27282
Gulf Coast Community College, Panama City, FL 32401-1041
Gupton Jones College of Funeral Service, Decatur, GA 30035
Gustavus Adolphus College, St. Peter, MN 56082-1498
Gwinnett Technical Institute, Lawrenceville, GA 30246-1505
Gwynedd-Mercy College, Gwynedd Valley, PA 19437
Hagerstown Business College, Hagerstown, MD 21742-2752
Hagerstown Junior College, Hagerstown, MD 21742-6590
Halifax Community College, Weldon, NC 27890
Hallmark Institute of Technology, San Antonio, TX 78230-1737
Hamilton College, Clinton, NY 13323-1293
Hamilton Technical College, Davenport, IA 52807
Hamline University, St. Paul, MN 55104-1284
Hampden-Sydney College, Hampden-Sydney, VA 23943
Hampshire College, Amherst, MA 01002-9988
Hampton University, Hampton, VA 23668
Hannibal-LaGrange College, Hannibal, MO 63401
Hanover College, Hanover, IN 47243-0108
Harcum College, Bryn Mawr, PA 19010-9849
Harding University, Searcy, AR 72149
Hardin-Simmons University, Abilene, TX 79698
Harford Community College, Bel Air, MD 21015
Harrington Institute of Interior Design, Chicago, IL 60605
Harris Stowe State College, St. Louis, MO 63103-2199
Harrisburg Area Community College, Harrisburg, PA 17110-2999
Harry M. Ayers State Technical College, Anniston, AL 36202
Hartnell College, Salinas, CA 93901
Hartwick College, Oneonta, NY 13820-9989
Harvard and Radcliffe Colleges, Cambridge, MA 02138
Harvey Mudd College, Claremont, CA 91711-5901
Haskell Indian Junior College, Lawrence, KS 66046-4800
Hastings College, Hastings, NE 68901
Haverford College, Haverford, PA 19041-1392
Hawaii Pacific University, Honolulu, HI 96813
Hawkeye Community College, Waterloo, IA 50704-8015
Haywood Community College, Clyde, NC 28721-9454
Hazard Community College, Hazard, KY 41701
Heald Business College
    Concord, Concord, CA 94520
    Fresno, Fresno, CA 93704-1706
    San Jose, San Jose, CA 95130
Heald Business College: Hayward, Hayward, CA 94545
Heald Business College: Honolulu, Honolulu, HI 96814-3715
Heald Business College: Oakland, Oakland, CA 94607

Heald Business College-Salinas, Salinas, CA 93906
Heald Business College-Stockton, Stockton, CA 95210
Heald College
    Sacramento, Rancho Cordova, CA 95670
    Santa Rosa, Santa Rosa, CA 95403
Heald Institute of Technology, Martinez, CA 94553-4000
Heald Institute of Technology-Hayward, Hayward, CA 94545
Heald Institute of Technology-Sacramento, Sacramento, CA 95821
Heald Institute of Technology-San Francisco, San Francisco, CA 94134
Heald Institute of Technology-San Jose, San Jose, CA 95130
Hebrew College, Brookline, MA 02146
Hebrew Union College: Jewish Institute of Religion, Los Angeles, CA 90007
Heidelberg College, Tiffin, OH 44883-2462
Helena College of Technology of the University of Montana, Helena, MT 59601-3098
Helene Fuld College of Nursing, New York, NY 10035
Hellenic College, Brookline, MA 02146
Henderson Community College, Henderson, KY 42420
Henderson State University, Arkadelphia, AR 71999-0001
Hendrix College, Conway, AR 72032-3080
Henry Cogswell College, Kirkland, WA 98033
Henry Ford Community College, Dearborn, MI 48128
Heritage College, Toppenish, WA 98948-9599
Herkimer County Community College, Herkimer, NY 13350-1598
Herzing College of Technology, Madison, WI 53704
Hesser College, Manchester, NH 03103-9969
Hesston College, Hesston, KS 67062-2093
Hibbing Community College, Hibbing, MN 55746
Hickey School, St. Louis, MO 63146
High Point University, High Point, NC 27262-3598
Highland Community College, Freeport, IL 61032-9341
Highland Community College, Highland, KS 66035-0068
Highland Park Community College, Highland Park, MI 48203
Highline Community College, Des Moines, WA 98198-9800
Hilbert College, Hamburg, NY 14075-1519
Hill College, Hillsboro, TX 76645
Hillsborough Community College, Tampa, FL 33631-3127
Hillsdale College, Hillsdale, MI 49242
Hinds Community College, Raymond, MS 39154-9799
Hiram College, Hiram, OH 44234
Hiwassee College, Madisonville, TN 37354-6099
Hobart and William Smith Colleges, Geneva, NY 14456-3385
Hobe Sound Bible College, Hobe Sound, FL 33475-1065
Hocking Technical College, Nelsonville, OH 45764-9588
Hofstra University, Hempstead, NY 11550-1090
Hollins College, Roanoke, VA 24020-1707
Holmes Community College, Goodman, MS 39079
Holy Apostles College and Seminary, Cromwell, CT 06416
Holy Cross College, Notre Dame, IN 46556-0308
Holy Family College, Philadelphia, PA 19114-2094
Holy Names College, Oakland, CA 94619-1699
Holy Trinity Orthodox Seminary, Jordanville, NY 13361
Holyoke Community College, Holyoke, MA 01040
Hood College, Frederick, MD 21701-8575
Hope College, Holland, MI 49422-9000
Hopkinsville Community College, Hopkinsville, KY 42241-2100
Horry-Georgetown Technical College, Conway, SC 29526-1966
Houghton College, Houghton, NY 14744-9989
Housatonic Community-Technical College, Bridgeport, CT 06608
Houston Baptist University, Houston, TX 77074-3298
Houston Community College, Houston, TX 77270
Howard College, Big Spring, TX 79720
Howard Community College, Columbia, MD 21044
Howard Payne University, Brownwood, TX 76801-2794
Howard University, Washington, DC 20059
Hudson Valley Community College, Troy, NY 12180
Huertas Junior College, Caguas, PR 00726
Humacao Community College, Humacao, PR 00792
Humboldt State University, Arcata, CA 95521-8299
Humphreys College, Stockton, CA 95207-3896
Huntingdon College, Montgomery, AL 36106-2148
Huntington College, Huntington, IN 46750
Huntington Junior College of Business, Huntington, WV 25701
Huron University, Huron, SD 57350
Hussian School of Art, Philadelphia, PA 19107-3679
Husson College, Bangor, ME 04401
Huston-Tillotson College, Austin, TX 78702
Hutchinson Community College, Hutchinson, KS 67501
ICPR Junior College, San Juan, PR 00919-0304
Idaho State University, Pocatello, ID 83209
Illinois Central College, East Peoria, IL 61635
Illinois College, Jacksonville, IL 62650-9990

Illinois Eastern Community Colleges
    Frontier Community College, Fairfield, IL 62837-9801
    Lincoln Trail College, Robinson, IL 62454-5707
    Olney Central College, Olney, IL 62450
    Wabash Valley College, Mount Carmel, IL 62863-2657
Illinois Institute of Technology, Chicago, IL 60616
Illinois State University, Normal, IL 61790-2200
Illinois Valley Community College, Oglesby, IL 61348-9693
Illinois Wesleyan University, Bloomington, IL 61702-9965
Immaculata College, Immaculata, PA 19345-0901
Imperial Valley College, Imperial, CA 92251-0158
Incarnate Word College, San Antonio, TX 78209-6397
Independence Community College, Independence, KS 67301
Indian Hills Community College, Ottumwa, IA 52501
Indian River Community College, Fort Pierce, FL 34981-5599
Indiana Business College, Indianapolis, IN 46204
Indiana Institute of Technology, Fort Wayne, IN 46803
Indiana State University, Terre Haute, IN 47809
Indiana University
    Bloomington, Bloomington, IN 47405-7700
    East, Richmond, IN 47374-1289
    Kokomo, Kokomo, IN 46904-9003
    Northwest, Gary, IN 46408
    South Bend, South Bend, IN 46634-7111
    Southeast, New Albany, IN 47150-6405
Indiana University of Pennsylvania, Indiana, PA 15705-1088
Indiana University—Purdue University
    Fort Wayne, Fort Wayne, IN 46805-1499
    Indianapolis, Indianapolis, IN 46202-5143
Indiana Wesleyan University, Marion, IN 46953-4999
Institute of American Indian Arts, Santa Fe, NM 87504
Institute for Christian Studies, Austin, TX 78705
Institute of Design and Construction, Brooklyn, NY 11201-5380
Institute of Electronic Technology, Paducah, KY 42001
Inter American University of Puerto Rico
    Aguadilla Campus, Aguadilla, PR 00605
    Arecibo Campus, Arecibo, PR 00614-4050
    Barranquitas Campus, Barranquitas, PR 00794
    Bayamon Campus, Bayamon, PR 00959
    Fajardo Campus, Fajardo, PR 00738-7003
    Guayama Campus, Guayama, PR 00784
    Metropolitan Campus, San Juan, PR 00919
    Ponce Campus, Mercedita, PR 00715
    San German Campus, San German, PR 00683
Interboro Institute, New York, NY 10019
International Academy of Merchandising and Design, Chicago, IL 60602
International Academy of Merchandising and Design, Tampa, FL 33634
International Bible College, Florence, AL 35630
International Business College, Fort Wayne, IN 46804
International College, Naples, FL 33962
International Fine Arts College, Miami, FL 33132
Inver Hills Community College, Inver Grove Heights, MN 55076-3209
Iona College, New Rochelle, NY 10801-1890
Iowa Central Community College, Fort Dodge, IA 50501
Iowa Lakes Community College, Estherville, IA 51334
Iowa State University, Ames, IA 50011-2010
Iowa Wesleyan College, Mount Pleasant, IA 52641-1398
Iowa Western Community College, Council Bluffs, IA 51502-3004
Irvine Valley College, Irvine, CA 92720
Isothermal Community College, Spindale, NC 28160
Itasca Community College: Arrowhead Region, Grand Rapids, MN 55744
Itawamba Community College, Fulton, MS 38843
Ithaca College, Ithaca, NY 14850-7020
ITT Technical Institute
    Hoffman Estates, Hoffman Estates, IL 60195
    Youngstown, Youngstown, OH 44509
Ivy Tech State College
    Central Indiana, Indianapolis, IN 46206-1763
    Columbus, Columbus, IN 47203
    Eastcentral, Muncie, IN 47307
    Kokomo, Kokomo, IN 46903-1373
    Lafayette, Lafayette, IN 47903
    Northcentral, South Bend, IN 46619
    Northeast, Fort Wayne, IN 46805
    Northwest, Gary, IN 46409-1499
    Southcentral, Sellersburg, IN 47172
    Southeast, Madison, IN 47250
    Southwest, Evansville, IN 47710
    Wabash Valley, Terre Haute, IN 47802-4898
    Whitewater, Richmond, IN 47374
J. F. Drake State Technical College, Huntsville, AL 35811-3421
J. Sargeant Reynolds Community College, Richmond, VA 23285-5622

Jackson Community College, Jackson, MI 49201
Jackson State Community College, Jackson, TN 38301-3797
Jackson State University, Jackson, MS 39217
Jacksonville College, Jacksonville, TX 75766-4759
Jacksonville State University, Jacksonville, AL 36265-9982
Jacksonville University, Jacksonville, FL 32211
James H. Faulkner State Community College, Bay Minette, AL 36507
James Madison University, Harrisonburg, VA 22807
James Sprunt Community College, Kenansville, NC 28349-0398
Jamestown Business College, Jamestown, NY 14702-0429
Jamestown College, Jamestown, ND 58405-0001
Jamestown Community College, Jamestown, NY 14702-0020
Jamestown Community College: Olean, Olean, NY 14760-5901
Jarvis Christian College, Hawkins, TX 75765-9989
Jefferson College, Hillsboro, MO 63050-2441
Jefferson Community College, Louisville, KY 40202
Jefferson Community College, Steubenville, OH 43952
Jefferson Community College, Watertown, NY 13601
Jefferson Davis Community College, Brewton, AL 36426
Jefferson State Community College, Birmingham, AL 35215-3098
Jersey City State College, Jersey City, NJ 07305-1597
Jewish Theological Seminary of America, New York, NY 10027
John A. Gupton College, Nashville, TN 37203-2920
John A. Logan College, Carterville, IL 62918
John Brown University, Siloam Springs, AR 72761
John Carroll University, University Heights, OH 44118-4581
John F. Kennedy University, Orinda, CA 94563
John M. Patterson State Technical College, Montgomery, AL 36116
John Tyler Community College, Chester, VA 23831-5399
John Wesley College, High Point, NC 27265-3197
John Wood Community College, Quincy, IL 62301
Johns Hopkins University, Baltimore, MD 21218
Johns Hopkins University: Peabody Conservatory of Music, Baltimore, MD 21202
Johnson Bible College, Knoxville, TN 37998
Johnson C. Smith University, Charlotte, NC 28216-5398
Johnson State College, Johnson, VT 05656
Johnson Technical Institute, Scranton, PA 18508-1495
Johnson & Wales University, Providence, RI 02903-3703
Johnston Community College, Smithfield, NC 27577-2350
Joliet Junior College, Joliet, IL 60431-9352
Jones College, Jacksonville, FL 32211
Jones County Junior College, Ellisville, MS 39437
Judson College, Marion, AL 36756
Judson College, Elgin, IL 60123
Juilliard School, New York, NY 10023-6590
Juniata College, Huntingdon, PA 16652-2119
Kalamazoo College, Kalamazoo, MI 49006-3295
Kalamazoo Valley Community College, Kalamazoo, MI 49003-4070
Kankakee Community College, Kankakee, IL 60901
Kansas City Art Institute, Kansas City, MO 64111-1762
Kansas City Kansas Community College, Kansas City, KS 66112
Kansas Newman College, Wichita, KS 67213-2097
Kansas State University, Manhattan, KS 66506
Kansas Wesleyan University, Salina, KS 67401-6196
Kaskaskia College, Centralia, IL 62801
Katharine Gibbs School, Norwalk, CT 06851
Katharine Gibbs School
    Boston, Boston, MA 02116
    Melville, Melville, NY 11747
    Montclair, Montclair, NJ 07042
    New York, New York, NY 10166
Kean College of New Jersey, Union, NJ 07083-7131
Keene State College, Keene, NH 03431-4183
Kehilath Yakov Rabbinical Seminary, Brooklyn, NY 11211
Keiser College of Technology, Fort Lauderdale, FL 33309
Kellogg Community College, Battle Creek, MI 49016-3397
Kelsey-Jenney College, San Diego, CA 92101
Kemper Military School and College, Boonville, MO 65233
Kendall College, Evanston, IL 60201-2899
Kendall College of Art and Design, Grand Rapids, MI 49503-3194
Kennebec Valley Technical College, Fairfield, ME 04937
Kennesaw State College, Kennesaw, GA 30144-5591
Kent State University
    East Liverpool Regional Campus, East Liverpool, OH 43920
    Kent, Kent, OH 44242-0001
    Salem Regional Campus, Salem, OH 44460
    Stark Campus, Canton, OH 44720-7599
    Trumbull Campus, Warren, OH 44483-1998
    Tuscarawas Campus, New Philadelphia, OH 44663-9447
Kentucky Christian College, Grayson, KY 41143-2205
Kentucky College of Business, Lexington, KY 40508

Kentucky Mountain Bible College, Vancleve, KY 41385
Kentucky State University, Frankfort, KY 40601
Kentucky Wesleyan College, Owensboro, KY 42302-1039
Kenyon College, Gambier, OH 43022-9623
Kettering College of Medical Arts, Kettering, OH 45429
Keuka College, Keuka Park, NY 14478-0098
Keystone College, La Plume, PA 18440-0200
Kilgore College, Kilgore, TX 75662-3299
Kilian Community College, Sioux Falls, SD 57102-0316
King College, Bristol, TN 37620-2699
King's College, Wilkes-Barre, PA 18711-0801
Kings River Community College, Reedley, CA 93654
Kirkwood Community College, Cedar Rapids, IA 52406
Kirtland Community College, Roscommon, MI 48653
Kishwaukee College, Malta, IL 60150-9699
Knox College, Galesburg, IL 61401-4999
Knoxville Business College, Knoxville, TN 37917
Knoxville College, Knoxville, TN 37921
Kutztown University of Pennsylvania, Kutztown, PA 19530
La Roche College, Pittsburgh, PA 15237
La Salle University, Philadelphia, PA 19141-1199
La Sierra University, Riverside, CA 92515-8247
Labette Community College, Parsons, KS 67357
Laboratory Institute of Merchandising, New York, NY 10022-5268
Laboure College, Boston, MA 02124
Lac Courte Oreilles Ojibwa Community College, Hayward, WI 54843
Lackawanna Junior College, Scranton, PA 18505
Lafayette College, Easton, PA 18042-1770
LaGrange College, LaGrange, GA 30240-2999
Lake Area Technical Institute, Watertown, SD 57201-0730
Lake City Community College, Lake City, FL 32025
Lake Erie College, Painesville, OH 44077-3389
Lake Forest College, Lake Forest, IL 60045-2399
Lake Land College, Mattoon, IL 61938-9366
Lake Michigan College, Benton Harbor, MI 49022-1899
Lake Superior State University, Sault Ste. Marie, MI 49783-1699
Lake Tahoe Community College, South Lake Tahoe, CA 96150-4524
Lake Washington Technical College, Kirkland, WA 98034
Lakeland College, Sheboygan, WI 53082-0359
Lakeland Community College, Kirtland, OH 44094
Lakeshore Technical College, Cleveland, WI 53015-9761
Lake-Sumter Community College, Leesburg, FL 34788-8751
Lakeview College of Nursing, Danville, IL 61832
Lakewood Community College, White Bear Lake, MN 55110
Lamar Community College, Lamar, CO 81052-3999
Lamar University at Orange, Orange, TX 77630
Lamar University at Port Arthur, Port Arthur, TX 77641-0310
Lamar University—Beaumont, Beaumont, TX 77710
Lambuth University, Jackson, TN 38301-5296
Lamson Junior College at Mesa, Mesa, AZ 85201
Lancaster Bible College, Lancaster, PA 17601
Lander University, Greenwood, SC 29649
Landmark College, Putney, VT 05346
Lane College, Jackson, TN 38301
Lane Community College, Eugene, OR 97405
Laney College, Oakland, CA 94607
Langston University, Langston, OK 73050
Lansdale School of Business, North Wales, PA 19454
Lansing Community College, Lansing, MI 48901-7210
Laramie County Community College, Cheyenne, WY 82007
Laredo Community College, Laredo, TX 78040-4395
Las Positas College, Livermore, CA 94550
Lasell College, Newton, MA 02166
Lassen College, Susanville, CA 96130
Laurel Business Institute, Uniontown, PA 15401
Lawrence Technological University, Southfield, MI 48075-1058
Lawrence University, Appleton, WI 54912-0599
Lawson State Community College, Birmingham, AL 35221-1717
LDS Business College, Salt Lake City, UT 84111-1392
Le Moyne College, Syracuse, NY 13214-1399
Lebanon Valley College of Pennsylvania, Annville, PA 17003-0501
Lee College, Cleveland, TN 37311-3450
Lee College, Baytown, TX 77522-0818
Lees-McRae College, Banner Elk, NC 28604
Lehigh Carbon Community College, Schnecksville, PA 18078-2598
Lehigh University, Bethlehem, PA 18015-3094
LeMoyne-Owen College, Memphis, TN 38126
Lenoir Community College, Kinston, NC 28501
Lenoir-Rhyne College, Hickory, NC 28603
Lesley College, Cambridge, MA 02138-2790
LeTourneau University, Longview, TX 75607-7001
Lewis & Clark College, Portland, OR 97219-7899

Lewis and Clark Community College, Godfrey, IL 62035-2466
Lewis College of Business, Detroit, MI 48235
Lewis University, Romeoville, IL 60446-2298
Lewis-Clark State College, Lewiston, ID 83501-2698
Lexington College, Chicago, IL 60643-3294
Lexington Community College, Lexington, KY 40506-0235
Liberty University, Lynchburg, VA 24506-8001
LIFE Bible College, San Dimas, CA 91773-3298
Lima Technical College, Lima, OH 45804
Limestone College, Gaffney, SC 29340
Lincoln Christian College and Seminary, Lincoln, IL 62656-2111
Lincoln College, Lincoln, IL 62656
Lincoln Land Community College, Springfield, IL 62794-9256
Lincoln Memorial University, Harrogate, TN 37752
Lincoln School of Commerce, Lincoln, NE 68501-2826
Lincoln Technical Institute, Allentown, PA 18104
Lincoln University, Lincoln University, PA 19352-0999
Lincoln University, San Francisco, CA 94118
Lincoln University, Jefferson City, MO 65102-0029
Lindenwood College, St. Charles, MO 63301-1695
Lindsey Wilson College, Columbia, KY 42728
Linfield College, McMinnville, OR 97128-6894
Linn-Benton Community College, Albany, OR 97321-3779
Little Big Horn College, Crow Agency, MT 59022
Little Hoop Community College, Fort Totten, ND 58335
Livingstone College, Salisbury, NC 28144-5213
Lock Haven University of Pennsylvania, Lock Haven, PA 17745
Loma Linda University, Loma Linda, CA 92350
Lon Morris College, Jacksonville, TX 75766
Long Beach City College, Long Beach, CA 90808
Long Island College Hospital School of Nursing, Brooklyn, NY 11201
Long Island University
    Brooklyn Campus, Brooklyn, NY 11201
    C. W. Post Campus, Brookville, NY 11548-1300
    Southampton College, Southampton, NY 11968
Longview Community College, Lee's Summit, MO 64081-2105
Longwood College, Farmville, VA 23909-1898
Lorain County Community College, Elyria, OH 44035-1697
Loras College, Dubuque, IA 52001
Lord Fairfax Community College, Middletown, VA 22645
Los Angeles City College, Los Angeles, CA 90029-3589
Los Angeles Harbor College, Wilmington, CA 90744
Los Angeles Mission College, Sylmar, CA 91342
Los Angeles Pierce College, Woodland Hills, CA 91371
Los Angeles Southwest College, Los Angeles, CA 90047
Los Angeles Trade and Technical College, Los Angeles, CA 90015-4181
Los Angeles Valley College, Van Nuys, CA 91401-4096
Los Medanos College, Pittsburg, CA 94565
Louisburg College, Louisburg, NC 27549
Louise Salinger Academy of Fashion, San Francisco, CA 94105
Louisiana College, Pineville, LA 71359-0560
Louisiana State University
    Agricultural and Mechanical College, Baton Rouge, LA 70803-2750
    Alexandria, Alexandria, LA 71302-9633
    Eunice, Eunice, LA 70535
    Medical Center, New Orleans, LA 70112-2223
    Shreveport, Shreveport, LA 71115-2399
Louisiana Tech University, Ruston, LA 71272
Louisville Technical Institute, Louisville, KY 40218-4524
Lourdes College, Sylvania, OH 43560-2898
Lower Columbia College, Longview, WA 98632-0310
Loyola College in Maryland, Baltimore, MD 21210-2699
Loyola Marymount University, Los Angeles, CA 90045-8350
Loyola University of Chicago, Chicago, IL 60611
Loyola University New Orleans, New Orleans, LA 70118-6143
Lubbock Christian University, Lubbock, TX 79407-2099
Lurleen B. Wallace State Junior College, Andalusia, AL 36420-1418
Luther College, Decorah, IA 52101-1042
Lutheran Bible Institute of Seattle, Issaquah, WA 98027
Lutheran College of Health Professions, Fort Wayne, IN 46807-1698
Luzerne County Community College, Nanticoke, PA 18634-9804
Lycoming College, Williamsport, PA 17701
Lynchburg College, Lynchburg, VA 24501-3199
Lyndon State College, Lyndonville, VT 05851
Lynn University, Boca Raton, FL 33431-5598
Lyon College, Batesville, AR 72503-2317
Macalester College, St. Paul, MN 55105-1899
MacCormac Junior College, Chicago, IL 60605
Machzikei Hadath Rabbinical College, Brooklyn, NY 11204
MacMurray College, Jacksonville, IL 62650-2590
Macomb Community College, Warren, MI 48093-3896
Macon College, Macon, GA 31297

Madison Area Technical College, Madison, WI 53704-2599
Madison Junior College of Business, Madison, WI 53703-3110
Madisonville Community College, Madisonville, KY 42431
Madonna University, Livonia, MI 48150-1173
Magnolia Bible College, Kosciusko, MS 39090
Maharishi University of Management, Fairfield, IA 52557-1155
Maine College of Art, Portland, ME 04101-3987
Maine Maritime Academy, Castine, ME 04420-5000
Malone College, Canton, OH 44709-3897
Manatee Community College, Bradenton, FL 34206-1849
Manchester College, North Manchester, IN 46962-0365
Manchester Community-Technical College, Manchester, CT 06040-1046
Manhattan Christian College, Manhattan, KS 66502
Manhattan College, Riverdale, NY 10471
Manhattan School of Music, New York, NY 10027-4698
Manhattanville College, Purchase, NY 10577
Mankato State University, Mankato, MN 56002-8400
Mannes College of Music, New York, NY 10024
Manor Junior College, Jenkintown, PA 19046-3399
Mansfield University of Pennsylvania, Mansfield, PA 16933
Maple Woods Community College, Kansas City, MO 64156-1299
Maranatha Baptist Bible College, Watertown, WI 53094
Maria College, Albany, NY 12208
Marian College, Indianapolis, IN 46222
Marian College of Fond du Lac, Fond du Lac, WI 54935-4699
Marian Court College, Swampscott, MA 01907-2896
Marietta College, Marietta, OH 45750-4005
Marion Military Institute, Marion, AL 36756-0420
Marion Technical College, Marion, OH 43302-5694
Marist College, Poughkeepsie, NY 12601-1387
Marlboro College, Marlboro, VT 05344-0300
Marquette University, Milwaukee, WI 53201-1881
Mars Hill College, Mars Hill, NC 28754
Marshall University, Huntington, WV 25755-2020
Martin Community College, Williamston, NC 27892-9988
Martin Luther College, New Ulm, MN 56073-3300
Martin Methodist College, Pulaski, TN 38478-2799
Martin University, Indianapolis, IN 46218
Mary Baldwin College, Staunton, VA 24401
Mary Holmes College, West Point, MS 39773-1257
Mary Washington College, Fredericksburg, VA 22401-5358
Marygrove College, Detroit, MI 48221
Maryland College of Art and Design, Silver Spring, MD 20902
Maryland Institute College of Art, Baltimore, MD 21217-9986
Marylhurst College, Marylhurst, OR 97036
Marymount College, Tarrytown, NY 10591-3796
Marymount College, Rancho Palos Verdes, CA 90275-6299
Marymount Manhattan College, New York, NY 10021-4597
Marymount University, Arlington, VA 22207-4299
Maryville College, Maryville, TN 37804-5907
Maryville University of Saint Louis, St. Louis, MO 63141-7299
Marywood College, Scranton, PA 18509-9989
Massachusetts Bay Community College, Wellesley Hills, MA 02181
Massachusetts College of Art, Boston, MA 02115-5882
Massachusetts College of Pharmacy and Allied Health Sciences, Boston, MA 02115
Massachusetts Institute of Technology, Cambridge, MA 02139
Massachusetts Maritime Academy, Buzzards Bay, MA 02532-1803
Massasoit Community College, Brockton, MA 02402
Master's College, Santa Clarita, CA 91322-0878
Mater Dei College, Ogdensburg, NY 13669-9699
Mayland Community College, Spruce Pine, NC 28777
Maysville Community College, Maysville, KY 41056
Mayville State University, Mayville, ND 58257
McCann School of Business, Mahanoy City, PA 17948
McCook Community College, McCook, NE 69001
McDowell Technical Community College, Marion, NC 28752
McGregor School of Antioch University, Yellow Springs, OH 45387
McHenry County College, Crystal Lake, IL 60012-2761
McIntosh College, Dover, NH 03820-3990
McKendree College, Lebanon, IL 62254
McLennan Community College, Waco, TX 76708
McMurry University, Abilene, TX 79697-0001
McNeese State University, Lake Charles, LA 70609-2495
McPherson College, McPherson, KS 67460-1402
Meadows College of Business, Columbus, GA 31906
Medaille College, Buffalo, NY 14214
Medcenter One College of Nursing, Bismarck, ND 58501
Median School of Allied Health Careers, Pittsburgh, PA 15222-3400
Medical College of Georgia, Augusta, GA 30912
Medical College of Pennsylvania and Hahnemann University, Philadelphia, PA 19102-1192

Medical University of South Carolina, Charleston, SC 29425-2970
Memphis College of Art, Memphis, TN 38104-2764
Mendocino College, Ukiah, CA 95482
Menlo College, Atherton, CA 94027-4301
Mennonite College of Nursing, Bloomington, IL 61701
Merced College, Merced, CA 95348-2898
Mercer County Community College, Trenton, NJ 08690-1099
Mercer University
    Atlanta, Atlanta, GA 30341-4115
    Macon, Macon, GA 31207-0001
Mercy College, Dobbs Ferry, NY 10522
Mercyhurst College, Erie, PA 16546-0001
Meredith College, Raleigh, NC 27607-5298
Meridian Community College, Meridian, MS 39307
Merrimack College, North Andover, MA 01845
Merritt College, Oakland, CA 94619
Mesa Community College, Mesa, AZ 85202
Mesa State College, Grand Junction, CO 81502-2647
Mesabi Community College: Arrowhead Region, Virginia, MN 55792-3448
Mesivta Torah Vodaath Seminary, Brooklyn, NY 11218
Messiah College, Grantham, PA 17027-0800
Methodist College, Fayetteville, NC 28311-1420
Metropolitan Community College, Omaha, NE 68103-3777
Metropolitan State College of Denver, Denver, CO 80217-3362
Metropolitan State University, St. Paul, MN 55106-5000
Miami University
    Hamilton Campus, Hamilton, OH 45011
    Middletown Campus, Middletown, OH 45042
    Oxford Campus, Oxford, OH 45056
Miami-Dade Community College, Miami, FL 33132-2297
Miami-Jacobs College, Dayton, OH 45401
Michigan Christian College, Rochester Hills, MI 48307-2764
Michigan State University, East Lansing, MI 48824-0590
Michigan Technological University, Houghton, MI 49931-1295
Microcomputer Technology Institute, Houston, TX 77036
Mid Michigan Community College, Harrison, MI 48625
Mid Plains Community College, North Platte, NE 69101-0001
Mid-America Bible College, Oklahoma City, OK 73170
MidAmerica Nazarene College, Olathe, KS 66062-1899
Mid-Continent Baptist Bible College, Mayfield, KY 42066-0357
Middle Georgia College, Cochran, GA 31014-1599
Middle Tennessee State University, Murfreesboro, TN 37132
Middlebury College, Middlebury, VT 05753-6002
Middlesex Community College, Bedford, MA 01730
Middlesex Community-Technical College, Middletown, CT 06457
Middlesex County College, Edison, NJ 08818-3050
Midland College, Midland, TX 79705
Midland Lutheran College, Fremont, NE 68025
Midlands Technical College, Columbia, SC 29202
Midstate College, Peoria, IL 61602-9990
Mid-State Technical College, Wisconsin Rapids, WI 54494
Midway College, Midway, KY 40347-1120
Midwestern State University, Wichita Falls, TX 76308
Miles College, Fairfield, AL 35064
Miles Community College, Miles City, MT 59301
Millersville University of Pennsylvania, Millersville, PA 17551-0302
Milligan College, Milligan College, TN 37682
Millikin University, Decatur, IL 62522-2084
Mills College, Oakland, CA 94613
Millsaps College, Jackson, MS 39210
Milwaukee Area Technical College, Milwaukee, WI 53233
Milwaukee Institute of Art & Design, Milwaukee, WI 53202
Milwaukee School of Engineering, Milwaukee, WI 53202-3109
Mineral Area College, Park Hills, MO 63601-1000
Minneapolis College of Art and Design, Minneapolis, MN 55404
Minneapolis Community College, Minneapolis, MN 55403-1779
Minnesota Bible College, Rochester, MN 55902
Minot State University, Minot, ND 58707-5002
MiraCosta College, Oceanside, CA 92056-3899
Mirrer Yeshiva Central Institute, Brooklyn, NY 11223
Miss Wade's Fashion Merchandising College, Dallas, TX 75258
Mission College, Santa Clara, CA 95054-1897
Mississippi College, Clinton, MS 39058
Mississippi County Community College, Blytheville, AR 72316-1109
Mississippi Delta Community College, Moorhead, MS 38761
Mississippi Gulf Coast Community College
    Jackson County Campus, Gautier, MS 39553
    Jefferson Davis Campus, Gulfport, MS 39507-3894
    Perkinston, Perkinston, MS 39573
Mississippi State University, Mississippi State, MS 39762-5268
Mississippi University for Women, Columbus, MS 39701
Mississippi Valley State University, Itta Bena, MS 38941-1400

Missouri Baptist College, St. Louis, MO 63141
Missouri Southern State College, Joplin, MO 64801-1595
Missouri Technical School, St. Louis, MO 63132-2907
Missouri Valley College, Marshall, MO 65340
Missouri Western State College, St. Joseph, MO 64507-2294
Mitchell College, New London, CT 06320
Mitchell Community College, Statesville, NC 28677
Mitchell Technical Institute, Mitchell, SD 57301
Moberly Area Community College, Moberly, MO 65270
Modesto Junior College, Modesto, CA 95350
Mohave Community College, Kingman, AZ 86401
Mohawk Valley Community College, Utica, NY 13501-5394
Molloy College, Rockville Center, NY 11570
Monmouth College, Monmouth, IL 61462-9989
Monmouth University, West Long Branch, NJ 07764-1898
Monroe College, Bronx, NY 10468-5907
Monroe Community College, Rochester, NY 14623
Monroe County Community College, Monroe, MI 48161
Montana State University
    Billings College of Technology, Billings, MT 59102
    College of Technology-Great Falls, Great Falls, MT 59405
    Billings, Billings, MT 59101-0298
    Bozeman, Bozeman, MT 59717-0016
    Northern, Havre, MT 59501
Montana Tech of The University of Montana, Butte, MT 59701-8997
Montana Tech of the University of Montana: College of Technology, Butte, MT 59701
Montcalm Community College, Sidney, MI 48885-0300
Montclair State University, Upper Montclair, NJ 07043-1624
Monterey Institute of International Studies, Monterey, CA 93940
Monterey Peninsula College, Monterey, CA 93940-4799
Montgomery College
    Germantown Campus, Germantown, MD 20876
    Rockville Campus, Rockville, MD 20850
    Takoma Park Campus, Takoma Park, MD 20912
Montgomery Community College, Troy, NC 27371-0787
Montgomery County Community College, Blue Bell, PA 19422-0758
Montreat College, Montreat, NC 28757-9987
Montserrat College of Art, Beverly, MA 01915
Moody Bible Institute, Chicago, IL 60610-3284
Moore College of Art and Design, Philadelphia, PA 19103-1179
Moorhead State University, Moorhead, MN 56563
Moorpark College, Moorpark, CA 93021
Moraine Park Technical College, Fond du Lac, WI 54935
Moraine Valley Community College, Palos Hills, IL 60465-0937
Moravian College, Bethlehem, PA 18018
Morehead State University, Morehead, KY 40351
Morehouse College, Atlanta, GA 30314
Morgan Community College, Fort Morgan, CO 80701
Morgan State University, Baltimore, MD 21239
Morningside College, Sioux City, IA 51106-1751
Morris Brown College, Atlanta, GA 30314
Morris College, Sumter, SC 29150-3599
Morrison College: Reno, Reno, NV 89503
Morrison Institute of Technology, Morrison, IL 61270-2959
Morton College, Cicero, IL 60650
Motlow State Community College, Tullahoma, TN 37388-8100
Mott Community College, Flint, MI 48503
Mount Aloysius College, Cresson, PA 16630
Mount Angel Seminary, St. Benedict, OR 97373
Mount Holyoke College, South Hadley, MA 01075-1488
Mount Hood Community College, Gresham, OR 97030
Mount Ida College, Newton Centre, MA 02159
Mount Marty College, Yankton, SD 57078-3724
Mount Mary College, Milwaukee, WI 53222-4597
Mount Mercy College, Cedar Rapids, IA 52402-4797
Mount Olive College, Mount Olive, NC 28365
Mount St. Clare College, Clinton, IA 52732
Mount St. Mary College, Newburgh, NY 12550
Mount St. Mary's College, Los Angeles, CA 90049-1597
Mount St. Mary's College, Emmitsburg, MD 21727-7796
Mount San Antonio College, Walnut, CA 91789
Mount San Jacinto College, San Jacinto, CA 92583-2399
Mount Senario College, Ladysmith, WI 54848
Mount Union College, Alliance, OH 44601-3993
Mount Vernon College, Washington, DC 20007-1199
Mount Vernon Nazarene College, Mount Vernon, OH 43050
Mount Wachusett Community College, Gardner, MA 01440-1000
Mountain Empire Community College, Big Stone Gap, VA 24219
Mountain View College, Dallas, TX 75211-6599
MTI Business College, Cleveland, OH 44115
Muhlenberg College, Allentown, PA 18104-5586

Multnomah Bible College, Portland, OR 97220-5898
Murray State College, Tishomingo, OK 73460
Murray State University, Murray, KY 42071
Muscatine Community College, Muscatine, IA 52761-5396
Muskegon Community College, Muskegon, MI 49442
Muskingum Area Technical College, Zanesville, OH 43701
Muskingum College, New Concord, OH 43762
NAES College, Chicago, IL 60659
Napa Valley College, Napa, CA 94558
Naropa Institute, Boulder, CO 80302
Nash Community College, Rocky Mount, NC 27804-7488
Nashville State Technical Institute, Nashville, TN 37209
Nassau Community College, Garden City, NY 11530-6793
National Business College, Roanoke, VA 24017-0400
National College, Denver, CO 80222
National College, Kansas City, MO 64133-1612
National College, St. Paul, MN 55108
National College, Albuquerque, NM 87110-3156
National College, Rapid City, SD 57709-1780
National College of Chiropractic, Lombard, IL 60148
National Education Center
    Brown Institute Campus, Minneapolis, MN 55407
    National Institute of Technology Campus, Cross Lanes, WV 25313
    Spartan School of Aeronautics, Tulsa, OK 74158-2833
National University, San Diego, CA 92108-4107
National-Louis University, Evanston, IL 60201-1796
Naugatuck Valley Community-Technical College, Waterbury, CT 06708-3089
Navajo Community College, Tsaile, AZ 86556
Navarro College, Corsicana, TX 75110
Nazarene Bible College, Colorado Springs, CO 80935
Nazareth College of Rochester, Rochester, NY 14618-3790
Nebraska Christian College, Norfolk, NE 68701
Nebraska College of Technical Agriculture, Curtis, NE 69025-0069
Nebraska Indian Community College, Winnebago, NE 68071
Nebraska Methodist College of Nursing and Allied Health, Omaha, NE 68114
Nebraska Wesleyan University, Lincoln, NE 68504
NEI College of Technology, Minneapolis, MN 55421-9990
Neosho County Community College, Chanute, KS 66720
Nettleton Junior College, Sioux Falls, SD 57104
Neumann College, Aston, PA 19014-1297
New Castle School of Trades, Pulaski, PA 16143-9721
New College of California, San Francisco, CA 94110
New College of the University of South Florida, Sarasota, FL 34243-2197
New England Banking Institute, Boston, MA 02111
New England College, Henniker, NH 03242-0792
New England Conservatory of Music, Boston, MA 02115
New England Culinary Institute, Montpelier, VT 05602
New England Institute of Technology
    Warwick, Warwick, RI 02886
    West Palm Beach, West Palm Beach, FL 33407
New Hampshire College, Manchester, NH 03106-1045
New Hampshire Technical College
    Berlin, Berlin, NH 03570
    Claremont, Claremont, NH 03743-9707
    Laconia, Laconia, NH 03246-9204
    Manchester, Manchester, NH 03102-8518
    Nashua, Nashua, NH 03061-2052
    Stratham, Stratham, NH 03885-2297
New Hampshire Technical Institute, Concord, NH 03301
New Jersey Institute of Technology, Newark, NJ 07102-1982
New Mexico Highlands University, Las Vegas, NM 87701
New Mexico Institute of Mining and Technology, Socorro, NM 87801
New Mexico Junior College, Hobbs, NM 88240
New Mexico Military Institute, Roswell, NM 88201-5173
New Mexico State University
    Alamogordo, Alamogordo, NM 88310
    Carlsbad, Carlsbad, NM 88220
    Grants, Grants, NM 87020
    Las Cruces, Las Cruces, NM 88003-8001
New Orleans Baptist Theological Seminary: School of Christian Education, New Orleans, LA 70126-4858
New River Community College, Dublin, VA 24084
New School of Architecture, San Diego, CA 92101
New York Institute of Technology, Old Westbury, NY 11538
New York School of Interior Design, New York, NY 10021
New York University, New York, NY 10011-9108
Newberry College, Newberry, SC 29108
Newbury College, Brookline, MA 02146

Newport Business Institute
    Lower Burrell, Lower Burrell, PA 15068
    Williamsport, Williamsport, PA 17701
Niagara County Community College, Sanborn, NY 14132
Niagara University, Niagara University, NY 14109-2011
Nicholls State University, Thibodaux, LA 70310
Nichols College, Dudley, MA 01570-5000
Nicolet Area Technical College, Rhinelander, WI 54501
Nielsen Electronics Institute, Charleston, SC 29405
Norfolk State University, Norfolk, VA 23504
Normandale Community College, Bloomington, MN 55431
North Adams State College, North Adams, MA 01247
North Arkansas Community/Technical College, Harrison, AR 72601
North Carolina Agricultural and Technical State University, Greensboro, NC 27411
North Carolina Central University, Durham, NC 27707
North Carolina School of the Arts, Winston-Salem, NC 27117-2189
North Carolina State University, Raleigh, NC 27695-7103
North Carolina Wesleyan College, Rocky Mount, NC 27804
North Central Bible College, Minneapolis, MN 55404
North Central College, Naperville, IL 60566-7065
North Central Michigan College, Petoskey, MI 49770
North Central Missouri College, Trenton, MO 64683
North Central Technical College, Mansfield, OH 44901-0698
North Central Texas College, Gainesville, TX 76240
North Country Community College, Saranac Lake, NY 12983
North Dakota State College of Science, Wahpeton, ND 58076
North Dakota State University
    Bottineau, Bottineau, ND 58318-1198
    Fargo, Fargo, ND 58105
North Florida Junior College, Madison, FL 32340
North Georgia College, Dahlonega, GA 30597
North Greenville College, Tigerville, SC 29688-1892
North Harris Montgomery Community College District, Houston, TX 77060-2000
North Hennepin Community College, Minneapolis, MN 55445
North Idaho College, Coeur d'Alene, ID 83814-2199
North Iowa Area Community College, Mason City, IA 50401
North Lake College, Irving, TX 75038-3899
North Park College, Chicago, IL 60625-4987
North Seattle Community College, Seattle, WA 98103-3599
North Shore Community College, Danvers, MA 01923-0840
Northampton County Area Community College, Bethlehem, PA 18017
Northcentral Technical College, Wausau, WI 54401
Northeast Alabama Community College, Rainsville, AL 35986
Northeast Community College, Norfolk, NE 68702-0469
Northeast Iowa Community College, Calmar, IA 52132
Northeast Louisiana University, Monroe, LA 71209-1160
Northeast Mississippi Community College, Booneville, MS 38829
Northeast State Technical Community College, Blountville, TN 37617-0246
Northeast Texas Community College, Mount Pleasant, TX 75455-1307
Northeast Wisconsin Technical College, Green Bay, WI 54307-9042
Northeastern Illinois University, Chicago, IL 60625
Northeastern Junior College, Sterling, CO 80751
Northeastern Oklahoma Agricultural and Mechanical College, Miami, OK 74354-6497
Northeastern State University, Tahlequah, OK 74464
Northeastern University, Boston, MA 02115-9959
Northern Arizona University, Flagstaff, AZ 86011-4084
Northern Essex Community College, Haverhill, MA 01830-2399
Northern Illinois University, DeKalb, IL 60115-2854
Northern Kentucky University, Highland Heights, KY 41099-7010
Northern Maine Technical College, Presque Isle, ME 04769
Northern Michigan University, Marquette, MI 49855
Northern New Mexico Community College, Espanola, NM 87532
Northern Oklahoma College, Tonkawa, OK 74653-0310
Northern State University, Aberdeen, SD 57401
Northern Virginia Community College, Annandale, VA 22003-3723
Northland College, Ashland, WI 54806
Northland Community & Technical College, Thief River Falls, MN 56701
Northland Pioneer College, Holbrook, AZ 86025
Northwest Christian College, Eugene, OR 97401-3727
Northwest College, Kirkland, WA 98083-0579
Northwest College, Powell, WY 82435
Northwest College of Art, Poulsbo, WA 98370
Northwest Indian College, Bellingham, WA 98226
Northwest Iowa Community College, Sheldon, IA 51201
Northwest Mississippi Community College, Senatobia, MS 38668
Northwest Missouri State University, Maryville, MO 64468-6001
Northwest Nazarene College, Nampa, ID 83686
Northwest State Community College, Archbold, OH 43502-9542
Northwest Technical Institute, Eden Prairie, MN 55344-5351

Northwestern Business College, Chicago, IL 60630-2298
Northwestern College, Lima, OH 45805
Northwestern College, St. Paul, MN 55113-1598
Northwestern College, Orange City, IA 51041
Northwestern Connecticut Community-Technical College, Winsted, CT 06098-1798
Northwestern Michigan College, Traverse City, MI 49686
Northwestern Oklahoma State University, Alva, OK 73717-2799
Northwestern State University, Natchitoches, LA 71497
Northwestern University, Evanston, IL 60204-3060
Northwest-Shoals Community College, Muscle Shoals, AL 35662
Northwood University, Midland, MI 48640
Northwood University: Texas Campus, Cedar Hill, TX 75104-0058
Norwalk Community-Technical College, Norwalk, CT 06854-1655
Norwich University, Northfield, VT 05663-1097
Notre Dame College, Manchester, NH 03104-2299
Notre Dame College of Ohio, South Euclid, OH 44121-4293
Nova Southeastern University, Fort Lauderdale, FL 33314
Nunez Community College, Chalmette, LA 70043
Nyack College, Nyack, NY 10960
Oak Hills Bible College, Bemidji, MN 56601
Oakland City University, Oakland City, IN 47660
Oakland Community College, Bloomfield Hills, MI 48304-2266
Oakland University, Rochester, MI 48309-4401
Oakton Community College, Des Plaines, IL 60016
Oakwood College, Huntsville, AL 35896
Oberlin College, Oberlin, OH 44074
Oblate College, Washington, DC 20017-1587
Occidental College, Los Angeles, CA 90041-3393
Ocean County College, Toms River, NJ 08754-2001
Odessa College, Odessa, TX 79764-7127
Oglala Lakota College, Kyle, SD 57752
Oglethorpe University, Atlanta, GA 30319-2797
Ohio Dominican College, Columbus, OH 43219-2099
Ohio Institute of Photography and Technology, Dayton, OH 45439
Ohio Northern University, Ada, OH 45810-1599
Ohio State University
    Agricultural Technical Institute, Wooster, OH 44691-4099
    Columbus Campus, Columbus, OH 43210-1200
    Lima Campus, Lima, OH 45804-3596
    Mansfield Campus, Mansfield, OH 44906
    Marion Campus, Marion, OH 43302
    Newark Campus, Newark, OH 43055
Ohio University
    Athens, Athens, OH 45701-2979
    Chillicothe Campus, Chillicothe, OH 45601
    Eastern Campus, St. Clairsville, OH 43950
    Lancaster Campus, Lancaster, OH 43130
    Southern Campus at Ironton, Ironton, OH 45638
    Zanesville Campus, Zanesville, OH 43701
Ohio Valley Business College, East Liverpool, OH 43920
Ohio Valley College, Parkersburg, WV 26101-9975
Ohio Wesleyan University, Delaware, OH 43015-2398
Ohlone College, Fremont, CA 94539-0390
Ohr Somayach Tanenbaum Education Center, Monsey, NY 10952
Okaloosa-Walton Community College, Niceville, FL 32578
Oklahoma Baptist University, Shawnee, OK 74801
Oklahoma Christian University of Science and Arts, Oklahoma City, OK 73136-1100
Oklahoma City Community College, Oklahoma City, OK 73159
Oklahoma City University, Oklahoma City, OK 73106
Oklahoma Panhandle State University, Goodwell, OK 73939-0430
Oklahoma State University
    Oklahoma City, Oklahoma City, OK 73107
    Stillwater, Stillwater, OK 74078
    Okmulgee, Okmulgee, OK 74447-3901
Old Dominion University, Norfolk, VA 23529-0050
Olean Business Institute, Olean, NY 14760-2691
Olivet College, Olivet, MI 49076
Olivet Nazarene University, Kankakee, IL 60901-0592
Olympic College, Bremerton, WA 98337-1699
O'More College of Design, Franklin, TN 37064-0908
Onondaga Community College, Syracuse, NY 13215
Oral Roberts University, Tulsa, OK 74171
Orange Coast College, Costa Mesa, CA 92628-5005
Orange County Community College, Middletown, NY 10940-0115
Orangeburg-Calhoun Technical College, Orangeburg, SC 29118-8299
Oregon Health Sciences University, Portland, OR 97201
Oregon Institute of Technology, Klamath Falls, OR 97601-8801
Oregon Polytechnic Institute, Portland, OR 97214
Oregon State University, Corvallis, OR 97331-2130
Otero Junior College, La Junta, CO 81050

Otis College of Art and Design, Los Angeles, CA 90057-3304
Ottawa University, Ottawa, KS 66067-3399
Otterbein College, Westerville, OH 43081
Ouachita Baptist University, Arkadelphia, AR 71998-0001
Our Lady of Holy Cross College, New Orleans, LA 70131-7399
Our Lady of the Lake University of San Antonio, San Antonio, TX 78207-4689
Owens Technical College
    Findlay Campus, Findlay, OH 45840
    Toledo, Toledo, OH 43699-1947
Owensboro Community College, Owensboro, KY 42303
Owensboro Junior College of Business, Owensboro, KY 42303
Oxford College of Emory University, Oxford, GA 30267-1328
Oxnard College, Oxnard, CA 93033
Ozark Christian College, Joplin, MO 64801
Ozarks Technical Community College, Springfield, MO 65802
Pace University, New York, NY 10038-1598
Pacific Christian College, Fullerton, CA 92631
Pacific Lutheran University, Tacoma, WA 98447-0003
Pacific Northwest College of Art, Portland, OR 97205-2486
Pacific Oaks College, Pasadena, CA 91103
Pacific Union College, Angwin, CA 94508
Pacific University, Forest Grove, OR 97116-1797
Paducah Community College, Paducah, KY 42002-7380
Paier College of Art, Hamden, CT 06514-3902
Paine College, Augusta, GA 30901-3182
Palm Beach Atlantic College, West Palm Beach, FL 33416-4708
Palm Beach Community College, Lake Worth, FL 33461-4796
Palo Alto College, San Antonio, TX 78224
Palo Verde College, Blythe, CA 92225
Palomar College, San Marcos, CA 92069-1487
Pamlico Community College, Grantsboro, NC 28529
Panola College, Carthage, TX 75633
Paradise Valley Community College, Phoenix, AZ 85032
Paris Junior College, Paris, TX 75460
Park College, Parkville, MO 64152-9970
Parkland College, Champaign, IL 61821-1899
Parks College, Albuquerque, NM 87102
Parsons School of Design, New York, NY 10011
Pasadena City College, Pasadena, CA 91106
Pasco-Hernando Community College, Dade City, FL 34654-5199
Patrick Henry Community College, Martinsville, VA 24115-5311
Patten College, Oakland, CA 94601-2699
Paul D. Camp Community College, Franklin, VA 23851-0737
Paul Quinn College, Dallas, TX 75241
Paul Smith's College, Paul Smiths, NY 12970-0265
Peace College, Raleigh, NC 27604-1194
Pearl River Community College, Poplarville, MS 39470
Peirce College, Philadelphia, PA 19102
Pellissippi State Technical Community College, Knoxville, TN 37933-0990
Pembroke State University, Pembroke, NC 28372
Peninsula College, Port Angeles, WA 98362
Penn State
    Allentown Campus, Fogelsville, PA 18051-9733
    Altoona Campus, Altoona, PA 16601-3760
    Beaver Campus, Monaca, PA 15061
    Berks Campus, Reading, PA 19610-6009
    Delaware County Campus, Media, PA 19063
    Du Bois Campus, Du Bois, PA 15801
    Erie Behrend College, Erie, PA 16563-0195
    Fayette Campus, Uniontown, PA 15401
    Harrisburg Capital College, Middletown, PA 17057-4898
    Hazleton Campus, Hazleton, PA 18201
    McKeesport Campus, McKeesport, PA 15132
    Mont Alto Campus, Mont Alto, PA 17237
    New Kensington Campus, New Kensington, PA 15068
    Ogontz Campus, Abington, PA 19001
    Schuylkill Campus, Schuylkill Haven, PA 17972
    Shenango Campus, Sharon, PA 16146
    University Park Campus, University Park, PA 16802
    Wilkes-Barre Campus, Lehman, PA 18627
    Worthington-Scranton Campus, Dunmore, PA 18512
    York Campus, York, PA 17403
Penn Technical Institute, Pittsburgh, PA 15222
Penn Valley Community College, Kansas City, MO 64111
Pennco Tech, Bristol, PA 19007
Pennsylvania College of Technology, Williamsport, PA 17701-5799
Pennsylvania Institute of Culinary Arts, Pittsburgh, PA 15222
Pennsylvania Institute of Technology, Media, PA 19063-4098
Pensacola Junior College, Pensacola, FL 32504
Pepperdine University, Malibu, CA 90263-4392
Peru State College, Peru, NE 68421-0010

Pfeiffer College, Misenheimer, NC 28109
Philadelphia College of Bible, Langhorne, PA 19047-2990
Philadelphia College of Pharmacy and Science, Philadelphia, PA 19104-4495
Philadelphia College of Textiles and Science, Philadelphia, PA 19144-5497
Philander Smith College, Little Rock, AR 72202
Phillips Beth Israel School of Nursing, New York, NY 10010
Phillips College Inland Empire Campus, Riverside, CA 92506
Phillips County Community College, Helena, AR 72342
Phillips Junior College
    Jackson, Jackson, MS 39216
    New Orleans, New Orleans, LA 70121
    Salt Lake City Campus, Salt Lake City, UT 84106
    San Fernando Valley Campus, Van Nuys, CA 91406-4203
    Springfield, Springfield, MO 65807
Phillips Junior College: Las Vegas Campus, Las Vegas, NV 89121
Phillips University, Enid, OK 73701-6439
Phoenix College, Phoenix, AZ 85013
Piedmont Bible College, Winston-Salem, NC 27101-5197
Piedmont College, Demorest, GA 30535-0010
Piedmont Community College, Roxboro, NC 27573-1197
Piedmont Technical College, Greenwood, SC 29648
Piedmont Virginia Community College, Charlottesville, VA 22902-8714
Pierce College, Tacoma, WA 98498-1999
Pikes Peak Community College, Colorado Springs, CO 80906-5498
Pikeville College, Pikeville, KY 41501-1194
Pillsbury Baptist Bible College, Owatonna, MN 55060
Pima Community College, Tucson, AZ 85709-1120
Pine Manor College, Chestnut Hill, MA 02167
Pitt Community College, Greenville, NC 27835-7007
Pittsburg State University, Pittsburg, KS 66762
Pittsburgh Institute of Mortuary Science, Pittsburgh, PA 15206-3706
Pittsburgh Technical Institute, Pittsburgh, PA 15222
Pitzer College, Claremont, CA 91711-6101
Plaza Business Institute, Jackson Heights, NY 11372
Plymouth State College of the University System of New Hampshire, Plymouth, NH 03264
Point Loma Nazarene College, San Diego, CA 92106-2899
Point Park College, Pittsburgh, PA 15222-1984
Polk Community College, Winter Haven, FL 33881-4299
Polytechnic University
    Brooklyn, Brooklyn, NY 11201-2999
    Long Island Campus, Farmingdale, NY 11735-3995
Pomona College, Claremont, CA 91711-6312
Pontifical Catholic University of Puerto Rico, Ponce, PR 00731-6382
Pontifical College Josephinum, Columbus, OH 43235-1498
Porterville College, Porterville, CA 93257
Portland Community College, Portland, OR 97219-0990
Portland State University, Portland, OR 97207-0751
Potomac State College of West Virginia University, Keyser, WV 26726
Prairie State College, Chicago Heights, IL 60411
Prairie View A&M University, Prairie View, TX 77446
Pratt Community College, Pratt, KS 67124
Pratt Institute, Brooklyn, NY 11205
Presbyterian College, Clinton, SC 29325-9989
Prescott College, Prescott, AZ 86301
Presentation College, Aberdeen, SD 57401
Prestonsburg Community College, Prestonsburg, KY 41653
Prince George's Community College, Largo, MD 20774-2199
Prince William Sound Community College, Valdez, AK 99686
Princeton University, Princeton, NJ 08544-0430
Principia College, Elsah, IL 62028-9799
Providence College, Providence, RI 02918-0001
Pueblo College of Business and Technology, Pueblo, CO 81004
Pueblo Community College, Pueblo, CO 81004
Puget Sound Christian College, Edmonds, WA 98020-3171
Purdue University
    Calumet, Hammond, IN 46323-2094
    North Central Campus, Westville, IN 46391-9528
    West Lafayette, West Lafayette, IN 47907-1080
Queen of the Holy Rosary College, Fremont, CA 94539-0391
Queens College, Charlotte, NC 28274
Quincy College, Quincy, MA 02169
Quincy University, Quincy, IL 62301-2699
Quinebaug Valley Community-Technical College, Danielson, CT 06239-1440
Quinnipiac College, Hamden, CT 06518-1908
Quinsigamond Community College, Worcester, MA 01606
Rabbinical Academy Mesivta Rabbi Chaim Berlin, Brooklyn, NY 11230
Rabbinical College of America, Morristown, NJ 07960
Rabbinical College Bobover Yeshiva B'nei Zion, Brooklyn, NY 11219
Rabbinical College Ch'san Sofer of New York, Brooklyn, NY 11204
Rabbinical College of Long Island, Long Beach, NY 11561
Rabbinical College of Telshe, Wickliffe, OH 44092-2584

Rabbinical Seminary Adas Yereim, Brooklyn, NY 11211
Rabbinical Seminary of America, Forest Hills, NY 11375
Radford University, Radford, VA 24142-6903
Rainy River Community College, International Falls, MN 56649
Ramapo College of New Jersey, Mahwah, NJ 07430-1680
Rancho Santiago Community College, Santa Ana, CA 92706
Randolph Community College, Asheboro, NC 27204-1009
Randolph-Macon College, Ashland, VA 23005-5505
Randolph-Macon Woman's College, Lynchburg, VA 24503-1526
Ranger College, Ranger, TX 76470
Ranken Technical College, St. Louis, MO 63113
Rappahannock Community College, Glenns, VA 23149
Raritan Valley Community College, Somerville, NJ 08876-1265
Rasmussen College-Minnetonka, Minnetonka, MN 56001
Ray College of Design, Chicago, IL 60654
Reading Area Community College, Reading, PA 19603-1706
Red Rocks Community College, Golden, CO 80401-5398
Redlands Community College, El Reno, OK 73036
Reed College, Portland, OR 97202-8199
Reformed Bible College, Grand Rapids, MI 49505-9749
Regis College, Weston, MA 02193-1571
Regis University, Denver, CO 80221-1099
Reid State Technical College, Evergreen, AL 36401
Reinhardt College, Waleska, GA 30183
Remington Education Center: Vale Campus, Blairsville, PA 15717
Rend Lake College, Ina, IL 62846
Rensselaer Polytechnic Institute, Troy, NY 12180-3590
Renton Technical College, Renton, WA 98056-4195
Research College of Nursing, Kansas City, MO 64110-2508
RETS
    Electronic Institute, Louisville, KY 40219
    Tech Center, Centerville, OH 45459
Rhode Island College, Providence, RI 02908
Rhode Island School of Design, Providence, RI 02903-2791
Rhodes College, Memphis, TN 38112-1690
Rice University, Houston, TX 77005
Rich Mountain Community College, Mena, AR 71953
Richard Bland College, Petersburg, VA 23805
Richard Stockton College of New Jersey, Pomona, NJ 08240-0000
Richland College, Dallas, TX 75243-2199
Richland Community College, Decatur, IL 62521
Richmond Community College, Hamlet, NC 28345
Ricks College, Rexburg, ID 83460-4104
Rider University, Lawrenceville, NJ 08648-3099
Ringling School of Art and Design, Sarasota, FL 34234
Rio Hondo College, Whittier, CA 90601-1699
Rio Salado Community College, Phoenix, AZ 85003
Ripon College, Ripon, WI 54971
Riverside Community College, Riverside, CA 92506-1299
Rivier College, Nashua, NH 03060-5086
Roane State Community College, Harriman, TN 37748
Roanoke Bible College, Elizabeth City, NC 27909
Roanoke College, Salem, VA 24153-3794
Roanoke-Chowan Community College, Ahoskie, NC 27910-9522
Robert Morris College, Coraopolis, PA 15108-1189
Robert Morris College: Chicago, Chicago, IL 60601
Roberts Wesleyan College, Rochester, NY 14624-1997
Robeson Community College, Lumberton, NC 28359
Rochester Business Institute, Rochester, NY 14622
Rochester Community College, Rochester, MN 55904-4999
Rochester Institute of Technology, Rochester, NY 14623-5604
Rock Valley College, Rockford, IL 61114-5699
Rockford Business College, Rockford, IL 61103
Rockford College, Rockford, IL 61108-2393
Rockhurst College, Kansas City, MO 64110-2508
Rockingham Community College, Wentworth, NC 27375-0038
Rockland Community College, Suffern, NY 10901
Rocky Mountain College, Billings, MT 59102-1796
Rocky Mountain College of Art & Design, Denver, CO 80224-2359
Roger Williams University, Bristol, RI 02809-2923
Rogers State College, Claremore, OK 74017-2099
Rogue Community College, Grants Pass, OR 97527
Rollins College, Winter Park, FL 32789-4499
Roosevelt University, Chicago, IL 60605-1394
Rosary College, River Forest, IL 60305-1099
Rose State College, Midwest City, OK 73110-2799
Rose-Hulman Institute of Technology, Terre Haute, IN 47803-3999
Rosemont College, Rosemont, PA 19010
Rowan College of New Jersey, Glassboro, NJ 08028
Rowan-Cabarrus Community College, Salisbury, NC 28145-1595
Roxbury Community College, Roxbury Crossing, MA 02120-3400
Rush University, Chicago, IL 60612

Russell Sage College, Troy, NY 12180-4115
Rust College, Holly Springs, MS 38635-2328
Rutgers, The State University of New Jersey
    Camden College of Arts and Sciences, Camden, NJ 08102
    College of Engineering, New Brunswick, NJ 08903-2101
    College of Nursing, Newark, NJ 07102-1896
    College of Pharmacy, New Brunswick, NJ 08903-2101
    Cook College, New Brunswick, NJ 08903-2101
    Douglass College, New Brunswick, NJ 08903-2101
    Livingston College, New Brunswick, NJ 08903-2101
    Mason Gross School of the Arts, New Brunswick, NJ 08903-2101
    Newark College of Arts and Sciences, Newark, NJ 07102-1896
    Rutgers College, New Brunswick, NJ 08903-2101
Sacramento City College, Sacramento, CA 95822
Sacred Heart Major Seminary, Detroit, MI 48226
Sacred Heart University, Fairfield, CT 06432-1000
Saddleback College, Mission Viejo, CA 92692-3635
Sage Junior College of Albany, Albany, NY 12208
Saginaw Valley State University, University Center, MI 48710-0001
St. Ambrose University, Davenport, IA 52803-2898
St. Andrews Presbyterian College, Laurinburg, NC 28352-9151
St. Anselm College, Manchester, NH 03102-1310
St. Augustine College, Chicago, IL 60640-3501
St. Augustine's College, Raleigh, NC 27610-2298
St. Bonaventure University, St. Bonaventure, NY 14778-2284
St. Catharine College, St. Catharine, KY 40061
St. Charles Borromeo Seminary-Overbrook, Wynnewood, PA 19096-3099
St. Charles County Community College, St. Peters, MO 63376
St. Clair County Community College, Port Huron, MI 48061-5015
St. Cloud State University, St. Cloud, MN 56301-4498
St. Cloud Technical College, St. Cloud, MN 56303
St. Edward's University, Austin, TX 78704-6489
St. Francis College, Fort Wayne, IN 46808
St. Francis College, Brooklyn Heights, NY 11201
St. Francis College, Loretto, PA 15940-0600
St. Francis Medical Center College of Nursing, Peoria, IL 61603-3783
St. Gregory's College, Shawnee, OK 74801
St. Hyacinth College and Seminary, Granby, MA 01033-9742
St. John Fisher College, Rochester, NY 14618-3597
St. John Vianney College Seminary, Miami, FL 33165
St. John's College, Santa Fe, NM 87501-4599
St. John's College, Annapolis, MD 21404-2800
St. Johns River Community College, Palatka, FL 32177-3897
St. John's Seminary College, Brighton, MA 02135
St. John's Seminary College, Camarillo, CA 93012-2599
St. John's University, Jamaica, NY 11439
St. John's University, Collegeville, MN 56321
St. Joseph College, West Hartford, CT 06117-2700
St. Joseph College of Nursing, Joliet, IL 60435
St. Joseph Seminary College, St. Benedict, LA 70457-9990
St. Joseph's College, Rensselaer, IN 47978
St. Joseph's College, Standish, ME 04084-5263
St. Joseph's College
    Brooklyn, Brooklyn, NY 11205-3688
    Suffolk Campus, Patchogue, NY 11772-2603
St. Joseph's Hospital Health Center School of Nursing, Syracuse, NY 13203
St. Joseph's University, Philadelphia, PA 19131
St. Lawrence University, Canton, NY 13617-1447
St. Leo College, St. Leo, FL 33574-2008
St. Louis Christian College, Florissant, MO 63033
St. Louis College of Pharmacy, St. Louis, MO 63110
St. Louis Community College
    Florissant Valley, St. Louis, MO 63135
    Forest Park, St. Louis, MO 63110
    Meramec, St. Louis, MO 63122-5799
St. Louis University, St. Louis, MO 63103-2097
St. Luke's College, Kansas City, MO 64111
St. Martin's College, Lacey, WA 98503-1297
St. Mary College, Leavenworth, KS 66048-5082
St. Mary-of-the-Woods College, St. Mary-of-the-Woods, IN 47876-0068
St. Mary's College, Orchard Lake, MI 48324-0515
St. Mary's College, Raleigh, NC 27603-1689
St. Mary's College of California, Moraga, CA 94575-4800
St. Mary's College of Maryland, St. Mary's City, MD 20686-9998
St. Mary's University, San Antonio, TX 78228-8503
St. Mary's University of Minnesota, Winona, MN 55987-1399
St. Meinrad College, St. Meinrad, IN 47577-1030
St. Michael's College, Colchester, VT 05439
St. Norbert College, De Pere, WI 54115-2099
St. Olaf College, Northfield, MN 55057-1098
St. Paul Technical College, St. Paul, MN 55102-9913
St. Paul's College, Lawrenceville, VA 23868

St. Peter's College, Jersey City, NJ 07306-5944
St. Petersburg Junior College, St. Petersburg, FL 33733
St. Philip's College, San Antonio, TX 78203-2098
St. Thomas Aquinas College, Sparkill, NY 10976
St. Thomas University, Miami, FL 33054
St. Vincent College, Latrobe, PA 15650-2690
St. Xavier University, Chicago, IL 60655
Saint Mary's College, Notre Dame, IN 46556-5001
Salem College, Winston-Salem, NC 27108-0548
Salem Community College, Carneys Point, NJ 08069-2799
Salem State College, Salem, MA 01970
Salem-Teikyo University, Salem, WV 26426
Salisbury State University, Salisbury, MD 21801-6862
Salish Kootenai College, Pablo, MT 59855
Salt Lake Community College, Salt Lake City, UT 84130-0808
Salve Regina University, Newport, RI 02840-4192
Sam Houston State University, Huntsville, TX 77341-2418
Samford University, Birmingham, AL 35229-0000
Sampson Community College, Clinton, NC 28328
Samuel Merritt College, Oakland, CA 94609-9954
San Antonio College, San Antonio, TX 78212-4299
San Bernardino Valley College, San Bernardino, CA 92410
San Diego City College, San Diego, CA 92101
San Diego Mesa College, San Diego, CA 92111
San Diego Miramar College, San Diego, CA 92126-2999
San Diego State University, San Diego, CA 92182-0771
San Francisco Art Institute, San Francisco, CA 94133-2299
San Francisco College of Mortuary Science, San Francisco, CA 94110
San Francisco Conservatory of Music, San Francisco, CA 94122-4498
San Francisco State University, San Francisco, CA 94132
San Jacinto College
    Central Campus, Pasadena, TX 77501-2007
    North, Houston, TX 77049
San Joaquin Delta College, Stockton, CA 95207
San Joaquin Valley College Inc., Visalia, CA 93291-9283
San Jose Christian College, San Jose, CA 95112-2381
San Jose City College, San Jose, CA 95128-2798
San Jose State University, San Jose, CA 95192-0009
San Juan College, Farmington, NM 87402
Sandhills Community College, Pinehurst, NC 28374
Santa Barbara City College, Santa Barbara, CA 93109-2394
Santa Clara University, Santa Clara, CA 95053
Santa Fe Community College, Santa Fe, NM 87502-4187
Santa Fe Community College, Gainesville, FL 32602
Santa Monica College, Santa Monica, CA 90405-1628
Santa Rosa Junior College, Santa Rosa, CA 95401
Sarah Lawrence College, Bronxville, NY 10708
Sauk Valley Community College, Dixon, IL 61021-9110
Savannah College of Art and Design, Savannah, GA 31402-3146
Savannah State College, Savannah, GA 31404
Savannah Technical Institute, Savannah, GA 31499
Sawyer College, Inc., Hammond, IN 46320
Sawyer School, Pittsburgh, PA 46320
Schenectady County Community College, Schenectady, NY 12305
Schiller International University, Dunedin, FL 34698-4964
School of the Art Institute of Chicago, Chicago, IL 60603
School for International Training, Brattleboro, VT 05301
School of the Museum of Fine Arts, Boston, MA 02115
School of Visual Arts, New York, NY 10010-3994
Schoolcraft College, Livonia, MI 48152-2696
Schreiner College, Kerrville, TX 78028
Schuylkill Business Institute, Pottsville, PA 17901
Scott Community College, Bettendorf, IA 52722-6804
Scottsdale Community College, Scottsdale, AZ 85250-2699
Scripps College, Claremont, CA 91711-3948
Seattle Central Community College, Seattle, WA 98122
Seattle Pacific University, Seattle, WA 98119-1997
Seattle University, Seattle, WA 98122-4460
Selma University, Selma, AL 36701
Seminole Community College, Sanford, FL 32773-6199
Seminole Junior College, Seminole, OK 74818-0351
Seton Hall University, South Orange, NJ 07079-2689
Seton Hill College, Greensburg, PA 15601-1599
Shasta College, Redding, CA 96049
Shaw University, Raleigh, NC 27601
Shawnee Community College, Ullin, IL 62992
Shawnee State University, Portsmouth, OH 45662
Shelby State Community College, Memphis, TN 38174-0568
Sheldon Jackson College, Sitka, AK 99835
Shelton State Community College, Tuscaloosa, AL 35405
Shenandoah University, Winchester, VA 22601-5195
Shepherd College, Shepherdstown, WV 25443-1569

Sheridan College, Sheridan, WY 82801-1500
Shimer College, Waukegan, IL 60079-0500
Shippensburg University of Pennsylvania, Shippensburg, PA 17257
Shor Yoshuv Rabbinical College, Far Rockaway, NY 11691
Shoreline Community College, Seattle, WA 98133
Shorter College, Rome, GA 30165-4298
Shorter College, North Little Rock, AR 72114
Siena College, Loudonville, NY 12211-1462
Siena Heights College, Adrian, MI 49221-1796
Sierra College, Rocklin, CA 95677
Sierra Nevada College, Incline Village, NV 89450-4269
Silver Lake College, Manitowoc, WI 54220-9391
Simmons College, Boston, MA 02115-5898
Simon's Rock College of Bard, Great Barrington, MA 01230
Simpson College, Redding, CA 96003-8606
Simpson College, Indianola, IA 50125-1299
Sinclair Community College, Dayton, OH 45402-1460
Sinte Gleska University, Rosebud, SD 57570
Sisseton-Wahpeton Community College, Sisseton, SD 57262-0689
Skagit Valley College, Mount Vernon, WA 98273
Skidmore College, Saratoga Springs, NY 12866-1632
Skyline College, San Bruno, CA 94066-1698
Slippery Rock University of Pennsylvania, Slippery Rock, PA 16057
Smith College, Northampton, MA 01063
Snead State Community College, Boaz, AL 35957
Snow College, Ephraim, UT 84627
Sojourner-Douglass College, Baltimore, MD 21205
Solano Community College, Suisun City, CA 94585
Somerset Community College, Somerset, KY 42501
Sonoma State University, Rohnert Park, CA 94928
South Arkansas Community College, El Dorado, AR 71731-7010
South Carolina State University, Orangeburg, SC 29117-0001
South College
　　Palm Beach Campus, West Palm Beach, FL 33409
　　Savannah, Savannah, GA 31406
South Dakota School of Mines and Technology, Rapid City, SD 57701-3995
South Dakota State University, Brookings, SD 57007-0649
South Florida Community College, Avon Park, FL 33825
South Georgia College, Douglas, GA 31533-5098
South Hills Business School, State College, PA 16801
South Mountain Community College, Phoenix, AZ 85040
South Plains College, Levelland, TX 79336
South Puget Sound Community College, Olympia, WA 98512-6218
South Seattle Community College, Seattle, WA 98106-1499
South Suburban College of Cook County, South Holland, IL 60473
Southeast Community College, Cumberland, KY 40823
Southeast Community College
　　Beatrice Campus, Beatrice, NE 68310
　　Lincoln Campus, Lincoln, NE 68520
　　Milford Campus, Milford, NE 68405
Southeast Missouri State University, Cape Girardeau, MO 63701
Southeast Technical Institute, Sioux Falls, SD 57107
Southeastern Baptist College, Laurel, MS 39440
Southeastern Baptist Theological Seminary, Wake Forest, NC 27587-1889
Southeastern Bible College, Birmingham, AL 35243-4181
Southeastern Business College, Chillicothe, OH 45601-1038
Southeastern Business College, Gallipolis, OH
Southeastern Business College, Lorain, OH 44055
Southeastern College of the Assemblies of God, Lakeland, FL 33801
Southeastern Community College, Whiteville, NC 28472
Southeastern Community College
　　North Campus, West Burlington, IA 52655-0605
　　South Campus, Keokuk, IA 52632-6007
Southeastern Illinois College, Harrisburg, IL 62946
Southeastern Louisiana University, Hammond, LA 70402-0752
Southeastern Oklahoma State University, Durant, OK 74701-0609
Southeastern University, Washington, DC 20024
Southern Arkansas University
　　Magnolia, Magnolia, AR 71753-5000
　　Tech, Camden, AR 71701
Southern California College, Costa Mesa, CA 92626-9601
Southern California Institute of Architecture, Los Angeles, CA 90066
Southern Christian University, Montgomery, AL 36117-3553
Southern College, Orlando, FL 32807
Southern College of Seventh-day Adventists, Collegedale, TN 37531
Southern College of Technology, Marietta, GA 30060-2896
Southern Connecticut State University, New Haven, CT 06515
Southern Illinois University
　　Carbondale, Carbondale, IL 62901-4710
　　Edwardsville, Edwardsville, IL 62026-1600
Southern Maine Technical College, South Portland, ME 04106
Southern Methodist University, Dallas, TX 75275-0296

Southern Nazarene University, Bethany, OK 73008-2694
Southern Ohio College, Cincinnati, OH 45237
Southern Oregon State College, Ashland, OR 97520-5032
Southern State Community College, Hillsboro, OH 45133
Southern Union State Community College, Wadley, AL 36276
Southern University
　　New Orleans, New Orleans, LA 70126
　　Shreveport, Shreveport, LA 71107
Southern University and Agricultural and Mechanical College, Baton Rouge, LA 70813
Southern Utah University, Cedar City, UT 84720
Southern Vermont College, Bennington, VT 05201
Southern Wesleyan University, Central, SC 29630-1020
Southern West Virginia Community and Technical College, Mount Gay, WV 25637
Southside Virginia Community College, Alberta, VA 23821
Southwest Baptist University, Bolivar, MO 65613-2496
Southwest Institute of Merchandising & Design, El Paso, TX 79925-6744
Southwest Mississippi Community College, Summit, MS 39666
Southwest Missouri State University, Springfield, MO 65804-0094
Southwest School of Electronics, Austin, TX 78735-8800
Southwest State University, Marshall, MN 56258-1598
Southwest Texas Junior College, Uvalde, TX 78801
Southwest Texas State University, San Marcos, TX 78666-5709
Southwest Virginia Community College, Richlands, VA 24641-1510
Southwest Wisconsin Technical College, Fennimore, WI 53809
Southwestern Adventist College, Keene, TX 76059
Southwestern Assemblies of God College, Waxahachie, TX 75165
Southwestern Christian College, Terrell, TX 75160
Southwestern College, Chula Vista, CA 91910
Southwestern College, Phoenix, AZ 85032-7042
Southwestern College, Winfield, KS 67156-1812
Southwestern College of Business, Dayton, OH 45402
Southwestern College of Christian Ministries, Bethany, OK 73008
Southwestern Community College, Sylva, NC 28779
Southwestern Community College, Creston, IA 50801
Southwestern Indian Polytechnic Institute, Albuquerque, NM 87184
Southwestern Oklahoma State University, Weatherford, OK 73096
Southwestern Oregon Community College, Coos Bay, OR 97420-2956
Southwestern University, Georgetown, TX 78626
Spalding University, Louisville, KY 40203
Sparks State Technical College, Eufaula, AL 36072-0580
Spartanburg Methodist College, Spartanburg, SC 29301
Spartanburg Technical College, Spartanburg, SC 29305
Spelman College, Atlanta, GA 30314-4399
Spencer School of Business, Grand Island, NE 68802
Spokane Community College, Spokane, WA 99207-5399
Spokane Falls Community College, Spokane, WA 99204-5288
Spoon River College, Canton, IL 61520
Spring Arbor College, Spring Arbor, MI 49283-9984
Spring Hill College, Mobile, AL 36608
Springfield College, Springfield, MA 01109
Springfield College in Illinois, Springfield, IL 62702-2694
Springfield Technical Community College, Springfield, MA 01105-1296
Standing Rock College, Fort Yates, ND 58538
Stanford University, Stanford, CA 94305
Stanly Community College, Albemarle, NC 28001
Stark Technical College, Canton, OH 44720
State Community College, East St. Louis, IL 62201
State Fair Community College, Sedalia, MO 65301-2199
State Technical Institute at Memphis, Memphis, TN 38134

State University of New York
  Albany, Albany, NY 12222
  Binghamton, Binghamton, NY 13902-6001
  Buffalo, Buffalo, NY 14260
  Oswego, Oswego, NY 13126-3599
  Purchase, Purchase, NY 10577-1400
  Stony Brook, Stony Brook, NY 11794-1901
  College of Agriculture and Technology at Cobleskill, Cobleskill, NY
    12043
  College of Agriculture and Technology at Morrisville, Morrisville, NY
    13408
  College at Brockport, Brockport, NY 14420-2915
  College at Buffalo, Buffalo, NY 14222-1095
  College at Cortland, Cortland, NY 13045
  College of Environmental Science and Forestry, Syracuse, NY 13210-
    2779
  College at Fredonia, Fredonia, NY 14063
  College at Geneseo, Geneseo, NY 14454-1471
  College at Old Westbury, Old Westbury, NY 11568-0307
  College at Oneonta, Oneonta, NY 13820-4016
  College at Plattsburgh, Plattsburgh, NY 12901
  College at Potsdam, Potsdam, NY 13676-2294
  College of Technology at Alfred, Alfred, NY 14802-1196
  College of Technology at Canton, Canton, NY 13617-1098
  College of Technology at Delhi, Delhi, NY 13753-1190
  College of Technology at Farmingdale, Farmingdale, NY 11735-1021
  Empire State College, Saratoga Springs, NY 12866-4390
  Health Science Center at Brooklyn, Brooklyn, NY 11203-2098
  Health Science Center at Syracuse, Syracuse, NY 13210
  Health Sciences Center at Stony Brook, Stony Brook, NY 11794-8276
  Institute of Technology at Utica/Rome, Utica, NY 13504-3050
  Maritime College, Throggs Neck, NY 10465-4198
  New Paltz, New Paltz, NY 12561-2499
Stautzenberger College, Toledo, OH 43614
Stenotype Academy, New York, NY 10038
Stephen F. Austin State University, Nacogdoches, TX 75962-3051
Stephens College, Columbia, MO 65215-9986
Sterling College, Craftsbury Common, VT 05827-0072
Sterling College, Sterling, KS 67579-9989
Stetson University, DeLand, FL 32720
Stevens Institute of Technology, Hoboken, NJ 07030-5991
Stevens-Henager College of Business, Provo, UT 84606-6157
Stillman College, Tuscaloosa, AL 35403
Stone Child College, Box Elder, MT 59521-9796
Stonehill College, North Easton, MA 02357-5610
Stratton College, Milwaukee, WI 53202-2608
Strayer College, Washington, DC 20005
Sue Bennett College, London, KY 40741
Suffolk County Community College
    Eastern Campus, Riverhead, NY 11901
    Selden, Selden, NY 11784
    Western Campus, Brentwood, NY 11717
Suffolk University, Boston, MA 02108-2772
Sul Ross State University, Alpine, TX 79832
Sullivan College, Louisville, KY 40232
Sullivan County Community College, Loch Sheldrake, NY 12759-4002
Suomi College, Hancock, MI 49930
Surry Community College, Dobson, NC 27017-0304
Susquehanna University, Selinsgrove, PA 17870-1040
Sussex County Community College, Newton, NJ 07860
Swarthmore College, Swarthmore, PA 19081-1397
Sweet Briar College, Sweet Briar, VA 24595
Syracuse University, Syracuse, NY 13244-1120
Tabor College, Hillsboro, KS 67063
Tacoma Community College, Tacoma, WA 98466-9971
Taft College, Taft, CA 93268
Talladega College, Talladega, AL 35160
Tallahassee Community College, Tallahassee, FL 32304-2895
Talmudic College of Florida, Miami Beach, FL 33139
Talmudical Academy of New Jersey, Adelphia, NJ 07710
Talmudical Institute of Upstate New York, Rochester, NY 14607
Talmudical Seminary Oholei Torah, Brooklyn, NY 11213-3397
Talmudical Yeshiva of Philadelphia, Philadelphia, PA 19131
Tampa College, Tampa, FL 33614
Tarleton State University, Stephenville, TX 76402
Tarrant County Junior College, Fort Worth, TX 76102-6599
Taylor Business Institute, New York, NY 10119-0118
Taylor University, Upland, IN 46989-1001
Technical Career Institutes, New York, NY 10001
Technical College of the Lowcountry, Beaufort, SC 29902-1288
Technical Trades Institute, Colorado Springs, CO 80909
Technological College of the Municipality of San Juan, Hato Rey, PR 00936

Teikyo Marycrest University, Davenport, IA 52804-4096
Teikyo-Post University, Waterbury, CT 06723-2540
Telshe Yeshiva-Chicago, Chicago, IL 60625
Temple College, Temple, TX 76504-7435
Temple University, Philadelphia, PA 19122-1803
Tennessee Institute of Electronics, Knoxville, TN 37918
Tennessee State University, Nashville, TN 37203
Tennessee Technological University, Cookeville, TN 38505
Tennessee Temple University, Chattanooga, TN 37404
Tennessee Wesleyan College, Athens, TN 37371-0040
Terra Community College, Fremont, OH 43420-9670
Texarkana College, Texarkana, TX 75599
Texas A&M International University, Laredo, TX 78041-1999
Texas A&M University
    College Station, College Station, TX 77843-0100
    Galveston, Galveston, TX 77553-1675
Texas A&M University-Corpus Christi, Corpus Christi, TX 78412
Texas A&M University-Kingsville, Kingsville, TX 78363-8201
Texas Christian University, Fort Worth, TX 76129
Texas College, Tyler, TX 75712-2404
Texas Lutheran College, Seguin, TX 78155
Texas Southern University, Houston, TX 77004
Texas Southmost College, Brownsville, TX 78520
Texas State Technical College
    Amarillo, Amarillo, TX 79111
    Harlingen, Harlingen, TX 78550-3697
    Sweetwater, Sweetwater, TX 79556
    Waco, Waco, TX 76705
Texas Tech University, Lubbock, TX 79409-5005
Texas Wesleyan University, Fort Worth, TX 76105-1536
Texas Woman's University, Denton, TX 76204-5679
Thaddeus Stevens State School of Technology, Lancaster, PA 17602
Thiel College, Greenville, PA 16125
Thomas Aquinas College, Santa Paula, CA 93060
Thomas College, Waterville, ME 04901-9986
Thomas College, Thomasville, GA 31792-7499
Thomas Jefferson University: College of Allied Health Sciences,
    Philadelphia, PA 19107
Thomas More College, Crestview Hills, KY 41017
Thomas More College of Liberal Arts, Merrimack, NH 03054
Thomas Nelson Community College, Hampton, VA 23670-0407
Three Rivers Community College, Poplar Bluff, MO 63901-1308
Three Rivers Community-Technical College, Norwich, CT 06360-2479
Tidewater Community College, Portsmouth, VA 23703
Tiffin University, Tiffin, OH 44883
Toccoa Falls College, Toccoa Falls, GA 30598-0368
Tompkins-Cortland Community College, Dryden, NY 13053-0139
Torah Teminah Talmudical Seminary, Brooklyn, NY 11218
Tougaloo College, Tougaloo, MS 39174
Towson State University, Towson, MD 21204-7097
Transylvania University, Lexington, KY 40508-1797
Treasure Valley Community College, Ontario, OR 97914
Trenton State College, Trenton, NJ 08650-4700
Trevecca Nazarene University, Nashville, TN 37210
Triangle Tech: Pittsburgh Campus, Pittsburgh, PA 15214-3897
Tri-County Community College, Murphy, NC 28906
Tri-County Technical College, Pendleton, SC 29670
Trident Technical College, Charleston, SC 29423-8067
Trinidad State Junior College, Trinidad, CO 81082
Trinity Bible College, Ellendale, ND 58436-7150
Trinity Christian College, Palos Heights, IL 60463
Trinity College, Hartford, CT 06106
Trinity College, Washington, DC 20017-1094
Trinity College of Vermont, Burlington, VT 05401
Trinity International University, Deerfield, IL 60015
Trinity International University, Miami, FL 33101-9674
Trinity University, San Antonio, TX 78212-7200
Trinity Valley Community College, Athens, TX 75751
Tri-State University, Angola, IN 46703-1764
Triton College, River Grove, IL 60171-1995
Trocaire College, Buffalo, NY 14220
Troy State University
    Dothan, Dothan, AL 36304-0368
    Montgomery, Montgomery, AL 36103-4419
    Troy, Troy, AL 36082
Truckee Meadows Community College, Reno, NV 89512
Truett-McConnell College, Cleveland, GA 30528
Truman State University, Kirksville, MO 63501-9980
Tufts University, Medford, MA 02155-5555
Tulane University, New Orleans, LA 70118-5680
Tulsa Junior College, Tulsa, OK 74135-6198
Tunxis Community-Technical College, Farmington, CT 06032-3187

Turabo University, Gurabo, PR 00778
Turtle Mountain Community College, Belcourt, ND 58316-0340
Tusculum College, Greeneville, TN 37743
Tuskegee University, Tuskegee, AL 36088
Tyler Junior College, Tyler, TX 75711-9020
Ulster County Community College, Stone Ridge, NY 12484
Umpqua Community College, Roseburg, OR 97470
Union College, Barbourville, KY 40906
Union College, Schenectady, NY 12308-2311
Union College, Lincoln, NE 68506-4300
Union County College, Cranford, NJ 07016-1599
Union Institute, Cincinnati, OH 45206-1947
Union University, Jackson, TN 38305-3697
United States International University, San Diego, CA 92131-1799
United States Merchant Marine Academy, Kings Point, NY 11024-1699
United Tribes Technical College, Bismarck, ND 58504
Unity College, Unity, ME 04988-0532
Universidad Adventista de las Antillas, Mayaguez, PR 00681
Universidad Metropolitana, Rio Piedras, PR 00928
Universidad Politecnica de Puerto Rico, Hato Rey, PR 00918
University of Akron
    Akron, Akron, OH 44325-2001
    Wayne College, Orrville, OH 44667
University of Alabama
    Birmingham, Birmingham, AL 35294-1150
    Huntsville, Huntsville, AL 35899
    Tuscaloosa, Tuscaloosa, AL 35487-0132
University of Alabama at Birmingham: Walker College, Jasper, AL 35501
University of Alaska
    Anchorage, Anchorage, AK 99508-8046
    Fairbanks, Fairbanks, AK 99775
    Southeast, Juneau, AK 99801
University of Arizona, Tucson, AZ 85721-0040
University of Arkansas
    Fayetteville, Fayetteville, AR 72701
    Little Rock, Little Rock, AR 72204
    Medical Sciences, Little Rock, AR 72205-7199
    Monticello, Monticello, AR 71655
    Pine Bluff, Pine Bluff, AR 71601-2799
University of the Arts, Philadelphia, PA 19102
University of Baltimore, Baltimore, MD 21201-5779
University of Bridgeport, Bridgeport, CT 06601
University of California
    Berkeley, Berkeley, CA 94720-5800
    Davis, Davis, CA 95616
    Irvine, Irvine, CA 92717
    Los Angeles, Los Angeles, CA 90024
    Riverside, Riverside, CA 92521
    San Diego, La Jolla, CA 92093-0021
    San Francisco, San Francisco, CA 94143-0404
    Santa Barbara, Santa Barbara, CA 93106
    Santa Cruz, Santa Cruz, CA 95064
University of Central Arkansas, Conway, AR 72035-0001
University of Central Florida, Orlando, FL 32816
University of Central Oklahoma, Edmond, OK 73034-0151
University of Central Texas, Killeen, TX 76540-1416
University of Charleston, Charleston, WV 25304-1099
University of Chicago, Chicago, IL 60637
University of Cincinnati
    Access Colleges, Cincinnati, OH 45221-0091
    Cincinnati, Cincinnati, OH 45221-0091
    Clermont College, Batavia, OH 45103-0162
    Raymond Walters College, Cincinnati, OH 45236
University of Colorado
    Boulder, Boulder, CO 80309-0030
    Colorado Springs, Colorado Springs, CO 80933-7150
    Denver, Denver, CO 80217-3364
    Health Sciences Center, Denver, CO 80262
University of Connecticut, Storrs, CT 06269-3088
University of Dallas, Irving, TX 75062-4799
University of Dayton, Dayton, OH 45469-1611
University of Delaware, Newark, DE 19716-6210
University of Denver, Denver, CO 80208-0132
University of Detroit Mercy, Detroit, MI 48219-0900
University of the District of Columbia, Washington, DC 20008
University of Dubuque, Dubuque, IA 52001-5050
University of Evansville, Evansville, IN 47722
University of Findlay, Findlay, OH 45840-3695
University of Florida, Gainesville, FL 32611-4000
University of Georgia, Athens, GA 30602
University of Great Falls, Great Falls, MT 59405
University of Hartford, West Hartford, CT 06117-0395

University of Hawaii
    Hawaii Community College, Hilo, HI 96720-4091
    Hilo, Hilo, HI 96720-4091
    Honolulu Community College, Honolulu, HI 96817
    Kapiolani Community College, Honolulu, HI 96816-4421
    Kauai Community College, Lihue, HI 96766
    Leeward Community College, Pearl City, HI 96782
    Manoa, Honolulu, HI 96822-9978
    Maui Community College, Kahului, HI 96732
    West Oahu, Pearl City, HI 96782
    Windward Community College, Kaneohe, HI 96817
University of Houston
    Clear Lake, Houston, TX 77058-1080
    Downtown, Houston, TX 77002
    Houston, Houston, TX 77204-2161
    Victoria, Victoria, TX 77901-4450
University of Idaho, Moscow, ID 83844-3133
University of Illinois
    Chicago, Chicago, IL 60680
    Springfield, Springfield, IL 62794-9243
    Urbana-Champaign, Urbana, IL 61801
University of Indianapolis, Indianapolis, IN 46227-3697
University of Iowa, Iowa City, IA 52242-1396
University of Judaism, Los Angeles, CA 90077
University of Kansas
    Lawrence, Lawrence, KS 66045
    Medical Center, Kansas City, KS 66160
University of Kentucky, Lexington, KY 40506-0054
University of La Verne, La Verne, CA 91750-4443
University of Louisville, Louisville, KY 40292-0001
University of Maine
    Augusta, Augusta, ME 04330-9410
    Farmington, Farmington, ME 04938-1994
    Fort Kent, Fort Kent, ME 04743-1292
    Machias, Machias, ME 04654
    Orono, Orono, ME 04469-5713
    Presque Isle, Presque Isle, ME 04769-2888
University of Mary, Bismarck, ND 58504-9652
University of Mary Hardin-Baylor, Belton, TX 76513
University of Maryland
    Baltimore, Baltimore, MD 21201
    Baltimore County, Baltimore, MD 21228-5398
    College Park, College Park, MD 20742-5235
    Eastern Shore, Princess Anne, MD 21853-1299
    University College, College Park, MD 20742-1672
University of Massachusetts
    Amherst, Amherst, MA 01003
    Boston, Boston, MA 02125-3393
    Dartmouth, North Dartmouth, MA 02747-2300
    Lowell, Lowell, MA 01854
University of Medicine and Dentistry of New Jersey: School of Nursing, Newark, NJ 07107-3006
University of Memphis, Memphis, TN 38152
University of Miami, Coral Gables, FL 33124
University of Michigan
    Ann Arbor, Ann Arbor, MI 48109-1316
    Dearborn, Dearborn, MI 48128-1491
    Flint, Flint, MI 48502-2186
University of Minnesota
    Crookston, Crookston, MN 56716
    Duluth, Duluth, MN 55812-2496
    Morris, Morris, MN 56267-2199
    Twin Cities, Minneapolis-St. Paul, MN 55455-0213
University of Mississippi
    Medical Center, Jackson, MS 39216
    University, University, MS 38677
University of Missouri
    Columbia, Columbia, MO 65211
    Kansas City, Kansas City, MO 64110-2499
    Rolla, Rolla, MO 65401
    St. Louis, St. Louis, MO 63121
University of Mobile, Mobile, AL 36663-0220
University of Montana-Missoula, Missoula, MT 59812
University of Montana College of Technology, Missoula, MT 59801
University of Montevallo, Montevallo, AL 35115-6030
University of Nebraska
    Medical Center, Omaha, NE 68198-4230
    Kearney, Kearney, NE 68849
    Lincoln, Lincoln, NE 68588-0417
    Omaha, Omaha, NE 68182-0005

University of Nevada
  Las Vegas, Las Vegas, NV 89154-1021
  Reno, Reno, NV 89557-0002
University of New England, Biddeford, ME 04005
University of New Hampshire
  Durham, Durham, NH 03824
  Manchester, Manchester, NH 03102
University of New Haven, West Haven, CT 06516
University of New Mexico, Albuquerque, NM 87131-2006
University of New Orleans, New Orleans, LA 70148
University of North Alabama, Florence, AL 35632-0001
University of North Carolina
  Asheville, Asheville, NC 28804-3299
  Chapel Hill, Chapel Hill, NC 27599-2200
  Charlotte, Charlotte, NC 28223-0001
  Greensboro, Greensboro, NC 27412-5001
  Wilmington, Wilmington, NC 28403-3297
University of North Dakota
  Grand Forks, Grand Forks, ND 58202-8357
  Lake Region, Devils Lake, ND 58301-1598
  Williston, Williston, ND 58802-1326
University of North Florida, Jacksonville, FL 32224-2645
University of North Texas, Denton, TX 76203-6797
University of Northern Colorado, Greeley, CO 80639
University of Northern Iowa, Cedar Falls, IA 50614-0018
University of Notre Dame, Notre Dame, IN 46556-5602
University of Oklahoma
  Health Sciences Center, Oklahoma City, OK 73190
  Norman, Norman, OK 73069-0520
University of Oregon
  Eugene, Eugene, OR 97403-1217
  Robert Donald Clark Honors College, Eugene, OR 97403-1293
University of Osteopathic Medicine and Health Sciences, Des Moines, IA 50312
University of the Ozarks, Clarksville, AR 72830
University of the Pacific, Stockton, CA 95211-0197
University of Pennsylvania, Philadelphia, PA 19104-6376
University of Phoenix, Phoenix, AZ 85072-2069
University of Pittsburgh
  Bradford, Bradford, PA 16701-2898
  Greensburg, Greensburg, PA 15601-5898
  Johnstown, Johnstown, PA 15904
  Pittsburgh, Pittsburgh, PA 15260
  Titusville, Titusville, PA 16354-9990
University of Portland, Portland, OR 97203-5798
University of Puerto Rico
  Aguadilla, Aguadilla, PR 00604-0160
  Arecibo Campus, Arecibo, PR 00613
  Bayamon Technological University College, Bayamon, PR 00959-1919
  Carolina Regional College, Carolina, PR 00984-4800
  Cayey University College, Cayey, PR 00633
  Humacao University College, Humacao, PR 00791
  La Montana Regional College, Utuado, PR 00641-2500
  Mayaguez Campus, Mayaguez, PR 00681-5000
  Medical Sciences Campus, Rio Piedras, PR 00936-5067
  Ponce Technological University College, Ponce, PR 00732
  Rio Piedras Campus, Rio Piedras, PR 00931-1907
University of Puget Sound, Tacoma, WA 98416-0003
University of Redlands, Redlands, CA 92373-0999
University of Rhode Island, Kingston, RI 02881-0806
University of Richmond, Richmond, VA 23173
University of Rio Grande, Rio Grande, OH 45674
University of Rochester, Rochester, NY 14627-0251
University of the Sacred Heart, Santurce, PR 00914
University of St. Thomas, St. Paul, MN 55105-1096
University of St. Thomas, Houston, TX 77006-4696
University of San Diego, San Diego, CA 92110
University of San Francisco, San Francisco, CA 94117-1080
University of Science and Arts of Oklahoma, Chickasha, OK 73018
University of Scranton, Scranton, PA 18510-4699
University of Sioux Falls, Sioux Falls, SD 57105-1699
University of the South, Sewanee, TN 37383-1000
University of South Alabama, Mobile, AL 36688
University of South Carolina
  Aiken, Aiken, SC 29801
  Beaufort, Beaufort, SC 29902
  Columbia, Columbia, SC 29208
  Lancaster, Lancaster, SC 29721
  Salkehatchie Regional Campus, Allendale, SC 29810
  Spartanburg, Spartanburg, SC 29303
  Sumter, Sumter, SC 29150-2498
  Union, Union, SC 29379

University of South Dakota, Vermillion, SD 57069-2390
University of South Florida, Tampa, FL 33620-6900
University of Southern California, Los Angeles, CA 90089-0911
University of Southern Colorado, Pueblo, CO 81001-4901
University of Southern Indiana, Evansville, IN 47712
University of Southern Maine, Gorham, ME 04038
University of Southern Mississippi, Hattiesburg, MS 39406-5166
University of Southwestern Louisiana, Lafayette, LA 70504
University of the State of New York: Regents College, Albany, NY 12203-5159
University of Tampa, Tampa, FL 33606-1490
University of Tennessee
  Chattanooga, Chattanooga, TN 37403
  Knoxville, Knoxville, TN 37996-0230
  Martin, Martin, TN 38238
  Memphis, Memphis, TN 38163
University of Texas
  Arlington, Arlington, TX 76019-0088
  Austin, Austin, TX 78712-1157
  Brownsville, Brownsville, TX 78520
  Dallas, Richardson, TX 75083-0688
  El Paso, El Paso, TX 79968
  Health Science Center at San Antonio, San Antonio, TX 78284-7702
  Medical Branch at Galveston, Galveston, TX 77555-1305
  Pan American, Edinburg, TX 78539
  Permian Basin, Odessa, TX 79762
  San Antonio, San Antonio, TX 78249-0617
  Southwestern Medical Center at Dallas, Dallas, TX 75235-9096
  Tyler, Tyler, TX 75701-6699
  Houston Health Science Center, Houston, TX 77225
University of Texas Health Science Center at Houston, Houston, TX 77225
University of Toledo, Toledo, OH 43606-3398
University of Tulsa, Tulsa, OK 74104-3189
University of Utah, Salt Lake City, UT 84112
University of Vermont, Burlington, VT 05401-3596
University of Virginia, Charlottesville, VA 22906
University of Washington, Seattle, WA 98195-5840
University of West Alabama, Livingston, AL 35470
University of West Florida, Pensacola, FL 32514-5750
University of West Los Angeles, Inglewood, CA 90301
University of Wisconsin
  Eau Claire, Eau Claire, WI 54701
  Green Bay, Green Bay, WI 54311-7001
  La Crosse, La Crosse, WI 54601
  Madison, Madison, WI 53706-1490
  Milwaukee, Milwaukee, WI 53201
  Oshkosh, Oshkosh, WI 54901-8602
  Parkside, Kenosha, WI 53141-2000
  Platteville, Platteville, WI 53818
  River Falls, River Falls, WI 54022-5001
  Stevens Point, Stevens Point, WI 54481
  Stout, Menomonie, WI 54751
  Superior, Superior, WI 54880
  Whitewater, Whitewater, WI 53190-1791
University of Wisconsin Center
  Baraboo/Sauk County, Baraboo, WI 53913-1098
  Barron County, Rice Lake, WI 54868
  Fond du Lac, Fond du Lac, WI 54935-2998
  Fox Valley, Menasha, WI 54952-8002
  Manitowoc County, Manitowoc, WI 54220-6699
  Marathon County, Wausau, WI 54401-5396
  Marinette County, Marinette, WI 54143
  Marshfield/Wood County, Marshfield, WI 54449
  Richland, Richland Center, WI 53581
  Rock County, Janesville, WI 53546-5699
  Sheboygan County, Sheboygan, WI 53081-4789
  Washington County, West Bend, WI 53095
  Waukesha, Waukesha, WI 53188-2799
University of Wyoming, Laramie, WY 82071-3435
Upper Iowa University, Fayette, IA 52142-1859
Urbana University, Urbana, OH 43078-2091
Ursinus College, Collegeville, PA 19426-1000
Ursuline College, Pepper Pike, OH 44124-4398
Utah State University, Logan, UT 84322-1600
Utah Valley State College, Orem, UT 84058
Utica College of Syracuse University, Utica, NY 13502-4892
Utica School of Commerce, Utica, NY 13501
Valdosta State University, Valdosta, GA 31698
Valencia Community College, Orlando, FL 32802-3028
Valley City State University, Valley City, ND 58072-4098
Valley Forge Christian College, Phoenixville, PA 19460-2399
Valley Forge Military College, Wayne, PA 19087-3695

Valparaiso University, Valparaiso, IN 46383-6493
Vance-Granville Community College, Henderson, NC 27536
Vanderbilt University, Nashville, TN 37203-1700
VanderCook College of Music, Chicago, IL 60616-3886
Vassar College, Poughkeepsie, NY 12601
Vennard College, University Park, IA 52595
Ventura College, Ventura, CA 93003
Vermilion Community College, Ely, MN 55731-9989
Vermont Technical College, Randolph Center, VT 05061-0500
Vernon Regional Junior College, Vernon, TX 76384-4092
Victor Valley College, Victorville, CA 92392-9699
Victoria College, Victoria, TX 77901
Villa Julie College, Stevenson, MD 21153-9999
Villa Maria College of Buffalo, Buffalo, NY 14225-3999
Villanova University, Villanova, PA 19085-1672
Vincennes University, Vincennes, IN 47591
Virginia College, Birmingham, AL 35234
Virginia Commonwealth University, Richmond, VA 23284-2526
Virginia Highlands Community College, Abingdon, VA 24210-0828
Virginia Intermont College, Bristol, VA 24201-4298
Virginia Marti College of Fashion and Art, Lakewood, OH 44107
Virginia Military Institute, Lexington, VA 24450-9967
Virginia Polytechnic Institute and State University, Blacksburg, VA 24061-0202
Virginia State University, Petersburg, VA 23806-9018
Virginia Union University, Richmond, VA 23220
Virginia Wesleyan College, Norfolk, VA 23502-5599
Virginia Western Community College, Roanoke, VA 24038
Vista Community College, Berkeley, CA 94704
Viterbo College, La Crosse, WI 54601
Volunteer State Community College, Gallatin, TN 37066
Voorhees College, Denmark, SC 29042
Wabash College, Crawfordsville, IN 47933-0352
Wadhams Hall Seminary-College, Ogdensburg, NY 13669-9308
Wagner College, Staten Island, NY 10301-4495
Wake Forest University, Winston-Salem, NC 27109
Wake Technical Community College, Raleigh, NC 27603
Waldorf College, Forest City, IA 50436
Walla Walla College, College Place, WA 99324-1198
Walla Walla Community College, Walla Walla, WA 99362-9267
Wallace State College at Hanceville, Hanceville, AL 35077-2000
Walsh College of Accountancy and Business Administration, Troy, MI 48007-7006
Walsh University, North Canton, OH 44720-3396
Walters State Community College, Morristown, TN 37813-6899
Warner Pacific College, Portland, OR 97215-4026
Warner Southern College, Lake Wales, FL 33853-8725
Warren County Community College, Washington, NJ 07882-9605
Warren Wilson College, Ashville, NC 28815-9000
Wartburg College, Waverly, IA 50677
Washburn University of Topeka, Topeka, KS 66621
Washington Bible College, Lanham, MD 20706-3599
Washington College, Chestertown, MD 21620-1197
Washington and Jefferson College, Washington, PA 15301
Washington and Lee University, Lexington, VA 24450
Washington State Community College, Marietta, OH 45750
Washington State University, Pullman, WA 99164-1036
Washington University, St. Louis, MO 63130-4899
Washtenaw Community College, Ann Arbor, MI 48106-1610
Waubonsee Community College, Sugar Grove, IL 60554-9799
Waukesha County Technical College, Pewaukee, WI 53072
Waycross College, Waycross, GA 31503
Wayland Baptist University, Plainview, TX 79072-6998
Wayne Community College, Goldsboro, NC 27533-8002
Wayne County Community College, Detroit, MI 48226
Wayne State College, Wayne, NE 68787
Wayne State University, Detroit, MI 48202
Waynesburg College, Waynesburg, PA 15370
Weatherford College, Weatherford, TX 76086
Webber College, Babson Park, FL 33827-0096
Weber State University, Ogden, UT 84408-1015
Webster University, Webster Groves, MO 63119-3194
Welder Training and Testing Institute, Allentown, PA 18103-1263
Wellesley College, Wellesley, MA 02181-8292
Wells College, Aurora, NY 13026
Wenatchee Valley College, Wenatchee, WA 98801
Wentworth Institute of Technology, Boston, MA 02115-5998
Wentworth Military Academy, Lexington, MO 64067-1799
Wesley College, Florence, MS 39073-0070
Wesley College, Dover, DE 19901-3875
Wesleyan College, Macon, GA 31297-4299
Wesleyan University, Middletown, CT 06459

West Chester University of Pennsylvania, West Chester, PA 19383
West Coast University, Los Angeles, CA 90020-1765
West Georgia College, Carrollton, GA 30118-0001
West Hills Community College, Coalinga, CA 93210
West Liberty State College, West Liberty, WV 26074
West Los Angeles College, Culver City, CA 90230
West Shore Community College, Scottville, MI 49454-0277
West Side Institute of Technology, Cleveland, OH 44102
West Suburban College of Nursing, Oak Park, IL 60302
West Texas A&M University, Canyon, TX 79016
West Valley College, Saratoga, CA 95070-5698
West Virginia Business College, Nutter Fort, WV 26301
West Virginia Institute of Technology, Montgomery, WV 25136-2436
West Virginia Northern Community College, Wheeling, WV 26003
West Virginia State College, Institute, WV 25112-1000
West Virginia University
    Morgantown, Morgantown, WV 26506-6009
    Parkersburg, Parkersburg, WV 26101-9577
West Virginia Wesleyan College, Buckhannon, WV 26201-2998
Westark Community College, Fort Smith, AR 72913-3649
Westbrook College, Portland, ME 04103
Westchester Business Institute, White Plains, NY 10602
Westchester Community College, Valhalla, NY 10595-1698
Western Baptist College, Salem, OR 97301-9392
Western Carolina University, Cullowhee, NC 28723
Western Connecticut State University, Danbury, CT 06810
Western Dakota Technical Institute, Rapid City, SD 57701
Western Illinois University, Macomb, IL 61455-1390
Western International University, Phoenix, AZ 85021
Western Iowa Tech Community College, Sioux City, IA 51102-5199
Western Kentucky University, Bowling Green, KY 42101
Western Maryland College, Westminster, MD 21157-4390
Western Michigan University, Kalamazoo, MI 49008-5120
Western Montana College of the University of Montana, Dillon, MT 59725-3598
Western Nebraska Community College, Scottsbluff, NE 69361
Western Nevada Community College, Carson City, NV 89703
Western New England College, Springfield, MA 01119-2688
Western New Mexico University, Silver City, NM 88062
Western Oklahoma State College, Altus, OK 73521
Western Oregon State College, Monmouth, OR 97361-1394
Western Piedmont Community College, Morganton, NC 28655-9978
Western State College of Colorado, Gunnison, CO 81231
Western Texas College, Snyder, TX 79549
Western Washington University, Bellingham, WA 98225-9009
Western Wisconsin Technical College, La Crosse, WI 54602-0908
Western Wyoming Community College, Rock Springs, WY 82901
Westfield State College, Westfield, MA 01086
Westmar University, Le Mars, IA 51031
Westminster Choir College of Rider University, Princeton, NJ 08540-3899
Westminster College, New Wilmington, PA 16172-0001
Westminster College, Fulton, MO 65251-1299
Westminster College of Salt Lake City, Salt Lake City, UT 84105-3697
Westmont College, Santa Barbara, CA 93108-1099
Westmoreland County Community College, Youngwood, PA 15697
Wharton County Junior College, Wharton, TX 77488-0080
Whatcom Community College, Bellingham, WA 98226
Wheaton College, Wheaton, IL 60187-5593
Wheaton College, Norton, MA 02766
Wheeling Jesuit College, Wheeling, WV 26003-6295
Wheelock College, Boston, MA 02215-4176
White Pines College, Chester, NH 03036-4331
Whitman College, Walla Walla, WA 99362-2085
Whittier College, Whittier, CA 90608-0634
Whitworth College, Spokane, WA 99251-0002
Wichita State University, Wichita, KS 67260-0124
Widener University, Chester, PA 19013
Wilberforce University, Wilberforce, OH 45384-1091
Wiley College, Marshall, TX 75670
Wilkes Community College, Wilkesboro, NC 28697-0120
Wilkes University, Wilkes-Barre, PA 18766-0001
Willamette University, Salem, OR 97301-3922
William Carey College, Hattiesburg, MS 39401-5499
William Jewell College, Liberty, MO 64068
William Paterson College of New Jersey, Wayne, NJ 07470
William Penn College, Oskaloosa, IA 52577
William Rainey Harper College, Palatine, IL 60067-7398
William Tyndale College, Farmington Hills, MI 48331-9985
William Woods University, Fulton, MO 65251-1098
Williams Baptist College, Walnut Ridge, AR 72476
Williams College, Williamstown, MA 01267
Williamsburg Technical College, Kingstree, SC 29556-4197

Williamson Free School of Mechanical Trades, Media, PA 19063-5299
Willmar Community College, Willmar, MN 56201
Willmar Technical College, Willmar, MN 56201-1097
Wilmington College, Wilmington, OH 45177
Wilmington College, New Castle, DE 19720
Wilson College, Chambersburg, PA 17201-1285
Wilson Technical Community College, Wilson, NC 27893
Wingate University, Wingate, NC 28174-0157
Winona State University, Winona, MN 55987
Winston-Salem State University, Winston-Salem, NC 27110
Winthrop University, Rock Hill, SC 29733
Wisconsin Indianhead Technical College, Shell Lake, WI 54871
Wisconsin Lutheran College, Milwaukee, WI 53226-4699
Wittenberg University, Springfield, OH 45501-0720
Wofford College, Spartanburg, SC 29303-3663
Wood College, Mathiston, MS 39752
Wood Tobe-Coburn School, New York, NY 10016-0190
Woodbury University, Burbank, CA 91510-7846
Worcester Polytechnic Institute, Worcester, MA 01609-2280
Worcester State College, Worcester, MA 01602-2597
Worthington Community College, Worthington, MN 56187
Wor-Wic Community College, Salisbury, MD 21804
Wright State University
    Dayton, Dayton, OH 45435
    Lake Campus, Celina, OH 45822
Wytheville Community College, Wytheville, VA 24382
Xavier University, Cincinnati, OH 45207-5311
Xavier University of Louisiana, New Orleans, LA 70125-1098
Yakima Valley Community College, Yakima, WA 98907
Yale University, New Haven, CT 06520-8234
Yavapai College, Prescott, AZ 86301
Yeshiva Beth Yehuda-Yeshiva Gedolah of Greater Detroit, Oak Park, MI 48237
Yeshiva Derech Chaim, Brooklyn, NY 11218
Yeshiva Gedolah Zichron Moshe, South Fallsburg, NY 12779
Yeshiva Ohr Elchonon Chabad/West Coast Talmudical Seminary, Los Angeles, CA 90046
Yeshiva Shaar Hatorah, Kew Gardens, NY 11418
Yeshiva Toras Chaim Talmudical Seminary, Denver, CO 80204
Yeshiva University, New York, NY 10033-3299
Yeshivath Beth Moshe, Scranton, PA 18505
York College, York, NE 68467-2699
York College of Pennsylvania, York, PA 17405-7199
York Technical College, Rock Hill, SC 29730
Yorktowne Business Institute, York, PA 17404
Young Harris College, Young Harris, GA 30582-0116
Youngstown State University, Youngstown, OH 44555-0001
Yuba College, Marysville, CA 95901

CSS/FINANCIAL AID PROFILE™

123-45-6789
SUSAN T POWELL

This 1996-97 form is similar to the form that will be available for 1997-98

— **1996-97**   06100614   **Application 0**

> Complete all sections of this PROFILE Application except Questions 1, 2, 24, and 25. Be certain that everyone giving information on the application signs it.

Section A — Student's Information

1. How many family members will the student (and spouse) support in 1996-97? Always include the student and spouse. List their names and give information about them in Section M. See instructions.

2. Of the number in 1, how many will be in college at least half-time for at least one term in 1996-97? Include yourself.

3. What is the student's state of legal residence?

4. What is the student's citizenship status?

a.
1 ☐ U.S. citizen (Skip to Question 5.)
2 ☐ Permanent resident (Skip to Question 5.)
3 ☐ Neither of the above (Answer "b" and "c" below.)

b. Country of citizenship?

c. Visa classification?
1 ☐ F1   2 ☐ F2   3 ☐ J1   4 ☐ J2   5 ☐ G   6 ☐ Other

Section B — Student's 1995 Income & Benefits

If married, include spouse's information in Sections B, C, D, and E.

5. The following 1995 U.S. income tax return figures are (Mark only one box.)

1 ☐ estimated. Will file IRS Form 1040EZ or 1040A. Go to 6.
2 ☐ estimated. Will file IRS Form 1040. Go to 6.
3 ☐ from a completed IRS Form 1040EZ or 1040A. Go to 6.
4 ☐ from a completed IRS Form 1040. Go to 6.
5 ☐ a tax return will not be filed. Skip to 10.

6. 1995 total number of exemptions (IRS Form 1040, line 6e or 1040A, line 6e or 1040EZ — see instructions)

7. 1995 Adjusted Gross Income from IRS Form 1040, line 31 or 1040A, line 16 or 1040EZ, line 4 (Use the worksheet in the instructions.) $ _____.00

8. 1995 U.S. income tax paid (IRS Form 1040, line 46 or 1040A, line 25 or 1040EZ, line 10) $ _____.00

9. 1995 itemized deductions (IRS Form 1040, Schedule A, line 28. Write in "0" if deductions were not itemized.) $ _____.00

10. 1995 income earned from work by student (See instructions.) $ _____.00

11. 1995 income earned from work by student's spouse $ _____.00

12. 1995 dividend and interest income $ _____.00

13. 1995 untaxed income and benefits (Give total amount for year.)

a. Social security benefits (See instructions.) $ _____.00

b. Aid to Families with Dependent Children $ _____.00

c. Child support received for all children $ _____.00

d. Earned Income Credit (IRS Form 1040, line 57 or 1040A, line 29c or 1040EZ, line 8) $ _____.00

e. Other - write total from worksheet, page 4. $ _____.00

14. 1995 earnings from Federal Work-Study or other need-based work programs plus any grant and scholarship aid required to be reported on your U.S. income tax return $ _____.00

Section C — Student's Assets

15. Cash, savings, and checking accounts $ _____.00

16. Total value of IRA, Keogh, 401k, 403b, etc. accounts as of December 31, 1995 $ _____.00

	What is it worth today?	What is owed on it?
17. Investments (Including Uniform Gifts to Minors. See instructions.)	$ ____.00	$ ____.00
18. Home (Renters write in "0.")	$ ____.00	$ ____.00
19. Other real estate	$ ____.00	$ ____.00
20. Business and farm	$ ____.00	$ ____.00

21. If a farm is included in 20, is the student living on the farm?   Yes ☐1   No ☐2

22. If student owns home, give

a. year purchased   1 9 __ __

b. purchase price $ _____.00

Section D — Student's Trust Information

23. a. Total value of all trust(s) $ _____.00

b. Is any income or part of the principal currently available?   Yes ☐1   No ☐2

c. Who established the trust(s)?
1 ☐ Student's parents   2 ☐ Other

Section E — Student's 1995 Expenses

24. 1995 child support paid by student $ _____.00

25. 1995 medical and dental expenses not covered by insurance (See instructions.) $ _____.00

SAMPLE

Section F — Student's Expected Summer/School-Year Resources for 1996-97

	Amount per month	Number of months
26. Student's veterans benefits (July 1, 1996 — June 30, 1997)	$_____.00	☐☐

27. Student's (and spouse's) resources
(Don't enter monthly amounts.)

	Summer 1996 (3 months)	School Year 1996-97 (9 months)
a. Student's wages, salaries, tips, etc.	$_____.00	$_____.00
b. Spouse's wages, salaries, tips, etc.	$_____.00	$_____.00
c. Other taxable income	$_____.00	$_____.00
d. Untaxed income and benefits	$_____.00	$_____.00
e. Grants, scholarships, fellowships, etc. from other than the colleges or universities to which the student is applying (List sources in Section P.)		$_____.00
f. Tuition benefits from the parents' and/or the student's or spouse's employer		$_____.00
g. Contributions from the student's parent(s)		$_____.00
h. Contributions from other relatives, spouse's parents, and all other sources		$_____.00

Section G — Parents' Household Information — See page 5 of the instruction booklet.

28. How many family members will your parents support in 1996-97? Always include the student and parents.
List their names and give information about them in Section M. ☐☐

29. Of the number in 28, how many will be in college at least half-time for at least one term in 1996-97? Include the student. ☐

30. How many parents will be in college at least half-time in 1996-97? (Mark only one box.)
1 ☐ Neither parent   2 ☐ One parent   3 ☐ Both parents

31. What is the current marital status of your parents? (Mark only one box.)
1 ☐ single   3 ☐ separated   5 ☐ widowed
2 ☐ married   4 ☐ divorced

32. What is your parents' state of legal residence? ☐☐

Section H — Parents' Expenses

	1995	Expected 1996
33. Child support paid by the parent(s) completing this form	$_____.00	$_____.00
34. Repayment of parents' educational loans (See instructions.)	$_____.00	$_____.00
35. Medical and dental expenses not covered by insurance (See instructions.)	$_____.00	$_____.00
36. Total elementary, junior high school, and high school tuition paid for dependent children		
a. Amount paid (Don't include tuition paid for the student.)	$_____.00	$_____.00
b. For how many dependent children? (Don't include the student.)	☐	☐

Section I — Parents' Assets — If parents own all or part of a business or farm, write in its name and the percent of ownership in Section P.

		What is it worth today?	What is owed on it?
37. Cash, savings, and checking accounts	$_____.00		
38. Monthly home mortgage or rental payment (If none, explain in Section P.)	$_____.00		
41. Business		$_____.00	$_____.00
42. a. Farm		$_____.00	$_____.00

42. b. Does family live on the farm? Yes ☐1   No ☐2

	What is it worth today?	What is owed on it?
39. Investments	$_____.00	$_____.00
40. a. Home (Renters write in "0".)	$_____.00	$_____.00
43. a. Other real estate	$_____.00	$_____.00

40. b. year purchased 1 9 ☐☐   c. purchase price $_____.00

43. b. year purchased 1 9 ☐☐   c. purchase price $_____.00

Section J — Parents' 1994 Income & Benefits

4. 1994 **Adjusted Gross Income** (IRS Form 1040, line 31 or 1040A, line 16 or 1040EZ, line 3) $ _____ .00

5. 1994 **U.S. income tax paid** (IRS Form 1040, line 46, 1040A, line 25 or 1040EZ, line 9) $ _____ .00

6. 1994 **itemized deductions** (IRS Form 1040, Schedule A, line 29. Write "0" if deductions were not itemized.) $ _____ .00

7. 1994 **untaxed income and benefits** (Include the same types of income & benefits that are listed in 55 a-k.) $ _____ .00

Section K — Parents' 1995 Income & Benefits

48. The following 1995 U.S. income tax return figures are (Mark only one box.)

1 ☐ estimated. Will file IRS Form 1040EZ or 1040A. Go to 49.
2 ☐ estimated. Will file IRS Form 1040. Go to 49.
3 ☐ from a completed IRS Form 1040EZ or 1040A. Go to 49.
4 ☐ from a completed IRS Form 1040. Go to 49.
5 ☐ a tax return will not be filed. Skip to 53.

(Tax Filers Only)

49. 1995 **total number of exemptions** (IRS Form 1040, line 6e or 1040A, line 6e or 1040EZ - see instructions)   **49.** ☐☐

50. 1995 **Adjusted Gross Income** (IRS Form 1040, line 31 or 1040A, line 16 or 1040EZ, line 4)   **50.** $ _____ .00

Breakdown of income in 50

a. **Wages, salaries, tips** (IRS Form 1040, line 7 or 1040A, line 7 or 1040EZ, line 1)   **50.** a. $ _____ .00

b. **Interest income** (IRS Form 1040, line 8a or 1040A, line 8a or 1040EZ, line 2)   b. $ _____ .00

c. **Dividend income** (IRS Form 1040, line 9 or 1040A, line 9)   c. $ _____ .00

d. **Net income (or loss) from business, farm, rents, royalties, partnerships, estates, trusts, etc.** (IRS Form 1040, lines 12, 17, and 18) If a loss, enter the amount in (parentheses).   d. $ _____ .00

e. **Other taxable income such as alimony received, capital gains (or losses), pensions, annuities, etc.** (IRS Form 1040, lines 10, 11, 13, 14, 15b, 16b, 19, 20b, and 21 or 1040A, lines 10b, 11b, 12, and 13b or 1040EZ, line 3)   e. $ _____ .00

f. **Adjustments to income** (IRS Form 1040, line 30 or 1040A, line 15c)   f. $ _____ .00

51. 1995 **U.S. income tax paid** (IRS Form 1040, line 46, 1040A, line 25 or 1040EZ, line 10)   **51.** $ _____ .00

52. 1995 **Itemized deductions** (IRS Form 1040, Schedule A, line 28. Write in "0" if deductions were not itemized.)   **52.** $ _____ .00

53. 1995 **Income earned from work by father**   **53.** $ _____ .00

54. 1995 **Income earned from work by mother**   **54.** $ _____ .00

55. 1995 **untaxed income and benefits** (Give total amount for the year. Do not give monthly amounts.)

a. **Social security benefits**   **55.** a. $ _____ .00

b. **Aid to Families with Dependent Children**   b. $ _____ .00

c. **Child support received for all children**   c. $ _____ .00

d. **Deductible IRA and/or Keogh payments** (See instructions.)   d. $ _____ .00

e. **Payments to tax-deferred pension and savings plans** (See address page.)   e. $ _____ .00

f. **Amounts withheld from wages for dependent care and medical spending accounts**   f. $ _____ .00

g. **Earned Income Credit** (IRS Form 1040, line 57 or 1040A, line 29c or 1040EZ, line 8)   g. $ _____ .00

h. **Housing, food and other living allowances** (See instructions.)   h. $ _____ .00

i. **Tax-exempt interest income** (IRS Form 1040, line 8b or 1040A, line 8b)   i. $ _____ .00

j. **Foreign income exclusion** (IRS Form 2555, line 43)   j. $ _____ .00

k. **Other** — write in the total from the worksheet in the instructions, page 8.   k. $ _____ .00

WRITE ONLY IN THE ANSWER SPACES. DO NOT WRITE ANYWHERE ELSE.

Section L — Parents' 1996 Expected Income & Benefits
(If the expected total income and benefits will differ from the 1995 total income and benefits by $3,000 or more, explain in Section P.)

56. 1996 **income earned from work by father** $ _____ .00

57. 1996 **income earned from work by mother** $ _____ .00

58. 1996 **other taxable income** $ _____ .00

59. 1996 **untaxed income and benefits** (See 55a-k.) $ _____ .00

Section M—Family Member Listing — Give information for all family members but don't give information about yourself. List up to seven other family members here. If there are more than seven, list first those who will be in school or college at least half-time. List the others in Section P.

60.

	Full name of family member / You — the student applicant	Use codes from below.	Age	Claimed by parents as tax exemption in 1995? Yes?	No?	1995-96 school year / Name of school or college	Year in school	Scholarships and grants	Parents' contri-bution	1996-97 school year / Attend college at least one term full-time 1	half-time 2	Name of school or co
1	You — the student applicant											
2		☐		☐	☐					1 ☐	2 ☐	
3		☐		☐	☐					1 ☐	2 ☐	
4		☐		☐	☐					1 ☐	2 ☐	
5		☐		☐	☐					1 ☐	2 ☐	
6		☐		☐	☐					1 ☐	2 ☐	
7		☐		☐	☐					1 ☐	2 ☐	
8		☐		☐	☐					1 ☐	2 ☐	

Write in the correct code from the right. ⌐ 1 = Student's parent, 2 = Student's stepparent, 3 = Student's brother or sister, 4 = Student's husband or wife, 5 = Student's son or daughter, 6 = Student's grandparent, 7 = Other

Section N — Parents' Information

61. Mark one: ☐ Father ☐ Stepfather ☐ Legal guardian ☐ Other (Explain in P.)

a. Name _____ Age ☐☐

b. Mark if: ☐ Self-employed ☐ Unemployed - Date: _____

c. Occupation _____

d. Employer _____ No. years _____

e. Work telephone ☐☐☐ – ☐☐☐ – ☐☐☐☐

f. Retirement plans: ☐ Social security ☐ Union/employer ☐ Civil service/state ☐ IRA/Keogh/tax-deferred ☐ Military ☐ Other

62. Mark one: ☐ Mother ☐ Stepmother ☐ Legal guardian ☐ Other (Explain in

a. Name _____ Age

b. Mark if: ☐ Self-employed ☐ Unemployed - Date: _____

c. Occupation _____

d. Employer _____ No. years _____

e. Work telephone ☐☐☐ – ☐☐☐ – ☐☐☐☐

f. Retirement plans: ☐ Social security ☐ Union/employer ☐ Civil service/state ☐ IRA/Keogh/tax-defer ☐ Military ☐ Other

Section O — Divorced, Separated, or Remarried Parents

(to be answered by the parent who completes this form if the student's natural or adoptive parents are divorced, separated, or remarried)

63. a. Year of separation ☐☐ Year of divorce ☐☐

b. Other parent's name: _____

Home address _____

_____

Occupation/Employer _____

c. According to court order, when will support for the student end? ☐☐ Month ☐☐ Year

d. Who last claimed the student as a tax exemption? _____

_____ Year? ☐☐

e. How much does the other parent plan to contribute to the student's education for the 1996-97 school year? $_____.0

f. Is there an agreement specifying this contribution for the student's education? Yes ☐ No ☐

Section P — Explanations/Special Circumstances
Use this space to explain any unusual expenses such as high medical or dental expenses, educational and other debts, child care, elder care, or special circumstances. Also, give information for any outside scholarships you have been awarded.

Certification:
All the information on this form is true and complete to the best of my knowledge. If asked, I agree to give proof of the information that I have given on this form. I realize that this proof may include a copy of my U.S., state, or local income tax returns. I certify that all information is correct at this time, and that I will send timely notice to my schools/programs of any significant change in family income or assets, financial situation, college plans of other children, or the receipt of other scholarships or grants.

1 _____ Student's signature

2 _____ Student's spouse's signature

3 _____ Father's (stepfather's) signature

4 _____ Mother's (stepmother's) signature

Date completed:
☐☐ ☐☐ Month Day
1 ☐ 19
2 ☐ 19
3 ☐ 19

06100614

ection Q - Institutional Questions

e following questions are being collected at the request of one or more of the colleges and schools listed on your PROFILE
gistration to receive your information. These colleges are listed on the last page in this section along with the codes
 the questions they requested. Question codes are the numbers next to the answers. They are for references purposes
d are not necessarily in numeric order.

Question(s)		Give your answer below.
f your parents have been approved for a home equity loan, write in the amount that was approved.	107.	$ _____ .00
Write in the amount owed, if any, on a second mortgage or home equity loan on your parents' home. (Explain the purpose of the loan in Section P.)	108.	$ _____ .00
Does either of your parents receive free housing or food as a job benefit? (If yes, be sure to include the value in questi on 55h of the PROFILE Application.)	110.	Yes ☐ ₁ No ☐ ₂
f your parents own real estate other than their home, write in the number of properties that they own. (For each property, write the year of purchase, purchase price , current value, and amount owed in Section P. Also, be sure to include the total value of all the real estate and the total amount owed in question 43 he PROFILE Application.)	111.	☐
Write in the cash value of your parents' single premium life nsurance holdings.	112.	$ _____ .00
Do your parents participate in a tax-deferred pension plan? (Check only one box. If yes, be sure to include the amount withheld for 1995 in question 55e of the PROFIL E Application.)	115.	₁ ☐ Yes, both parents ₂ ☐ Yes, father only ₃ ☐ Yes, mother only ₄ ☐ No
Write in the total monthly amount your parents actually contribute to their retirement plans.	118.	$ _____ .00
Write in the current value of all of your parents' IRA/Keogh plans.	121.	$ _____ .00
Does either parent hold an interest in a corporation, partnership, or Schedule C business? (If yes, include the value and debt owed in question 41 of the PROFILE Application. Also, give the name, the amount invested, and the percent of ownership in each venture in Section P.)	122.	Yes ☐ ₁ No ☐ ₂
Do you or your parents no longer own assets that generated interest/dividend income in 1995? (If yes, explain the purpose for which the assets were expended in Section P.)	127.	Yes ☐ ₁ No ☐ ₂
If your parents own a business or farm, write in the amount of untaxed income they received from the business or farm during 1995.	207.	$ _____ .00
Are your parents paying debt service for educational loans? (If yes, please specify in Section P for whom t he payments are made, the type of loan, the current amount owed , and the expected 1996 payments.)	214.	Yes ☐ ₁ No ☐ ₂

(Questions continue on the back of this page.)

Write in the amount your parents will contribute from income toward your 1996-97 educational expenses.	**303.**	$ _____ .00
Write in the amount your parents will contribute from assets toward your 1996-97 educational expenses.	**304.**	$ _____ .00
Is the college authorized to discuss the family's information with the student or to release the family's information to outside agencies and donors?	**318.**	Yes ☐₁ No ☐₂
If the student's parents are divorced or separated, is the college authorized to discuss the student's information with the student's non-custodial parent?	**319.**	Yes ☐₁ No ☐₂
Write in the cash value of the student's (and spouse's) single premium life insurance holdings.	**515.**	$ _____ .00
Write in the current total value of the student's (and spouse's) Zero Coupon Bonds.	**516.**	$ _____ .00
Is the college authorized to release the name of the student, if a scholarship recipient, to the student's hometown media?	**778.**	Yes ☐₁ No ☐₂

(Questions continue on the next page.)

123-45-6789   06100614   SUSAN   T   POWELL

Is the student a finalist for a National Merit, National Achievement, or National Hispanic Award?	773. Yes ☐ 1 No ☐ 2

College(s) below:	Will receive answers to the following question codes
LOYOLA UNIV CHICAGO UNIV OF NORTH CAROLINA CHAPEL HILL WESLEYAN UNIVERSITY	111 121 122 207 303 304 318 319 773 778 No Section Q questions requested. 107 108 110 111 112 115 118 122 127 214 303 515 516

Order Form

Mail order form to: College Board Publications, Department W21, Box 886, New York, New York 10101-0886

Qty.	Item No.	Title	Price	Amount
___	005260	Summer on Campus	$ 15.00	$_____
___	004000	The College Board Guide to 150 Popular College Majors	$ 16.00	$_____
___	005422	The College Handbook, 1997	$ 21.95	$_____
___	005430	Index of Majors and Graduate Degrees, 1997	$ 17.95	$_____
___	005449	College Costs and Financial Aid Handbook, 1997	$ 16.95	$_____
___	239402	3-Book Set: College Handbook, Index of Majors/Graduate Degrees, College Costs and Financial Aid Handbook, 1997+	$ 39.00	$_____
___	239403	Int'l 3-Book Set: College Handbook Foreign Student Supplement, College Handbook, Index of Majors/Graduate Degrees, 1997+	$ 39.00	$_____
___	005465	The College Handbook for Transfer Students, 1997	$ 17.95	$_____
___	005457	The College Handbook Foreign Student Supplement, 1997	$ 16.95	$_____
___	004671	The College Board Guide to Jobs and Career Planning, Second Edition	$ 14.00	$_____
___	004736	ABC's of Eligibility for College-Bound Student Athletes video, Revised & Updated	$ 49.95	$_____
___	004744	The College Guide for Parents, Third Edition	$ 14.00	$_____
___	005503	8 Real SATs	$ 16.95	$_____
___	004418	Breaking the Science Barrier: How to Explore and Understand the Sciences	$ 14.00	$_____
___	003330	Choosing a College: The Student's Step-By-Step Decision Making Workbook	$ 9.95	$_____
___	004280	Your College Application	$ 9.95	$_____
___	004299	Writing Your College Application Essay	$ 9.95	$_____
___	002601	Campus Visits and College Interviews	$ 9.95	$_____
___	002261	The College Admissions Organizer	$ 16.95	$_____
___	003047	College Bound: Getting Ready, Moving In, and Succeeding on Campus	$ 9.95	$_____
___	003357	Countdown to College: Getting the Most Out of High School	$ 9.95	$_____
___	003179	Campus Health Guide	$ 14.95	$_____
___	003837	Inside College: New Freedom, New Responsibility	$ 10.95	$_____
___	003535	The Student's Guide to Good Writing	$ 9.95	$_____
___	002598	Succeed with Math: Every Student's Guide to Conquering Math Anxiety	$ 12.95	$_____
___	005481	The Internet Guide for College Bound Students	$ 15.95	$_____
___	004396	Paying For College	$ 14.00	$_____
___	005139	One-on-One with the SAT (Home Version, Windows)	$ 49.95	$_____
___	005570	College Cost Explorer FUND FINDER, 1997* (Single Computer License -MS-DOS)	$ 295.00	$_____
___	239613	College Cost Explorer FUND FINDER, 1997* (Multicomputer License - MS-DOS)	$ 495.00	$_____
___	005589	College Explorer PLUS, 1997* (Single Computer License - MS-DOS)	$ 195.00	$_____
___	221819	College Explorer PLUS, 1997* (Multicomputer License - MS-DOS)	$ 295.00	$_____

*Available September   +No other discounts apply.

Payment must accompany all orders not submitted on an institutional purchase order or charged to a credit card. **Unless otherwise noted, orders for 5 or more of a single title receive a 20% discount. College Board members receive an automatic 15% discount when order is submitted with an institutional purchase order. Discounts may not be combined. The College Board pays regular ground postage on credit card and prepaid orders. Postage is charged on all orders received on purchase orders or requesting faster than UPS ground shipment. Allow two weeks from receipt of order for delivery.

Add Sales Tax:
CA 7.25%, GA 5%, D.C. 5.75%, PA 6%,
Canadian residents 7% GST $_____
** Subtotal $_____
Handling charge $___3.95
Total $_____

☐ Enclosed is my check or money order made payable to the College Board
☐ Enclosed is an institutional purchase order (for orders of $25 or more)
☐ Please charge my   ☐ MasterCard   ☐ Visa   ☐ American Express   ☐ Discover

My credit card number is: _____   Card expiration date: _____/_____
                                                                          month/year

Cardholder's Signature:_____

Credit card holders only can place orders by calling toll-free 1-800-323-7155 Monday through Friday, 8am to 11pm EST. Please have your credit card number ready when you call and give operator the department number **W21**. This special 800 number is for credit cards only. For other information or assistance, call (212) 713-8165, Monday through Friday, 9am to 5pm EST, FAX (212) 713-8143.

SHIP TO:

Name _____   City _____

Street Address _____   State _____   Zip _____
(NO P.O. BOX NUMBERS)

_____   Telephone _____

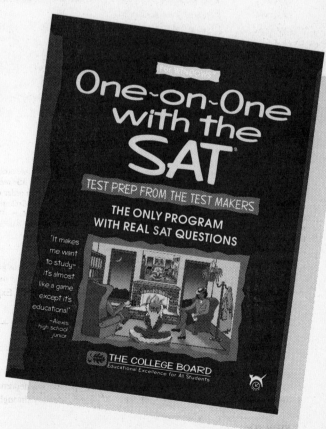

Order Form

Mail order form to: College Board Publications, Department W21, Box 886, New York, New York 10101-0886

Qty.	Item No.	Title	Price	Amount
___	005260	Summer on Campus	$ 15.00	$_____
___	004000	The College Board Guide to 150 Popular College Majors	$ 16.00	$_____
___	005422	The College Handbook, 1997	$ 21.95	$_____
___	005430	Index of Majors and Graduate Degrees, 1997	$ 17.95	$_____
___	005449	College Costs and Financial Aid Handbook, 1997	$ 16.95	$_____
___	239402	3-Book Set: College Handbook, Index of Majors/Graduate Degrees, College Costs and Financial Aid Handbook, 1997+	$ 39.00	$_____
___	239403	Int'l 3-Book Set: College Handbook Foreign Student Supplement, College Handbook, Index of Majors/Graduate Degrees, 1997+	$ 39.00	$_____
___	005465	The College Handbook for Transfer Students, 1997	$ 17.95	$_____
___	005457	The College Handbook Foreign Student Supplement, 1997	$ 16.95	$_____
___	004671	The College Board Guide to Jobs and Career Planning, Second Edition	$ 14.00	$_____
___	004736	ABC's of Eligibility for College-Bound Student Athletes video, Revised & Updated	$ 49.95	$_____
___	004744	The College Guide for Parents, Third Edition	$ 14.00	$_____
___	005503	8 Real SATs	$ 16.95	$_____
___	004418	Breaking the Science Barrier: How to Explore and Understand the Sciences	$ 14.00	$_____
___	003330	Choosing a College: The Student's Step-By-Step Decision Making Workbook	$ 9.95	$_____
___	004280	Your College Application	$ 9.95	$_____
___	004299	Writing Your College Application Essay	$ 9.95	$_____
___	002601	Campus Visits and College Interviews	$ 9.95	$_____
___	002261	The College Admissions Organizer	$ 16.95	$_____
___	003047	College Bound: Getting Ready, Moving In, and Succeeding on Campus	$ 9.95	$_____
___	003357	Countdown to College: Getting the Most Out of High School	$ 9.95	$_____
___	003179	Campus Health Guide	$ 14.95	$_____
___	003837	Inside College: New Freedom, New Responsibility	$ 10.95	$_____
___	003535	The Student's Guide to Good Writing	$ 9.95	$_____
___	002598	Succeed with Math: Every Student's Guide to Conquering Math Anxiety	$ 12.95	$_____
___	005481	The Internet Guide for College Bound Students	$ 15.95	$_____
___	004396	Paying For College	$ 14.00	$_____
___	005139	One-on-One with the SAT (Home Version, Windows)	$ 49.95	$_____
___	005570	College Cost Explorer FUND FINDER, 1997* (Single Computer License -MS-DOS)	$ 295.00	$_____
___	239613	College Cost Explorer FUND FINDER, 1997* (Multicomputer License - MS-DOS)	$ 495.00	$_____
___	005589	College Explorer PLUS, 1997* (Single Computer License - MS-DOS)	$ 195.00	$_____
___	221819	College Explorer PLUS, 1997* (Multicomputer License - MS-DOS)	$ 295.00	$_____

*Available September   +No other discounts apply.

Payment must accompany all orders not submitted on an institutional purchase order or charged to a credit card. **Unless otherwise noted, orders for 5 or more of a single title receive a 20% discount. College Board members receive an automatic 15% discount when order is submitted with an institutional purchase order. Discounts may not be combined. The College Board pays regular ground postage on credit card and prepaid orders. Postage is charged on all orders received on purchase orders or requesting faster than UPS ground shipment. Allow two weeks from receipt of order for delivery.

Add Sales Tax:
CA 7.25%, GA 5%, D.C. 5.75%, PA 6%,
Canadian residents 7% GST $_____

** Subtotal $_____

Handling charge $___3.95

Total $_____

☐ Enclosed is my check or money order made payable to the College Board
☐ Enclosed is an institutional purchase order (for orders of $25 or more)
☐ Please charge my   ☐ MasterCard   ☐ Visa   ☐ American Express   ☐ Discover

My credit card number is: _____   Card expiration date: ____/____
                                                                                      month/year

Cardholder's Signature: _____

Credit card holders only can place orders by calling toll-free 1-800-323-7155 Monday through Friday, 8am to 11pm EST. Please have your credit card number ready when you call and give operator the department number **W21**. This special 800 number is for credit cards only. For other information or assistance, call (212) 713-8165, Monday through Friday, 9am to 5pm EST, FAX (212) 713-8143.

SHIP TO:

Name _____   City _____

Street Address _____   State _____   Zip _____
(NO P.O. BOX NUMBERS)

Telephone _____

Selected Books, Software, and Videos from the College Board

Summer on Campus: College Experience for High School Students, Introduction by Shirley Levin. Comprehensive information on more than 450 academic summer programs at over 350 institutions nationwide. 321 pages, paperbound. $15.00

The College Board Guide to 150 Popular College Majors. One-of-a-kind reference to majors in 17 fields, with related information on typical courses, high school preparation, much more. 377 pages, paperbound. $16

The College Handbook, 1997. "Still the best resource of its kind, the bible of college description guides." -- *Randax Education Guide.* Over 1.5 million copies sold. The only one-volume guide to the nation's 3,300 two- and four-year guides. 1,700 pages, paperbound. $21.95

Index of Majors and Graduate Degrees, 1997. "A comprehensive, no-nonsense guide" -- *The New York Times.* Covers 580 undergraduate majors, 470 master's degree programs, 380 doctoral programs, 10 professional programs, including law, medicine, and dentistry. 682 pages, $17.95

College Costs and Financial Aid Handbook, 1997. "...an excellent resource" -- *Randax Education Guide.* Covers 3,100 two- and four-year institutions; includes indexed information on scholarships. 336 pages, paperbound. $16.95

The College Handbook for Transfer Students, 1997. The basic reference for detailed facts about transfer policies and services at over 2,600 two- and four-year colleges. 551 pages, paperbound. $17.95

The College Handbook Foreign Student Supplement, 1997. Provides students outside the U.S. with information they need to apply for study at 3,000 U.S. colleges, including costs, required tests, availability of financial aid, ESL programs. 320 pages, paperbound. $16.95

The College Board Guide to Jobs and Career Planning, Second Edition, Joyce Slayton Mitchell. Detailed descriptions of more than 100 occupations, with educational requirements, income range, more. 331 pages, paperbound. $14

ABCs of Eligibility for College-Bound Student Athletes, Michael D. Koehler. "...should be required viewing for students who want to play sports in college." -- *Library Journal.* Solid advice from a longtime counselor and coach, covering NCAA regulations, academic requirements, recruiting pressures, sports careers, much more. VHS videotape. 33 minutes. $49.95

The College Guide for Parents, Third Edition, Charles J. Shields. Helps parents guide their teenagers through the entire college admission process, from taking the right courses to applying for financial aid. 187 pages, paperbound. $14

8 Real SATs. From the College Board, official source of the SAT: 8 real, complete SATs for student practice, including the one administered in May 1996. With test-taking tips from the test makers themselves. 600 pages, paperbound. $16.95

Breaking the Science Barrier: How to Explore and Understand the Sciences, Sheila Tobias and Carl T. Tomizuka. "Excellent" -- *Voice of Youth Advocates.* Ideal for both high school and college students. 163 pages, paperbound. $14

Choosing a College: The Student's Step-by-Step Decision-Making Workbook, Gordon Porter Miller. "...an excellent tool..." -- *Tri-State YA Book Review Committee, Drexel University.* With exercises, quizzes, and worksheets. 165 pages, paperbound. $9.95

Your College Application, Revised and Updated, Scott Gelband, Catherine Kubale, and Eric Schorr. Practical advice from admission professionals on how to document strong points, demonstrate abilities, interests, goals, character, more. 139 pages, paperbound. $9.95

Writing Your College Application Essay, Sarah Myers McGinty. Application essay policies of more than 180 institutions, types of questions asked, plus 40 actual questions and analyses of 6 essays. 131 pages, paperbound. $9.95

Campus Visits and College Interviews, Zola Dincin Schneider. "...mu reading for students and parents." -- *The Book Report.* Why they a important, when to visit, what to look for, questions usually asked, muc more. 126 pages, paperbound. $9.95

The College Admissions Organizer. Three-ring binder with sections f each stage of the admission process, plus 12 pockets to store importa materials. $16.95

College Bound: Getting Ready, Moving In, and Succeeding o Campus, Evelyn Kaye and Janet Gardner. All about how to live with roommate, find and use campus services, manage money, cope wit freshman shock, more. 159 pages, paperbound. $9.95

Countdown to College: The Student's Handbook for Getting th Most Out of High School, Zola Dincin Schneider and Phyllis B. Kal Encourages students to improve reading, writing, speaking skills; ask fc help when needed; use summer productively; more. 140 page paperbound. $9.95

Campus Health Guide, Carol L. Otis, M.D., and Roger Goldinga "...sensible, practical advice based on sound medical science." -- Jane I Brody, *The New York Times.* Stresses the link between a healthy life-sty and a productive college experience. Covers birth control, AID! alcoholism, suicide, eating disorders, stress, much more. 460 page paperbound. $14.95

Inside College: New Freedom, New Responsibility, Henry C. Mose A seasoned dean of freshmen helps students explore the social, ethica and academic challenges of going to college. 234 pages, paperbound $10.95

The Student's Guide to Good Writing: Building Writing Skills fo Success in College, Rick Dalton and Marianne Dalton. How to meet th challenges of writing assignments for all college courses. 166 pages paperbound. $9.95

Succeed with Math: Every Student's Guide to Conquering Mat Anxiety, Sheila Tobias. "...an eye-opening and nonthreatening look at th world of mathematics..." -- *Library Journal.* The tools for mastering th subject in high school and college courses, and in the world of work. 25 pages, paperbound. $12.95

The Internet Guide for College-Bound Students, Kenneth E. Hartman How to surf the net to get insider opinions as well as official facts abou colleges, evaluate college information, find sources of scholarships, muc more. 250 pages, paperbound. $15.95

Paying for College: A Guide for Parents, Gerald Krefetz. Exper advice from a well-known investment analyst and financial consultant o covering college costs, with case studies. 158 pages, paperbound. $14

One-on-One with the SAT®. Invaluable advice and test-taking strategie from the SAT test makers themselves, plus the opportunity to take a real complete SAT on computer. (Home Version--Windows) $49.95

College Cost Explorer FUND FINDER®, 1997. An annually updated data base of over 3,300 sources of private and public scholarships internships, and loans; a separate data base of current costs and financia aid availability at 2,700 two- and four-year colleges; interactive electronic worksheets that automatically calculate the expected family contribution; much more. Single computer license (MS-DOS) $295.00. Multicomputer license (MS-DOS) $495.00

College Explorer PLUS®, 1997. Students can match their needs with specific offerings at 2,700 two- and four-year colleges, 1,200 graduate and professional schools, and 10 professional degree programs, including law, medicine, and dentistry. Over 800 options. Single computer license (MS-DOS) $195.00. Multicomputer license (MS-DOS) $295.00

Order Form

Qty.	Item No.	Title	Price	Amount
___	005260	Summer on Campus	$ 15.00	$_____
___	004000	The College Board Guide to 150 Popular College Majors	$ 16.00	$_____
___	005422	The College Handbook, 1997	$ 21.95	$_____
___	005430	Index of Majors and Graduate Degrees, 1997	$ 17.95	$_____
___	005449	College Costs and Financial Aid Handbook, 1997	$ 16.95	$_____
___	239402	3-Book Set: College Handbook, Index of Majors/Graduate Degrees, College Costs and Financial Aid Handbook, 1997+	$ 39.00	$_____
___	239403	Int'l 3-Book Set: College Handbook Foreign Student Supplement, College Handbook, Index of Majors/Graduate Degrees, 1997+	$ 39.00	$_____
___	005465	The College Handbook for Transfer Students, 1997	$ 17.95	$_____
___	005457	The College Handbook Foreign Student Supplement, 1997	$ 16.95	$_____
___	004671	The College Board Guide to Jobs and Career Planning, Second Edition	$ 14.00	$_____
___	004736	ABC's of Eligibility for College-Bound Student Athletes video, Revised & Updated	$ 49.95	$_____
___	004744	The College Guide for Parents, Third Edition	$ 14.00	$_____
___	005503	8 Real SATs	$ 16.95	$_____
___	004418	Breaking the Science Barrier: How to Explore and Understand the Sciences	$ 14.00	$_____
___	003330	Choosing a College: The Student's Step-By-Step Decision Making Workbook	$ 9.95	$_____
___	004280	Your College Application	$ 9.95	$_____
___	004299	Writing Your College Application Essay	$ 9.95	$_____
___	002601	Campus Visits and College Interviews	$ 9.95	$_____
___	002261	The College Admissions Organizer	$ 16.95	$_____
___	003047	College Bound: Getting Ready, Moving In, and Succeeding on Campus	$ 9.95	$_____
___	003357	Countdown to College: Getting the Most Out of High School	$ 9.95	$_____
___	003179	Campus Health Guide	$ 14.95	$_____
___	003837	Inside College: New Freedom, New Responsibility	$ 10.95	$_____
___	003535	The Student's Guide to Good Writing	$ 9.95	$_____
___	002598	Succeed with Math: Every Student's Guide to Conquering Math Anxiety	$ 12.95	$_____
___	005481	The Internet Guide for College Bound Students	$ 15.95	$_____
___	004396	Paying For College	$ 14.00	$_____
___	005139	One-on-One with the SAT (Home Version, Windows)	$ 49.95	$_____
___	005570	College Cost Explorer FUND FINDER, 1997* (Single Computer License -MS-DOS)	$ 295.00	$_____
___	239613	College Cost Explorer FUND FINDER, 1997* (Multicomputer License - MS-DOS)	$ 495.00	$_____
___	005589	College Explorer PLUS, 1997* (Single Computer License - MS-DOS)	$ 195.00	$_____
___	221819	College Explorer PLUS, 1997* (Multicomputer License - MS-DOS)	$ 295.00	$_____

*Available September   +No other discounts apply.

Add Sales Tax:
CA 7.25%, GA 5%, D.C. 5.75%, PA 6%, Canadian residents 7% GST $_____

** Subtotal $_____

Handling charge $ 3.95

Total $_____

Payment must accompany all orders not submitted on an institutional purchase order or charged to a credit card. **Unless otherwise noted, orders for 5 or more of a single title receive a 20% discount. College Board members receive an automatic 15% discount when order is submitted with an institutional purchase order. Discounts may not be combined. The College Board pays regular ground postage on credit card and prepaid orders. Postage is charged on all orders received on purchase orders or requesting faster than UPS ground shipment. Allow two weeks from receipt of order for delivery.

☐ Enclosed is my check or money order made payable to the College Board
☐ Enclosed is an institutional purchase order (for orders of $25 or more)
☐ Please charge my   ☐ MasterCard   ☐ Visa   ☐ American Express   ☐ Discover

My credit card number is: _____   Card expiration date: ____/____
                                                              month/year
Cardholder's Signature: _____

Credit card holders only can place orders by calling toll-free 1-800-323-7155 Monday through Friday, 8am to 11pm EST. Please have your credit card number ready when you call and give operator the department number W21. This special 800 number is for credit cards only. For other information or assistance, call (212) 713-8165, Monday through Friday, 9am to 5pm EST, FAX (212) 713-8143.

SHIP TO:

Name _____   City _____

Street Address _____   State _____ Zip _____
(NO P.O. BOX NUMBERS)

Telephone _____

*Visit our
home page
on the
World Wide Web!*